ITALY AND THE VATICAN AT WAR

ITALY AND
THE VATICAN AT WAR

*A Study of Their Relations from
the Outbreak of the Franco-Prussian War
to the Death of Pius IX*

+

By S. WILLIAM HALPERIN

GREENWOOD PRESS, PUBLISHERS
NEW YORK

PREFACE

THE story of Italo-papal relations, from the spectacular and far-reaching developments of 1870 to our own times, constitutes one of the most absorbing and significant phases of recent history. The clash and interplay of institutions, issues, and personalities lend to this story a suggestiveness and a dramatic quality which are its constant attributes. Domestic and international problems, spiritual and temporal claims, the pretensions of church and state—all these and still other elements combine to fashion the texture of this Italo-papal epic. And the men on either side who come and go as the story unfolds represent not only individual drives and programs but powers and forces that are at the very core of contemporary life.

The years surveyed in this volume—one of several projected by the author—constitute a momentous phase of this protracted drama. From the summer of 1870 until the death of Pope Pius IX in February, 1878, the basic issues of Italo-papal relations emerge in all their intensity and significance. The questions, both internal and international, raised during this period, the controversies accompanying them, and the solutions attempted or consummated, touch upon the very bedrock of a feud that was followed with unflagging interest throughout the world. And the subsequent history of that feud was colored in no small measure by the developments of these initial years.

In preparing this study, the author has made use of a large assortment of variegated materials. Unpublished diplomatic documents from the Archives du Ministère des Affaires étrangères in Paris and from the Haus-, Hof-, und Staatsarchiv in Vienna have been of paramount value. Contemporary newspaper material, especially Italian and French, has likewise been exceedingly useful. Contemporary periodicals, parliamentary debates, official reports, documentary collections, memoirs, letters, diaries, speeches, and yearbooks have been thoroughly canvassed. All these sources, unpublished and printed, together with the vast array of secondary works on this subject, have contributed in varying degree to the reconstruction of the account which follows.

The author takes this opportunity to express his warmest appreciation to the Social Science Research Committee of the University of Chicago, whose generous financial assistance made possible the publication of this study. He is extremely grateful to his colleagues, Professors Bernadotte E. Schmitt and Louis Gottschalk, who read the entire manuscript. He is heavily indebted to the archivists at Paris and Vienna for their courtesies in giving him access to the unpublished documents mentioned above. He is likewise grateful to Miss Diane Greeter and Miss Mapes, members of Dean Redfield's staff, for innumerable kindnesses. To Miss Mary D. Alexander and Miss Olive Mills, of the University of Chicago Press, the author extends his deepest appreciation for helpful advice and assistance throughout the process of publication. And to his wife, without whose aid and companionship the writing of this book would have been a vastly less exhilarating undertaking, he expresses thanks which words alone can scarcely convey.

TABLE OF CONTENTS

INTRODUCTION

ON APRIL 29, 1848, Pope Pius IX proclaimed his refusal to join the national "crusade" against Austria. This gesture produced one of the gravest crises of the Italian Risorgimento. It destroyed the neo-Guelfist dream and sowed dissension among Italians by placing religion and church in opposition to country. In its wake came a republican uprising in Rome, Pius' flight to Gaeta, and his eventual restoration by the French. The latter's protracted occupation of the papal capital thrust the so-called Roman question into the foreground as one of the most formidable barriers to the unification of the peninsula. The once liberal and patriotic pontiff was now the archadversary of the Italian national program. Until 1859 his extensive domain in central Italy was unmolested. But in that year France and Sardinia waged a successful war against Austria. There ensued a series of revolutions and military occupations which resulted in the transfer of large portions of the peninsula to the Sardinian kingdom. Pius was one of the principal victims. He saw the ancient papal provinces of Romagna, Umbria, and the Marches pass into the hands of the House of Savoy. In 1860 only Rome and the surrounding territory known as the Patrimony of St. Peter remained in the possession of the Holy See.

It was at this rather inauspicious juncture that Count Camillo di Cavour, the Piedmontese statesman whose consummate diplomacy had brought into being a united Italy, turned to the embittered pontiff in the hope of inducing him to relinquish Rome itself. He offered, in return for the surrender of the Eternal City, to recognize the pope as a nominal and inviolable sovereign, guarantee his spiritual independence, and bestow upon the Italian clergy complete immunity from governmental interference. Success would have fittingly climaxed his brilliant career, for the establishment at Rome of the capital of Italy and the separation of church and state were among his supreme ambitions. But the intransigence of the Vatican, which refused categorically to recognize the new state of affairs, foredoomed his overtures. Cardinal Antonelli, the all-powerful papal secretary of state, hoped for foreign intervention and adjured his master to remain firm. The pope's Jesuit advisers played upon his fears of what would happen to the Italian church were the proposals of Cavour accepted. The fate that had overtaken Francis II of Naples fanned to a white heat the Curia's hatred of the Piedmontese. The proffered olive branch was spurned. In his strongly worded allocution of March 18, 1861, Pius served notice that he would make no peace with the government at Turin as long as its troops continued to occupy any of his territories. Cavour replied in two great addresses before the Sardinian parliament. He insisted that Rome would have to become the capital of Italy and proclaimed, as the goal of his ecclesiastical policy, "a free church in a free state." The chamber of deputies rewarded his efforts by voting on March 27 in favor of the union of Rome with Italy.

Convinced that an accord with the pope was unattainable, Cavour turned to Paris. His principal objective now was to secure the recall of the French garrison from Rome. But Napoleon III, whose Roman policy was dictated by the clerical party in France, offered to withdraw his troops only if Italy guaranteed the integrity of the papal patrimony. Cavour knew that such a pledge would be deeply resented by his countrymen. There was little he could do, however, except assent to the emperor's terms, and this he quickly did. Only certain preliminary formalities remained to be hurdled when, in June, 1861, he was fatally stricken.

The French government, after some hesitation, renewed its offer to Baron Bettino Ricasoli, the distinguished Tuscan statesman who had succeeded Cavour. But the new premier, who had already put forward a plan similar to the one Cavour had broached to the Vatican, bluntly refused to lend himself in any way to the preservation of the temporal power. An internal crisis precipitated his resignation early in 1862, and a ministry was formed by Urbano Rattazzi, the veteran parliamentarian who drew his support mainly from the party of the left, the Sinistra. The outlook for an Italo-papal reconciliation was at this moment far from cheering. Father Passaglia, the famous theologian who had been one of Cavour's principal collaborators in the negotiations of 1860–61, infuriated the Vatican by publishing a brochure assailing the doctrine of the temporal power. Pius' reply was a solemn declaration that territorial sovereignty had been conferred upon the pontiff by divine will and that it was indispensable to the free and complete exercise of his spiritual functions. The specter of a Garibaldian incursion into papal territory, momentarily laid at Aspromonte in the summer of 1862, did not improve the Holy Father's temper.

Rattazzi gave way to Marco Minghetti, a leader of the moderate rightist party, the Destra, and during the next two years the skilful hand of this statesman was at the helm of Italian affairs. He had been one of Cavour's most intimate and trusted associates, and he possessed something of the sober realism and suppleness of his erstwhile chief. He broached the subject of evacuation in the summer of 1863, and the emperor, after considerable procrastination, countered by reviving the offer originally made to Cavour. However, he now insisted that Italy agree to transfer her capital to a city other than Rome as an earnest of her sincerity in pledging herself to respect the inviolability of the papal dominion. The Minghetti government reluctantly assented to this hard condition. A convention was finally signed on September 15, 1864. Italy undertook "not to attack the present territory of the Holy Father, and to prevent, by force if necessary, any attack on the said territory coming from without." She further bound herself, in an appended protocol, to move the capital from Turin. France, in return, engaged to withdraw her garrison from Rome. In a subsequent exchange of notes, the two governments stipulated that, in the event of "exceptional contingencies," each would be entitled to resume its freedom of action.

Minghetti and his ministerial colleagues entertained few illusions about the probable reaction of Italian public opinion. They anticipated a violent outcry against the transfer of the capital to Florence, which had been selected as the new seat of the government. In an effort to soften the blow and forestall charges that they were yielding to foreign pressure, they pictured the transfer as a purely voluntary action based on weighty strategic considerations. They sought to create the impression that Florence was but a step toward Rome. The national program, they said, would have to be achieved piecemeal and by moral means, as the only other alternative, a war with France, was unthinkable. But these explanations and assurances failed of their purpose. The indignation of the Turinese at seeing their city divested of its supreme rank exceeded even the government's apprehensions. There were demonstrations, riots, and shouts of "Down with the ministry!" Soldiers had to be called out to disperse the mobs, and there were numerous casualties. The Minghetti cabinet was forced to resign, but its successors had no choice but to comply with the terms of the September convention. A law naming Florence the capital was signed by the king in December, 1864. In June, 1865, the transfer was an accomplished fact, and in December of the following year the French garrison abandoned Rome.

In circles friendly to the government the September convention was hailed as a prelude to the acquisition of Rome. It was claimed that the evacuation of the city would be followed by a spontaneous rising of its inhabitants and plebiscitary annexation to Italy. The radicals of the Sinistra opposition bitterly assailed the pact. They charged that it might defer indefinitely the realization of the national program. The Vatican was furious with Napoleon III. It charged him with desertion of the historic role which all rulers of France, without exception, had faithfully discharged. It was distrustful of the Italians. It placed little confidence in their promise to respect the territorial integrity of the Holy See. The Syllabus of Errors, which appeared on December 8, 1864, served the incidental purpose of conveying its keen dissatisfaction with the recent turn of affairs. Especially significant was the condemnation of the separation of church and state.

The Vatican's fears were destined speedily to be verified. No sooner had the French garrison departed than the Mazzinian Committee of Action called on all patriotic Romans to prepare for an insurrection against papal rule. When Rattazzi, whose personal sympathies were unmistakably with the exponents of a march on Rome, formed a cabinet in April, 1867, Garibaldi resolved to take matters into his own hands. The ensuing sequence of events was swift and dramatic. Late in September the hero was arrested on his way to the papal frontier and transported to Caprera, his island retreat. With half the Italian fleet detailed to watch him, he escaped to the mainland. The irresolute Rattazzi resigned, and, amid the confusion caused by the reluctance of party leaders to assume the premiership, Garibaldi decided to strike. He assembled a band of hastily recruited volunteers and launched the attack which, he hoped, would forever destroy the temporal power. In France the ultramontane party clamored for immediate military intervention. Napoleon held out for a time in the hope that the Italian government, in accordance with its obligations under the September convention, would disperse the Garibaldians. But he finally yielded, and late in October a strong force sailed from Toulon for Civita Vecchia. The Battle of Mentana, early in November, brought the campaign to a sudden close. The undisciplined, poorly equipped troops of Garibaldi wilted before the murderous fire of the new French *chassepots* and fled in confusion. Rome was reoccupied by the victors, and, in the

Corps législatif, Rouher, the spokesman of the French ministry, declared: "Never will Italy seize Rome, never will France tolerate such a violence to her honor and to Catholicism."

The temporal power had been saved, and Napoleon was once again the darling of his clerical subjects. But he did not altogether relish the responsibility which he had resumed. He now sought to throw some of it upon his fellow-sovereigns. He proposed a conference of the powers to arbitrate between the Vatican and Italy. It was his aim to secure an international guarantee of the papal territory which would effectually restrain Italy and permit France to recall her soldiers from Civita Vecchia. His overtures, however, met with no success, largely because of Bismarck's opposition. The latter, who had rejected the emperor's earlier suggestion that France and Prussia jointly undertake to safeguard the temporal power, had no desire to help the French disentangle themselves from the Roman imbroglio.

The Roman question had indeed become Napoleon's nemesis. During the next two years it contributed heavily to defeat his own efforts to induce Austria and Italy to join France in a triple alliance against Prussia. The refusal of Count Beust, the Austrian chancellor, to bind his government except in the event of a war arising out of a clash of interests in the Near East, was one insurmountable obstacle. The other was Napoleon's unwillingness to surrender Rome. The Italians made the withdrawal of the French garrison the condition of their participation in the proposed alliance. The emperor, however, did not feel that he could afford an open break with his ultramontane subjects. He needed their support more than ever after the liberal reforms of 1869. This was the situation until the summer of 1870, when the candidacy of Prince Leopold of Hohenzollern-Sigmaringen to the Spanish throne precipitated the long-impending Franco-Prussian crisis. The prince, who was a cousin of King William of Prussia, withdrew after strong protests by the French.

But the affair did not end there. The imperial government resolved to exploit the situation to inflict an even more resounding diplomatic defeat upon Prussia. It demanded of King William a promise never to allow a Hohenzollern to become a candidate for the throne of Spain. There followed the momentous interview at Ems. The carefully edited report of it, which appeared in the Parisian press on July 14, evoked tremendous indignation in France. The emperor, yielding to the popular clamor and the counsels of his ministers, agreed to make the incident a *casus belli*. On the following day the French parliament voted a declaration of war against Prussia by overwhelming majorities.

CHAPTER I
THE RENEWAL OF THE SEPTEMBER
CONVENTION

THE impending struggle with Prussia spurred Napoleon to renew his overtures to Vienna and Florence for an alliance *à trois*. Warned that the presence of his troops in papal territory would continue to preclude Italian participation,[1] he determined to lose little time in rectifying the situation.[2] His hopes soared when he was assured by Count Vimercati, the Italian military attaché who served as the special emissary of King Victor Emmanuel, that the latter was ready to join France in return for the prompt evacuation of Civita Vecchia.[3] The emperor was further encouraged by the attitude of Beust, who made it clear that Austrian assistance would be easier to obtain after Italy's aid had been purchased by the withdrawal of the garrison.[4] On July 16 he telegraphed Victor Emmanuel that he

[1] On July 9 the French minister at Florence, Malaret, pointed out that Italy was virtually disarmed and in financial straits and that her natural desire under these circumstances to remain neutral could be overcome only by recalling the garrison (*Les Origines diplomatiques de la guerre de 1870–1871* [Paris, 1910–32], XXVIII, No. 8362, 173–76 [hereafter cited as *OD*]).

[2] Napoleon hoped that the recall of the occupation corps would dispose Italy favorably to the idea of intervention (cf. Emile Bourgeois, *Manuel historique de politique étrangère* [Paris, 1924], III, 721). Moreover, the small contingent at Civita Vecchia, completely cut off from reinforcement after the outbreak of war, could be of little real value to the pope. Finally, the ecumenical council at Rome was nearing its close and would no longer need protection (cf. Emile Ollivier, *L'Empire libéral* [Paris, 1895–1915], XV, 443).

[3] On Vimercati's interview with Napoleon see *OD*, XXVIII, 143; Hermann Oncken, *Die Rheinpolitik Kaiser Napoleons III von 1863 bis 1870 und der Ursprung des Krieges von 1870–71* (Berlin and Leipzig, 1926), III, No. 868, 418; Henry Salomon, *L'Ambassade de Richard de Metternich à Paris* (Paris, 1931), p. 250; Emile Bourgeois and E. Clermont, *Rome et Napoléon III, 1849–1870* (Paris, 1907), p. 252; M. Mazziotti, *Napoleone III e l'Italia* (Milano, 1925), p. 293.

[4] Oncken, *op. cit.*, III, No. 871, 425–26.

1

wished to renew the September convention and would recall his occupation corps if the king would personally guarantee the safety of the papal frontier.[5] At the same time, Vimercati and Count Vitzthum, the Austrian minister at Brussels who had been conferring with Napoleon, undertook to secure the adhesion of their governments to the proposed triple alliance.

Vitzthum's mission proved utterly hopeless. Public opinion in both Austria[6] and Hungary[7] was strongly opposed to intervention. The views of Count Andrássy, the Hungarian premier,[8] prevailed over those of Beust, who favored an active anti-Prussian policy.[9] Fear of what Russia might do overshadowed all else. On July 18 unconditional neutrality was decided upon in a ministerial conference at the Hofburg.[10]

[5] *OD*, XXIX, No. 8571, 11. This demand for Victor Emmanuel's personal guarantee, which the French government subsequently dropped, was inspired by the fear that nothing less would suffice to meet the danger of an imminent coup against Rome. Genuine alarm had been produced by reports from the French consul at Leghorn that men were being recruited there for an incursion into papal territory, and the matter had been brought to the attention of the Italian government (*ibid.*, No. 8604, pp. 39–40).

[6] Cf. the dispatch, dated July 14, of General von Schweinitz, the Prussian minister at Vienna, in Robert H. Lord, *The Origins of the War of 1870* (Cambridge, 1924), p. 241.

[7] Magdolna M. Kégel, *Die Beurteilung der deutschen Frage in der ungarischen Presse, 1866–1871* (Budapest, 1934), p. 34.

[8] On July 14, Andrássy had emphasized in the Hungarian chamber of deputies the necessity of maintaining strict neutrality. His attention was centered on Russia, which, he knew, would not brook Austrian intervention on the side of France.

[9] Cf. Wilhelm Alter, "Deutschlands Einigung und die Österreichische Politik," *Deutsche Rundschau*, October, 1910, p. 114.

[10] Cf., on the famous *Kronrat* of July 18, Eduard von Wertheimer, *Graf Julius Andrássy: sein Leben und seine Zeit* (Stuttgart, 1910), I, 510–20, and "Zur Vorgeschichte des Krieges von 1870," *Deutsche Rundschau*, January, 1921, pp. 56–57; Friedrich Ferdinand Graf von Beust, *Aus drei viertel-jahrhunderten* (Stuttgart, 1887), II, 392; Heinrich von Sybel, *Die Begründung des deutschen Reiches durch Wilhelm I* (München and Leipzig, 1899), VII, 384–86; Giuseppe Gallavresi, *Italia e Austria, 1859–1914* (Milano, 1922), p. 115; Ottokar Lorenz, *Kaiser Wilhelm und die Begründung des Reichs, 1866–1871* (Jena, 1902), pp. 317–18. On July 20, Hofmann, the *Sektionschef* of the Austrian foreign office, explained to Schweinitz that his government's policy was one of "passivity as long as our safety permits" (*Denkwürdigkeiten des Botschafters General v. Schweinitz* [Berlin, 1927], I, 263).

Beust, however, refused to acknowledge defeat.[11] "We consider the cause of France as our own," he wrote two days later to Prince Metternich, the Austrian ambassador at Paris, "and we will contribute to the success of her arms within the limits of the possible." He explained his government's declaration of neutrality as a means of "completing our armaments without exposing ourselves to a sudden attack by Prussia or Russia."[12] He pointed out that, though armed neutrality was not an alliance, it could be a step toward one.[13] He persuaded his imperial master to write in this sense to Napoleon III.[14]

The Italian government welcomed Napoleon's announcement that the French garrison would be recalled and the September convention renewed. Despite the unpopularity of that pact and the widespread demand that it be forthwith denounced, official circles were fully alive to the advantages of a peaceful and voluntary withdrawal of the occupation corps. True to the principles laid down by Cavour, they held that a solution of the Roman question would have to be effected in agreement with France and that the departure of her troops should be the immediate objective.[15] Even Quintino Sella, the minister of finance, who, among the members of the cabinet, had most vehemently opposed the convention, was acquiescent now. Victor Emmanuel therefore lost little time in informing Napoleon that Italy had never denounced

[11] Alter, *op. cit.*, p. 117; Sybel, *op. cit.*, VII, 386.

[12] Oncken, *op. cit.*, III, No. 911, 464–66; Wertheimer, "Zur Vorgeschichte des Krieges von 1870," *op. cit.*, p. 58.

[13] Oncken, *op. cit.*, III, No. 913, 470; Wertheimer, "Zur Vorgeschichte des Krieges von 1870," *op. cit.*, pp. 59–60. Beust's efforts to convert Andrássy to this point of view proved futile (Wertheimer, *Andrássy*, I, 520–21).

[14] In a letter of July 25 to the French emperor, Francis Joseph alluded to Austrian neutrality as "benevolent toward France." He added that Napoleon could count on him, especially if a third power (meaning Russia) should intervene in the war. He declared that his efforts were aimed at "completing my armaments in order to be able to defend the solidarity of our interests and aid your Majesty in giving Europe the permanent peace which we all desire" (Oncken, *op. cit.*, III, No. 920, 475–76).

[15] Alessandro Guiccioli, *Quintino Sella* (Rovigo, 1887), I, 265.

the September convention and that she would continue to fulfil her obligations under it.[16] The way was now cleared for formal action by the French cabinet. On July 25, after a spirited discussion, it indorsed the emperor's decision to recall the garrison.[17]

In assenting to the renewal of the September convention, the Italian government intended only to set the stage for a more satisfactory solution of the Roman question. And it deemed the intervention of Beust indispensable to the success of this program.[18] Even while it was telling Napoleon III that it accepted its obligations under the pact of 1864, it requested the Austrian government to secure French acquiescence in an arrangement permitting Italian troops to occupy certain points in papal territory.[19] Beust, who believed that a Franco-Italian accord on the Roman question would enhance the possibility of an anti-Prussian coalition, needed little urging. On July 20, in a long letter to Metternich, he argued that only by boldly discarding the September conven-

[16] *OD*, XXIX, No. 8686, 129; Bourgeois and Clermont, *op. cit.*, p. 278.

[17] The French cabinet meeting on July 25 was presided over by Empress Eugénie. Two of the ministers present, Plichon and Louvet, opposed the evacuation on the ground that it would leave the pope at the mercy of his enemies. They were convinced that, once the French troops were gone, the Garibaldians would lose little time in attacking the papal state. They insisted that the Italian troops which would be charged with the defense of Rome were not to be trusted. They would use the pretext of halting the Garibaldians to march into the papal capital ahead of them. But Eugénie was equal to the occasion. She warned that France, bereft of an alliance with Italy and Austria, could not dispense with the aid which even the modest force at Civita Vecchia could afford her. She declared that any Italian aggression against the papal territory would have only temporary success because a victorious France would experience little difficulty in restoring the pontiff to his former position (Ollivier, *op. cit.*, XV, 450–51).

[18] Visconti-Venosta subsequently explained to the Austrian minister in Florence that Italy, in accepting the September convention as the sole means of securing the immediate evacuation of papal territory, had not renounced the hope of obtaining more from France. It was with this in mind that the Italian government had requested the good offices of Vienna (cf. Kübeck to Beust, August 13, 1870, Haus-, Hof-, und Staatsarchiv, Politisches Archiv [Florenz], Fasz. XI/74, Bericht 63A, fols. 309*b*–310*a*). (The Haus-, Hof-, und Staatsarchiv is hereafter cited as HHSA.)

[19] Cf., on this Italian *démarche*, Beust's dispatches in the HHSA, Politisches Archiv (Rome, Expeditions, Varia), Fasz. XI/225, fols. 172*a*–173*a*, 184*b*–188*a*, 195*a*–195*b*.

tion could the French hope to secure Italy's aid. Clearly, the pope could not rely for protection upon his own troops. The choice lay between Victor Emmanuel and Garibaldi, and the former was the lesser evil. "The day the French leave the papal states," he wrote, "it is necessary that the Italians should be able to enter them with full right and with the assent of Austria and France. Never will we have the Italians with us heart and soul if we do not remove their Roman thorn." Such a solution of the Roman question, he argued, would facilitate co-operation between the three countries.[20]

In the meantime, Napoleon's overtures for a triple alliance were faring rather badly at Florence. The Italian government, even had it been so disposed, could hardly have embarked upon any costly military preparations. Its recently inaugurated financial policy was predicated upon the uninterrupted maintenance of peace during the next few years. The treasury was depleted, and credit was far from abundant. To climax matters, the army was grossly inadequate, and the transition from a peace to a war footing was necessarily slow.[21] Giovanni Lanza, the then Italian premier, remarked in later years to Gadda, who had served in his cabinet as minister of public works: "Yes . . . . we were lucky. The very deficiency of our armaments . . . . redounded to the ad-

[20] Oncken, op. cit., III, No. 911, 466–67; OD, XXIX, 441–44; Bourgeois and Clermont, op. cit., pp. 282–85. "It was easy to foresee," Beust wrote in later years, "that after the outbreak of the war, the safety and independence of the papal government, which was protected by the French garrison, would be endangered, even if France should be victorious. In view of the invasion already attempted by Garibaldi at Mentana, which was frustrated only by the timely intervention of the French troops, it was certain that a similar attempt would be repeated with greater energy, and that this would necessitate an increase in the French garrison. . . . . A timely agreement by France with Italy on the one hand, and with Rome on the other, might have led to a compromise permitting Italy to occupy several points in the papal states, with the exception of Rome. Only in this way would the papal troops have been strong enough to keep Rome; and if Italy had been true to her engagements, a basis might have been found for an understanding between Rome and Florence" (Beust, op. cit., II, 411).

[21] Cf. Uberto Govone, Il Generale Giuseppe Govone (Torino, 1902), pp. 366–67, 376; Guiccioli, op. cit., I, 251; Francesco Crispi, Politica interna (Milano, 1924), p. 64; OD, XXIX, 21; Ugo Pesci, Firenze capitale (1865–1870) (Firenze, 1904), p. 209.

vantage of Italy. It made it evident . . . . that in the European conflict no military action by us was possible."[22] The situation was further complicated by the agitated state of public opinion. While there was considerable pro-French sentiment among the upper classes,[23] the bulk of the nation supported the Sinistra leaders in their violent opposition to intervention on the side of the perpetrators of Mentana.[24] Most Italians could not see why Italy should help bring about a victory whose effect would only be to obstruct the realization of the national program.[25] Their reasoning was simple and conclusive. The French barred the way to Rome. To aid them was to postpone indefinitely the acquisition of the coveted city. An influential section of the moderate Destra press did not disguise its pro-Prussian sympathies, while the organs of the Sinistra gave free vent to their Francophobia. One leftist newspaper caustically referred to the Italian and French governments as "servant" and "master," respectively.[26] To some Italians the idea of making war on the ally of 1866 was nothing short of monstrous.[27] Demonstrations had occurred in various cities, and there resounded such cries as "Long live Prussia!" "Long live Rome, capital of Italy!" "Down with French tyranny!" The anti-French sentiment was nowhere stronger than in Sicily. The Austrian consul general in Palermo reported on July 17 that the clamor for an immediate solution of the Roman question had become more intense. The Garibaldian sheets, he noted, were passionately ranging themselves on the side of Prussia. They were invoking a Prussian victory in order that Rome might be obtained

---

[22] G. Gadda, "Roma capitale ed il Ministero Lanza-Sella," *Nuova antologia*, September 16, 1897, p. 217.

[23] Cf., e.g., Walburga, Lady Paget, *Embassies of Other Days* (London, 1923), I, 260.

[24] The Prussian chargé d'affaires at Florence reported on July 15 that Italian public opinion was favorable to the maintenance of peace (Lord, *op. cit.*, p. 256).

[25] Govone, *op. cit.*, p. 360.

[26] Paolo Maria Arcari, *La Francia nell'opinione pubblica italiana dal '59 al '70* (Roma, 1934), p. 125.

[27] *Ibid.*, p. 123.

and the French yoke lifted.[28] At Florence a proclamation had been issued by the leaders of the opposition denouncing France and warning the country that the government was traitorously negotiating an alliance with her.[29] Patriotic citizens were urged to protest against this contemplated betrayal of national interests. They were reminded of the many grievances against France and the advantages reaped from the alliance with Prussia. The cryptic formula, "Neutrality: Rome," was broadcast as the imperative alpha and omega of Italian policy.[30] The Sinistra, which now styled itself the "party of action," published the following manifesto:

Whereas the services rendered by the Second Empire to Italy in a just cause . . . . do not obligate Italy to co-operate in an unjust one, all the more so as those services . . . . have been requited at a usurious rate . . . . with blood, money and territories; whereas the consummation of the alliance in question would profoundly shock the national sentiment mindful of so many bloody humiliations and insults; whereas an aggrandizement of French power would strengthen our yoke for many years; whereas the French alliance would never be based upon the recognition of Rome but would, instead, perpetuate the renunciation of it . . . . , we hold that Italy must observe neutrality.[31]

The sympathies of Victor Emmanuel lay with France. He was entirely sincere in his desire to aid her.[32] Confident that she would win,[33] he believed that Italy would secure what she wanted, and especially a solution of the Roman question, by intervening in her behalf. He therefore demanded immediate participation in the war[34] and rejected neutrality as both inglorious and unprofitable.[35] His ministers, however, showed

[28] Cf. the annex to Bericht 54A, HHSA, Politisches Archiv, Fasz. XI/74, fol. 111a.

[29] Alfredo Comandini and Antonio Monti, *L'Italia nei cento anni del secolo XIX giorno per giorno illustrata* (Milano, 1918–29), IV, 1226.

[30] Cf. Malaret's report of July 17, 1870, in *OD*, XXIX, No. 8598, 35.

[31] Arcari, *op. cit.*, p. 126.

[32] Giuseppe Massari, *La Vita ed il regno di Vittorio Emanuele II di Savoia* (Milano, 1910), II, 514.

[33] Cf. Attilio Simioni, *Vittorio Emanuele II* (Milano, 1911), p. 140.

[34] Govone, *op. cit.*, p. 361.   [35] Guiccioli, *op. cit.*, I, 259.

little enthusiasm for the proposed alliance. Its principal opponent was Sella, who was among the few to predict a Prussian victory.[36] He claimed that the cause of France was really that of the Vatican. Consequently, Italy could expect no equitable solution of the Roman question from a partnership in arms with Napoleon III.[37] Lanza supported Sella against the king.[38] The Francophil group in the cabinet was headed by the influential and respected foreign minister, Emilio Visconti-Venosta.[39] But though he shared Victor Emmanuel's belief that the French would win, he was cool to their overtures.[40] He did not feel that the evacuation of Civita Vecchia would place Italy under any special obligation to France. He remarked to Sir Augustus Paget, the British minister at Florence, that "if the French troops were withdrawn now, he should regard it simply as the fulfilment by France of the terms of the September convention, and not as an act entailing any corresponding compensation to be given to her by Italy."[41] He feared that the projected triple alliance might involve Italy in war "prematurely and contrary to public opinion." He was determined to do nothing to compromise his freedom of action. Above all, he wished in advance to come to an understanding with Austria "directly and without the intervention of France."[42] In the course of a discussion of

[36] Arcari, *op. cit.*, p. 130; Guiccioli, *op. cit.*, I, 252; cf. also, for Sella's attitude, Giuseppe Paladino, *Storia d'Italia dal 1861 al 1871 con particolare riguardo alla questione romana* (Milano, 1932), p. 104.

[37] Guiccioli, *op. cit.*, I, 260–62.   [38] *Ibid.*, p. 266.

[39] *OD*, XXIX, 22; Bourgeois and Clermont, *op. cit.*, p. 276.

[40] Guiccioli, *op. cit.*, I, 263.

[41] *Correspondence Respecting the Affairs of Rome, 1870–71* (London, 1871), No. 1, p. 1 (hereafter cited as *Blue Book*).

[42] Oncken, *op. cit.*, III, No. 902, 457–58 and note on p. 457. From the outset the Italian government attached paramount importance to the attitude of the Viennese cabinet. On July 17, Victor Emmanuel wrote Napoleon III: "I desire with all my heart to be agreeable to Your Majesty, while seeking the real interest of the Italian nation. I should like to know what are the intentions of Austria and whether there are any engagements on her part" (*OD*, XXIX, No. 8617, 53; Ollivier, *op. cit.*, XV, 445; Bourgeois and Clermont, *op. cit.*, p. 277).

foreign affairs in the chamber on July 18, he found opportunity to state the attitude of the government. The latter, he declared, was anxious to preserve peace. Its policy, like that of all other nonbelligerent powers, was directed toward the localization of the impending war.[43] Lanza, however, was careful to add that Italy might not escape the repercussions of the current crisis. It was as yet impossible, he observed, to indicate her course of action, but there could be no doubt that changes in the European situation would affect the government's decision. For the time being, the cabinet could assume no obligations vis-à-vis the country or restrict its liberty in the slightest degree. But parliament could rest assured that nothing would be left undone to meet the exigencies of the moment.[44] Visconti-Venosta himself later that day impressed upon the Austrian minister that his remarks in the chamber had in no way prejudiced Italy's freedom of action.[45]

The guarded declarations of Lanza and Visconti-Venosta failed to shake Gramont's confidence in the ultimate success of the negotiations for an alliance.[46] The duke's exaggerated optimism blinded him to the real significance of what was transpiring in the Italian capital. On July 19 he wrote to Beust: "The news which I receive from Florence is excellent. They are ready to conclude, and already the government has informed the chamber of its resolution to call two classes to the colors, that is to say, one hundred thousand men."[47] Reassuring indeed was the news conveyed by Vimercati, who reported that he had found Victor Emmanuel busily engaged in trying to persuade his cabinet to accept Napoleon's proposals. Conversations with leading ministers led the ubiquitous envoy to predict that Austria's acquiescence in the treaty à trois would make Italian participation a certainty.[48]

[43] Atti del parlamento italiano, CLIX (July 18, 1870), 3421 (hereafter cited as Atti).

[44] Ibid., p. 3423.   [45] Oncken, op. cit., III, 457 n.

[46] Cf. Salomon, op. cit., p. 259. The Duke of Gramont was the French foreign minister at this time.

[47] OD, XXIX, No. 8659, 104–5.

[48] Ibid., No. 8666, pp. 111–12; Bourgeois and Clermont, op. cit., pp. 277–78.

The king himself continued to use very brave language. He declared his readiness to sign a treaty of alliance with France whenever Prussia should reject Austro-Italian mediation in the conflict. Vimercati, who was about to depart for Vienna, did what he could to second Victor Emmanuel's efforts. The cabinet, however, was still far from tractable. On July 21 the king confessed in a telegram to Napoleon that "to arrive at a realization of our projects, I am obliged to indulge the susceptibilities of a ministry formed with a pacific purpose" and that "the rapidity of events has prevented me from carrying our old plans into effect as promptly as I would have desired."[49] A ministerial crisis was averted only after Vimercati had promised Lanza and Visconti-Venosta that he would follow them in enlisting the services of Austria to obtain far-reaching concessions from France in the Roman question.[50] The recalcitrant cabinet now agreed to something of a compromise. Vimercati was to apprise the Austrian government that Italy wished to reach an understanding with it regarding the triple alliance; but he was to add that a treaty was first to be concluded between France and Austria, to which Italy would subsequently adhere.[51]

In the meantime, it was necessary to follow the Viennese cabinet in announcing a "hands-off" policy toward the Franco-Prussian War. The attitude of Lanza and his colleagues had been profoundly affected by the Austrian decision of July 18. They were now more than ever convinced of the wisdom of their policy of watchful waiting.[52] Only the opposition of

[49] OD, XXIX, No. 8705, 154; Ollivier, op. cit., XV, 448; Bourgeois and Clermont, op. cit., pp. 278-79.

[50] Cf. Oncken, op. cit., III, 484; Wertheimer, "Zur Vorgeschichte des Krieges von 1870," op. cit., p. 65; Bourgeois and Clermont, op. cit., pp. 280-81.

[51] Oncken, op. cit., III, No. 918, 474; Bourgeois and Clermont, op. cit., p. 279.

[52] Without Austria they were most reluctant to act. On February 27, 1871, Visconti-Venosta wrote in a retrospective vein to Nigra, the Italian minister at Paris: "The attitude of Russia paralyzed Austria; and Italy, alone, felt and was powerless" (C. Nigra, "Ricordi diplomatici, 1870," Nuova antologia, March 1, 1895, p. 25).

the king stood in the way of an unambiguous declaration of neutrality.[53] But he too finally yielded. A bit of salutary pressure exerted by Bismarck helped to overcome the monarch's scruples. Anxious to provoke Italy to a clear enunciation of her noninterventionist position, the resourceful Prussian instructed his minister at Florence, Brassier de St. Simon, to leave immediately for Berlin.[54] The stratagem worked. On July 24, Sella assured Brassier that he would rather resign than consent to a war against Prussia.[55] The following day Visconti-Venosta formally stated in the chamber of deputies that the government was pursuing a policy of strict neutrality. He added that as yet no official communications had been exchanged between Paris and Florence on the Roman question. He was careful to emphasize that France might expect no reward for her belated compliance with the terms of the September convention. Any decision reached by her with respect to the garrison at Civita Vecchia was to be considered "independent of the line of conduct which Italy might be called upon to take in the present circumstances." But it would be improper, he concluded, to add to France's embarrassments by threatening the use of violence in the Roman question.[56]

The outbreak of the Franco-Prussian War was unwelcome news to the papal government. It feared that Napoleon, in order to secure the alliance of Italy, might agree to concessions detrimental to the Holy See.[57] Reports of Italo-French negotiations on the Roman question, the rumor that Rattazzi

[53] The king endeavored in vain to convert Sella, the archapostle of nonintervention, to his point of view. There ensued at times some sharp verbal exchanges, with the minister having much the better of them (cf. Guiccioli, *op. cit.*, I, 267–68; Luigi Luzzatti, *Memorie autobiografiche e carteggi* [Bologna, 1931], I, 306–7; Paladino, *op. cit.*, p. 115).

[54] Bismarck, *Die gesammelten Werke* (Berlin, 1924–35), VI*b*, No. 1698, 413–14 and note. This great collection, hereafter cited as *GW*, contains many hitherto unpublished documents.

[55] Guiccioli, *op. cit.*, I, 273.   [56] *Atti*, CLIX (July 25, 1870), 3673.

[57] Palomba to Beust, July 21, 1870, HHSA, Politisches Korrespondenz (Rom), Fasz. XI/224, Bericht 85*B*, fol. 135*a*.

might soon return to power, the recruiting of Garibaldian volunteers, and the language of the Sinistra press which was clamoring for an immediate occupation of the papal capital, evoked grave apprehensions at the Vatican.[58] Within Rome itself there were strong pro-Prussian sympathies. All those who hoped for the completion of Italian unity favored an alliance with Prussia, which would guarantee to Italy the possession of Rome. Equally significant was the fact that a part of the sacred college, the prelates in general, the lower clergy, and the rabid ultramontanes came out openly in favor of Prussia because, they said, King William was the representative of legitimacy and the protector of Catholics.[59]

Following Vimercati's departure for Vienna, the Italian government had resolved to demand nothing less than the formal abrogation of the September convention as the *sine qua non* of an alliance. Visconti-Venosta, however, was reluctant to put forward any official proposals until the French government had been carefully sounded. Not he, therefore, but a friend of his submitted to Malaret a plan similar to the one the Italian government had already suggested to Beust. Italy was to be permitted to occupy Civita Vecchia and Viterbo as a precautionary measure against possible Garibaldian coups aimed at Rome. The pope's sovereignty was to be respected until the termination of the war, when a definitive settlement would be sought. It was urged that this plan would safeguard peace in the peninsula and enable the Italian government to have at its disposal the bulk of its forces for co-operative action with France.[60] It had the further merit of excluding Rome from the zone of occupation.[61] Visconti-Venosta himself intimated to the French minister that the Italian government was exceedingly anxious to make the proposed triple alliance the *point de départ* of negotiations for a solution of the Roman question.[62] Malaret needed little

[58] *Ibid.*, fols. 135*b*–136*a*.

[59] *Ibid.*, fols. 137*b*–138*a*.

[60] *OD*, XXIX, 182.

[61] *Ibid.*, No. 8797, pp. 258–59.

[62] *Ibid.*, pp. 182–83.

prompting. He warned Gramont that the Italian cabinet attached the greatest importance to these concessions.[63] He pointed out that even Victor Emmanuel was becoming very much preoccupied with the difficulties created by the Roman problem.[64] He reported a conversation with the king which revealed the latter's troubled state of mind. Malaret had asked him whether the proposed triple alliance "might be seriously compromised if the emperor should refuse to assume any new engagement in the Roman affair." Victor Emmanuel had replied that he hoped not and that he "wished to go the limit." But he had alluded to the danger of revolution and civil war in Italy and insisted that it would be advantageous to both countries to have certain points in the papal territory occupied by Italian troops should the Holy Father require military protection.[65]

While the Italian government was thus pushing the fate of the papal state into the foreground of its conversations with France, Vimercati was making the most of his visit to Vienna. On July 24 he had a long conference with Beust. The discussion revolved about the Italian suggestion that Austria first conclude a treaty with France. The chancellor proposed instead an Austro-Italian pact of armed neutrality which would leave the way open for assistance to Napoleon III.[66] The result of their joint labors was a draft treaty which was to be submitted for approval to the Italian and French governments. Article VII of this document ran as follows: "From now on, the emperor of Austria . . . . engages to use his good offices with the emperor of the French to obtain not only the immediate evacuation of the papal states . . . . but also the execution thereof in accordance with the wishes and interests of Italy and in a manner to assure the internal peace

[63] *Ibid.*, p. 197.   [64] *Ibid.*, No. 8741, pp. 197–98.

[65] *Ibid.*, No. 8758, pp. 220–21.

[66] Oncken, *op. cit.*, III, 483–84; Wertheimer, "Zur Vorgeschichte des Krieges von 1870," *op. cit.*, p. 64; Nigra, *op. cit.*, p. 14; Sybel, *op. cit.*, VII, 399; Bourgeois and Clermont, *op. cit.*, p. 287.

of the kingdom."[67] French acceptance of this article would have paved the way for that definitive solution of the Roman question which Italy was making the price of her participation in the triple alliance.

Vienna and Florence were destined to be speedily disabused. On July 24, Metternich gave Gramont a copy of Beust's letter of July 20. The chancellor's suggestion that Italy be permitted to occupy certain points in papal territory upon the departure of the French was indignantly rejected.[68] Gramont had very unkind things to say about the "Huguenot."[69] Ollivier, the premier, wrote a strong letter to Napoleon declaring that the idea "of handing Rome over to the Italians is pitiful, impracticable." He warned that it would be impossible to muster a majority for such a program and that its adoption would precipitate a crisis in France. "With Italy," he insisted, "we have only one honorable, sure thesis, accepted by all: the Convention of September 15. If, in fighting the Prussians, we do not wish to become like them, without faith or law, we must adhere to it. No alliance is worth a breach of our honor. Honor forbids us to leave Rome except with the promise of Italy to respect the Convention of September 15."[70] The emperor, yielding to Eugénie's insistence,[71] promptly voiced his approval of this position.[72] On

[67] Cf. the text of the Austro-Italian draft treaty in Oncken, *op. cit.*, III, 488–89.

[68] Beust's position was weakened by the attitude of Metternich. The latter did not share his chief's views on the Roman question. He confessed that he could not find "in his convictions arguments to show the need of abandoning Rome to the Italians." His lack of enthusiasm in submitting Beust's proposals helped to foredoom them (cf. Salomon, *op. cit.*, pp. 260–62).

[69] Bourgeois, *op. cit.*, III, 723. Beust was a Protestant.

[70] *OD*, XXIX, No. 8745, 204–5; Ollivier, *op. cit.*, XV, 481–82.

[71] The empress suspected the existence of "a little conspiracy between the chancelleries" to dispose of the Roman question (Salomon, *op. cit.*, pp. 263–64). To her has been attributed the remark: "Better the Prussians at Paris than the Italians at Rome!" According to Ollivier, however, she did not provoke the rejection of Beust's scheme, although she was admittedly fiercely opposed to it. The initiative, he insists, came not from her but from Gramont and himself (*op. cit.*, XV, 523).

[72] "Is it possible," Napoleon asked Metternich, "that the emperor of Austria demands the abandonment of the pope?" (Salomon, *op. cit.*, p. 260; Oncken, *op. cit.*, III, No. 928, 480–81).

July 25 the French cabinet formally pronounced Beust's suggestion unacceptable.[73] Gramont immediately instructed his
diplomatic representatives at Florence and Vienna to declare
in the most emphatic terms that France would never agree to
scrap the September convention.[74] The ire of the French government was enhanced by a report that Beust had given his
blessing to an Italian occupation not only of certain strategic
points in papal territory but of Rome itself.[75] "If Count
Beust," Gramont wrote to the French ambassador at Vienna,
"believes that we will weaken under the pressure of circumstances, he knows neither our character nor our position."[76]
In vain Vimercati warned Gramont that, if Austria were discouraged from taking any initiative in a solution of the
Roman question, it would be difficult, if not impossible, to
bring about the triple alliance.[77] The French government,
Gramont retorted, was not to be cajoled or intimidated. It
was prepared to renounce the triple alliance rather than
repudiate the September convention. "The mere idea," he
wrote Malaret, "of betraying the pope in exchange for the
assistance of our allies would cover us with shame, and nothing would be more frightful for Italy and for the king than to
enter the papal territory in consequence of a bargain of this
kind."[78] France could hardly barter away her honor at Rome
while taking up arms to defend it elsewhere.[79] To subsequent
warnings of friends and well-wishers that Italy's help could
be secured only by consenting to drastic concessions in the
Roman question, Gramont turned a deaf ear.[80]

---

[73]Ollivier, *op. cit.*, XV, 482; Bourgeois and Clermont, *op. cit.*, pp.295-300;
OD, XXIX, 205 n.

[74]*OD*, XXIX, Nos. 8747, 8749, and 8750, 206-7.

[75]*Ibid.*, p. 221.   [77]*Ibid.*, No. 8783, p. 242.

[76]*Ibid.*, No. 8770, pp. 228-29.   [78]*Ibid.*, No. 8786, pp. 245-46.

[79]*Ibid.*, p. 248.

[80]Cf. Gramont's reply to the warning from General Türr, an honorary aide
de camp to Victor Emmanuel, in *ibid.*, No. 8827, pp. 293-94 and note on p. 294;
c.f also Jerome Napoleon Bonaparte, ''Les Alliances de l'Empire en 1869 et
1870,'' *Revue des deux mondes*, April 1, 1878, p. 497; Ollivier, *op. cit.*, XV,
513 n.

The tone of Gramont's communications left Beust no choice but to submit.[81] Information relayed by his minister in Florence, Kübeck, further convinced him of the hopelessness of the situation. He learned that confidential messages from Napoleon and Gramont to Nigra, the Italian minister in Paris, indicated France's inability to go beyond the terms of the September convention. Beust learned too that Visconti-Venosta had declared himself satisfied with the turn of affairs and had voiced his unwillingness to create any embarrassments for the French government.[82] The chancellor, however, could not refrain from reiterating his warning that France's obduracy would cost her dear.[83] "We ask," he wrote Metternich on July 27, "that Emperor Napoleon and his government take note of our profound conviction that without an equitable, immediate and practical solution of the Roman question, it will hardly be possible to attain the double objective . . . . of assuring the safety of the Holy See and enabling the king of Italy to make common cause with us and France."[84] And indeed the Italians made it clear to Vitzthum that France's attitude more than justified their noninterventionist course. Visconti-Venosta told the roving Austrian envoy that only concessions in the Roman question could have induced Italy to participate in the war. And now that such concessions had been declared impossible at Paris, his government preferred "to await events."[85] For the moment, there was nothing to do except give formal assent to the renewal of the September convention. On July 29 Visconti-Venosta au-

[81]OD, XXIX, Nos. 8782 and 8804, 241-42 and 267.

[82]Kubeck to Beust, July 27 ,1870, HHSA, Politisches Archiv, Fasz. XI/74, No. 1459/523, fols. 185a-185b.

[83]Cf. Salomon, op. cit., pp. 259-60.

[84]Oncken, op. cit., III, No.930, 485-86. In his memoirs Beust complains that his "good" advice to the French evoked only great indignation against the "heretic" (op. cit., II, 366).

[85]Oncken, op. cit., III, No. 939, 496-500; Sybel, op. cit., VII, 402-3; Wertheimer, "Zur Vorgeschitchte des Krieges von 1870," op. cit., p. 68.

thorized Nigra to declare that his government would faithfully adhere to the terms of that pact.[86]

While the refusal of France to abandon the September convention was closing the door to Italian participation in the triple alliance, the Sinistra, supported by the bulk of Italian public opinion,[87] was conducting a furious campaign in favor of the immediate seizure of Rome. The *Riforma*, the organ of the Sinistra chieftain, Francesco Crispi, stood well in the van of this agitation. Its thesis, which all the lesser party sheets faithfully echoed, was that the September convention signified the recognition and maintenance of the temporal power, the renunciation of Rome. France, it insisted, must withdraw unconditionally from Civita Vecchia.[88] The temper of the actionists was aggravated by the fear that the government might be misled into allying itself with France against Prussia.[89] Such an alliance, according to the *Riforma*, would be "an irremediable misfortune."[90] Bismarck sought to make the most of this fear.[91] An opportunity presented itself when a certain Angelo de Angeli of Bologna wrote him in the name of a committee which was planning the formation of an Italian legion of three thousand men for service in behalf of Prussia. Bismarck, who was ready to make funds available for the organization of such a corps,[92] sent legation-secretary

[86] *OD*, XXIX, No. 8830, 297–98.

[87] On August 1, Malaret reported that the majority of Italians regarded the obligations imposed by the September convention as "a charge without compensations" (*ibid.*, No. 8868, p. 346).

[88] *Riforma*, July 24 and 30, 1870.   [89] Paladino, *op. cit.*, p. 111.

[90] *Riforma*, July 24, 1870.

[91] As early as July 17, Malaret had warned his government that Prussia would spare no effort and expense to prejudice Italian public opinion against the French cause. Recalling the role played by Prussian agents in October, 1867, he had observed that they would now utilize the Roman question "to create in Italy a situation which might become very difficult even for our friends" (*OD*, XXIX, No. 8618, 55). As a matter of fact, Bismarck did not neglect to work on Italian public opinion. And some Italian "irredentists" were already dreaming of retaking Savoy and Nice (cf. Paul Matter, *Bismarck et son temps* [Paris, 1908], III, 119).

[92] Cf. *GW*, VI*b*, No. 1707, 421.

Fritz von Holstein to contact De Angeli and ascertain the possibility of an attack on Rome or Nice. De Angeli, however, failed to appear, and Holstein went on to Florence to see the leaders of the party of action.[93] He conferred with Crispi and General Fabrizi, another conspicuous actionist, but they could not give him the assurances he wanted. They declared that a freebooters' expedition against Rome or Nice would compromise the Sinistra in the eyes of the country.[94] They were, however, ready to engineer a revolutionary rising as soon as an Italo-French alliance should appear probable. They would, in such an eventuality, need money and arms. Francesco Cucchi, a well-known Garibaldian, was sent to discuss this matter with Bismarck.[95] The latter reiterated his readiness to aid the Sinistra radicals whenever Victor Emmanuel should take the sword against Prussia.[96] While he was bargaining with the leftists, the chancellor was careful to assure the Italian government that he would not oppose a *modus vivendi* between Florence and Rome. "We have, in previous years, advised an understanding," he explained to Brassier de St. Simon early in August, "but for a long time we have made no overtures at Rome. The proclamation of infallibility can certainly not increase our zest for such overtures."[97] The Prussian government, Visconti-Venosta was informed, had no interest in the question of the temporal power. It desired only to see the pope free in the exercise of

[93] Friedrich von Holstein, *Lebensbekenntnis* (Berlin, 1932), p. 201.

[94] *GW*, VI*b*, No. 1717, 430-31.

[95] *Ibid.*, No. 1719, p. 432 and note; Holstein, *op. cit.*, p. 88; Francesco Crispi, *Politica estera* (Milano, 1912), p. 325 n.

[96] Otto Fürst von Bismarck, *Gedanken und Erinnerungen* (Stuttgart, 1898), p. 451. Many years later, Cucchi asserted that Bismarck had agreed to sanction the occupation of the papal capital, prevent foreign intervention in behalf of the Holy Father, and facilitate international recognition of Rome as the Italian capital. This the chancellor sharply denied, whereupon Cucchi admitted that no "formal treaty" had been concluded.

[97] *GW*, VI*b*, No. 1729, 438-39.

his spiritual authority.[98] To further this strategy, Bismarck was prepared to resort to a characteristic diplomatic trick. In 1866, Napoleon III had submitted to him a draft treaty designed to guarantee the integrity of the papal territory. Bismarck now played with the idea of publishing this treaty. But though he finally decided against it, he suggested to the legation at Florence that it might allow certain Prussophils there to see the document.[99]

The authorities at Paris were in the meantime making ready to recall the garrison from Civita Vecchia. On July 27, Antonelli was officially informed by Banneville, the French ambassador to the Vatican, that the occupation corps would depart on August 5.[100] The cardinal was unable to conceal his consternation. He had hoped, he said, that France, without undue sacrifice of her military strength, would continue to protect the pope. The latter, in the light of past experience, could place no credence in Italy's promises. In the circumstances, the Holy See would employ the inadequate resources at its disposal to provide for its own defense.[101] Banneville, who was without information as to the pledges exacted from Italy by his government, replied that he understood perfectly the cardinal's distrust. He was sure, however, that his superiors on this occasion had demanded guarantees which would suffice to prevent a recurrence of the events of 1867. Moreover, he added, the Italian government was in circumstances more normal than those which had prevailed then. Consequently, it would now be able to fulfil its obligations.[102] Antonelli, though unconvinced, was well aware of the futility

[98] Malaret to Gramont, August 14, 1870, Archives du Ministère des Affaires étrangères (Italie, août-décembre, 1870), Tome 379, fol. 104 (hereafter cited as AMAE).

[99] GW, VIb, 439 n.

[100] OD, XXIX, No. 8790, 252; Blue Book, No. 3, p. 1; Michele Rosi, Vittorio Emanuele II (Bologna, 1930), II, 151.

[101] Ollivier, op. cit., XV, 501.

[102] Palomba to Beust, July 30, 1870, HHSA, Politisches Korrespondenz (Rom), Fasz. XI/224, Bericht 87A, fols. 147a–147b.

of diplomatic overtures. Nevertheless, he instructed the nuncio at Paris to attempt to elicit from Napoleon a promise to keep the French garrison in Rome.[103] The Vatican's reaction disturbed the imperial government, and, in a long dispatch to Banneville, Gramont reviewed the considerations which had prompted the emperor's decision. He contended that the fulfilment by France of the terms of the September convention and the resultant good relations with Italy offered the Holy See its one chance of salvation in the current European crisis. He wrote:

> We are engaged in a formidable war, and to be able to count on the preservation of tranquillity on the Roman frontiers, we must win the goodwill of the Italian cabinet. . . . . The material guarantees which the occupation of its territory by a French brigade gives the Holy See are inadequate if we are in disagreement with the government of Victor Emmanuel. It is therefore necessary, for the duration of the war, to replace them with political guarantees, and these can be secured only by reviving the stipulations by which Italy is bound to us. In a word, occupation becomes ineffective and harmful, evacuation opportune and really advantageous to the papal states.[104]

In communicating these observations to Antonelli, Banneville remarked that the status of the Holy See could be definitively fixed only by a congress of the powers at the close of the war. He added that, should France emerge victorious, she would exert her great influence at this congress in behalf of the papacy. The wily cardinal was but little impressed. He again alluded to the Vatican's lack of faith in the guarantees proffered by the Italian government. He pointed out that the Florentine authorities would be unable for long to resist the pressure of the actionists.[105] He readily admitted,

---

[103] *Ibid.*, fols. 148a–148b.

[104] *OD*, XXIX, No. 8848, 316–20. In his *La France et la Prusse avant la guerre* (Paris, 1872), p. 349, Gramont explains that the recall of the garrison was "a very great sacrifice" dictated by imperative considerations. "The occupation corps," he writes, "was a moral rather than a material force. It possessed value only in so far as it represented the advance-guard of the French army. Now, it lost this significance from the moment that the entire French army found itself engaged elsewhere."

[105] Palomba to Beust, August 6, 1870, HHSA, Politisches Korrespondenz (Rom), Fasz. XI/224, Bericht 89B, fols. 173b–174b.

however, that the defeat of France would be followed by
chaos and the complete dispossession of the papacy.[106]

Notified that everything was in readiness for the resuscitation of the September convention, Visconti-Venosta assumed
the thankless role of breaking the news to the country. The
Italian government, he declared in the chamber on July 31,
had no choice but to take note of France's desire to renew the
treaty of 1864 and indicate its willingness to accept the concomitant obligations.[107] This evoked the loud displeasure of
the Sinistra. One of its spokesmen, La Porta, charged that
the government was undertaking to protect the pope in order
that Italian guns might be substituted for *chassepots* in dealing out death to Italians. He accused the cabinet of con-
templating an alliance with France against Prussia. This
policy, he warned, would provoke revolution. He intimated
that the Second Empire's reoccupation of Rome entitled
Italy to reject the renewal of the burdensome convention.[108]
Lanza intervened in the debate to emphasize that neither the
ministry nor parliament would ever make difficulties for
France while she was involved in war. They were inflexibly
resolved to accomplish the national program, but under no
circumstances would they permit private initiative to be substituted for theirs.[109] The Sinistra emerged from this encounter more than ever convinced that the foreign policy of
Italy was not safe in the hands of a Destra government. It
proceeded to make much of the widespread belief that an
alliance with France had been secretly concluded.[110] The cabinet contented itself with solemn reiterations of its position.
Thus, on August 3, Visconti-Venosta told the senate that he
and his colleagues felt it expedient to acquiesce in the revival
of the September convention. They rejected violence as
wholly inapposite for the solution of this purely moral question. Accordingly, they would not allow the direction of na-

---

[106] *Archives diplomatiques, 1874* (Paris, n.d.), II, 9 (hereafter cited as *AD, 1874*).

[107] *Atti*, CLIX (July 31, 1870), 3925.   [109] *Ibid.*, pp. 3926 and 3929.

[108] *Ibid.*, pp. 3925–26.   [110] Cf. *Riforma*, August 6, 1870.

tional affairs to slip out of their hands.[111] The premier again
followed with a spirited affirmation of the cabinet's resolve to
observe the utmost respect for legality.[112]

The leading organ of the Destra, the *Opinione*, vigorously
defended the official thesis. The departure of the French garrison, it urged, would serve to avert further conflicts. It reminded its readers that the reoccupation of Civita Vecchia by
the minions of Napoleon III was clearly illegal. It was this
fact and not the aid afforded by the occupation corps or the
desire to acquire Italy's sympathy that moved France to
order the evacuation of the papal port. It was equally indis-
putable that account would have to be taken of the moral
interests of the powers, and notably France, at Rome if
foreign intervention was to be forestalled. There could be no
gainsaying the necessity of reassuring the Catholic world
that the papacy, in this altered situation, would be able to
preserve its independence and freedom. Germane always to
the present issue, the journal concluded, was the attitude of
Cavour, who had decried the use of violence in dealing with
the Roman question.[113] This was all very well, retorted the
Riforma, but it was quite another matter to agree to the
resuscitation of the September convention as a condition of
the recall of the French garrison. A more resolute government, it contended, would have taken cognizance only of the
projected evacuation and would have ignored completely the
pact of 1864. Instead, the Lanza cabinet had indicated that
it regarded that pact as still in existence. This unquestionably was a serious error.[114]

The renewal of the September convention was officially
consummated with an exchange of notes between Paris and
Florence. Gramont's communiqué reminded Italy that she
"obliged herself not to attack, and if necessary to defend
against aggression, the papal territory."[115] In his reply, Vis-

[111] *Atti*, CLX (August 3, 1870), 998.   [113] *Opinione*, August 1 and 2, 1870.

[112] *Ibid.*, p. 1001.   [114] *Riforma*, August 7, 1870.

[115] *OD*, XXIX, No. 8884, 362–63; *AD, 1874*, II, 6–7.

conti-Venosta reaffirmed his government's determination to abide by the terms of the convention.[116] The evacuation, as promised, occurred on August 5.[117] Antonelli promptly prepared to meet the danger of invasion[118] with an army that was far below the requisite strength.[119] France, however, was not disposed to leave the Holy Father altogether defenseless. At the request of Banneville, the imperial government sent the man-of-war "Orénoque" to Civita Vecchia to assist the pope if necessary and to transport him elsewhere should he feel obliged to leave Rome.[120] "However grave the events which absorb our attention," Gramont's successor, Prince de la Tour d'Auvergne, assured Banneville on August 23, "we do not lose sight of the difficult situation of the pontifical government."[121] This gesture did not pass unchallenged. Certain moderate elements in France decried the dispatch of the "Orénoque" as a violation of the September convention. They insisted that the interests of the country should be given precedence over those of the Holy Father. The clericals made short shrift of these objections. The government's critics were unaware, they retorted, that "to protect the pope was to halt Prussia." And they failed to realize too that, if Pius should be compelled to leave Rome, the disasters of the

[116] OD, XXIX, No. 8900, 385-86; AD, 1874, II, 8.

[117] Cf. Palomba to Beust, August 6, 1870, HHSA, Politisches Korrespondenz (Rom), Fasz. XI/224, fol. 171a.

[118] Cf. Raffaele de Cesare, Roma e lo stato del papa dal ritorno di Pio IX al XX settembre (Roma, 1907), II, 433.

[119] Cf. the appraisal of the British minister at Rome in Blue Book, No. 4, p. 2, and that of the Austrian chargé d'affaires in HHSA, Politisches Korrespondenz (Rom), Fasz. XI/224, fols. 152a–155a.

[120] Cf. Palomba to Beust, September 3, 1870, HHSA, Politisches Korrespondenz (Rom), Fasz. XI/224, Bericht 97, fols. 258b–259a; De Cesare, op. cit., II, 432; Paladino, op. cit., p. 116; Saverio Cilibrizzi, Storia parlamentare politica e diplomatica d'Italia (Milano, 1925), I, 575 n. The vessel arrived at Civita Vecchia late in August (cf. the Univers of September 2, 1870).

[121] AMAE (Rome, juin-septembre, 1870), Tome 1047, fol. 208.

war would become infinitely greater.[122] In the meantime, the British cabinet, fearful lest the withdrawal of the French corps be followed by disturbances which might jeopardize the safety of its subjects and force the pope to flee, had decided to emulate the imperial government. On August 21, Granville, the British foreign secretary, wrote his minister in Rome:

> It is not improbable that . . . . His Holiness may turn his thoughts towards a temporary refuge in some possession of the British Crown, and that a communication may be made to you on his part, in order to ascertain whether he would be likely there to obtain it. I need scarcely say that Her Majesty's Government have no desire for such a result, and would not wish spontaneously to offer to receive the Pope in any place of Her Majesty's dominions; but, at the same time, Her Majesty's Government would certainly not refuse, if requested by the Pope, to afford His Holiness an immediate asylum on board one of her Her Majesty's ships of war, and having ascertained his wishes as to the place he would desire to proceed to, they would consider how far those wishes, if they pointed to his temporary residence in any place within Her Majesty's dominions, could properly be complied with. In order to provide for such an emergency a powerful ship of war has been ordered to proceed at once to Civita Vecchia, with the primary object of affording protection and a place of refuge for any subjects of Her Majesty who may seek to escape the dangers which any popular outbreak may threaten them with. But this ship will also be available as a place of refuge for the Pope if he should be compelled to seek one; and on board of it His Holiness would be in safety, and might securely await the reply of Her Majesty's Government to the expression conveyed to them through you of his wishes in regard to his future movements.[123]

The Beust-Vimercati treaty of armed neutrality evoked little enthusiasm at Florence and none at all at the French headquarters in Metz. Napoleon, at the behest of the empress, demanded the suppression of Article VII.[124] On August 3 he wrote Eugénie that despite the pleas of his cousin, Prince Jerome, he would not yield on Rome.[125] Vitzthum, who had

[122] Cf. *Univers*, August 30, 1870.

[123] *Blue Book*, No. 9, pp. 4–5.

[124] *OD*, XXIX, No. 8893, 381; Nigra, *op. cit.*, pp. 15–16; Bourgeois and Clermont, *op. cit.*, pp. 325 and 329.

[125] Bourgeois, *op. cit.*, III, 726.

come to Florence to secure Italy's acceptance of the treaty, was presented on August 6 with a counterdraft. Article IV of this document marked the beginning of the diplomatic offensive which was to clear the way for the Italian occupation of the papal capital. It pledged the Austrian emperor to support the principle that foreign powers were not to intervene in Roman territory. It further obligated him to advocate the application there of measures "most in accord with the wishes and interests of the Romans and Italy."[126] Visconti-Venosta explained that his government had accepted the September convention as a *pis aller*. It was the only way of getting rid of the French garrison and preventing another Mentana. Italy, he continued, was determined to adhere to old alignments, and she sympathized with France in the present conflict. But the country would refuse to take up arms without good reason. Vitzthum was inclined to believe that the defeat of the French at Wissembourg two days earlier had stiffened the Italians' attitude. He thought he discerned a fear to incur obligations on the eve of another battle which might well prove decisive.[127] Malaret, who had been informed of the conversations, urged his government to accept the Italian version. "In my opinion," he wrote Gramont, "the only effective part of this plan would be to assure Italy the moral support of Austria in the Roman question. We do not have the right to prevent these two powers from holding the same view on this point or on any other."[128] The minister's advice was not kindly received by his superiors.[129] But the sudden eclipse of French arms dealt a lethal blow to these negotiations.

[126] *OD*, XXIX, 487; Nigra, *op. cit.*, p. 16.

[127] *OD*, XXIX, 483–86; Oncken, *op. cit.*, III, No. 950, 514.

[128] *OD*, XXIX, No. 8932, 243.

[129] Ollivier writes: "This clause [Article IV of the Italian counterdraft] was even more contrary to the will of the emperor than article VII" (*op. cit.*, XV, 519).

News of the decisive Prussian victory at Wörth on August 6 reached Florence early the following day. The first feeling of astonishment[130] quickly gave way to the conviction that the French cause was now hopeless.[131] The Sinistra triumphantly renewed its demand for neutrality.[132] Even the most ardent Francophils were converted to the necessity of nonintervention.[133] Victor Emmanuel himself was little inclined to dispute the issue any further.[134] "We have happily escaped," he told Vitzthum. "We knew since 1859 that the French had no generals. But this flight from Wörth is incomprehensible. Militarily, there is nothing we can do. I will see whether I can help poor Napoleon diplomatically."[135] The Austrian envoy was informed that the conversations with Vienna were to be indefinitely suspended, and Beust was requested to disregard the Italian counterdraft.[136] An urgent appeal from Paris to join the war without Austria[137] met with a definite refusal.[138] The Italian government made its position doubly clear by joining a league of neutrals organized under British auspices.[139] This step was vigorously ap-

[130] The great majority of Italians had assumed that the French would win the war (cf. Vittorio Bersezio, *Il Regno di Vittorio Emanuele II: trent'anni di vita italiana* [Torino, 1878–95], VIII, 361; Pesci, *op. cit.*, p. 221). In Austria, too, the victors of Magenta and Solferino had been considered invincible (cf. Schweinitz, *op. cit.*, I, 268).

[131] Cf. Rosi, *op. cit.*, II, 151–52.

[132] Cf. the *Riforma*, August 9, 1870.

[133] Cf. Arcari, *op. cit.*, pp. 129–30.

[134] Luzzatti, *op. cit.*, I, 307.

[135] Sybel, *op. cit.*, VII, 404.   [136] Oncken, *op. cit.*, III, No. 954, 519.

[137] OD, XXIX, Nos. 8931 and 8936, 422 and 426; Nigra, *op. cit.*, p. 19 and notes on pp. 19–20; Bourgeois and Clermont, *op. cit.*, pp. 331–32.

[138] OD, XXIX, No. 8953, 437–38. Malaret refused, however, to admit defeat. The intentions of the Italian cabinet, he wrote Gramont on August 12, were "not at all such as to discourage our hopes" (AMAE [Italie, août-décembre, 1870], Tome 379, fol. 96).

[139] Cf. Guiccioli, *op. cit.*, I, 287–88; Nigra, *op. cit.*, p. 20 and note; Gallavresi, *op. cit.*, p. 117; cf. also Visconti-Venosta's defense of Italian participation in the league of neutrals in Ollivier, *op. cit.*, XVI, 532–34. For additional information on the

plauded by Italian public opinion. No qualms were felt about leaving France to face unaided the irresistible military might of Prussia.[140]

---

league itself see Dora N. Raymond, *British Policy and Opinion during the Franco-Prussian War* (New York, 1921), p. 124; A. W. Ward and G. P. Gooch, *The Cambridge History of the British Foreign Policy, 1783–1919* (New York, 1923), III, 41-42; Kurt Rheindorf, *England und der deutsch-französische Krieg, 1870–1871* (Bonn and Leipzig, 1923); Horst Michael, *Bismarck, England und Europa* (München, 1930), p. 306; Paul Knaplund, *Gladstone's Foreign Policy* (New York and London, 1935), p. 50.

[140] Ollivier himself, who went to Italy immediately after the fall of his ministry, quickly discovered the hopelessness of imploring assistance from the government of Florence (*op. cit.*, XVI, 538).

CHAPTER II
THE OCCUPATION OF ROME

THE situation created by the French military disasters was one which admitted of no dilatory tactics. Of this the government at Florence was well aware. A special session of parliament was announced for August 16, and the ministerial experts promptly busied themselves with the preparation of measures demanded by the unexpected turn of affairs. Precautions were taken to prevent irresponsible revolutionary bands from precipitating a crisis. Mazzini was unceremoniously clapped into the prison-fortress of Gaeta, while the other *enfant terrible*, Garibaldi, was kept under strict surveillance at Caprera.[1] The *Opinione* warned the Sinistra extremists to cease agitating for immediate action. It counseled prudence in order that episodes like that of Mentana might be averted.[2] But under the mounting pressure of public opinion, which hailed the French reverses as the signal for a descent on Rome,[3] the ministry was compelled to envisage expedients which only a few weeks before it had dismissed as premature. Victor Emmanuel himself was disinclined to temporize. He told Vitzthum, who was about to return to Vienna, that he might be compelled to take account of Italy's national aspirations in the Roman question, even if a republican France should attempt to prevent him from occupying the papal capital.[4] At a sign from him, sixty thou-

---

[1] Enrico Tavallini, *La Vita e i tempi di Giovanni Lanza* (Torino and Napoli, 1887), II, 4–9; Stefano Castagnola, *Da Firenze a Roma: diario storico-politico del 1870–71* (Torino, 1896), p. 15.

[2] *Opinione*, August 8, 1870.

[3] Cf. J. B. Bury, *History of the Papacy, 1864–1878* (London, 1930), pp. 147–48.

[4] *OD*, XXIX, 496; Eduard von Wertheimer, "Zur Vorgeschichte des Krieges von 1870," *Deutsche Rundschau*, January, 1921, p. 70.

sand men were ready to cross the Roman frontier, and it was
obvious that so formidable a force had not been mobilized
solely for the purpose of dealing with Garibaldian incursions.[5]
But Lanza and his colleagues were anxious to proceed carefully, preferring to strike only when the terrain seemed absolutely clear. At the same time they were ready to exploit
the general unrest to convince foreign powers that it might
become necessary to march troops into Roman territory in
order to maintain tranquillity and afford the pope adequate
protection.[6] According to Visconti-Venosta, Italian policy in
the Roman question had undergone no change. The rumors
of an immediate entry of Italian troops into papal territory
were, he said, without foundation. The mobilization of three
divisions along the papal frontier was designed only to prevent raids by armed bands and to repress revolutionary
movements in that troubled area.[7] The niceties of this waiting policy were summarily dismissed as absurd and criminal
by the leftist opposition. The *Riforma* contended that the
immediate occupation of Rome, executed in the name of
"unitary right" and "internal order," could not be considered
inconsistent with the policy of neutrality. And there was apparently nothing to fear, it added, from the victorious Prussians. The latter could have no objection to an Italian occupation of the papal capital. On the contrary, they had every
reason to desire the triumph of the unitary principle in
Italy.[8]

At the opening session of the chamber of deputies, Lanza
demanded an appropriation of forty million lire to enable the
government to call two more classes to the colors.[9] In the

[5] G. Gadda, "Roma capitale ed il Ministero Lanza-Sella," *Nuova antologia*, September 16, 1897, p. 204.

[6] Michele Rosi, *Vittorio Emanuele II* (Bologna, 1930), II, 152.

[7] Kübeck to Beust, August 17, 1870, HHSA, Politisches Archiv, Fasz. XI/74,
No. 65, fols. 359*b*–360*a*.

[8] *Riforma*, August 19 and 20, 1870.

[9] *Atti*, CLIX (August 16, 1870), 3979–80.

course of the general debate which began on August 19, Pasquale Stanislao Mancini, an internationally famous jurist and one of the foremost Sinistra spokesmen, denounced the renewal of the September convention in language of extraordinary virulence. He declared that the government of Napoleon III read into that pact "the renunciation of Rome by Italy, the implicit abrogation of the Italian parliament's memorable vote of March 27, 1861, the perpetual mutilation of Italian unity, the indefinite maintenance of the temporal sovereignty of the pope, the right of France to intervene whenever that sovereignty should be in danger." So interpreted, he contended, the convention had lost all validity and was nothing short of a "monstrous aberration, a political suicide." He urged that Italy's salvation lay in a prompt disavowal of the obnoxious agreement. The opportunity offered by the existing situation in Europe, he warned, should not be allowed to go unutilized. Italy's national interests demanded a drastic solution of the Roman question, and only *faits accomplis* could expect to receive the sanction of the powers assembled in peace conference at the close of the war. He concluded by addressing the following questions to the government:

Do you wish to go to Rome, proclaimed the capital of Italy, yes or no? Do you wish to complete by some legitimate means . . . . the national unity, yet respecting and protecting the absolute independence of the pope's spiritual power, and offering to Catholic Europe all the guarantees which could be demanded and desired by the interests of Catholicism? If you reply yes . . . . I will ask you, when do you propose to go to Rome, and by what means?[10]

Mancini's stirring address elicited a vigorous rejoinder from Visconti-Venosta. The course suggested by the Sinistra, the foreign minister insisted, was devoid of both foresight and generosity. The government had no intention of exploiting France's difficulties to repudiate obligations which it had solemnly assumed. However, should unforeseen eventualities arise, the provisions of the September convention would not

[10] *Ibid.*, August 19, 1870, pp. 4004-19.

operate to restrict its freedom of action. The country could rest assured that national interests would be fully safeguarded and that the independence of the pope would be effectively guaranteed. But Italy had nothing to gain from an isolated action based upon force. Rather, she had to do what she could to win the sympathy and confidence of Europe.[11] On the following day, Lanza eloquently defended the policy set forth by his foreign minister. He enlarged upon the insuperable difficulties which the violent dispossession of the pope would create. The proposal to effect an immediate and forcible occupation of the papal territory was, he bluntly declared, entirely unacceptable. He sought to placate the government's critics by reminding them that the September convention was subject to changing conditions and circumstances and that therefore it could hardly be regarded as a permanent factor in the situation. However, any modification of its terms would have to take place in the proper diplomatic way. The cabinet was fully alive to the necessity of solving the Roman question, but it was likewise convinced that any solution which disregarded existing treaties would prove unsatisfactory.[12] A vote was taken, and the Destra majority adopted an order of the day indorsing the government's Roman policy.

Not at all disheartened, the opposition prepared to carry its case to the country. The Italian parliament, trumpeted the *Riforma*, had abandoned Rome. It reiterated Mancini's warning that only a *fait accompli*, which found Italy at Rome by virtue of her own rights and not as the pope's guardian, would receive the sanction of a congress of the powers.[13] A

---

[11] *Ibid.*, pp. 4023–29. These views were echoed by the *Opinione*. The Roman question, it contended on August 19, was a political rather than a military one. The papal government was recognized by all the powers, Italy included. Therefore, the occupation of Rome could not occur except as a consequence of acts of war which would not receive popular approval. The attitude of the other powers had to be kept in mind. And it would not do to break with France or take advantage of her present predicament.

[12] *Atti*, CLIX (August 20, 1870), 4086–88

[13] *Riforma*, August 22, 1870.

committee consisting of the party's leading members unanimously adopted a resolution calling for the resignation en masse of the Sinistra deputies as a protest against the inaction of the cabinet. However, in response to a personal appeal from Sella, who alone among the ministers enjoyed its confidence, the committee relented. It was impressed above all by Sella's pledge that he would resign if his colleagues should persist in their refusal to go to Rome without delay.[14] Nevertheless, it intensified its agitation in the hope of forcing the hand of the government. "Only at Rome," maintained the *Riforma*, "can there be the complete affirmation of our right; from Rome alone can Italy say to Europe: I am and wish to be a sovereign nation . . . . ; only at Rome can Italy close the era of foreign domination." It never wearied of repeating that "the interests of order—of true, legitimate juridical order—call the government without further delay to Rome."[15] It charged that the army which had been sent to the papal frontier was detailed to defend the Holy See. "This," it proclaimed, "is a challenge, a provocation to civil war."[16] But the moderates of the Destra, paying scant heed to these admonitions and accusations, continued to temporize.[17]

The Lanza cabinet's emphatic repudiation of violence did not lessen the fears of the Vatican, where Prussian aid against Italy was impatiently awaited.[18] Antonelli admitted

[14] Jessie White Mario, *Agostino Bertani e i suoi tempi* (Firenze, 1888), II, 353–54; Francesco Crispi, *Politica interna* (Milano, 1924), p. 66; Alessandro Guiccioli, *Quintino Sella* (Rovigo, 1887), I, 297–98; Saverio Cilibrizzi, *Storia parlamentare politica e diplomatica d'Italia* (Milano, 1925), I, 582; Giuseppe Paladino, *Storia d'Italia dal 1861 al 1871 con particolare riguardo alla questione romana* (Milano, 1932), p. 118.

[15] *Riforma*, August 24 and 26, 1870.   [16] *Ibid.*, August 27, 1870.

[17] Cf. M. Albertone, "Ricordi dell'impresa di Roma nel 1870," *Nuova antologia*, September 16, 1920, p. 20.

[18] No sooner had the French garrison been recalled from Civita Vecchia than a strongly pro-Prussian party made its appearance at the Vatican (cf. Ernesto Vercesi, *Pio IX* [Milano, 1930], p. 229). Early in August, Rome was host to a rumor that Prussia had interceded at Florence in the pope's behalf. A prompt *démenti* by Vis-

to the British minister that he was quite satisfied with the conduct and public utterances of the Italian government. But the future was fraught with grim uncertainties. He pointed out that the fall of the Second Empire and the proclamation of a republic in France could not fail to react materially upon both Italy and Rome. While the present rulers of the country were perhaps sincere in disavowing the use of force, their successors might be otherwise-minded. In any case, an invasion of Roman territory would be resisted by the papal forces.[19] The Holy See was aware, remarked the *Osservatore romano*, the Vatican's influential daily, that back of the Italian government was the revolution which at any moment might overthrow it. "Rome," it continued, "awaits tranquilly the hour of justice," confident that the might of right would ultimately triumph.[20] The prospect of an Italian incursion made the pope's immediate plans the focal point of a lively debate. Some of Pius' most intimate counselors urged him to flee. But Antonelli was vigorously opposed to such a course, and in this he was supported by the great majority of the sacred college.[21]

On August 21, at the very crescendo of the controversy over the when and how of solving the Roman question, Prince Jerome Napoleon arrived in Florence.[22] He came as the emissary of the French emperor to demand Italian military assistance against Prussia—he refused to discuss diplomatic in-

---

conti-Venosta followed. The Roman clericals were extremely hopeful of securing King William's protection (cf. Palomba to Beust, August 13, 1870, HHSA, Politisches Korrespondenz [Rom], Fasz. XI/224, Bericht 91B, fols. 195a–196a). On August 16, Jervoise, the British minister in Rome, reported: "It is remarkable to hear how confidently support is expected to come to the Papacy from the Protestant Powers, whose Catholic populations are supposed to be sufficiently powerful to exact for it from their governments more or less active protection against its enemies" (*Blue Book*, No. 7, p. 3).

[19] *Blue Book*, No. 16, p. 9.   [20] *Osservatore romano*, August 22, 1870.

[21] Palomba to Beust, August 27, 1870, HHSA, Politisches Korrespondenz (Rom), Fasz. XI/224, Bericht 96A, fols. 232b–233b.

[22] Cf. Malaret to Foreign Office, August 21, 1870, AMAE (Italie, août-décembre, 1870), Tome 379, fol. 141.

tervention—and to assure the king and his ministers that they were free to dispose as they pleased of the Eternal City.[23] As one writer puts it, he was there "to exchange the temporal power of the popes for Italian aid in France."[24] He designated Munich as the "natural objective" of the Italian army, once the latter had been thrown into the fray.[25] He quickly discovered that his task was indeed a herculean one. The very day of his arrival, he reported to the emperor that Italy would take no military action without Austria.[26] Two days later, he wrote that the ministers were ill-disposed and that an answer was being awaited from Vienna. He declared, however, that he had not yet abandoned hope of inducing Italy to intervene.[27] The Italian government, obviously sparring for time, appointed Minghetti to the legation at Vienna[28] with instructions to sound out Beust.[29] The former premier was also to forestall difficulties on the part of Austria should it be decided to occupy Rome.[30] Victor Emmanuel, even at this late date, professed the hope that Austria would join France if Italy did. Hence, he insisted that a decision be withheld until the intentions of the Viennese cabinet had

[23] Jérôme Napoléon Bonaparte, "Les Alliances de l'Empire en 1869 et 1870," *Revue des deux mondes,* April 1, 1878, p. 499; Malaret to Foreign Office, August 27, 1870, AMAE (Italie, août-décembre, 1870), Tome 379, fol. 171; M. Mazziotti, *Napoleone III e l'Italia* (Milano, 1925), p. 297; E. Bourgeois and E. Clermont, *Rome et Napoléon III, 1849-1870* (Paris, 1907), p. 333; Castagnola, *op. cit.,* pp. 3, 9-10, and notes on pp. 10 and 17-20.

[24] Paul Matter, *Bismarck et son temps* (Paris, 1908), III, 118.

[25] Malaret to De la Tour d'Auvergne, August 23, 1870, AMAE (Italie, août-décembre, 1870), Tome 379, fols. 148-50.

[26] "Correspondance inédite de Napoléon III et du Prince Napoléon," *Revue des deux mondes,* March 15, 1924, p. 337.

[27] *Ibid.,* pp. 337-38.

[28] This post had been vacant since March, 1870 (cf. *Carteggio tra Marco Minghetti e Giuseppe Pasolini* [Torino, 1930], IV, 193 n.; Augusto Sandonà, *L'Irredentismo nelle lotte politiche e nelle contese diplomatiche italo-austriache* [Bologna, 1932], I, 67).

[29] Giuseppe Gallavresi, *Italia e Austria, 1859-1914* (Milano, 1899), p. 117.

[30] Cf. Giovanni Maioli, *Marco Minghetti* (Bologna, 1926), p. 215.

been ascertained.[31] Beust's reply, as the Italian cabinet fore-saw, was unfavorable to military action.[32] The prince was thereupon informed that Italy could be of service to France by co-operating diplomatically with other powers, but that a military alliance was out of the question.[33] On August 27 he reported that Italian intervention was unlikely before the arrival of fresh news from the theater of war and inquired whether he should remain in Florence. The emperor, how-ever, advised him to continue the negotiations.[34] The Sinis-tra, which had viewed the prince's arrival with undisguised alarm, was impatient to see him go. The *Riforma* maliciously observed:

> We are assured that Prince Napoleon, mindful of the singular situation which his presence in Florence . . . . creates for the government of the king, has decided to depart. A most laudable decision, and one which the government of the king, without failing in its duties of hospitality, can only highly approve.[35]

Unruffled by the clamor of the actionists, Lanza and Vis-conti-Venosta were not yet ready to concede that the use of violence was ineluctable. They clung to the hope that the papacy might be induced to come to an understanding which would make possible a peaceable occupation of Rome. They were encouraged by the formation among the cardinals of a party favorable to such an understanding. Heartening, too, was the possibility of a spontaneous rising of the Roman population.[36] Should the pontiff be overthrown by his own

[31] Tavallini, *op. cit.*, II, 31, 34; Vittorio Bersezio, *Il Regno di Vittorio Emanuele II: trent'anni di vita italiana* (Torino, 1878–95), VIII, 366.

[32] Cf. "Correspondance inédite de Napoléon III et du Prince Napoléon," *op. cit.*, p. 338.

[33] Castagnola, *op. cit.*, p. 21; C. Nigra, "Ricordi diplomatici, 1870," *Nuova antologia*, March 1, 1895, p. 22.

[34] "Correspondance inédite de Napoléon III et du Prince Napoléon," *op. cit.*, pp. 338–39.

[35] *Riforma*, August 28, 1870; cf. also Crispi, *Politica interna*, p. 67.

[36] This possibility, however, failed to materialize. The memory of previous repressions, the activity of the local police, disagreement between the various parties, and the devotion of many citizens to the pope, accounted for this (Carlo Tivaroni, *L'Italia degli italiani* [Torino, 1897], III, 126–27).

subjects and the union of the city with Italy proclaimed, the hands of the government would be clean and an indignant Catholic world would have to look elsewhere for a scapegoat. A false step at this critical moment would have played into the hands of the Jesuits, who were reputed to be urging Pius to abandon Rome. Moreover, decisive developments at the theater of war and in Paris, which was seething with revolutionary discontent, were hourly awaited, and it seemed rash to precipitate matters while these were impending.

But the situation in Italy was threatening to get out of hand. The party of action prated freely of appealing to the sovereign will of the people, while expatriates from the papal domain proclaimed their readiness to embark upon any expedition, however perilous. The Sinistra press was unwearied in censuring the government's military measures, charging that their sole purpose was to sustain the faltering temporal power. The cabinet, though determined as before to adhere to its international obligations, was now ready to concede that its hand might be forced. The same prudence which dictated a policy of watchful waiting seemed also to recommend the issuance of a warning to the various powers that the *status quo* could not continue indefinitely. On August 29, Visconti-Venosta wrote Nigra:

Let France have no illusions; the situation of Italy is grave. The attitude of the papal government, the preparations of the party of disorder, the danger which the more than hazardous conditions in the Roman territory might create for us, from one moment to the next, in the present state of Europe, are of a nature to arouse the preoccupations of all those who bring a disinterested solicitude to the affairs of Rome.[37]

In another dispatch of the same date addressed to the diplomatic representatives of Italy abroad, Visconti-Venosta contended that the September convention was not a solution of the Roman question. It was, he claimed, only a transitional arrangement designed to facilitate a definitive settlement. He accused the Vatican of conspiring to restore, with the aid

[37] *Documenti diplomatici relativi alla questione romana* (Firenze, 1870), No. 1, pp. 7–9 (hereafter cited as *Libro verde*).

of foreign armies, the old order of things in the peninsula. The consequences of all this were such that Italy had no choice but to contemplate a breaking of the vicious circle. "It is the force of circumstances," he urged, "which with every new phase of European affairs makes it more imperatively necessary to resolve the Roman problem. We believe that it is wise and prudent to put aside the transitory considerations which until now have delayed a solution and to approach practically . . . . a question which affects the destinies of a nation and the greatness of Catholicism."[38]

This practical approach was set forth in the famous memorandum, likewise dated August 29, which the Italian foreign minister addressed to the governments of Europe. The purpose of this document was to show that, even in the event of an Italian occupation of Rome, the independence of the pope would be secure.[39] In it were listed the terms of an Italo-papal understanding based upon the surrender by the Holy See of its temporal power and generally in harmony with projects worked out under Cavour and Ricasoli. The pope was to retain the attributes of sovereignty and enjoy precedence over the king of Italy and other princes. The district of Rome known as the Leonine City was to remain subject to his authority.[40] The cabinet pledged itself to guarantee his freedom of communication with the governments, clergy, and faithful of other countries. His representatives at foreign courts and the ministers of foreign countries at the Vatican were promised diplomatic immunity. The Italian government further undertook to preserve all ecclesiastical "institu-

---

[38] *Libro verde*, No. 2, pp. 9–12.   [39] Castagnola, *op. cit.*, p. 22.

[40] The Leonine City was bounded on the south by the bastions of S. Spirito. It comprised the Vatican and the castle of S. Angelo with their annexes and dependencies. Also included in the Leonine City were the Borgo and the greater part of the Trastevere. It enjoyed a fairly extensive frontage on the right or west bank of the Tiber. The government was much criticized for offering the pontiff the Leonine City, though even Sella, the most antipapal member of the cabinet, interposed no objections. But this concession was made contingent upon acquiescence by the Vatican in a reconciliation with Italy (Guiccioli, *op. cit.*, I, 304; Castagnola, *op. cit.*, p. 27 and note).

tions, offices and bodies" at Rome, though specifically denying them civil or criminal jurisdiction. The property of religious corporations in the city was to remain intact and exempt from special taxation. There was to be no governmental interference with either the discipline of ecclesiastical
bodies or the exercise by the clergy of its spiritual functions.
The right of royal patronage over church benefices, both
major and minor, was to be renounced by the king. The
Holy See was to receive from Italy an annual civil list not
inferior in amount to the sums then being allocated for the
purpose in the papal budget. These terms, the memorandum
concluded, "would be considered a bilateral public contract
and would form the object of an agreement with those powers
that have Catholic subjects."[41] In thus inviting the sanction of the Catholic states, the Lanza cabinet was departing
from the position taken by Cavour, who had emphatically
rejected any international guarantee.[42] But moderate opinion in the country was quite prepared to accept such a settlement. Ruggiero Bonghi, the leading journalist of the Destra
and an exceptionally lucid thinker who was destined to take a
prominent part in the parliamentary debates on the ecclesiastical problem,[43] expressed the feeling of his party when he
wrote in the *Nuova antologia*[44] that the Roman question possessed an international character which excluded a unilateral
solution. The concurrence of the Holy Father and of the interested powers, he contended, was requisite. The Sinistra,
at this juncture, likewise declared itself favorable to an international guarantee of the pope's spiritual authority. Indeed,
according to the *Riforma*, an international pact sanctifying,

---

[41] *AD*, *1874*, II, 37-38.

[42] See Cavour's comment on Clause IX of the Pantaleoni-Passaglia memorandum
in Lynn M. Case, *Franco-Italian Relations, 1860-1865* (Philadelphia, 1932), p. 34.
Ricasoli, however, had envisaged an accord with the Catholic powers (cf. Mario
Falco, *La Politica ecclesiastica della Destra* [Torino, 1914], p. 10).

[43] Lady Paget alludes to him as "certainly the most learned and perhaps the
cleverest of our friends" (*Embassies of Other Days* [London, 1923], I, 277).

[44] September, 1870, p. 216.

"as the common obligation of civilized peoples, the guardianship of religious liberty" would constitute a great step forward.[45]

Having thus presented its case to the world, the Italian government discreetly proceeded to sound out the Prussians. On September 2, Sella inquired of Brassier de St. Simon whether Bismarck would agree to a secret treaty with Italy whereby the latter was neither to abandon her neutrality nor to join other powers in exerting pressure on Prussia regarding the terms of peace. Prussia, in turn, was not to oppose the occupation of Rome. And she was also to secure, as a condition of the peace, renunciation by France of the idea of garrisoning the city. Bismarck, who had already assured the Italian government that he had no intention of meddling in the affairs of the peninsula,[46] thereby tacitly abandoning Rome to the Italians,[47] turned down this proposal. He failed to understand, he wrote, how Italians could believe that Prussia would intervene in the domestic concerns of other nations.[48] This reply was scarcely cheering, but Sella and his colleagues had little time for useless regrets. Their attention was focused on more urgent matters. Tidings from Paris and from the theater of war indicated that momentous events were imminent, and certain members of the cabinet began to fret over the continued inaction.[49] But Lanza saw little reason as yet to alter his course. He was in no hurry. National sentiment, he felt, required more time to gain irresistible

[45] *Riforma*, September 2, 1870. The Sinistra journal was careful, however, to distinguish between the guarantees to be enacted after the occupation of Rome and the act of occupation itself. As regards the latter, it would tolerate neither the interference nor the concurrence of the powers. For this, it insisted, was a purely internal question, "a question of nationality, subject only to the national sovereignty." Rome was the capital of Italy, and the pleasure of foreign governments did not have to be consulted.

[46] Cf. *GW*, VI*b*, No. 1756, 455.

[47] Cf. the discussion of Bismarck's policy in the Roman question, following the withdrawal of the French garrison, in Julius Clausen, *Bismarck und der Katholizismus in den Jahren 1851–1871* (Hamburg, 1934), p. 57.

[48] *GW*, VI*b*, No. 1775, 470.   [49] Cf. Castagnola, *op. cit.*, p. 28 and note.

momentum. He knew, moreover, that efforts were being made to provoke pro-Italian demonstrations on papal territory. At the beginning of September, Govone, the minister of war, wrote to General Cadorna, who commanded the army stationed at the papal frontier: "Present political circumstances daily strengthen the belief that the Italian government will not have to depart from the prudent reserve hitherto maintained in order to protect public order and national rights."[50] The ministry was served by an able and vigilant press which continued to insist that Italy had most to gain by respecting treaty obligations and shunning violence. On the other hand, the columns of the opposition journals were more than ever alive with the theme that procrastination would be fatal to the country's interests. Thus, the *Riforma* warned that the present possibility of going to Rome ought not to be overlooked. It was a matter "not of days, but of hours." Any pause in the Franco-Prussian War—whether it be an armistice or a convention—would rob Italy of her golden opportunity. Haste would have to be the *mot d'ordre* in fulfilling the national program. Only when the city had been made part of the national domain, it declared, would Italy be able to convince the world that her unity was indestructible. The Gordian knot had to be severed by an immediate occupation, even in defiance of possible international complications.[51]

On September 3 news of the overwhelming French defeat at Sedan reached Florence.[52] The actionists in the ministry and in the country at large were galvanized into a spirited reiteration of their thesis. But the exponents of moderation held back. It was above all Visconti-Venosta, Kübeck reported, who wished "to resist as long as possible within the

[50] Raffaele Cadorna, *La Liberazione di Roma nell'anno 1870 ed il plebiscito* (Torino, 1898), p. 81.

[51] *Riforma*, September 3 and 4, 1870; Crispi, *Politica interna*, pp. 67–68.

[52] Victor Emmanuel, whose Francophil sympathies had persisted, received this announcement with real sorrow (Giuseppe Massari, *La Vita ed il regno di Vittorio Emanuele II di Savoia* [Milano, 1910], II, 515).

terms of the September convention."[53] The cabinet hastily closeted itself to examine the situation. A lively discussion ensued. Immediate occupation of the papal patrimony was demanded by Sella. He dangled before the eyes of his colleagues the specter of a republican insurrection in Rome. He even intimated that the Prussians might take it into their heads to occupy the city in order to protect themselves against an Italian revolutionary movement sympathetic with the French cause. The country, in his opinion, would fall a prey to civil disorder and undergo the humiliation of foreign intervention unless it discarded the September convention without further ado. But the majority was not yet ready to act.[54] On this, as on other occasions, the views of Lanza and Visconti-Venosta prevailed.[55] The clamor of the opposition failed to move them. The government could now be told, raged the *Riforma*, that if it did not, "after today's tragic news," march at once to Rome, it would be betraying the country.[56] "Woe to Italy," it wailed, "if she halted in esctatic stupor to contemplate the fall of an empire while her own edifice is not yet complete."[57] A delegation of Sinistra deputies, headed by Rattazzi and Crispi, handed the premier an address which reiterated that further delay would be tantamount to treason. The Battle of Sedan, it urged, "traces for the government the easy fulfilment of its duty: the immediate occupation of Rome." The cabinet was warned that failure to act quickly in the present crisis would compel the country to take its salvation into its own hands.[58] Lanza im-

---

[53] Kübeck to Beust, September 3, 1870, HHSA, Politisches Archiv (Florenz), Fasz. XI/75, No. 1347/66, fol. 1*a*.

[54] Guiccioli, *op. cit.*, I, 300–301; Paolo Boselli, "Roma e Quintino Sella," *Nuova antologia*, September 16, 1927, p. 143; Castagnola, *op. cit.*, pp. 29–30; Tivaroni, *op. cit.*, III, 128.

[55] Gadda, *op. cit.*, p. 211.   [56] *Riforma*, September 4, 1870.

[57] *Ibid.*, September 5, 1870.

[58] *Ibid.*; cf. also Luigi Chiala, *Giacomo Dina e l'opera sua nelle vicende del Risorgimento italiano* (Torino and Roma, 1903), III, 252 (hereafter cited as Chiala, *Dina*); Crispi, *Politica interna*, p. 68; Paolo Maria Arcari, *La Francia nell'opinione pubblica italiana dal '59 al '70* (Roma, 1934), p. 133; Castagnola, *op. cit.*, p. 29.

mediately replied that the government would not deviate from its previously announced policy.[59] It was imperative, the *Opinione* explained, to act with complete freedom and without regard for the pressure of any party.[60]

But overnight the complexion of things changed. Word was received that a republic had been proclaimed at Paris. This, Kübeck noted, "impresses and decides" the king. The latter gave the Austrian envoy to understand that he could master the movement provoked by the Roman issue only by placing himself in its van. He hoped, he said, that Austria would create no difficulties for him in this matter. He did not doubt that Prussia would refrain from interfering.[61] Victor Emmanuel's attitude portended a speedy occupation of the papal patrimony, and other indications were not wanting that a showdown was near. The revolution in France and the alleged fear of a republican uprising in Rome and in Italy, Kübeck observed, had aided the actionist program. Italians now appeared to be looking only for a more or less legal pretext. "Even the resistance of Visconti-Venosta seems to be giving way."[62] A legal pretext was not hard to find, thanks to the September convention. That treaty was pronounced dead. It constituted, the Italian government claimed, a bilateral pact with Napoleon III; obligations assumed under it lapsed with the disappearance of his regime.[63] Moreover, the fall of the Second Empire was classified as one of those "exceptional contingencies" which restored freedom of action to the signatories of the convention.[64] "At the city hall of Paris," the *Riforma* joyfully announced, "we have all the guarantees for the consolidation of our unity." The cabinet, it continued, would have to act quickly to exploit the pro-

---

[59] Crispi, *Politica interna*, p. 69.   [60] *Opinione*, September 6, 1870.

[61] Kübeck to Beust, September 5, 1870, HHSA, Politisches Archiv (Florenz), Fasz. XI/75, No. 2093/190, fol. 5*b*.

[62] *Ibid.*, No. 2242/262, fol. 7*a*.

[63] Cf. Castagnola, *op. cit.*, p. 14.   [64] Paladino, *op. cit.*, p. 119.

Italian attitude of the members of the French provisional government.[65]

Victor Emmanuel urged his ministers to delay no longer, and this time they were not loath to obey.[66] They invited Prince Napoleon to leave the country.[67] Alleging an imminent disruption of public order, they formally decided to occupy the papal domain.[68] It was also voted to send Count Ponza di San Martino, a prominent Piedmontese conservative, to Rome to notify the pope of the impending invasion and to assure him that his religious freedom would be amply guaranteed.[69] The cautious Visconti-Venosta intimated to Paget that the establishment of a republic in France "might make it necessary to occupy certain portions of the Roman territory, and possibly a part of Rome itself, should there be disturbances there." He disingenuously insisted that no decision had as yet been reached by his government. In any case, he added, the solution of the Roman question would ultimately be reserved for "deliberation with other Powers." Plebiscites would be held in the papal territory, and the outcome would have to be taken into account by the various governments when they considered a definitive settlement.[70]

Formal notice of the forthcoming expedition was served on the powers in the circular note which Visconti-Venosta addressed to the Italian diplomatic representatives on September 7. This document stated that in view of the serious turn taken by the Franco-Prussian War and the agitated state of public feeling throughout the peninsula, the government would be obliged to occupy certain points in the papal territory in order to safeguard the interests of the Holy See as well as those of Italy. It acknowledged the right of the Ro-

[65] *Riforma*, September 6, 1870.   [66] Bury, *op. cit.*, pp. 148–49.

[67] Tavallini, *op. cit.*, II, 32–33; Castagnola, *op. cit.*, p. 29; Ugo Pesci, *Firenze capitale (1865–1870)* (Firenze, 1904), p. 228.

[68] Massari, *op. cit.*, II, 517; Paladino, *op. cit.*, p. 120.

[69] Chiala, *Dina*, III, 254–55; Michele Rosi, *I Cairoli* (Bologna, 1929), I, 232.

[70] *Blue Book*, No. 23, pp. 12–13.

mans to determine their own fate. Most important of all, it reiterated the readiness of the ministry "to enter into arrangements with the powers concerning the conditions to be decided upon by common agreement in order to insure the spiritual independence of the pope."[71] On this very crucial point the program of the Italian cabinet seemed entirely unchanged. On September 8, Lanza himself wrote to his intimate friend and adviser, Michelangelo Castelli, that the definitive solution of the Roman question "will be the work of a congress of the Catholic powers."[72] The premier was likewise convinced—and the cabinet quite agreed with him—that it would be well to defer the invasion until overtures for an understanding had been made to the Vatican. Count San Martino was instructed to offer the pope the terms contained in the memorandum of August 29. Should these overtures prove successful, the occupation of Rome would be accomplished without violence and bloodshed. Visconti-Venosta attached supreme importance to this point. He told his colleagues on September 8 that, in the existing state of affairs, he would resign rather than agree to a forcible entry. It was at his instance that General Cadorna was ordered to refrain from occupying the city if violence should have to be employed.[73] All this afforded the foreign minister an excellent talking-point. He told Paget, among others, that the fact of the occupation would settle nothing. Everything was being reserved for future negotiations with the powers. Rome would not be attacked except "under very extreme circumstances." Italian troops were not to set foot in the Leonine City unless the pope assented thereto.[74] The *Opinione* warmly lauded the government's attitude. "The Roman ques-

[71] *Libro verde*, No. 3, pp. 12–13.

[72] Castelli, however, professed no desire to see Italy assume the initiative in urging such a conference upon foreign governments (Luigi Chiala, *Ricordi di Michelangelo Castelli* [Torino and Napoli, 1888], pp. 187–88).

[73] Crispi, *Politica interna*, p. 70; Castagnola, *op. cit.*, pp. 38–39.

[74] *Blue Book*, No. 24, p. 13.

tion," it reiterated, "is a political and moral one. We cannot wish to solve it by force." Firmness, however, was urgently requisite. It was the duty of the cabinet to inform the pope of its intentions "without hesitation and without bravado."[75] San Martino conferred with Antonelli on September 9. He enlarged upon his antecedents as a Catholic and a conservative to emphasize the conciliatory character of his mission. But his assurances fell on deaf ears. The cardinal insisted that the papacy could not renounce any of its rights. The action contemplated by the Italian authorities constituted a villainy which the pope refused to condone.[76] He declared that any transaction which left the Leonine City in the pope's possession was entirely unacceptable. The Italian government could not expect the Vatican to do anything which might be interpreted as a "tacit assent of the one despoiled to the resolution of the cabinet of Florence."[77] On the following day, San Martino had an audience with Pius. The conversation started off very inauspiciously. "Fine loyalty!" exclaimed the irate pontiff. "You are all a set of vipers, whited sepulchers, wanting in faith!" When this explosion of wrath had somewhat subsided, San Martino attempted to convince His Holiness of the reasonableness of the terms offered by the cabinet. He made much of the concessions which were to be lavished upon the Holy See. There was the sovereignty over the Leonine City, with the prospect of securing territory on the left bank of the Tiber as far as Ostia, where the government would build a port. Not to be overlooked were the retention of the papal guards, the generous civil list, the pledge that the proceeds from the sale of ecclesiastical property in Rome would be turned over to the expropriated religious orders, and the offer to give due consideration to the interests of nationals now in the service of the papal government.

[75] *Opinione*, September 10, 1870; cf. also Chiala, *Dina*, III, 255.

[76] Cadorna, *op. cit.*, p. 41; Rosi, *Vittorio Emanuele II*, II, 157; Cilibrizzi, *op. cit.*, I, 592; Castagnola, *op. cit.*, p. 43 and note.

[77] Cf. Jules Favre, *Rome et la République française* (Paris, 1871), p. 44.

Pius, however, was adamant. He had no great confidence, he said, in these promises. The acts of one ministry could be disavowed by the next. He would never sanction an Italian occupation of Rome. He professed no real apprehension. "I am neither a prophet nor the son of one," he was reported to have said, "but I tell you, you will never enter Rome!"[78] In reply to a touching request from Victor Emmanuel that he come to an understanding with the Italian monarchy,[79] he wrote: "I am unable to admit the demands expressed in your letter, nor can I adhere to the principles which it contains."[80] Informed that the Vatican would enter into no negotiations with the Italian government, San Martino left for Florence.[81] The failure of his mission was officially announced in the *Giornale di Roma*, an organ of the papal authorities. The aim of the king's letter, so ran the communiqué, "is to make known that, in view of the inability to resist . . . . the *party of action* and the so-called *national aspiration*, it has been decided to take possession of what remains of the territory of the Holy See. Any comment on this unqualifiable act is

[78] Cadorna, *op. cit.*, p. 42; *AD, 1874*, II, 60–61, 69; Raffaele de Cesare, *Roma e lo stato del papa dal ritorno di Pio IX al XX settembre* (Roma, 1907), II, 436; Castagnola, *op. cit.*, pp. 44–45; Cilibrizzi, *op. cit.*, I, 593.

[79] The king's letter, dated September 8, was couched in respectful and affectionate terms. He pointed to the dangers which were threatening all Europe as well as Italy and the papacy as a result of the activity of the "party of international revolution." He explained that the crown felt obliged to assume responsibility for the maintenance of order and the safety of the Holy See. Accordingly, troops were to be sent into papal territory. His Holiness was not to regard this gesture as a hostile one. "My government and my forces," the king continued, "will absolutely confine themselves to a conservative action designed to protect the rights of the Roman population, rights which are easily reconcilable with the inviolability of the Supreme Pontiff, his spiritual authority and the independence of the Holy See." By satisfying the national aspirations, the Holy Father, "surrounded by the devotion of the Italian people, would retain on the banks of the Tiber a glorious seat independent of all human sovereignty." He would restore peace to the church and demonstrate to Europe that "great battles could be won and immortal victories gained by an act of justice and with a word of affection" (cf. Rosi, *Vittorio Emanuele II*, II, 154–56).

[80] Cadorna, *op. cit.*, p. 43; Rosi, *Vittorio Emanuele II*, II, 158–59; Cilibrizzi, *op. cit.*, I, 593.

[81] Cf. Palomba to Beust, September 11, 1870, HHSA, Politisches Korrespondenz (Rom), Fasz. XI/224, No. 14987/1437, fol. 299a.

superfluous, and it is needless to say that the Holy Father declared himself sharply opposed to any proposal."[82]

In the meantime, the cabinet had decided that General Cadorna should cross the papal frontier on September 11.[83] An insurrection in Roman territory would have furnished an excellent pretext for invasion, and the Florentine authorities had been waiting impatiently for just such an eventuality.[84] But the failure of the pope's subjects to stage an uprising was deemed no deterrent to immediate military action. In any case, the road seemed clear. No real opposition was to be expected from foreign governments, whose attitude was partly influenced by the proclamation of the dogma of papal infallibility.[85] On September 6, Nigra had sounded out Jules Favre, the foreign minister of the embattled French republic. Though the latter had refused to denounce the September convention, he had made it clear that his government would not invoke the moribund pact. He was unable and unwilling "to prevent anything," he had told the Italian envoy. "I believe like you," he had continued, "that if you do not go there, Rome will fall into the power of dangerous agitators. I would rather see you there. But it is well understood that France gives no consent, and that you execute this enterprise exclusively on your own responsibility."[86] Simultaneously, he had instructed his representatives in Florence and Rome

[82] Cf. *Osservatore romano*, September 13, 1870; Rosi, *Vittorio Emanuele II*, II, 158 n.; cf. also, on Ponza's mission, Tavallini, *op. cit.*, II, 35–36, 41–45.

[83] Generale Cesare Ricotti, *Osservazioni al libro di Raffaele Cadorna: la liberazione di Roma nell'anno 1870* (Novara, 1889), p. 61 (Ricotti's volume contains documents from the archives of the war ministry); cf. also Castagnola, *op. cit.*, p. 41.

[84] Cf. Kübeck to Beust, September 10, 1870, HHSA, Politisches Archiv (Florenz), Fasz. XI/75, No. 4520/4177, fol. 64a.

[85] Paladino, *op. cit.*, p. 121. As Luigi Salvatorelli points out, the proclamation of papal infallibility had contributed to the political and diplomatic isolation of Pius IX in September, 1870, "an isolation without comparison in history" (cf. his "De la brèche de Porta Pia aux accords du Latran," *L'Esprit international*, July, 1929, p. 351).

[86] *Libro verde*, No. 6, pp. 16–17; Favre, *op. cit.*, pp. 5–7. Favre himself explains this refusal to denounce the September convention as "a simple act of inoffensive neutrality."

to maintain "an attitude of complete abstention" in this matter.[87] The French government, he wrote four days later, "can neither approve nor recognize the temporal power of the Holy See." But, inasmuch as its paramount duty for the time being was to repel the foreigner, it was reserving all questions which did not require immediate solution.[88] "You know our opinion," he recapitulated in a dispatch to Malaret. "The temporal power has been a scourge to the world, it is prostrate, we will not resurrect it. But we feel too unhappy to trample on it." France would be pleased to see the Italian government go to Rome, for its going there was a necessity. The order and peace of the world were at stake.[89] Favre's reply to Nigra, despite its obvious evasiveness, was regarded as satisfactory by the Florentine authorities.[90] And nothing disquieting had been reported by the Italian representatives in other European capitals. Thile, the Prussian secretary of state for foreign affairs, refused to commit himself in the absence of instructions from Bismarck,[91] whose noninterventionist attitude, in any case, scarcely required reiteration.[92] Austria indicated she had no intention of obstructing an Italian occupation of papal territory and of Rome itself.[93] Count Bray, the Bavarian foreign minister, declared that his government would not intervene if Italy should find it necessary to take action. Its attitude in such an eventuality would be

[87] Favre to Lefebvre de Béhaine and to Malaret, September 6, 1870, AMAE (Rome, juin-septembre, 1870), Tome 1047, fol. 266.

[88] Favre to Lefebvre de Béhaine, September 10, 1870, *ibid.*, fol. 273.

[89] Cf. Favre's dispatch to Malaret in *ibid.* (Italie, août-décembre, 1870), Tome 379, fols. 227–28. On September 12, when informed by Nigra that the invasion of the papal domain was being launched, Favre replied that France would, "with sympathy," allow Italy to proceed (*Libro verde*, No. 12, p. 24; Nigra, *op. cit.*, p. 23).

[90] Kübeck to Beust, September 8, 1870, HHSA, Politisches Archiv (Florenz), Fasz. XI/75, No. 3590/779, fol. 54*a*.

[91] *Libro verde*, No. 14, pp. 25–26.

• [92] According to Matter (*op. cit.*, III, 122), Bismarck "was too happy to see the Florentine cabinet turn southward (toward Rome) to intervene."

[93] *Libro verde*, No. 8, pp. 18–19.

one of noncommittal reserve.[94] The head of the Belgian foreign office, D'Anethan, contented himself with an allusion to the necessity of safeguarding the pope's spiritual freedom by means of a collective guarantee of the Catholic powers.[95]

Cadorna was equipped with elaborate instructions. He was to declare that the mission of his troops was purely "conservative and protective." He was to try to enter Rome without violence. He was not to occupy the Leonine City. He was to afford the pope and the cardinals complete freedom of movement. He was to show Pius every deference and endeavor to dissuade him from leaving Rome. However, should he insist on going, no obstacles were to be placed in his way, and sovereign honors were to be paid him.[96] On the eleventh, at the head of fifty thousand men, the general crossed the papal frontier. It was obvious that so powerful a force was hardly necessary to overcome the feeble opposition of the pontifical army. But Lanza and Visconti Venosta, who had not yet despaired of achieving a bloodless conquest of Rome,[97] were hopeful that this demonstration of superior might would convince the Vatican of the futility of armed resistance. A longer and more difficult line of march had been selected in order to postpone a frontal attack on Rome until all attempts to negotiate a peaceful entry had failed.[98] The additional days of grace thus allotted the papal government might prove conducive to a more dispassionate appraisal on its part of the realities of the situation.[99] They might, too, furnish time for a popular rising in Rome.[100] In accordance with a preconcerted

[94] *Ibid.*, No. 4, p. 14.   [95] *Ibid.*, No. 16, p. 27.

[96] Ricotti, *op. cit.*, pp. 49–50; Cadorna, *op. cit.*, pp. 105, 112–14.

[97] Cf. the war minister's instructions of September 10 to Cadorna in Ricotti, *op. cit.*, p. 63.

[98] *Ibid.*, p. 3.   [99] Paladino, *op. cit.*, p. 135.

[100] To the end, the Italian government hoped for such a rising (De Cesare, *op. cit.*, II, 448). Thus, on September 13, Cadorna was informed that, though he was not to attack Rome without an explicit order to do so, he was to forego no opportunity to take the city by surprise or stratagem and with the aid of an insurrection within the papal capital (Ricotti, *op. cit.*, p. 71).

plan, Cadorna issued from Terni a proclamation calling upon
the inhabitants of the Roman provinces to show Europe that
the exercise of their rights was entirely compatible with respect for the spiritual authority of the pope. "The independence of the Holy See," the manifesto continued, "will remain
more inviolate amid civil liberties than it ever was under
foreign protection."[101] The inauguration of the campaign did
not fail to gratify the actionists, but they promptly reminded
the government that the major objective still remained to be
attained. "It is not enough," declared the *Riforma*, "to have
crossed the frontier. The capital must be at Rome."[102]

The Lanza cabinet was careful to place the issue squarely
before the dignitaries of the ecclesiastical hierarchy. On September 12, Raeli, the minister of public worship and justice,
dispatched a circular to all Italian bishops expressing the government's readiness to insure the freedom of the papacy.
"Let us hope," he wrote, "that the Holy Father will accept
our proposals. Whatever his decision may be, the government will never allow anyone to offend or insult the church or
its ministers." But duty to the Italian nation, he went on,
left the authorities no choice but to forbid the clergy to do or
say anything which might provoke disregard of the laws and
contempt for the institutions of the state. Severe penalties
were to be visited upon all members of the ecclesiastical
hierarchy guilty of such treasonable behavior. Appealing to
their love of country, Raeli adjured them to refrain from disturbing the public order.[103] The episcopate, however, refused
to take these injunctions seriously. Foremost in the brigade
of rebels was Mgr. Ghilardi, the Bishop of Mondovì. He boldly protested against the circular and decried the intentions of
the cabinet as revealed in it. He also sent a letter to the pope
expressing his sympathy with the latter in the present crisis.

---

[101] Cadorna, *op. cit.*, p. 120; Castagnola, *op. cit.*, p. 41 and note.

[102] *Riforma*, September 13, 1870.

[103] Pietro Vigo, *Storia degli ultimi trent'anni del secolo XIX* (Milano, 1908), I,
53–54; *AD, 1874*, II, 62–63.

Pius rewarded him with a warm commendation of his fearlessness. The Vatican itself did not conceal its resentment. Through the columns of the *Civiltà cattolica*, its famous Jesuit organ, it charged that Raeli's gesture was motivated only by the desire to silence the clergy.[104] In the meantime, Pius had turned to Austria and Bavaria in the hope of inducing them to bestir themselves in his behalf. The Hapsburg monarchy was still high in his esteem for services rendered the papal state in the past.[105] Now, at this critical juncture, Antonelli asked the Austrian chargé d'affaires to inform Beust that the Holy See reposed hope solely in a "benevolent action" by the imperial and royal government—an action calculated to deter the Italian cabinet from going ahead with the invasion.[106] Simultaneously, the nuncio at Vienna requested the Austrian government to voice its displeasure at the outrage about to be committed by the Italians.[107] But the Vatican's entreaties failed to move the cabinet of Vienna. Beust, after conferring with the emperor and with the Austrian and Hungarian premiers, vouchsafed a negative reply. Austria, he declared, had repeatedly informed the pontifical government that she was unable to replace the armed protection of France with her own. The Holy See had always understood the exigencies of her position, and the present *démarche* therefore was doubtless not motivated by demands of that nature. But even the censure requested by the papal government would be exceedingly detrimental to the dignity of Austria if it were unaccompanied by a firm determination to back it up. Moreover, any attempt by Austria to exert real pressure upon the decisions of the Italian government would involve her in "a serious

[104] *Civiltà cattolica*, I (8th ser.; January 8, 1871), 224–26 (hereafter cited as *CC*).

[105] Cf. Antonio Monti, *Pio IX nel Risorgimento italiano* (Bari, 1928), p. 182.

[106] Palomba to Beust, September 11, 1870, HHSA, Politisches Korrespondenz (Rom), Fasz. XI/224, No. 14987/1437, fols. 299a–299b.

[107] Beust to Palomba, September 13, 1870, *ibid.*, Politisches Archiv (Rome, Expeditions, Varia), Fasz. XI/225, fol. 184a.

conflict" which her interests forbade her to provoke. "The establishment of peaceful and friendly relations with the kingdom of Italy," he continued, "was hailed with rejoicing throughout the Hapsburg empire. The benefits of proximity and the community of important interests oblige us to cultivate good relations with a power with whom we have had every reason to be satisfied ever since the *rapprochement*. The Imperial and Royal government . . . . would certainly be disavowed by public opinion if today it should break the entente with Italy." Furthermore, a strong line by Austria would hardly be a service to the papacy. It would only aggravate Italy's attitude. Resistance to foreign pressure would give further impetus to existing passions and would unite all the parties in the peninsula. And the Italian government would be compelled to show the pope less indulgence in order to give proof of its independence. All these considerations counseled against an "inefficacious" and hence "compromising" *démarche*. They also weighed against a more serious *démarche* which would prove prejudicial to the interests of the Holy Father as well as to those of Austria. It had to be understood, however, that the emperor and his government were keenly concerned about the position of the Roman pontiff. The latter's personal safety and spiritual independence were the object of their "most active solicitude." If Pius, while awaiting more favorable circumstances, should want to conclude a temporary *modus vivendi* with the Italians, the imperial and royal government would hasten to place its good offices at his disposal. "Our relations with the cabinet of Florence," Beust pointed out, "would certainly permit us in such a case to act with success in removing more than one difficulty. All our efforts would be directed toward assuring the Holy Father the guarantees compatible with a state of affairs which . . . . is the inevitable result of events that can no longer be halted." The Italian government, one had a right to believe, fully realized that the Roman question involved great interests which no one power alone could handle. Whenever the various governments should be called upon to examine the new situation of the Holy See, Austria would not fail to demand in its behalf "the conditions inseparable from its high mission."[108] Simultaneously, Beust summoned the Lanza cabinet to exhibit the utmost forbearance in its dealings with the pope. "At a time when the Italian troops are crossing the Roman frontier," he wrote to Kübeck, "we cannot refrain from appealing to the honorable sentiments of the Italian government and from expressing the firm hope that it will treat the Holy Father with the maximum indulgence consistent with the measures adopted." The Austrian government's friendliness to Italy, he observed, could not be doubted. It had, in the past, willingly helped to render Italy's situation less embarrassing. Now, too, it was not seeking to trammel her freedom of decision. But the Roman question was one which greatly interested the cabinet of Vienna. The emperor, out of deference to his personal feelings as well as to the religious convictions of the majority of his subjects, felt obliged to show the keenest solicitude in everything that affected the position of the Holy See. Consequently, the Austrian government would have to insist upon securing "tranquillizing assurances" from the Italian authorities. "We can certainly count on the spirit of moderation which animates the cabinet of Florence and on its oft-announced intention of not proceeding alone to a solution of the Roman question," the chancellor continued. "We have faith in its promises, but we owe it to our conscience and to our sympathies for the Holy Father to call the Florentine cabinet's most serious attention to the necessity of not augmenting the alarm experienced at this moment by all Catholics." In taking upon itself the responsibility of entering papal territory, the Italian government, it was to be hoped, would realize the importance of "restraining all passions hostile to the Holy See" and of "observing the greatest respect for the

[108] *Ibid.*, fols. 189a–192a.

person of the Holy Father."[109] A copy of this dispatch was
sent to the Austrian chargé d'affaires in Rome with instructions to bring it to the notice of Antonelli. The latter was to
be told that Beust expected Florence to heed his counsels.[110]
This expectation was not belied. Vienna's friendly warning
elicited from Visconti-Venosta the assurances demanded.
Especially noteworthy was the foreign minister's declaration
that his government had in no way modified its intention of
inviting the co-operation of the interested powers.[111]

The Vatican found Bavaria no more helpful. On receipt of
the papal inquiry, Bray hastened to ascertain the attitude of
the Prussian government. This *démarche* elicited a reply
which boded ill for the pontiff's expectations. Bismarck reiterated the impossibility of intervention. He alluded to the
war with France, the recent Austro-Italian conversations, the
anti-Prussian activity of the ultramontane party in France,
Belgium, Luxemburg, and Germany, and the infallibility
dogma as reasons for his aloofness from the Italo-papal conflict.[112] Thile, however, suggested that Prussia might make
some gesture at Florence to demonstrate her solicitude for
the pope's personal safety. "The effect on our Catholics," he
urged, "would be excellent. Also on the South Germans, in
contrast with the indifference of Austria." Bismarck could
not gainsay the force of this observation. He authorized
Thile to inform the Italian government that the King of
Prussia was compelled to take account of the desire of his
Catholic subjects to see the pope free and respected.[113] At
the same time, however, Brassier de St. Simon was instructed
to assure Visconti-Venosta that Bismarck's policy was un-

---

[109] Beust to Kübeck, September 13, 1870 (copy), *ibid.*, fols. 195*a*–196*b*.

[110] Beust to Palomba, September 13, 1870, *ibid.*, fols. 194*a*–194*b*. As a further
token of its solicitude for the Holy Father, the Austrian government ordered its
ambassador to the Vatican to cut short his leave of absence and return to Rome
(cf. Beust to Kübeck, September 17, 1870, *ibid.*, Politisches Archiv [Weisungen
nach Florenz, 1870], Fasz. XI/76, fol. 202*a*).

[111] *AD, 1874,* II, 78–79.

[112] *GW*, VI*b*, No. 1798, 491–92.   [113] *Ibid.*, VI*b*, No. 1803, 496–97.

changed and that his sympathies for the pope "have their natural limit in the good relations between Prussia and Italy which prevent the cabinet of Berlin from creating any difficulties for Italy or entering any combinations hostile to her."[114] The Italian foreign minister received other indications of Berlin's benevolence. Count Arnim, the Prussian ambassador to the Vatican, was quite explicit. While in Florence, en route to his post in Rome, he told Visconti-Venosta that he had been given no instructions other than to return at once to the papal capital. There was no question, he said, of protesting against the Italian invasion.[115] Count Launay, the Italian minister to Prussia, relayed similar information to his chief. The circumspect Thile was reported to have repudiated all thought of intervening against the projected occupation of Rome.[116] In these circumstances, Bavaria had no choice but to vouchsafe a negative reply to the papal inquiry.

While the Italian government solemnly disclaimed any intention of disavowing its pledges, its legions were pursuing their steady march toward Rome. Cadorna proceeded with a slowness which bespoke the importance attached by his superiors to the possibility of a peaceful occupation of the city.[117] Such a possibility seemed greatly enhanced by the decision of the French government to recall those of its nationals who were in the military service of foreign powers.[118] Hopelessly outnumbered and handicapped by inferior equip-

---

[114] *Libro verde*, No. 18, p. 29; Jean Lulvès, "Bismarck und die römische Frage," *Hochland*, June, 1929, p. 267.

[115] Cf. Kübeck to Beust, September 17, 1870, HHSA, Politisches Archiv (Florenz), Fasz. XI/75, No. 76D, fols. 120a–120b.

[116] *Ibid.*, fol. 121a.

[117] Cf. Palomba to Beust, September 21, 1870, *ibid.*, Politisches Korrespondenz (Rom), Fasz. XI/224, No. 101H, fol. 351a.

[118] The authorities at Florence were hopeful that this decision, which robbed the Vatican of many of its most valiant warriors, would help eliminate the likelihood of serious resistance on the part of the papal forces (cf. Kübeck to Beust, September 14, 1870, *ibid.*, Politisches Archiv [Florenz], Fasz. XI/75, No. 6065/843, fol. 104a).

ment, the pontifical army, some eight thousand strong, re-
treated in the direction of Rome.[119] But General Kanzler, its
commander-in-chief, would not hear of surrender. On September 15 he brusquely rejected Cadorna's plea for an unop-
posed occupation of the papal capital. "His Holiness," he declared, "desires to see Rome occupied by his own troops and
not by those of other sovereigns. Consequently, I have the
honor to respond that I am determined to resist with all the
means at my disposal, as duty and honor dictate."[120] The
following day Civita Vecchia surrendered to Nino Bixio, the
fiery Garibaldian and anticlerical who commanded one of the
Italian divisions.[121] Kanzler was asked a second time to open
the gates of Rome to the steadily advancing Italians, but
again his reply was a flat refusal.[122] His superiors professed
no apprehension over the ultimate outcome. In an article
entitled "Portae inferi non praevalebunt," the *Osservatore
romano* predicted that the revolution headed by Victor Emmanuel and his battalions would result in miserable discomfiture.[123]

The failure of Cadorna's overtures clarified the situation.
But a brief pause ensued when Count Arnim offered his
mediation.[124] Though well aware of the hopelessness of direct

[119] On the pontifical army in September, 1870, see Paladino, *op. cit.*, pp. 126–27;
Giuseppe Leti, *Roma e lo stato pontificio dal 1849 al 1870* (Roma, 1909), II, 341.

[120] Cadorna, *op. cit.*, p. 149; Ricotti, *op. cit.*, p. 76; Giacomo Emilio Curàtulo, *La
Questione romana da Cavour a Mussolini* (Roma, 1928), p. 63; cf. also Albertone,
op. cit., p. 102.

[121] The cabinet, eager to curtail the possibility of foreign military intervention,
attached great importance to the occupation of this port (cf. Giuseppe Cesare
Abba, *La Vita di Nino Bixio* [Torino, 1912], p. 185).

[122] Cadorna, *op. cit.*, pp. 152–54; Curàtulo, *op. cit.*, pp. 66.

[123] *Osservatore romano*, September 17, 1870.

[124] Arnim was very much in the thick of the papacy's counsels at this moment.
He had conferred with Pius on September 15. The latter had asked him to urge
Cadorna to retire with his entire force. Arnim had replied that, in the absence of
any such instructions from his sovereign, he could scarcely execute a *démarche* of
this nature. Whereupon the pope had asked that he request King William to induce the Italian government to spare Rome. Arnim had acquiesced and had added
that, if the Vatican should wish to arrive at some understanding with Florence, he

appeals to the Holy Father,[125] he visited Cadorna on September 17 and requested him to wait twenty-four hours before giving the signal for the attack. Arnim proposed to urge the diplomatic corps at the Vatican to press for a peaceful surrender,[126] and Cadorna agreed to this delay. The Prussian minister promptly busied himself with the drafting of a note which the diplomatic corps was to be invited to address to Antonelli; but the French, Belgian, and Bavarian representatives flatly refused to participate in this *démarche*, and the matter was dropped.[127] On the eighteenth, therefore, Arnim, who subsequently insisted that he had repeatedly advised the pope to offer no armed resistance to the Italians,[128] informed Cadorna that his efforts had proved futile.[129] The count's gesture had been made without authorization from Berlin;[130] but Bismarck, with an eye to the good will of his Catholic compatriots, ordered his foreign office to play up the incident as proof that the Prussian ambassador, alone among the diplomatic representatives in Rome, was active in behalf of

---

would deem himself authorized to initiate negotiations with General Cadorna. Pius, however, had indignantly rejected this suggestion, asserting that he could not traffic with usurpers. And King William, in reply to Arnim's inquiry, had indicated his inability to intervene in this question (cf. Palomba to Beust, September 21, 1870, HHSA, Politisches Korrespondenz [Rom], Fasz. XI/224, Bericht 101E, fols. 330b–332a).

[125] He was reported to have said that the military element was master of the situation in Rome and that consequently resistence was inevitable (cf. Kübeck to Beust, September 18, 1870, *ibid.*, Politisches Archiv [Florenz], Fasz. XI/75, fol. 139a).

[126] Palomba to Beust, September 21, 1870, *ibid.*, Politisches Korrespondenz (Rom), Fasz. XI/224, Bericht 101H, fol. 355a.

[127] *Ibid.*, fols. 356b–357a; Lefebvre de Béhaine to Favre, September 17, 1870, AMAE (Rome, juin-septembre, 1870), Tome 1047, fols. 302–5.

[128] Cf. Blanc to Visconti-Venosta, September 30, 1870 (copy), HHSA, Politisches Archiv (Weisungen nach Florenz), Fasz. XI/76, fols. 262a–262b.

[129] Cadorna, *op. cit.*, pp. 164–65, 166–67; Curàtulo, *op. cit.*, pp. 67–68.

[130] *GW*, VIb, 514; *Libro verde*, Nos. 21, 27, 33, pp. 32, 39, 45; HHSA, Politisches Archiv (Varia, Berlin), Fasz. III/104, fols. 183a–183b; Lulvès, *op. cit.*, pp. 266–67. Visconti-Venosta himself informed Kübeck that he had ascertained at Berlin that Arnim had acted without instructions (Kübeck to Beust, September 19, 1870, HHSA, Politisches Archiv [Florenz], Fasz. XI/75, No. 560/404, fol. 144a).

the pope.[131] On receiving word of Arnim's action, the Italian government reviewed the whole question in the light of this new situation. Visconti-Venosta was still the archexponent of moderation. Rome, he suggested, should not be occupied in the event that Arnim were successful in persuading the pope to disarm and disband his troops. But the majority of his colleagues were less sanguine. Anticipating that nothing would come of the Prussian ambassador's eleventh-hour intercession, they empowered General Ricotti, who had succeeded Govone as minister of war,[132] to issue orders for an attack on Rome. Cadorna was to be informed that the government, in view of the repeated failures to arrive at an understanding with the Vatican, had decided to take the city by force. However, he was to be reminded that "political conditions require, more than ever, prudence, moderation, and speed."[133] These instructions were sent to Cadorna on September 18, when the failure of Arnim's mediation had convinced even Visconti-Venosta that a peaceful solution was out of the question.[134] On the following day the necessity of resorting to force was proclaimed to the country in the *Gazzetta ufficiale*.[135] Simultaneously, Ricotti warned Cadorna that, "from the political point of view, delay might be fatal." Cadorna promptly replied, "I attack tomorrow morning."[136] The Italian government would have preferred to see the firing commenced by the defenders of Rome, and it was still very much embarrassed by the resistance which the papal forces were prepared to offer.[137] But the situation was now deemed

[131] *GW*, VI*b*, No. 1827, 514–15.

[132] Govone had resigned on September 7 (cf. Uberto Govone, *Il Generale Giuseppe Govone* [Torino, 1902], p. 388; Massari, *op. cit.*, II, 517-18).

[133] Crispi, *Politica interna*, p. 71; Castagnola, *op. cit.*, pp. 52–53.

[134] Ricotti, *op. cit.*, p. 79.

[135] Guiccioli, *op. cit.*, I, 307; Cadorna, *op. cit.*, pp. 168–69; Rosi, *Vittorio Emanuele II*, II, 163.

[136] Ricotti, *op. cit.*, p. 81.

[137] Cf. Kübeck to Beust, September 19, 1870, HHSA, Politisches Archiv (Florenz), Fasz. XI/75, Nos. 480/356 and 560/404, fols. 141*a* and 144*a*.

to be one which the military authorities alone were competent to handle.

The Holy Father watched the swift approach of the denouement with unshakable fortitude. The impending extinction of his temporal sovereignty could not disturb his serene faith in the ultimate triumph of his cause. He had been ejected from Rome in 1848, but he had returned to resume his sway over the papal patrimony. What had happened once could happen again. His course was now clear. From the very outset he had resolved to make only a show of resistance—just enough to demonstrate beyond any doubt that he was the victim of force. At no time did he intend to prolong the hopeless struggle.[138] On September 19 he sent the following instructions to Kanzler: "As regards the duration of the defense, I am obliged to order that it should consist only of a protest which will make clear the violence done and nothing more, that is to say, you are to open negotiations for a surrender at the first cannon shot."[139] It is not surprising that under these cheerless circumstances he should have played with the idea of quitting the city. He was reported to have said to Arnim a day or so before the occupation: "There, you see all my things are packed up. I depart as soon as they enter."[140] The persistent rumors of his imminent departure had it that Malta, Trent, and Innsbruck were being given the most consideration as possible places of refuge. Transportation was always available in the "Orénoque," which the government of the Third Republic had retained in the waters of Civita Vecchia.[141] The proponents of flight were confident that the prevailing regime in Italy would not be of

---

[138] On September 12, Kübeck wrote to Beust: "I learn from a reliable source that Count San Martino . . . . found His Holiness resigned to the idea of undergoing violence and opposed to any bloodshed" (*ibid.*, No. 5262/319, fol. 94*a*).

[139] De Cesare, *op. cit.*, II, 450; cf. also Paladino, *op. cit.*, p. 136; Leti, *op. cit.*, II, 346-47.

[140] *Times*, September 30, 1870.

[141] R. P. Lecanuet, *Les dernières années du pontificat de Pie IX, 1870–1878* (Paris, 1931), p. 89.

long duration and that by leaving Rome the pope would hasten its demise.[142]

September 19 passed amid the greatest tension. The Italian military command momentarily expected to receive word of some incident in Rome which would justify intervention. But nothing of the sort happened. There was no popular rising, and the papal troops had no thought of betraying their sovereign. Accordingly, Cadorna proceeded with the projected attack early on the morning of the twentieth. Mindful of the admonition contained in Ricotti's instructions, he was careful to provide beforehand for an orderly occupation of the city.[143] The attack was launched at 5:30 A.M.[144] Cadorna directed the main operations between Porta Pia and Porta Salara, leaving Bixio to create a diversion in the vicinity of Porta S. Pancrazio. The irrepressible Garibaldian, whose presence in the attacking forces had given the Holy See not a few anxious moments, lost little time in justifying these apprehensions. Disregarding Cadorna's explicit orders, he let loose an indiscriminate artillery fire which endangered the Vatican and St. Peter's.[145] There was excessive zeal on the other side, too. Defying the pope's instructions to Kanzler, the foreign commanders of the pontifical forces refused to surrender after the enemy's first salvos.[146] More than four hours of cannonading were required to breach Porta Pia. It was only then that the defenders, complying with orders from the pope, who did not wish it to be said that "the vicar of Jesus Christ, although unjustly attacked, assented to great bloodshed," raised the white flag.[147] During these trying mo-

---

[142] Cf. Humphrey Johnson, *The Papacy and the Kingdom of Italy* (London, 1926), pp. 29–30.

[143] Rosi, *Vittorio Emanuele II*, II, 163.

[144] Cf. Cadorna's dispatch to the war minister in Ricotti, *op. cit.*, p. 83.

[145] De Cesare, *op. cit.*, II, 454. Bixio's reckless behavior on this occasion was subsequently defended by Ricotti, who declared that the general had operated with "sane military judgment" (Ricotti, *op. cit.*, p. 42; cf. also Abba, *op. cit.*, pp. 188–89).

[146] Cf. De Cesare, *op. cit.*, II, 456–57.   [147] Cf. Albertone, *op. cit.*, p. 105.

ments, the Holy Father's sense of humor did not forsake him. While the cannon thundered, he calmly sat down at his writing table and composed a charade on the word *tremare*.[148] The Italian troops proceeded to occupy strategic points in various parts of the city in order to prevent disturbances by returning *emigrés* and adventurers who poured into Rome in the wake of Cadorna's men.[149] Kanzler promptly opened negotiations for the conclusion of a truce. He met his victorious adversary at Villa Albani, and an agreement was quickly reached. The pope was allowed to retain the Leonine City, although Kanzler had put forward no such demand.[150] The pontifical army was to be immediately disarmed and disbanded. Italians serving in it were to be allowed to retain their rank and salary, while foreign officers and men were to be repatriated without the loss of any rights which they at the moment enjoyed. The guards assigned to the personal service of the Holy Father were to be unmolested.[151] The capitulation was signed on the afternoon of the twentieth and was immediately put into effect. It was nominally an armistice, but more than half a century was to elapse before it was replaced by a formal treaty. The legal formalities disposed of,

---

[148] Meaning "to tremble" (Curàtulo, *op. cit.*, p. 75). Rarely did Pius' mordant humor fail him. In 1867, after the Battle of Mentana, he had greeted the triumphant General Kanzler by loudly declaiming the first eight lines of *Gerusalemme liberata*, much to the amusement of those present. In January, 1875, Garibaldi, the high priest of Italian anticlericalism, came to Rome to take his seat as a member of the chamber of deputies. The pontiff was reported to have remarked: "It was said that the two of us [he and Victor Emmanuel] could not stay in Rome. Now we are three" (cf. Leroy-Beaulieu "Un Roi et un pape: II. Pie IX et le Saint-Siège," *Revue des deux mondes*, May 15, 1878, p. 403). For further examples of Pius' sense of humor see Giambattista Casoni, *Pio IX e Vittorio Emanuele II* (Bologna, 1910), note on pp. 7–8.

[149] Cf. Ugo Pesci, *Come siamo entrati in Roma* (Milano, 1895), pp. 81–156.

[150] The fact that Pius had apparently authorized Kanzler to accept papal sovereignty over the Leonine City occasioned intense surprise in diplomatic circles (cf. Palomba to Beust, September 21, 1870, HHSA, Politisches Korrespondenz [Rom], Fasz. XI/224, Bericht 101L, fol. 381*b*).

[151] Cadorna, *op. cit.*, p. 199; Curàtulo, *op. cit.*, pp. 69–71; De Cesare, *op. cit.*, II, 461–62; Paladino, *op. cit.*, pp. 138–39; Albertone, *op. cit.*, pp. 111–12; Andrea Piola, *La Questione romana nella storia e nel diritto* (Padova, 1931), pp. 97–98.

Cadorna issued a ringing proclamation to the Romans. "Strengthened by your free votes," he announced, "Italy will have the glory of finally solving that great problem which so grievously burdens modern society. . . . . The morning of September 20, 1870, marks one of the most memorable dates of history. Rome again and forever has become the great capital of a great nation!"[152]

Patriotic Italians greeted the occupation of their future capital with boundless jubilation. Even the Florentines, who knew that the days of their city as the seat of the government were now numbered, participated wholeheartedly in the national rejoicing.[153] Turinese liberals were no less ready to put aside municipal jealousies on this unique occasion. The *Gazzetta del popolo*, one of their principal journals, summoned the old Piedmontese capital to make the nation's joy its own. "We have witnessed," it observed, "the realization of the principal and most popular part of our program. . . . . The national unity is complete. City of Turin! The celebration of the entry into Rome has for you a special and very precious significance. Be worthy of Rome and of yourself."[154] The *Riforma* triumphantly proclaimed: "The Italian nation, represented by its army, today has entered its Rome, the sacred city of its unity. It will never leave it. This is the oath which every Italian heart takes today. We hail the event. Today Italian might begins to exist."[155] Another leading Sinistra sheet, the *Diritto*, welcomed the fall of the temporal power as "the dawn of a profound religious transformation."[156] The ministerial *Opinione* was scarcely less fervent. "This is one of the most memorable events of our times and of our Risorgimento," it declared, "and we should be happy that it was accomplished without much conflict and opposi-

---

[152] Leti, *op. cit.*, II, 353–54.

[153] Pesci, *Firenze capitale (1865–1870)*, pp. 232–35; *Riforma*, September 21, 1870.

[154] Cf. Ermanno Amicucci, *G. B. Bottero giornalista del Risorgimento* (Torino, 1935), p. 186.

[155] *Riforma*, September 21, 1870.   [156] *Diritto*, September 22, 1870.

tion."[157] A less sanguine note was struck by Bonghi's Milanese organ, the *Perseveranza*. Its rejoicing was tempered by anxiety over the complications which the consummation of the national program was certain to bring.[158] It pointed out that it would be very difficult to remain in Rome. The government, it feared, might now be prevailed upon to pursue a policy detrimental to the peace and security of the state. And the Roman campaign, it warned, had so far not been opposed by the other powers only because they had had as yet no opportunity to do so.[159] The newspapers loyal to the papal cause gave the freest vent to their indignation. The *Unità cattolica* of Turin, one of the peninsula's most authoritative clerical dailies, declared that the adversaries of the pope's temporal power were not distinguishable from the foes of his spiritual authority. It predicted that before long the Italians, like all their predecessors in church-baiting, would be forced to abandon Rome. "Now the Roman question begins!" it reminded Lanza and his colleagues.[160] Following the lead given by this stalwart defender of the papacy, which published an article from the pen of an eminent ultramontane spokesman, Count Edoardo Crotti of Costigliole, the Italian clerical press opened its columns to innumerable protests against the seizure of Rome.[161]

The Romans were beside themselves with joy. Apprised, immediately after the entry of Cadorna's troops, that a plebiscite would soon be held to determine the fate of their city, they made no secret of their patriotic proclivities. Doubtless mindful of the part played by Parisian mobs during the many revolutions in the French capital, they were clearly determined to have a hand in forthcoming events. An opportunity to display their temper was not slow in presenting itself. No sooner had the capitulation of Villa Albani

[157] *Opinione*, September 21, 1870.   [158] Cf. Arcari, *op. cit.*, p. 135.

[159] *Perseveranza*, September 20 and 22, 1870.

[160] *Unità cattolica*, September 22, 23, and 24, 1870.

[161] *Ibid.*, September 22 and 25, 1870; *CC*, I (8th ser.; January 9, 1871), 161.

been signed than the news leaked out that the Leonine City was to be divorced from the rest of Rome and allotted to the pope. The inhabitants of the district were incensed. They protested violently against this transaction and clamored for union with Italy. They threatened to make trouble if their demand should be disregarded. Some of them did not bother to wait. During the night of September 20 they proceeded to attack the papal guards. Apprehension was felt for the safety of the Vatican, and on the following day Kanzler, at the pope's behest, formally requested Cadorna to send some troops into the Leonine City.[162] Antonelli likewise urged Arnim to intercede with Cadorna in the same sense.[163] The latter was somewhat reluctant to comply with this request, since he had received strict orders to refrain from setting foot in the district.[164] But the urgent tone of Kanzler's communication, coupled with Arnim's good offices, induced him to take the step.[165] However, he reminded the Vatican that the eight hundred men who composed the papal guards were entirely adequate to insure the Holy Father's personal safety. He was also careful to state that he intended to recall his troops at the earliest possible moment.[166] It was under these circumstances that the Italian troops, on September 21, crossed to the west bank of the Tiber and occupied the Leonine City.[167] Only the Vatican and the Lateran in Rome and the villa of Castel Gandolfo in the Alban hills remained in the possession

[162] Cadorna, *op. cit.*, p. 218; Rosi, *Vittorio Emanuele II*, II, 165; Pesci, *Come Siamo entrati in Roma*, p. 175. The Vatican had never asked for the Leonine City and was quite ready to surrender it. Its *mot d'ordre* at this juncture was: "All of the Patrimony of St. Peter or nothing" (cf. Paladino, *op. cit.*, p. 142).

[163] Palomba to Beust, September 21, 1870, HHSA, Politisches Korrespondenz (Rom), Fasz. XI/224, Bericht 101L, fol. 382a.

[164] On September 19, Ricotti had instructed Cadorna to respect the Leonine City, even if papal soldiers should withdraw to it (Ricotti, *op. cit.*, p. 82).

[165] Castagnola, *op. cit.*, p. 58; Palomba to Beust, September 21, 1870, HHSA, Politisches Korrespondenz (Rom), Fasz. XI/224, Bericht 101L, fols. 382a–382b.

[166] Lanza, however, instructed the general to wait until he had received a request in this sense from the pope himself (Cadorna, *op. cit.*, p. 257).

[167] Cf. the *Blue Book*, No. 35, p. 37.

of the Holy Father. This *de facto* "armistice line," inclosing the tiny papal enclave, was destined to endure until the accords of 1929.[168] For the time being, at least, the Vatican felt it had no reason to regret the invitation which Cadorna had finally accepted. On September 25, Antonelli himself made the papacy's position in this matter clear to Baron Blanc, the secretary-general of the Italian foreign office, who had been assigned to Cadorna's staff by Visconti-Venosta to handle all questions of a diplomatic nature. The cardinal remarked that the difficulties presented by the Italian government's plan to allow the Holy See to retain the Leonine City were at the moment "insoluble." The Leonine City had become the rendezvous of all the *mascalzoni* of Rome. It was therefore his desire, Antonelli concluded, that Cadorna should establish in that district a regular police and military administration.[169]

With the occupation of Rome, the Risorgimento hurdled one of its most formidable barriers. In accomplishing this result by violence, the Italian government exposed itself to the charge of flagrant inconsistency. But deviation from the course originally contemplated was forced upon it by circumstances which even a less vacillating cabinet would have been powerless to control. This was justly appreciated by Paget. On September 29 he wrote to Lord Granville, the British foreign minister:

The Italian Government started with very reasonable and moderate intentions when they invaded the Roman territory; Rome was not to be attacked, and the authority of the Pope was to be preserved; the occupation was to be a purely military one confined to certain strategical points necessary for the preservation of order. . . . . The Government has not acted in bad faith, but it has been carried away by the force of circumstances, and by the popular current resistance to which might have produced revolution.[170]

[168] Johnson, *op. cit.*, pp. 31–32; Arnold J. Toynbee, *Survey of International Affairs, 1929* (London, 1930), pp. 426–27; Benedict Williamson, *The Treaty of the Lateran* (London, 1929), p. 11.

[169] Blanc to Visconti-Venosta, September 25, 1870 (copy), HHSA, Politisches Archiv (Varia de Rome), Fasz. XI/225, fols. 55*a*–55*b*.

[170] *Blue Book*, No. 51, p. 58.

CHAPTER III

THE PRISONER OF THE VATICAN

THE Vatican lost no time in replying to the occupation of Rome. While Cadorna and Kanzler were negotiating an armistice at Villa Albani, Antonelli addressed a strong note to the diplomatic corps at the papal court. This document was the first of a long series inveighing against the "robbery" of September 20. It declared that the destruction of the temporal power in no way prejudiced the sovereign rights of Pius and of his successors. It pictured the pontiff as bereft of the freedom and independence without which he could not properly exercise his spiritual authority. The hope was expressed that the governments would interest themselves in his fate, and allusion was even made to the recovery in due time of his territorial domain.[1] The warlike mood which inspired this utterance did not blur the pontiff's perception of the realities of the situation. Speaking with impressive dignity, he told several members of the diplomatic corps that he had humbly resigned himself to the dictates of Providence. He went on to say that he had discharged his duty. He had done nothing to provoke "this atrocious and barbaric war" waged by a Catholic monarch against the head of the church.[2] Informed that the terms of the capitulation had been executed, he wrote to his nephew, Luigi: "All is over! Without liberty it is impossible to govern the church. Pray for me, all of you. I bless you."[3]

[1] Annex to Bericht 101C, HHSA, Politisches Korrespondenz (Rom), Fasz. XI/224, fols. 319a–321b; AD, 1874, II, 86–88; Giuseppe Leti, Roma e lo stato pontificio dal 1849 al 1870 (Roma, 1909), II, 350–52.

[2] Palomba to Beust, September 21, 1870, HHSA, Politisches Korrespondenz (Rom), Fasz. XI/224, Bericht 101I, fol. 362b.

[3] Raffaele de Cesare, Roma e lo stato del papa dal ritorno di Pio IX al XX settembre (Roma, 1907), II, 475.

The papal note of September 20 evoked from the Destra a reiteration of the official thesis that the occupation of Rome would only enhance the authority of the Holy See.[4] Pius' indignation and bitterness were indeed altogether too natural to be resented by the Italian government. But it was determined to give him no legitimate cause for further complaint. Cadorna was cautioned to assume a most deferential and conciliatory attitude in his dealings with the Vatican.[5] More than that, he was authorized to make the pontiff some very attractive offers. A separate telegraph and postal office was to be placed at the latter's exclusive disposal. It was to be run by officials of his own choice. He was to be given direct communication with the sea. A special coach was to be reserved for his use in any train that he might board. Special relays were to serve him wherever railways were not available. His couriers were to enjoy all the diplomatic immunities.[6] The Italian government was certain that these offers would demonstrate beyond any doubt that the events of September 20 involved no change in the pope's position vis-à-vis the Catholic world.

Pius, however, was in no mood for transactions with his despoilers. On September 29 he poured forth his many grievances in a letter to the sacred college. The loss of his territorial sovereignty, he proclaimed, had deprived him of the freedom to discharge his religious duties.[7] This eloquent pronouncement served notice upon the world that he was a "prisoner" within the confines of the Vatican.[8] Thereafter, he never ventured outside this rigidly circumscribed zone. To have gone about in the streets of Rome would have been

---

[4] Cf. the *Opinione* of September 24, 1870.

[5] Raffaele Cadorna, *La Liberazione di Roma nell'anno 1870 ed il plebiscito* (Torino, 1898), p. 256.

[6] *Ibid.*, p. 261.　　　　[7] *CC*, I (8th ser.; January 9, 1871), 215-16.

[8] "Protest, voluntary imprisonment, hope of foreign aid—these comprise the attitude for which the pontiff, after long meditation, had prepared himself" (cf. Francesco Salata, *Per la storia diplomatica della questione romana* [Milano, 1929], I, 133).

to acquiesce in his subjection to the power whose lawlessness he was denouncing. He proscribed for himself and his entourage all official or secular relations with the usurper, his courtiers, and his functionaries. He declared himself opposed to the coming of Catholic rulers or heads of governments to Rome, regarding as unfriendly their eventual visit to the Italian royal family. In assuming this position, Pius encircled his "prison" with a spiritual cordon more difficult to traverse than walls or moats. Antonelli did not dissemble the purely "moral" nature of his master's imprisonment. The cardinal admitted, in conversation with Blanc, that if Pius were to venture outside the Vatican, he would be very well received everywhere. But the point of the matter was that he could scarcely resume his pontifical functions in the very place where his sovereignty was being violated.[9] The *Osservatore romano* was equally candid. The Vatican, it explained, constituted "a moral prison." Bayonets did not bar the pope's exit, but his honor and dignity did.[10] This self-imposed incarceration opposed to the seizure of Rome "a continuous attitude of protest in order to safeguard a right."[11] It was designed to galvanize into an irresistible force the moral indignation of the Catholic world. It was also to implement the policy of watchful waiting which the Holy See had resolved to pursue.[12] The Italian government was in-

---

[9] Leti, *op. cit.*, II, 363.

[10] *Osservatore romano*, March 13, 1871.

[11] Cf. Antonio Monti, *Pio IX nel Risorgimento italiano* (Bari, 1928), p. 199.

[12] "I am loth to suspect the good intentions of your King or even of his Ministry," Antonelli explained to a member of parliament, "but how long are these men likely to remain in office? Who can answer for their successors? Was not the Government the first to promise us protection, and was it not the first to invade our territory? . . . . Believe me, neither your Sovereign nor his Ministers are able to make any promise on which we can rely. . . . . Why should the Holy Father quit the basis of his rights, international as well as private, and enter into transactions, when he is sure he can only lose by them. . . . . We had far better wait patiently till circumstances allow us to regain possession of what belongs to us, or till time shall have arranged matters" (*Times*, October 11, 1870). The cardinal's slogan then and later was: "Protest and Wait!" (cf. Ugo Pesci, *I primi anni di Roma capitale* [*1870–1878*] [Firenze, 1907], pp. 21–22).

censed at the pope's representation of his situation.[13] In a note issued to its diplomatic agents on October 11, it disclosed the postal and telegraphic concessions which it had offered him. These proposals, it declared,

should completely reassure not only the Holy Father but also the Catholic world as to the scrupulous care we are taking to preserve the existing relations between Catholic Christendom and its venerable head. We reject as insulting and absurd the accusation of wishing to keep the pope a prisoner in the Vatican. . . . .[14]

Pius' intransigent attitude, symbolized in his self-imprisonment, split the Roman aristocracy into Whites and Blacks. The former accepted the *status quo* and professed national and liberal sentiments.[15] The Blacks, who comprised some of the city's most illustrious names, were unreservedly and unalterably loyal to the dispossessed pontiff and his cause. Indeed, they were on the whole more papal than the pope himself. Many of them signified their state of mourning after September 20 by closing the shutters of their palace windows and vowing not to reopen them until the incarceration of the Holy Father had been happily terminated. In other Black mansions the throne reserved for the use of His Holiness when visiting his princely friends was turned to the wall. The hatred of Blacks for Whites achieved almost incredible

[13] Visconti-Venosta, Kübeck reported to Beust on October 8, 1870, seemed much pained by the reproaches contained in the papal letter of September 29 (cf. HHSA, Politisches Archiv [Florenz], Fasz. XI/75, No. 82, fol. 210b).

[14] *Libro verde*, No. 47, pp. 58–60. It should be noted that, despite its intransigent attitude, the Vatican accepted from the Italian government, early in October, the amount allocated in the papal civil list for the current month—50,000 scudi. This sum afterward served as the basis for the revenue allotted the Holy See in the great book of the public debt (Michele Rosi, *Vittorio Emanuele II* [Bologna, 1930], II, 167; Alessandro Guiccioli, *Quintino Sella* [Rovigo, 1887], I, 319; Stefano Castagnola, *Da Firenze a Roma: diario storico-politico del 1870–71* [Torino, 1896], note on pp. 66–67). This was, however, the only money which the Vatican consented to take from the Italian authorities. All payments subsequently proffered under the terms of the law of guarantees were spurned.

[15] On October 8, 1870, the Austrian ambassador in Rome reported that a considerable section of the aristocracy had openly accepted the new order of things (cf. HHSA, Politisches Korrespondenz [Rom], Fasz. XI/224, Bericht 108A, fol. 457a).

proportions. Marriages between members of the two groups were likely to be forbidddn by parents of the Black persuasion in order to preserve undefiled their allegiance to pope and church. The cleavage cast its shadow even over harmless social functions, and occasional diplomatic incidents served to give it an international flavor. This feud severely taxed the common sense and tact of the government. It frequently found itself obliged to hold the balance between the rival factions. The situation was aggravated by the plight of many Roman youths of noble ancestry. Assured by self-styled prophets that the existing regime would soon be extinguished by crusaders come from abroad to rescue the pope, they abruptly abandoned their university studies and even renounced imminent degrees. Their cue, they were told, was to wait for the deliverance, when they would be more than recompensed for their sacrifices.[16]

The events of September 20 evoked the greatest indignation among the faithful everywhere. The papacy, to its profound satisfaction,[17] received communications from every part of the world professing the deepest commiseration with the Holy Father. Lay and ecclesiastical leaders of the church vied with each other in proclaiming their unflinching devotion to the "prisoner" of the Vatican and in berating his alleged jailers.[18] In France the episcopate rallied sharply to the cause of the pope-king.[19] Monarchists and clericals were loud in their outcry against Italy. The *Union*, a leading legitimist organ, seized the opportunity to flay the Roman policy of Napoleon III and of the government of September 4. "The man who encompassed the misfortune of France," it trumpeted, "encompassed the misfortune of the church.

[16] Cf., in connection with this division into Whites and Blacks, the discussion of the Roman aristocracy in Pesci, *I primi anni*, pp. 155–72.

[17] Cf. "Un Conforto ai cattolici," in the *Osservatore romano*, December 26, 1870.

[18] Cf. "La grande manifestazione dell'Europa cattolica nel 1870," *CC*, I (8th ser.; December 24, 1870), 44–61.

[19] A. Debidour, *L'Eglise catholique et l'état sous la Troisième République* (Paris, 1906), I, 4–5.

He surrendered the pope in order to assure himself of the alliance of the Florentine government. He authorized the assault, and the reward of his treason has been denied him." The present rulers of the country had remained inactive, though all the world knew that France regarded the defense of the papacy as one of her first duties. From the moment of her failure to discharge this sacred obligation, she had been lost. With the pope a prisoner in his own palace, the journal continued, the proper government of the church was impossible. And only the shortsighted could believe that the Roman question had been solved. On the contrary, that question had only begun to exist.[20] "A great iniquity has been perpetrated," wailed the clerical *Monde*. "Rome has fallen into the power of Italy. . . . . May God take pity on France and pardon her for not having forbidden this outrage!" The new government, it dared to hope, would not wrap itself in a silence which Italy would interpret as encouragement. The present embarrassments of France or the acts of the fallen emperor could not be adduced in extenuation of a *fainéant* attitude. Were Paris itself to be in the hands of the Prussians, France would not abandon her mission. For "the indestructible solidarity which unites . . . . Rome and France does not depend on the accidents of war." It was therefore necessary to inform Italy that she could not occupy Rome without offending her Latin neighbor. The pope's despoilers, the Catholic sheet ominously concluded, held their prey for the moment. But the day of retribution would come. "God will know how to take his revenge. May he deign to do so by the sword of a purified and regenerated France!"[21] No less spirited was the language of the violently ultramontane *Univers*. It too enlarged upon the nexus between events in France and Rome. In its opinion, the independence of the pope was an absolute necessity for the eldest daughter of the church. The capture of Rome and the ensuing imprisonment of the Holy Father were victories for those enemies of France and of society: Bismarck and Blanqui.[22] While outraged religious sensibilities helped to account for much of this resentment, they were by no means the sole factor. Even more important was the realization that the fall of Rome meant a loss in power and influence for France.[23] Coming on the heels of the disastrous experience with Prussia, the extinction of the temporal power seemed to Frenchmen of conservative sympathies an added insult and sorrow.[24] Fulda was the scene of an important protest gathering of German Catholics. Many notables, some of them from outlying regions, were present. A resolution denouncing the occupation of Rome and demanding intervention by the powers was enthusiastically adopted. "To protect right against force," it declared, "is the duty of all governments of Europe which have recognized . . . . the sovereignty of the Holy See." The faithful were exhorted to elect to their legislatures men who could be relied upon to serve the papal cause.[25] In Prussia leading Catholics fomented an agitation which, in view of the approaching elections to the Landtag, gave the authorities at Berlin no little concern. Much was made of King William's pledge, vouchsafed in a speech from the throne in October, 1867, to do what he could to safeguard the spiritual independence of the Holy Father.[26] The Prussian ultramontanes accused the ministry of having violated that pledge. They pointed to the official silence on the occupation of Rome and intimated that further inaction would

[22] *Univers*, October 1, 1870.

[23] Many Frenchmen saw in the synchronism of the national *débâcle* and the events of September 20 a severe blow to their country (cf. C. Nigra, "Ricordi diplomatici, 1870," *Nuova antologia*, March 1, 1895, p. 24).

[24] Cf. Vicomte de Meaux, *Souvenirs politiques, 1871–1877* (Paris, 1905), p. 59; Charles Chesnelong, *Derniers jours de l'empire et le gouvernement de M. Thiers* (Paris, 1932), pp. 54–55.

[25] *Europäischer Geschichtskalender, 1870*, ed. H. Schulthess (Nördlingen, 1871), p. 118 (hereafter cited as *Schulthess, 1870*).

[26] Cf. Ed. Hüsgen, *Ludwig Windthorst: sein Leben, sein Wirken* (Köln, 1911), p. 100.

compel the Catholics of the country to take matters into their own hands. The Bishop of Hildesheim addressed himself directly to King William, imploring him to protect the pope's temporal throne. The rulers of other German states were the recipients of similar pleas. The excitement was particularly intense in devout Bavaria. There zealots talked of a crusade to rescue the head of their church.[27]

In Austria leading bishops and nobles depicted as intolerable the position of the Holy Father. They argued that the spoliation of the papacy jeopardized the existence of all legitimate thrones. More than that, Austria, by allowing this outrage to go unprotested, was exposing herself to the possibility of Italian depredations in certain of her own territories.[28] Countless petitions and addresses deploring the government's passive attitude poured into the foreign office. These documents were at one in demanding prompt and vigorous intervention.[29]

English Catholics found an effective spokesman in Archbishop Manning. This strong-willed prelate denounced Victor Emmanuel as "another Pontius Pilate for allowing himself, against his conviction, to be borne along by the tide of revolution."[30] The agitation which Manning personally launched and over which he presided was climaxed by a great meeting in St. James Hall in London on December 9. On this occasion he outdid himself in flaying the Italian government. He defended the Vatican's position on the temporal power and impugned with gusto the Cavourian heresy of a free church in a free state.[31] No less outspoken were the Irish Catholics. They sent the pope an address which read in part:

In the face of the recent usurpation, we proclaim, together with all the Catholics of the world, that to Your Holiness alone belongs the full and

---

[27] Cf. *Schulthess, 1870*, p. 118.   [28] Cf. *Libro verde*, No. 105, pp. 113–14.

[29] Cf. Friedrich Ferdinand Graf von Beust, *Aus drei viertel-jahrhunderten* (Stuttgart, 1887), II, 412.

[30] *Times*, October 5, 1870.   [31] *Ibid.*, December 10, 1870.

entire sovereignty over every part of the provinces which were occupied from the very beginning of the invasion, and to you alone belongs the fidelity of their inhabitants. . . . .[32]

While European Catholics were thus venting their wrath upon the despoilers of the Holy Father, their governments were speaking a very different language. The French cabinet, whose energies were engaged elsewhere, had not wavered in its resolve to maintain a guarded reserve in all matters affecting Italo-papal relations. It was therefore with no little bewilderment that it learned of the action taken by its inexperienced envoy at Florence, Sénard.[33] The latter, without explicit authorization from his government,[34] sent Victor Emmanuel a somewhat dithyrambic letter warmly felicitating him on the success of the recent campaign and on the moderation he had displayed in dealing with the religious phase of the Roman question.[35] The Italian government was very much touched by the friendly tone of this communication. "It is worthy of the present government of France," Visconti-Venosta wrote in reply, "to associate itself spontaneously with a policy which, after breaking down the last remnants of the temporal power, will proclaim at Rome the separation of church and state."[36] But in France a very different view was taken of Sénard's gesture. To his monarchist

---

[32] Cf. *Libro verde*, No. 94, pp. 99–100.

[33] Kübeck on one occasion alluded to Sénard's "complete lack of experience" in diplomatic affairs (cf. the Austrian minister's dispatch of October 8, 1870, to Beust in HHSA, Politisches Archiv [Florenz], Fasz. XI/75, No. 82D, fol. 224*b*).

[34] Frantz Despagnet, *La République et le Vatican, 1870–1906* (Paris, 1906), p. 18. It was probable, Kübeck caustically noted, that an "improvised" diplomatist like Sénard acted on his own initiative (Kübeck to Beust, November 3, 1870, HHSA, Politisches Archiv [Florenz], Fasz. XI/75, No. 88D, fol. 345*a*).

[35] *Libro verde*, No. 30, pp. 41–42. Sénard's letter, which was subsequently published by the Italian government, evoked considerable indignation at the Vatican. The *Civiltà cattolica* reproduced it in full in order that republican France "might be known for what she is and for what she is worth." This document, the Jesuit organ continued, sufficed to prove that the Italian government, before turning its artillery against Porta Pia, had assured itself of French noninterference (*CC*, I [8th ser.; January 21, 1871], 345).

[36] *Libro verde*, No. 31, pp. 42–43.

compatriots it seemed "a gratuitous humiliation."[37] But his republican superiors, too, were irked. Sénard's line of action had been agreed upon prior to his departure for Florence. He was to tell the Italian authorities that the French government had not officially denounced the September convention because of a sentiment of personal dignity and because it had been understood by the two governments that the convention had virtually ceased to exist with the fall of the empire.[38] Such an oblique imprimatur was one thing. Sénard's offensive pronouncement was quite another. The cabinet could scarcely forgive him for overstepping the bounds of the noncommittal attitude which it had scrupulously imposed upon itself. Even Gambetta, who was destined to become the country's foremost anticlerical, found Sénard's action imprudent. Before long, the unfortunate envoy was recalled, and the chargé d'affaires at Florence was cautioned against similar indiscretions. The French government, he was told, had taken no "absolute decision" in the Roman question. For the time being, the greatest reserve would have to be observed.[39] Sénard's place was eventually taken by Rothan, an experienced career diplomatist.[40] Favre, though his personal sympathies were with the Italians in their quarrel with the Roman Curia, was determined to preserve for France complete freedom of action. Moreover, with an eye to placating the clericals at home, he did not hesitate to proclaim himself the "zealous and resolute defender" of the church. It was his aim to steer a middle course and to abstain from taking sides. He would thus avoid becoming embroiled with the Catholic

---

[37] Meaux, op. cit., p. 59.

[38] Sénard to Crémieux, September 27, 1870, AMAE (Italie, août-décembre, 1870), Tome 379, fol. 259.

[39] Chaudordy to Cléry, November 24, 1870, ibid., fol. 356.

[40] Charles du Moüy, Souvenirs et causeries d'un diplomate (Paris, 1909), p. 21; R. P. Lecanuet, Les dernières années du pontificat de Pie IX, 1870–1878 (Paris, 1931), p. 90; Luigi Chiala, Dal 1858 al 1892; pagine di storia contemporanea (Torino, 1892–93), I, 75–76 (hereafter cited as Chiala, Pagine); Curàtulo, op. cit., p. 74.

party in France while retaining the friendship of Italy.[41] The range and scope of his Roman policy were circumscribed, however, by the *fait accompli* of September 20. The finality of that historic event was for him beyond question. In his opinion, the question of the temporal power had ceased to be the legitimate concern of the European powers.[42] But the French government was prepared to exert its influence to protect the spiritual freedom of the Holy Father.[43]

No less guarded was the position taken by the Prussian government. Thile refused to comment when he was officially apprised of the occupation of Rome. He explained to Count Launay that he had received no instructions from Bismarck in this matter.[44] The plight of the pope evoked little sympathy in influential quarters. Crown Prince Frederick believed the papacy "endlessly compromised" by the loss of its temporal sovereignty so soon after Pius IX's "self-deification."[45] "The miserable regime of priestly domination is at an end," he wrote in his diary on September 22, "and once more the triumph of German arms has done the Italians good service."[46] Bismarck himself appreciated the attitude of his Catholic compatriots, though their tactics strongly displeased him.[47] But he had his own reasons for taking their clamor for intervention coolly. Late in September he re-

---

[41] Maurice Reclus, *Jules Favre* (Paris, 1912), pp. 494–95.

[42] On September 28 the French chargé d'affaires at the Vatican wrote Favre: "I feel that the developments at Rome since the royal troops took possession of it have entered into the exclusive domain of Italian internal policy and should be withdrawn from the action of the diplomatic corps at the Holy See." Favre fully concurred in this view (Jules Favre, *Rome et la République française* [Paris, 1871], p. 53).

[43] Cf. Léopold Bastide, *Relations diplomatiques de la France et du Saint-Siège de 1804 à 1904* (Montpellier, 1909), p. 166.

[44] *Libro verde*, No. 29, pp. 40–41.

[45] Kaiser Friedrich III, *Das Kriegstagebuch von 1870–71* (Berlin and Leipzig, 1926), p. 156; Friedrich Fuchs, "Der römische Friede: seine Propheten, Pseudopropheten, Vorläufer u. Märtyrer," *Hochland*, June, 1929, p. 235.

[46] Kaiser Friedrich III, *op. cit.*, p. 134.

[47] Georges Goyau, *Bismarck et l'église; le culturkampf* (Paris, 1911–13), I, 41–42.

marked: "Yes, sovereign he [the pope] must remain, only there arises the question, how? More could be done for him if the ultramontanes were not everywhere so active against us. I am accustomed to paying people back in their own coin."[48] Bismarck was here alluding to the enemies of Prussia in Bavaria and Austria, to the Polish agitators, and to the Catholic party in France which at the moment was active in whipping up sentiment in favor of prolonging the war. In any case, the patent exigencies of the moment constrained him to continue to assure the Italian government that Prussia remained entirely alien to the occupation of the Roman territory and that she regarded this question as a purely internal one.[49] But there were weighty reasons for championing the cause of the Holy Father. The latter might be induced to exert pressure upon the French clergy in favor of an early peace. Such a service, in Bismarck's opinion, was more than enough to compensate for the ill feeling which Prussian intervention would engender among German Protestants and Italians.[50] His position was also influenced by the menacing language of his Catholic compatriots, who were altogether too formidable a force to be ignored with impunity. Conse-

[48] Moritz Busch, *Tagebuchblätter* (Leipzig, 1899), I, 243.

[49] Such was the language repeatedly employed by the Prussian minister in Florence after September 20 (cf. Kübeck to Beust, December 5, 1870, HHSA, Politisches Archiv [Florenz], Fasz. XI/75, No. 95C, fols. 515b–516a).

[50] Bismarck, *Gedanken und Erinnerungen* (Stuttgart, 1898), p. 470; Jean Lulvès, "Bismarck und die römische Frage," *Hochland*, June, 1929, p. 268. There was a tendency among Germans to hold the strength of Italy in low esteem, and the occupation of Rome had done nothing to discourage it. Joseph von Radowitz, who was destined to become one of Bismarck's most trusted adjutants at the foreign office, believed that the Italians had bitten off more than they could chew. They had always to be given courage by others, he asserted, and their most recent military exploit had not added to their luster (*Aufzeichnungen und Erinnerungen aus dem Leben des Botschafters Joseph Maria von Radowitz*, ed. Hajo Holborn [Berlin and Leipzig, 1925], I, 209). Heinrich von Treitschke, the famous historian and publicist, shared the belief that the Italians might prove unequal to the magnitude of their task. No friend of Italy, he wrote on September 25, could wish to see her king and parliament establish themselves in Rome. For they would scarcely be able to elude "the fine nets of clerical policy." More than that, the weak dynasty would be completely undermined and the country's sufferings perpetuated (cf. Treitschke's observations in "Friedenshoffnungen," *Preussische Jahrbücher*, XXVI, 500).

quently, despite previous and repeated affirmations of a
hands-off policy in the Roman question, he wrote to the
Prussian minister at Florence early in October:

> His Majesty the King does not consider the North German Confedera-
> tion called upon to interfere unasked in the political affairs of other coun-
> tries, yet he considers it a duty owed to the North German Catholics to take
> part in maintaining the dignity and independence of the head of the Catho-
> lic church.[51]

Thile spoke in the same sense to Launay.[52] The unceasing
flow of Catholic petitions imploring William's intervention
spurred the chancellor to study the question more carefully.
He asked Mühler, the Prussian minister of public worship,
for a memorandum indicating the conditions which would
secure the pope's spiritual freedom and which could be insisted upon in negotiations with the Italian government. He
also suggested that Mühler might request the petitioners or
some of the local dignitaries of the Catholic church to formu-
late their mimimum demands and specify just how they
might be satisfied.[53] There, for the time being, matters
rested.

Despite the clamor of the clerical party in Austria, Beust
steadfastly refused to protest against the occupation of
Rome. But he sought to make amends by counseling moderation at Florence.[54] He likewise hurried to place the services
of the Austrian ambassador at Rome at the disposal of the
Holy Father. The envoy was authorized to act as mediator
in eventual Italo-papal negotiations for a *modus vivendi*.[55] The
Vatican, however, betrayed not the slightest desire to avail
itself of his good offices.[56] Beust's position was rendered more
difficult by the fact that he was a Protestant. His adversaries
did not hesitate to attribute to his faith his alleged lack of

[51] *GW*, VI*b*, No. 1852, 537.   [53] *GW*, VI*b*, No. 1876, 553–54.

[52] *Libro verde*, No. 53, pp. 66–68.   [54] Cf. Beust, *op. cit.*, II, 416.

[55] *AD, 1874*, II, 120.

[56] Cf. Trauttmansdorff to Beust, October 8, 1870, HHSA, Politisches Korrespondenz (Rom), Fasz. XI/224, Bericht 108A, fol. 455*a*.

interest in the plight of the Holy See. The *Civiltà cattolica* spoke of the abject state into which the Hapsburg empire had fallen because it allowed itself to be governed by a man who was not only a heretic but a Mason as well.[57] The chancellor pleaded that he could not censure the Italian government for acts which it regarded as indispensable to the national well-being. But his critics would not be persuaded. Early in October a Catholic deputation called on him and submitted an address demanding that every opportunity be taken "to work for the restoration of the violated rights, the liberty and independence of the pope." In his reply, Beust underlined the futility of a demonstration which was not backed by force. Its sole result, he warned, would be to compromise the dignity of Austria. He did, however, promise to do what he could to safeguard the pope's spiritual position.[58] The Vatican, which was making every effort to remain on the friendliest terms with the Austrian authorities, professed satisfaction with the chancellor's declaration.[59] Italians felt that they had better reason to rejoice. Minghetti, who still headed the legation at Vienna, pointed out in a letter to his friend, Senator Giuseppe Pasolini, that the friendly attitude of the Austrian government had persisted despite the presence of numerous clericals in the imperial court. "If the Apostolic Empire," he triumphantly queried, "is satisfied with the end of the pope's temporal government, who would dare to take up its defense?"[60] In Italy, Minghetti's friends and admirers were ready to believe that Vienna's passivity was largely the result of his efforts.[61]

Lord Granville, the British foreign secretary, received word of the occupation of Rome with the utmost reserve.

[57] *CC*, I (8th ser.; December 24, 1870), 39.

[58] *Libro verde*, No. 49, pp. 61–62.

[59] Cf. Trauttmansdorff to Beust, October 15, 1870, HHSA, Politisches Korrespondenz (Rom), Fasz. XI/224, Bericht 112B, fols. 503*a*–503*b*.

[60] *Carteggio tra Marco Minghetti e Giuseppe Pasolini* (Torino, 1897), IV, 195.

[61] Cf. Luigi Luzzatti, *Memorie autobiografiche e carteggi* (Bologna, 1931), I, 309.

But, records the Italian minister who saw him on September 21, "his countenance, the expression of his benevolent sentiments and the very topics of our conversation left no doubt that the news . . . . was very agreeable to him."[62] Less circumspect was the attitude of Granville's chief, Gladstone. The Roman question caught up with the premier in the form of a memorial from a Catholic community requesting British diplomatic intervention in behalf of the Holy Father. Gladstone reassuringly replied that he and his colleagues in the cabinet regarded all questions relating to the pope's spiritual freedom and independence as within their province. This remark promptly embroiled him with some of his followers in the liberal party. They intimated that they would continue to support his ministry only if he explained away the objectionable statement.[63] But Gladstone refused to be intimidated. On February 21, 1871, he declared in the house of commons:

> The Government do not . . . . wish to have the spiritual functions of the Pope recognized or meddled with by us in any way; but the Government believe that the liberty of the head of the religion of many millions of our fellow-subjects—his liberty and personal independence—is a legitimate matter for the notice of this Government. That is the proposition we maintain and that we mean to adhere to. . . . .[64]

The events of September 20 gave rise to a host of rumors concerning the Holy Father's immediate plans. According to the most persistent of these, he was on the point of taking to his heels. True it was that numerous members of the papal entourage were again urging him to flee. They argued that Pius, by remaining in Rome, was making it easier for the Italians to claim that the future capital could properly house both sovereigns. In the event of a post-war international congress, Italy's chance of retaining Rome might be enhanced by this *de facto* coresidence. Furthermore, inaction by the pontiff would constitute a very great concession to his

---

[62] *Libro verde*, No. 32, pp. 43–45.   [63] Cf. *Times*, January 23, 1871.

[64] *Hansard's Parliamentary Debates*, CCIV, 649.

enemies, who feared his departure above all else and would move heaven and earth to prevent it. But Antonelli continued to frown on the idea of flight.[65] A spirited duel ensued between the cardinal and the proponents of immediate departure, who were led by the Jesuits. The outcome of this contest was a matter of no little concern to the authorities at Florence. Visconti-Venosta himself remarked to Paget that the efforts being made to persuade the pope to leave were worrying him. His government, he added, would regret the pontiff's going; but, should the latter decide to take this step, he would be given an escort and conducted with sovereign honors to his destination.[66] A like assurance was given Count Trauttmansdorff, the Austrian ambassador to the Holy See, who had been instructed by his government to interrupt his leave of absence and resume his post in Rome. During his brief stay in Florence, the envoy conferred with the Italian foreign minister. The latter emphasized his desire to see the pope remain in Rome. But if His Holiness, Visconti-Venosta continued, should wish to depart, no obstacle would be placed in his way. On the contrary, he would receive all the consideration and honors due him.[67] Convinced that the situation was exceedingly serious, the Italian cabinet attempted to counteract the influence of the Jesuits. It availed itself of the services of Emilio Diamilla-Müller, an engineer who was friendly with Mgr. Pasquale Badia, one of the pope's domestic prelates.[68] More effective was Visconti-Venosta's request that the powers advise the reputedly vacillating inmate of the Vatican against quitting his present abode. This

[65] Palomba to Beust, September 21, 1870, HHSA, Politisches Korrespondenz (Rom), Fasz. XI/224, Bericht 101D, fols. 326a–327b; Lefebvre de Béhaine to Favre, September 22, 1870, AMAE (Rome, août-décembre, 1870), Tome 1047, fol. 314.

[66] *Blue Book*, No. 49, p. 57.

[67] Cf. Kübeck to Beust, October 8, 1870, HHSA, Politisches Archiv (Florenz), Fasz. XI/75, No. 82, fol. 208b.

[68] Giuseppe Paladino, *Storia d'Italia dal 1861 al 1871 con particolare riguardo alla questione romana* (Milano, 1932), p. 146.

most of them readily agreed to do.[69] But the Belgian government refused to commit itself,[70] while Beust, though agreeing that the pope would do better to remain in Rome, declined to influence his decision in any way. At the same time, the chancellor informed His Holiness that he would be offered a refuge in Austria should he feel obliged to seek new quarters.[71]

This burning of the wires proved quite unnecessary, however. Pius, despite periodic allusions to the subject, had never seriously entertained the idea of quitting Rome.[72] His advanced age was one deterrent. The hardships of travel and a profound abhorrence for ocean voyages were others. Finally, there was the influence of Antonelli and Don Giovanni Bosco, the saintly founder of the Salesian Society.[73] The latter reminded Pius that "the Sentinel, the angel of Israel, remained at his post to guard the Rock of God and the Holy Ark."[74] On September 23, Antonelli assured the Austrian chargé d'affaires in the most positive fashion that the Holy Father had no thought of leaving the city.[75] A few days later, the cardinal informed Trauttmansdorff and Lefeb-

[69] *Blue Book*, No. 59, p. 61; *Libro verde*, No. 37, pp. 47–48; *GW*, VI*b*, No. 1840, 527. Cf. the description of the Prussian government's attitude on this question in Wimpffen to Beust, October 13, 1870, HHSA, Politisches Archiv (Rapports de Berlin), Fasz. III/103, fol. 167*b*.

[70] *Libro verde*, No. 40, pp. 49–50.

[71] *Das Staatsarchiv. Sammlung der officiellen Actenstücke zur Geschichte der Gegenwart* (Hamburg, 1861———), XIX, No. 4178, 355 (hereafter cited as *Staatsarchiv*); *AD, 1874*, II, 119–20; Salata, *op. cit.*, I, 129–30. Beust for a time considered the idea of placing Trent at the pope's disposal (Eduard von Wertheimer, *Graf Julius Andrássy: Sein Leben und seine Zeit* [Stuttgart, 1910], II, 194).

[72] Salata, *op. cit.*, I, 123–24, 132. Pius, according to the testimony of Mgr. Pacca, a member of the papal entourage, had from the outset refused to abandon the city (cf. Pesci, *I primi anni*, p. 17).

[73] On the work of Bosco see H. L. Hughes, *The Catholic Revival in Italy, 1815–1915* (London, 1935), pp. 49–66; Ernesto Vercesi, *Don Bosco: il santo italiano del secolo XIX* (Milano, 1929); Paolo Mattei-Gentili, "Don Bosco Santo d'Italia," *Nuova antologia*, March 16, 1934, pp. 214–24.

[74] Ernesto Vercesi, *Pio IX* (Milano, 1930), pp. 227–28.

[75] Palomba to Beust, September 24, 1870, HHSA, Politisches Korrespondenz (Rom), Fasz. XI/224, Bericht 102A, fol. 376*b*.

vre de Béhaine, the French chargé, that his master was re-solved not to abandon Rome.[76] On September 28, Pius him-self remarked to Trauttmansdorff that he had decided to stay where he was as long as it should prove possible for him to do so.[77] Baron Blanc received a similar assurance from the papal secretary of state.[78] Visconti-Venosta's emissary was told that, for the present, the pope did not contemplate departure. Nothing, Antonelli quickly added, could be guar-anteed for the future, because the difficulties might increase.[79] The mood which inspired this reservation inspired too a sig-nificant diplomatic gesture. As a precautionary measure, and to avoid the annoyance of a secret departure, in the im-probable eventuality that Pius should feel obliged to go, the Vatican requested the various governments to indicate whether they would use their influence at Florence to insure a free and safe exit.[80] The replies received were in the affirma-tive,[81] much to the gratification of Antonelli.[82] Visconti-Venosta himself, in a circular note of October 14, reassured the powers on this score. Should the Holy Father decide to abandon Rome, he wrote, the Italian government, though

[76] Lefebvre de Béhaine to Favre, September 28, 1870, AMAE (Rome, juin-septembre, 1870), Tome 1047, fol. 338; Trauttmansdorff to Beust, September 27, 1870, HHSA, Politisches Korrespondenz (Rom), Fasz. XI/224, No. 4447/72, fol. 396a.

[77] Trauttmansdorff to Beust, September 28, 1870, HHSA, Politisches Korre-spondenz (Rom), Fasz. XI/224, Bericht 103B, fols. 411a–411b.

[78] Cadorna, op. cit., p. 439; Vercesi, Pio IX, p. 228; Salata, op. cit., I, 124; Leti, op. cit., II, 357.

[79] Blanc to Visconti-Venosta, September 28, 1870 (copy), HHSA, Politisches Archiv (Weisungen nach Florenz), Fasz. XI/76, fol. 258a.

[80] Chaudordy to Sénard, October 13, 1870, AMAE (Italie, août-décembre, 1870), Tome 379, fol. 299; Trauttmansdorff to Beust, October 8, 1870, HHSA, Politisches Korrespondenz (Rom), Fasz. XI/224, Bericht 108B, fols. 466a–467b; AD, 1874, II, 124, 125–26; Favre, op. cit., pp. 56–57.

[81] Cf. Beust to Trauttmansdorff, October 13, 1870, HHSA, Politisches Archiv (Rome, Expeditions, Varia), Fasz. XI/225, fol. 207a; AD, 1874, II, 128, 159–60.

[82] The cardinal was careful to explain to Trauttmansdorff that the pope's de-parture was an eventuality which, it was to be hoped, would not arise (Trautt-mansdorff to Beust, October 14, 1870, HHSA, Politisches Korrespondenz [Rom], Fasz. XI/224, No. 102, fol. 495a).

deploring this resolution, would give him complete liberty to do as he pleased and would show him every possible courtesy and respect.[83] This declaration, vouchsafed with an eye to the attitude of Vienna, was well received. Beust, who once again was reminding the Italian government that it had pledged itself to respect the pope's freedom of decision,[84] found Visconti-Venosta's note entirely satisfactory. It was now clear, he observed, that Pius could safely leave Rome and travel across Italian territory.[85] The chancellor's peace of mind was enhanced by the Florentine cabinet's specific rejoinder to his representations. Visconti-Venosta very formally renewed to Kübeck the assurances contained in the circular of October 14. He told the Austrian minister that the Italian government was anxious to be informed in advance of the pope's intentions so as to be able to take all precautions to insure a proper exit.[86]

This diplomatic interlude was accompanied by the customary contradictory reports regarding the Holy Father's immediate plans. Authoritative papal quarters did what they could to discourage this rumormongering. Thus, on October 18, the *Osservatore romano* sharply denied that Pius was about to pack up and leave for Innsbruck. But popular skepticism persisted, and no less a personage than Arnim was widely suspected of being among the proponents of flight.[87] This

[83] *Libro verde*, No. 51, p. 64.

[84] Cf. Kübeck to Beust, October 22, 1870, HHSA, Politisches Archiv (Florenz), Fasz. XI/75, No. 86A, fol. 291a; Beust to Trauttmansdorff, October 16, 1870, *ibid*. (Rome, Expeditions, Varia), Fasz. XI/225, fols. 209a–209b.

[85] Beust to Trauttmansdorff, October 22, 1870, *ibid*. (Rome, Expeditions, Varia), Fasz. XI/225, fol. 215b.

[86] Kübeck to Beust, October 22, 1870, *ibid*. (Florenz), Fasz. XI/75, No. 86A, fols. 291a–292a.

[87] Arnim's alleged activity in this sense had been reported by the Austrian and French chargés d'affaires (cf. Palomba to Beust, September 21 and 24, October 1, 1870, *ibid*. [Rom], Fasz. XI/224, Nos. 101L, 102A, 104A, fols. 374a, 375a–376a, 382b–383a, 421a; Lefebvre de Béhaine to Favre, September 22, 26, 1870, AMAE [Rome, juin-septembre, 1870], Tome 1047, fols. 314 and 333).

suspicion was shared by the Florentine authorities.[88] The indefatigable diplomatist did indeed inform his government that the Holy Father might decide to seek refuge in Prussia. But the response from Berlin could scarcely have been to his liking. Bismarck advised the ambassador to say nothing about this matter. He told him, for his personal information, that it would be impossible to find the pope a suitable asylum in Germany.[89] This had been the chancellor's position from the very beginning,[90] and it was shared by King William and Crown Prince Frederick.[91]

Bismarck's real intentions were the subject of considerable speculation in Rome. It was bruited about that the redoubtable statesman, in order to induce the Bavarian Catholics to unite with the rest of Germany, had declared himself willing to intervene in behalf of the Holy Father. This story was never verified, but the Prussian party at the Vatican had not yet despaired of seeing the new colossus of the North assume the role of savior. Aid from other quarters seemed out of the question, for the Holy Father was involved in an ecclesiastical quarrel with Austria, and France had just abandoned him to the Italians.[92] And it was a fact that Italy had aroused the ire of Prussia by permitting Garibaldi to join

[88] Cf. Kübeck to Beust, October 8, 1870, HHSA, Politisches Archiv (Florenz), Fasz. XI/75, No. 82E, fol. 229b.

[89] GW, VIb, No. 1846, 531.

[90] On September 19, Thile had informed him that Arnim was being cautioned against inviting the pope to come to Prussia. "But," the foreign secretary had queried, "should not Fulda now be kept in mind?" Bismarck's reply had been most explicit. "No," he had written, "the migration of the pope to Prussia would be an embarrassment and a political danger for us. Therefore, no initiative is to be taken in this matter."

[91] On September 22 the latter had recorded in his diary the hope that Pius would be wise enough to remain in Rome and recognize the new state of affairs in Italy. Were the pontiff to leave his capital, he had written, it was doubtful whether a return could easily be effected. It was reported, he had noted further, that Berlin had taken steps to offer the pope a refuge in Fulda. "God preserve us from ever having these people settled in our country! That would be the last straw!" (Kaiser Friedrich III, op. cit., p. 134).

[92] Cf. Julius Clausen, Bismarck und der Katholizismus in den Jahren 1851–1871 (Hamburg, 1934), p. 57.

the fighting forces of France. This circumstance did indeed encourage the Prussophils in Pius' entourage to believe that King William would not object to diplomatic intervention.[93] They were very soon disabused, however, thanks to Archbishop Ledochowski of Posen and Gnesen. The latter—so his secretary subsequently reported to the Holy Father—believed he could turn to good advantage his cordial relations with William by presenting personally to that monarch the address of his diocese on the affairs of Rome.[94] Accordingly, he wrote Bismarck that he wished to come to Versailles. This gesture, which the Vatican claimed was due exclusively to the initiative of the distinguished ecclesiastic and was neither suggested nor commanded by the Holy See,[95] was very kindly received. The chancellor replied that he would welcome the opportunity to discuss methods of guaranteeing the freedom and independence of the Holy Father.[96] The prelate, who arrived on November 6, had more immediate business to transact. It became speedily apparent that he was charged with the mission of imploring King William to protest against the occupation of Rome and to offer the pope an asylum, should he need one, in the Prussian monarchy.[97] William, as a Protestant ruler, declined to make such a protest. That, he felt, was the concern of the Catholic powers. He observed that Prussia, for the time being, had every reason to remain

[93] Ottocar Lorenz, *Kaiser Wilhelm und die Begründung des Reichs, 1866–1871* (Jena, 1902), p. 487.

[94] Trauttmansdorff to Beust, November 30, 1870, HHSA, Politisches Korrespondenz (Rom), Fasz. XI/224, Bericht 123, fols. 624*a*–624*b*.

[95] Cf. Trauttmansdorff to Beust, November 14, 1870, *ibid.*, No. 120, fols. 586*a*–586*b*.

[96] *GW*, VI*b*, No. 1880, 555–56.

[97] Hermann Oncken, *Grossherzog Friedrich I von Baden und die deutsche Politik von 1854–1871* (Berlin and Leipzig, 1927), II, 189; Kaiser Friedrich III, *op. cit.*, p. 215; *Denkwürdigkeiten des Fürsten Chlodwig zu Hohenlohe-Schillingsfürst* (Stuttgart and Leipzig, 1906), II, 27. In requesting a Prussian protest against the occupation of Rome, Ledochowski contended that the pope's temporal power was guaranteed by the treaties of Vienna (Paul Matter, *Bismarck et son temps* [Paris, 1908], III, 123).

on good terms with Italy. He deplored, he said, the pontiff's plight. He was keenly interested in the propapal sympathies of his Catholic subjects. But it was necessary, he went on, to await an opportune moment for action which for the present he could not undertake. He did allude, however, to the possibility of a post-war international conference to consider the question of Italo-papal relations.[98] On this issue, the king and Bismarck were entirely at one. The latter agreed that it was the duty of the Catholic states to protest against the events of September 20. And it was impossible to say, he remarked, whether Prussia would co-operate in such a démarche.[99] A more categorical refusal to accede to the request for a protest was shunned out of deference, perhaps, to the susceptibilities of the Bavarian ultramontanes.[100] But monarch and chancellor differed sharply on the question of an asylum. William, supported by the crown prince and the Grand Duke of Baden,[101] would not hear of establishing the pope and his court on German soil. Bismarck, executing a volte-face, now declared himself in favor of offering Pius a refuge in Köln or Fulda. He pointed out that ultramontanism was as strong as it was in Germany only because the faithful did not have a correct picture of the papacy. An opportunity to see this institution at close range would rectify the situation. Protestants, too, would be enlightened and disillusioned. The sight of the old man, eating and drinking like everyone else, taking his pinch of snuff and smoking a cigar, would cure them of any desire to embrace Catholicism. And important political interests would be served. Prussia would gain in the esteem of Catholics as the only power which

[98] Trauttmansdorff to Beust, November 30, 1870, HHSA, Politisches Korrespondenz (Rom), Fasz. XI/224, Bericht 123, fol. 624b; Oncken, Grossherzog Friedrich I von Baden, pp. 179 and 191; Denkwürdigkeiten des Fürsten Chlodwig zu Hohenlohe-Schillingsfürst, II, 27–28.

[99] Oncken, Grossherzog Friedrich I von Baden, pp. 189–90.

[100] Cf. Matter, op. cit., III, 123.

[101] Oncken, Grossherzog Friedrich I von Baden, p. 164; Kaiser Friedrich III, op. cit., p. 215.

could protect their head. The Poles would be won over. And
a grateful and necessarily subservient pope would be highly
serviceable in persuading the Bavarian ultramontanes to accept the treaties establishing the German empire. Above all,
he could make himself distinctly invaluable by exerting pressure on the French clergy in behalf of a speedy termination
of the war.[102] The pope never availed himself of Bismarck's hospitality
and evinced no desire to do so.[103] Nevertheless, rumors of an
imminent flight from Rome persisted, and Antonelli himself
helped to keep them alive by assuring Lefebvre de Béhaine
that, if circumstances should compel Pius to depart, he would
go to Corsica.[104] This projected honor had been well earned
by France. Her government, more than any other and despite its many pressing cares, was giving the matter in question its unremitting attention. Its position was an interesting compound which combined the hospitality of a prospective host with the detachment of the inveterate realist. It
declared itself prepared to grant the Holy Father an asylum;[105] but it coupled this offer with the suggestion that he
would do better to remain where he was. If it should prove
impossible to prevent the pope's departure, Favre wrote
Lefebvre de Béhaine on March 15, 1871, it would be the duty
of France to receive him with "respectful warmth." But it
would be her duty, too, to indicate to him the complications
involved. With the country divided into two hostile camps,

---

[102] Lulvès, op. cit., pp. 267–68; Denkwürdigkeiten des Fürsten Chlodwig zu Hohenlohe-Schillingsfürst, II, 28; Busch, op. cit., I, 372–73; Bismarck, op. cit., p. 470;
Oncken, Grossherzog Friedrich I von Baden, pp. 163–64; Kaiser Friedrich III, op.
cit., p. 215; GW, VIb, 556 n.; Lorenz, op. cit., pp. 487–88; Hubert Bastgen, Die römische Frage (Freiburg i.B., 1919), III (1), note on pp. 12–13; Karl Bachem,
Vorgeschichte Geschichte und Politik der deutschen Zentrumspartei (Köln, 1927), III,
195; Vercesi, Pio IX, p. 234.

[103] Cf. Trauttmansdorff's observations on the subject of the pope's departure in
his dispatch of December 16, 1870, to Beust, HHSA, Politisches Archiv (Varia de
Rome), Fasz. XI/225, fol. 44b.

[104] Lefebvre de Béhaine to Chaudordy, January 1, 1871, AMAE (Rome, janvier-
février, 1871), Tome 1049, fol. 1.

[105] Cf. Chaudordy to Lefebvre de Béhaine, January 10, 1871, ibid., fols. 34–35.

there was reason to fear that his sojourn would be troubled by intrigues injurious to his interests and to those of his hosts. It was therefore necessary to apprise the Vatican of the "delicacy" of France's situation.[106] In another dispatch to Lefebvre de Béhaine later that month, Favre returned to this theme with increased emphasis. It was regrettable, he observed, that the cabinet of Florence did not appreciate all the advantages of a more moderate policy. Not that the law of guarantees was excessively harsh. On the contrary, it granted fairly generous concessions to the Holy Father. "It is in the matter of detail and application," he contended, "that there is manifested a petty, quarrelsome and persecutory spirit which makes impossible a serious and lasting rapprochement." Such a rapprochement, however, was very much to be desired.

Everyone would gain by it: the pope, by retaining the prestige of a territorial tie which goes back almost two thousand years; Italy, by not losing this great figure; . . . . finally, the power on whose soil the pope would demand refuge. The Italian government would have more authority, the pope, more security and peace, the allied power, more freedom of action and internal tranquillity. The Holy Father should therefore remain in Rome. . . . . Tell Cardinal Antonelli that we are ready to receive him with all due respect in Corsica, at Pau, in Algiers . . . . but that we continue to believe that the reconciliation which will permit him to stay in the Vatican is still the best solution.[107]

Pius, however, scarcely needed any urging. His reluctance to leave had in no way diminished since the previous September. His aversion for the trials of exile was as great as ever. He

---

[106] *Ibid.* (Rome, mars-avril, 1871), Tome 1050, fols. 89–90.

[107] Favre to Lefebvre de Béhaine, March 26, 1871, *ibid.*, fol. 163. Favre gave similar instructions to his envoy in Florence. "Your role," he wrote, "must be that of an impartial and firm protector of the spiritual authority of the Holy Father and of a defender of all measures which will assure his free and dignified sojourn at Rome." The departure of the pope would be deleterious both to Italy and to the papacy and therefore everything would have to be done to prevent it. "In asking us for an asylum," Favre added, "the Holy Father will create a real embarrassment for us. We would receive him properly, but we would be unable to halt the inopportune zeal of his friends and the excesses of his enemies. We would be placing the Roman question in the thick of our national passions, to the great detriment of our internal peace and of the dignity of our guest" (Favre to Choiseul, April 20, 1871, *ibid.* [Italie, mars-avril, 1871], Tome 381, fol. 435).

realized, moreover, that it would be much easier to leave than to return. And he could think of no really suitable place to go to. Conditions in France definitely excluded her. Belgium was far away. He doubted whether he would find adequate protection in Austria. In any case, a long sea voyage was required to get to Trieste, and sea voyages were of course anathema to him. And travel was hardly the thing for an old, ailing man.[108] On one occasion, he remarked: "I am not moving and I shall not move. I am too old to imitate Pius VII, and Victor Emmanuel is not Napoleon."[109] But the possibility that he might change his mind and decide to establish himself elsewhere continued, nevertheless, to preoccupy the Italian government. Indicative of the latter's frame of mind was Visconti-Venosta's candid admission in May, 1871, that Pius' departure would be very embarrassing for Italy as well as for everyone else.[110]

On October 9, Victor Emmanuel announced the appointment of the veteran soldier-statesman, General Alfonso La Marmora, as governor pro tem of Rome.[111] This action caused no surprise. The idea of sending him there in this capacity had been urged for weeks by Sella;[112] and late in September the *Opinione* had discussed his appointment as a *fait accompli*.[113] His choice was violently assailed by the Sinistra. The *Riforma* charged that he was wilful and obstinate and a failure both as a soldier and as a statesman.[114] The bulk of public opinion, however, took a different view of the general's appointment. The utmost tact and delicacy

---

[108] Camillo Manfroni, *Sulla soglia del Vaticano* (Bologna, 1920), I, 58, 287–89.

[109] *Ibid.*, p. 72.

[110] Kálnoky to Beust, May 19, 1871, HHSA, Politisches Archiv (Rom), Fasz. XI/226, No. 29D, fols. 462b–463a.

[111] His official title was "royal lieutenant-general."

[112] Cf. Paolo Boselli, "Roma e Quintino Sella," *Nuovo antologia*, September 16, 1927, p. 144.

[113] Cf. the *Opinione* of September 28, 1870.

[114] *Riforma*, October 13, 1870.

were required to deal with the situation created by the occupation, and these he reputedly possessed in ample degree.
It was assumed that he would succeed in holding the balance
between anticlerical and clerical extremists.[115] His name, it
was believed, would be "a challenge hurled at the republican
party." Inasmuch as he had taken no part in the occupation
of Rome and had even disapproved of it in principle, he would
be giving proof of "abnegation" and "devotion to his country" by accepting this mandate. It was supposed that he,
more than anyone else, was "fitted to support the cause of
order and reconciliation."[116] His presence in Rome, in the
opinion of ministerialists, would attest the government's sincerity in promising to protect the freedom and independence
of the Holy Father. It would signify, his biographer tells us,
that "the servitude of the church was over and that Italy, in
becoming mistress of her capital, did not come to offend
against religion, but rather to surround it with reverence, respect and freedom."[117] And indeed the selection of La Marmora did reassure the Vatican a little.[118] His appointment
was also made with an eye to the reaction of foreign governments. On September 22, Paget wrote to Granville: "The
great object of the Government now is to reassure the Pope
and Europe as to their intentions; and General La Marmora's
appointment is the best guarantee which could be given in
this respect."[119] On September 29, Paget again alluded to the

[115] Vittorio Bersezio, *Il Regno di Vittorio Emanuele II: trent'anni di vita italiana*
(Torino, 1878–95), VIII, 389.

[116] Cf. Kübeck to Beust, September 26, 1870, HHSA, Politisches Archiv (Florenz), Fasz. XI/75, No. 79A, fols. 181*b*–182*a*.

[117] Giuseppe Massari, *Il Generale Alfonso La Marmora* (Firenze, 1880), pp..411–
12. On January 8, 1878, Sella declared in the course of a funeral service in honor of
the general: "In 1870, when Italy, after having finally arrived at Rome, wished to
show . . . . with what loyalty and moderation she intended to solve the arduous
questions which now presented themselves, she chose La Marmora to represent the
king" (Guiccioli, *op. cit.*, I, 318).

[118] Cf. Trauttmansdorff to Beust, October 1, 1870, HHSA, Politisches Korrespondenz (Rom), Fasz. XI/224, No. 104A, fol. 416*b*.

[119] *Blue Book*, No. 35, p. 37.

significance of La Marmora's appointment. "The general's well-known character and political sentiments," he observed, "are a certain pledge that he will omit no means of conciliation in the execution of his duties; that he will do all that can be done to reassure the Pope; and that he will deal with a firm hand with the propagators of violent doctrines and revolution."[120] High hopes were entertained that he would do much to pave the way for an Italo-papal *modus vivendi*. The general himself was confident, on the eve of his departure for Rome, that these hopes would not be disappointed. The Roman correspondent of the *Times* reported: "General La Marmora, from what I hear, is very sanguine in his conviction that by his own personal influence he shall be able to win over the Pope and effect that reconciliation which no one has yet been able to accomplish."[121]

La Marmora arrived in Rome on October 11 and at once took charge of his post. His first official act was to issue a proclamation in which he sang the praises of the recently achieved Italian unity and alluded very pointedly to the upright policy which the government intended to pursue toward the Holy See. The acquisition of Rome, he declared, imposed serious obligations upon Italy, and her rulers were resolved to fulfil them by enacting guarantees which would render the papacy free and independent in the exercise of all its rights and functions. "We could not," he continued, "fail to discharge this duty without seriously offending the conscience of Catholics and falling short of our principles." But the national sentiment was as sacred as the religious, and the two had to be blended harmoniously. Whoever, by rejecting all overtures for a reconciliation, created a gulf between these sentiments, would be shouldering a grave responsibility.[122] Language of this sort could scarcely fail to wound and embitter the Vatican.[123] The *Unità cattolica* sharply informed the

---

[120] *Ibid.*, No. 51, p. 58.   [121] *Times*, October 17, 1870.

[122] *CC*, I (8th ser.; January 9, 1871), 222–23.

[123] Cf. Trauttmansdorff to Beust, October 12, 1870, HHSA, Politisches Korrespondenz (Rom), Fasz. XI/224, No. 111, fol. 488a.

general that it was impossible for Catholicism to be nation al.[124] According to the *Civiltà cattolica*, the concluding words of his manifesto seemed a threat addressed to the Holy Father,[125] and Antonelli, as if to reply to them, declared in a note of October 17 to the nuncios that the usurpations committed at the expense of the pontiff and the imprisonment forced upon him after September 20 were without parallel in the history of the civilized world.[126] Undeterred by this indirect warning, La Marmora attempted to persuade the Holy See to permit employees of the former papal administration to take an oath of loyalty to the new regime. But the pope's reply was a categorical refusal.[127] The general drew another rebuff when Antonelli politely but firmly turned down his request for an interview.[128] This was hardly an auspicious beginning, and ensuing developments were to aggravate the situation and render La Marmora's mission utterly hopeless.

On October 19 the Italian government issued two important decrees. One of them provided that existing laws against abuses of the press were to be inapplicable to the printing establishments used by the pope. They were likewise to be inoperative with respect to printed documents emanating from the Holy See or from the congregations and ecclesiastical offices dependent upon it.[129] The other decree was likewise intended as a conciliatory gesture. It extended to the person of the pope the safeguards conferred upon the king by the edict of March 26, 1848. The Holy Father was thereby protected not only against incitements to attempts upon his life but also against press attacks and insults directed at his

[124] *Unità cattolica*, October 13, 1870.

[125] *CC*, I (8th ser.; January 9, 1871), 223.

[126] Annex to Beust's dispatch of November 27, 1870, to Trauttmansdorff, HHSA, Politisches Archiv (Rome, Expeditions, Varia), Fasz. XI/225, fol. 251*b*.

[127] Guiccioli, *op. cit.*, I, 320.

[128] Cf. Trauttmansdorff to Beust, October 15, 1870, HHSA, Politisches Korrespondenz (Rom), Fasz. XI/224, No. 112A, fol. 497*a*.

[129] *CC*, I (8th ser.; January 21, 1871), 349.

person or at foreign ambassadors accredited to his court. But the Vatican was unimpressed. The *Civiltà cattolica* sarcastically remarked:

> Here, for the first time, by the kindness of Signor Raeli, the life of the pope in Rome is made safe! . . . . Breathe freely, therefore, Italian and foreign Catholics! Not only is life guaranteed the pope, but he is also promised a respect which forbids journalists to demand that he be handcuffed and imprisoned.

Continuing in this vein, the Curia's Jesuit organ informed its readers that the purpose of this decree was evidently to show that "the liberty introduced into Rome on September 20 by the bombs of Cadorna and Bixio . . . . will more efficaciously than ever safeguard the majesty and inviolability of the pope." This "precious document," it went on derisively, would probably be utilized to edify European diplomacy as to the zeal with which the government of Florence was protecting the freedom and dignity of the Holy See.[130] While the Vatican scoffed, the Sinistra fumed. The opposition press charged that the decrees were reactionary in character, that they were the "despotic acts of an arbitrary, uncontrolled ministry," inasmuch as parliament had not been consulted. Furthermore, they outraged the principle of civic equality by granting "exorbitant privileges to a priest and his subordinates in office." The special safeguards conferred upon the person of the pontiff were lashed as part of a "conspiracy against the freedom of conscience." Their effect was to set up in Italy a "second executioner" who was unrestrained even by the most ordinary scruples.[131]

Whatever expectations the government may have attached to these decrees were dissipated overnight by Pius himself. On October 20 he issued a bull (*Postquam Dei munere*) suspending indefinitely the ecumenical council which had been in session since the close of the previous

---

[130] *Ibid.*, pp. 348–49.

[131] Cf., e.g., the furious tirade in the *Riforma* of October 24, 1870. Cf. also Kübeck to Beust, November 3, 1870, HHSA, Politisches Archiv (Florenz), Fasz. XI/75, fol. 335*a*.

year. The occupation of Rome, this document announced, had created an impossible situation. The Holy See, placed under a hostile rule, was seriously hindered in the discharge of its religious functions. In such a state of affairs, the council could not enjoy the "necessary freedom, safety and tranquillity."[132] The government hastened to reply to these allegations. On October 21 the *Gazzetta ufficiale* published a strongly worded note denying that the spiritual freedom of the Holy Father had in any way been restricted. In support of this contention, it was pointed out that the bull had been published and posted without the slightest interference from the authorities. Not content with this pungent rejoinder, the cabinet submitted its case to the powers. On October 22, Visconti-Venosta declared, in a circular to his diplomatic representatives, that the fears expressed by the pontiff were wholly groundless. He pointed out that the churchmen participating in the deliberations of the council were, by the very nature of their office and mission, placed beyond the reach of political influence. They were entirely free to resume their sittings in Rome, if they should so desire.[133] The ministerial thesis was reiterated in the columns of the *Opinione*. The Destra daily ridiculed Pius' assertion that he was under the sway of enemies. Such a charge, it observed, did not accord with the liberty, unquestionably his, to assail publicly those very enemies.[134] Visconti-Venosta's contentions were sharply controverted by Antonelli. In a circular note to the nuncios dated November 5 the cardinal insisted that it was vain to speak of liberty and independence when every branch of the public administration was in the hands of the "usurping" government. "It is necessary to reaffirm," he went on, "that the authority of the pope has become nil. . . . . Confined within the circle of the Vatican, surrounded on every side by Italian authorities and soldiers, he cannot

---

[132] *CC*, I (8th ser.; December 24, 1870), 63; Saverio Cilibrizzi, *Storia parlamentare politica e diplomatica d'Italia* (Milano, 1925), II, 2.

[133] *Libro verde*, No. 61, pp. 74–75.   [134] *Opinione*, October 28, 1870.

be free and is obliged to resort to expedients in order to communicate with the faithful on the most important matters."[135]

The problem of finding a suitable residence in Rome for Victor Emmanuel produced further tension. The choice of the government fell on the Quirinal, the erstwhile summer abode of the popes which had been unoccupied since 1850.[136] The papal authorities were incensed. Antonelli told Blanc that the terms of the capitulation of September 20 did not embrace the Quirinal, which, like the Vatican and the Castel Gandolfo, was rightfully considered the private property of each pontiff.[137] The cabinet, however, was not daunted and calmly proceeded with its plans. To justify the seizure of the palace, it secured from three noted jurists a legal opinion to the effect that the Quirinal was state property and therefore could be used by the king without detriment to the rights of the papacy. On November 7, La Marmora formally requested Antonelli to hand over the keys of the palace and announced that occupation would take place the following day. The cardinal was apprised that the Italian government, after careful study, had come to the conclusion that the Quirinal was not the private property of the popes. The authorities' examination of title had convinced them that the palace belonged to the state and that consequently it was to be included in the category of buildings specified in the capitulation of Villa Albani.[138] Antonelli's point-blank refusal to comply with La Marmora's request was of no avail. Entry was duly effected by force on November 8.[139] The Vatican promptly retaliated by placing the Quirinal under interdic-

[135] Annex to Beust's dispatch of November 27, 1870, to Trauttmansdorff, HHSA, Politisches Archiv (Rome, Expeditions, Varia), Fasz. XI/225, fol. 246*b*.

[136] Castagnola, *op. cit.*, p. 86.

[137] Cf. Trauttmansdorff to Beust, October 8, 1870, HHSA, Politisches Korrespondenz (Rom), Fasz. XI/224, No. 108C, fols. 470*b*–471*a*.

[138] Trauttmansdorff to Beust, November 8, 1870, *ibid.*, No. 117B, fols. 547*a*–547*b*.

[139] Pesci, *Come Siamo entrati in Roma* (Milano, 1895), pp. 246–47; Tavallini, *op. cit.*, II, 417.

tion.[140] The Jesuits in the pope's entourage seized the opportunity to renew their agitation in favor of flight.[141] Antonelli, who continued to frown on the idea of running away, resorted to a more dignified expedient. He addressed a solemn protest to the powers.[142] He explained to Trauttmansdorff that he had taken this action in order to safeguard the rights of the Holy See. The entire incident, he remarked, was not at all surprising. It only helped to confirm his belief that no reliance could be placed in the Italian government's assurances. He knew, he went on, that the time had not yet arrived to count on foreign aid. And the situation of the Holy Father in the meantime would grow steadily worse. He feared that the Italians would even find a pretext to come as far as the Vatican. But so much was certain, current rumors notwithstanding: the pope had to remain where he was to the very last, until his own chamber should be invaded.[143]

The Lanza cabinet was seriously alarmed. It learned from Vienna that the papal protest had put the Austrian government in a difficult position.[144] The Viennese authorities had indeed obtained a most disturbing picture of what had taken place. Trauttmansdorff had written his superiors that the seizure of the Quirinal was an "inexcusable atrocity." It constituted, in his opinion, "a revolting absence of regard for the person of the pope, ... a flagrant violation of assurances solemnly vouchsafed, a proof of the pressure being ex-

[140] Paladino, op. cit., p. 147.

[141] Cf. The Roman Journals of Ferdinand Gregorovius, 1852–1874 (London, 1907), p. 390.

[142]Cf. Antonelli's note of November 9, 1870, to the nuncios in HHSA, Politisches Archiv (Weisungen an Florenz), Fasz. XI/79 (annex to Beust's dispatch of November 27, 1870, to Kubeck), fols. 333a-334a. Cf. also Antonelli to Trauttmansdorff, November 9, 1870, ibid. (Rom), Fasz. XI/224 (annex to No. 119A), fols. 559a-560b; Trauttmansdorff to Beust, November 10, 1870, ibid., No. 118B, fol. 554b; AD, 1874, II, 185-86.

[143]Trauttmansdorff to Beust, November 12, 1876, HHSA, Politisches Korrespondenz (Rom), Fasz. XI/224, No. 119A, fols. 561a-562a.

[144]Castagnola, op. cit., p. 106.

erted on the Italian government."[145] Beust found himself
obliged to intervene. Taking the papal circular notes of
October 17 and November 5 as his *point de départ,* he ordered
Kübeck to call attention to the discrepancy between the actions of the Italian government and the assurances it had repeatedly given regarding the consideration to be shown the
Holy Father and the church. Documents in the possession of
the Austrian government, the chancellor wrote to his envoy
in Florence, made it apparent that the events taking place
at Rome did not entirely correspond with the expectations
aroused by the declarations of the Lanza cabinet. He continued:

> We have always shown ourselves disposed to take account of the diffi-
> culty which confronts the cabinet of Florence in the Roman question. We
> do not wish at this time to augment its embarrassment, but we believe
> . . . . that we are acting in its behalf as well as in our own when we call its
> attention to . . . . the drawbacks of actions which are likely to revive
> among Catholics the sentiment of sorrow and fear. It is only by observing
> a scrupulous regard for the person of the Holy Father and for everything
> connected with the exercise of his spiritual functions that the Italian gov-
> ernment will efface the impression created by the occupation of Rome. We
> had strongly recommended the adoption of such a line of conduct, and the
> assurances given by the cabinet of Florence had permitted us to hope that
> it would carefully avoid anything which might violate further the religious
> beliefs and rights of the church. We regret to see that such is not the case.

After alluding, at this point, to the "violent occupation of one
of the principal papal residences," Beust went on:

> All this constitutes a state of affairs which will not have the effect of
> reconciling the sentiment of Catholics to the necessities invoked by the
> Italian government in the name of political interests. I fear that the cabi-
> net of Florence is in this way making more complicated the difficult prob-
> lem which it has undertaken to solve. It is alarming consciences instead of
> calming them, and the church sees its liberty menaced. . . . .

The conduct of Lanza and his associates, he complained, was
likewise placing the Austrian government in a false position
because it had manifested complete confidence is the promises of the cabinet of Florence. If ensuing developments

[145]Trauttmansdorff to Beust, November 12, 1870, HHSA, Politisches Korrespondenz (Rom), Fasz. XI/224, No. 119A, fals. 562*a*-562*b,* 564*a*-564*b.*

should not be entirely in accord with those promises, the Austrian government would find itself exposed to irksome reproaches. Consequently, it felt "authorized" to raise this question at Florence and to recall to the Italian authorities the importance which it attached to the fulfilment of promises made. In conclusion, Beust requested Kübeck to be careful to couch his remarks in the friendly terms consistent with the good relations between the Austrian and Italian governments.[146] Simultaneously, Trauttmansdorff was instructed to inform Antonelli that the Austrian government had made representations at Florence apropos of the recent regrettable incidents.[147]

The Italian cabinet, in the meantime, had discovered no better way to justify its action than to argue, in a pretentiously worded memorandum, that the Quirinal, considered both historically and juridically, was lay property and consequently eligible for civil use.[148] But Beust's remonstrances, when relayed to the Florentine authorities by Kübeck, were not without effect. The Austrian envoy noted that Visconti-Venosta seemed much moved by the chancellor's appraisal of Italy's actions. With unwonted bitterness, the taciturn foreign minister complained to Kübeck of the Vatican's resistance to all the administrative measures taken by La Marmora. He denied the truth of Antonelli's assertion that the pope was not free. Pius' refusal to make use of his complete liberty, he contended, could not be laid at the door of the Italian government. The forthcoming law of papal guarantees, he stated in conclusion, would insure the Holy Father's spiritual independence.[149] Beust took note of these "satis-

---

[146] Beust to Kübeck, November 27, 1870, *ibid.*, Politisches Archiv (Weisungen an Florenz), Fasz. XI/79, fols. 312*b*–315*b*.

[147] Beust to Trauttmansdorff, *ibid.* (Rome, Expeditions, Varia), Fasz. XI/225, fols. 245*a*–245*b*.

[148] *Libro verde*, No. 97 and inclosed *mémoire*, pp. 101–7; cf., also, Humphrey Johnson, *The Papacy and the Kingdom of Italy* (London, 1926), pp. 32–33.

[149] Kübeck to Beust, December 3, 1870, HHSA, Politisches Archiv (Florenz), Fasz. XI/75, fols. 449*a*, 450*b*, 451*b*.

factory assurances." The Austrian government, he informed Kübeck, was disposed to believe that the Lanza cabinet had every intention of manifesting the regard due the person of the pontiff as well as the high functions which he discharged. Nevertheless, the chancellor continued, the repeated complaints from the Vatican seemed to indicate that at Rome influences hostile to the papacy were often being allowed to prevail. In the circumstances the Austrian cabinet could only reiterate its desire to see the Italian government maintain the principles which the latter itself had laid down in earlier utterances.[150]

The moderation of this position could scarcely fail to escape the authorities at Florence, but the Austrian government was by no means inclined to accept the verbal gratitude of Lanza and his colleagues as its sole recompense. Rather, it was determined to make the Italians pay a handsome diplomatic price for its benevolence. Kübeck had been instructed to make this very clear to the Italian foreign office even before the dispatch of Beust's reply to Visconti-Venosta's latest assurances. The envoy had been told that, in view of the forthcoming convocation of the international conference at London to deal with Russia's repudiation of the Black Sea clauses of the Treaty of Paris, the Viennese authorities had to know exactly where Italy would stand. If they should not find her frankly on their side, if she, together with Prussia, should support Russia, they would no longer find it possible to consider her an ally whose interests were dear to them and in whose behalf they could expose themselves to parliamentary attacks. The Austrian government had been reproached in the delegations because of its attitude in the Roman question. If it could not adduce, in justification of its present policy in that question, any community of political interests between Austria and Italy, it would be deprived of its best argument in opposing the adversaries of the Italian govern-

---

[150] Beust to Kübeck, December 22, 1870, *ibid.* (Weisungen an Florenz), Fasz. XI/79, fols. 362*b* and 363*b*.

ment. In such a case, the continuance of the policy hitherto pursued vis-à-vis Italy could not be guaranteed. Indeed, Italy would risk a cooling-off in the Hapsburg monarchy's relations with her. And yet the attitude of the Austrian government in the Roman question was necessarily of great importance to her. Furthermore, it was evident that in the Near Eastern question, the interests of the two countries were almost identical. Here, therefore, was a double reason why Italy ought not to deviate from the policy she would have to pursue if she wished the Austro-Italian alignment to be of any significance.[151]

The sensation produced by the seizure of the Quirinal had scarcely subsided when another bombshell was dropped into the arena of Italo-papal relations. On November 21 the clerical *Unità cattolica* of Turin published an extraordinary document which the other newspapers of the peninsula promptly reproduced. It was the encyclical *Respicientes ea omnis* and bore the date of November 1. In it Pius reaffirmed, in language of unprecedented vigor, the claims of the papacy to its sequestered patrimony. He declared that the temporal power had been "granted by divine Providence to the Apostolic See in order that the blessed successors of Peter might freely and safely exercise their spiritual powers." He pronounced null and void everything that the Italian government had done and proposed to do. The familiar refrain that he was languishing in a state of capitivity, bereft of freedom and independence, was repeated. Reconciliation based on the *status quo* was pronounced forever impossible. No arrangement would be assented to "which destroys or diminishes our rights; similarly, despite our advanced age, we prefer, ... with divine aid, to drink the cup to the dregs rather than accept the iniquitous proposals which have been made to us." Resorting to the most telling weapon in his spiritual arsenal, he imposed the major excommunication upon all

[151] Beust to Kübeck, December 10, 1870, *ibid.*, fols. 357*b*–359*b*.

those who had perpetrated the seizure of Rome or in any way abetted it.[152]

The government was incensed by this outburst. It ordered the confiscation of all newspapers, without distinction of party, which had published the text of the document. Even the *Opinione*, the cabinet's principal mouthpiece, was not spared.[153] But this Draconian measure was speedily recognized to be a clumsy mistake. It evoked a storm of disapproval throughout the country.[154] The press, irrespective of political affiliations or sympathies, was unanimous in condemning it as politically inopportune.[155] From the clerical sheets there went up a loud and unisonal cry of "I told you so!" They triumphantly declared that the worthlessness of the government's assurances now stood starkly revealed.[156] "This is the kind of freedom the pope enjoys in the kingdom of Italy," the *Unità cattolica* announced with emphatic finality. "He cannot speak, or at least his words cannot be reported and transmitted to the faithful!"[157] Antonelli himself protested in a note to the nuncios which left no doubt that the painful incident had strengthened the hand of the intransigent party at the Vatican.[158] The cabinet, impressed by the sharp dissent of Visconti-Venosta, in whose absence the action against the culpable newspapers had been decided

---

[152] *AD, 1874,* II, 167–76.

[153] Chiala, *Dina,* III, 283.

[154] Italian public opinion in general and Destra circles in particular took an exceedingly critical view of the government's action (cf. Kübeck to Beust, November 23, 1870, HHSA, Politisches Archiv [Florenz], Fasz. XI/75 [postscript to No. LXII/ P.P.], fol. 435*a*).

[155] The *Opinione* remarked that the inviolability and freedom of the pope were incomplete without the right to publish encyclicals (issue of November 24, 1870). The *Riforma*, in the course of a slashing attack upon the "incoherences of the present ministry," complained that the sequestration would serve to justify the pope's lament that he was not free (issues of November 23 and 24, 1870).

[156] *CC,* I (8th ser.; January 21, 1871), 354.

[157] *Unità cattolica,* November 23, 1870.

[158] *CC,* I (8th ser.; January 21, 1871), 364.

upon,[159] admitted its blunder, although Correnti, the minister of public instruction, argued that the sequestration was defensible on the ground that the encyclical had been clandestinely published abroad and secretly distributed. Raeli, whose signature had been affixed to the decree of confiscation, offered himself as the scapegoat and announced his readiness to resign. But Lanza would not hear of this.[160] Instead, he made belated amends. The encyclical was published in the *Gazzetta ufficiale* on December 4. It was accompanied by a communiqué which lamely exculpated the authorities by averring that they were now convinced of the document's authenticity. The episode had its sequel in the senate when a member of that body made light of the ministry's reiterated promises to respect the Holy Father's spiritual freedom. Raeli was intrusted with the thankless task of defending the cabinet. Though his apologia was not altogether effectual in meeting the pungent criticism leveled at his colleagues and himself, it was accepted by the Destra-packed upper house.[161] It carried no conviction, however, to the clericals, who were all disdain. It was no longer possible, declared the *Civiltà cattolica* in saturnine tones, to be deceived about the value of the government's highly touted guarantees.[162] The misstep had cost the Italian authorities much sympathy both at home and abroad and was long remembered with bitterness by the champions of papal liberties.

[159] The decree of confiscation, which Visconti-Venosta regarded as inopportune, almost led to the latter's withdrawal from the cabinet (cf. Kübeck to Beust, December 3, 1870, HHSA, Politisches Archiv [Florenz], Fasz. XI/75, fols. 448*b*, 451*a*).

[160] Castagnola, *op. cit.*, pp. 99, 104–5.

[161] *Atti*, CLXVIII (December 27, 1870), 53–57.

[162] *CC*, I (8th ser.; January 21, 1871), 356.

CHAPTER IV
THE LAW OF GUARANTEES

THE occupation of Rome brought with it a host of urgent problems. Few of these, however, proved more trying than that of arranging the plebiscite scheduled for October 2. The text of the plebiscite formula gave rise to fierce controversy. On September 15 the cabinet had agreed upon the following wording:

> In the certainty that the Italian government will assure the spiritual independence of the pope, we declare our union with the kingdon of Italy under the constitutional monarchical government of King Victor Emmanuel and his successors.[1]

The Roman municipal council, the Giunta, flatly rejected the preamble. It refused to attach any conditions to the annexation of Rome. It was all very well, it said, to guarantee the independence of the pope, but that issue was wholly alien to the plebiscite. If anxiety was felt abroad for the future status of the Holy Father, it was the duty of the Italian government and not of the Romans to dissipate it.[2] The Giunta could see no reason to accept any formula which differed from that used in effecting the territorial annexations of 1859 and 1860. Accordingly, it declared in all finality that it would tolerate no reference to the pope's spiritual authority.[3] The Romans were vigorously supported by the Sinistra. The *Riforma* challenged the government's wish to inject a religious issue into these proceedings. To compel respect for the pontiff through a plebiscite would be, in the opinion of the leftist journal, an insult to Italian dignity and a gesture of

---

[1] Stefano Castagnola, *Da Firenze a Roma: diario storico-politico del 1870–71* (Torino, 1896), p. 48; Francesco Crispi, *Politica interna* (Milano, 1924), pp. 70–71.

[2] Castagnola, *op. cit.*, p. 148 n.

[3] Camillo Manfroni, *Sulla soglia del Vaticano* (Bologna, 1920), I, 12.

contempt for the national sentiment. "The Romans," it urged, "should persist in this position. It is their right and their duty."[4]

So heated did the quarrel become that two members of the Giunta went to Florence to warn the government that it would be impossible to induce the Romans to accept the ministerial version.[5] Sella supported the Giunta.[6] He agreed with it that the question of papal guarantees was strictly the government's own affair and ought not therefore to be made a plebiscitary issue.[7] The cabinet finally consented to drop the preamble.[8] The Giunta could now afford to be magnanimous. It added the following sentence to its proclamation inviting the Romans to participate in the plebiscite: "Under the aegis of free institutions, we leave to the judgment of the Italian government the care of assuring the independence of the pope's spiritual authority."[9]

The outcome of the controversy evoked jubilation only in the Sinistra camp. Catholics pointed to it as further proof of the illusory character of the government's assurances. Moderate opinion did not dissemble its disappointment. A cabinet, wrote Bonghi, which had demonstrated such boldness in embarking upon the Roman expedition should have acquired sufficient authority to prevent its counsels from being so speedily discarded. He contended that this incident, together with the occupation of the Leonine City—even

[4] *Riforma*, September 28, 1870.

[5] Castagnola, *op. cit.*, pp. 48–49, 69–70.

[6] Paolo Boselli, "Roma e Quintino Sella," *Nuova antologia*, September 16, 1927, p. 144; Alessandro Guiccioli, *Quintino Sella* (Rovigo, 1887), I, 313.

[7] Cf. Ugo Pesci, *Come Siamo entrati in Roma* (Milano, 1895), pp. 198–99.

[8] Raffaele Cadorna, *La Liberazione di Roma nell'anno 1870 ed il plebiscito* (Torino, 1898), pp. 265–66; Guiccioli, *op. cit.*, I, 314; Enrico Tavallini, *La Vita e i tempi di Giovanni Lanza* (Torino and Napoli, 1887), II, 51; Vittorio Bersezio, *Il Regno di Vittorio Emanuele II: trent'anni di vita italiana* (Torino, 1878–95), VIII, 385; CC, I (8th ser.; January 9, 1871), 220; Saverio Cilibrizzi, *Storia parlamentare politica e diplomatica d'Italia* (Milano, 1925), I, 494–95.

[9] Cf. Robert von Nostitz-Rieneck, "Wie Neuitalien auf das Garantiegesetz kam," *Stimmen der Zeit*, April, 1917, p. 35; Castagnola, *op. cit.*, p. 49 n.

though the latter had occurred at the request of the Vatican
—signalized the ministry's failure to fulfil the promises contained in Visconti-Venosta's memorandum of August 29. He
observed that two parties stood opposed to the ministerial
Destra. One of these wished to subject the church to the
state, the other desired to destroy the church altogether. The
triumph of either would bring sad days to Italy. Consequently, it behooved the Destra, which had been somewhat de-
flated by its bungling policy in the Roman question, to be on
the alert to prevent the situation from slipping into the control of its revolutionary adversaries.[10]

The Giunta now proceeded to set the stage for the plebiscite. On September 29 it reminded the Romans that, at this
solemn moment, "history will register in ineffaceable char-
acters the great event which consecrates this fruitful principle: *a free church in a free state.*"[11] This pronouncement was
received with enthusiasm by the Roman populace. But the
government found its path beset with another formidable
complication. In accordance with its announced intention of
allotting the Leonine City to the pope, it now sought to exclude the residents of that district from participation in the
plebiscite. The latter, however, would not hear of this, and
they manifested their disapproval in no equivocal terms.[12]
The government was equally emphatic in its refusal to deviate from its original program. It reiterated that the occupation of the Leonine City, executed under special circumstances and on the strength of a transfer of papal authority,
was purely temporary in character.[13] But the looming im-
passe was resolved by Cadorna. Acting on his own responsibility, he granted the inhabitants of the Leonine City per-

[10] *Nuova antologia*, October, 1870, pp. 457–58.

[11] *AD, 1874*, II, 110–11; Giuseppe Leti, *Roma e lo stato pontificio dal 1849 al 1870*
(Roma, 1909), II, 358.

[12] Cf. Manfroni, *op. cit.*, I, 11.

[13] Giuseppe Paladino, *Storia d'Italia dal 1861 al 1871 con particolare riguardo alla
questione romana* (Milano, 1932), p. 144.

mission to vote.[14] The ultimate fate of the district proved the
source of much dissension in ministerial circles. On September 30 the cabinet discussed the text of the royal edict decree-
ing the union of Rome and Italy and scheduled to be promulgated after the plebiscite. It was debated whether reference
should be made in that edict to "territorial franchises," i.e.,
the Leonine City, as part of the guarantees to be offered the
Holy Father. Some of the ministers wished to see the district go to the pontiff even if he should refuse to exercise sovereignty over it. Others urged a simple acceptance of the
outcome of the plebiscite without allusion to territorial or
other guarantees. No formal decision was reached.[15] But
Lanza's influence was on the side of fulfilment by the government of its original pledge. On October 1 he wrote to Giacomo Dina, the editor of the *Opinione*, who had declared
himself opposed to any territorial concessions:[16] "If the retention by the pope of this strip of earth could lead to a settlement, you favor rejecting it and *vada todos?* It is impossible that, after having well reflected on it, you would wish to
persist in this idea."[17] And on the same day, the premier
wired Cadorna that it was important not to prejudice the
question of the Leonine City. He reminded the general that
the military occupation of this part of Rome was to be understood as having occurred through a delegation of the pope's
authority.[18]

The government's position was rendered no easier by the
violent antipapal campaign conducted by the opposition.
The pontiff, the leftists were insisting, ought not to be endowed with any political sovereignty. For to admit that such
sovereignty was indispensable to his office was to imply that
he would have to be given territorial dominion. And the

---

[14] Cf. Cadorna, *op. cit.*, pp. 273 and 560.

[15] Castagnola, *op. cit.*, pp. 76–77.

[16] Cf. the strong editorial on this subject in the *Opinione* of October 1, 1870.

[17] Chiala, *Dina*, III, 270–71.   [18] Castagnola, *op. cit.*, p. 77.

cession of the Leonine City was absolutely out of the question. The Sinistra likewise announced itself uncompromisingly opposed to any negotiations with the Vatican. All overtures to the Holy See, it predicted, would receive the same reply: *Non possumus!* They would founder upon the futility of attempting "to reconcile the irreconcilable." All this was easy to see. But the cabinet was altogether too much concerned about the pope and not enough about the state and the interests of civil society.[19]

It was in this somewhat troubled atmosphere that the plebiscite duly took place on October 2. The most perfect order was maintained despite the prevailing excitement.[20] Some fifteen hundred inhabitants of the Leonine City crossed the bridge of S. Angelo, set up their own polling-place, and cast a unanimous vote in favor of annexation to Italy. They then apprised the authorities of the result.[21] On the evening of the third, all the ballot boxes were brought to the Campidoglio. Some embarrassment ensued when an old resident of the Leonine City, accompanied by a large number of fellow-Trasteverians, presented the votes of his district. The Giunta appealed to Baron Blanc, who represented the government at these rites, and someone expressed the opinion that, for diplomatic reasons, it might be advisable to follow a special procedure in this instance. But the baron unhesitatingly replied: "Forward, Romans of the Trastevere," and their votes were registered with all the others.[22] The tabulation of the results showed an overwhelming triumph for the national cause. Of the 135,291 votes cast, 133,681 were in favor of

[19] Cf. the *Riforma*, October 1, 2, and 5, 1870.

[20] Trauttmansdorff to Beust, October 3, 1870, HHSA, Politisches Korrespondenz (Rom), Fasz. XI/224, No. 1098/206, fol. 436a.

[21] M. Albertone, "Ricordi dell'impresa di Roma nel 1870," *Nuova antologia*, September 16, 1920, pp. 113–14.

[22] G. E. Curàtulo, *La Questione romana da Cavour a Mussolini* (Roma, 1928), p. 90.

union, 1,507 were against, and 103 were classified as invalid.[23] The Florentine authorities had ample reason to rejoice, but the more moderate elements in the cabinet betrayed no exaggerated optimism. Visconti-Venosta, in particular, did not disguise the difficulties of the new situation. According to Kübeck, the Italian statesman attributed these difficulties to "political necessities" and to "a certain fatalism." He was disturbed above all by the complete passivity of the pope, who was rejecting all overtures for a settlement or a *modus vivendi*.[24] Kübeck himself sought to convince Beust that the Roman question, far from having been solved, was only in an initial phase.[25]

On October 9, Victor Emmanuel received a deputation of Romans who had come to Florence to apprise him of the outcome of the plebiscite.[26] In his reply the king declared that the position of the pope would be properly safeguarded. It was still his firm intention, he said, "to assure the liberty of the church and the independence of the supreme pontiff."[27] Simultaneously, the cabinet issued an edict proclaiming the incorporation of the former papal territory into the Italian kingdom.[28] Article II of this edict stated: "The supreme pontiff retains the dignity, the inviolability and all the personal prerogatives of a sovereign." Article III held out the promise of "territorial franchises" to the pope.[29] This was interpreted to mean that the cabinet, even after the king's ac-

[23] For a graphic account of the plebiscite see Pesci, *Come Siamo entrati in Roma*, pp. 202–16.

[24] Kübeck to Beust, October 8, 1870, HHSA, Politisches Archiv (Florenz), Fasz. XI/75, No. 82, fols. 209b and 210a.

[25] *Ibid.*, fol. 209b.

[26] Cf. Pesci, *Firenze capitale (1865–1870)* (Firenze, 1904), pp. 493–94.

[27] Giuseppe Massari, *La Vita ed il regno di Vittorio Emanuele II di Savoia* (Milano, 1910), II, 520.

[28] This decree was converted into law by the Italian parliament at the close of December, 1870.

[29] *CC*, II (8th ser.; May 6, 1871), 440; cf. the discussion of Article III in Paladino, *op. cit.*, p. 145.

ceptance of the result of the plebiscite, still clung to the idea of divorcing the Leonine City from the rest of Italy. But the instant reaction of public opinion was so hostile to the proposed "territorial franchises"[30] that the government hurried to disavow them. Even before the full impact of public indignation could make itself felt, the *Opinione* authoritatively declared that Article III of the edict had been misconstrued. Not temporal sovereignty, but immunities, were being contemplated.[31] A week later, Sella assured a deputation of anxious Romans that there was no longer any question of detaching the Leonine City. Other means, he said, would have to be found to safeguard the pope's spiritual authority.[32]

A similar fate befell the Italian government's promise to act in concert with the powers in defining the rights of the papacy. On the morrow of the occupation of Rome, the Lanza cabinet had, it is true, evinced no change of heart. In an important dispatch to Minghetti, dated September 21, Visconti-Venosta had again welcomed the collaboration of the various governments. He had even suggested that they themselves might intervene to negotiate satisfactory guarantees if the pope should reject Italy's terms.[33] A few days later he had informed Paget that he would seek to reach an agreement with the Catholic governments regarding "measures to be taken in common for securing for the future the spiritual independence . . . . of the Pope."[34] The attitude of the Italian government did evoke, moreover, warm praise in Vienna. Beust instructed Kübeck to thank Visconti-Venosta for his friendly dispatch of September 21 and for the promptness with which he had reassured the Austrian government. The latter, the chancellor declared, took due note of all this and observed "with satisfaction" the extent to which the Italian

---

[30] The *Riforma* led in this outcry against the idea of ceding the Leonine City (cf. the issues of October 11 and 12, 1870).

[31] *Opinione*, October 11, 1870; cf. also Chiala, *Dina*, III, 271.

[32] Cf. Guiccioli, *op. cit.*, I, 322.

[33] *Libro verde*, No. 24, pp. 37–38.   [34] *Blue Book*, No. 50, p. 58.

government revealed itself "disposed to recognize the necessity of assuring the independence and personal safety of the
Holy Father." However, the moment had not yet arrived to
enter into "an exhaustive discussion of the grave questions
associated with the position of the Holy See." Visconti-
Venosta's explanations, Beust concluded, "allow us to believe that the Italian government, despite the difficulties of
the present crisis, will show all the consideration due the situation of Pius IX and the sacred character with which he is
clothed."[35] But the idea of internationally defined papal
guarantees had at this moment few really enthusiastic champions. No less a personage than Gladstone did indeed propose
to Antonelli the convocation of an international conference
to deal with the position of the papacy. But the cardinal did
not regard this proposal as either opportune or advantageous.[36] And it became quickly apparent too that the powers, Belgium excepted,[37] were in no hurry to negotiate. They
were altogether too much preoccupied with the course of the
Franco-Prussian War to give any extended attention to the
Italo-papal conflict. They made it clear that they preferred
to see Italy assume sole responsibility, reserving the right to
judge the adequacy of the guarantees to be enacted by her.[38]
The Lanza cabinet was not loath to comply, for it knew that
a purely unilateral solution would meet with universal approval throughout the peninsula. Moderates, who had agreed
to an international solution when the possibility of foreign
intervention had seemed more real, were taking a different
line now. The *Opinione* voiced their feeling when it insisted

[35] Beust to Kübeck, October 2, 1870, HHSA, Politisches Archiv (Weisungen an Florenz), Fasz. XI/79, No. 3, fols. 210*b*–212*a*.

[36] Cf. Lefebvre de Béhaine to Chaudordy, January 31, 1871, AMAE (Rome, janvier-février, 1871), Tome 1049, fols. 160–61.

[37] D'Anethan, the Belgian foreign minister, continued to urge an international sanction for the papal guarantees (cf. *Libro verde*, No. 93, pp. 98–99).

[38] Cf. Visconti-Venosta's remarks in the chamber of deputies on December 21, 1870, in *Atti*, CLXV, 145; cf. also Hubert Bastgen, *Die römische Frage* (Freiburg i.B., 1917), II, 634; Tavallini, *op. cit.*, II, 194.

that Italy, in dealing with the Roman question, was bound by no obligations vis-à-vis other countries.[39] Particularly significant was the Sinistra's sharp reversal of position. The *Riforma* was now arguing that church-state relations could be defined only by domestic legislation. The question of safeguarding the freedom of the papacy, it was saying, was a purely Italian one. To invite international co-operation would be to open the door to "a new kind of dependence" upon the other powers. It was time "to close the era of foreign influence and to set ourselves up as masters in our own house." And Europe would be satisfied with such a solution.[40] On October 18 the government announced in a note to its diplomatic representatives that Italy's task was "to apply the idea of law, in its largest and highest sense, to the relations of church and state."[41] Nothing was said about a conference of the powers. The fate of the Roman question was thus to rest exclusively with Italy.

The Vatican protested in no uncertain terms. It was not the implied repudiation of an international conference, for which it had little enthusiasm, that drew its ire. It was incensed by the complacent passages in the note which alluded to the freedom and correct impartiality of the plebiscite and to the pope's decision to remain in Rome.[42] It denounced the "political stupidity" and the "almost incredible disregard of the most obvious and simple dictates of reason and conscience" which it saw revealed in the document.[43] The Italian *volte-face* caused scarcely a ripple in foreign capitals.[44] Beust, who had all along insisted on international guaran-

---

[39] *Opinione*, October 11, 1870.

[40] *Riforma*, September 27, 1870. During the ensuing weeks the influential Sinistra organ forcefully reiterated this view.

[41] *Libro verde*, No. 56, pp. 69–71.

[42] Trauttmansdorff to Beust, November 5, 1870, HHSA, Politisches Korrespondenz (Rom), Fasz. XI/224, Bericht 116A, fols. 535a–535b.

[43] Cf. *Osservatore romano*, November 3, 1870.

[44] Cf. *AD, 1874*, II, 159, 161, 188–89.

tees, agreed that the policy proclaimed by the Lanza government was "reasonable and just and likely to lead to an equitable solution."[45] The Prussian government noted the change, but contented itself with a position of complete reserve.[46]

There was little time to be lost, and of this the Italian cabinet was well aware. But the precise nature and scope of the concessions to be granted the Holy See and the church could not fail to evoke spirited controversy among the ministers. Visconti-Venosta, on the side of moderation, as usual, pleaded in behalf of generous terms, while Sella, the inveterate champion of the state's prerogatives, argued in favor of exiguous concessions.[47] The cabinet quickly evinced a decided preference for the views of the foreign minister. On November 2 it issued a decree dissolving the chamber of deputies and ordering new elections. The next day it published in the *Gazzetta ufficiale* an elaborate statement of its ecclesiastical program. "With the abolition of the territorial sovereignty of the pontiff," it declared, "it is necessary to assure to the Apostolic See . . . . such economic and juridical conditions[48] as will remove any reasonable suspicion of direct or indirect interference by the Italian kingdom in the government of the church." In order to render the Holy See truly independent and fulfil in this regard the expectations of Europe and the Catholic world, it was imperative to give the church "that complete freedom which, in the famous formula advanced by Count Cavour, is the counterpart of civil liberty." But while freedom, as defined by Italian law, was likely to satisfy Italian Catholics, it might seem inadequate to the faithful of other lands. Consequently, Italy acknowledged the necessity of recognizing the sovereignty and personal inviolability of the pontiff and of bestowing upon his function-

---

[45] *Libro verde*, No. 79, pp. 87–88.   [46] Cf. *GW*, VI*b*, No. 1904, 575–77.

[47] Cf. Kübeck to Beust, November 3, 1870, HHSA, Politisches Archiv (Florenz), Fasz. XI/75, fol. 336*a*.

[48] Note the omission of "territorial" conditions.

aries all the immunities enjoyed by foreign embassies. But the property of the Holy See in Rome was to be placed on precisely the same footing as that of ecclesiastical bodies in the rest of Italy. It was to be subject to the laws forbidding mortmain and regulating the disposition of lands and buildings belonging to religious associations.[49]

This manifesto was well received by both the Destra and the Sinistra. The former was gratified by the ministry's fidelity to the Cavourian formula,[50] while the Sinistra rejoiced over the silence on "territorial franchises"—a silence generally interpreted as a definitive disavowal of the pledge to leave the Leonine City in the possession of the Holy See. The watchful papal secretary of state could hardly allow this pronouncement to go unchallenged. In a circular note issued on November 8, he took sharp issue with it. He reiterated that freedom and independence for his master were impossible without temporal sovereignty. The guarantees offered by the Italian government were a very inadequate substitute for that sovereignty. To all the schemes of the cabinet, Pius was prepared to offer steadfast resistance. Rather than fall short in the performance of his sacred duty, he would undergo "a more severe captivity and even death." The world must know that Italy was bent on undermining the foundations of the church and destroying Catholicism itself.[51]

These words carried with them an unequivocal finality. They seemed to close all roads to compromise. But the Italian government pretended to ignore them and proceeded serenely with its self-appointed task. At a banquet of the

---

[49] Cadorna, *op. cit.*, pp. 297–98; Robert von Nostitz-Rieneck, "Rom, Italien, Europa, 1870 (August bis Dezember)," *Stimmen der Zeit*, April, 1917, pp. 93–94; *CC*, I (8th ser.; January 21, 1871), 351–52.

[50] Cf., e.g., the *Opinione* of November 5, 1870. Kübeck reported to Beust on November 5, 1870, that moderate opinion saw in the manifesto a realization of that famous formula (HHSA, Politisches Archiv [Florenz], Fasz. XI/75, No. 89A, fol. 352b).

[51] *AD, 1874*, II, 179–84; Pietro Vigo, *Storia degli ultimi trent'anni del secolo XIX* (Milano, 1908), I, 56–57.

Patriotic Society of Milan on November 11, Visconti-Venosta spoke optimistically of the future. He dwelt on the advantages of moderation. It was to be hoped, he said, that the chamber of deputies soon to be elected would establish good relations with the papacy. Europe had left Italy to her own responsibility and was waiting to see if she would measure up to it.[52]

The elections took place on November 20, and the Destra emerged with a convincing majority.[53] The Sinistra took its discomfiture with ill-grace and loudly deplored the failure of large numbers of qualified voters to exercise their franchise.[54] The lightness of the vote[55] was due in no small measure to the refusal of faithful Catholics to serve as candidates and go to the polls.[56] No other course seemed open to them after the seizure of Rome. To take the oath of office required of all deputies was tantamount to acceptance of the regime which had destroyed the temporal power. And to exercise the franchise under the auspices of that regime was scarcely less shocking to the Catholic conscience. Moreover, the policy of abstention was no new one. It had been inaugurated in Piedmont in 1860 and was epitomized in the famous formula, *Nè eletti nè elettori*,[57] coined by the clerical publicist, Don Giacomo Margotti. The latter, however, had subsequently experienced a change of heart. In January, 1868, he had urged mass voting in the columns of his *Unità cattolica*. His argument had been that the papal cause would be best served by returning the largest possible number of Catholic

[52] *Times*, November 14, 1870.

[53] Cf. Robert von Nostitz-Rieneck, "Der Parlamentskampf ums Garantiegesetz," *Stimmen der Zeit*, July, 1917, p. 387.

[54] Cf. the *Riforma*, December 3, 1870.

[55] Cf. Lefebvre de Béhaine to Chaudordy, January 18, 1871, AMAE (Rome, janvier-février, 1871), Tome 1049, fol. 77; Kübeck to Beust, November 23, 1870, HHSA, Politisches Archiv (Florenz), Fasz. XI/75, No. LXII/P.P., fol. 430b.

[56] Cf., on this abstentionist policy, Lefebvre de Béhaine to Chaudordy, January 25, 1871, AMAE (Rome, janvier-février, 1871), Tome 1049, fols. 121-22.

[57] "Neither elected nor electors."

deputies. Other clerical sheets had promptly seconded Margotti's suggestion. But the *Osservatore romano* and the *Giornale di Roma* had authoritatively declared that the Vatican saw no reason to drop the boycott.[58] The *Civiltà cattolica* had reminded its readers that the anticlerical and fraudulent policies of the Italian government made it impossible for Catholics to participate in the parliamentary elections.[59] On February 27 the Holy See itself had officially recommended abstention in the famous *non-expedit*.[60] This advice, which was dictated by the fear that voting by Catholics might be interpreted as concurrence in the dismemberment of the papal state, had for a time not been rigidly followed. But after the events of September 20, 1870, the attitude of the faithful hardened, and Margotti's formula became their *mot d'ordre*.[61] The *Unità cattolica* signalized its reconversion to its original position by defending the Catholic boycott of the polls on November 20.[62]

The new parliament convened in Florence on December 5 and listened to an inspiring speech from the throne. In ringing tones, the king declared:

With Rome the capital of Italy, I have fulfilled my promise and crowned the undertaking which twenty-three years ago was begun by my magnanimous father. . . . . Italy is free and united; it now depends only on us to make her great and happy. . . . . We entered Rome in the name of national right, in the name of the pact which binds all Italians in national unity. We will remain there, maintaining at the same time the promises we have solemnly made to ourselves: freedom of the church, complete independ-

[58] *CC*, I (7th ser.; January 18, 1868), 361–62.

[59] "I Pericoli dell'Italia e l'aiuto dei cattolici" (*ibid.*, I [7th ser.; February 1, 1868], 385–93).

[60] Cf. the article on the *non-expedit* in the *Enciclopedia italiana*, XXIV, 907–8.

[61] Cf. "Ueber das politische Verhalten der Katholiken in Italien," *Historisch-Politische Blätter für das katholische Deutschland*, LXXXI (1878), 597–99. In reply to numerous inquiries, the Sacred Penitentiary of the Holy See had declared that membership in the Italian parliament was permissible only on the condition that to the oath taken by deputies the following reservation be added: *Salvis legibus divinis et ecclesiasticis*.

[62] *Unità cattolica*, November 23, 1870.

ence for the pontifical see in the exercise of its religious ministry, in its relations with the Catholic world.[63]

Four days later the cabinet presented to parliament the long-awaited bill on papal guarantees. This measure, prepared by Visconti-Venosta and Raeli, followed the lines of the earlier projects worked out under Cavour and Ricasoli.[64] As finally voted, the law consisted of two sections. The first dealt with the prerogatives of the pope and the Holy See, the second, with the relations of church and state in Italy.[65] The articles on the rights and immunities of the pope bespoke the generally conciliatory attitude of the Italian government in juridical matters—an attitude inspired in no small degree by the hope of pacifying foreign governments[66] and placating the pontiff.[67] This dual objective remained uppermost in the minds of ministerialists throughout the critical months which followed. Official circles were more than ever obsessed with the fear that, once the Franco Prussian War was over, the possibility of international intervention would have to be seriously reckoned with. The French minister to Italy, Rothan, pointed out on February 14, 1871:

In presenting the law of guarantees, the government had hoped that parliament would agree with it on the necessity of calming . . . . the apprehensions of the great Catholic powers by offering the pope . . . . complete

[63] Massari, La Vita ed il regno di Vittorio Emanuele II di Savoia, II, 528-29.

[64] Paladino, op. cit., p. 151. The text of the original ministerial bill is in Atti, CLXI, No. 31, pp. 8-11.

[65] The classic study on the law of guarantees is Francesco Scaduto's Guarentigie pontificie e relazioni tra stato e chiesa (Torino, 1884). The famous statute has been analyzed and appraised in innumerable monographs, articles, and treatises on ecclesiastical law (cf., e.g., the bibliographies in Andrea Piola, La Questione romana nella storia e nel diritto [Padova, 1931], and in Burchard Neuhaus, Die völkerrechtliche Stellung des Heiligen Stuhles nach den Lateranverträgen vom 11. Februar 1929 [Würzburg, 1932]).

[66] In the words of Minghetti, the law of guarantees was designed "to assure the Catholic governments and peoples that the end of the temporal power of the pope does not involve the spiritual servitude of the church" (Piola, op. cit., p. 121). On the Italian government's preoccupation with the international aspect of the Roman question see Lefebvre de Béhaine to Chaudordy, January 20, 1871, AMAE (Rome, janvier-février, 1871), Tome 1049, fols. 84-85.

[67] Mario Falco, La Politica ecclesiastica della Destra (Torino, 1914), p. 24.

immunity of person and wide liberty in the exercise of his spiritual authority. It sought, by acting while Europe was distracted by the war, to prevent intervention later. . . . .[68]

No less anxious was the Italian cabinet to leave the way open
for a *modus vivendi* with the Vatican, much to the disgust of
the Sinistra. Thus, one of the latter's principal organs, the
Diritto, insisted that an Italo-papal reconciliation was impossible. It decried as futile, in the face of the alleged ob-
stinacy and intransigence of the ultramontanes, the government's efforts to arrive at an accord with them.[69]

The section of the law dealing with the papal guarantees
was designed to regularize the position of the stateless pontiff. By way of compensation for the loss of his territorial
dominion, and in order that the Catholic world might be
convinced that the territoryless head of the church would retain his spiritual freedom and independence, he was invested
with sovereign attributes and honors.[70] His person was declared sacred and inviolable. He was thus to be rendered irresponsible and immune from arrest, trial, and all repressive
jurisdiction. He was likewise to be protected against personal
attacks and incitements to attacks, and the penalties prescribed for such misdemeanors were to be the same as those

[68] Gustave Rothan, *Souvenirs diplomatiques: l'Allemagne et l'Italie* (Paris, 1884–85), II, 255–56.

[69] *Diritto*, January 28 and February 11, 1871.

[70] The nature of the sovereignty conferred upon the pope by the law of guarantees has been the subject of much discussion among jurists and students of ecclesiastical law. Typical of the attitude of Catholic scholars is the position taken by Benedict Williamson (*The Treaty of the Lateran* [London, 1929], p. 16): "The only independent sovereignty of which we have cognizance is a territorial sovereignty." A similar view is expounded by Neuhaus. He holds that, with the fall of the temporal power, the concept of sovereignty, strictly speaking, was no longer applicable to the Holy See, despite the immunities vouchsafed it in the law of guarantees. Only a *state* could be sovereign (*op. cit.*, pp. 20–22). In the view of this school, no real sovereignty can exist apart from the exercise of supreme jurisdiction over a given territorial do-main. Some jurists have termed the territoryless sovereignty conferred by the law of guarantees a *jus singolare*. Others have named it a sovereignty *sui generis*, a per-sonal, spiritual, or honorary sovereignty (cf. Piola, *op. cit.*, pp. 116–17). Professor Mario Falco, a leading authority on Italian ecclesiastical law, holds that after 1870 the pope retained sovereignty "in the international sphere" (*The Legal Position of the Holy See before and after the Lateran Agreements* [Oxford, 1935], p. 17).

covering attacks against the person of the king. He was to be
free to maintain diplomatic relations with foreign governments. And, in order that the safety and secrecy of his communications with those governments might be insured, the
diplomatic representatives accredited to the Vatican were to
enjoy in Italy all the immunities conferred upon diplomatic
agents by international law. His freedom of communication
with parties abroad was to be further guaranteed by providing him with separate postal and telegraph offices and special
couriers. He was to receive in perpetuity an annual payment
of 3,225,000 lire, a sum equal to that formerly allocated in the
papal budget for the maintenance of his court.[71] He was to retain his guards and enjoy the use of the Vatican, the Lateran,
and the villa of Castel Gandolfo. These enclaves, which remained the property of the state, were to be exempt from
taxation and immune from intrusion by agents of the civil
authorities. A notable feature of this section was Article VI,
which stipulated that the cardinals meeting in conclave to
elect a successor to the throne of St. Peter were to be free
from all interference. Significant too was the provision that
Catholic seminaries in Rome and in the suburbicarian sees
were to continue under the exclusive aegis of the Holy See.[72]

The second section of the law was based on the separatist
principle.[73] It represented an attempt to approximate the
Cavourian ideal which, in matters ecclesiastical, was the
guiding star of Lanza and most of his colleagues.[74] Complete

[71] In the course of the parliamentary debate on this article, the suggestion was
made that the Catholic powers be invited to share with Italy the burden of paying
this annuity. But nothing came of it (cf. Piola, *op. cit.*, p. 51).

[72] Cf. the excellent discussion of Sec. I of the law of guarantees in Piola, *op. cit.*,
pp. 42–52, and in Scaduto, *op. cit.*, pp. 111–217.

[73] Cf. Falco, *The Legal Position of the Holy See before and after the Lateran Agreements*, p. 10; Scaduto, *op. cit.*, pp. 217–18.

[74] R. Bonghi, "Le Gouvernement italien et la papauté," *Revue des deux mondes*,
May 1, 1873, p. 125; cf. Lanza's elaborate defense of the separatist thesis in Tavallini, *op. cit.*, II, 59–62; cf. also the chapter on "Post-Cavourian Separatists" in S.
William Halperin, *The Separation of Church and State in Italian Thought from Cavour
to Mussolini* (Chicago, 1937), pp. 18–39.

freedom of assembly was to be vouchsafed the clergy. The state surrendered its right to nominate bishops, who were no longer to take an oath of allegiance to the king. The civil courts were denied appellate jurisdiction in cases against ecclesiastics charged with abusing their spiritual powers. The *exequatur* and *placet*, traditionally required for the promulgation of acts of the ecclesiastical authorities, were in principle abolished; but they were retained for the allocation of benefices.[75] This arrangement, in flagrant contradiction with the principle of freedom, was theoretically a provisional one, pending the definitive disposal of ecclesiastical properties.[76] But a measure determining the fate of those properties, promised in Article XVIII of the law of guarantees, was never enacted, and this weapon of control over the clergy remained in the possession of the civil authorities.[77] The concessions contained in this section of the law, unlike those in Section I, were inspired not so much by fear of foreign complications as by "scientific conviction"[78]—an abiding faith in the efficacy of the separatist principle.

Accompanying the bill was a memorandum explaining and defending its provisions. It declared that the two sections of the measure could not be divorced because "it would do little or no good to make the supreme head of the church free and independent when the church itself and its ministers . . . . remained . . . . subject to some other power." It emphasized the necessity of enacting guarantees that would "remove from the conscience of Catholics any reasonable suspicion of interference, direct or indirect, by the kingdom of Italy in

---

[75] The ministry had favored the unconditional abolition of the *exequatur*, but the parliamentary reporting committee successfully insisted on this reservation (cf. Falco, *La Politica ecclesiastica della Destra*, pp. 28–30; Castagnola, *op. cit.*, pp. 132–33).

[76] Bonghi, *op. cit.*, p. 131; Michele Rosi, *Vittorio Emanuele II* (Bologna, 1930), II, 184; Paladino, *op. cit.*, p. 151.

[77] Cf. Scaduto, *op. cit.*, pp. 385–86; Biagio Brugi, "Giurisprudenza e codici," *Cinquanta anni di storia italiana* (Milano, 1911), II, 19.

[78] Scaduto, *op. cit.*, p. 79.

the government of the church." The immunities conferred upon the pope in no way detracted from the territorial sovereignty of the Italian state. Papacy and monarchy moved in spheres "entirely diverse and distinct," meeting only to promote the common good. Turning to the second section of the bill, the document denied that the church, to be truly free, had to be so isolated from the civil power that it ceased to have any relation or contact with it. In Italy, where church and state were "composed . . . . almost of the same elements," such a total severence would be "a social impossibility." Rather, freedom for the church meant that in purely religious matters the latter was to be independent of the state. It signified that each was to have its own province and enjoy every liberty compatible with harmonious coexistence. This was not only possible but inherent in the very nature of the two institutions.[79]

The proposed papal guarantees, which were hailed by moderate opinion as the fulfilment of the government's oft-repeated promise to safeguard the spiritual authority of the Holy Father,[80] evoked a withering barrage from the Sinistra press. The *Riforma* was the spearhead of this agitation. It charged that the bill created "a pontifical sovereignty without parallel" and that Italy, in enacting it, would be recognizing the Syllabus as "the emanation of an inviolable and infallible sovereignty." The state, it contended, would be foregoing its principal duties in favor of a power "acknowledged to be superior and essentially hostile to it." This situation could not fail to be the source of "new complications and infinite difficulties."[81] In like fashion, the *Diritto* assailed the conferment of sovereignty upon the pope. It warned against the creation in Italy of "a fatal dualism" between the king and the head

---

[79] *Atti*, CLXI, No. 31, 1–7. The reader will note that the *absolute* separation of church and state, which this official memorandum disavowed, was nevertheless eulogized as the ideal objective of Italian ecclesiastical policy by ministerial spokesmen (see below, p. 124).

[80] Cf. the typical observations of the *Opinione* of December 16, 1870.

[81] *Riforma*, December 14, 15, and 18, 1870.

of the church. The immunities with which the government proposed to invest the pontiff constituted a revival of the "barbaric" medieval right of asylum. The permission to maintain separate papal guards would redound to the jeopardy of public order. And there was no reason whatever to allow the retention of a diplomatic corps at the Vatican. The latter could communicate freely with the entire world without such ambassadorial intermediaries.[82]

The bill was scrutinized in committee, and on January 16 the chamber of deputies was regaled with an elaborate report. The first question to be decided, the document declared, was whether the provisions of the contemplated measure could be enacted without damage to any of the "civil criteria which inform the legislation of all states." The answer was clearly in the affirmative. The separation of the ecclesiastical from the civil was a matter of internal public law and therefore within the competency of every state. So, too, the country which happened to harbor the supreme pontiff could make statutory provision for his honorable sojourn. But the sovereign attributes which he continued to possess after the loss of his temporal power were recognized in international law, and care had to be taken to leave them intact. Only those rights which were inseparable from territorial dominion had fallen away. Consequently, the honors and immunities accorded the pope were altogether defensible. There remained, however, the hostility of the Catholic hierarchy, which made it unwise to renounce all the traditional regalist safeguards.[83] At the instance of its anticlerical members, the committee proposed modifications in this sense,[84] and some of them were enacted. But the remainder of the bill was not seriously tampered with.

The general debate in the chamber began on January 23, and it was not until March 21 that the bill was finally voted there. The chief opposition to the ministerial program came

---

[82] *Diritto*, January 8, 1871.

[83] *Atti*, CLXI, No. 31A, 1–3.   [84] Cf. Scaduto, *op. cit.*, p. 276.

from the extreme conservatives and the Sinistra jurisdiction-alists.[85] The former minced no words. Their principal spokes man, Toscanelli, declared that the guarantees offered the pope were a poor substitute for territorial sovereignty. They were utterly inadequate to safeguard his freedom and inde-pendence. It was therefore a foregone conclusion that the proposed law would not satisfy the Catholic world.[86] The anticlericals of the left made no secret of their hostility to the measure. Inasmuch as there was no danger of foreign com-plications, they contended, there was no reason to treat the pope and the church so leniently.[87] Their great orator on this occasion was again Mancini.[88] His blasts against the govern-ment's ecclesiastical policy were never more withering. He decried the intention of endowing the pope with sovereignty. Certain concessions to the dispossessed pontiff, yes. But to attempt to make him a sovereign when he had ceased to be one was altogether too much. In any case, parliament lacked the power to create or grant the prerogatives of sovereignty. He warned against excessive zeal in lavishing immunities upon the Holy See and the church. He did concede, how-ever, the justice of endowing the pope with personal inviola-bility, but he insisted that this privilege be denied lesser ec clesiastical dignitaries. He reminded the chamber that civil society also possessed rights and that these required protec-tion. He apotheosized the national state as the sole reposi-tory of absolute authority. Within its borders there could be no rival power.[89] Some of Mancini's leading colleagues were even more intractable. La Porta perceived in the proposed inviolability of the pope a "hypocrisy" and a "lie."[90] Crispi

---

[85] *Ibid.*, p. 87.   [86] *Atti*, CLXV (January 23, 1871), 285, 291–92.

[87] Scaduto, *op. cit.*, pp. 76–77.

[88] For a general evaluation of his role in the parliamentary debates on the law of guarantees see Falco, *La Politica ecclesiastica della Destra*, pp. 23–24.

[89] *Atti*, CLXV (January 28, 1871), 407, 408–10, 412, 414.

[90] Cf. Nostitz-Rieneck, "Der Parlamentskampf ums Garantiegesetz," *op. cit.*, p. 397.

argued that Italian law recognized no personal sovereign. It acknowledged only one sovereignty—the collective sovereignty of the people, whose chosen mandatory was the king. Consequently, the pope was being endowed with something that did not exist in Italy, where there were no sovereigns and subjects but simply citizens who constituted in their totality the sole possessors of sovereignty. The Sinistra chieftain went on to contend that it was suicidal to confer personal inviolability upon the pontiff. The latter, he predicted, would exploit his position to plot against the state, whereupon the authorities would be compelled "to arrest and perhaps to shoot him."[91] And the *Riforma*, taking its cue from these strictures, argued that the dispossessed Holy See was being vouchsafed a vaster domain—the kingdom of Italy.[92] But in the opinion of the great majority of the deputies, the concessions stipulated in Section I represented an indispensable minimum, and the opposition to them proved numerically unimportant.[93]

No less serious was the divergence of opinion on the second section. This part of the law, according to Destra spokesmen, was the necessary complement of the papal guarantees. The goal to be achieved, they explained, was the absolute separation of church and state.[94] A very different line was taken by the militant leaders of the Sinistra. They claimed that Section II was altogether gratuitous. Neither necessity nor expediency could be invoked in vindication of this surrender of powers traditionally exercised over the church.[95] It was imprudent, to say the least, to leave the clergy to their own unsavory devices. Indeed, the state, in disarming itself, was subjecting the nation "to the conspiracy of a hostile political power."[96] As understood and applied by the Destra, the

---

[91] *Ibid.*; Crispi, *Politica interna*, p. 72; Falco, *La Politica ecclesiastica della Destra*, p. 25.

[92] *Riforma*, March 14, 1871.   [94] Cf. the *Opinione* of February 19, 1871.

[93] Cf. Guiccioli, *op. cit.*, I, 335.   [95] Cf. Scaduto, *op. cit.*, pp. 96–99.

[96] Cf. the *Riforma* of December 14, 1870.

freedom of the church was nothing less than "an odious privilege" proffered the Catholic hierarchy. It signified "the supremacy of the Catholic church over political society"— in short, a new kind of Roman theocracy.[97] The *Diritto* was no less emphatic in scoring the alleged shortcomings of this portion of the measure. It likewise enlarged upon the folly of granting too much liberty to the church and even managed to cite Cavour in support of its position.[98] The fate of the *exequatur* and the *placet* figured heavily in this controversy. The *Riforma*, in urging the retention of these regalist safeguards, lauded them as "guarantees which restrain the absolute power of the Catholic hierarchy." And if anything, concluded Crispi's sheet, they were insufficient for the purpose.[99] This opposition to Section II converged into the refrain that civil society, in order to protect its highest interests, had no choice but to keep the liberty of the church within very narrow limits. It was under no circumstances to countenance the surrender of rights which in the past had given the state a certain security against clerical abuses and aggression.[100] A number of Destra moderates took a similar position.[101] Among them was Sella. He, too, denounced the ministerial program because he felt the state, in self-defense, ought to retain some of its ancient powers over the church.[102]

The bill was eloquently defended by Sella's colleagues. Raeli explained that the government was attempting to ascertain which of the existing restrictions on the liberty of the church—restrictions imposed at a time when protection was needed against the overbearing pretensions of the ecclesiastical hierarchy—could be removed without damage to the state. What was now being proposed had been whittled

[97] *Ibid.*, January 11, 1871.

[98] *Diritto* of January 8, 1871. [99] *Riforma*, March 18, 1871.

[100] Cf. Bersezio, *op. cit.*, VIII, 399; cf., for a general discussion of the views of the Sinistra jurisdictionalists, Halperin, *op. cit.*, pp. 40–41.

[101] Falco, *La Politica ecclesiastica della Destra*, p. 26.

[102] Guiccioli, *op. cit.*, I, 336; Piola, *op. cit.*, p. 40.

down to conform to that criterion. Only that which conflicted with the principle of freedom was being discarded.[103] Lanza painted the situation in very realistic colors. The Holy See, he declared, was an institution which the government could neither alter nor destroy. The powers, moreover, would never permit the pope to be treated as an ordinary citizen. He took up the cudgels in behalf of Article I of the *Statuto*, whose suppression had been demanded by some of the opposition speakers.[104] He argued that, since its promulgation, this article, though it was in conflict with the separatist principle, had never proved an obstacle to complete freedom of conscience and worship. He also dealt sharply with the suggestion of certain Sinistra deputies that the two sections of the bill be considered independently. The inviolability of the pope and the freedom of the church, he asserted, could not be separated. With an eye to the reaction of the Catholic world, he hailed the Holy Father as "an international entity, dependent on no state and the subject of no government."[105]

Visconti-Venosta was easily the most effective of the ministerial orators. In cogency and elegance of expression, he was second to none. He began by acknowledging himself a convinced partisan of the separation, or rather, the "absolute distinction," of church and state. He felt that, under existing social conditions, harmony and peace were possible only by divorcing the two institutions. The church would then learn to seek its strength not in the support of the government but in "the sentiment of humanity." Liberty would produce a salutary change within the church. It would stimulate a movement of ideas altogether different from the absolutism which the civil authorities, by their meddlesome policy, had unwittingly engendered. From this it followed that the freedom of the church was the "true and great solution of the

---

[103] *Atti*, CLXV (January 27, 1871), 391.

[104] This clause of the Italian constitution proclaimed Roman Catholicism the official religion of the state.

[105] *Atti*, CLXV (February 2, 1871), 506-7, 509.

Roman question."[106] The government, he continued, had always striven to spare the sentiments of the Catholic world and the legitimate interests of the powers. But it was clear that damage would accrue to those sentiments and interests were the pope to become a subject of the king of Italy. And it was equally clear that "whoever is not a subject is a sovereign." The sovereignty of the pope existed by the force of circumstances, and this the Italian government was unable to gainsay.[107] The law of guarantees could not be discussed as a contract with the pope because the latter had rejected a bilateral arrangement. Furthermore, it was not the last word on the Roman question. Only time could provide a definitive settlement. In the meantime, however, care had to be taken to reassure the Catholic world that the pope was to be immune from any kind of pressure on the part of Italy.[108] He was at great pains to explain why no international solution had been resorted to. "We declared," he said, "that we were ready to examine, in concert with the other governments, the guarantees necessary to safeguard the spiritual independence of the supreme pontiff. We also indicated the means we intended to employ to insure this independence. The governments allowed us to assume responsibility . . . . and reserved the right to pass judgment upon the result of our labors." It therefore behooved Italy to treat the pope with generosity and moderation, if she wished to spare herself the necessity of discussing the guarantees with a hostile Europe.[109]

The senate's deliberations were less prolonged and acrimonious. Certain modifications were proposed which the chamber readily accepted. One of these was the suppression of an article, voted as an amendment by the lower house, declaring the papal museums and libraries national property. Pius had been incensed by the action of the chamber. Had it

---

[106] *Ibid.*, January 30, 1871, pp. 441–42. [108] *Ibid.*, February 13, 1871, p. 756.

[107] *Ibid.*, p. 442. [109] *Ibid.*, January 30, 1871, p. 444.

gone unchallenged, he would have been unable to use the papal archives without permission from the state librarian. He had threatened to forego his walks in the Vatican gardens, which could not be reached without going through one of the museums. The French government had come to his aid. Favre had invited Beust to act with him in pressing for the elimination of the objectionable article[110] and had made strong representations to the Italian government.[111] Visconti-Venosta, who was much irked by the chamber amendment,[112] had acted to comply with Favre's request and had secured its defeat in the senate.[113] The debate in the upper house had been further enlivened by one of the foreign minister's major oratorical efforts. On this occasion he had underlined the futility of arguing whether the Roman question was a national or international one. With reference to the rights of Italy and the Romans, it was purely national. But it was true nonetheless that the papacy was a universal institution which had relations with the Catholics of all nations. Consequently, account had to be taken of the attitude of the powers in the formulation of papal guarantees. They had to be reassured that the Italian nation's sense of loyalty and

[110] Cf. the allusion to the joint Austro-French *démarche* at Florence in Zaluski to Beust, April 30, 1871, HHSA, Politisches Archiv (Berichte aus Florenz), Fasz. XI/78, No. 22B, fol. 697a.

[111] Cf. Favre to Lefebvre de Béhaine, March 15, 1871, AMAE (Rome, mars-avril, 1871), Tome 1050, fols. 89–90; Favre to Rothan, April 12, 1871, *ibid.* (Italie, mars–avril, 1871), Tome 381, fol. 409; Favre to Choiseul, April 20, 1871, *ibid.*, fol. 434; J. Favre, *Rome et la République française* (Paris, 1871), pp. 100–101; Rothan, *op. cit.*, II, 388; *AD, 1874,* II, 222; Bastgen, *op. cit.*, II, 787; Maurice Reclus, *Jules Favre* (Paris, 1912), p. 496.

[112] Castagnola, *op. cit.*, p. 144.

[113] On April 6, Rothan reported to Favre that Italian fear of international intervention "is salutary and will encourage a reaction against the activities of the left." The Italian government, he observed, "is more willing to listen to protests and has asked the senate to revise the most regrettable features of the law of guarantees." Visconti-Venosta took every precaution to pacify the French cabinet. "What European government," he declared to Rothan, "could furnish the pope . . . . such full guarantees both for his person . . . . and for the exercise of his ministry? Add to all these guarantees . . . . our firm intention to show the Holy Father the most respectful deference, and you will agree that he could nowhere find a better asylum than Rome" (Rothan, *op. cit.*, II, 383–85).

responsibility could be relied upon to protect those guarantees.[114] Fortunately, they realized the impossibility of undoing the accomplished facts. They were aware that the
difficulties which the ultramontanes might create for them
were less dangerous than the complications attendant upon
intervention.[115] These and other ministerial observations
were not lost on the senators, who from the outset had been
favorably disposed toward the government's program. On
May 2 they formally approved the bill. Eleven days later the
king affixed his signature to it.

Moderate opinion received the outcome of the prolonged
debates with satisfaction. It felt that the statute was adequate, in the existing circumstances, to safeguard the pope's
spiritual position. Under the law of guarantees, the *Opinione*
asserted, the Holy Father was freer than he had been when
the Austrians were at Bologna and the French at Rome.[116]
The *Libertà* lauded the generous terms accorded the Holy
See. They sprang, it insisted, from the realization that liberty and independence had to be substituted for violence and
compulsion.[117] Anticlericals were in high dudgeon. They reiterated the charge that the Holy See was being treated much
too leniently.[118] Present always in their minds was the oft-
expressed fear that the enactment of the papal guarantees
would signify the restoration of a Roman theocracy.[119] Foremost among the critics of the law was Garibaldi, to whom
anything short of the complete subjugation of the priesthood
was anathema.[120] From the Catholic party came an endless
stream of denunciations and the familiar refrain that only
territorial sovereignty could insure the pope's freedom and
independence. From the moment of its presentation to par-

[114] *Atti*, CLXVIII (April 22, 1871), 776.

[115] *Ibid.*, p. 781.

[116] Chiala, *Dina*, III, 290.

[117] *Libertà*, May 11, 1871.

[118] Cf. J. B. Bury, *History of the Papacy, 1864–1878* (London, 1930), p. 156.

[119] The *Riforma's* obsession with this theme can be gathered from a perusal of its
issues of January and February, 1871.

[120] Cf. Vigo, *op. cit.*, I, 58, 92.

liament, the law, which certain members of Pius' entourage were exploiting to urge a precipitate departure,[121] had been mercilessly flayed by the clerical press. "The barbarians use barbaric words," the *Unità cattolica* had taunted. "*Guarantee* does not belong to the Italian language. . . . . They consider Rome a store and offer to safeguard the goods in it."[122] The government, moreover, was seeking to handcuff the pope in his own domicile.[123] In the past, Italy had consistently breached her pledges and contracts. How then, queried the Turinese journal, could any faith be reposed in her present promises?[124] The *Osservatore romano* had editorialized in like vein. The "so-called guarantees," it had warned, were considered "an insult" and "an indecent mockery" by Catholics.[125] Such governmental concessions would not modify the real situation, since transactions of this nature could have no validity without the pope's explicit and formal consent.[126] The tone of the *Civiltà cattolica* had been especially virulent. It had alluded to the guarantees as the "monstrous outcome of revolutionary jurisprudence" and adduced every possible argument against their acceptance. It had never wearied of repeating that the pope could not at one and the same time be free and dependent; that he could not become the subject of any state; that sovereignty without territorial dominion was a crude joke; that the sovereignty offered the pope was really "privileged subjection" to the Italian monarchy; that independence which rested upon concessions could at any time be destroyed by the stroke of a pen; that guarantees not founded on territorial sovereignty were designed only to hoodwink foreign governments and the Catholic world; that they would always remain subordinated to *raison d'état*, especially in the event of war, when Italy might be tempted

---

[121] Francesco Salata, *Per la storia diplomatica della questione romana* (Milano, 1929), I, 133.

[122] *Unità cattolica*, December 13, 1870.

[123] *Ibid.*, January 22, 1871.   [125] *Osservatore romano*, December 15, 1870.

[124] *Ibid.*, April 29, 1871.   [126] *Ibid.*, December 26, 1870.

to scrap the fiction of papal freedom and independence; that in a parliamentary state the government which today respected the church and the papacy might on the morrow abandon this restraint.[127] It had declared that even internationally sanctioned guarantees would be no satisfactory substitute for the temporal power.[128] These contentions were echoed and re-echoed in clerical brochures and pamphlets. With much show of learning, these tracts set forth the reasons why, with things as they were, reconciliation between Italy and the Holy See was impossible.[129]

Antonelli and Pius spurned the law of guarantees. Shortly after its submission to parliament, the cardinal remarked to Trauttmansdorff: "That is of no concern at all to us, we accept nothing."[130] Late in December the pontiff himself, in the course of an audience with the Austrian ambassador, reiterated the absolute impossibility of coming to an understanding with Italy.[131] The effect of the proposed law, he was led to believe, would be to make him "a permanent and honoured guest of the King of Italy," and acquiescence "would have fatally compromised his position in the eyes of Europe."[132] He objected strongly to the unilateral character of the settlement, even though the government had intimated that the law might conceivably serve as a basis for Italo-papal negotiations.[133] Especially galling was Article V, which accorded him the use but not the ownership of the apostolic

---

[127] Cf. *CC* (8th ser.), Vols. I and II.

[128] "Le Guarentigie saranno date al Papa per Legge o per Trattato," *ibid.*, I (8th ser.; February 18, 1871), 513–24.

[129] Cf. *ibid.*, I (8th ser.; March 5, 1871), 701–7; II (8th ser.; May 6, 1871), 441.

[130] Trauttmansdorff to Beust, December 16, 1870, HHSA, Politisches Korrespondenz (Rom), Fasz. XI/224, Bericht 127A, fol. 646*b*.

[131] Trauttmansdorff to Beust, December 27, 1870, *ibid.*, No. 131, fol. 716*a*.

[132] Humphrey Johnson, *The Papacy and the Kingdom of Italy* (London, 1926), p. 120.

[133] The Vatican held that issues between two sovereign powers could only be resolved by bilateral arrangements. The Italian government exculpated itself by pointing to the pope's refusal to negotiate.

palaces.[134] He gave free vent to his indignation in his encyclical of May 15. On this occasion he pronounced the proffered guarantees absolutely unacceptable. Insisting that no privileges or immunities could replace the temporal sovereignty, he exhorted the governments of Europe to unite in restoring the Holy See to its former status.[135] When the Italian government subsequently placed at his disposal the first instalment of the annuity assigned to him under the law, he was all defiance. "Yes," he said on this occasion, "I need money badly . . . . but you, what do you bring me . . . . ? A part of what you stole from me? Never will I accept it from you by way of reimbursement and you will obtain no signature which might seem to imply an acquiescence in or a resignation to the spoliation."[136] Antonelli informed Sella that the pope would do nothing to prejudice the imprescriptible rights of the Holy See. He could therefore accept no payments from the Italian government.[137] And so this instalment and succeeding ones were credited to the account of the papacy in the great book of the public debt.

From the date of its promulgation until 1929, the law of guarantees remained the charter of church-state relations in Italy. It has been the object of very divergent appraisals.[138] These have ranged from undiluted praise to utter and absolute condemnation. There is scarcely an Italian jurist, historian, or politician of any consequence who has not ventured

---

[134] Cf. Piola, *op. cit.*, p. 50. Clericals have made much of this as proof of the utterly dependent status of the pope under the law of guarantees. The latter, they urged, was "without so much as a foot of earth upon which to rest his sovereignty. It was not then a question of a greater or less amount of territory, but of there being no territory at all upon which to base the Papal Sovereignty, that made any settlement impossible" (Williamson, *op. cit.*, p. 16).

[135] Cf. the text of the encyclical in *CC*, II (8th ser.; June 9, 1871), 719–29; cf. also Joseph Schmidlin, *Papstgeschichte der neuesten Zeit* (München, 1933–34), II, 96.

[136] Cilibrizzi, *op. cit.*, III, 289.

[137] Cf. Luigi Luzzatti, *Dio nella libertà: studi sulle relazioni tra lo stato e la chiesa* (Bologna, 1926), p. 596; Manfroni, *op. cit.*, I, 106.

[138] Cf. Piola, *op. cit.*, pp. 132–34; Falco, *The Legal Position of the Holy See before and after the Lateran Agreements*, p. 12.

an evaluation.[139] One of its warmest defenders was the well-known statesman and philosopher, Luigi Luzzatti. He found it "a monument of Latin wisdom" which had solved Italy's oldest and most formidable problem and had contributed to her greatness as well as to that of the papacy.[140] The measure has likewise been extolled by such noted scholars as Francesco Ruffini[141] and Mario Falco.[142] Conspicuous among the law's earliest critics was Professor Guido Padelletti, of the University of Rome. This brilliant student of ecclesiastical law branded it a "juridical monster" which would speedily be cast into the discard.[143] Professor Luigi Palma, a leading authority on Italian constitutional law, expressed the feeling of many moderates when he wrote only four years after the enactment of the measure:

> Esau for a pot of lentils despoiled himself of primogeniture. Italy, to assure herself of the peaceful possession of Rome, has guaranteed to the supreme pontiff . . . . the personal prerogatives of a sovereign and the most ample immunity. . . . . By this policy . . . . she has achieved her political objective. But she has thrown away almost all the rights of the state vis-à-vis the Catholic church.[144]

Catholic publicists continued to insist upon the inadequacy of a unilateral solution.[145] They likewise enlarged upon the

---

[139] Cilibrizzi, *op. cit.*, II, 24.

[140] Luzzatti, *Memorie autobiografiche e carteggi* (Bologna, 1931), I, 339–40, and *Dio nella libertà*, p. 143.

[141] Cf. his remarks in his "La Questione romana e l'ora presente," *Nuova antologia*, June 1, 1921, pp. 198, 202, and 205.

[142] According to Falco, the law of guarantees "has been fully effective in that it has enabled the Pope to carry on in complete liberty his high mission throughout the entire world without any hindrance or the possibility of any hindrance from the Italian authorities" (*The Legal Position of the Holy See before and after the Lateran Agreements*, pp. 13–14).

[143] Cf. his "La Politica ecclesiastica in Italia," *Nuova antologia*, February 15, 1878, p. 654.

[144] Cf. his "L'Insegnamento religioso nelle scuole primarie e i seminarii ecclesiastici," *Nuova antologia*, June, 1875, pp. 356–57.

[145] Typical is the attitude of Abbé Edouard Devoghel, who alludes to this unilaterality as the "essential vice" of the law of guarantees (cf. his *La Question romaine sous Pie XI et Mussolini* [Paris, 1929], p. 4).

impossibility of any bilateral settlement which did not resurrect the temporal power. Had the pope been amenable, they invariably argued, he would have become in the eyes of non-Italians a "chaplain of the House of Savoy."[146] The year 1929, which witnessed the signing of the Lateran Accords, brought with it a host of uncomplimentary fascist allusions to the law of guarantees. Mussolini himself declared in the course of his address in the senate on May 25:

> It is a law of compromise and transition which was voted after a long, often chaotic and confused discussion . . . . a law which did not even please those who had devised it. . . . . Not the law of guarantees, of and by itself, but rather the often accommodating policy of the two parties, brought it about that, despite the law, there were no fearful and dangerous crises.[147]

Certain German jurists have contended that the law of guarantees was in the nature of an international treaty which placed upon Italy definite obligations toward the powers.[148] There can be little doubt, however, that from a juridical point of view it was a purely internal statute which could be modified or repealed in the customary legislative manner by the state which had enacted it.[149] It has been urged that the

[146] Cilibrizzi, *op. cit.*, II, 25.

[147] *Scritti e discorsi di Benito Mussolini* (Milano, 1934), VII, 114.

[148] Cf., e.g., Neuhaus, *op. cit.*, p. 16.

[149] The position taken by Falco is the one most generally accepted by Italian authorities on ecclesiastical law. "It is impossible," he writes, "to review . . . . the various theories about the juristic nature of the Law of Guarantees. According to the opinion which I think should be accepted there is no difference between it and any other internal law. Its subject-matter invests it with peculiar importance and may be said to give it the character of a fundamental constitutional law, inasmuch as it regulated the legal position of the Pope, the Church, and religion in Italy, and therefore could not be abrogated or modified without special and weighty consideration; but it had no greater legal force than any other law—and could therefore be abrogated or modified through the ordinary legislative channels. Moreover, it could be abrogated or modified by the unilateral action of Italy, since it was not, although several writers have maintained the contrary, the fulfilment of an international legal obligation incumbent on Italy" (*The Legal Position of the Holy See before and after the Lateran Agreements*, pp. 12–13). French scholars are substantially in agreement in emphasizing the point that juridically speaking the law of guarantees was a purely Italian, i.e., internal, statute (cf. Raoul Bompard, *La Papauté en droit international* [Paris, 1888], p. 190; Frantz Despagnet, *Cours de droit international public* [Paris, 1910], p. 212; Pierre Dilhac, *Les Accords du Latran: leurs origines, leur contenu, leur portée* [Paris, 1932], pp. 66–68).

purely Italian character of the papal guarantees proved a blessing to Europe. Had they been internationally sanctioned, so runs this argument, the Roman question might have been even more disturbing to the internal peace of Italy and of other Catholic states than it actually was. The church, too, would have found its position endangered by the temptation thus offered the powers to intervene in its affairs. Moreover, it was exceedingly improbable that Italy, of her own accord, would abrogate the law. She had little to gain and much to lose by reopening the entire question. Nor was she likely to denude the pope of his sovereign attributes. To do so would be to assume responsibility for his language and actions and thus to expose herself to serious international risks.[150]

[150] Cf. A. Leroy-Beaulieu, "Un Roi et un pape: Pie IX et le Saint-Siège," *Revue des deux mondes*, May 15, 1878, pp. 405-6.

CHAPTER V

THE TRANSFER OF THE CAPITAL

NO SOONER had Cadorna's troops filed through the breach at Porta Pia than a great cry went up for the immediate transfer of the capital to Rome.[1] The Sinistra placed itself in the van of this agitation,[2] but the issue quickly transcended party lines. To the average Italian, nothing seemed simpler than to move the seat of the government. Rome belonged to the House of Savoy. The pope could offer no effective resistance. Why, therefore, delay? But wiser heads knew better. They did not underestimate the difficulty of domiciling within the same city the sovereign of a modern state and the head of a medieval church. There were serious Italians, Paget reported on September 22, who favored keeping the capital where it was and allowing Rome to continue as the exclusive residence of the Holy Father. The British minister himself appreciated the inherently anomalous character of the situation. He pointed out to Granville that the establishment in Rome of "a constitutional and excommunicated King by the side of an infallible Pope; of a Representative Parliament by the side of an absolute authority; of a liberty of the press and freedom of discussion by the side of the Inquisition .... is giving a legal sanction to a state of things which can hardly be expected to work harmoniously."[3]

The opposition to *Roma capitale* came from clericals, certain influential Florentines, and a small number of Destra moderates. The latter would have been satisfied to see Rome

---

[1] Giuseppe Gadda, "Roma capitale ed il Ministero Lanza-Sella," *Nuova antologia,* September 16, 1897, p. 214.

[2] Cf., e.g., the *Riforma* of September 27, 1870.

[3] *Blue Book*, No. 35, p. 38.

become a sort of honorary capital.[4] But public opinion was heavily against them, and they would have courted certain repudiation at the polls. The press of their own party was on the popular side in this controversy and joined the Sinistra sheets in urging compliance with the national will.[5] But the cabinet itself could not furnish the necessary leadership. Before the occupation it had been divided on this as on other questions.[6] A few of its members had doubted the wisdom of moving the seat of the government. The question of when such action should be taken had been more hotly contested. Lanza and most of his colleagues had counseled delay, alleging that precipitateness in so delicate a matter might do much damage.[7] After September 20 dissension within the cabinet persisted.[8] Again the question of whether, as well as when, the transfer should be effected proved a source of spirited controversy. Several of the ministers were anxious to cut short all contests for primacy among the cities of the peninsula. They invoked the axiom, consecrated by several votes of the Italian parliament, that Rome had to be the capital. They were unwilling to wait until the pope's future status had been defined by international diplomatic arrangements. They wished in effect to avail themselves of the argument of the *fait accompli*.[9] Again it was Sella who assumed the leadership in advocating the course demanded by popular sentiment. It was not demagoguery which impelled him to take this position. He sincerely believed that no government could refuse to fulfil the program to which all Italian statesmen since Cavour had solemnly committed themselves

[4] Robert von Nostitz-Rieneck, "Wie Neuitalien auf das Garantiegesetz kam," *Stimmen der Zeit*, April, 1917, p. 18.

[5] Chiala, *Dina*, III, 267–68.

[6] Stefano Castagnola, *Da Firenze a Roma: diario storico-politico del 1870–71* (Torino, 1896), p. 22.

[7] Cf., for Lanza's position, Chiala, *Dina*, III, 611–12.

[8] Cf. Attilio Simioni, *Vittorio Emanuele II* (Milano, 1911), p. 143.

[9] Kübeck to Beust, September 22, 1870, HHSA, Politisches Archiv (Florenz), Fasz. XI/75, No. 78A, fols. 163*a*–163*b*.

and which the Italian parliament, speaking for the nation, had enthusiastically indorsed. The establishment of the capital at Rome was an issue too dear to the Italian people to admit of compromise. The cabinet, he told Paget on September 24, could not hesitate. The coresidence of pope and king in the former papal capital would create difficulties no greater than those which would ensue were the existing situation to be left undisturbed.[10] The destruction of the temporal power, he insisted, was incomplete as long as the status of Rome remained unchanged. The immediate transfer of the capital was therefore dictated by every consideration of patriotism and expediency.[11]

Lanza, and with him Visconti-Venosta, continued to caution against haste, much to Sella's disgust.[12] They understood the impatience of their countrymen, but they firmly believed that the solution of a question which bristled with so many formidable complications could not be hurried. In this they were supported by Ricasoli, who agreed that the removal of the capital would have to be a gradual process.[13] For a time the rift in the cabinet seemed likely to produce a ministerial crisis.[14] Minghetti, with his shrewd appreciation of political realities, deplored the possibility of a definitive break between Sella and Visconti-Venosta. He felt that the two men admirably complemented each other. Sella could always be relied upon for the forceful if indiscreet gesture, while the foreign minister excelled in the *suaviter in modo*. He feared that their parting at this moment would be a calamity for the Destra, which might thus be robbed of the fruits of its Roman policy.[15]

[10] *Blue Book*, No. 40, pp. 44–45.

[11] Alessandro Guiccioli, *Quintino Sella* (Rovigo, 1887), I, 312.

[12] Correnti, who saw eye to eye with Lanza and Visconti-Venosta on this issue, was dubbed by the irate Sella "that blessed canon" (Giovanni Giolitti, *Memoirs of My Life* [London, 1923], p. 38).

[13] Aurelio Gotti, *La Vita del Barone Bettino Ricasoli* (Firenze, 1898), p. 381.

[14] Luigi Luzzatti, *Memorie autobiografiche e carteggi* (Bologna, 1931), I, 308–9

[15] *Ibid.*, p. 309.

The apparent indecision of Florence irked the Romans no end.[16] But they knew that the trumps were in their possession. The chief of these was public opinion.[17] The others were the strong sectional jealousies which rendered impossible the selection of any other city as the capital and the widespread fear that failure to move the seat of the government to Rome would encourage revolutionary movements there.[18] The Sinistra was more vociferous than ever in its support of the Romans' demand for an immediate transfer.[19] But the authorities at Florence still hesitated to concede the inevitable. Even after Victor Emmanuel's formal acceptance of the result of the plebiscite, Lanza continued "uncertain" and Visconti-Venosta "perplexed."[20] Journals hostile to the cabinet intimated that some of the ministers were held back by religious scruples.[21] Other deterrents were operative in the case of certain Destra die-hards. The attitude of Senator Giuseppe Pasolini, Minghetti's close friend, was typical of this school. The establishment of the capital in Rome, he feared, would prove "another most serious crisis for Italy." It would entail a policy of decentralization, the wisdom of which he was inclined to doubt. "In the solution of this problem," he warned, "lies perhaps the salvation or ruin of Italy."[22] Minghetti did his best to reassure Pasolini. With the bestowal upon the pope of all possible guarantees, he argued, the program of the government as regards Italy would have to be politically conservative and favorable to decentralization in the administrative sphere. "In any case and despite all

---

[16] Castagnola, *op. cit.*, p. 75.

[17] On September 30 the Rome correspondent of the *Times* reported: "What seems clear as noonday to me is that it is quite impossible to resist and go against the unanimous and overpowering current of feeling in Italy in favour of the capital being transferred to Rome" (*Times*, October 8, 1870).

[18] J. B. Bury, *History of the Papacy, 1864–1878* (London, 1930), p. 158.

[19] Cf. the *Riforma* of October 5 and 8, 1870.

[20] Chiala, *Dina*, III, 272.   [21] Luzzatti, *op. cit.*, I, 309 n.

[22] *Carteggio tra Marco Minghetti e Giuseppe Pasolini* (Torino, 1924–30), IV, 193–94.

conceivable difficulties," he concluded, "*Roma capitale* is still the lesser evil in view of the internal dangers which would arise upon the abandonment of this idea."[23] Late in October the cabinet finally reached the same conclusion. At Lanza's insistence, however, it was decided to postpone the actual transfer until the following summer.[24] The date selected for parliament's approval was July 1, 1871. Lanza's decision to defer the transfer was influenced by the representations of certain foreign governments[25] and the desire "to make a last loop-hole for reconciliation."[26] Other factors were the difficulty of securing adequate quarters in Rome for the various governmental bureaus and the immense cost of a hurried transfer.[27]

There remained the corollary problem of setting a date for the king's first visit to his future capital. Again Sella found himself at loggerheads with his colleagues. Mindful of the growing impatience of public opinion, he urged that Victor Emmanuel ought to lose little time in presenting himself to the Romans.[28] Any delay, he contended, would prove prejudicial to the king's popularity and to the interests of Italy.[29] But his plea encountered the stubborn resistance of Lanza. The premier was of the opinion that the step should not be taken until parliament had sanctioned the proposed papal guarantees.[30] He shrank from inflicting a gratuitous affront upon the Vatican by hastening the king's arrival. He feared

[23] *Ibid.*, pp. 195-96.

[24] Enrico Tavallini, *La Vita e i tempi di Giovanni Lanza* (Torino, 1887), II, 52.

[25] Notably Great Britain and Bavaria (*Libro verde*, No. 41, pp. 50–53; *AD, 1874,* II, 115-16, 127).

[26] Bolton King, *A History of Italian Unity* (London, 1899), II, 378-79.

[27] Kübeck attributed to these factors the decline in the enthusiasm of the proponents of an immediate transfer (cf. his dispatch of October 8, 1870, to Beust in HHSA, Politisches Archiv [Florenz], Fasz. XI/75, No. 82, fol. 212*b*).

[28] On Sella's position in this matter see Kübeck to Beust, October 22, 1870, *ibid.*, No. 86C, fol. 296*a*.

[29] Cf. Kübeck to Beust, November 3, 1870, *ibid.*, No. 88C, fols. 339*b*–340*a*.

[30] Tavallini, *op. cit.*, II, 53–55.

that the latter's presence might prove the signal for the pope's departure, and he was anxious to give the moderate party at the Vatican time to persuade the pontiff to abandon thoughts of flight and resign himself to this additional trial.[31] It was of paramount importance to do nothing to prejudice the chances of an Italo-papal understanding. Victor Emmanuel himself did not relish the idea of going to Rome at this time. The delicacy of his position vis-à-vis the pope rather than religious scruples accounted for this attitude.[32] Sella, however, showed no inclination to yield. Even the advice of the highly respected General La Marmora, who adduced many formidable arguments in support of the premier's position,[33] failed to move him. He had never believed, he insisted, in the possibility of a reconciliation with the papacy. The next few months, far from improving the temper of the Holy See, would only aggravate it. With the termination of the Franco-Prussian War and the release of the powers from the anxiety occasioned by it, the Vatican would redouble its complaints. It would be encouraged to perpetrate acts of hostility against the king in the hope of precipitating international complications. At the moment, Victor Emmanuel's entry into Rome could take place without damage to Italian interests. Before very long, however, it might be fraught with real danger.[34] Sella was supported by a section of the Destra press,[35] but Lanza too was obdurate. He was not yet ready to concede that the outlook for an Italo-papal reconciliation was hopeless. He could also point, in vindication of his position, to the unwillingness of certain foreign governments to permit their

[31] Raffaele Cadorna, *La Liberazione di Roma nell'anno 1870 ed il plebiscito* (Torino, 1898), pp. 286–87.

[32] Cf. Kübeck to Beust, October 8, 1870, HHSA, Politisches Archiv (Florenz), Fasz. XI/75, No. 82, fol. 212a.

[33] Guiccioli, *op. cit.*, I, 324–25; Tavallini, *op. cit.*, II, 413; Vittorio Bersezio, *Il Regno di Vittorio Emanuele II: trent'anni di vita italiana* (Torino, 1878–95), VIII, 390–91.

[34] Guiccioli, *op. cit.*, I, 325–27.

[35] Notably the *Opinione* (cf. the issue of November 2, 1870).

ministers at Florence to accompany the king on a premature visit to Rome.[36] Of particular importance, in this connection, was the attitude of Beust. The latter admitted that it would be difficult for the diplomatic corps to reject a formal invitation from the Italian government. But the Florentine authorities, he averred, would afford proof of their tact by not having the king come to Rome before the questions relating to the future position of the papacy had been definitively settled.[37] Evidently at Sella's suggestion, the *Opinione* on November 7 published a note announcing that the king was to go to Rome on the thirtieth. Lanza promptly denied the truth of this statement. In a letter to Michelangelo Castelli, he insisted that no decision had as yet been arrived at. Were the visit to occur before parliament had approved the outcome of the plebiscite, both he and La Marmora would resign. "The important thing," he wrote, "is that it be positively known that the king will go to Rome and that preparations to house him in the Quirinal will be begun."[38] At a cabinet meeting on the twelfth, the Lanza-Sella feud flared anew. The premier threatened to resign, whereupon the majority of his colleagues rallied to his support in a formal vote on the question.[39] They decided that the king's visit was to be postponed until parliament had disposed of the bills dealing with

[36] The Bavarian foreign office arranged that its minister in Florence was not to follow Victor Emmanuel were the latter to decide to go to Rome at this time (cf. Georges Goyau, *Bismarck et l'église; le culturkampf* [Paris, 1911–13], I, 45). Brassier de St. Simon advised the Italian government against inviting the diplomatic corps to accompany the king. Bismarck entirely agreed with his minister. Hitherto, he observed, Prussia had scrupulously refrained from any interference unwelcome to the Italians. But she ought not, in his opinion, participate in a step which would certainly alienate German Catholics (*GW*, VI*b*, No. 1924, 595). Kübeck proclaimed himself ready to tell Visconti-Venosta that he was opposed to the idea of having the diplomatic corps at Florence join Victor Emmanuel on the latter's entry into Rome (Kübeck to Beust, October 22, 1870, HHSA, Politisches Archiv [Florenz], Fasz. XI/75, No. 86C, fols. 297*b*–298*a*).

[37] Beust to Kübeck, October 30, 1870, HHSA, Politisches Archiv (Weisungen an Florenz), Fasz. XI/79, No. 3, fols. 255*a*–255*b*.

[38] Chiala, *Dina*, III, 274

[39] Castagnola, *op. cit.*, pp. 89–90; Bersezio, *op. cit.*, VIII, 389–90.

the annexation of Rome and the papal guarantees.[40] The cabinet's action was inspired by a realistic appreciation of the situation. Of considerable moment was the report that preparations to house the king in Rome were still in arrears. Furthermore, the complications precipitated by the seizure of the Quirinal enhanced the difficulties which stood in the way of an early royal entry. Finally, there was Victor Emmanuel's obvious reluctance to make the trip at this time.[41] It was now Sella's turn to pout. He declared he could not share responsibility for this resolution and presented his resignation. But he was induced to withdraw it when he was reminded that his departure would lead to the fall of the Lanza ministry.[42] The cause of peace within the cabinet was further served by the finance minister's decision to reject the Romans' offer to name him as one of their candidates in the forthcoming chamber elections.[43] Thus the affair was happily settled, and the ministry, with its unity unimpaired, could devote all its attention to the busy legislative program ahead.

On December 9 parliament was presented with a bill providing for the transfer of the capital not later than six months from the date of its enactment. The reporting committee of the chamber gave its unconditional approval,[44] but public opinion was sharply divided. The opposition, supported by certain dissident Destra elements, feared that delay might lead to the renunciation of *Roma capitale*. It argued that even a short postponement was a matter of real political importance.[45] In its impatience to see this part of the national program accomplished, it refused to take seriously the difficulties alleged by ministerial spokesmen.[46] The clericals pro-

[40] Cf. Kübeck to Beust, November 16, 1870, HHSA, Politisches Archiv (Florenz) Fasz. XI/75, No. 1715/109, fol. 391a.

[41] Kübeck to Beust, November 19, 1870, *ibid.*, No. 92A, fols. 395b–396a.

[42] Guiccioli, *op. cit.*, I, 327–28; Chiala, *Dina*, III, 275–76.

[43] Cf. Giuseppe Paladino, *Storia d'Italia dal 1861 al 1871 con particolare riguardo alla questione romana* (Milano, 1932), p. 150.

[44] Cf. *Atti*, Vol. CLXI, No. 30C.

[45] *Riforma*, December 23, 1870.   [46] Paladino, *op. cit.*, p. 150.

fessed to regard this impatience as a hopeful symptom. It sprang, they said, from fear of foreign intervention.[47] The *Opinione* stoutly defended the government's position. Everything possible was being done, it asserted, to facilitate a speedy transfer. It would be inexpedient, however, to move the seat of the government before the question of papal guarantees had been dealt with.[48] The general debate in the chamber began on the twenty-second. Various substitute proposals were promptly put forward. One of these specified March 31, 1871, as a suitable transfer date. Another recommended May 31. A third urged that no action be taken until November 1. The Sinistra deputies were unanimous in railing against the long delay and pressing for an earlier transfer. Precautions had to be taken, one of them warned, against certain unpredictable dangers that might materialize in the immediate future to jeopardize Italy's national existence. If six months were allowed to slip by before going to Rome, the city would be lost to Italy. He alluded to the world-wide activity of the ultramontane party on behalf of a restoration of the temporal power. He reminded the house that the attitude of the powers was not altogether clear. In the circumstances, the transfer ought to be effected before some unexpected difficulty should arise to impede it. Immediate action was therefore imperative.[49] Toscanelli spoke against the bill. He urged the government to separate the question of an Italian Rome from that of *Roma capitale*. By making Rome the capital, he contended, Italy would complicate her position and render more probable the departure of the Holy Father.[50] The subsequent discussion continued to center on the Sinistra's demand for a speedier transfer. Lanza made much of the material difficulties which allegedly stood in the

[47] *Osservatore romano*, December 21, 1870.

[48] *Opinione*, December 10 and 12, 1870.

[49] *Atti*, CLXV (December 22, 1870), 173–74.

[50] *Ibid.*, p. 175.

way of prompt action.[51] But he conceded that six months were the maximum and promised that the government, alive to the political realities of the situation, would endeavor to shorten the period.[52] Sella, though his sympathies were still with the opposition, came to the rescue of his colleagues. He insisted that the question of confidence could not be dissociated from the issue at hand. The government, he declared, would know how to interpret an adverse vote.[53] The Destra majority heeded this warning and passed the bill without further ado. The Sinistra had been worsted again, but it knew that its plea for haste had not been ill-received by large sections of public opinion, for increasing numbers of Italians were anxious to see the government firmly ensconced in Rome before the termination of the Franco-Prussian War.[54] The clericals professed to know that the chamber had rendered Italy a distinct disservice. The *Civiltà cattolica* observed that the coresidence in Rome of pope and king would be a source of unmixed grief for the latter. The sovereignty of the pope would completely overshadow that of his rival. The royal court would, as a result, be rife with jealousy and quarrelsomeness. And, to cap it all, the hostility of the Catholic world would be an ever present menace to the very existence of the monarchy.[55]

[51] Cf., on these material difficulties, Ugo Pesci, *I primi anni di Roma capitale* (Firenze, 1907), p. 93.

[52] *Atti*, CLXV (December 23, 1870), 197–99.

[53] *Ibid.*, pp. 210–11.

[54] On January 2, 1871, the correspondent of the *Times* reported from Florence: "A firm persuasion is . . . . gradually gaining ground day by day in this country that France will not fail to vent her resentment in a second Italian war as soon as she has sufficiently recruited her strength after peace has been signed to enable her to do so, and it will be her object this time to undo all that she did during the first war, and to restore the Papal Government" (*Times*, January 7, 1871).

[55] *CC*, I (8th ser.; January 21, 1871), 257–67. This prognosis was sharply challenged by the *Opinione*. It insisted that the church would adjust itself to the new situation once it realized that the state was sincere in wishing to give it complete freedom and independence. While the pope, it conceded, could hardly be expected to make a formal renunciation of his claims, a satisfactory *modus vivendi* would in time be attained.

While the transfer bill was awaiting action by the senate, an unexpected occurrence brought the king to the future capital. On December 27 the Tiber rose and flooded half of Rome. The clericals promptly explained this disaster as a divine visitation upon the despoilers of the Holy Father.[56] The destruction of life and property horrified the entire country, and aid for the destitute was at once organized on a national scale. Victor Emmanuel, accompanied by leading members of the cabinet, rushed to the lugubrious scene and dispensed charity with a generous hand.[57] It was during this brief stay in the city—he arrived on the morning of December 31 and left that night—that he signed the law incorporating the Patrimony of St. Peter into the Italian kingdom.[58] He found time, too, to remark to the officers of the Roman national guard: "Finally we are in Rome. . . . . Now no one will take her from us."[59] He remembered to send his aide de camp, Marquis Giacomo Spinola, to the Holy Father as a mark of his filial deference and devotion. But Pius refused to receive him, although Antonelli was careful to say that his master was grateful for this gesture.[60] The king's visit, according to the French chargé d'affaires, seemingly made no very deep impression upon the Romans. It was remarked by some, and not without bitterness, that Victor Emmanuel saw but little of his subjects and nothing at all of the Tiber.[61] Trauttmansdorff likewise noted the lack of popular enthusi-

[56] F. Gregorovius, *The Roman Journals of Ferdinand Gregorovius, 1852–1874* (London, 1907), p. 393.

[57] Cf. the reports in the *Blue Book*, Nos. 119 and 120, p. 135. The idea of making the trip to Rome was suggested by Visconti-Venosta and adopted by the cabinet (cf. Kübeck to Beust, December 30, 1870, HHSA, Politisches Archiv [Florenz], Fasz. XI/75, No. 103A, fols. 643*a*–643*b*).

[58] Pietro Vigo, *Storia degli ultimi trent'anni del secolo XIX* (Milano, 1908), I, 52.

[59] *CC*, I (8th ser.; February 6, 1871), 483.

[60] Giuseppe Massari, *La Vita ed il regno di Vittorio Emanuele II di Savoia* (Milano, 1910), II, 530–31.

[61] Lefebvre de Béhaine to Chaudordy, January 4, 1871, AMAE (Rome, janvier-février, 1871), Tome 1049, fols. 9–10.

asm.[62] Nevertheless, the brief royal sojourn had its panegyr-
ists. Gregorovius, the famous historian of the city of Rome,
was prompted to note in his diary: "What a memorable end-
ing of the year for Rome is the sight of the King of United
Italy! It closes the Middle Ages."[63] Victor Emmanuel's presence, the *Libertà* proclaimed, "will render more sacred and
precious the ties which unite the people with their sovereign."[64] Even the strongly propapal Austrian ambassador,
who continued to insist that the reception accorded the royal
visitor had been devoid of enthusiasm, admitted that Victor
Emmanuel, by coming to aid the victims of the flood, "has
acquired a claim to popularity in Rome."[65]

On January 27 the transfer bill received the senate's imprimatur. The debate was brief but spirited. The attenuated
opposition found a fiery spokesman in Jacini, a conservative
of considerable reputation. His contentions were pithy, but
they grated on ears attuned to more heroic utterances. He
thought the transfer unwise in view of the bad state of the
national finances. Florence, he said, had a more salubrious
climate, and Rome was not strategically safe. He warned
that the government would not gain in strength by going to
Rome. Moreover, the notion that Rome had to be the seat
of the government was not "an essentially liberal or patriotic
idea." It was, rather, a distinctly antiquated one, "adopted
by patriots and liberals in good faith but without adequate
reason."[66] Another of the die-hards, Alfieri, alluded to the
contemplated transfer as "sudden and premature."[67] Whatever truth these observations contained mattered little to the
majority of the senators. They could no more resist the

---

[62] Trauttmansdorff to Beust, December 31, 1870, HHSA, Politisches Korrespondenz (Rom), Fasz. XI/224, No. 98/386, fols. 720a–720b.

[63] *Op. cit.*, p. 394.   [64] *Libertà*, January 1, 1871.

[65] Trauttmansdorff to Beust, January 4, 1871, HHSA, Politisches Archiv (Rom),
Fasz. XI/226, Bericht 1A, fol. 3b.

[66] *Atti*, CLXVIII (January 23, 1871), 117–23.

[67] *Ibid.*, January 24, 1871, p. 133.

magic of *Roma capitale* than their friends in the lower house. Nor would they hear of making the transfer contingent upon the enactment of the law of guarantees. They applauded Lanza when he declared that such a proviso was wholly un-called for. They agreed with him that the sequence of events would more than satisfy all scruples on this score.[68] A few slight modifications introduced by the senate were readily approved by the chamber on February 1, and two days later the law was promulgated. Especially galling to the clericals was the provision authorizing the expropriation of buildings belonging to religious corporations.[69] There was little they could do, however, except reiterate their prophecies of woe. The *Civiltà cattolica* did not hesitate to warn the government against the disastrous consequences of its policy. It even ad-duced the argument that the overwhelming majority of Rome's residents were loyal to the pope.[70] But not even the liberals were unanimous in believing the law opportune. Many of them feared that its enactment at this particular juncture might provoke reprisals from certain foreign sup-porters of the Holy See. The country most feared in this con-nection was France.[71] The cabinet itself was not free from misgivings.[72] This pessimism, however, was only one side of the national picture. The enthusiasm of large numbers of Italians at the prospect of seeing Rome become, before long, the capital of their country, was voiced by the *Nazione* of Florence. "We are going to Rome," it declared late in April, "to make a great experiment—so great, in fact, that we be-lieve it has no parallel in history. We are making it with the pope; we are making it with a city which resembles no other

---

[68] *Ibid.*, January 25, 1871, p. 170.

[69] *CC*, I (8th ser.; February 23, 1871), 621-23. Cf., on the actual work of trans-ferring the capital, Giuseppe Gadda, *Relazione del r. commissario governativo sui lavori del trasferimento* (Roma, 1872).

[70] *CC*, II (8th ser.; May 6, 1871), 391.   [71] Vigo, *op. cit.*, I, 38.

[72] Cf. Rothan to Favre, February 24, March 22, 1871, AMAE (Italie, janvier-février, mars-avril, 1871), Tome 380, fols. 277-79, Tome 381, fols. 208-9; Gustave Rothan, *Souvenirs diplomatiques: l'Allemagne et l'Italie* (Paris, 1884-85), II, 349-50.

in Italy; we are making it with the Catholic world, with the whole world."[73]

While the Italian cabinet busily speculated on the dangers ahead, the Vatican was not idle. It replied to the enactment of the transfer law with a concerted attempt to keep the diplomatic representatives accredited to Victor Emmanuel away from Rome. It was clear even to the most intransigent papalists that the coming of the king to the new capital was inevitable. But the powers, they hopefully reasoned, could scarcely permit their ministers to accompany him and thus bestow a tacit sanction upon the sacrilege perpetrated by the House of Savoy. The attitude of the two leading Catholic states, France and Austria, was of course of paramount importance. It was therefore to them that the pope made his initial overtures.[74] It was unlikely, he remarked in the course of a conversation with Lefebvre de Béhaine on February 16, that the new regime in Rome would be overthrown by force. It was consequently necessary to ascertain how it would be possible "to reserve the future" and to safeguard the principle of papal independence against impairment or destruction as a result of the transfer of the capital. This transfer, serious in itself, would be even more deplorable if the foreign representatives accredited to the king should install themselves in Rome. It was to be hoped that the powers would be in no hurry to make new concessions to Italy in this delicate matter.[75] Two days later Pius spoke in a similar vein to the Austrian ambassador. He appreciated, he said, the impossibility of armed intervention in his behalf, but he hoped that the governments would not authorize their ministers to follow Victor Emmanuel to Rome.[76] The pontiff returned to the charge in a subsequent conversation with

[73] Cf., in this connection, CC, II (8th ser.; May 6, 1871), 386–87.

[74] Jules Favre, Rome et la République française (Paris, 1871), pp. 124–25.

[75] Lefebvre de Béhaine to Chaudordy, February 18, 1871, AMAE (Rome, janvier-février, 1871), Tome 1049, fols. 240–41.

[76] Lefebvre de Béhaine to Favre, February 25, 1871, ibid., fols. 271–72.

Trauttmansdorff. He reiterated his belief that armed assistance was not to be expected. But there were other ways, he observed, of serving the papal cause. And above all it was the hope of the Holy See that the powers would refrain from transferring their Florentine legations to Rome.[77] The Vatican, which attached the greatest importance to an explicit Austro-French pledge to keep the legations in Florence even after the formal establishment of the capital in Rome,[78] backed up these *démarches* with others. It requested the French government to point out to Florence the complications which would attend the transfer.[79] The nuncio at Versailles exhorted Favre to intervene unofficially and invite the Lanza cabinet to abandon the idea of moving the capital to Rome.[80]

The Vatican's overtures were carefully studied in Vienna and Paris. Beust could hardly fail to be impressed by Trauttmansdorff's suggestion that some sort of Italo-papal deal might be possible if Italy were to renounce altogether her plan of making Rome the capital.[81] But information received from Florence indicated that Lanza and his colleagues were in no mood to yield on this issue. Kübeck reported Visconti-Venosta as saying that the choice of the capital was no longer subject to revision, that Italy could not retrace her steps, and that "any transaction on this terrain has become impossible."[82] Favre in the meantime thought hard to find a way out. The difficulty was to determine just how much of a

---

[77] Trauttmansdorff to Beust, February 24, 1871, HHSA, Politisches Archiv (Rom), Fasz. XI/226, Nos. 12A and 12B, fols. 95*a*, 97*b*–98*b*.

[78] Cf. Trauttmansdorff to Beust, March 10, 1871, *ibid.*, No. 15A, fols. 127*b*–128*b*.

[79] Lefebvre de Béhaine to Favre, March 17, 1871, AMAE (Rome, mars–avril, 1871), Tome 1050, fol. 126.

[80] Favre to De la Villestreux, April 2, 1871, *ibid.* (Italie, mars–avril, 1871), Tome 381, fols. 271–72.

[81] Trauttmansdorff to Beust, April 24, 1871, HHSA, Politisches Archiv (Rom), Fasz. XI/226, No. 26, fols. 410*b*–411*b*.

[82] Kübeck to Beust, April 14, 1871, *ibid.* (Berichte aus Florenz), Fasz. XI/78, No. 28A–C, fols. 596*a*–596*b*.

concession, if any, Italy would be willing to make. She might conceivably agree to renounce *Roma capitale* in return for international recognition of the city as an integral part of the kingdom. Acting on this assumption, he instructed Rothan to press for such a renunciation. The latter accordingly suggested to Visconti-Venosta that Florence be allowed to remain the seat of the government.[83] But this overture brought little satisfaction. Rothan reported to his chief that the Italian cabinet considered it exceedingly difficult to ignore the transfer law voted by parliament. Moreover, it contended that such disregard of the popular will would not improve the pope's position. He would find himself confronted not by a strong government animated by the best of intentions but by a prefect and by municipal authorities incapable of repressing the excesses of a disgruntled populace.[84] Favre, however, persisted in advising the retention of Florence as the seat of the government. Italy, he urged, would thereby be showing a commendable *justesse d'esprit*. It was an attractive prospect that he dangled before the Lanza cabinet. He wrote:

> Rome, placed under the Italians, subject to the royal power, an integral part of the Italian nation, but continuing to be . . . . sovereign in the domain of faith, would lose none of her prestige and would double that of Italy, and the reconciliation would come of its own accord, because the pope would learn to feel that he was in his own home. . . . .

Such an arrangement would represent "a victory for common sense and reason."[85] Favre wrote directly to Visconti-Venosta in a similar vein. He urged the wisdom of making Rome the honorary capital. "Governed simultaneously by a municipal administration and an Italian prefect," he observed, "the Eternal City would differ from the other cities of the peninsula only by virtue of its grandiose originality." Rome, Italy, and the Holy See would be the principal beneficiaries. But such a solution would also prove a great boon to all

---

[83] Rothan to Favre, April 13, 1871, AMAE (Italie, mars–avril, 1871), Tome 381, fol. 411.

[84] *Ibid.*, fols. 414–15.   [85] Rothan, *op. cit.*, II, 392–93.

Europe by removing from its conscience the weight of this perplexing problem. However, if such a compromise were impossible, the transfer of the capital could be delayed at least until November. Such a lapse of time, he felt, would do much to iron out many of the concomitant difficulties.[86] Favre's overtures came to nought. Visconti-Venosta made it clear to Rothan that concessions in this matter were out of the question.[87] Favre again broached the subject of postponement through Rothan's successor, Choiseul, toward the close of April.[88] But Visconti-Venosta's reply was the same. Acting on information from Nigra which indicated that the French government would not insist on the acceptance of its proposal,[89] he told Choiseul that there was nothing to gain by a delay. Rather, the agitation and widespread passions which it might provoke would constitute a danger for the pope, who would be regarded as an obstacle to the achievement of the national aspiration. On the other hand, the Italian government, once established in Rome, would be completely the master of the situation. And care would be taken to eschew irritating and inopportune gestures.[90] Favre's suggestion, he reiterated on another occasion, was impracticable and, from the Italian government's point of view, highly inexpedient. He reiterated in all finality that the transfer could not be delayed. Choiseul was informed that the various ministries would be moved to Rome in July.[91] And in order to forestall further overtures of this kind, Visconti-Venosta offi-

---

[86] Favre, *op. cit.*, pp. 125–27; Maurice Reclus, *Jules Favre* (Paris, 1912), pp. 496–97.

[87] Rothan, *op. cit.*, II, 395–98.

[88] Favre to Choiseul, April 26, 1871, AMAE (Italie, mars–avril, 1871), Tome 381, fol. 443.

[89] Zaluski to Beust, April 30, 1871, HHSA, Politisches Archiv (Berichte aus Florenz), Fasz. XI/78, No. 32B, fols. 700b–701a. The Austrian chargé d'affaires in Florence alluded to the French *démarche* as "much attenuated by explanations given to Nigra" (*ibid.*, No. 40, fol. 687a).

[90] *Ibid.*, No. 32B, fols. 701a–701b.

[91] Choiseul to Favre, May 6, 1871, AMAE (Italie, mai–août, 1871), Tome 382, fol. 44; Vigo, *op. cit.*, I, 52.

cially notified the powers on June 8 that the seat of the government would be installed in the new capital on the day fixed by the transfer law.[92] The Italian cabinet was hopeful that the entire diplomatic corps accredited to Victor Emmanuel would be in Rome on the occasion of his entry into the city, scheduled for July 2.[93] But the matter was far from simple, and this the government at Versailles well knew. It was Favre's opinion that the French minister could scarcely stay away. The choice, in a sense, lay between going to Rome and precipitating a rupture of Franco-Italian diplomatic relations. But there was the pope to consider. While strongly averse to a break with Italy, Favre was anxious to spare the Holy Father further humiliation. He therefore had to seek a middle course which would enable France to retain the good will of Italy without jeopardizing the friendly relations with the Vatican.[94] It was clear, in any case, that, after having urged the Italian government to retard the transfer of the capital, France could hardly be the first to go to Rome. "Our duty," Favre had already pointed out to Choiseul, "is to show in this matter the greatest reserve and to wait, before considering our departure [from Florence], until the transfer is a *fait accompli*."[95] The first concern of the French foreign office was to ascertain the intentions of Vienna.[96] Almost as urgent was the necessity of finding out whether the offices and bureaus of the Italian

---

[92] Choiseul to Favre, June 8, 1871, AMAE (Italie, mai–août, 1871), Tome 382, fol. 113; Favre, *op. cit.*, pp. 127–28; Luigi Chiala, *Dal 1858 al 1892; pagine di storia contemporanea* (Torino, 1892–93), I, 111.

[93] Augusto Sandonà, *L'Irredentismo nelle lotte politiche e nelle contese diplomatiche italo-austriache* (Bologna, 1932), I, 93.

[94] Favre, *op. cit.*, pp. 128–29.

[95] Favre to Choiseul, May 16, 1871, AMAE (Italie, mai–août, 1871), Tome 382, fol. 58.

[96] *Documents diplomatiques français, 1871–1914* (1st ser.; Paris, 1929), I, No. 6, 16 (hereafter cited as *DDF*). Favre had already broached to Beust the idea of an Austro-French entente in the Roman question (cf. Beust to Trauttmansdorff and Kübeck, March 24, 1871, HHSA, Politisches Archiv [Weisungen an Rom], Fasz. XI/228, fols. 32*a*–32*b*).

cabinet were actually being moved to Rome. If they were not being so moved, and if only a sort of simulacrum was being staged in order to consecrate the seizure of the city, there would be no obligation to follow Lanza and his colleagues on the day announced by the Italian government.[97] Favre's position met with the entire approval of Adolphe Thiers, the chief of the executive power. The latter agreed that France could not act alone and that the collective action of Europe would have to be governed by the extent to which the Italian foreign ministry was actually being transplanted.[98] Information received from Rome indicated that no complete transfer of Visconti-Venosta's department was in contemplation,[99] and Favre lost little time in underscoring this fact. But he was equally emphatic in insisting that the paramount consideration was the necessity of acting in concert with the Catholic powers, especially Austria. He was careful to have Antonelli informed that the French government's resolution to proceed in this fashion "will be in no way hostile to the Holy Father." It was, he wrote, "the ineluctable consequence of our diplomatic position vis-à-vis Italy. . . . . We will follow the Italian government when it goes to Rome in order to continue our relations with it."[100]

Beust was no less eager than Favre to see the French and Austrian ministers in Florence adopt a similar course of action. He proffered the assurance that, should Visconti-Venosta go to Rome unaccompanied by the various bureaus of his ministry, Kübeck would not follow him and the Austrian legation would remain in Florence.[101] The chancellor,

[97] Favre to Choiseul, June 9, 1871, AMAE (Italie, mai–août, 1871), Tome 382, fol. 115.

[98] Favre to Choiseul, June 10, 1871, ibid., fol. 119.

[99] Harcourt to Favre, June 9, 1871, ibid. (Rome, mai–juin, 1871), Tome 1051, fol. 151.

[100] Favre to Harcourt, June 12, 1871, ibid., fol. 152.

[101] Banneville to Favre, June 13, 1871, ibid. (Autriche, janvier–juin, 1871), Tome 504, fol. 275.

however, had already instructed Kübeck to proceed to Rome
a few days after Visconti-Venosta's arrival, pay the latter an
official visit in his new quarters, and present the Austrian
chargé d'affaires, who was to direct the legation during the
absence on leave of its titular head.[102] News of Beust's action
came as an unpleasant surprise to the Vatican, for reports
from Florence had created the impression that all the heads
of legations were about to depart on leaves of absence and
that none of them intended to be in Rome before the autumn.[103] Moreover, the papal government had been hopeful
that the cabinet of Vienna would not show Italy any excessive consideration in this matter.[104] The attitude of France
was now anxiously pondered, and it was with an eye to the
reaction of Favre and his associates that Antonelli proceeded
to issue a sharp warning. If the powers should permit their
ministers to come to Rome, the cardinal declared, they would
be consecrating the spoliation and accepting "a sort of complicity in the events that have taken place."[105] Favre found
Antonelli's position natural enough. But France, he demurred,
did not feel that the occupation of Rome obliged her to sever
relations with the Italian government. She was not disposed
to break with that government because it was doing something which was only a "strict consequence" of the occupation itself. She was in no sense an accomplice in this transaction. She was merely emulating the rest of Europe which
was following the Italian foreign minister to the new capital.
She had never desired to be the first to come to Rome, and
now the Austrian government had not hesitated to accept
that responsibility. The French minister at Florence had

[102] Beust to Kübeck, June 10, 1871 (copy), *ibid.* (Italie, mai–août, 1871), Tome
382, fol. 124.

[103] Kálnoky to Beust, June 16, 1871, HHSA, Politisches Archiv (Rom), Fasz.
XI/227, No. 39B, fols. 45b–46a.

[104] *Ibid.*, fol. 44a.

[105] Harcourt to Favre, June 14, 1871, AMAE (Rome, mai–juin, 1871), Tome
1051, fols. 155–56.

been instructed to act in accord with the other Catholic powers. The Holy Father could ask no more.[106] Antonelli received official notification of Beust's instructions to Kübeck with patent bitterness. He remarked to Count Kálnoky, who was directing the Austrian embassy in Rome during the absence of Trauttmansdorff:

> I find it impossible not to attach the greatest importance to this decision [of the Austrian government], and I cannot share the viewpoint of Count Beust, who would like to persuade himself that the fact of Baron Kübeck's official presence in Rome . . . . could in no way alter our situation. If it is a fact of no consequence, why does the Italian government attach so much importance to it? The semi-official newspapers interpret this step as a recognition and an approval of the transfer of the capital and consequently of the actions of the Italian government which have brought about the present state of affairs—and they are perfectly right. For the official presence in Rome of foreign representatives will have that significance for the entire world, and the Italian government will not fail to exploit it in that sense. I am unaware of the motives which induced your government to take the initiative in this question. . . . . The chancellor says that this action is indispensable to the maintenance of the good relations established between Austria and Italy, but what sort of relations can they be if they require such favors on the part of Austria . . . . ?

In conclusion, the cardinal said very despairingly:

> I greatly fear the extremely painful impression which this communication will make upon the Holy Father. . . . . I do not know what decision he will come to. To recognize officially the present state of affairs at Rome is to push us to the last extremity. We had decided to endure whatever we could, but I fail to see how the position of the Holy See can continue hereafter to be tenable at Rome. . . . . If the Holy Father should decide to leave Rome, Italy would not be solely responsible. You, as well as the other powers that recognized, by the official presence of their representatives, the acts of the Italian government, would be largely responsible.[107]

What angered the Vatican most of all, according to Kálnoky, was the circumstance that a Catholic power—Austria—had been the first to signify its desire to follow the Italian government to Rome. The papal authorities claimed to know that all the other legations in Florence had no precise instructions

---

[106] Favre to Harcourt, June 15, 1871, *ibid.*, fol. 157.

[107] Kálnoky to Beust, June 20, 1871, HHSA, Politisches Archiv (Rom), Fasz. XI/227, No. 40B, fols. 59a-63b.

in this matter and that none of them seemed anxious to move to the new capital before the autumn. Especially galling therefore was Beust's announced intention to transfer the Austrian legation to Rome when the necessary arrangements had been completed. However, all was not hopeless in Austro-papal relations, in the opinion of Kálnoky. The latter suggested that, if Kübeck were to come to Rome merely to pay his respects to Visconti-Venosta and were carefully to avoid doing anything which might be interpreted as a recognition of the state of affairs resulting from the events of September 20, the extremely painful impression created by Beust's action could be attenuated.[108]

The chancellor, nettled by Antonelli's stinging rejoinder, was inclined to believe that Kálnoky had failed to make clear to the Vatican the real nature of the instructions to Kübeck.[109] Scarcely more cheering to Beust was the pontiff's reaction. His Holiness refused to take the latest turn of affairs philosophically. He had hoped, he told Kálnoky, that the powers would abstain as long as possible from sanctioning, by the presence at Rome of their representatives to Victor Emmanuel, the acts committed by the Italian government. Such abstention, he continued, would have been "a great moral prop" for the Holy See. But now, to his great chagrin, he understood that the cabinet of Vienna had decided otherwise.[110] Kálnoky thereupon endeavored to explain Beust's action and to calm the pope's apprehension. The latter seemed willing to accept Beust's own interpretation of the Austrian government's gesture, but only on two conditions: all semblance of acquiescence in the existing state of affairs was to be avoided and the presence of Kübeck was not to coincide with Victor Emmanuel's arrival in Rome.[111] An-

---

[108] *Ibid.*, No. 40C, fols. 65a–67a.

[109] See Kálnoky's reaction to Beust's reproach on this score in *ibid.*, No. 41D, fols. 105a–108b.

[110] Kálnoky to Beust, June 24, 1871, *ibid.*, No. 4117, fols. 88a–90a.

[111] Kálnoky to Beust, June 21, 1871, *ibid.*, No. 5467/22, fols. 84a–84b.

tonelli now professed to take a somewhat calmer view of the
Austrian chancellor's behavior. This change of attitude was
due in part to a letter from the papal nuncio in Vienna re-
capitulating the reassuring declarations which Beust had appended to his much criticized instructions. The cardinal told
Kálnoky with evident satisfaction that the nuncio had mentioned the various precautions to be taken in order to cir-
cumscribe the political importance of Kübeck's stay in
Rome.[112]

The significance of Beust's instructions to Kübeck was not
lost on Favre. He ordered Choiseul to ascertain the plans of
his colleagues in Florence. If the other powers should emulate
Austria, he pointed out, the question would be settled.[113]
Choiseul replied that all the foreign diplomatic representatives in Florence were taking leaves of absence. The French
minister, he urged, could scarcely be the first and, for a time,
the sole representative of a foreign power in Rome. He suggested that he too be permitted to absent himself. He could
offer the very natural pretext of going off for a month to participate in the deliberations of the Versailles assembly.[114]
Favre promptly gave Choiseul the necessary authorization,
specifying that his departure from Florence was to synchro-
nize with that of the Austrian and British ministers. Visconti-
Venosta was to be informed that the French legation would
be moved to Rome at the same time as the others.[115] Favre
intended, however, that Choiseul should, like Kübeck, repair
to Rome to pay a visit to Visconti-Venosta before leaving
Italy.[116] But the strong-willed envoy, acting on his own interpretation of the course he was to pursue—and here he gave

[112] Kálnoky to Beust, June 24, 1871, *ibid.*, No. 41C, fols. 101a–102a.

[113] Favre to Choiseul, June 15, 1871, AMAE (Italie, mai–août, 1871), Tome 382,
fol. 128.

[114] Choiseul to Favre, *ibid.*, fol. 130. Choiseul had been elected a member of the
French national assembly in the contests of February, 1871.

[115] Favre to Choiseul, June 16, 1871, *ibid.*, fol. 131.

[116] Favre to Choiseul, June 21, 1871, *ibid.*, fol. 145.

frce play to his Italophobe sentiments—arranged to return
to France without first putting in an appearance at Rome.
He apprised the Italian foreign office of his plans. He explained that De la Villestreux, the French chargé d'affaires in
Florence, would be presented to Visconti-Venosta before the
latter's departure for Rome and would remain to direct the
work of the legation. According to Choiseul, the Italian foreign minister expressed satisfaction with this arrangement.[117]
Favre was no less gratified to learn that the Vatican seemed
pleased with the instructions imparted to Choiseul.[118] Beust
made no secret of his dissatisfaction. He complained that
France was failing to act in agreement with Austria. Choiseul, he pointed out, was planning to return to France without first presenting himself in Rome.[119] Favre replied that he
had approved Choiseul's plans and expressed the hope that
they would suit Beust. He likewise reiterated his desire for a
Franco-Austrian accord in this matter.[120] The chancellor,
however, insisted that he could not alter the instructions
given to Kübeck.[121] It was now Favre's turn to be disturbed.
He adjured Beust to take account of France's "infinitely delicate position vis-à-vis Italy." When France recalled her garrison from Rome, he observed, the Italian government promised not to profit by the war then in progress to establish itself
in the papal capital. The authorities at Florence would therefore understand why France was in no hurry now to follow
them to Rome.[122]

At this late juncture the French cabinet was shocked to
discover that Choiseul's description of the Italian foreign

---

[117] Choiseul to Favre, June 21, 1871, *ibid.*, fol. 144.

[118] Harcourt to Favre, June 25, 1871, *ibid.* (Rome, mai–juin, 1871), Tome 1051,
fol. 186.

[119] Banneville to Favre, June 21, 1871, *ibid.* (Autriche, janvier–juin, 1871), Tome
504, fols. 417–18.

[120] Favre to Banneville, June 22, 1871, *ibid.*, fol. 419.

[121] Banneville to Favre, June 24, 1871, *ibid.*, fol. 422.

[122] Favre to Banneville, June 25, 1871, *ibid.*, fol. 423.

minister's attitude was grossly misleading. "Nigra just left me," Favre wrote to his headstrong subordinate in Florence on June 27. "He seemed very excited by our determination not to go to Rome. He told me that Visconti-Venosta could not consent to this and that he had been constrained to submit to your decision."[123] Furthermore, Favre pointed out, Thiers was now inclined to attach great importance to the projected arrival of Victor Emmanuel in Rome. Accordingly, the minister of France would have no choice but to go to the new capital. But Choiseul betrayed no readiness to comply with these belated directions. He retorted that Visconti-Venosta, in alluding to the king's forthcoming presence in Rome, had stated that no invitations to follow him were being issued to members of the diplomatic corps in order that they might retain complete freedom of action in this matter. More than that, Visconti-Venosta had, according to Choiseul, expressed satisfaction with the French line of action in conversations with the other foreign diplomatic representatives in Florence.[124] Thiers, however, was not entirely reassured. On June 28 he wrote directly to Choiseul:

> Under no circumstances would I wish to add to the chagrin of the pope by following the Italian government to Rome, nor would I wish to throw Italy into the arms of Prussia. This policy is so natural that it requires no lengthy justification. But I ask myself whether you are quite sure of being in accord with Visconti-Venosta on the course you are going to pursue in the present circumstances. If you do not fear complaints and recriminations on the occasion of your return to Versailles, leave. But try also to learn what Austria will do, for . . . . we must endeavor to act as she does.[125]

Choiseul, who was at no loss for a reply, promptly explained:

> Our situation is excellent vis-à-vis the Italian cabinet. . . . . It is being compromised by an intrigue of which Prussia is the author and M. Nigra the instrument. The idea of having the king of Italy installed in Rome by the minister of France serves Prussia by humiliating us and flatters Italy.

[123] Favre to Choiseul, June 27, 1871, *ibid.* (Italie, mai–août, 1871), Tome 382, fol. 152.

[124] Choiseul to Favre, June 28, 1871, *ibid.*, fol. 155.

[125] Thiers to Choiseul, June 28, 1871, *ibid.*, fol. 156.

The policy which I have pursued for two months and the surrender of my powers[126] render . . . . the presence of the minister of France in Italy impossible at this moment.

Visconti-Venosta, he contended, "understood the reserve imposed upon us" and was "very grateful" to the French government for its decision to transfer its legation to Rome whenever the other powers should do likewise.[127] Choiseul's representations were reinforced by a highly significant dispatch from Rome. The pope, Favre was informed, had explicitly approved the proposed procedure. And the Italian press, though a little mortified by the announcement of the French minister's impending departure, had offered a plausible interpretation: Choiseul's duty to participate in the labors of the French national assembly. Were Choiseul now to come to Rome, the author of the dispatch continued, Italy would not be grateful and the pope would be so deeply offended that he might resort to extreme measures.[128] Thiers was still not entirely convinced. This question, he wrote Choiseul on June 30, "seriously involves our relations with Austria. Very probably I will confirm the decision you have taken, despite its drawbacks vis-à-vis Austria. But do not leave Florence without an order from me, which you will receive today."[129] While the chief executive was pondering the wisdom of alternative courses, his government was being implored by the Vatican to refrain from authorizing Choiseul to go to Rome. If, however, France should feel compelled to send her minister to the new capital, the nuncio at Versailles told Favre, it was the hope of the Holy Father that such action would be preceded or accompanied by declara-

[126] Choiseul had already presented Villestreux to the Italian government as interim director of the French legation in Florence.

[127] Choiseul to Thiers, June 29, 1871, AMAE (Italie, mai–août, 1871), Tome 382, fols. 159 and 161.

[128] Harcourt to Favre, June 29, 1871, ibid. (Rome, mai–juin, 1871), Tome 1051, fol. 209.

[129] Thiers to Choiseul, June 30, 1871, ibid. (Italie, mai–août, 1871), Tome 382, fol. 163.

tions and reservations disavowing any wish to sanction or approve the usurpations committed at the expense of the papacy.[130] Thiers failed to send further instructions to Choiseul, and the latter accordingly informed his government that he was leaving Florence forthwith.[131] After conferring with Nigra and Metternich, the French government decided to authorize Choiseul's departure.[132] But it reminded the impatient envoy that Villestreux was to be instructed to act in concert with Kübeck and to go to Rome with him to see Visconti-Venosta and the king.[133] In the course of the same day—the thirtieth—as the vanguard of Italian officialdom was making its way to the new capital, Choiseul left for France.[134] At the same time the Austrian government, acting on instructions from Emperor Francis Joseph,[135] apprised Kübeck that he was not to go to Rome before July 5.[136] The latter, in any case, was to arrive in the new capital only after Victor Emmanuel had come and gone.[137] Villestreux agreed with his Austrian and Belgian colleagues that they would make the trip together. But on reflection he thought it wiser to go a day later than Kübeck in order, so he averred, to avoid all ap-

[130] Chigi to Favre, June 30, 1871, *ibid.* (Rome, mai–juin, 1871), Tome 1051, fol. 215.

[131] Choiseul to Favre, June 30, 1871, *ibid.* (Italie, mai–août, 1871), Tome 382, fol. 164.

[132] See Favre to Harcourt, June 30, 1871, *ibid.* (Rome, mai–juin, 1871), Tome 1051, fol. 211.

[133] Favre to Choiseul, June 30, 1871, *ibid.* (Italie, mai–août, 1871), Tome 382, fol. 165.

[134] De la Villestreux to Favre, June 30, 1871, *ibid.*, fol. 166.

[135] On June 29 the Austro-Hungarian ruler commanded Beust to proceed in accord with France and indicated when Kübeck was to go to Rome (cf. Sandonà, *op. cit.*, I, 94).

[136] De la Villestreux to Favre, June 30, 1871, AMAE (Italie, mai-août, 1871), Tome 382, fol. 167.

[137] This explicit order was contained in the final instructions sent to Kübeck at the close of June (cf. HHSA, Politisches Archiv [Rom], Fasz. XI/227, fols. 156a–156b). It was known that Victor Emmanuel intended to spend only a few days in Rome.

pearance of a demonstration against the Italian government.[138] Favre readily agreed to this postponement.

While these negotiations were in progress, the prospect of
a tranquil coresidence of king and pope in Rome had been
further darkened by still another manifestation of papal intransigence. On June 16 the twenty-fifth anniversary of
Pius IX's accession was celebrated, and Victor Emmanuel,
as a dutiful son of the church, sent one of his aides de camp,
General Bertolè-Viale, to the Vatican with felicitations. The
pope alleged indisposition and refused to receive him.[139] He
was well enough, however, to receive many other distinguished personages who had come to pay their homage.[140]
The incident made things no easier for the champions of reconciliation.[141] But their cause, at no time a hope-inspiring
one, seemed irrevocably doomed now that the ancient seat
of the papacy was about to assume a new role in the political
life of the peninsula.

On July 1 the long-awaited transfer was duly effected, and
Rome was proclaimed the capital of Italy. The king, looking "stiff, and gloomy and ugly,"[142] arrived the next day.
He was received by the crown prince, the municipal council, the members of the cabinet, and the presidents of the two
houses of parliament. A great crowd cheered him wildly as
he made his way to the Quirinal, where he received the homage of delegations from all sections of the country.[143] In reply to an address from the representatives of one hundred
municipalities, he said: "Yes, we are in Rome and we will

[138] De la Villestreux to Favre, July 2, 1871, AMAE (Italie, mai-août, 1871),
Tome 382, fol. 168.

[139] Massari, *La Vita ed il regno di Vittorio Emanuele II di Savoia*, II, 533.

[140] It was said at the time that Pius would have received the king's emissary but
that he was prevented from doing so by his entourage (cf. Castagnola, *op. cit.*, p.
124 n.).

[141] Cf. Camillo Manfroni, *Sulla soglia del Vaticano* (Bologna, 1920), I, 67.

[142] Gregorovius, *op. cit.*, p. 404.

[143] Cf., on the enthusiastic reception accorded the king, Pesci, *I primi anni di
Roma capitale*, p. 65.

stay there. I am certain that, if any trouble should arise, all Italy will be ready to defend Rome, because the cause of Rome is the cause of Italy."[144] He was reported to have assured the Roman Giunta: "I have come to Rome with the consent of every nation, France not excepted."[145] In response to greetings from a deputation representing the University of Rome, he complained that Pius had rejected his courteous and respectful overtures.[146]

The Holy See witnessed these proceedings with understandable mortification. A number of cardinals, quick to exploit the explosive possibilities of the situation, had been urging the pope to quit the city, and during the days immediately preceding the king's arrival, the question had been seriously debated at the Vatican. But once again the moderate counsels of Antonelli had prevailed, and this drastic course had been eschewed.[147] Not to be outdone by their liberal adversaries, staunch papalists now hurried to the Vatican to signalize their loyalty to the Holy Father. Gloom pervaded the great halls of the papal residence. The long-dreaded moment had at last arrived, the usurper was taking his place as sovereign of the city that housed the exalted ruler of Catholic consciences. "The Italian revolution," wailed the *Civiltà cattolica*, "has exceeded the expectations of friends and foes and infinitely increased the consternation of the good, the wild joy of the wicked, the stupor of all." The Jesuit organ took some solace, however, in the reflection that the coresidence of the two sovereigns could not be of indefinite duration.[148] The mood of the Vatican was mirrored in its peremptory dismissal of two noted professors of the Col-

---

[144] Vigo, *op. cit.*, I, 71; *CC*, III (8th ser.; July 29, 1871), 364; Manfroni, *op. cit.*, I, 73.

[145] *CC*, III (8th ser.; July 29, 1871), 361.   [146] *Ibid.*, p. 360.

[147] Harcourt to Favre, June 30, 1871, AMAE (Rome, mai–juin, 1871), Tome 1051, fol. 212; Kálnoky to Beust, June 28, 1871, HHSA, Politisches Archiv (Rom), Fasz. XI/227, No. 1734/31, fol. 116a; Kálnoky to Beust, July 1, 1871, *ibid.*, No. 43A, fol. 134a.

[148] *CC*, III (8th ser.; August 5, 1871), 385.

legio romano who had joined in welcoming Victor Emmanuel.[149] It was reported in anticlerical newspapers that the pope had already left Rome or was on the point of doing so.[150] The conspicuous absence of the French, Austrian, and Belgian ministers[151] evoked vitriolic comment in the Sinistra press. Semiofficial organs, however, were careful to shun violent language in alluding to this painful theme. Their forbearance on this occasion exposed them to uncharitable charges. But they could point, in vindication of their attitude, to the eminently satisfactory declaration of one of the culpable governments. On July 3 the Belgian foreign minister declared in the senate:

As regards the removal of the Italian government to Rome, the Belgian government was not called upon to express approval or disapproval of the Italian occupation of that city. All we had to do was to follow the usual diplomatic customs. The minister for foreign affairs gave instructions to the Belgian representative at Florence to follow the king of Italy wherever he might go to establish his capital. Belgium will have two legations in Italy, one accredited to the king, the other to the pope.[152]

The Italian government attached particular significance to the absence of the French minister,[153] and it was against France that the animus of the Sinistra was chiefly directed.[154] The *Riforma* admonished its political adversaries to take note of what had happened and to learn to choose their foreign friends more wisely. Specifically, it advocated an alliance with Germany as an escape from subjection to France.[155] It contrasted the behavior of Germany and France, stressing the former's alacrity in sending her minister to Rome. The government of Berlin had thereby vouchsafed an earnest of friendliness which France had been careful to withhold.[156]

---

[149] *Times*, July 24, 1871.   [150] Manfroni, *op. cit.*, I, 71.

[151] Cf. Bersezio, *op. cit.*, VIII, 404–5; Paladino, *op. cit.*, p. 156.

[152] *Times*, July 4, 1871.

[153] Cf. Michele Rosi, *Vittorio Emanuele II* (Bologna, 1930), II, 193–94.

[154] Chiala, *Pagine*, I, 111–12.

[155] *Riforma*, July 4, 1871.   [156] *Ibid.*, July 10, 1871.

The situation was momentarily eased when the representatives of France, Austria, and Belgium finally presented themselves. Kübeck and his Belgian colleague arrived on July 6. Villestreux came the following day and reported, on his return to Florence: "My mission to Rome was accomplished in as satisfactory a manner as possible. During the three days I was there, I saw Visconti three times; and I am certain that, as regards the Italian government, my visit has obtained the good result which we intended."[157] At the same time, calm and confidence were reappearing at the Vatican. On one occasion, Antonelli remarked to Kálnoky:

> The Italian government and press are attempting . . . . to create the impression that the temporary presence of the foreign representatives at Rome implies a consent to and an approval of the acts committed vis-à-vis the Holy See. I therefore note with much satisfaction the explanations which Count Beust gave verbally to the nuncio . . . . and which indicate that your government wished to make only a formal and inevitable gesture of courtesy toward the Italian cabinet and did not intend thereby to approve or sanction the conduct of Italy. . . . .

Kálnoky, though gratified by these observations, was careful to remind the papal secretary of state that any deviation by Austria from her friendly policy toward Italy was out of the question.[158] But the astute cardinal scarcely required such an admonition. He and his associates were well aware that the most determined champions of the temporal power were to be found not in Austria but in France, where a powerful clerical movement was preparing to cross swords with the government at Versailles in an effort to secure intervention on behalf of the Roman pontiff.

[157] Villestreux to Favre, July 10, 1871, AMAE (Italie, mai–août, 1871), Tome 382, fol. 204.

[158] Kálnoky to Beust, July 14, 1871, HHSA, Politisches Archiv (Rom), Fasz. XI/227, No. 45A, fols. 157a–158b, 159b–160a.

CHAPTER VI

INTERNATIONAL HANDS OFF IN THE ROMAN QUESTION

WHILE the task of steering the law of guarantees through parliament and the preparations for the transfer of the capital were taxing the energies of Italian officialdom, the idea of a conference of the powers to determine the future status of the Holy See was revived. The Italian government, anticipating something of the sort, had taken all possible precautions to strengthen its position. Speed in executing its ecclesiastical program was its principal preoccupation. On February 24, Rothan reported that Visconti-Venosta and Sella were agreed on the necessity of finishing at any cost with the law of guarantees before Europe should turn its attention to the affairs of the peninsula. The king himself, the envoy noted, was reputed to be disturbed by the length of the parliamentary debates.[1] On this occasion the role of instigator fell to Bray. The Bavarian statesman, who came to Versailles late in February for the signing of the peace preliminaries, discussed the Roman question with Bismarck. The latter stated that he intended to come to an understanding with the powers.[2] Thus encouraged, Bray proceeded during the next few weeks to explore the diplomatic terrain. Hoping above all for a commitment from Berlin, he suggested that Prussia seek Austria's collaboration in this matter. Bismarck, however, declined to assume the initiative and wrote in this sense to his ministers in Munich and Vienna. He insisted that it was

[1] Rothan to Favre, February 24, 1871, AMAE (Italie, janvier–février, 1871), Tome 380, fols. 277–79.

[2] Cf. Lefebvre de Béhaine to Favre, March 17, 1871, *ibid.* (Rome, mars–avril, 1871), Tome 1050, fol. 124.

more fitting for Catholic Austria and Bavaria to take the lead, though he expressed a willingness to examine any proposals they might make. Late in March, Bray renewed his overtures. His objective, he explained, was to get Germany, Austria, and eventually France to help the pope regain a more worthy position. Bismarck replied that his government would come to no decision until the attitude of the other German states and of German public opinion had been ascertained. He was reluctant, he said, to discuss in the abstract questions which were not yet ripe for solution.[3] In the meantime, Bray had formally broached the subject of a conference to the other governments. In so doing, he had expressed the hope that they would agree to this proposal in order to assure the success of their efforts without recourse to force.[4]

Beust, egged on by urgent admonitions from Trauttmansdorff,[5] supported Bray in this *démarche*. He believed that a conference of the Catholic powers could most advantageously define the future relations between the Holy Father and the Italian monarchy.[6] The Vatican, which had already voiced its opposition to any deal between the powers and Italy in the Roman question,[7] did not in advance spurn

[3] *GW*, VIc, No. 2, 2–3.

[4] Cf. Lefebvre de Béhaine to Favre, March 17, 1871, AMAE (Rome, mars–avril, 1871), Tome 1050, fols. 124–25.

[5] The latter for some time had been telling his chief that neither the pope nor the powers could assent to a purely Italian, unilateral solution of the Roman question. Any legislative action that might be taken by the Italian parliament, he had been arguing, would be wholly unacceptable. Moreover, the projected law of guarantees was replete with shortcomings. It was very superficial. It disclosed the ignorance of its authors. It contained obvious incongruities. Under the circumstances, the Austrian government would do well to inform the authorities at Florence that an act of the Italian parliament could not, in the light of the Lanza cabinet's earlier pledges, be considered decisive in settling the papal issue (Trauttmansdorff to Beust, December 20 and 24, 1870, HHSA, Politisches Korrespondenz [Rom], Fasz. XI/224, Berichte 128 and 130A, fols. 672b–674a, 693a–693b, 696a–696b).

[6] Cf. Favre to Rothan, April 5, 1871, AMAE (Italie, mars–avril, 1871), Tome 381, fol. 344.

[7] Early in January, 1871, Lefebvre de Béhaine suggested to Antonelli that the powers might agree to designate the "minimum guarantees" to be demanded of the

Bray's suggestion. Antonelli expressed the hope that France, now that the war was over, would not refuse to co-operate with the other powers.[8] Italy was clearly worried by the possibility of an international gathering.[9] She foresaw many difficulties in connection with such a conference, particularly if recognition of the *fait accompli* of September 20 were not accepted as the condition precedent of its convocation. She professed herself ready, however, to welcome a congress of the powers provided such a condition was in advance agreed upon and the program rigidly delimited.[10] Visconti-Venosta did not, therefore, formally accept or reject the Bavarian proposal. Before Italy could commit herself, he said, she would have to obtain from the Catholic governments reassuring declarations regarding the occupation of Rome. But he made no secret of the cabinet's reluctance to appear before the bar of Europe to vindicate the papal guarantees. And it seemed, he observed, that due account was not being taken of the feeling which a conference would stir up and of the hopes it would awaken at the Vatican and throughout

---

Italian government. The cardinal replied that the Holy See could exact nothing less than the complete restoration of its rights. Nor could it desire to have the powers "solicit concessions for which they would have to pay by recognizing, more or less formally, a state of affairs against which it has protested and will continue to protest" (Lefebvre de Béhaine to Chaudordy, January 4, 1871, *ibid.* [Rome, janvier-février, 1871], Tome 1049, fols. 17–18). A few weeks later, Antonelli again declared that the Holy See could not allow the Roman question to become the object of negotiation between Italy and the powers. "Never," the cardinal stated on this occasion, "would the Holy See recognize the right of any power to fix, define and limit the spiritual jurisdiction of the supreme chief of the church" (Lefebvre de Béhaine to Chaudordy, January 25, 1871, *ibid.*, fols. 111–12).

[8] Lefebvre de Béhaine to Favre, March 17, 1871, *ibid.* (Rome, mars–avril, 1871), Tome 1050, fols. 125–26.

[9] Rothan to Favre, April 1, 1871, *ibid.* (Italie, mars–avril, 1871), Tome 381, fols. 265–67.

[10] Rothan, who came to Rome after he had relinquished his post at Florence, told Antonelli that the Italian government regarded an international congress as "the anchor of safety" (Trauttmansdorff to Beust, April 24, 1871, HHSA, Politisches Archiv [Rom], Fasz. XI/226, No. 26, fol. 404a). What the Italian government had in mind was a congress commissioned to ratify without further ado the occupation of Rome.

the Catholic world.[11] In a subsequent allusion to this subject, he spoke with less reserve. He declared that international transactions regarding the re-establishment of the temporal power were impossible and that any discussion of the papal guarantees would be premature.[12]

Italy's anxiety proved needless, thanks to the strong line taken by the French government. Favre made short shrift of Bray's suggestion. It was inconceivable that the pope should desire a conference, he wrote Lefebvre de Béhaine on March 26, for a consecration of the *status quo* could scarcely be avoided. If Pius were represented, he would raise the question of the temporal power. The other conferees would balk, and further proceedings would become impossible. Furthermore, discussion of an Italo-papal *modus vivendi* was replete with "inextricable difficulties." Were the conference to content itself with a declaration that the pope's spiritual freedom should be guaranteed, it would be giving only "a purely sentimental assistance." Were it to attempt anything more, it would be coming to grips with the impossible. A conference, Favre concluded, might prove feasible only if its purpose were in advance precisely defined and its means of action clearly delimited. In the absence of such precautions, the French government would refuse to consider the question unless the papacy should desire otherwise.[13]

These observations were not lost on the Vatican. Early in April, Antonelli assured Lefebvre de Béhaine that the Holy See would oppose any conference "implying on its part an abandonment of principles." The pope, he said, refused to have his rights appraised in a conclave of the powers concurrently with those of Italy.[14] The cardinal subsequently reiterated that his master would not allow his relations with

[11] Rothan to Favre, April 7 and 13, 1871, AMAE (Italie, mars–avril, 1871), Tome 381, fols. 361–62, 411, 414.

[12] Zaluski to Beust, April 30, 1871, HHSA, Politisches Archiv (Florenz), Fasz. XI/78, No. 32A, fol. 693a.

[13] AMAE (Rome, mars–avril, 1871), Tome 1050, fol. 164.

[14] Lefebvre de Béhaine to Favre, April 4 and 5, 1871, *ibid.*, fols. 217, 218–19.

Italy to become "the object of a transaction."[15] Antonelli made his position very clear to Trauttmansdorff too. The Vatican, the latter reported to Beust, feared that a congress in which the powers would treat with Italy regarding the settlement of the Roman question might endanger the principle of nonrecognition (of the occupation of Rome) and admit Italy's right to that city. The Holy See desired international intervention only if it were based on the maintenance of the temporal rights of the pontiff and on "the recognition of that entire independence of the papacy and of the spiritual power which does not admit of guarantees proffered by the secular power." There could be no acceptance of the results of an international conclave "whose aim it would be to sanction the . . . . present state affairs."[16] Finally, the French ambassador at the Vatican was given to understand that the Holy See had never favored the conference proposal because it regarded the moment as unpropitious to raise so crucial a question and because it refused to consecrate the *fait accompli*.[17] Favre's attitude likewise did not fail to impress Beust, who now hastened to modify his position.[18] Bray, however, was not yet ready to admit defeat. In the course of a conversation with the Austrian chancellor, who was passing through Munich on his return from Switzerland, he again urged co-operative action by the powers in behalf of the Holy Father—an action, he added, with which Bismarck keenly desired to associate France. But Beust showed no enthusiasm.[19] And Favre, who watched the Bavarian's maneuvers with deep misgivings, hurried to restate

[15] Lefebvre de Béhaine to Favre, April 21, 1871, *ibid.*, fols. 331–32.

[16] Trauttmansdorff to Beust, April 24, 1871, HHSA, Politisches Archiv (Rom), Fasz. XI/226, No. 26, fols. 404*b*–405*a*, 407*a*–408*a*.

[17] Harcourt to Favre, May 13, 1871, AMAE (Italie, mai–juin, 1871), Tome 1051, fols. 32–33.

[18] Cf. Favre to Rothan, April 5, 1871, *ibid.* (Italie, mars–avril, 1871), Tome 381, fol. 344.

[19] Lefebvre de Béhaine to Favre, April 21, 1871, *ibid.* (Rome, mars–avril, 1871), Tome 1050, fol. 331; Augusto Sandonà, *L'Irredentismo nelle lotte politiche e nelle contese diplomatiche italo-austriache* (Bologna, 1932), I, 98.

his government's position in the most unequivocal terms. Bismarck's anxiety to have France participate in an international action, he observed in a dispatch to Lefebvre de Béhaine on April 27, constituted an additional reason for rejecting the conference idea. The German chancellor, in his opinion, wished "to embroil us at one and the same time with Florence and Rome." Furthermore, France was obliged to refrain from encouraging the papacy in its belief that it would soon recover the temporal power. And an international gathering would only provide an opportunity to air "untimely claims" and "theological quarrels."[20] Bray thereafter held his peace, for Beust, in whom he had reposed his greatest hopes, continued to show no more interest in the conference proposal.[21]

The idea of convoking a conclave of the powers was seemingly dead, much to the relief of the Italian government. But there were other clouds on the peninsula's horizon. The most formidable of these was the perennial danger that certain governments might yet yield to the relentless pressure of their Catholic subjects and intervene on behalf of the "prisoner" of the Vatican. The Lanza cabinet kept its eyes fixed on Austria and France, where papal intrigues seemed most likely to create trouble.[22] But Austrian and French clericals were not the only mischief-makers. The activity of German ultramontanes during the first months of 1871 proved to be a source of constant and acute preoccupation.

The Vatican had been much taken aback by Ledochowski's failure to get King William to protest against the occupation of Rome, but it had not ceased to repose faith in Prussia.[23] Nor had the rebuff at Versailles discouraged the

[20] AMAE (Rome, mars–avril, 1871), Tome 1050, fols. 358–59.

[21] Cf. Harcourt to Favre, May 13, 1871, *ibid.* (Rome, mai–juin, 1871), Tome 1051, fol. 33.

[22] Cf. Italicus, *Italiens Dreibundpolitik, 1870–1896* (München, 1928), p. 17; Michele Rosi, *Vittorio Emanuele II* (Bologna, 1930), II, 199–200.

[23] Cf. Ottocar Lorenz, *Kaiser Wilhelm und die Begründung des Reichs, 1866–1871* (Jena, 1902), pp. 488–89.

German Catholics. On November 28, 1870, the Bavarian ultramontane leader, Jörg, had published in his journal, the *Historisch-politische Blätter*, a manifesto declaring that his coreligionists were awaiting "an energetic disapproval by Prussia of the recent events in Rome."[24] The cabinet of Berlin was at the moment very much concerned about the result of the recent elections to the Prussian diet. The Catholics had substantially increased the number of their seats and had become a much more formidable factor in the domestic political situation. Thile made no secret of his uneasiness. He remarked to Launay that he hoped the Italian government would take account of the Prussian cabinet's "delicate position" and would endeavor to ease it by treating the pope with greater indulgence.[25] The Prussian clericals knew their own strength and were determined to make the most of it. On February 8 a delegation of Silesian Knights of Malta formally requested the German emperor to intervene in the Roman question. William declared that his attitude toward the pope as the spiritual head of his Catholic subjects was unchanged; that he saw in the occupation of Rome "an act of violence." But, he went on, "we must wait and see what Italy will do; we must ascertain how she will guarantee the freedom of the pope. I am ready to join other princes in a *démarche*, but not until the war is over."[26] On February 18, Bishop von Ketteler of Mainz appeared in Versailles with an address signed by fifty-six Catholic members of the Prussian diet. This strongly worded document implored the emperor to come to the rescue of the dispossessed pontiff. "May the

---

[24] *Schulthess, 1870*, p. 221. For additional information on Jörg see Heinrich von Sybel, *Die Begründung des deutschen Reiches durch Wilhelm I* (München and Leipzig, 1899), VII, 362.

[25] *Libro verde*, No. 102, pp. 110–11.

[26] Cf. Ed. Hüsgen, *Ludwig Windthorst: sein Leben, sein Wirken* (Köln, 1911), p. 100; Karl Bachem, *Vorgeschichte Geschichte und Politik der deutschen Zentrumspartei* (Köln, 1927), III, 196; Hubert Bastgen, *Die römische Frage* (Freiburg i.B., 1917), II, 771 and 839; Jean Lulvès, *"Bismarck und die römische Frage,"* Hochland, June, 1929, p. 269; Georges Goyau, *Bismarck et l'église; le culturkampf* (Paris, 1911–13), I, 54–55.

new year of peace," it declared, "bring the necessary restoration of the temporal authority of the Holy See, for which your father, Friedrich Wilhelm III, worked so outstandingly at the congress of Vienna."[27]

In the same month Cardinal Bonnechose of Rouen arrived at the imperial headquarters bent upon succeeding where Ledochowski had failed. He spoke to the emperor, Bismarck, Crown Prince Frederick, and the Grand Duke of Baden. He envisaged nothing less than the complete undoing of Italian unity through the action of a congress of the powers. The pope was to recover his territorial possessions; the Italian kingdom was to comprise only Lombardy and Venetia; Naples and Tuscany were to be restored to their former rulers.[28] He remarked that Germany, in befriending the pope, would do herself an invaluable service. She would gain in power, prestige, and unity. She would benefit from the tranquilization of Catholic consciences which would come with the restoration of the papal state. Moreover, she could have no tenderness for Italy, now that Garibaldi had been permitted to fight against the Prussians.[29] Bismarck somewhat caustically declared that Prussia could hardly do two things at once and that therefore for the present a war against Italy was unthinkable. He also reminded the prelate that it would be too much to expect German Protestants to shed their blood in the service of the Roman Curia. However, he assured Bonnechose that there were other ways of serving the pope's cause and of bringing it to a successful issue and that the German government would make use of them once the

[27] Bastgen, *op. cit.*, III (1), 15 n.; Bachem, *op. cit.*, 135; Ludwig Hahn, *Geschichte des "Kulturkampfes" in Preussen* (Berlin, 1881), pp. 41–42.

[28] Kaiser Friedrich III, *Das Kriegstagebuch von 1870–71* (Berlin and Leipzig, 1926), p. 380; cf. the allusion to Bonnechose's plan in Moritz Busch, *Tagebuchblätter* (Leipzig, 1899), II, 2–3. Mgr. Chigi, the papal nuncio in Paris, had laid a similar scheme before Crown Prince Frederick (cf. Kaiser Friederich III, *op. cit.*, p. 172).

[29] Hermann Oncken, *Grossherzog Friedrich I von Baden und die deutsche Politik von 1854–1871* (Berlin and Leipzig, 1927), II, 378–79.

war was over.[30] The chancellor was apparently toying with the idea of diplomatic intervention. He was indeed furious with the Italians for having allowed Garibaldi to aid the French,[31] and he was as anxious as before to ingratiate himself with his Catholic compatriots.[32] But other considerations prevailed. There was the danger of involving Germany in foreign complications from which she had little to gain and everything to lose. In order to keep France isolated, the friendship of Italy, weak as she was, had to be courted. And already Bismarck began to think of the young kingdom as a weapon with which to strike, if need be, at Austria's flank in the event of war.[33] Moreover, having acceded to Ledochowski's request for a papal asylum in Germany, he had hoped that Pius would intervene more energetically in France in favor of an early peace.[34] Understandably enough, therefore, the pontiff's failure to fulfil this hope had been a keen disappointment to him. It had led him to believe, he himself tells us, that the papacy was either unable or unwilling to aid Prussia.[35] And it was to the second of these hypotheses that he was more inclined to subscribe.[36] To make matters worse, he distrusted the Vatican. He feared that it might exploit the dogma of infallibility to interfere in Germany's domestic affairs and impede the consolidation of the empire. The triumph of the liberal parties in the Reichstag elections of March 3, 1871,[37] furnished added reason to ignore the cleri-

[30] Mgr. Louis Besson, *Vie du cardinal de Bonnechose archevêque de Rouen* (Paris, 1887), II, 144; Lulvès, *op. cit.*, p. 269; Bastgen, *op. cit.*, II, 772; Lorenz, *op. cit.*, p. 518; Goyau, *op. cit.*, I, 55.

[31] Bismarck's irritation over the consistently pro-French attitude of a good many Italians rendered him willing to do more for the pope than might otherwise have been the case (cf. Julius Clausen, *Bismarck und der Katholizismus in den Jahren 1851–1871* [Hamburg, 1934], p. 57).

[32] Goyau, *op. cit.*, I, 56–57.   [33] Lulvès, *op. cit.*, p. 270.

[34] Cf. Clausen, *op. cit.*, pp. 57–58.

[35] Bismarck, *Gedanken und Erinnerungen* (Stuttgart, 1898), p. 470.

[36] Cf. Clausen, *op. cit.*, p. 46.

[37] Cf. Johannes Ziekursch, *Politische Geschichte des neuen deutschen Kaiserreiches* (Frankfurt-am-Main, 1925), II, 217–19.

cals' clamor for intervention.[38] He knew, of course, that adhesion to a noninterventionist course would be none too easy to defend before his ultramontane compatriots. It was therefore imperative that he bolster his own case by helping to remove in advance some of the clericals' grounds for complaint. With this in mind, he proceeded to proffer the Italian government some very judicious advice. He sought to impress upon the Florentine authorities that adoption by them of the *suaviter in modo* would make it easier for the Catholic world to reconcile itself to the new situation in Rome. Severity, he cautioned, would only retard the establishment of tolerable relations with the pope and render more improbable his continued sojourn in the future capital.[39]

The speech from the throne which opened the first German Reichstag on March 21 made Bismarck's position indubitably clear. It proclaimed that the German government intended to mind its own business. The significant passage ran:

> The spirit which lives in the German people, ... the constitution of the empire and its military organization safeguard Germany, in the midst of her successes, against any temptation to abuse the power she has gained through unification. She has for the independence of all other states and peoples . . . . the very same regard which she demands for her own.[40]

This utterance evoked considerable satisfaction in Italy, where it was hailed as pledging Germany to a hands-off policy in the Roman question.[41] There could be no principle more just than that of nonintervention, declared the *Libertà*. And it was certain, it continued, that Germany would give "the best earnest of her intentions."[42] On March 29, Rothan

[38] Robert von Nostitz-Rieneck, "Die römische Frage im Frühjahr 1871," *Stimmen der Zeit*, August, 1917, pp. 559 and 561; Bastgen, *op. cit.*, II, 773.

[39] *GW*, VIc, 6.

[40] *Stenographische Berichte über die Verhandlungen des deutschen Reichstages*, XIX (March 21, 1871), 2 (hereafter cited as *SB*).

[41] Cf. Rothan to Favre, March 24, 1871, AMAE (Italie, mars-avril, 1871), Tome 381, fol. 250; Luigi Chiala, *Dal 1858 al 1892; pagine di storia contemporanea* (Torino, 1892-93), I, 109; Bastgen, *op. cit.*, II, 766.

[42] *Libertà*, March 26, 1871.

wrote to Favre: "The cabinet of Florence has re-entered the good graces of Prussia. The German emperor has sanctioned the reconciliation at the opening of the Reichstag with a few pacifying words addressed indirectly to Italy."[43] The Reichstag voted an address, in reply to the royal pronouncement, which reiterated even more emphatically that there would be no intervention in the domestic concerns of other countries. The deputies of the Catholic Centrist party sought unsuccessfully to secure the adoption of an address of their own in which action on behalf of the pope was portended. The debate, which occurred on March 30, demonstrated the profound divergence of views between them and the Reichstag majority. The chief Catholic spokesmen were Reichensperger, one of the most respected leaders of the Centrist party, Bishop Ketteler, and Ludwig Windthorst, destined for many years to be Bismarck's most formidable parliamentary antagonist. The burden of their remarks was that they did not want war but were not opposed to armed intervention in favor of the Holy See; that the new German empire ought to make itself the protector of religion and morality; and that failure to come to the aid of the prisoner of the Vatican would constitute a gross disregard for the most vital interests of German Catholics.[44]

The outcome of the Reichstag debate was received with loud applause in Italy. Ministerial circles interpreted the majority address as "an act of homage to the principles of modern public law."[45] The Sinistra was no less elated. The Reichstag, declared the *Riforma*, "has fittingly replied to the expectations of the liberals of Europe."[46] The Holy See seemed very little concerned. The adoption of the address, observed the *Osservatore romano*, had only the validity of a

---

[43] Gustave Rothan, *Souvenirs diplomatiques: l'Allemagne et l'Italie* (Paris, 1884–85), II, 365.

[44] *SB*, XIX (March 30, 1871), 49–71; cf. also Bachem, *op. cit.*, II, 193–95; Hüsgen, *op. cit.*, pp. 99–100.

[45] Cf. the *Libertà*, April 8, 1871.   [46] *Riforma*, April 2, 1871.

chamber vote. It placed no obligation whatever upon the government, which remained free to intervene or not, in accordance with the maintenance of those interests "which affect all monarchies and all thrones."[47] But the papal organ's rather nonchalant attitude was not indicative of the Vatican's real reaction. "The reverses suffered by the Catholic party in the parliament of Berlin," Trauttmansdorff reported to Beust, "have made a keen impression here and brought about disillusionment in many circles, for much had been made of the importance and effectiveness of the Catholic movement in Germany." The Vatican had expected, he continued, that the Catholic party would exert a decisive influence upon the attitude and decisions of the German government.[48] That expectation had been resoundingly belied, much to the discomfiture of the now thoroughly discredited Prussophil group in Pius' entourage. Another savior had to be found, and France, as we shall see, had already begun to loom as the most likely candidate for this role.

Though worsted in this initial skirmish, the German Centrists continued to press for intervention. Their spokesmen enlarged upon the "hypocrisy" of the guarantees offered the Holy Father by Italy and voiced their confidence in the ultimate success of his cause.[49] Inasmuch as the papal monarchy, they argued, was the oldest and most legitimate in Europe, every state was under obligation to restore and preserve it.[50] At the general assembly of German Catholics in September, 1871, some strong resolutions were adopted. The occupation of Rome, the law of guarantees, and the alleged indifference

[47] *Osservatore romano*, April 4, 1871.

[48] Trauttmansdorff to Beust, April 15, 1871, HHSA, Politisches Archiv (Rom), Fasz. XI/226, No. 24A, fols. 387*b*–388*a*. A few weeks later, Kálnoky, who directed the Austrian embassy in Rome during Trauttmansdorff's absence, reported that Germany seemed to inspire "only a mediocre confidence" in the pope (Kálnoky to Beust, May 6, 1871, *ibid.*, No. 28A, fol. 430*b*).

[49] Cf. A. Schmitz, "Das Jubiläum des heiligen Vaters am Juni 1871," *Stimmen aus Maria-Laach*, July, 1871, pp. 44–53.

[50] Pachtler, "Das 'Princip' der Nicht-Intervention," *Stimmen aus Maria-Laach*, August, 1871, pp. 107–20.

of the powers to the plight of the pontiff were roundly denounced.[51]

Bismarck himself had taken no part in the Reichstag debate of March 30. He was loath to prejudice further the possibility of establishing a friendly and co-operative relationship between the German government and the Center.[52] He even claimed to know that Antonelli had deplored the action of the Catholic deputies.[53] He also sought to ease his own position vis-à-vis the German Catholics by renewing his friendly admonitions to the Italian government. He wrote on May 1 to Brassier de St. Simon: "The sympathies of the Catholic world for the pope have been greatly increased by commiseration with his personal sufferings and distress and by anxiety about his freedom and dignity." This was especially true, he continued, of the faithful in Germany. The emperor could scarcely disregard the attitude of so important a section of the nation. Italy had to remember that in this question she had to deal not only with her own parliament and her political parties but with the Catholic church outside her own borders. By treating the pontiff with great consideration, she would enable those powers now friendly to her to continue on the same footing without outraging the

---

[51] Bastgen, *op. cit.*, III (1), 131–32.

[52] Cf. *GW*, VIc, No. 3, 3–4.

[53] Freiherr Lucius von Ballhausen, *Bismarck-Erinnerungen* (Stuttgart and Berlin, 1921), p. 9. The cardinal, in a conversation with the Bavarian envoy, Count Tauffkirchen, had as a matter of fact observed that the Reichstag address of the Centrist deputies was "inopportune" (cf. Harcourt to Favre, June 30, 1871, AMAE [Rome, mai-juin, 1871], Tome 1051, fol. 220). In June the German papers published a letter from Bismarck stating that Antonelli had disapproved of the conduct of the Centrists in the Reichstag. Bishop Ketteler thereupon produced a letter from the cardinal which attempted to explain away the incident. Relying on newspaper reports, Antonelli was quoted as saying, he had supposed that the aim of the Centrist deputies was to provoke an expression of opinion on the question of intervention in Italy. He had, he admitted, remarked that their action was premature. But he had stated this confidentially and had in no way intended to make an official declaration (*Staatsarchiv*, XXIV, 351–53; Hüsgen, *op. cit.*, pp. 86–87; Ziekursch, *op. cit.*, II, 233–34). Pius too had expressed regret that a somewhat untimely zeal on the part of the German Centrists should have provoked the recent debates in the Reichstag (cf. Kálnoky to Beust, May 6, 1871, HHSA, Politisches Archiv [Rom], Fasz. XI/226, No. 28A, fol. 432a).

sensibilities of their Catholic subjects.[54] But the feud between the German government and the Centrists became
more intense during the succeeding months. It was the anti-
imperial, particularist attitude of the Centrists, their identi-
fication, as Bavarians, Poles, Alsatians, and Lorrainers, with
the cause of separatism, that deeply alarmed the chancellor.
This situation constituted a serious danger to the recently
achieved imperial unity, and Bismarck, to ward it off, sought
to enlist the aid of the pope, whose power in these and other
matters he did not underestimate.[55] He attempted to curry
favor with the Curia by requesting Antonelli to indicate the
bases upon which the Holy See would agree to negotiate a
settlement of the Roman question.[56] He endeavored, on the
other hand, to intimidate the Vatican by warning it that, if it
did not compel the Centrists to desist from further attacks on
the German government, the latter would disavow all responsibility for the consequences.[57] He summoned Pius to
show that he disapproved of this "aggression against the
state."[58] He assured the pontiff that he sincerely desired
peace with the Catholic church, and explained that he was
fighting the Centrists only because they comprised elements
hostile to the existing political regime in Germany.[59] He instructed Arnim to say that such a peace would be possible
as soon as the clericals should cease to promote separatism.[60]
He authorized the ambassador to offer the Holy Father not

[54] *GW*, VIc, No. 5, 6. In August he returned to this subject in the course of a
conversation with Launay. He remarked that Italy would be well-advised to show
the pope every indulgence (cf. Gaetano Salvemini, "La Politica estera della Destra,
1871–1876," *Rivista d'Italia*, February 15, 1925, p. 186).

[55] On February 13, 1871, the chancellor had remarked: "Nothing can be more
stupid than to consider me an enemy of the Roman see. In my opinion, the pope is
first of all a political figure, and I have an inborn respect for all real powers. . . . . A
man who disposes of the consciences of 200 million people is a great monarch in my
estimation" (cf. Clausen, *op. cit.*, pp. 59–60).

[56] Cf. Kálnoky to Beust, July 1, 1871, HHSA, Politisches Archiv (Rom), Fasz.
XI/227, No. 43B, fols. 138a–138b.

[57] *GW*, VIc, No. 9, 9.   [59] *Ibid.*, No. 18, p. 16.

[58] *Ibid.*, p. 15.   [60] *Ibid.*, p. 16 n.

only an asylum in Germany but friendship and alliance as
well. In return, Pius was to induce the Centrists to abandon
their particularist position and rally loyally to the banner
of imperial unity. But the Vatican rejected these offers.[61]
Bismarck retaliated with a series of anti-Catholic measures
which were designed to inaugurate a fight to the finish against
the coalition of separatist forces within the empire.[62] On
the international side the ensuing Kulturkampf represented
a phase of the chancellor's attempt to isolate France and forestall the creation of an anti-German bloc of powers.[63]

The equally persistent agitation of Austrian clericals impelled Beust to renew his friendly admonitions to Florence.
The alarm and grief evoked throughout the Catholic world
by the occupation of Rome, he wrote Kübeck in March,
1871, could be allayed only by showing greater consideration
for the person of the pontiff and for the interests of religion.
Despite the Italian government's reassuring declarations,
which Vienna had always received with confidence, many
things were happening in Rome which were giving rise to

[61] Cf. *Memoirs and Letters of the Right Hon. Sir Robert Morier* (London, 1911),
II, 251–52; William L. Langer, *European Alliances and Alignments, 1871–1890* (New
York, 1931), p. 36. The Vatican could scarcely have given any other answer, for
Italy would have been the chief beneficiary of an acceptance of Bismarck's proposals.
Sir Robert Morier, the British minister in Munich, to whom Arnim gave an account
of his mission, pointed this out. He noted that the alliance offered the Holy See "was
in its nature one not only not hostile to, but necessarily friendly, to Italy, and there-
fore one which could be offered not only without any breach of faith towards the
Italian Government, but with the most considerate regard for the interests of that
Government. For what were the conditions of the alliance? What was the 'service'
which the Chancellor asked in return for such services as Germany might render to
Rome? It was that the Pope should join Germany in her crusade against Ultramontanism and Jesuitism and therefore *pro tanto* side with Germany against France.
But what Power would gain more than Italy from a domesticated Pope, won back
from the errors of Ultramontanism to a purified Catholicism, and lending the prestige of his spiritual supremacy to modern and liberal ideas?" (*Memoirs and Letters
. . . . Morier*, II, 256–57).

[62] Hans Herzfeld, *Deutschland und das geschlagene Frankreich, 1871–1873* (Berlin, 1924), p. 195; Franz Xaver Schmitt, *Bismarcks Abkehr vom Kulturkampf* (Neu-
Ulm, 1931), p. 2.

[63] Langer, *op. cit.*, p. 37; Schmitt, *op. cit.*, p. 3; Adalbert Wahl, *Deutsche Geschichte
von der Reichsgründung bis zum Ausbruch des Weltkriegs* (Stuttgart, 1926), I, 145.

just complaints. As a result, the uneasiness and dissatisfaction of Catholics were increasing, and the governments involved could scarcely avoid taking account of the sentiment of so important a section of their populations. The friendship which united Austria and Italy obliged the cabinet of Vienna once again to call attention to this matter and to the grave inconveniences which would ensue for all governments if the new situation at Rome should lapse into ever sharper conflict with the interests of Catholics.[64] The contents of this dispatch evoked repeated expressions of gratitude from Antonelli,[65] much to Beust's relief. The latter, prepared to go no farther, instructed Kálnoky to remind the Vatican that Austria's position in the Roman question had undergone no change.

> We have not deviated from the views which guided us then [shortly before the occupation of Rome], and we intend to adhere to them now. We do not wish to enter into an examination of accomplished facts. . . . . The relations of sincere friendship which we maintain and desire to continue to maintain with the Italian government, as well as the higher political interests with which we must concern ourselves, compel us to abstain from hindering the execution of measures which the Italian government declares to be the indispensable conditions of its existence.[66]

It was therefore with growing anxiety that Beust noted the maneuvers of the Austrian Catholic party. In May, twenty-eight archbishops addressed a petition to Francis Joseph imploring him to express, through his foreign minister, his disapproval of Italy's entire Roman policy. They reminded their monarch that the temporal power was indispensable to the pope's spiritual freedom.[67] The document elicited from the chancellor the terse reply that Austria had no intention of altering the course she had hitherto pursued in this question.

[64] Beust to Kübeck, March 10, 1871 (annex to Beust's dispatch of same date to Trauttmansdorff), HHSA, Politisches Archiv (Weisungen an Rom), Fasz. XI/228, fols. 23a–24b.

[65] Cf. ibid. (Rom), Fasz. XI/226, No. 22A, fols. 364a–364b.

[66] Beust to Kálnoky, April 24, 1871, ibid. (Weisungen an Rom), Fasz. XI/228, fols. 45a–46b.

[67] Stimmen aus Maria-Laach, July, 1871, p. 89.

The prelates, however, were not without vociferous supporters. Catholics throughout the country hastened to affix their
signatures to an address demanding that the government
make effective provision for the complete liberty and independence of the Holy Father. The *Vaterland*, a leading clerical organ, solemnly asserted that this gesture was intended
to serve as a nation-wide protest against the unspeakable policy of the Protestant chancellor.[68] The hard-pressed statesman endeavored to hold the balance between liberals and
ultramontanes, but there was little he could say to satisfy
the latter. Thus, at the opening meeting of the delegations
in June, he declared that Austria, true to the principle of
nonintervention, would remain Italy's friendly neighbor.[69] In
reply to inquiries from members of the foreign affairs committee of the Hungarian delegation, he advocated the retention of the embassy at the Vatican, but promptly added that,
in doing so, his government would not be undermining the
friendly relations with Italy. The latter, he explained, desired the continuance of foreign embassies at the papal court
in order to demonstrate the groundlessness of the charge that
the Holy Father was a prisoner and bereft of sovereign attributes.[70] He spoke in a similar vein in a much applauded
address on foreign policy before the plenum of the Austrian
delegation.[71] He subsequently explained to the emperor that
he favored a hands-off policy in the Roman question solely
because of Austria's political situation. He denied that his
attitude was in any way due to a lack of understanding of religious problems. Hostility to Italy, he added, would only
result in a restoration of the Italo-Prussian alliance.[72]

The activities of German and Austrian ultramontanes did
indeed evoke profound misgiving throughout the peninsula.

[68] *CC*, II (8th ser.; May 6, 1871), 637-38.

[69] Ludwig Ritter von Przibram, *Erinnerungen eines alten Oesterreichers* (Stuttgart and Leipzig, 1910), I, 298; Friedrich Ferdinand Graf von Beust, *Aus drei viertel-
jahrhunderten* (Stuttgart, 1887), II, 471.

[70] *Schulthess, 1871*, p. 279.   [71] *Ibid.*, p. 284.   [72] Beust, *op. cit.*, II, 487.

But France continued to be the principal source of concern. Many Italians, particularly of the Destra persuasion, would have welcomed a renewal of the old friendship with that country. As a matter of fact, immediately after the occupation of Rome, Italian public opinion had become much more favorable to France.[73] The resentment against Napoleon III's Roman policy had been somewhat assuaged by the advent of a republican regime. But, try as they might, the exponents of such a *rapprochement* could not overlook the disconcerting fact that the cause of the temporal power continued to have many influential friends in France. The clerical party, despite the disappearance of its Bonapartist puppet, was still a very formidable force. It was feared that France, under its influence, might reverse the neutral policy inaugurated by the Government of National Defense.[74] Italy, it was felt in some quarters, would never be forgiven for violating the September convention, exploiting France's military reverses to seize Rome, and refusing to come to her aid against Prussia.[75] The Sinistra fretted over the likelihood of a speedy termination of the Franco-Prussian War. It pointed an ominous finger at the French clericals who had not been converted to a saner view by their country's disasters and who, perhaps in six months, would be reminding their rulers of the occupation of Rome and of the treaty which bound Italy vis-à-vis France.[76]

Current political developments in France afforded little comfort to Italian observers. The elections of February 8, 1871, to the national assembly were fought on the issue of war or peace. The anticlerical republicans favored war à

[73] C. Nigra, "Ricordi diplomatici, 1870," *Nuova antologia*, March 1, 1895, p. 24. On January 14, 1871, the French minister in Florence called the attention of his government to this *volte-face* (cf. AMAE [Italie, janvier–février, 1871], Tome 380, fol. 60).

[74] Rothan, *op. cit.*, II, 160–61.

[75] Cf. the *Gazzetta d'Italia*, February 9, 1871.

[76] Cf. Lefebvre de Béhaine to Chaudordy, February 8, 1871, AMAE (Rome, janvier–février, 1871), Tome 1049, fol. 188.

outrance, while the propapal conservative-monarchist candidates campaigned for an early cessation of the hopeless struggle with Prussia.[77] The rightists won a signal victory. Four hundred seats went to the legitimists and the Orleanists and thirty to the Bonapartists. The republicans emerged with only two hundred.[78] This conservative majority, however it might differ on other questions, was agreed on the necessity of protecting the pope.[79] The Vatican exulted,[80] while Italy, naturally enough, found much cause for gloom.[81] Fear of an eventual French intervention in the Roman question was appreciably augmented.[82] The *Riforma*, speaking on behalf of its leftists friends, sounded a very unoptimistic note. It recalled France's long-standing role as the guardian of the Holy See. It adjured the government to reckon always with one grim possibility: the restoration in France of a monarchy traditionally hostile to Italian unity and independence.[83] The language of the greatly heartened legitimists was particularly alarming. These champions of a Bourbon restoration went so far as to accuse Italy of planning to regain Nice and Savoy.[84]

The selection of Thiers on February 17 as provisional chief of the executive power, far from allaying Italian uneasiness, served only to intensify it. The veteran statesman and historian had always opposed the unification of Italy. Moreover, he was known as a defender of the temporal power.

[77] Gabriel Hanotaux, *Histoire de la France contemporaine* (Paris, 1903–8), I, 30–31.

[78] *Ibid.*, p. 39; Paul Deschanel, *Gambetta* (London, 1920), pp. 137–38; R. P. Lecanuet, *Les dernières années du pontificat de Pie IX, 1870–1878* (Paris, 1931), p. 93; Herzfeld, *op. cit.*, p. 7.

[79] Cf. Chiala, *Pagine*, I, 96.

[80] Cf. the *Osservatore romano*, February 9, 1871.

[81] Cf. Rothan, *op. cit.*, II, 269–70, 291–92.

[82] Cf. Rothan to Favre, February 27, 1871, AMAE (Italie, janvier–février, 1871), Tome 380, fol. 286.

[83] *Riforma*, February 16 and 17, 1871.

[84] Cf. the *Union*, February 20, 1871.

This reputation, which partly explained his popularity with the conservative deputies,[85] gave rise to anxious speculation throughout the peninsula.[86] The *Riforma* insisted that the dictates of prudence constrained Italians always to remember what Thiers thought of them and of their accomplishments. They would do well to repeat to themselves the Cromwellian admonition: "Pray to God and keep your powder dry." Certain people were saying, the journal continued, that the new chief executive had altered his views on Italian unity. But it was difficult, it argued, to believe that a man seventy-four years of age could divest himself of ancient prejudices.[87] The *Diritto*, in equally censorious tones, flayed those Italians who failed to realize that Thiers was their country's greatest enemy.[88] Even the *Libertà*, which had made bold to ridicule the Italian clericals' hope of French intervention,[89] alluded to his accession as one of the clouds on the national horizon.[90] A few days of reflection brought an improvement in perspective in ministerial circles and a tendency, exemplified in the columns of the *Libertà* and the *Nuova antologia*, to deride the idea that France or any other European power would be willing to come to blows with Italy merely because she had occupied Rome and was establishing her capital there.[91] But a deep undercurrent of alarm persisted. Even the Francophil Visconti-Venosta showed himself very reserved, after the election of Thiers, on the subject of the future relations between the two countries.[92]

Italian clericals made no effort to conceal their elation. The *Unità cattolica* recalled with satisfaction Thiers's views

[85] A. Debidour, *L'Eglise catholique et l'état sous la Troisième République* (Paris, 1906), I, 29. On the reaction of the French ultramontanes to the election of Thiers see the *Univers*, February 20, 1871.

[86] Rothan, *op. cit.*, II, 271–73; Pietro Vigo, *Storia degli ultimi trent'anni del secolo XIX* (Milano, 1908), I, 16.

[87] *Riforma*, February 20 and 22, 1871.   [89] *Libertà*, February 8, 1871.

[88] *Diritto*, February 21, 1871.   [90] *Ibid.*, February 28, 1871.

[91] *Ibid.*, March 4, 1871; *Nuova antologia*, March, 1871, p. 746.

[92] Chiala, *Pagine*, I, 96.

on the temporal power. Should Italy, it predicted, present to him her law of guarantees, she would receive the following answer: "There is no independence for the papacy other than sovereignty itself." A part of his work, the Turinese sheet continued, would consist of settling with those powers that had concluded pacts with France and had then taken advantage of her misfortunes to violate them. And the Italian government would be the first to be called to account.[93] The *Osservatore romano* took delight in noting that Italians were now beginning to be fearful lest France, once restored to peace and stable government, should refuse to tolerate any longer the scrapping of the September convention. Indeed, the papal organ went on, Thiers's repute as a champion of the temporal power was causing so much apprehension throughout the peninsula that even the retention of Favre at the French foreign office did not suffice to dissipate it. The world well knew that "cowardly transactions" were not to be expected of men of Thiers's fiber.[94] The *Osservatore romano*'s jubilation was shared in the highest quarters. Pius himself, according to Antonelli, received word of Thiers's election with "real pleasure."[95]

The signing of peace preliminaries between France and Germany at the close of February—an event to which the Vatican had hopefully looked forward[96]—provided further grist for the mill of Italian alarmists and scaremongers. Much was made of the fact that French papalists would now be free

[93] *Unità cattolica*, February 21 and 24, 1871.

[94] *Osservatore romano*, February 21, 1871.

[95] Antonelli to Lefebvre de Béhaine, February 20, 1871, AMAE (Rome, janvier-février, 1871), Tome 1049, fol. 257.

[96] The Holy See believed that a speedy peace between France and Germany would make possible some kind of propapal diplomatic action. Antonelli seemed certain that the Roman question would be touched upon in the *pourparlers* between the negotiators. He felt that the Catholic movement in Prussia might force the German government to show some consideration for the Holy Father. He figured that Bismarck might wish to impel France to place herself in the van, so that she might be the first to espouse the papal cause (cf. Trauttmansdorff to Beust, February 24, 1871, HHSA, Politisches Archiv [Rom], Fasz. XI/226, No. 12B, fols. 98*b*–100*a*).

to direct their attention and energies elsewhere. A cry went up for military reforms and increased army appropriations to meet the eventual danger of a French attack on Rome.[97] There arose, too, a clamor for an alliance with Germany.[98] The *Diritto* remarked that everyone was now convinced of the identity of interests which united Italy and the powerful Hohenzollern empire.[99] Moderates as well as radicals began to see in Germany a bulwark of defense against the Third Republic. There was even a desire for a *rapprochement* with Austria. All possible alliances were envisaged, except one with France.[100] Bonghi expressed the general feeling in ministerial circles when he declared that Italy would abandon Rome only if compelled to do so by force. Her position, he conceded, had been rendered less favorable by the termination of the Franco-Prussian War. She could now expect to have "more or less obstinate enemies" who would encourage the pretensions of the Holy See. It was therefore incumbent upon her to take the necessary precautions.[101] A similar note was sounded by the *Libertà*, which now rejoined the alarmist camp. Italy, it asserted, entertained no unfriendly feeling toward France. But if the latter should persist in her hostile designs, the sentiment of Italians would change and they would resist "the odious aggression."[102]

True it was that Antonelli, unlike his Prussophil colleagues, was now beginning to repose his hopes for the future in France,[103] but the Versailles government had no intention

[97] Chiala, *Pagine*, I, 103.

[98] As Herzfeld points out (*op. cit.*, p. 194), the composition of the French national assembly was in itself enough to cause Italy to gravitate toward Germany.

[99] *Diritto*, March 8, 1871.

[100] Rothan to Favre, March 11, 1871, AMAE (Italie, mars-avril, 1871), Tome 380, fols. 136–37; Rothan, *op. cit.*, II, 253, 309–10, 317–19; Chiala, *Pagine*, I, 102.

[101] *Nuova antologia*, March, 1871, p. 747.   [102] *Libertà*, March 31, 1871.

[103] Cf. Trauttmansdorff to Beust, March 10, 1871, HHSA, Politisches Archiv (Rom), Fasz. XI/226, No. 15A, fols. 126*b*–127*a*. In the course of a recent conversation with Thiers, the papal nuncio, Mgr. Chigi, had underlined the importance to France of coming to the pope's rescue (cf. Trauttmansdorff to Beust, February 24, 1871, *ibid.*, No. 12B, fol. 100*b*).

of emulating Napoleon III. Though Thiers had not modified his views on the necessity of the temporal power and the fateful consequences to France of Italian unification,[104] he was too much of a realist to wish another descent on Rome. He honored in the person of Pius IX the supreme chief of the Catholic church, but he was mindful too of the claims of Victor Emmanuel. It was, above all, the general European situation which determined his attitude on the Roman question.[105] He knew it would be suicidal for France, still prostrate from the blows of her Prussian conquerors, to take up arms against Italy. On March 11 he wrote:

> I am very decided, for my part, not to resurrect the Roman question, which we are in no position to bring to a happy solution. Infinite regard for the pope, earnest entreaties that he be spared further torments—that is our natural and honorable role; but to embroil ourselves with Italy at this moment would be an imprudence and a folly.[106]

Six days later he and his ministerial colleagues declared that they were "resolutely hostile to any *démarche* calculated to encourage the hopes of the defenders of the temporal power."[107] The chief executive did not hesitate to inform the pontiff himself that, though his own opinions were unchanged, his government could not dissociate itself from the other powers in its policy toward Italy.[108] As one of his liberal contemporaries tells us, Thiers "had witnessed the occupation of Rome by the Italians with regret; but he was too wise not to accept the *fait accompli*."[109] He was also wise enough to see that a less tractable attitude would drive Italy into the arms of Germany, and it was one of the axioms of his diplomacy

---

[104] On March 14, Prince Metternich reported to his government that Thiers's sympathies for Italy were "very mediocre" (Henry Salomon, *L'Ambassade de Richard de Metternich à Paris* [Paris, 1931], p. 295).

[105] *Ibid.*, p. 296.

[106] *Thiers au Pouvoir, 1871–1873: texte de ses lettres annoté et commenté par Gaston Bouniols* (Paris, 1921), pp. 46–47 (hereafter cited as *Bouniols*).

[107] Emile Bourgeois, *Manuel historique de politique étrangère* (Paris, 1924) III, 770.

[108] Henri Hauser (ed.), *Histoire diplomatique de l'Europe* (Paris, 1929), I, 83.

[109] Jules Simon, *The Government of M. Thiers* (New York, 1879), II, 492.

that nothing should be left undone to forestall such an alliance.[110] He himself repeatedly stated that he had not made Italian unity and was powerless to abolish it. But he did profess his readiness to do what he could to insure the complete independence of the papacy.[111] He felt that France, as a leading Catholic power, was entitled to protect the personal safety and freedom of the Holy Father. Acting on this conviction, the new head of the state, shortly after his assumption of office, assured Pius that his government would be honored to give him an asylum should Rome cease to be a suitable place of residence.[112] His agile mind was busy with possible international alignments which might enable France to exert a salutary pressure in behalf of the Holy See without involving herself in serious complications. One device which appealed to him was an all-Catholic alliance of France, Austria-Hungary, and Italy which would make it possible to exercise a moderating influence upon the last-named. His hope for Austria's co-operation in this matter was more than mere wishful daydreaming, in view of that power's well-known anxiety to see the spiritual authority of the pope properly safeguarded.[113]

Favre, whose continued presence at the foreign office was bitterly resented by the clericals,[114] persisted in his demand for a policy of complete reserve in the current phase of Italo-papal relations.[115] A crusade to restore the temporal power, he kept insisting, was utterly out of the question. He believed that a solution of the Roman question could only come about, "so to speak, of itself." In his opinion, all "shocks" had to be avoided.[116] He was particularly careful to dissipate

[110] See *DDF* (1st ser.), I, No. 13, 29.

[111] Cf. Mme Juliette Adam, *Mes Angoisses et nos luttes, 1871–1873* (Paris, 1907), pp. 182–83; Hanotaux, *op. cit.*, I, 246.

[112] Daniel Halévy, *Le Courrier de M. Thiers* (Paris, 1921), p. 477.

[113] Cf. Langer, *op. cit.*, p. 33.   [114] Cf. Lecanuet, *op. cit.*, p. 94.

[115] Cf. Favre to Rothan, February 19, 1871, AMAE (Italie, janvier-février, 1871), Tome 380, fol. 251.

[116] Salomon, *op. cit.*, p. 296.

whatever false hopes the election of Thiers might have induced at the Vatican.[117] He described the situation very clearly in a dispatch to Lefebvre de Béhaine on March 15. It was true, he wrote, that Thiers, once the brilliant defender of the pontifical authority, was surrounded by deputies whose antecedents and views would make them the pillars of a propapal policy. But these elements in the new regime were held in check by other and stronger ones. The chief executive was well aware that, as long as he, Favre, directed the foreign ministry, nothing would be done, written, or said which might encourage "a policy of pontifical restoration." At the same time, no stone would be left unturned to protect the person and spiritual authority of the Holy Father. The majority of the national assembly, Favre continued, frowned not only on "efficacious action" in favor of the temporal power but on any "serious demonstration" as well. Moreover, even an otherwise-minded majority would scarcely wish, in the existing state of affairs, to risk an adventure. Weighed down by excruciating difficulties, how could France complicate the situation by taking up questions "which an inexorable power seems to have resolved"? Had the temporal power fallen "in an hour of surprise," its speedy re-establishment might be hoped for. But no one could deny that it fell bit by bit under the double pressure of political opinion and interests. France could not enter the lists to undo the *fait accompli*. She was restrained by her impotence and by an appreciation of her interests. She would therefore carefully refrain from pronouncing herself on this delicate issue.[118] Favre held similar language to Florence in an effort to assuage Italian alarm which had recently taken shape in plans for a reorganization of the army and in the strengthening of the country's fortifications.[119] Visconti-Venosta welcomed this

[117] Jules Favre, *Rome et la République française* (Paris, 1871), p. 65.

[118] Favre to Lefebvre de Béhaine, March 15, 1871, AMAE (Rome, mars–avril, 1871), Tome 1050, fols. 89–90; cf. also Favre, *op. cit.*, pp. 70–72; Maurice Reclus, *Jules Favre* (Paris, 1912), p. 495.

[119] Rothan, *op. cit.*, II, 355.

friendly overture. It would, he hopefully observed, facilitate an Italo-papal *modus vivendi*.[120]

An opportunity to display its solicitude for the bereaved pope now presented itself to the French government. The former ambassador to the Holy See, Banneville, had left his post late in September, 1870, and no successor had as yet been appointed when Thiers assumed his new office. The void was keenly felt at the Vatican, where the arrival of a French envoy had been impatiently awaited; and shortly after Thiers's accession the papal nuncio in France broached the subject to the veteran statesman.[121] Early in March, Antonelli spoke in a similar vein to the French chargé d'affaires. He alluded to the importance which Pius attached to the appointment of a new French ambassador to the Holy See.[122] Thiers knew that compliance with this request would greatly increase the unpopularity of France in Italy. Indeed, the press of the peninsula, as if at a signal from the government, had already addressed itself to this theme. It had sounded the warning that the presence of a French ambassador would constitute an insult and a challenge. More than that—so ran this journalistic refrain—it could be viewed as a step toward eventual intervention on behalf of the temporal power. The Sinistra was already clamoring for further military preparations as a reply to the supposedly impending appointment of Banneville's successor.[123] The report that Thiers had asked the Vatican to suggest a *persona grata* as the future ambassador was zestfully exploited by the *Riforma*. This request, the influential leftist organ charged, was an admonition as well as an act of devotion. "The great Catholic nation, the people of the crusades, cannot forget either Pippin

---

[120] *Ibid.*, pp. 359–61.

[121] Cf. Trauttmansdorff to Beust, February 24, 1871, HHSA, Politisches Archiv (Rom), Fasz. XI/226, No. 12B, fol. 100*b*.

[122] Lefebvre de Béhaine to Favre, March 8, 1871, AMAE (Rome, mars–avril, 1871), Tome 1050, fol. 37.

[123] *Ibid.*, fol. 38.

or Charlemagne." It was therefore incumbent upon Italy to be on the alert and ready to provide for future contingencies.[124] The editorial effusions of Rome's ultramontane newspapers made matters no easier. Their recurrent motif was hope of speedy redemption. High Vatican officials were indiscreet enough to hail the arrival of a French ambassador as a pledge of forthcoming action in favor of a papal restoration.[125] There was even talk of a Catholic crusade to liberate the pope.[126] The situation was further complicated by the Italian government's long-standing desire to have a single diplomatic representation in Rome accredited to both pope and king.[127] Inspired articles in ministerial journals were now advancing the argument that the agents accredited to the king were qualified to handle whatever business there was with the Vatican and that, in any case, ecclesiastics would suffice for this work.[128] These contentions, ardently seconded by the Sinistra,[129] were repudiated in the strongest terms by Antonelli. Acceptance of the government's thesis, he held, would be tantamount to a recognition of the occupation of Rome. He told the French chargé d'affaires that any representative accredited to Victor Emmanuel would never, on the strength of the same credentials, be admitted to the Vatican. And the pope would not hear of ecclesiastical agents in lieu of the customary diplomatic ones.[130] The powers were

[124] *Riforma*, February 26, 1871. [125] Favre, *op. cit.*, p. 76.

[126] F. Gregorovius, *The Roman Journals of Ferdinand Gregorovius* (London, 1907), p. 398.

[127] Cf. Lefebvre de Béhaine to Favre, March 21, 1871, AMAE (Rome, mars–avril, 1871), Tome 1050, fol. 135.

[128] Cf., on the question of a dual diplomatic representation in Rome, Favre, *op. cit.*, pp. 77–78; Robert von Nostitz-Rieneck, "Der Ausgang des Parlamentskampfs ums Garantiegesetz und dessen europäische Begleiterscheinungen (Februar-Juli, 1871)," *Stimmen der Zeit*, August, 1917, p. 488.

[129] Throughout 1871 the *Diritto* kept pointing to the dangers which would accrue to Italy from a dual diplomatic representation in Rome (cf. especially the issues of May 22 and November 13, 1871).

[130] Lefebvre de Béhaine to Favre, March 21, 1871, AMAE (Rome, mars–avril, 1871), Tome 1050, fol. 136; Favre, *op. cit.*, pp. 78–81; *AD, 1874*, II, 218–19.

subsequently informed in very emphatic language that they would either have a double representation in Rome or suffer a severance of diplomatic relations with the Holy See.[131]

The outcry in the Italian press proved of no avail. Favre informed Rothan that, under existing circumstances, it would be better to have ambassadors accredited separately to the royal and papal courts. The prevailing antagonism between Pius and Victor Emmanuel excluded the possibility of a common diplomatic representation. France, consequently, was resolved to maintain her embassy at the Vatican. But the government at Versailles had every intention of adhering to its policy of reserve vis-à-vis the question of the temporal power. Rothan was to make this clear to the authorities at Florence in order to dispel in advance any fears which the French ambassador's arrival might engender.[132] Thiers, though he deplored the attitude of the Italian press, was not to be swerved from his determination to demonstrate his filial devotion to the church. So signal an act of deference toward the Holy Father could not fail, with political conditions in France as they were, to strengthen his position internally. He appointed the Count of Harcourt, a staunch Catholic and a *persona gratissima* at the Vatican,[133] to the post in Rome. However, in compliance with a request from the Italian government, which sought thereby to salvage its own prestige, the appointment of Choiseul as Rothan's successor was announced simultaneously with that of Harcourt.[134] The ambassadorial rank conferred upon the latter was designed to be a mark of special consideration for the

[131] Cf., on this papal communication, *CC*, III (8th ser.; June 17, 1871), 5.

[132] Favre to Rothan, March 26, 1871, AMAE (Italie, mars–avril, 1871), Tome 381, fol. 234.

[133] The selection of Harcourt was viewed with satisfaction by the papacy (cf. Lefebvre de Béhaine to Favre, March 28, 1871, AMAE [Rome, mars–avril, 1871], Tome 1050, fol. 166).

[134] Favre, *op. cit.*, p. 82; Reclus, *op. cit.*, p. 496. The Italian government, in making this request, acted with an eye to the reaction of public opinion in the peninsula (cf. Rothan to Favre, April 1, 1871, AMAE [Italie, mars–avril, 1871], Tome 381, fol. 261).

Holy Father in his hour of misfortune. To have given Harcourt an inferior rank would have been, in Favre's opinion, "a regrettable mistake."[135] Pius and the Vatican were distinctly gratified,[136] while Italian public opinion seethed with resentment.[137] The Roman clericals were the special object of ire. Destra and Sinistra joined in accusing them of working to provoke foreign intervention. And the French were warned that they would not find Italy weak and divided were they to undertake a crusade against her.[138] The Lanza cabinet was nettled. It regarded Thiers's haste in naming an ambassador to the Holy See as a manifestation of ill will.[139] His action, it complained, had prejudiced the very controversial subject of diplomatic representation at the Vatican.[140] It was small comfort to receive assurances from Nigra that Thiers was not one to create difficulties for Italy in the Roman question and that he was an eminently practical person who readily adjusted himself to accomplished facts.[141] The prestige of the Italian monarchy had been dealt a severe blow, and the immediate future seemed fraught with dangerous complications.

Harcourt arrived in Rome on April 22, and at once the clerical press of the city regaled its readers with prophecies of woe for Italy. Typical were the observations and tone of the *Voce della verità*, the official organ of the Roman Society for

---

[135] *DDF* (1st ser.), I, 15.

[136] Antonelli to Lefebvre de Béhaine, April 1, 1871, AMAE (Rome, mars–avril, 1871), Tome 1050, fol. 205; Lefebvre de Béhaine to Favre, April 1, 1871, *ibid.*, fols. 196–97; *CC*, II (8th ser.; May 6, 1871), 469.

[137] Certain sections of the ministerial press, after the first outburst of rage, sought to minimize the importance of Thiers's action. Thus, according to the *Libertà* of May 19, 1871, the Catholic powers were moved by a purely personal sense of deference to the wishes of the Holy Father in the matter of a double diplomatic representation in Rome. They were unwilling to displease a poor old man.

[138] Cf. *Diritto* of April 14, 1871, and *Opinione* of April 17, 1871.

[139] Chiala, *Pagine*, I, 107–8.

[140] Rothan, *op. cit.*, II, 369–70.

[141] See Stefano Castagnola, *Da Firenze a Roma: diario storico-politico del 1870–71* (Torino, 1896), p. 167.

Catholic Interests.[142] The arrival of Harcourt, it remarked, was an event which derived from existing circumstances "a significance doubtless more grave" than the cabinet of Florence cared to admit. Thiers, it continued, would certainly not have sent so eminent a representative to the Holy See "if France were not in a position to speak loudly." Italy had 1,600 kilometers of exposed and defenseless littoral. She could not, therefore, "throw down the gage to a power which disposes of a considerable maritime material that is still intact." Although it confessed ignorance of Harcourt's instructions, the journal found it easy to suppose that this scion of "one of the most illustrious and Catholic families of France .... would not come to Rome in order to aid the despoilers of the Holy See in the execution of their designs."[143] On April 26, Harcourt was received in private audience by Pius. The latter professed to appreciate France's difficulties. His only request now, he said, was that she give counsels of moderation to the Italian government. "Sovereignty is not to be sought in times like these," he went on. "I know this better than anyone. All that I desire is a small corner of land where I will be master." He did not mean, he added, that, if his former dominions were offered to him, he would reject them. But he insisted that, so long as he did not have this modicum of territorial sovereignty, he would be hampered in the discharge of his spiritual functions.[144] In speaking thus, Pius sought to indicate that he might be satisfied with the Leonine City.[145] The delicacy of the situation did not escape Har-

[142] The founding of this society is discussed in chap. ix.

[143] *Voce della verità*, April 23, 1871.

[144] Harcourt to Favre, April 26, 1871, AMAE (Rome, mars–avril, 1871), Tome 1050, fols. 351–52.

[145] Ernesto Vercesi, *Pio IX* (Milano, 1930), p. 237. The pontiff spoke in much the same fashion to Kálnoky. He was accused, he said, of demanding the impossible because he maintained his rights over all the provinces which formerly constituted the pontifical monarchy. But that, he continued, was a duty which he was obliged by his vows to discharge. "Nevertheless," he remarked at this point, "I would content myself with the strictly necessary, but it is indispensable that the sovereign pontiff be free and in no way dependent on any power, and that will never come to

court. In reporting this conversation to his government, he ventured the following observation: "If we declare formally to the pope that we have decided not to intervene under any circumstances, even to assure him the small corner of land of which he spoke to me today, we will lose much of our standing with him. . . . . To retain our influence over him, we must keep our attitude vague and indeterminate."[146] The moderation and resignation of the pontiff's language on this occasion did not fail to impress Favre. But as the "convinced adversary" of the temporal power,[147] he was perturbed by the allusion to "a small corner of land." Determined to shun all discussion of a restoration, however attenuated, of the Holy See's territorial sovereignty, he promptly warned his envoy to maintain complete reserve on this point in further conversations with Pius or Antonelli.[148] The pontiff, who continued to repose his hopes in France,[149] came away from the interview with Harcourt somewhat dissatisfied. He had the impression, he said, that the French ambassador had arrived without instructions to make any *démarches* or precise declarations. "I have seen the ambassador of France," he remarked to Trauttmansdorff. "He has absolutely nothing to say." It was obvious to the Austrian envoy that Harcourt's failure to make his debut with a heartening promise or assurance for the future had evoked disappointment at the Vatican.[150]

---

pass unless the pope possesses, as a sovereign, the territory on which he resides together with the numerous religious institutions and establishments which are necessary for the exercise of his functions" (Kálnoky to Beust, May 6, 1871, HHSA, Politisches Archiv [Rom], Fasz. XI/226, No. 28A, fols. 431a–432a).

[146] Harcourt to Favre, April 26, 1871, AMAE (Rome, mars–avril, 1871), Tome 1050, fol. 355.

[147] So Favre described himself in his dispatch of April 27, 1871, to Lefebvre de Béhaine (cf. *ibid.*, fol. 357).

[148] Favre to Harcourt, May 4, 1871, *ibid.* (Rome, mai–juin, 1871), Tome 1051, fol. 19; *AD, 1874*, II, 226–27; Favre, *op. cit.*, pp. 110–11; Bastgen, *op. cit.*, II, 785.

[149] Cf. Trauttmansdorff to Beust, May 3, 1871, HHSA, Politisches Archiv (Rom), Fasz. XI/226, No. 22A, fol. 414b; cf. also *ibid.*, No. 29, fol. 452b.

[150] *Ibid.*, No. 27B, fols. 418a–419a.

Favre's endeavors to mollify the Italians were in the meantime being nullified by the behavior of the French reactionaries, with whom the pope had allied himself in the hope of attaining through them his territorial objectives.[151] In the midst of the civil strife precipitated by the rising of the Paris commune, the French clergy, supported by the ultramontane press, initiated a campaign in favor of restoring the temporal power.[152] These developments were closely watched by the Vatican, which impatiently awaited the triumph of its legitimist-clerical minions.[153] In May the agitation became more pronounced. The *Monde* provided its Catholic readers with a resounding battle cry when it proclaimed: "Our disasters began the day we abandoned Rome. They will not end until we resume the defense of the Holy See. . . . . France succumbed twice. She rose in 1814 with the restoration of Pius VII. She will rise in 1871 only after restoring Pius IX."[154] Simultaneously, the legitimist pretender to the French throne, the Count of Chambord, declared in a widely publicized letter to one of his followers:

It is said that the independence of the papacy is dear to me, and that I am determined to obtain effective guarantees for it. That is true. The liberty of the church is the first condition of the spiritual peace and order of the world. To protect the Holy See was always the honor of our country and the most incontrovertible cause of its greatness among the nations. It is only in time of great misfortune that France has abandoned this glorious patronage.[155]

The degradation of Europe, echoed the *Union*, was evidenced by the plight of the church. For Europe had ceased to be

[151] Cf. E. L. Woodward, "The Diplomacy of the Vatican," *Journal of the British Institute of International Affairs*, May, 1924, p. 128; cf., on the pro-French orientation of Antonelli's policy after the events of 1870, Ugo Pesci, *I primi anni di Roma capitale* (Firenze, 1907), p. 19.

[152] Cf. Edmond de Pressensé, "L'Ultramontanisme et la politique française," *Revue des deux mondes*, May 1, 1872, p. 137.

[153] Camillo Manfroni, *Sulla soglia del Vaticano* (Bologna, 1920), I, 54–55.

[154] *Monde*, May 8, 1871.

[155] *Ibid.*, May 13, 1871; Hanotaux, *op. cit.*, I, 245–46; Lieutenant-Colonel Rousset, *La République conservatrice* (Paris, 1914), I, 307; Lecanuet, *op. cit.*, p. 149.

Christian; it was finding no fault with the subjection of the church to the Italian monarchy. The duty of restoring Europe to Christianity belonged to France. The Continent would then be rescued from "the materialist policy of usurpations, annexations and accomplished facts."[156]

Chambord's pronouncement, which some of his sympathizers deplored because it created the impression that the royalists, if successful, would drag the country into a war with Italy,[157] greatly bolstered the morale of the Holy See. It was the "true monarchy" which this Bourbon prince wished to restore, the *Osservatore romano* triumphantly announced.[158] The Curia made no effort to conceal its belief in an imminent deliverance at the hands of France.[159] It was freely predicted in Vatican circles that, on the forthcoming silver jubilee of Pius' elevation to the pontifical throne, Rome would be restored to the church. The French ambassador, who made no secret of his papal sympathies,[160] was widely regarded as the principal instrument of these machinations.[161] Gregorovius noted on May 21: "Harcourt appears to be the enemy of Italy. Should the monarchy be restored in France, it will harass Italy in favor of the pope, and will necessarily put Italy to the proof of whether or not she is independent."[162] The unpopular envoy, whose behavior evoked from the *Opinione* only polite expressions of regret over the deterioration of Franco-Italian relations,[163] quickly found

---

[156] *Union*, May 23, 1871.

[157] Cf. Vicomte de Meaux, *Souvenirs politiques, 1871–1877* (Paris, 1905), p. 63.

[158] *Osservatore romano*, May 20, 1871.   [159] Manfroni, *op. cit.*, I, 65.

[160] Shortly after his arrival in Rome, Harcourt unburdened himself on the subject to Trauttmansdorff. He was convinced, he told the Austrian envoy, that for him, as ambassador to the pope, there was no other attitude to assume than that of abstaining from all relations with the Italian authorities, with official circles, and with the court of Victor Emmanuel (Trauttmansdorff to Beust, May 3, 1871, HHSA, Politisches Archiv [Rom], Fasz. XI/226, No. 27B, fol. 419*b*).

[161] The Sinistra denounced him as the spearhead of the clerical opposition in Italy (cf. Kálnoky to Beust, May 22, 1871, *ibid.*, No. 31, fol. 483*a*).

[162] Gregorovius, *op. cit.*, p. 400.   [163] *Opinione*, May 25, 1871.

himself the target of spirited diatribes in the columns of less circumspect sheets.[164] The *Riforma* accused him of openly repudiating the new order of things in Rome.[165] The *Diritto* complained that his conduct constituted a provocation to the Italian government and revealed contempt for its authority in the future capital.[166] The *Libertà*, spurning the restraint displayed by the *Opinione*, did not hesitate to warn Harcourt against making himself the tool of the Jesuits.[167] These newspaper assaults had been preceded by even more vituperative ones, and the indignant ambassador had felt constrained to bring the matter to the attention of his government. He had suggested to Favre the idea of eliciting from the Italian government a disavowal of all complicity in these attacks.[168] The foreign minister did ask Visconti-Venosta to put a stop to the scurrilous language of the Italian press.[169] But he most emphatically cautioned Harcourt against overstepping the bounds of the reserve to which the French government was resolved to adhere. He reminded the count that France had two precepts of conduct. She was unwilling to participate, "directly or indirectly, diplomatically or militarily, in any action aimed at the re-establishment of the temporal power," and she wished, at the same time, to continue at the Vatican in her role as "respectful protector" of the pope's person and religious freedom.[170]

The nervousness of official circles in Florence was reflected in the chamber debate on May 27. The deputies had before them a memorandum, prepared by Sella, justifying the cabi-

---

[164] Cf. Harcourt's own account of some of these press attacks in his dispatch of May 20, 1871, to Favre, AMAE (Rome, mai–juin, 1871), Tome 1051, fols. 51–53.

[165] *Riforma*, May 23, 1871.   [166] *Diritto*, May 22, 1871.

[167] *Libertà* of May 24, 1871.

[168] Harcourt to Favre, May 22, 1871, AMAE (Rome, mai–juin, 1871), Tome 1051, fol. 74.

[169] Favre to Harcourt, May 28, 1871, *ibid.*, fol. 107; cf. also Favre, *op. cit.*, p. 117.

[170] Favre to Harcourt, May 27, 1871, AMAE (Rome, mai–juin, 1871), Tome 1051, fol. 95.

net's demand for increased military appropriations. Italy, the document observed, had to arm because she had de-throned the pope. The danger confronting her did not come from within but from foreign supporters of the papal cause. No country was named, but this omission deceived no one. In the ensuing discussion of the government's financial proposals, one Sinistra spokesman, eschewing the caution shown by the ministry, minced no words. A war against Italy, he pointed out, would unite all those parties in France that were eager to rehabilitate their country's military prestige. He even recalled the well-known views of Thiers on Italian unity and the temporal power.[171] These unguarded remarks brought a sharp reprimand from Sella. He declared that such excursions into the past were rendered inopportune by the French government's recent assurances of good will. He paid a graceful compliment to Thiers, pointing out that all sagacious statesmen knew how to modify their opinions in the face of accomplished facts. "At this moment," he continued, "when everyone should feel grateful to the man who has restored Paris to civilization[172] and peace to France, it is impossible not to resent this citation of utterances which tend to cast suspicion of Italophobia upon .... that very great historical figure, M. Thiers."[173]

The Versailles cabinet was perturbed by the distrust with which Italians continued to view its foreign policy, but it saw little to do except reiterate its pacific intentions. "The French government," Favre wrote on June 1 to the ambassador in Vienna, "wishes neither to menace Italian unity nor re-establish the temporal power." The majority of Frenchmen were admittedly favorable to the papal cause. In the absence, however, of any mandate from the national assembly, there would be no departure from the policy of strict neutrality. Were the temporal power still in existence, the French gov-

[171] *Atti*, CLXVII (May 27, 1871), 2418.
[172] Sella was alluding to the suppression of the Paris commune.
[173] *Atti*, CLXVII (May 27, 1871), 2424.

ernment would be disposed to maintain it. But it had no intention of reviving it, and "to engage in an enterprise having such a restoration as its object would be to misjudge its interests and wishes. The pope therefore cannot count on us." Only in matters pertaining to the personal and religious freedom of the Holy Father would France resume her traditional protective role.[174]

Very different, however, was the language of Favre's clerical compatriots. Their campaign in favor of intervention was daily assuming more formidable proportions. Catholic members of the national assembly presented to that body an address which urged immediate diplomatic action. This document was couched in the strongest language.

Amid the disasters of our country, Rome was invaded and the sovereign pontiff despoiled of the . . . . territory which European public law had guaranteed to him as the safeguard of his spiritual independence. Violation of treaties, contempt for the rights of peoples, scandalous abuse of force, sacrilegious defiance of the most august of authorities: all these odious things are joined in this onslaught. It is also a murderous insult to France, whose honor and faith it affects. All French hearts have keenly sensed this outrage, and despite the most painful preoccupations of the war, thousands of voices were raised in protest. It is up to you . . . . to renew . . . . this solemn protest. . . . . You must proclaim the necessity of the temporal government from the viewpoint of freedom of conscience.[175]

High church dignitaries were very much in the thick of this agitation. A number of eminent bishops organized a vast petition movement[176] in an effort to force the hand of the government. Their demands were exceedingly explicit. The minister at the court of Victor Emmanuel was to be recalled; two warships were to be placed at the disposal of Colonel Baron de Charette and his Zouaves to enable them to go to the pope's defense; and the temporal power was to be forthwith restored.[177] The bishops, nevertheless, insisted that their intentions were peaceful and that they had no desire

[174] DDF (1st ser.), I, 15 and 16.　　[176] Cf. Pressensé, op. cit., p. 139.

[175] Union, June 26, 1871.　　[177] Lecanuet, op. cit., pp. 146–47.

to involve their country in hostilities with Italy.[178] But they were also untiring in their contention that, so long as the pope was not free, there could be liberty for no one. And never for a moment did they cease to belabor the necessity of terminating the Holy Father's intolerable situation without delay. Passages from earlier speeches by Thiers were extensively quoted in order to recall to the country the chief executive's long-standing hostility to Italian unity. One of the many addresses which poured into Versailles bore the signatures of Cardinal Bonnechose and of a distinguished company of prelates. The pope, it stated, was being held captive by the Italian government. The Catholic world, whose freedom of conscience was thereby being violated, was unanimous in demanding independence for its august head. And that independence was inseparable from the exercise of temporal sovereignty. In language reminiscent of Pius' encyclicals and of Antonelli's circulars, it argued that the oft-repeated promises of the Italian government were destined to remain unfulfilled. With the church degraded and the Holy Father a prisoner, glory and freedom were impossible for France. It alluded to the country's traditional protectorate over the Holy See and inferred from this the duty to rectify the present situation in Rome. It invited the national assembly to induce the French government to co-operate with the other powers in restoring the pope to the kind of position that was indispensable to his freedom.[179] Other groups of prelates, headed, respectively, by the Cardinal-Archbishop of Chambéry and the archbishops of Tours, Auch, Rennes, Bourges, and Toulouse, likewise petitioned the national assembly to promote an international diplomatic intervention directed to-

---

[178] Meaux, *op. cit.*, pp. 59–60; Bastgen, *op. cit.*, II, 773–74. Thus Cardinal Donnet and his episcopal subordinates of the ecclesiastical province of Bordeaux emphatically asserted that they were not asking France to go to war. They wanted only, they said, an official declaration to the effect that the pope's temporal rights had remained intact (cf. the *Univers*, July 22, 1871).

[179] *Univers*, June 14, 1871.

ward the resurrection of the papal sovereignty.[180] The Bishop
of Versailles addressed a letter to the national assembly in
which he dwelt upon the alleged sufferings of the Holy Father
and declared that the French republic had no choice but to
protest in the name of justice against the behavior of Italy.
He charged that the guarantees offered the pope were "a bitter mockery" and "an additional outrage" inflicted upon the
august successor of St. Peter. "Your silence," he warned,
"will fall back on you like a curse. By imprinting upon the
forehead of a predatory and perfidious government an in-
delible brand, you will be accomplishing an act of high policy
and helping to strengthen the principles whose victory alone
can give us protection against the fearful dangers which
threaten the world."[181] A few of the prelates intimated that
something more than diplomatic co-operation with the powers was requisite. The Bishop of Nîmes was among those
calling for stronger nostrums. He urged that protests were
futile and that action was imperative; but he was careful to
say that he could not specify the kind of action which would
be appropriate in the circumstances.[182] The bishops of the
province of Sens indulged in similar language. They agreed
with their colleagues that it was time to put an end to the
state of affairs in Rome. "You will intervene in the measure
of the possible," they counseled in their address to the national
assembly, "and your intervention will take the forms which
your wisdom will suggest."[183] The legitimist newspapers did
what they could to abet this movement. They sponsored an
address of their own which was to be presented to Pius on
his forthcoming pontifical jubilee. It closed with the *vœu:*
"May France, restored and regenerated, soon lend once more
the aid of her avenging arm to her oppressed Father." Accounts with Italy would be squared, the *Union* reassured its

---

[180] *Ibid.*, June 21 and 28, and July 3, 7, 14, and 15, 1871.

[181] *Ibid.*, July 15, 1871.

[182] *Ibid.*, July 8, 1871; Lecanuet, *op. cit.*, pp. 147–48.

[183] *Univers*, July 17, 1871.

readers. But with an eye to the reaction of its republican adversaries, who might easily be encouraged to exploit this show of belligerence, it proceeded to clarify its position. It explained that the national assembly, "in our present state of humiliation," could not ask the executive power "to chastise the insolent invader of Rome who has profited by our defeats to complete his criminal work against the pope." The sovereign body at Versailles was unable to do more than commission the government to negotiate a diplomatic understanding with the powers for the specific purpose of "delivering the pope from the Italian yoke."[184]

The bitterness against Italy was intensified by that country's apparent determination to displace France as the guardian of Catholic interests in the Levant.[185] "The desire and ambition of Italians at this moment," Harcourt wrote Thiers on May 31, "seems to be to substitute their influence for ours everywhere. This objective is pursued at Rome and in the East with great persistence." The Italian government, he warned, was exploiting the presence of its nationals in a great many outlying establishments and communities to pose as the natural protector of the church. He alluded to the view of impartial observers that "the evident propensity of the new kingdom is to profit by our embarrassments and, in many places, to covet our heritage."[186] Harcourt addressed a similar warning to Favre.[187] The strongly propapal ambassador had already observed in this connection that a direct Italo-papal understanding, which Favre was seeking to promote,[188] would work harm to French interests. He had point-

---

[184] *Union*, June 29 and July 15, 1871.

[185] As early as December, 1870, the Austrian ambassador in Rome had alluded to Italian attempts to supplant France as the protector of Catholicism throughout the Near East (cf. Trauttmansdorff to Beust, December 24, 1870, HHSA, Politisches Korrespondenz [Rom], Fasz. XI/224, Bericht 130C, fols. 705b–706a).

[186] Halévy, *op. cit.*, pp. 477–78.

[187] Harcourt to Favre, June 15, 1871, AMAE (Rome, mai–juin, 1871), Tome 1051, fol. 159.

[188] Cf. Favre to Lefebvre de Béhaine, April 27, 1871, *ibid.* (Rome, mars–avril, 1871), Tome 1050, fols. 357–58.

ed out that one of the principal impediments to Italian success in displacing France as the guardian of Catholic interests was the Holy See's loyalty to its former protectors. He
had warned that this obstacle would disappear the day the
Holy See, disheartened by its isolation and despairing of securing support from the great Catholic powers, should decide to cast its lot with Italy. And the latter would then affect to regard as vacated the great position which France in
the course of years had created for herself through her solicitude for Catholic interests.[189] But even the very unclerical
foreign minister was seriously disturbed by Italian maneuvers
in the Near East. He noted that the claims of the Italian
cabinet had become more pretentious since the occupation of
Rome. In a dispatch to Choiseul late in May, he declared
that he could not accept "with indifference the language and
attitude of Italy's consular agents in the Levant." Everywhere, he wrote, "they announce the eclipse of our influence
and the supremacy of that of their nation."[190] On June 12
he unburdened himself in a similar vein to the French ambassador at Constantinople, the Marquis de Voguë. Italy's
representatives in the Orient, he observed, "aim at nothing
less than to place themselves on a level of complete equality
with us." More than that, they were insinuating that their
country, by succeeding to the temporal power of the papacy,
had acquired rights over the Catholic church in the Levant
which were better than those of France. He anticipated disputes between French and Italian consuls arising out of rival
claims to the role of defender of the religious interests of
Catholic Christendom.[191]

Louis Veuillot, the editor of the *Univers*, played a most
conspicuous part in the anti-Italian agitation. Day after

[189] Harcourt to Favre, May 5, 1871, *ibid.* (Rome, mai–juin, 1871), Tome 1051,
fols. 20–23.

[190] Favre to Choiseul, May 25, 1871, *ibid.* (Italie, mai–août, 1871), Tome 382,
fol. 76.

[191] DDF (1st ser.), I, No. 8, 22–23.

day, he announced the impending rehabilitation of legitimate thrones overthrown by atheist conspirators. He never wearied of summoning his country to embark upon a new Roman expedition.[192] Before long, he proclaimed, France would settle her accounts with Italy.[193] "We do not say," he wrote early in July, "that France should *hic* and *nunc* make war on Italy, but we think that . . . . a war against Italy to restore the pope to his provinces would be the best road to the return of Alsace and Lorraine to France."[194] He joyfully predicted that the silver jubilee of Pius IX, "captive but invincible," was one miracle which foreshadowed another, that of his deliverance by a restored Bourbon king of France who would confine Victor Emmanuel to his subalpine principality.[195] The virulence of Veuillot's effusions on this as on other questions was without parallel in the French journalism of his day. "The limits of scurrilous abuse, of deliberate misrepresentation, of the spirit of unscrupulous controversy at its worst," were reached in his columns.[196] His close connection with the Holy See gave his utterances a special significance. Pius frequently referred to him as "caro Veuillot" and on one occasion called him "vero defensore del mio pontificato."[197] The *Monde* was scarcely less vitriolic and persistent in championing the papal cause. "The present situation of the head of the church," it declaimed, "cannot continue. He cannot remain the prisoner of Italy, at the mercy of the first cutthroat who will take it into his head to force the doors of the Vatican. It is not only his liberty which is being violated, but ours as well. . . . . We have a right to his independence, because it is an integral part of ours." This, it continued, was what the national assembly was being asked to say. "Let

[192] Daniel Halévy, *La Fin des notables* (Paris, 1930), p. 24.

[193] *Univers*, June 29, 1871.

[194] Lecanuet, *op. cit.*, pp. 150–51.   [195] *Ibid.*, p. 149.

[196] Roger Soltau, *French Political Thought in the Nineteenth Century* (London, 1931), p. 75.

[197] *Ibid.*, p. 183.

the assembly protest against the injustice while awaiting the moment to terminate it: if its sword is not free, it at least has the weapon of speech, the Catholic weapon par excellence. Let it declare to Italy that the Roman question is a Catholic question . . . . and especially a French one." All the Catholic powers could act in concert, and Italy, confronted by their "unanimous and energetic representations," would regain her reason.[198]

The transfer of the Italian capital to Rome gave fresh impetus to the ultramontane-monarchist campaign. The *Monde* hotly declared that "the simultaneous existence at Rome of two independent sovereigns is impossible." It reminded its readers that "the apostate seized Rome in defiance of treaties with France and of European public law." It argued that the great powers were sanctioning a crime which some day would recoil upon themselves. For the end of papal liberty was the end of civilization.[199] The festivities at Rome, the *Union* acidly observed, could not obscure the fact that that city still belonged to the pontiffs. Europe had to remember that it would incur disaster if it should persist in its passive attitude vis-à-vis this "victorious iniquity."[200] Another leading legitimist sheet, the *Gazette de France*, insisted that the Roman question was more acute now than ever before. The transfer of the capital constituted no solution at all. The pope was "morally" a prisoner in the Vatican. The "derisive" guarantees offered him were proof of the degradation and humiliation to which his enemies wished to reduce him. France was invested with the special mission of defending the Holy See; and she would fulfil it once she had recovered her old status.[201] The impotence of the country was bitterly lamented by the *Français*, a conservative journal destined before long to become an important Orleanist mouthpiece. It ruefully remarked that France, in her present state of exhaustion, was condemned to witness "the violation of rights for which she

[198] *Monde*, June 15 and 16, 1871.   [200] *Union*, July 8, 1871.

[199] *Ibid.*, July 4, 6, and 7, 1871.   [201] *Gazette de France*, July 14, 1871.

had so often given . . . . the blood of her sons." Regardless
of the future behavior of the Italians, it continued, the pope
would remain a captive in the eyes of the world. And the
Quirinal might easily become another prison for its royal inmate, who would find himself hemmed in by the "embarrassment of an odious role and the redoubtable proximity of his
victim."[202]

Moderates keenly deplored the campaign against Italy.
The language of the *Temps*, which shared with certain other
organs the self-imposed duty of representing this section of
French opinion, was especially significant.[203] Its like-minded
confrere, the *Journal des débats*, gave free vent to its indignation and disgust. There were certain people, it observed, who
seemed anxious to justify the accusation that France was in
a demented state. Was it possible that some Frenchmen
were still clamoring for a new Roman expedition? These individuals, it continued ironically, wanted a war with Italy in
order that France might recover from the struggle with
Prussia. "We are apparently neither sufficiently vanquished
nor bled of wealth and blood, and the best remedy for our
ills is to risk still further adventures."[204] It dealt unsparingly
with the bellicose petitions of the episcopate. "One imagines
one's self dreaming when one reads of such things," it asserted. "To preach a holy war at a moment like this to a
nation bereft of strength, money, and everything else—is that
not the height of mockery?" But the ultramontanes did not
look at the situation in this way. They cared little about the
fate of France when it was a question of satisfying "their
passions and their rancors." It would not, it went on, do the
authorities the unkindness of believing that they would take
the petitions seriously. "The place of a government which
attached any importance to such documents would be
marked out in advance. It would be necessary to prepare an

---

[202] *Français*, July 4, 1871.

[203] Cf. *Temps* of June 28, 1871.   [204] *Journal des débats*, June 8, 1871.

insane asylum as its residence."[205] Charles de Mazade, the
political commentator of the *Revue des deux mondes* and a
competent student of Italian affairs,[206] likewise presented
the moderates' case. He pointed out that the bishops had not
chosen their moment well. If they desired only to demonstrate their fidelity to the pope, a pastoral would have been
enough. Did they wish to involve France in a new war in
order to effect the restoration of the temporal power and expel
Italy from Rome? The important thing, he insisted, was that
the fall of the temporal power was irrevocable. France, like
the other powers, had only one request to make of Italy: that
the law of guarantees be applied with the utmost liberal-
ity.[207]

The republicans viewed the activity of their clerical-monarchist rivals with undisguised alarm. Gambetta pronounced
the episcopal petitions sheer madness. His friend, Challemel,
complained that France, powerless even to retain Alsace and
Lorraine, was being summoned to restore the papal states.
Spuller, another of Gambetta's most trusted collaborators,
observed that Italy was being driven into the arms of Germany.[208] In a manifesto issued on June 14, leading leftist
spokesmen charged that their political adversaries had
breached the Pact of Bordeaux.[209] The republican *Siècle* accused the legitimists of meditating another Roman expedition. "At the close of a disastrous war with Germany," it
fumed, "they can think of nothing better than to engage in a
struggle with Italy."[210] In its opinion, the clerical agitators
were employing "the most illegal and reprehensible means"
to attain their objective. And they were enjoying, so it intimated, the clandestine encouragement of the Thiers gov-

---

[205] *Ibid.*, June 15, 1871.   [206] He published a life of Cavour.

[207] *Revue des deux mondes*, July 15, 1871, p. 453.

[208] Adam, *op. cit.*, p. 182.

[209] An agreement between the French political parties to defer all questions which
might divide the nation.

[210] *Siècle*, June 6, 1871.

ernment.[211] The radical press was unanimous in urging that
the question of the temporal power had been satisfactorily
settled and that, in any case, it was not the concern of France.
The petitioning bishops, these journals repeatedly charged,
were leading the country to the brink of war with Italy.
To this Veuillot replied: "Yes, it is a crusade, and we shall
not cease to preach it."[212]

The Vatican and its Italian adherents followed the developments in the neighboring republic with the utmost satisfaction. France, averred the *Civiltà cattolica*, was once more
becoming mindful of her role as the eldest daughter of the
church and as the protector of the vicar of Christ.[213] It was,
of course, a delusion, the *Unità cattolica* conceded, to believe
that France would make war on Italy within a day or two.
But so much was certain: France, once she had set up a stable government, would lose no time in ordering Lanza to get
out of Rome.[214] Italian public opinion, paced by the Sinistra,
was thoroughly outraged by the attitude of the French ultramontanes, and in the ensuing press barrage[215] the charge was
advanced that the Versailles cabinet was abetting the petitioners. Favre countered with a spirited denial. On July 11
he addressed a strong note to Nigra calling attention to the
language of the Italian newspapers and of certain Italian
politicians. These fomenters of trouble, he declared, were
imputing to the French government the design of preparing
"a movement, perhaps an expedition, in favor of the temporal power of the Holy Father." This, he said, was not so.
France was unalterably opposed to a resuscitation of the
question of the temporal power. She was inspired solely by a
desire to protect "the personal independence and spiritual

---

[211] *Ibid.*, June 17 and 18, 1871.　　　[212] Lecanuet, *op. cit.*, pp. 149–50.

[213] *CC*, III (8th ser.; July 29, 1871), 378.

[214] *Unità cattolica*, July 16, 1871.

[215] The *Diritto* was very much in the thick of this tumult. It warned the country
that, should the clericals triumph in France, they would almost certainly declare
war on Italy (cf. the issue of June 11, 1871).

freedom of the sovereign pontiff." He reproached the Italian
government for pandering to the scaremongers by strengthening its armaments and defenses. It was thus helping to
perpetuate the prevailing antagonism between the two countries.[216] Favre's assurances, however, seemed belied by the
unabated ultramontane agitation in France. The alleged existence of some understanding between the authorities at
Versailles and the reactionary parties continued to give Italians many uneasy moments. The *Opinione* noted with no
little anxiety that Thiers was seeking to ingratiate himself
with his clerical compatriots. Inasmuch as the ultramontane
party was steadily losing ground throughout Europe, the
authoritative journal observed, the chief executive would be
well advised to take a more realistic view of French interests.
If he were able to justify Choiseul's absence from Rome on
the ground that he could not alienate the Catholic party, he
would find it more difficult to explain to Europe any surrender now to the claims of that party. France, the Destra sheet
continued, had to guard against complete isolation. But her
bishops thought otherwise. Their petitions were ridiculous.
It was plain indeed that clericals were wholly devoid of any
sense of country and of right. In Italy they were busy inviting foreign intervention. In France they were seeking to
poison the relations between the two nations.[217] It reminded
the French that the occupation of Rome had not been accomplished in order to vex them. That event was an "inevitable historical" one dictated by "ineluctable necessities."
The Italophobe episcopate would do well to remember, too,
that no authoritative voice had been raised in any European
parliament on behalf of a restoration of the temporal power.[218] The *Diritto*, in equally vigorous language, summoned
the French government to drop all subterfuge and clarify,
once and for all, its position on the Roman question.[219] More
and more, the conviction gained currency among Italians

---

[216] *DDF* (1st ser.), I, No. 23, 44-45.

[217] *Opinione*, July 12 and 13, 1871.

[218] *Ibid.*, July 21 and 23, 1871.

[219] *Diritto*, July 17, 1871.

that an alliance with Germany was the only road to national
salvation. Foremost among the proponents of such an alliance was Launay. He went so far as to suggest a preventive
war against France. In his opinion, the moment was a propitious one to make her understand that Italy wished to be
unmolested.[220] The *Riforma* editorialized in a similar vein.
It counseled Italy and Germany to unite and exploit for their
own purposes the provocative language of the French conservatives.[221]

The fate of the episcopal petitions continued to give rise to
much speculation in both countries. The reporting committee of the national assembly adopted a resolution declaring
the Roman question the proper subject of diplomatic negotiation and demanding that the petitions be turned over to the
foreign minister for official action.[222] The legitimist-clerical
deputies clamored for an immediate full-dress debate. Favre,
fearful of international complications, advised Thiers to postpone the discussion for three months. But the chief execu-
tive, though he deplored the attitude of the rightist members,[223] decided against so long a delay. On July 22, in the
course of a protracted and stormy session, he explained his
position on the very delicate question at issue. Without in
any way repudiating his well-known views on the necessity
of the temporal power, and though reiterating his undimin-
ished veneration for the person of the pontiff, he called the
attention of the assembly to the grave difficulties with which
the path of the government was beset in dealing with the
problem raised by the petitions. He began by severely cas-
tigating the Italian policy of the Second Empire. The unification of Italy, he declared, had rendered possible that of
Germany and paved the way for the destruction of the temporal power. It was with this troublesome legacy that France

---

[220] Salvemini, *op. cit.*, November 15, 1924, p. 362.

[221] *Riforma*, July 7, 1871.   [222] Hanotaux, *op. cit.*, I, 246.

[223] He warned the conservative deputies that the discussion demanded by the
bishops constituted "a real danger" (Salomon, *op. cit.*, p. 297).

had now to deal. Catholics were indeed justified in asking themselves whether their pontiff was free in his Vatican refuge. But now they were demanding too much of the French government. He reminded his listeners that he had done nothing to facilitate Italian unification. As a matter of fact, he had contributed less to that result than any of his contemporaries. But a united Italy existed, and she was now one of the greater powers of Europe. The other states—Protestant, schismatic, and Catholic—were on the best of terms with her. France had no choice but to emulate them. He conceded that his conscience, too, rebelled against an acceptance of the *fait accompli* at Rome. But when the rest of the world was seeking Italy's friendship, France could scarcely do otherwise. The aim of his government was peace, and neither his prudence nor his patriotism would permit him to sanction a policy which might jeopardize it by alienating a neighboring power. At the same time, Pius could count on France's whole-hearted respect and devotion. Were he ever to choose the road of exile, the republic would always be open to him. It would never fail in its duty to maintain the spiritual independence of the Holy See. France had never ceased to demand that that independence be properly guaranteed, and she was ready even now to join other Catholic nations in its defense. But his duty as a Frenchman, a citizen, and a representative of the government was to maintain good relations with Italy and to provoke no issue which might becloud them.[224] A noisy debate followed, and finally an order of the day assigning the petitions to the foreign office was adopted.[225]

[224] *Discours parlementaires de M. Thiers* (Paris, 1879–83), XIII, 406–24.

[225] Charles Chesnelong, a Catholic-legitimist leader, contends that the national assembly observed in this matter "a circumspection which to it seemed dictated by the situation of the country" (cf. his *L'Avènement de la République, 1873–1875* [Paris, 1934], pp. 206–7).

CHAPTER VII

ROME, VERSAILLES, AND THE VATICAN: THE QUESTION OF FRENCH DIPLOMATIC REPRESENTATION AT THE QUIRINAL

THE general reaction of French moderates and radicals to the outcome of the debate of July 22 was that the clerical-monarchist coalition had obtained merely a nominal victory, that in actuality it had gained nothing, and that the status of the Roman question had been left unchanged.[1] The *Journal des débats* observed that Thiers's declaration denuded the assembly's vote of all significance. Though it sharply rejected the chief executive's views on the temporal power and Italian unification, it had warm words of praise for his frank opposition to a policy which could only lead to warlike complications. It was clear, it went on, that the foreign minister would take no action on the petitions. The aim of the petitioners could be realized only through a war against Italy, and the head of the government had unequivocally declared himself in favor of peace. Certain it was that the temporal power had been "pompously but definitively buried" by the national assembly. France was in no position to embark upon adventures in order that the pope might recover his modicum of territory.[2] The *Temps* agreed that no political results were to be expected from the assembly's deliberations. A question which had become "so completely futile and platonic" could scarcely affect the government's relations with the various parties. And even less

---

[1] Even the Viscount of Meaux, a leading royalist, admits that the resolution of July 22 did not strengthen the position of his party (cf. his *Souvenirs politiques, 1871–1877* [Paris, 1905], p. 61).

[2] *Journal des débats*, July 24, 25, and 26, 1871.

could it serve as a pretext for war with Italy.[3] The *Revue politique* took a somewhat more alarmist view of the situation. It reiterated the warning that any attempt by France to restore the temporal power would increase her isolation by alienating Italy and pushing that country into the arms of Germany.[4] Mazade sharply decried the demands of the ultramontanes. Their only effect, he predicted, would be to bring additional difficulties and embarrassments. The petitioners, he sarcastically remarked, disclaimed any desire to provoke a war; they asked only for diplomatic intervention. But who would collaborate in staging such intervention? What power had not recognized the *fait accompli* in Italy? And what was the sense of diplomatic intervention unless more active measures were likewise in contemplation? Thiers was therefore to be lauded for his skilful leadership on this occasion.[5] The *Siècle* was equally emphatic in its praise of the veteran statesman. "France," it declared, "counted on the good sense and patriotism of the chief of the executive power. . . . . He has not deceived this expectation." And his statement of policy had in no way been prejudiced by the consignment of the petitions to the foreign minister. This session of the assembly, it concluded, would be remembered as "a desperate appeal of the partisans of the temporal power to a country taught by its misfortunes and prudent by necessity. France has pronounced her *non possumus*."[6]

The reaction of the rightist press was by no means uniform. The Bonapartist *Pays* minimized the importance of the assembly's proceedings. The petitions, it averred, were destined to evoke, sooner or later, a "heated and dangerous" discussion. But only "words and demonstrations" could come of all this. It was clear that the freedom of the pope was not adequately guaranteed so long as the Italian government

---

[3] *Temps*, July 24, 25, and 26, 1871.   [4] *Revue politique*, July 29, 1871.

[5] *Revue des deux mondes*, August 1, 1871, pp. 676–77.

[6] *Siècle*, July 24, 1871.

remained in the Quirinal. And it was irritating that Italy should have profited by French misfortunes to complete her unification so swiftly. She had acted with a "precipitancy" which offended France. It was necessary, however, to tell the petitioners that nothing could be done. No one thought of using force, and, in the event of negotiations, France would very probably find herself isolated. "It was indeed a sterile satisfaction," the journal continued, "to make threats which cannot be executed, demands which will not be heeded, protests which will remain in the files of the chancelleries and in the columns of the newspapers." True, Thiers had promised to guard the freedom of the Holy See. But this was something which was to be expected of him in any case, and no very great significance could be attached to it. In short, Frenchmen had to content themselves with "the pleasure of loudly condemning a usurpation which could not have been prevented."[7] The *Union* deplored the *fainéant* attitude of Thiers and demanded greater firmness and warmth in vindicating the rights of the Holy Father. This session of the assembly, it conceded, was in one sense a "good" one: it had affirmed the Catholic sentiment of the great majority of the deputies. But the dismal fact remained that nothing was to be expected of the present government of France.[8] The *Gazette de France* was kinder to Thiers. It even applauded his language. The assembly, it said, found in his declarations "reliable guarantees of an intervention favorable to the Holy Father within the bounds of the possible."[9] The Orleanist *Journal de Paris* joined its legitimist confrere in expressing satisfaction with the outcome of the debate. Thiers, in its opinion, had placed the Roman question "on its true terrain." He had set forth the policy which circumstances and considerations of dignity inescapably imposed on France. It was fortunate that he had thus dissipated the illusions of the more ardent defenders of the Holy See. His was the merit of

[7] *Pays*, July 24, 1871.

[8] *Union*, July 24, 1871.   [9] *Gazette de France*, July 24, 1871.

facing this issue courageously and of removing all equivocation. For it would indeed be perilous for France to turn
against accomplished facts.[10] The *Français* likewise registered its approval.[11] The *Presse*, a journal of kindred sympathies, paid an exceptionally fervid tribute to the conservative members of the assembly:

> The Holy Father can count on our inviolable respect and our firm and
> vigilant solicitude. If he should seek a refuge on our territory, he will be
> welcomed as the head of the church. If he should remain in Rome, France
> . . . . will support his independence. If necessary, she will remind Italy of
> her obligations and Europe of its duties. Such will be the attitude of the
> government. It is neither weak nor resigned. It must reconcile the dic-
> tates of prudence with the obligations of devotion. It is in this sense that
> one must interpret the order of the day. This vote . . . . gives satisfaction
> to Catholic consciences without creating any present complication.[12]

The *Monde* found Thiers's speech "an exercise in oratorical
tight-rope walking." It reiterated that the fate of France as
well as of Europe hinged on the treatment of the Roman
question. But it, too, managed to rejoice in the vote of the
assembly. It was of course true, it explained, that France
could not forgive her chief executive for having "lowered the
national honor before the despoilers of Christianity." But
the defense of the Holy See had been imposed upon the government "by the patriotism and courage of the Catholics."
Frenchmen accordingly could congratulate themselves.[13]
Veuillot alone refused to be consoled. He was furious with
the *vieillard frivole* who had "betrayed" the Holy See. "The
cause of the temporal power," he wrote in his *Univers*, "has
been defeated in the national assembly. . . . . All our hopes
have been deceived. The papacy has lost its last support in
the only nation on which it could count."[14] The outcome of
the debate was therefore an unmitigated and humiliating
disaster. "What political Sedans after the military one!" he
wailed.[15]

[10] *Journal de Paris*, July 24 and 27, 1871.

[11] *Français*, July 24, 1871.

[12] *Presse*, July 24, 1871.

[13] *Monde*, July 24, 28, and 30, 1871.

[14] *Univers*, July 24 and 25, 1871.

[15] *Ibid.*, July 28, 1871.

The Vatican, however, professed no such keen disappointment. It had not expected a more partisan declaration of policy from Thiers.[16] Antonelli even remarked to the Austrian ambassador: "In the present situation of France, if I had had to speak before a French chamber, I would have spoken no differently."[17] In the opinion of the Holy Father and of his secretary of state, the considerable majority which had sent the petitions to the foreign office attested the propapal attitude of the national assembly.[18] It was now clear, observed the *Osservatore romano*, that Thiers had not changed his views on the Roman question. He had admitted that his country had duties toward the Holy See and that the pope must be independent. France did not wish "to abdicate her privileged position as the eldest daughter of the church." She was again to become "that noble and generous nation which supported with its arms the Christian name."[19] The Vatican's optimism was shared by the Italian clericals, who now labored more zealously than ever to provoke French intervention.[20] The tone of the *Civiltà cattolica* was eloquent of this hopeful attitude.[21] Even more illuminating were the observations of the *Unità cattolica*. The Turinese organ came out openly in favor of Chambord's restoration.[22] It predicted that France, as represented by the national assembly, would not follow Thiers were he to agree to the abandonment of the sacrosanct rights of the pope. The deputies at Versailles did not share his fear of international complications. The debate and the vote had brought inestimable benefits. A so-called *fait accompli* had been called into question; the Holy Father's

---

[16] See, in this connection, the remarks in Stefano Castagnola, *Da Firenze a Roma: diario storico-politico del 1870–71* (Torino, 1896), p. 196 n.

[17] Henri Hauser (ed.), *Histoire diplomatique de l'Europe* (Paris, 1929), I, 83–84.

[18] *DDF* (1st ser.), I, No. 34, 52.

[19] *Osservatore romano*, July 25 and 28, 1871.

[20] Camillo Manfroni, *Sulla soglia del Vaticano* (Bologna, 1920), I, 78.

[21] Cf. *CC*, III (8th ser.; July 29, 1871), 378.

[22] *Unità cattolica*, August 2, 1871.

rights had been defended; and the destruction of the temporal power had been denounced.[23]

A section of the moderate press in Italy declared itself satisfied with the outcome of the debate. The vote of the Versailles assembly, in the opinion of the *Libertà*, was "far from being a declaration hostile to Italy." Rather, it was "the explicit and solemn condemnation of those who want France to engage in a war on behalf of the defunct temporal power." One could scarcely expect France to vouchsafe "an approval, pure and simple, of the accomplished facts in Italy." It was therefore unnecessary to speculate about certain phrases of Thiers's speech.[24] But the great majority of Italians refused to take so indulgent a view of the momentous debate. They were agreed in regarding it as a mark of implacable hostility to their country.[25] On August 11, Visconti-Venosta wrote to Robilant, the Italian minister at Vienna: "The language of M. Thiers was what I had expected. He reassured us with regard to impending difficulties. But the evident antipathies and the vote . . . . made a bad impression on public opinion."[26] The feeling was widespread that only the chaotic post-war conditions in France kept her from yielding to the demands of the ultramontanes. Even the invariably circumspect *Opinione* did not dissemble its dissatisfaction. It readily admitted that Thiers's address dealt a lethal blow to the lingering hopes of the clericals. The papacy had been courteously but firmly admonished to renounce forever the temporal power. What displeased Italians, however, was the reason advanced to justify the French attitude. The acceptance of a *fait accompli* dictated by sheer powerlessness to do otherwise was not a suitable basis on which to establish Franco-Italian amity. It would have been "far more noble and generous" to recognize the right of nations to achieve

---

[23] Cf. *ibid.*, July 25 and 28, 1871.   [24] *Libertà*, July 27 and 31, 1871.

[25] *DDF* (1st ser.), I, No. 35, 53.

[26] Gaetano Salvemini, "La Politica estera della Destra, 1871–1876," *Rivista d'Italia*, November 15, 1924, pp. 361–62.

unity and live by the precepts of freedom. "Now," it concluded, "we know the attitude of the French government
toward us. All equivocation has ceased."[27] Castelli, who was
an excellent barometer of ministerial opinion, complained of
"French impertinences."[28] Sinistra newspapers lashed out
furiously against Thiers, and some of them even alluded to
the possibility of a war in the immediate future.[29] The *Riforma* reminded its readers that Thiers was an adversary of
the principle of nationality and that consequently his remarks contained nothing new. It summoned the government to adopt a stronger policy and to be more conscious of
its independence, which all except France had recognized.[30]
The *Diritto*, though no less exasperated, took consolation in
the thought that France would not be so foolhardy as to incur the risk of even greater disasters.[31]   On all sides adequate
military and diplomatic precautions were urged. Less overt,
but no less profound, was the disquietude of the Italian government. The Versailles debate, in Lanza's opinion, obliged
Italy to strengthen her defenses, and especially her navy.[32]
Visconti-Venosta, too, was genuinely disturbed. He agreed
with his chief that the future of Franco-Italian relations
seemed decidedly cheerless. They both deplored this recrudescence of bad feeling which stood in the way of a perfect
accord. What was needed, they felt, was a steady effort on
the part of both countries to eliminate this mutual distrust
and hostility.[33] Sella complained that Thiers should have
been more explicit, that he should have repeated what he had
said in Florence the previous year, namely, that Italy, with

---

[27] *Opinione*, July 28, 1871; Chiala, *Dina*, III, 299–300.

[28] Enrico Tavallini, *La Vita e i tempi di Giovanni Lanza* (Torino and Napoli,
1887), II, 428–29.

[29] The episode was not quickly forgotten by the Sinistra leadership. As late as
1891, Crispi alluded to it with undisguised bitterness (cf. his article "Italy, France
and the Papacy," *Contemporary Review*, August, 1891, pp. 170–71).

[30] *Riforma*, July 28 and 30, 1871.

[31] *Diritto*, July 26, 1871.

[32] Castagnola, *op. cit.*, p. 197 and note.   [33] *DDF* (1st ser.), No. 35, 53.

the consummation of German unity, had become a factor making for equilibrium in Europe.[34] Castagnola, the minister of agriculture, industry, and commerce, noted in his diary:

It is clear that the French, though they say they do not wish to make war on us, harbor ill-feeling toward us; and therefore political prudence makes it advisable not to neglect our armaments and to conclude an alliance with the German empire.[35]

No very great faith was placed by the cabinet in assurances from Nigra that the national assembly was not at one with French public opinion.[36]

The only immediate result of the debate of July 22 was the advent of a new French foreign minister. Favre had repeatedly declared that he would not remain at his post should it ever be decided to turn the episcopal petitions over to the foreign office.[37] Such a gesture, in his opinion, constituted a commitment to diplomatic action and even conceivably to direct intervention on behalf of the temporal power. Its only effect, he felt, would be to antagonize Italy and encourage the ultramontanes to believe that France was about to resume her old role of armed defender of the Holy See.[38] Now, incensed by the outcome of the vote and irked by the persistent and vicious attacks of Bonapartists, Orleanists, and legitimists, he resigned.[39] Thiers endeavored to dissuade his irate subordinate.[40] "My very sincere feeling," he wrote him on July 25, "is that you exaggerate the situation."[41]

---

[34] Alessandro Guiccioli, *Quintino Sella* (Rovigo, 1887), I, 362.

[35] Castagnola, *op. cit.*, p. 195.   [36] *Ibid.*, p. 198.

[37] Maurice Reclus, *Jules Favre* (Paris, 1912), p. 497.

[38] Jules Favre, *Rome et la République française* (Paris, 1871), pp. 3–4.

[39] *Notes et souvenirs de M. Thiers, 1870–1873* (Paris, 1903), pp. 206–7.

[40] *Bouniols*, pp. 92–93.

[41] De Vogüé agreed with the president. "You have acted in this circumstance with your usual loyalty and sincerity," he wrote Favre on August 15, "but I am of Thiers's opinion that it is an exaggerated scruple which has carried you away. I cannot believe that any of those who voted in favor of consigning the petitions to the foreign office would have raised a finger on behalf of a more emphatic gesture. Sim-

But he finally desisted when he saw that Favre was not to be moved. The latter's departure evoked eulogistic effusions in the Italian press. Destra and Sinistra organs joined in showering him with fervid tributes. His noninterventionist attitude in September, 1870, was gratefully recalled. It was he, declared the *Opinione*, "who eased for us a most difficult moment of our political life and found in his liberalism the real and fair explanation of our conduct."[42] The *Riforma* reminded its readers that Favre had virtually repudiated the September convention. With his resignation, it warned, another of the obstacles which stood in the way of Italian subjection to the France of Thiers had been removed.[43] Very different, of course, was the reaction of the clericals. According to the *Osservatore romano*, Favre's disappearance signalized the supremacy of the conservatives in the political councils of France.[44] The *Civiltà cattolica* hailed the exit of the veteran republican as "perhaps the best result" of the July 22 debate.[45] The *Unità cattolica* likewise made no effort to conceal its exultation. It spoke in glowing terms of the "great service" which the deputies of the Versailles assembly had rendered the national cause.[46]

Favre's successor was Rémusat, a veteran politician of

---

ple good sense counsels prudence and silence at this moment." He shared, however, Favre's feeling that the clamor of the clericals was highly inopportune. "If there is anything worse than impotence," he observed, "it is the confirmation of that impotence by sterile wishes and ineffectual menaces" (Reclus, *op. cit.*, p. 501 n.).

[42] *Opinione*, August 2, 1871. The Destra journal admitted that the sentiment of the great majority of Frenchmen was too clearly averse to Favre to be flouted. It contended that the latter's resignation was important only for France's domestic affairs. Neither Italy nor the pope had any reason to lament or rejoice. The temporal power was interred and Italy's national rights denied: these were the conclusions to be drawn from the recent debate in the Versailles assembly, and they were not to be modified with a change in the person of the French foreign minister.

[43] *Riforma*, August 3, 1871.

[44] *Osservatore romano*, August 8, 1871.

[45] *CC*, III (8th ser.; August 5, 1871), 498.

[46] *Unità cattolica*, July 26, 1871.

considerable standing.[47] The new chief of the foreign office promptly professed a desire to cultivate friendly relations with Italy. He was reputed to share Favre's view that the question of the temporal power was *hors de cause*.[48] It is not therefore surprising that the *Opinione* hailed his appointment as of good augury for the future of Franco-Italian relations.[49] The *Diritto*, however, warned against excessive elation. Rémusat, it cautioned, would have no choice but to submit to the dictates of the clericals. The important thing to remember was the propapal and anti-Italian attitude of the French nation.[50] Rémusat's accession did not lessen the optimism of the Vatican.[51] Nor did it suffice to erase the painful impression created in Italy by the recent discussion in the national assembly. Rather, that impression was being further aggravated by the monotonously scurrilous language of the French ultramontanes. The latter now transferred their attack to another sector of the Italian front. On July 27 they addressed a new petition to the legislators at Versailles. Their objective now was a declaration stating that France would forever abstain from appointing a successor to the post which Choiseul had failed to resume.[52] The presence of a French minister at the Quirinal, explained the *Univers*, was equivalent to an official recognition of the existing order in Italy. The absence of a diplomatic representative constituted, on the other hand, "a permanent protest against the

[47] Rémusat had served for a time as minister of the interior under Louis Philippe. On his appointment as Favre's successor see *Notes et souvenirs de M. Thiers, 1870–1873*, pp. 207–8.

[48] Cf. Pietro Vigo, *Storia degli ultimi trent'anni del secolo XIX* (Milano, 1908), I, 79.

[49] *Opinione*, August 9, 1871.

[50] *Diritto*, August 10, 1871.

[51] The *Osservatore romano* contended that the defense of the papacy was essentially a matter of national moment for France and consequently one which concerned the entire country, regardless of party (cf. the issue of August 17, 1871).

[52] Cf. *Univers*, July 28, 1871.

fait accompli."[53] The petition was circulated in the dioceses
to the accompaniment of vitriolic attacks on Thiers.[54]

Italians looked on with patent concern. But elsewhere in
Europe their prospects seemed less bleak. In August, and
again in September, the Austrian and German emperors met
on Austrian soil in an atmosphere that seemed to presage
well for the future of Austro-German relations. No less noteworthy was the meeting of the Austrian and German chan-
cellors at Gastein. These events were hailed with great enthusiasm throughout the peninsula. The formation of an
Austro-German bloc in Europe, it was felt, would facilitate
Italy's quest for safeguards against clerical France. The
Libertà re-emphasized Italy's pacific outlook.[55] The *Opinione*
dwelt with satisfaction on the cordial relations between
Rome, Vienna, and Berlin, and the entire press of the kingdom made much of the idea of a triple entente for the maintenance of peace.[56] The *Diritto* insisted that such an entente
virtually existed, in so far as the interests of the three countries coincided.[57] The nature of the agreements arrived at in
Gastein was the subject of considerable speculation. Well-
informed persons professed to be vastly reassured. Though
no treaties had been concluded, Minghetti wrote Pasolini, it
was certain that Prussia would aid Italy should the latter be
the victim of an attempt by France to regain power and
prestige.[58] Actually, Bismarck had told Beust that, should
France take action against Italy and sound out Germany,
she would receive no reassuring reply.[59] A rumor that Italo-
papal relations had formed one of the subjects of conversa-

[53] *Ibid.*, July 30, 1871.

[54] R. P. Lecanuet, *Les dernières années du pontificat de Pie IX, 1870–1878* (Paris,
1931), pp. 156–57; *Temps*, July 29, 1871.

[55] *Libertà*, September 10, 1871.

[56] Cf. *DDF* (1st ser.), I, No. 53, 73.   [57] *Diritto*, September 5, 1871.

[58] *Carteggio tra Marco Minghetti e Giuseppe Pasolini* (Torino, 1924–30), IV, 206.

[59] Friedrich Ferdinand Graf von Beust, *Aus drei viertel-jahrhunderten* (Stuttgart,
1887), II, 487.

tion at Gastein was denied by the conservative *Kreuzzeitung* of Berlin.

We learn that the negotiators at Gastein avoided bringing into the discussion the regular Roman Question—that, namely, of the re-establishment of the Temporal Power. This question is to continue to be regarded as an affair concerning Italy alone, and the Italian government has not only not sought, but has, indeed, decisively declined any international settlement of the matter.[60]

Simultaneously, a report was circulated that Bismarck, in an effort to conciliate his ultramontane compatriots, had suggested an Austro-German *démarche* at Rome to induce the Italian government to make further concessions to the Holy Father. It was stated that Beust had lent a ready ear to this overture and that the Lanza cabinet had intimated its willingness to accept such advice in order to make sure of the friendship of the two empires.[61] This report remained unconfirmed; but its widespread dissemination bespoke the general tendency to link the fortunes of the Roman question with the future of Italy's relations with the central powers. The *Diritto* attached great importance to the reputed unwillingness of the two emperors to discuss the Roman question on the ground that it was a matter of Italian domestic concern. This, insisted the Sinistra journal, should open the eyes of French and Italian clericals who still dreamed of an armed intervention on behalf of the temporal power.[62] In France there were some who persisted in the belief that the Gastein conferees intended to draw Italy into the Austro-German orbit

[60] *Times*, September 6, 1871.

[61] *Ibid.*, September 9, 1871. The following item appeared in the *Annual Register: 1871* (London, 1872), p. 231: "But he [Bismarck] had other political objects also to attain by a face-to-face conference with Count Beust . . . . , and one of these was the arrangement of some joint representation—not by any means as a requisition, but as a friendly suggestion—to be made to the Italian Government for the amelioration, if possible, of the Pope's position at Rome. This was a sop by which he hoped to soften the feelings of the German Catholics against him, and to prevent Jesuit intrigues at home from representing him in too black colours. . . . . With regard to the Pope, it was promised that Austrian influence should be exerted to further the course proposed by Bismarck."

[62] *Diritto*, September 7, 1871.

by promising her the undisturbed possession of Rome.[63]
Mazade, however, contended that the Roman question
placed Italy under no pressure to seek allies. Indeed, that
question would be the very last to create Italo-French ill
feeling. In any case, it had ceased to exist, and with its disappearance there remained only reasons for friendly relations.[64]

Moderate Italians were not unwilling to meet the French
halfway. The forthcoming inauguration of the Mount Cenis
tunnel, scheduled for the middle of September, seemed an
excellent occasion for burying old animosities. The initiative
was taken by Sella. He sought to arrange a meeting between
Victor Emmanuel and Thiers in the hope of smoothing the
way for such a *rapprochement*. Thiers declared himself willing to come to Modane to meet the king at the dedication
ceremonies. But Victor Emmanuel proved utterly unamen-
able. The absence of the French minister on July 2, he told
Sella, was an affront he could scarcely forget. Thiers's anti-
Italian attitude and his offensive language of late were further reasons for shunning the projected meeting.[65] But at the
inaugural rites there were only the friendliest words from the
representatives of both nations. The festivities at Bardonecchia on September 17 brought together Visconti-Venosta,
Sella, Rémusat, and Le Franc, the French minister of agriculture.[66] "The piercing of the Mount Cenis," declared the
Italian foreign minister, "will be a work forever memorable.
Communication having been facilitated, the relations between Italy and France will become even more intimate."
Le Franc, in reply, complimented his Italian hosts on their

[63] Cf. *Revue des deux mondes*, September 15, 1871, p. 467.

[64] *Ibid.*, p. 470.

[65] Guiccioli, *op. cit.*, I, 360–61; Tavallini, *op. cit.*, II, 76–78; Luigi Chiala, *Dal 1858 al 1892; pagine di storia contemporanea* (Torino, 1892–94), I, p. 112 n.; Vittorio Bersezio, *Il Regno di Vittorio Emanuele II: trent'anni di vita italiana* (Torino, 1878–95), VIII, 411; cf. also Attilio Simioni, *Vittorio Emanuele II* (Milano, 1911), pp. 147–48.

[66] Guiccioli, *op. cit.*, I, 362–63; Castagnola, *op. cit.*, p. 202.

splendid political and scientific achievements. Amid great applause he proposed the following toast: "To the union of France and Italy."[67] Two days later, Rémusat arrived in Turin and was cordially received by Victor Emmanuel.[68] Speaking at a banquet in the presence of Visconti-Venosta and other Italian notables, he declared: "We are all of the Latin race and united. It is the true moment for calling to mind the advantages of union."[69] The French ministers, Minghetti recorded in a letter to Pasolini on September 20, "did not cease to make the most ample declarations of friendship. To suppose, they said, that France wishes at some time to make war on behalf of the temporal power is absurd. And such is also the opinion of Nigra."[70]

Moderate and leftist opinion in France applauded the remarks of Le Franc and Rémusat on this occasion. Mazade hailed the opening of the tunnel as an event which, "in appearance industrial, has had a political result: that of dissipating all the shadows by restoring Franco-Italian friendliness."[71] The *Siècle* expressed the hope that Rémusat's visit to the Piedmontese capital would remove all existing difficulties between the two governments. The foreign minister had spoken "in the name of France and in the name of the republic." His words would be welcomed by French liberal opinion because they indicated that France was extending to Italy "a frank and loyal hand." Italians could now rest assured that French arms would never again serve to restore papal rule in Rome. There was no more room for misunderstanding on this issue.[72] The Orleanists entirely shared the

[67] *Journal officiel de la République française*, CLXXXIV (September 22, 1871), 3617; *Times*, September 18, 1871.

[68] Cf. Michele Rosi, *Vittorio Emanuele II* (Bologna, 1930), II, 205 n.; Simioni, *op. cit.*, p. 148.

[69] *Journal officiel de la République française*, CLXXXIV (September 22, 1871), 3618.

[70] *Carteggio tra Marco Minghetti e Giuseppe Pasolini*, IV, 205.

[71] *Revue des deux mondes*, October 1, 1871, p. 704.

[72] *Siècle*, September 21, 1871.

views of their liberal compatriots. The union of France and Italy was, in the opinion of the *Journal de Paris*, "altogether natural." The two nations had no reason to hate each other. On the contrary, they had every reason to stand together. It was, however, for the Italians to take the steps necessary "to re-establish a really friendly understanding." Otherwise, the two nations would continue to be separated by a barrier more formidable than the Alps.[73] The *Presse* agreed that France and Italy had everything to gain from collaboration. It underlined the "happy importance" of the Mount Cenis rites as a factor which might pave the way for a "useful" and "necessary" alliance.[74]

Bonapartists, legitimists, and ultramontanes took a very different line. While French and Italian ministers were busy exchanging friendly speeches, the *Pays* observed, people were asking themselves whether Italy had made *démarches* at Gastein in an effort to enter the system of alliances which Bismarck was seeking to erect. It went on to point out that the reason for Italo-French friction was one which could not disappear overnight. France always remembered that Italian unity owed its origin to the will of a French sovereign and that it was completed thanks to the protection of the latter's enemies. "The House of Savoy entered Milan as a result of our victory. It entered Rome as a result of our defeat. Though the word 'ingratitude' is indeed harsh, it is in the minds of many Frenchmen."[75] The *Gazette de France* deplored the remarks of Le Franc and Rémusat. It found distasteful "their effusions of misplaced lyricism about the Italian statesmen and their political achievements." Had the recent misfortunes of France, it queried, made her politicians lose even "the sentiment of national honor"? They were doubtless hoping, through their subservient language, to secure the favor and perhaps the alliance of Italy. That hope was entirely futile. Italy had been won over to the enemies of

[73] *Journal de Paris*, September 19 and 20, 1871.

[74] *Presse*, September 19 and 21, 1871.   [75] *Pays*, September 20, 1871.

France. No illusions were to be entertained on that score.[76]
The *Union* likewise accused the two statesmen of betraying
the national honor. But retribution, it asserted, was on the
way. The Holy See would emerge triumphant from its trials.
"The martyrdom of Pius IX is preparing a liberator; and
God, in His mercy, seems to be awaiting the end of our
tribulations in order that the deliverance of the papacy might
be the signal for the French restoration."[77] The legitimist
organ was careful to remind its readers that the principal
grievances against Italy were three in number:

> In the moral sphere, the Italian revolution has struck at the pontifical
> independence which is necessary to the government of the universal church.
> In the political sphere, it has annihilated our influence beyond the Alps and
> created a power against us. In the sphere of material interests, it has made
> the peninsula a rival, opened transport routes which will be of no profit to
> us, and the future of Marseilles . . . . is seriously menaced.[78]

The *Union* was careful, too, to reiterate that its program was
an eminently peaceful one. "There is no need," it observed,
"to draw the sword against Italy. A precise and firm diplomatic note would put an end to her sacrilegious assaults."
The future could be trusted to provide for "the punishment
of past crimes."[79] The *Monde* was wild with rage. "As long
as Italy remains the persecutor of the Holy See," it thundered, "she will be the irreconcilable enemy of Catholic
France." Neither alliance nor peace was possible between
the two countries. All the tunnels that might be constructed
would only serve to afford passage to soldiers and cannon.[80]
The *Univers* unburdened itself in language of equal violence.
It berated the itinerant ministers for their pacific utterances
and protested loudly against a *modus vivendi* of any kind with
Italy. "The more we see of the Italians," Veuillot wrote,
"the less we like them. And the longer we see them chained to
the Prussians and hostile to the church and to Christ, the less

[76] *Gazette de France*, September 23, 1871.

[77] *Union*, September 23, 1871.   [79] *Ibid.*, September 26, 1871.

[78] *Ibid.*, September 21, 1871.   [80] *Monde*, September 20, 1871.

we hope and wish to make the peace of the world with them.
To make the peace of the world against them . . . . very soon!
Of this we do not despair."[81] This barrage in the legitimist-
clerical press came on the heels of a significant gesture by
forty-eight ultramontane members of the national assembly.
Only a day before the meeting at Bardonecchia, they had
sent an address to the pope declaring that the temporal power
was indispensable to the spiritual freedom of the Holy See
and invoking international action against Italy.[82]

The Mount Cenis rites and the apparent improvement in
the relations between the French and Italian governments,
which impressed even the Sinistra,[83] greatly disheartened the
Vatican. Its widely advertised belief that, before the close
of September, French intervention, diplomatic or military,
would ensue[84] now seemed a crude joke. Its gloom was deep-
ened by the impending occurrence of an event which patriots
throughout the peninsula were impatiently awaiting. The
first Italian parliament to sit in Rome was to be opened on
November 27. As the day drew near, Pius was reported to
be increasingly restive at the thought of having to witness
this culminating sacrilege. There had been of late a revival
of rumors that he was about to quit the city,[85] and it was
popularly supposed that the desire to spare himself this additional torment was the chief reason for his projected flight.

[81] *Univers*, September 23, 1871. Three days earlier, Veuillot had written in his
newspaper: "Let us pray to God to hasten the moment when France, delivered from
the Prussians, but above all from herself, will deliver Rome from the Italian mire."

[82] A. Debidour, *L'Eglise catholique et l'état sous la Troisième République* (Paris,
1906), I, 59.

[83] Cf. *Riforma* of September 25, 1871, and *Diritto* of September 22, 1871. The
latter sheet, however, did not fail (September 28, 1871) to remind the ministerialists,
whose hope for better relations with France had been greatly encouraged by the
Mount Cenis rites, that a Franco-Italian accord was possible only if Italy agreed to
accept French protection.

[84] Manfroni, *op. cit.*, I, 83.

[85] At a cabinet meeting on October 17, Visconti-Venosta stated that the question
of the pope's departure was again being discussed at the Vatican (cf. Castagnola,
op. cit., p. 207).

French newspapers were announcing his departure as im
minent, and France was most frequently mentioned as his
preferred haven of refuge. It was assumed in some quarters
that Thiers proposed to place Pau at the disposal of the
Holy Father.[86] Well-informed circles in Italy were not loath
to believe that the pope's counselors had asked the French
government for an asylum. They were inclined to attribute
this maneuver to the Vatican's hope of creating confusion and
of precipitating thereby a postponement in the opening of the
Italian parliament.[87] The Sinistra professed to view the reports of an imminent flight as a papal stratagem designed to
secure further concessions from the government. It insisted
that Pius really had no intention of leaving his present com-
fortable residence.[88] Were he ever to go, the *Diritto* observed,
he would do so in agreement with France. His departure
would therefore be equivalent to a French declaration of war
on Italy. The latter consequently had no choice but to prepare for all eventualities while awaiting the day when the
Versailles assembly should acclaim Henri V and the restoration of the temporal power.[89]

Thiers himself made his position clear in an interview with
a correspondent of the *Journal des débats*. He declared that
the French government, though it regarded the pope's departure as highly improbable and was determined to do
nothing to influence his decision in this matter, was ready to
receive him with every respect and solicitude should he wish
to come to France.[90] This offer produced no great enthusiasm among the ultramontanes. They professed to see in it a
sly evasion of the duty to give the pope more material aid.
"It is certainly quite enough for M. Thiers," Veuillot stated

[86] Cf. Vicomte de Gontaut-Biron, *Mon ambassade en Allemagne* (Paris, 1906),
p. 427.

[87] Cf. *Opinione*, November 14, 1871.

[88] Cf. *Riforma*, November 23, 1871.   [89] *Diritto*, November 20, 1871.

[90] *Journal des débats*, November 20, 1871. A few days later, instructions in this
sense were sent to Harcourt (cf. *DDF* [1st ser.], I, No. 83, 104–5).

in the *Univers*, "but it is little for France. . . . . If we wish to save ourselves, it is not France that must be opened to the pope; it is Rome that must be opened to France."[91] Ministerial circles in Italy viewed Thiers's gesture as an effort to influence the pope in favor of flight. The *Opinione* was moved to reiterate the official thesis that the Holy Father was absolutely free to do as he pleased. But it went on to contend that he would be submitting to the commands of one party were he to go, whereas it was his duty to take account of the spiritual interests of all the faithful. Moreover, the vicissitudes of French politics were not likely to be very gratifying to the pontifical guest. For, with a change of government, he might find himself face to face with less hospitable hosts.[92] In any case, the Destra journal concluded, Thiers's intervention in this matter served only to stimulate vain hopes at the Vatican and exacerbate Italo-papal relations. But there was one reassuring fact which ought not to be overlooked: in order to solve the Roman question in their own manner, the French would require an army of three hundred thousand men to fight Italy and another force to defend themselves against foes elsewhere; and they did not, at present, possess such military strength.[93]

The Italian parliament was duly opened on the twenty-seventh in the presence of the entire diplomatic corps accredited to the Quirinal. The French chargé d'affaires had been instructed to come in from Florence for the occasion,[94] much to the disgust of Veuillot, who protested against "this last insult to French honor."[95] The pope remained in Rome.

[91] *Univers*, November 23, 1871; Lecanuet, *op. cit.*, p. 157.

[92] *Opinione*, November 25, 1871.   [93] *Ibid.*, November 29, 1871.

[94] Cf. *DDF* (1st ser.), I, No. 84, 105.

[95] *Univers*, December 1, 1871; cf. also Lecanuet, *op. cit.*, p. 157. The *Union* alluded to the opening of the Italian parliament in Rome as the last phase of "this great and criminal usurpation begun a dozen years ago." It went on to declare the coresidence of the two sovereigns impossible. "We inscribe," it concluded, "the date of November 27 as a date of death for the kingdom of Italy. The Italian government believes that it has just taken possession of Rome: it has just dug its own grave" (issue of November 29, 1871).

But the *Osservatore romano* outdid itself in flaying this "new insult . . . . to the religion, the rights, the freedom and the honor of Romans,"[96] and the rumors that the Holy Father was on the point of leaving did not subside. So persistent were these rumors that Count Andrássy, who had succeeded Beust as head of the Austrian foreign office,[97] instructed his representative at the Vatican to do what he could to dissuade Pius from abandoning his residence.[98] Not long afterward, the same statesman made his position clear in reply to a request that the pope be invited to migrate to Austria. There was no Catholic state, he declared publicly, which was in a position to offer the Holy Father as attractive an asylum as the one he enjoyed in Rome.[99] The government at Versailles was even more concerned. It continued to assure the pope that if he should decide to desert Rome—a decision he would have to make entirely on his own responsibility—he would receive a suitable refuge in France.[100] At the same time it admonished the Lanza cabinet to treat the august inmate of the Vatican indulgently in order to deter him from quitting his abode. On April 6, 1872, Thiers wrote to his diplomatic representative in Italy:

What I ask of King Victor Emmanuel . . . . is that he render the life of the pope endurable by showing him the consideration which his misfortunes, his virtues, his dignity, his role as the head of Catholicism, and, I will say, the interests of the House of Savoy itself, merit. If this consideration is not shown, the pope will end by leaving Rome, and I do not know a greater danger to Italian unity. As for me, I have not urged him and I will not urge him to leave the Vatican. But others will urge him to it; and it is

96 *Osservatore romano*, November 28, 1871.

97 On the fall of Beust in November, 1871, see Eduard von Wertheimer, *Graf Julius Andrássy: Sein Leben und seine Zeit* (Stuttgart, 1910), I, 633; Beust, *op. cit.*, II, 515–16.

98 Augusto Sandonà, *L'Irredentismo nelle lotte politiche e nelle contese diplomatiche italo-austriache* (Bologna, 1932), I, 98.

99 Wertheimer, *Andrássy*, II, 194; *Schulthess, 1872*, p. 252.

100 *Bouniols*, pp. 152–56, 162–63. Arnim, who was in Rome at this time, subsequently remarked to Morier that Thiers was eager [?] to have the pope on French soil in order that France might replace Italy as the center of the Catholic world (cf. the *Memoirs and Letters of the Right Hon. Sir Robert Morier* [London, 1911], II, 255–56).

necessary that he be free, completely free, respected, even venerated, in order to keep Catholics both in France and in Europe from . . . . rebelling against the present situation.[101]

The Italian government was well aware of the harm that the flight of the pope might work,[102] and it was not loath to vouchsafe the necessary reassurances. Some weeks later a suitable opportunity to do so offered itself. A few Sinistra deputies, with a zeal worthy of a less hopeless cause, pressed the charge that the government was much too conciliatory toward the Vatican. They accused the ministry of trying to curry favor with the clericals rather than "satisfy the most legitimate demands of the nation." Even the overgenerous terms of the law of guarantees, they asserted, were not being enforced against the clergy.[103] In his reply, Visconti-Venosta sharply stated that his policy and that of his colleagues was not to render it impossible for the Holy Father and the Italian government to dwell together peaceably in Rome.[104] Not alone Catholic governments, but liberal statesmen who were among Italy's most trustworthy friends were counseling such moderation and indulgence.[105] This declaration satisfied Thiers. The latter, moreover, was not blind to the fact that the Kulturkampf, which was now reaching an acute stage in Germany, enhanced the perils of playing host to the pope.[106]

While the possibility that the Vatican might soon be without its prisoner continued to hold the attention of the French and Italian governments, the failure of Thiers to fill the post

[101] *DDF* (1st ser.), I, No. 120, 139-40.

[102] Cf. Sandonà, *op. cit.*, I, 99.

[103] *Atti*, CLXXXIII (May 14, 1872), 2105, 2109, 2110.

[104] *Ibid.*, p. 2118.   [105] *Ibid.*, p. 2119.

[106] On September 2, 1872, he wrote to Rémusat: "We have already offered our hospitality without urging departure. We have been listened to without enthusiasm. We need go no further. Without withdrawing our offer, we need not renew it. During the open war undertaken by Prussia against the papacy, the retreat of the pope into France would be a serious matter. Honor would not allow us to refuse, but it is not necessary to invite embarrassments" (Daniel Halévy, *Le Courrier de M. Thiers* [Paris, 1921], p. 478; *Bouniols*, p. 221).

formally vacated by Choiseul[107] was being bitterly resented
throughout the peninsula.[108] To many Italians this seemed
to signify a refusal to recognize the *fait accompli* at Rome.
Visconti-Venosta pressed with little success for a prompt
rectification of the situation.[109] Victor Emmanuel himself
had directed Rémusat's attention to this matter during the
latter's recent visit to Turin. The king had expressed the
hope that France would soon send a minister to his court.[110]
To make matters worse, French ultramontanes had not abandoned their campaign in favor of foregoing all diplomatic representation at the Quirinal.[111] The activity of the *Univers* in
promoting this campaign was the special target of Italian
ire and ridicule.[112] Thiers's position vis-à-vis his clerical compatriots was exceedingly delicate, but toward the close of
1871 he finally bestirred himself. Formal announcement was
made that Goulard, who was then serving as French plenipotentiary at Frankfort in the discussions with Germany,
had been appointed Choiseul's successor. The chargé d'affaires at Florence was authorized to inform the Italian government that his legation would definitely be transferred to
Rome on January 1, 1872.[113] But whatever favorable impression these gestures might have created in Italy was completely dissipated by the failure of Goulard to take charge of his
new post. It was reported that his departure from Paris was
to be postponed until the clerical petitions demanding a
diplomatic boycott of the Quirinal had been disposed of in the
national assembly. Italian irritation was further increased

[107] Choiseul resigned as minister to the Quirinal in November.

[108] Cf. the typically Francophobe attitude expressed in the *Riforma* of November 16, 1871.

[109] Castagnola, *op. cit.*, p. 197 n.

[110] Giuseppe Massari, *La Vita ed il regno di Vittorio Emanuele II di Savoia* (Milano, 1910), II, 535.

[111] Edmond de Pressensé, "L'Ultramontanisme et la politique française," *Revue
des deux mondes*, May 1, 1872, p. 139.

[112] Cf. the *Opinione* of October 25, 1871.

[113] *DDF* (1st ser.), I, No. 100, 119.

by the language of the Count of Chambord and his followers. On January 25 the pretender issued another manifesto proclaiming his loyalty to the Holy Father; and a few weeks later his adherents gathered about him in Antwerp and drank "to the health of the king and to the restoration of the pope."[114]

The Italian government was convinced that the French clericals were only waiting for an improvement in their country's international position to organize a descent upon Rome. The key to their behavior, it believed, was to be found in the policy of Vienna. The good will of Austria, Visconti-Venosta wrote Robilant early in January, was of vital importance. For as long as she refrained from resuscitating the Roman question, the ultramontane party in France could do nothing. Frenchmen themselves, he continued, rightly believed that Austria's friendly attitude toward Italy explained the passivity of their government. Were the latter, however, once assured of support from Vienna, it would act.[115] But Italian anxiety on this score was destined to be allayed by Andrássy himself. The latter's accession had been recognized by Italians as a great boon to their cause.[116] And they did not have long to wait to see their optimism vindicated. The new Austrian foreign minister, from the very outset, showed the greatest desire to make no difficulties for Italy in the Roman question.[117] Defying the opposition of the powerful clerical party, he made no secret of his determination to cultivate the most friendly relations with the neighboring kingdom.[118] In February he told a Catholic deputation that concern for the welfare of the country and for peace did not permit any devi-

---

[114] Debidour, *op. cit.*, I, 77; Lecanuet, *op. cit.*, p. 149 n.

[115] Salvemini, *op. cit.*, November 15, 1924, pp. 368-69.

[116] Thus the *Libertà* of December 4, 1871 had noted with intense satisfaction that the clericals, who had been heartened by the fall of Beust, were beginning to discover that Andrássy would not lend himself to their intrigues.

[117] Salvemini, *op. cit.*, November 15, 1924, p. 355.

[118] Wertheimer, *Andrássy*, II, 200-201.

ation from the Roman policy pursued under his predecessor.
He asked the deputation point-blank whether it thought it
was Austria's duty to march into Italy. To this the Catholic spokesman could give no clear answer.[119] Andrássy's repudiation of the interventionist thesis made a great impression throughout Europe.[120] It ran counter to the anti-Italian
attitude of the country's Catholic masses and the propapal
sentiment of the imperial family. But the astute Magyar
had no intention of retracting it. The following September
he informed the budget committee of the Austrian delegation that the cabinet attached great importance to the friendship with Italy. His government, he said, was trying, with
perfect frankness and honesty, to make its views acceptable
to the Quirinal without offending in any way the legitimate
national feeling of the Italians. Particular care had to be
taken to avoid anything which smacked of pressure. The
same unequivocal language had been held to both sides in the
belief that only thereby would it be possible to achieve a truly
useful solution.[121]

In the meantime, the question of French diplomatic representation at the Quirinal continued to cast a heavy pall over
the relations of the two Latin states. Italian radicals and
moderates alike complained bitterly of Goulard's failure to
assume his new post. The *Diritto* recalled Thiers's haste in
sending an ambassador to the Vatican; but it could think of
nothing better to do than to urge the Lanza cabinet to manifest complete indifference to the unworthy behavior of
France.[122] "It seems destined," declared the *Libertà*, "that
France, despite her great misfortunes, should offer the world
only comical spectacles which rob her of all sympathy."
Thiers and the national assembly apparently wished to embroil themselves irreconcilably with Italy. But France would
quickly discover that she was not strong enough to destroy
Italian unity and that she would have to accept that unity

---

[119] *Ibid.*, p. 194.

[120] *Ibid.*, pp. 194–95.

[121] *Schulthess, 1872*, p. 278.

[122] *Diritto*, January 24, 1872.

whether she liked it or not. All the powers had sent representatives to Rome. France alone had failed to do so because
of her hatred of Italy. The latter, the journal warned, would
have to prepare herself "morally and materially" to deal with
future difficulties. Specifically, her military program, which
was far from adequate, would have to be expanded.[123]

Thiers sought to make some amends by loudly insisting
that he would appoint a successor to the procrastinating
Goulard without delay.[124] He deplored as a grotesque error
the ultramontanes' demand that France sever all diplomatic
ties with the court of Victor Emmanuel. In a letter to Harcourt, he dismissed the clerical petitions as wholly unreasonable. "It is only from time and circumstances," he observed,
"that one can expect a change favorable to the power of the
popes."[125] Finally, on February 7, the *Journal officiel* announced the appointment of Goulard as minister of agriculture and commerce.[126] Nothing was said, however, about
naming a new minister to the Quirinal, much to the disgust
of the Italians. The *Opinione* remarked: "To give leave to
M. de Choiseul and accept his resignation, appoint M. Goulard and then intrust him with a portfolio, retard the choice
of his successor until it had pleased the national assembly to
discuss the clerical petitions, is the worst of policies because
it is no policy at all." Anything, it concluded, was preferable
to this unedifying and dishonest maneuvering—even the
frankly hostile attitude of the French clericals.[127] The *Riforma*, although proclaiming for the moment its scornful indifference to French animosity, pressed the government to
safeguard its dignity in its dealings with the rulers of the
neighboring republic.[128] The *Diritto* made Thiers's "prodi-
gious" ingenuity the butt of a long and ironic disquisition.

[123] *Libertà*, February 1 and 7, 1872.

[124] Lecanuet, *op. cit.*, pp. 159–60.   [125] *Bouniols*, pp. 161–62.

[126] Goulard subsequently became minister of finance.

[127] *Opinione*, February 14, 1872; Chiala, *Dina*, III, 315–16.

[128] *Riforma*, February 9, 1872.

Italy, according to this stalwart Sinistra sheet, found it quite convenient to dispense with a French minister to the Quirinal. She had, for the time being, many domestic problems to solve.[129]   The pinpricks administered by Versailles made the publicists and statesmen of the peninsula more acutely aware of the dangers of isolation, and once again their thoughts turned to Berlin. Prince Charles Frederick of Prussia was visiting Rome at this time, and his presence gave further impetus to the talk of a *rapprochement* with Germany—a *rapprochement* for which Visconti-Venosta was working in the belief that upon it the future safety of Italy might well depend.[130]   The organs of the two major parties were encouraged to re-examine, in this light, the basic objectives of the nation's diplomacy. Thus the *Libertà* was moved to reiterate that the quest for allies had to constitute one of the principal preoccupations of Italian foreign policy.[131]   After alluding to the cordial reception vouchsafed Charles Frederick, the *Diritto* went on to urge hearty acceptance of Germany's friendship.[132]   Italy had nothing to learn from France, it declared, but from Germany she could secure fruitful collaboration in the achievement of liberal reforms. The two recently unified states were combating reactionary clericalism, and both of them were intent upon peaceful economic and intellectual self-development.[133]   The *Riforma* continued to bewail the "connubium" between the French government and the clericals. As long as that partnership prevailed, it remarked, Franco-Italian amity would be impossible.[134]   And in some quarters, comparisons were even made of the armed forces which the two countries could throw against each other in the event of war.[135]

---

[129] *Diritto*, February 8, 1872.

[130] Salvemini, *op. cit.*, November 15, 1924, p. 364.

[131] *Libertà*, February 19, 1872.   [133] *Ibid.*, March 12, 1872.

[132] *Diritto*, February 21, 1872.   [134] *Riforma*, February 18, 1872.

[135] Cf. *DDF* (1st ser.), I, 130–31; *CC*, VI (8th ser.; April 13, 1872), 256; Vigo, *op. cit.*, I, 132; *Schulthess, 1872*, p. 446.

Observers in France did not underestimate the danger. It was true, Mazade admitted, that the Italians had not yet succumbed to Bismarck's blandishments. But they might very easily do so if the demonstrations against them should continue in France.[136] It was exceedingly regrettable, observed the *Journal des débats*, that the agitation of French champions of the temporal power should have alarmed Italy and induced her to turn to Germany.[137] The legitimists, not to be outdone in the matter of manifesting patriotic preoccupation, professed a righteous alarm over the Italo-German *rapprochement*. But their conclusions were hardly at one with those of their liberal and radical adversaries. Germany and Italy, the *Union* contended, were opposed to the Catholic hierarchy and fearful of a Bourbon restoration in France. The latter's reply must be: "Absolute devotion to the Roman church and return to the legitimate monarchy."[138] Thiers himself fully appreciated the reality of the danger. It was therefore with no little relief that he at last found himself able to announce the appointment of Fournier, the minister in Stockholm, to the post at the Quirinal. An Italo-German alliance was still the president's *bête noire*,[139] but it was apparent that his ultramontane countrymen were aborting all his calculations. Discussing with his French colleague the significance of Charles Frederick's visit to Italy, Count Károlyi, the Austro-Hungarian ambassador in Berlin, insisted that Germany had no warlike intentions. Her quest for an alliance with Italy was not inspired by a desire to attack France. Rather, it was in the nature of a precaution against a strengthening of the French clerical party should a restored Bourbon king decide to rescue the pope.[140] Bismarck's sen-

---

[136] *Revue des deux mondes* (March 15, 1872), pp. 482–83.

[137] *Journal des débats*, March 5, 1872.

[138] *Union*, March 24, 1872.

[139] Cf. Halévy, *op. cit.*, p. 479.   [140] Gontaut-Biron, *op. cit.*, pp. 74–75.

sational charges in the Prussian upper house on March 6[141] caused a tremendous stir in diplomatic circles. Gontaut-Biron, the French ambassador in Berlin, reported to his government that he was "not far from believing in the projection or even in the existence of a treaty between Germany and Italy assuring the latter the support of Germany's armies should France attempt to restore the temporal power."[142] This surmise seemed partially substantiated by the language of the *Opinione*. It was not necessary, the influential Destra sheet observed, to talk about formal treaties of alliance "to know that between Germany and Italy there is a community of ideas and interests which insures their friendly accord." The two countries were in complete agreement on such matters as the maintenance of the freedom of conscience and the extinction of the temporal power. The inescapable logic of the situation was that they had a common enemy, the clericals, and a common cause to defend against them.[143]

Thiers, who shared the prevailing belief in the existence of an understanding between the cabinets of Berlin and Rome,[144] was hopeful that the appointment of Fournier would diminish to some extent Italy's distrust of France and lessen her sense of dependence on Germany. This expectation was not altogether an idle one. The new envoy was extremely popu-

[141] Early in March an anticlerical school inspection law came up for discussion in the Prussian house of lords. In the course of the debate, Bismarck read passages from a dispatch he had recently received from one of his diplomatic representatives abroad as evidence that the German ultramontanes were fomenting denominational discord at home in order to facilitate a double objective: the overthrow of Germany by France and the restoration of the temporal power. French arms, according to this source, were to be turned against Italy after Germany had been paralyzed by the eruption of religious strife (*Stenographische Berichte über die Verhandlungen der durch die Allerhöchste Verordnung vom 16. November 1871 einberufenen beiden Häuser des Landtages. Herrenhaus* [March 6, 1872], p. 204). The author of the dispatch in question was Arnim (cf. Adalbert Wahl, *Deutsche Geschichte von der Reichsgründung bis zum Ausbruch des Weltkriegs* [Stuttgart, 1926], I, 161.

[142] *DDF* (1st ser.), I, No. 115, 134–35.

[143] *Opinione*, March 13, 1872; Chiala, *Dina*, III, 319–20.

[144] Cf. *Occupation et libération du territoire, 1871–1873: correspondances* (Paris, 1900), I, 213.

lar throughout the peninsula, where he was reputed to be a man of anticlerical and Italophil sympathies.[145] In authorizing the *Opinione* to confirm the news of Fournier's appointment, Visconti-Venosta was careful to emphasize that he was known for his liberal views and his eagerness to promote Franco-Italian amity. And the ministerial journal, taking its cue from the foreign office, observed that Thiers, in naming this admirable diplomatist, had given an unimpeachable earnest of his desire for friendly relations with Italy.[146] So elated were the Italians that a previously announced parliamentary interpellation on the relations between the two countries was unceremoniously dropped.[147] Even the *Riforma*, which had warned that France would have to send to the Quirinal a man who would betray no reserve anent Italy's right to Rome,[148] noted with satisfaction that the appointment of Fournier was intended by Thiers to prevent an aggravation of Franco-Italian relations.[149] The *Diritto*, though no less pleased, was careful to attribute the president's conciliatory gesture to the fact that France was finding herself more and more isolated in the Roman imbroglio.[150] The Vatican was incensed, and through its faithful journalistic mouthpieces it loudly decried the action of Thiers. The *Civiltà cattolica* roundly accused him of selling out to the Italian revolution.[151] The *Unità cattolica* reprimanded him for giving Fournier's appointment "the appearance of a new defeat suffered by France." It could now be said, according to the Turinese sheet, that "the republic of Thiers has had its Sedan."[152]

French moderates received Fournier's appointment with keen satisfaction. Some of them, however, could not refrain

---

[145] Vigo, *op. cit.*, I, 142–43.

[146] *Opinione*, February 29, 1872; Chiala, *Dina*, III, 316.

[147] Cf. DDF (1st ser.), I, No. 112, 131.

[148] *Riforma*, March 3, 1872.

[149] *Ibid.*, March 28, 1872.   [151] CC,VI (8th ser.; April 26, 1872), 357.

[150] *Diritto*, March 6, 1872.   [152] *Unità cattolica*, March 5, 1872.

from making certain caustic observations. It was to be
hoped, they said, that the new envoy would repair to his post
and would not be content to discharge his duties from Paris
or Versailles.[153] The liberal camp was agreed that all efforts
had to be bent toward improving the country's international
position by renewing the friendships with neighboring states.
The government, in its opinion, had therefore acted in the
best interests of France. It had terminated an anomalous
situation and had eased the tension with Italy.[154] The *Bien
public*, reputed to be Thiers's mouthpiece, vouchsafed a
most elaborate defense of the president's gesture. It emphasized the impossibility of suppressing the French legation in
Italy without good reason. "Diplomatic relations between
nations," it urged, "are so essential a reality that they cannot
be broken off without scandal and without bringing a serious
disturbance into that harmony of affairs which is the first
characteristic of international union." Italian irritation on
the score of the French government's procrastination was already considerable, and French national interests might be
endangered. The decision to send a representative to the
court of Victor Emmanuel would therefore "appear wise to
every impartial person." The hatreds and predilections of
France were necessarily circumscribed by her present state
of weakness.[155]

Fournier's appointment evoked emphatic applause from
the radical republican press. The *République française*, the
organ of Gambetta, announced that it was indeed time to
terminate "a very irregular state of affairs which seriously
prejudiced our diplomatic interests in Italy." All the powers,
it pointed out, had sent their representatives to the Quirinal.
France alone had failed to do so. She had thus created the
impression that she was protesting against the recognition of

---

[153] Cf. the remarks of the *Journal des débats* on March 2, 1872.

[154] Cf. the representative attitude of Mazade in the *Revue des deux mondes*, March
15, 1872, p. 479.

[155] *Bien public*, March 3, 1872.

a *fait accompli* which all Europe had hastened to accept.[156] The *Siècle*, stressing the need of winning over Italian public opinion, went so far as to urge the recall of Harcourt. It was ridiculous, it said, to have two ministers in Rome. A representative at the Quirinal was indispensable. But the functions of an ambassador to the Vatican defied definition. The pope was now merely a spiritual sovereign, and the termination of this "unacceptable dualism" would be a highly politic gesture. The imperative duty of France was not to encourage the pretensions of the pontiff but to contract with Italy "relations of solid and permanent friendship."[157] The royalist-clerical camp was split wide open on this issue. The Orleanists spoke kindly of Fournier.[158] But the Catholic party, backed by the legitimists, mercilessly flayed his appointment and the policy which inspired it. To fill the post at the court of Victor Emmanuel was bad enough; but to give it to an acknowledged foe of the church was intolerable.[159] Ultramontane sheets proclaimed that Fournier was not really the spokesman of France and that, far from carrying out her wishes, he would only do something to horrify her. They complained that the government had prejudiced the question of diplomatic representation at the Quirinal on the eve of a discussion of this theme in the national assembly. The sovereignty of that body had thus been shamelessly flouted. The resignation of Goulard as minister to Italy, they wailed, had furnished an opportunity "to take up a correct position without openly breaking with anyone." Neither Italy nor Germany would have gone to war over the failure to name a successor. But the French government was impervious to such considerations. The appointment of Fournier was "an act of fear, the pendant of the recall of the troops from

[156] *République française*, March 5, 1872.   [157] *Siècle*, March 2, 1872.

[158] The *Journal de Paris* of February 28, 1872, alluded to him as "one of our most experienced and learned diplomatic agents."

[159] The *Monde* (February 29, 1872) stressed Fournier's reputation as a "freethinker."

Rome." And his presence in the Eternal City would be "the last of the accomplished facts at Rome, the most shameful for us and the saddest for the pope."[160]

Veuillot and his friends confidently expected to have their inning when the Catholic petitions should come before the national assembly. They did indeed score an initial victory when the reporting committee brought in recommendations favorable to their cause. Discussion of the controversial documents had originally been set for March 2, but the government, in view of the many thorny issues which still remained to be dealt with before a plenum debate could be ventured, secured a fortnight's delay. These dilatory tactics did not enhance the government's popularity. The rightists were, of course, angry.[161] But so were the moderates. The *Journal des débats* complained that there would now ensue a painful suspense which would do Italo-French relations no good and would be all to Germany's profit. It was better, it urged, to have done with this question by listening to a report on the petitions and writing finis with an order of the day.[162] But on the fifteenth the assembly again voted to postpone the discussion, much to the indignation of the legitimist-clerical deputies. One of their principal spokesmen, Chesnelong, complained that the petitions had been kept waiting a long time. He was interrupted by shouts of "They can wait some more!" and "They will wait until the Prussians are no longer in France!" But Chesnelong went on to insist that the Roman question was not one which could be "suppressed or confiscated." It was not worthy of the assembly, he urged, to evade the issue by indefinite postponement.[163] And the *Union*, offering words of encouragement to the conservative contingent in the assembly, warned: "The burial of petitions

---

[160] *Univers*, March 2, 1872; *Monde*, March 3 and 5, 1872.

[161] Cf. *Union*, March 3 and 4, 1872.

[162] *Journal des débats*, March 3, 1872.

[163] *Annales de l'assemblée nationale*, VIII (March 15, 1872), pp. 360–61 (hereafter cited as *AAN*).

signed by more than three hundred thousand Frenchmen is impossible."[164] The behavior of the ultramontanes was sharply censured by Mazade. France, he wrote, would again have to reply to their dangerous agitation by doing nothing. Happily, even the sponsors of the petitions did not dare to carry their viewpoint to its logical conclusion. There was scarcely a French politician blind or capricious enough to propose a policy which could only lead to war with Italy or to a useless demonstration. "Before thinking of the temporal sovereignty of the pope," he admonished, "we might think of France." A discussion of the petitions in the national assembly, he added, would provoke recriminations with Italy. Difficulties between the two countries would be gratuitously created, and Bismarck would be the one to profit by them. The Catholic party was actually playing into his hands by doing its best to detach Italy from France.[165]

On March 22 the issue was finally liquidated. Mgr. Dupanloup, the bishop of Orléans, who had been scheduled to speak on the petitions, made way for Thiers at the latter's request. In characteristically felicitous phrases, the president explained and defended his position. The government, he stated,

has nothing to conceal. It made its policy clear to you last year, and in that policy it is resolved to persist . . . . . The cause of the independence of the Holy See . . . . is dear to it. . . . . But there is another cause which is no less dear, that of the state. I declare to you in all sincerity . . . . that under present circumstances, discussions such as these constitute a real embarrassment for France . . . . and will in no way promote the cause of papal independence.

He adjured the deputies to trust in him and his colleagues and forego debates "which at this moment are entirely inopportune."[166] Dupanloup, who had been advised by Mgr. Chigi, the papal nuncio to France, that the Holy Father's interests would not be served by a defeat in the assembly or

[164] *Union*, March 17, 1872.

[165] *Revue des deux mondes*, March 15, 1872, pp. 480–81, 483.

[166] *AAN*, VIII (March 22, 1872), 496–97.

by a victory achieved at the price of a dangerous conflict with Thiers,[167] agreed to an adjournment of the question. The *Bien public* again volunteered an extensive vindication of the chief executive's attitude.

> M. Thiers, in wishing to postpone the discussion of the Roman question, did not act from any fear . . . . of reprisals on the part of Italy. That country does not and will not dare to concoct any plans directed against us. The president of the republic . . . . wished to spare France a fruitless *démarche*. . . . . He points out that . . . . , at present, nothing can be done for the solution of this question . . . . and that even verbal intervention would still further envenom an already very serious controversy.

The role of France, the journal continued, would have to be entirely conciliatory. Her efforts would have to be directed toward rendering tolerable the relations between the Holy See and Italy. She could do no more than that. And even that she could do only if she did not weaken her action by sterile and irritating discussions. France was not powerless. She would never be powerless. But she was prudent, and prudence was "the duty and the law of all, even of the strongest, in the new world-situation."[168] This was the consensus of opinion among moderates and republicans, who were at one in lauding Thiers for having so skilfully averted a serious crisis.[169] The remarks of the *Siècle* on this occasion attracted much favorable attention outside the leftist camp. Despite the president's cautious language, it asserted, the question of the rights of the Holy See could now be considered terminated. The Catholic petitions had been "well buried," and it was doubtful whether they would ever be exhumed. Perhaps it would have been better to face the basic issues of the debate and to dispose of the ultramontanes' claims with a drastic order of the day. But such a discussion might have been dangerous, and Thiers had done well to discountenance it.[170]

---

[167] Lecanuet, *op. cit.*, p. 160.   [168] *Bien public*, March 24, 1872.

[169] Cf., e.g., the attitude expressed in the following: *Revue des deux mondes*, April 1, 1872, p. 733; *Journal des débats*, March 25, 1872; *République française*, March 23, 1872.

[170] *Siècle*, March 24, 1872.

The Orleanists likewise expressed satisfaction at seeing a
"heated and useless discussion" of the Roman question
shunted.[171] Even the legitimists were pleased. They congratulated Thiers for having made such a "clear" statement.
They pointed out that he had offered his record as a guarantee of his devotion to the papal cause. No one, they emphasized, had forgotten how energetically in years past he had
defended that cause against the empire and against the revolution. There was reason to be grateful to him for stating
that he had not changed his views on the Roman question.
Catholics would be justified in rejoicing, for they had secured
what they had demanded in their petitions.[172] As a matter of
fact, however, the ultramontanes were far from pleased. They
bitterly censured the monarchist members of the national assembly who had assented to the adjournment.[173] Mgr. Ma-
bile, the bishop of Versailles, found them a more shocking
lot than their predecessors under the empire, since the latter,
with all their faults, had not refused to concern themselves
with the Roman question. The *Monde*, charging that the
government and the assembly had committed "a great political mistake," demanded "a pacific declaration in favor of
what was right." It openly accused the deputies of being
fearful of wounding Italy. This equivocal and cowardly attitude, it somberly concluded, would benefit France not at all.
And Italy would only become bolder and more distrustful.[174]
The *Univers*, as usual, far outstripped its confreres in virulence. It compared the Bishop of Orléans to Pontius Pilate
and alluded to Thiers in scarcely less excoriating terms. "We
are tired," it proclaimed, "of these men without doctrine,
love, and resolution." The right of petition had been shamelessly violated, it insisted. And it was now abundantly clear
that Catholics counted for nothing under liberal governments. The clerical party was not, however, altogether

[171] Cf. *Journal de Paris*, March 24, 1872.

[172] Cf. *Gazette de France*, March 24, 1872.

[173] Debidour, *op. cit.*, I, 61.   [174] *Monde*, March 24, 1872.

blameless. It was "soft" and "pusillanimous."[175] Veuillot himself described the incident as disgraceful and expressed horror at seeing Mgr. Dupanloup mixed up in "this denial of justice."[176] Italian Catholic circles were no less chagrined over the "honorable burial" of the petitions.[177] They had been hoping that France, supported by Austria, would intervene on behalf of the Holy Father.[178] But the *Osservatore romano*, more mindful of the constraints imposed upon the president of the French republic, managed to profess a certain satisfaction with the tone of his speech. His remarks, it contended, contained "such reticences and ambiguities" that they were equivalent to "explicit declarations absolutely contrary to the Italian revolution and entirely favorable to the rights of the Holy See."[179] Ministerial opinion, however, had no patience with such subtleties of interpretation. It was now clear, the *Libertà* emphatically asserted, that Italy for the time being had no reason to feel herself threatened by France. If any danger did exist, it was comfortably remote.[180] Those Italians who were inclined to subscribe to this judgment found it easy to believe that the most critical phase of Italo-French relations had finally drawn to a close. But there were many others who viewed the future with no excessive optimism. The respite, they were persuaded, would prove to be a short-lived one.

[175] *Univers*, March 23, 1872; Lecanuet, *op. cit.*, p. 162.

[176] *Univers*, March 24, 1872. Veuillot continued to denounce the outcome of the March 22 discussion and the French government's decision to send a minister to the Quirinal. So abusive did his language become that Pius found it necessary to rebuke him for his excess of zeal (cf. Roger Soltau, *French Political Thought in the Nineteenth Century* [London, 1931], pp. 184–85; Joseph Schmidlin, *Papstgeschichte der neuesten Zeit* [München, 1933–34], II, 127).

[177] Cf. *CC*, VI (8th ser.; April 13, 1872), 256.

[178] Manfroni, *op. cit.*, I, 92.

[179] *Osservatore romano*, March 28, 1872.   [180] *Libertà*, March 28, 1872.

CHAPTER VIII

THE ROMAN QUESTION CONTINUES TO DISTURB ITALO-FRENCH RELATIONS

THE fate of the French petitions was some consolation to the Italian government. Equally gratifying was the arrival of Fournier. The latter, it was confidently believed, would relinquish his post rather than allow himself to be made the tool of ultramontane intrigue. The Sinistra did indeed continue to draw attention to Thiers's views on the Roman question and to the unabated agitation of the French clericals.[1] But moderates found the outlook much less cheerless. The *Opinione* could talk with apparent conviction about the political wisdom of France. It rejoiced that French liberals were beginning to come to life and predicted that this fact would help to restore complete harmony between the two nations.[2] Bonghi was hopeful that the French government, now that it had a minister at the Quirinal, would perceive the necessity of maintaining the *status quo* at Rome and would shape its policies accordingly.[3] The Vatican heavily discounted these prognostications. The *Osservatore romano* held that the presence of a diplomatic representative at the Quirinal portended no change in "the traditional inclinations" of France or in "the necessities of her national policy." Franco-Italian relations remained absolutely unaltered, because Fournier's mission was devoid of any real importance. Much more significant, in its opinion, was the attitude of French Catholics, who were saying that Fournier was not their representative but Thiers's.[4]

[1] *Diritto*, April 4, 1872.
[2] *Opinione*, March 24, 1872.
[3] *Nuova antologia*, April, 1872, p. 922.
[4] *Osservatore romano*, March 28, 1872.

251

On March 24, Fournier had his first interview with Visconti-Venosta. The event attracted wide and sympathetic notice. The *Libertà* observed: "If M. Fournier's mission has, as is announced, no other aim but to remove all misunderstanding and to maintain friendly relations between the two governments, no diplomatist ever had an easier mission." He could be sure, it continued, of obtaining "the most constant support" from Italy. For Italians had no thought of conquest or of war. They wanted only peace and repose. All would be well if France were to reciprocate this good feeling. Specifically, Thiers could render both countries a great service by ceasing to depict Italian unity as a disaster for France.[5] On the following day, Fournier was received by Victor Emmanuel. The king was exceedingly cordial. "I am very glad to see you," he said, "because I know that you are a man of honor, that you wish us well and have already proved it to us."[6] The warm reception accorded the new envoy encouraged Thiers and his entourage to believe that Franco-Italian friendship could still be salvaged. "All reports of an Italo-Prussian alliance," remarked the *Bien public*, "spring only from one source: the fear of Italy that we may intervene in her quarrel with the papacy." The imprudent language of certain French newspapers and the procrastination in filling the post at the Quirinal had given credence to this mistaken apprehension—so much so that Victor Emmanuel had played with the idea of a *rapprochement* and perhaps even a treaty with Germany. But the presence of Fournier in Rome, Thiers's reputed mouthpiece concluded, would terminate all such velleities.[7]

In the course of a conversation with Fournier early in April, Visconti-Venosta explained just why Italy distrusted

[5] *Libertà*, March 25, 1872.

[6] Giuseppe Massari, *La Vita ed il regno di Vittorio Emanuele II di Savoia* (Milano, 1910), II, 542; Pietro Vigo, *Storia degli ultimi trent'anni del secolo XIX* (Milano, 1908), I, 217.

[7] *Bien public*, March 27, 1872.

and feared France. The papacy, he said, dreamed of a territorial restoration to be achieved only with the aid of France.
It was this hope which sustained it in its ill will toward Italy.
Most Italians desired friendly relations with France. The
sole obstacle was the question of the temporal power. If the
French government, out of deference to the past and on suppositions of future expediency, were to make of this question
a national issue, it would be committing a colossal error. It
would be announcing that it did not recognize "Italy's right
to live as she believes indispensable to her destinies." These
were the fears, he concluded, which, "despite ourselves, your
ultramontane party, your legitimists, inspire in us."[8] The
foreign minister's observations were echoed in the *Libertà*.
The militant Destra sheet bluntly accused Thiers of pursuing
a tortuous policy similar to that of Napoleon III and volunteered the following advice to Versailles:

> France has not gained the sympathies of civilized nations. Let her
> government initiate an honest and sincere policy, inspired by the strength
> of her rights and by respect for those of others, a policy which unites order
> with freedom . . . . and she will acquire that prestige and influence which
> a misguided party pretends to find in the discussion of Catholic petitions
> or in the restoration of the House of Bourbon.[9]

Such an admonition, retorted the *Diritto*, would prove futile.
France was the common enemy of Italy and Germany. She
was determined to reconquer the Rhineland and re-establish
the pope as the sovereign of Rome. She was, to boot, the
champion of clericalism and reaction. She could not, therefore, be the friend of Italy.[10] But the leftist journal was hardly doing justice to Thiers's unfailing realism. On April 6 he
wrote Fournier: "I would not have made . . . . either Italian
or German unity. But it is another matter to make or un-
make. Italy exists as a national entity and I shall not bring
any trouble into Europe in order to abrogate events of such
importance." Fournier was to make this clear to Victor Emmanuel. At the same time the Italian monarch was to be

---

[8] *DDF* (1st ser.), I, No. 119, 138.

[9] *Libertà*, April 5, 1872.   [10] *Diritto*, April 19, 1872.

cautioned that a war against his ally of 1859 would be a piece of dangerous folly, since fortune was a variable thing and France "is or will be as strong as ever."[11] Visconti-Venosta lost little time in disabusing Thiers on this score. On April 19 he seized a propitious moment to declare in the chamber: "All the powers give us proof of a moderation which serves to facilitate the policy of peace to which the government strenuously adheres." Italy, he went on, "has endeavored to show . . . . that the religious independence of the pontiff was a reality in which all Europe could repose its faith." She wished to prove that she was steadfast in respecting the papacy as a spiritual institution even when her energies were engaged in consolidating her territorial unity. The Catholic governments had manifested their solicitude for the religious interests of the Holy See and were eager to see the pope treated with every indulgence. But their language had invariably been most friendly, and they had been unanimous in welcoming the possibility of cordial relations with Italy.[12]

The prevailing distrust of France was mirrored in the chamber debate of May 14 on the foreign office budget. The *enfant terrible* of the occasion was the Sinistra deputy, Miceli. He charged that France was supporting the clericals and exploiting Catholic sentiment in the hope of achieving supremacy in Europe. This policy, he continued, "is a challenge to us, a permanent threat to the existence of our country." As long as France remained wedded to it, Italy would have to seek safety in certain precautions. Happily, other nations were friendly. There was, of course, Germany. She, at the moment, was engaged in a war to the knife against that ultramontanism which was Italy's principal enemy. "Here we see," he continued, "an identity of interests and aims." France and Germany were destined some day to come to blows, and Italy could not avoid taking sides. Between the

[11] *DDF* (1st ser.), I, No. 120, 139.

[12] *Atti*, CLXXXIII (April 19, 1872), 1605.

clerical and liberal programs, there was no middle position.[13]
He blamed the weak policy of Visconti-Venosta for the long
delay of France in filling the post at the Quirinal. He called
on the foreign minister to explain the true nature of Franco-
Italian relations. He demanded to know whether the government at Versailles, in sending Fournier to Rome, had frankly
and unconditionally recognized the new political order in
Italy or had made the customary exasperating reservations.
He closed with a request for light on the relations with Germany, whose struggle against ultramontanism Italy would
some day be obliged to emulate.[14] With his usual tact and
economy of language, Visconti-Venosta replied that Italy's
relations with France were "friendly and quite satisfactory."
Fournier, on arriving in Rome, had declared that his government was eager to consolidate Franco-Italian amity. This
feeling was fully reciprocated by the Lanza cabinet. "Italy,"
the foreign minister proclaimed with impressive solemnity,
"is content, now that she has fulfilled her destinies. She demands nothing more. She entertains hostile plans against no
one. She needs above all peace, tranquillity, security, in
order to reorganize and develop the elements of her strength
and her prosperity. She cannot desire a policy which runs
directly counter to this supreme interest." Italy, he went on,
was on "excellent" terms with Germany. The common resistance of the two countries to the claims of the ultramontane party "offers a new basis for their friendly relations."[15]

Visconti-Venosta's remarks on this occasion were applauded by moderates in France. The Italian government, Mazade
observed, was avoiding an adventuresome policy because it
wished to remain in Rome. It had shown Europe that the
pope could safely reside in the capital of Italy. It was wisely
reluctant to heed the counsels of those who were demanding
a formal alliance with Germany directed against France.[16]

[13] *Ibid.*, May 14, 1872, pp. 2111-12.

[14] *Ibid.*, pp. 2113-14.   [15] *Ibid.*, pp. 2120-21.

[16] *Revue des deux mondes*, June 1, 1872, pp. 709-10.

The foreign minister's laconic address was treated with scant deference by the Sinistra;[17] but it was heartening to those of his compatriots who, despite the ominous and provocative activity of French clericals and legitimists, had persisted in espousing a *rapprochement* with the Third Republic. Conspicuous among these staunch Francophils was Carlo Bon-Compagni, a moderate of the Cavourian stamp. From September, 1871, to February, 1872, he had published in the *Opinione* a series of letters on Italo-French relations. His arguments in favor of amity between the two nations had ranged over a variety of themes. France, he had declared, could not recall either the legitimist, Orleanist, or Bonapartist dynasty because each of them would be unable to obtain universal confidence.[18] Moreover, the republic in France would be a threat to no one. Consequently, Italy's relations with the rulers of that country ought to be such as would not hinder them in their work of eliminating political reaction.[19] Bon-Compagni had also alluded to the "liberal and conciliatory policy" of Thiers and had urged that Italy do nothing to disturb that policy.[20] He had reminded his countrymen of the services rendered by France in 1859.[21] He had summoned the latter, in turn, to divest herself of old prejudices and resentments where Italy was concerned,[22] and he had strongly protested against the activity of his Francophobe compatriots who were picturing her as the inevitable foe of Italy. His aim, he had explained, was to show that between France and Italy no reason for enmity existed which could withstand dispassionate scrutiny.[23] Now, in the May and June issues of the *Nuova antologia*, he published two more letters on the same subject. In the second of these he asserted that there was now a strong inclination among his

---

[17] Cf. the *Riforma*, May 17, 1872.

[18] Carlo Bon-Compagni, *Francia e Italia: lettere politiche* (Torino, 1873), pp. 9–10.

[19] *Ibid.*, pp. 14–15.   [21] *Ibid.*, p. 28.

[20] *Ibid.*, p. 23.   [22] *Ibid.*, p. 44.   [23] *Ibid.*, p. 113.

countrymen to be friendly to France. He posed as the sole
condition of Italo-French amity the willingness of each of
these nations to recognize the right of the other to govern
itself. He found it quite natural that the French should concern themselves with the pope's fate, but he warned that
those who were kindling vain hopes at the Vatican were compromising the real interests of the Holy See. He expressed
the belief that France herself, as well as Italy and the rest of
Europe, stood to gain from a triumph of liberalism within
her borders.[24]

Italian public opinion, however, had turned momentarily
to the most recent phase of the conflict between Germany
and the Vatican. Early in May, Pius rejected the appointment of Cardinal Hohenlohe as German ambassador to the
Holy See.[25] The pontiff's drastic action was dictated by several considerations. The eminent German prelate, a brother of
Prince Hohenlohe, the future chancellor, was suspected of
harboring conciliatory views on the Roman question. He
passed as an opponent of the Jesuits, who were in the ascendant at the Vatican.[26] It was rumored that Bismarck hoped to
influence through him the deliberations of the next papal
conclave. Above all, the appointment of ecclesiastics as the
diplomatic representatives of foreign powers at the Vatican
was deemed prejudicial to the sovereign status of the Holy
See. The Curia professed to know that the Italian government, which was notoriously opposed to a double diplomatic
representation in Rome, had been attempting to persuade
the powers to accredit only one political agent to king and
pope. Were Bismarck's example to be followed by other governments, and were ecclesiastics instead of laymen to be accredited to the papal court, this object, it was feared, would

---

[24] *Nuova antologia*, June, 1872, pp. 309, 311, 312.

[25] Cf. Ed. Hüsgen, *Ludwig Windthorst: sein Leben, sein Wirken* (Köln, 1911),
pp. 122-23; Adalbert Wahl, *Deutsche Geschichte von der Reichsgründung bis zum
Ausbruch des Weltkriegs* (Stuttgart, 1926), I, 166.

[26] Wahl, *op. cit.*, I, 164.

ultimately be achieved.[27] The applause with which the Italian press greeted the report of Cardinal Hohenlohe's appointment seemed to confirm the Vatican's suspicions.[28] The
ministerial organs were unanimous in hailing Bismarck's
gesture as a first step toward the complete abolition of the
diplomatic corps accredited to the Holy See. The *Opinione*
declared that the chancellor, in naming a cardinal to this
post, had indicated the manner in which relations between
the powers and the papacy should hereafter be conducted.
Now that the Holy Father was no longer a temporal ruler, it
was better to send ecclesiastics to his court, for a foreign
legate to the Vatican was in no proper sense a diplomatic representative; his mission necessarily was confined to spiritual
matters.[29] The chagrin of the Italians on learning of the papal
veto of Hohenlohe's appointment can therefore be readily
surmised.[30] They blamed the Jesuits and the French.[31] But
they were still hopeful of making some political capital out
of the incident. They now hazarded the suggestion that the
ambassadors then accredited to the Holy See be replaced by
simple secretaries of legation. The clericals pounced upon
this proposal as another proof of the inadequacy of the law
of guarantees.[32]

[27] *CC*, VI (8th ser.; May 25, 1872), 614-19; Vigo, *op. cit.*, I, 155-56.

[28] According to the *Osservatore romano* (May 18, 1872), the very fact that it was
Bismarck who was proposing the appointment and that Italian liberalism was warmly seconding him in this matter, justified the assumption that a new blow at the
papacy was being prepared. That this blow has been parried signified, therefore, a
great triumph for Catholicism and the church.

[29] *Opinione*, May 10, 1872; cf. also Vigo, *op. cit.*, I, 155. The *Opinione* had for
some time been predicting that eventually the embassies at the Vatican would be
replaced by special agents for ecclesiastical affairs who would be attached to the
legations at the Quirinal (cf. the issues of September 7, 1871, and March 2, 1872).

[30] Cf., e.g., the *Diritto* of May 5, 1872. A year and a half later the Sinistra was
still lamenting the episode. The dispossessed pontiff, declared the *Diritto* on December 22, 1873, had no reason to maintain diplomatic relations with foreign states.

[31] Cf. Georges Goyau, *Bismarck et l'église; le culturkampf* (Paris, 1911-13), I,
283.

[32] Pius himself seized the opportunity to allude once again to the illusory character of the safeguards provided by that statute (Vigo, *op. cit.*, I, 170-71).

Bismarck deeply resented the papal rebuff. He had taken great pains to represent the appointment of Hohenlohe as an indication of his desire for peace with the Curia.[33] He now made no secret of his dissatisfaction. At his bidding, the German ministerial press made a great outcry over this latest instance of papal intractability. The more radical sheets went so far as to urge the government to do away entirely with the embassy at the Vatican. The chancellor, however, could see the drawbacks of such a step and publicly opposed it.[34] But there was another and more effective way of striking back. On May 27, Crown Prince Humbert of Italy and his consort arrived in Berlin to act as godparents at the baptism of the baby daughter of the German Crown Prince and Princess. The ceremony took place on June 4, and two days later the royal visitors departed. The government utilized their presence to proclaim the inevitability of Italo-German solidarity. The semiofficial *Norddeutsche Allgemeine Zeitung* pointed out that the German empire had no choice but to defend its unity against clerical aggression. Italy, which had granted the pope "maximum liberty," was confronted with a similar problem. This community of interests was fittingly signalized by the friendly reception accorded the distinguished guests. Other authoritative newspapers were even more explicit in their allusions to the danger which threatened the two states. These comments were reproduced with keen satisfaction by the Italian and notably the Sinistra press. The *Diritto* enlarged upon the cordial welcome which Berlin had extended to the princely couple. It emphasized that these manifestations of good will were addressed to Victor Emmanuel and to the Italian people. The latter, it went on, knew how to appreciate all this. But the same was not true of the Destra, which claimed to represent Italy and yet stood in continuous awe of France.[35] The Holy See was much annoyed. It pronounced the *rapprochement* of its principal

---

[33] *GW*, VI*c*, No. 23, 18.

[34] *SB*, XXIV (May 14, 1872), 355–56.   [35] *Diritto*, June 2, 1872.

foes not at all surprising, inasmuch as both of them were honeycombed with corruption and immorality.[36] But it professed to believe that their present intimacy would not be of long duration.[37] In any case—so reasoned high Vatican circles—the latest turn of affairs had helped to clarify the situation. "At last," the *Civiltà cattolica* remarked, "Italian liberalism has removed its mask. It has openly declared that its war is against Catholicism . . . . because it is against the authority of the pope." Italian eagerness to secure the alliance of Germany accounted for this unabashed disclosure of aims. The Jesuit organ went on to predict that the Italo-German understanding would bring disaster to both countries. Italy had definitely aligned herself with the enemies of France. Should war ensue, the latter would have little difficulty in wrecking the young kingdom, Germany notwithstanding. And after Italy had been disposed of, Germany's turn would come.[38]

If such a disconsolate fate awaited the adversaries of the Holy See, Bismarck apparently did not know it. He did know, however, that French ultramontanism was a menace to German as well as to Italian unity, and it was clear to him that Germany could not remain passive in the event of a Franco-Italian war.[39] He had the satisfaction of seeing Italy draw ever closer to Germany as the French clericals continued to importune their government. Heartening indeed to the chancellor was the mounting energy with which certain influential circles at Rome were pressing for a strengthening

---

[36] Cf. the *Osservatore romano*, June 2, 1872.

[37] The *Osservatore romano* had for some time been contending that there were too many disparities between the two nations to permit any sort of permanent alliance (cf. the issues of April 19 and 20, 1872). This the *Libertà* emphatically denied. It insisted that the Italo-German friendship would be lasting. Berlin and Rome were drawn together by "common interests and common aspirations." Their amity was that of two peoples "who wish only to fight the battle of civilization and progress" (cf. the issue of June 7, 1872).

[38] *CC*, VII (8th ser.; July 19, 1872), 243, 257–58, 261, 262, 269, 270.

[39] Cf. Karl Bachem, *Vorgeschichte Geschichte und Politik der deutschen Zentrumspartei* (Köln, 1927), III, 216–18.

of the Italian army by way of reply to the French threat.[40] He could afford to smile at the predicament of Thiers, whose ingenuity and resourcefulness seemed wasted on the arduous task of simultaneously placating the pope and currying favor with the Italian government. The veteran chief executive was repeatedly explaining now to one, now to the other, that France could be of service to both by counseling moderation. But his ultramontane countrymen made short work of his hope of securing a respite from this trying business. Rightist deputies were announcing to their constituencies that, within a year, France would take up arms to re-establish the territorial sovereignty of the Holy Father.[41] Bishops were once again sponsoring petitions demanding the restoration of the temporal power.[42] Early in October, Lourdes was the scene of the first of a series of national pilgrimages which turned out to be mighty demonstrations in behalf of the papal cause.[43] In a letter, which one of his followers made public at this time, the Count of Chambord again proclaimed the intimate nexus between legitimism and the Holy See.[44]

These manifestations created a painful impression in Italy, where for sometime the complaint had been voiced that the government at Versailles was once again resorting to a policy of pinpricks. The *Diritto* had been by far the loudest complainant. This mouthpiece of the Sinistra militants, accused by the Destra press of envenoming Franco-Italian relations, had accepted the challenge with gusto. It had strongly underlined its duty to combat the Italophobe maneuvers of France. It had reminded the country that the vote of July 22, 1871, had not been repudiated.[45] Its anti-

---

[40] The principal mouthpiece of these circles was the *Libertà* (cf. the issues of July 6 and August 18, 1872).

[41] Cf. *Revue des deux mondes*, September 15, 1872, p. 501.

[42] Gabriel Hanotaux, *Histoire de la France contemporaine* (Paris, 1903–8), I, 491.

[43] A. Debidour, *L'Eglise catholique et l'état sous la Troisième République* (Paris, 1906), I, 66.

[44] Cf. *Schulthess, 1872*, p. 424.   [45] *Diritto*, September 12, 1872.

French attitude, it had replied to critics, was due to the unceasing interference of the republic in Italian affairs.[46] Annoying indeed to sensitive Italians was the action of Thiers in assigning a military attaché to the Vatican. This gesture, which had the appearance of a poor joke at the expense of the armyless pontiff, was bitterly resented as an oblique recognition of the temporal power.[47] Even more exasperating was an incident which had just occurred in Paris. In June, 1870, the international metric commission had convened in that city. All the countries had sent delegates to it. Father Angelo Secchi, the famous astronomer, had represented the papacy. The outbreak of the Franco-Prussian War had brought a suspension of its sessions, which were not resumed until October, 1872. The French government had notified the Quirinal and the Vatican that the commission was to reconvene, and both sent their representatives. Father Secchi again served as the delegate of the Holy See, and he was treated by the French government in exactly the same manner as all the other delegates. The learned Jesuit, whose reappearance at this international gathering grated upon Italian sensibilities, made things no easier by styling himself the emissary of the "sovereign state of the church." Matters came to a head at the closing session when the various participants were invited to sign the record of the proceedings. The senior Italian delegate read a formal statement which declared in part:

Our government, in view of the fact that the Holy See is now only a spiritual power and not a state according to European public law, has ordered my colleague and myself to take no part in any act in which Father Secchi should figure as the representative of the Holy See.[48]

Nigra was instructed to demand an explanation from Rémusat. The latter sought to make amends in a conciliatory note addressed to the Italian minister. It was to be hoped, he

46 *Ibid.*, September 17, 1872.   47 Cf. Wahl, *op. cit.*, I, 25.

48 Cf. *Atti*, CLXXXV (November 27, 1872), 3391; cf. also, on the incident of the international metric commission, the *Libertà* of October 22, 1872.

wrote, that this incident, which in itself was of no great moment, would not be allowed to engender any misunderstanding between the two countries. The Italian government, he continued, was apparently fearful that the affair might be regarded as creating a precedent which could be invoked on similar occasions in the future. France, however, was ready to give the most positive assurances that she had not the slightest intention of viewing the episode in this light.[49]

The Italian government professed itself satisfied and declared the incident closed.[50] The *Opinione*, its faithful mouthpiece, had only words of praise for the line taken by Lanza and his colleagues.[51] But other moderate organs refused to be so easily satisfied. The *Libertà* alluded to the incident as ample proof of French hostility toward Italy. It conceded that such men as Fournier and Rémusat were friendly and that from time to time French newspapers adopted a friendly tone when speaking of their Italian neighbors. But, unfortunately, these were deceptive symptoms. France, which constituted in reality the center of a world-wide reactionary conspiracy, contained only a minority of Italophils. Under existing circumstances, an Italo-French clash was inescapable. And it therefore behooved Italy to make ready for the eventual conflict.[52] The Sinistra was not disposed to forego so golden an opportunity to berate France and the foreign policy of the cabinet. The government of Thiers was again assailed in the opposition press,[53] and leftist deputies aired their grievances in an acrimonious chamber debate late in November. Again it was Miceli who led the assault. He charged that the French government had "gratuitously inflicted a serious affront upon Italy." It had perpetrated an outrage which signified nothing less than "the negation of one of our

[49] *Atti*, CLXXXV (November 27, 1872), 3392.

[50] Luigi Chiala, *Dal 1858 al 1892: pagine di storia contemporanea* (Torino, 1892–93), I, 125–26; Vigo, *op. cit.*, I, 201.

[51] *Opinione*, October 22, 1872.

[52] *Libertà*, October 23, 1872.   [53] Cf., e.g., *Riforma*, October 23, 1872.

most sacred rights, that of our national integrity, of our possession of Rome, the capital of Italy." It was now clear even
to those who had hoped for a change of heart on the part of
France that their expectations were entirely vain. "All
Europe and our enemies were able to see," he wailed, "that
in the opinion of the French republic, Rome still belongs to
the pope." Visconti-Venosta and his lieutenant at Paris,
Nigra, were directly responsible for this deplorable state of
affairs. The foreign minister, he claimed, was docile and
yielding to the point of jeopardizing the interests of his country. In the end, this abjectness would only sow new seeds of
dissension between the two nations.[54] Addressing himself to
Italo-papal relations, Miceli censured the government for its
allegedly indulgent attitude toward the Vatican. The cabinet, he asserted, was seeking a reconciliation with the church
at any price, however ruinous. And, in courting the favor of
the clericals, it was transforming Italy into a satellite of ultramontane France.[55]

Miceli was followed by other unsparing critics of the government. But the language of Deputy Musolino surpassed in
virulence that of all his predecessors. He vehemently denied
that the attitude of France had undergone any change for
the better with the arrival of Fournier. He substantiated this
contention by enumerating some recent instances of French
hostility. He recalled Thiers's address of July 22, 1871. The
French national assembly, he warned, "has imposed upon
its cabinet the obligation of restoring the temporal power of
the pope. The president of the republic has accepted this
obligation, asking only for freedom in the choice of means and
time. . . . . The ultimatum which will be put to us will be:
evacuation of Rome or war!" Hostilities with France were
therefore inevitable. After she had rid herself of the German troops of occupation and set up a permanent govern-

54 *Atti*, CLXXXV (November 25, 1872), 3321-24.
55 *Ibid.*, pp. 3324-26.

ment, she would draw the sword. And Italy, rather than the Prussians, would be her first victim.[56]

Visconti-Venosta replied with his usual effectiveness. He began by reminding his adversaries that the Catholic governments had a very legitimate interest in the fate of the Roman question. The papacy had relations with the Catholics of all countries, and this fact could not be blinked. Italy, he went on, must not play into the hands of the ultramontanes by acting imprudently. It was her cue to force them into the open and bare their true objective: to precipitate a European war in order to restore the temporal power. The world must be made to see them as they really were—a political party bent upon exploiting religion to subjugate civil society. It was incumbent upon Italy to forestall their attempts to stir up trouble, to deprive them of such favorite talking-points as the "threatened" freedom of the pope. This she was actually doing. Such a policy, he caustically observed, could scarcely be termed a clerical one; and it very effectively disposed of the charge that the cabinet was overindulgent with the Vatican. Adverting to the major issue of the debate, he declared: "Our relations with all the powers are entirely satisfactory. All the governments . . . . have apprised us of their desire to continue on friendly terms with Italy." Peace, he proclaimed, "is and always will be" one of Italy's "great and permanent interests." Her cause "is identical with that of liberty in Europe."[57] His allusion to Italo-German solidarity vis-à-vis the threat of ultramontanism was received with approval on both sides of the house.

We . . . . are involved in a great question which . . . . has raised against us a formidable party in Europe, a party which seeks almost everywhere to seize power. There is a great nation . . . . which says to us: We watch with sympathy your work of political consolidation, we ask only that you continue to be the arbiters of your domestic problems and a pillar of peace and order in Europe. Our own troubles with the party that is your enemy enable us to appreciate your internal difficulties. . . . .

[56] *Ibid.*, November 26, 1872, pp. 3347–50; November 27, 1872, pp. 3357–8.

[57] *Ibid.*, November 27, 1872, pp. 3387–88.

It was therefore natural, Visconti-Venosta went on, that Italy should cultivate good relations with that nation. He dwelt with satisfaction on the recent visit of the Crown Prince and Princess to Berlin. The reception given them on that occasion constituted another testimonial of Italo-German cordiality.[58] Turning to Franco-Italian relations, he vigorously impugned the veracity of the press in reporting all sorts of serious difficulties between the two Latin nations. These stories, he charged, were "more or less fantastic inventions." Actually, France and Italy were on good terms. When incidents did occasionally arise, the two governments invariably handled them "in a spirit of conciliation." The French had utilized every suitable opportunity to impress upon Italy their desire to remove all grounds for misunderstanding and to consolidate the friendship with her. France, he admitted, had expressed the hope that the Italian government would continue to treat the pope with moderation, but this she had done with the utmost reserve and good will. Italy, too, was not animated by any hostility toward France. It was her aim to maintain "those good . . . . relations which conform to the memories of the past." Whatever uneasiness she experienced sprang solely from the fact that there was in France a clerical party more powerful than its counterparts elsewhere.[59]

One of Italy's principal grievances against the French government was the retention of the "Orénoque" in the waters of Civita Vecchia. It had originally been stationed there, as has already been related,[60] to aid the pontiff and take him aboard should he decide to abandon Rome. There it had remained ever since the summer of 1870, despite the plain determination of the Holy Father to stay where he was. As a result, the conviction had become general in the peninsula that the failure to recall the frigate was motivated more by a desire to annoy Italy than to serve the interests of the papa-

---

[58] *Ibid.*, p. 3389.   [59] *Ibid.*, pp. 3390–92.   [60] Cf. p. 23.

cy. This conviction found its strongest expression in the columns of the Sinistra press. The "Orénoque" had nothing to do at Civita Vecchia, the *Diritto* declared on one occasion. The pope was free to go where and when he pleased. True it was that the presence of the vessel in Italian waters did not violate international law. All the states, for example, maintained ships in South American ports. But this they were doing, the leftist journal pointed out, in order to protect citizens residing in revolution-torn areas. In Italy, on the other hand, there were no such interests to defend.[61] It was inescapable, therefore, that the "Orénoque" should become in the eyes of Italians the symbol of French hostility to their recently achieved unity. In the words of the *Diritto*, its protracted presence in Italian waters constituted "a permanent insult to our sovereignty and a continuous protest against the Italian character of Rome."[62] To some, indeed, this floating outpost of the republic was "a kind of recognition . . . . of the survival of the temporal power."[63] An incident late in 1872 revealed the explosive potentialities of the situation. The previous year, the officers of the "Orénoque" had gone to Rome during the Christmas holidays to call on the Holy Father. No similar courtesy had been shown the Quirinal, much to the annoyance of the Italians. The French government now decided to rectify matters. On December 21, Rémusat wrote to the French ambassador at the Vatican:

> The commander of the "Orénoque" will go first to present his respects to the Vatican and pay a visit to the embassy. Then he will put everything in order with the government of the king and the French legation. This is only the discharge of duties recognized everywhere. In a dual situation, there is a dual obligation.[64]

[61] *Diritto*, September 1, 1872.   [62] *Ibid.*, August 30, 1872.

[63] Veuillot, among others, helped to keep this attitude alive. He viewed the "Orénoque" as an arm of France extended protectingly toward the Vatican, as if to warn the Italians: "Non plus ultra" (Camillo Manfroni, *Sulla soglia del Vaticano* [Bologna, 1920], I, 185).

[64] DDF (1st ser.), I, No. 160, 192.

Count Bourgoing, Harcourt's successor at Rome, was incensed by this proposed deference to the Quirinal. He protested that the officers of the "Orénoque" were under no obligation to take any notice of Fournier. Insisting that he would be no party to this transaction, he announced his resignation. The Vatican was profoundly disturbed, and Antonelli assured the irate ambassador that Pius would refuse to make use of the frigate should the scheduled visit to the king take place. Impressed by the seriousness of the situation, the French government yielded. The instructions to the officers were revoked, and the latter were ordered to return immediately to Civita Vecchia.[65] But Bourgoing refused to be placated, and on December 28 he left Rome.

The news of Bourgoing's resignation created a considerable stir in Italian leftist and clerical circles. The *Riforma* charged that France, though compelled to recognize Italy as a great power, was hoping before long to take revenge and engineer the triumph of the papal cause.[66] The *Diritto* adduced the incident as further proof of French hatred. The identity of those who happened to govern the republic was inconsequential, it contended. For whoever ruled that restless state could be only the enemy of Italy.[67] The clericals hailed Bourgoing as a hero and master strategist in one. His resignation, remarked the *Voce della verità*, had frustrated the "little Nigra-Visconti-Fournier intrigue."[68] The *Osservatore romano* assured its readers that lovers of justice throughout Europe were unanimous in praising Bourgoing; and it published an address conveying to the count the gratitude and admiration of the Catholics of Rome.[69] The *Unità cattolica* lauded the former ambassador's "most noble conduct," which

[65] *Ibid.*, p. 192, n. 2; *Journal des débats*, December 28, 1872; R. P. Lecanuet, *Les dernières anneés du pontificat de Pie IX, 1870–1878* (Paris, 1931), p. 166.

[66] *Riforma*, January 5, 1873.

[67] *Diritto*, December 29, 1872.

[68] *Voce della verità*, January 1, 1873.

[69] *Osservatore romano*, January 3 and 5, 1873.

contrasted so markedly with Thiers's "act of weakness and
. . . . cruelty vis-à-vis the Holy Father."[70]

Bourgoing's gesture gave rise to widely different reactions
in France. According to the *Temps*, the incident demonstrated the difficulty, not to say the impossibility, of domiciling
in Rome two diplomatic representatives whose divergence of
outlook inevitably exposed them to incessant conflicts. As for
the "Orénoque," it was hard to see why it should be kept at
Civita Vecchia when the probability of the pope's departure
was becoming increasingly remote.[71] It would have been
contrary to all international usage, the *Journal des débats*
claimed, to deny the king of Italy the homage paid the pope
by the officers of the "Orénoque." Both Pius and Bourgoing
had refused to recognize this equality of attributes. So
much, however, was indubitable: the kingdom of Italy existed and the king of Italy was in Rome. This might displease certain parties, but the French government had no
choice but to acknowledge "an order of things which rests,
like itself, on the will and sovereignty of a nation."[72] Mazade
expressed little sympathy for Bourgoing. He pointed out
that, ever since the recognition by France of the *fait accompli*
at Rome, her ambassador to the pope had become simply a
species of honorary plenipotentiary, symbolizing the veneration of his country for the head of the Catholic church. The
real representation of French interests had passed to the legation at the Quirinal. In any case, Bourgoing was not in Rome
in order to play the game of the enemies of Italian unity.
And the French government would have to be careful to send
no more men of his ilk to the Vatican.[73] Moreover, it was
foolish to believe that the situation in the Italian capital
could be altered by a display of ill feeling. Bourgoing's rash

[70] *Unità cattolica*, December 28 and 31, 1872.

[71] *Temps*, December 28, 1872.

[72] *Journal des débats*, January 5, 1873.

[73] *Revue des deux mondes*, January 1, 1873, p. 219.

resignation could only be a source of embarrassment for his own government.[74]

The republicans were profuse in their declamations against the propapal sympathies of the self-removed envoy. No one, averred the *République française*, would regret the departure of a diplomatic agent who was so close to the clerical party.[75] "France cannot and does not wish to recommence the disastrous expedition of 1849," it proclaimed. "She does not intend to re-embark upon that fatal intervention .... which has been the origin and first cause of all our misfortunes."[76] The French embassy at the Vatican was "an altogether honorific burden." The minister to Victor Emmanuel ought to supplant his colleague at the Vatican in all political and diplomatic matters affecting Franco-Italian relations. There was only one sovereign in Italy—the king.[77] The *Siècle*, after vigorously defending Fournier, called the attention of its readers to the realities of the existing situation. "The temporal power no longer exists," it reiterated. Acceptance of this obvious fact also involved acceptance of its consequences. Bourgoing's resignation would not aid the papal cause. It would, however, serve the intrigues of monarchists in France.[78] Thiers could make but one reply: to send no other ambassador to the Holy See and to recall the members of the embassy there. Ambassadors, after all, were the political representatives of temporal governments. There was no longer a temporal government of the pope. And there were therefore no political relations to maintain with the Vatican.[79]

The Orleanists preferred not to go into the merits of the Bourgoing-Fournier controversy. This "regrettable incident," they permitted themselves to point out, ought to serve as a lesson. France was not justified in having two diplomatic agents abroad who spent their time quarreling

---

[74] *Ibid.*, January 15, 1873, p. 462.

[75] *République française*, December 29, 1872.

[76] *Ibid.*, January 2, 1873.

[77] *Ibid.*, January 3 and 4, 1873.

[78] *Siècle*, December 28, 1872.

[79] *Ibid.*, December 29, 1872.

with each other. It was the duty of the foreign office to settle
all such disputes privately. Certainly, they ought not to be
aired in public.[80] The clericals exploited the episode with
gusto. They deluged the former ambassador with congratu-
latory messages and loudly berated his superiors. The *Univers* renewed its attacks on Fournier and threatened the
government with dire reprisals. "All has not been said,"
Veuillot warned, "for the assembly will have to acquaint itself with this quarrel and pass judgment on it." The members
of that body had not been the ones to send to the Quirinal
this "deadly man whose slightest acts are a scandal." The
time had come to ascertain whether the government of the
"chivalrous and Catholic nation" was really on the side of
injustice.[81] One thing, however, was already clear. Bourgoing's "generous behavior" had thwarted the scheme of
Thiers and the Italian cabinet to liquidate the Roman question.[82] The *Monde*, which extolled the "Orénoque" as "a
last link between the sovereign pontiff and the civilized
world,"[83] enlarged upon the conflict between the "principles"
of Bourgoing and Fournier. The former represented the
"Christian policy," the latter, the "revolutionary policy."
The first, beloved of the pope, was being sacrificed. The second, an enemy of the Holy See, was being maintained at his
post. France was now giving the head of the church only "a
disarmed ambassador and a vessel on which to flee." This
was indeed very little, but it was still too much for the present rulers of the country.[84] The legitimists seized the opportunity to proclaim their solidarity with the ultramontanes.
They conceded that the disasters of the last war made it impossible for the time being to give more effective aid to the
pope. But they were most insistent that France eschew any
act or obligation which might imply approval of recent events

[80] Cf. *Journal de Paris*, December 29, 1872.

[81] *Univers*, December 28, 1872.

[82] *Ibid.*, January 1, 1873.   [83] *Monde*, December 28, 1872.

[84] *Ibid.*, December 29, 1872, and January 16, 1873.

in Italy. They accused the government of Thiers of wishing to emulate the underhanded policy of Napoleon III. In refusing to lend himself to that policy, they contended, Bourgoing had behaved as a "man of courage" and had furnished a "noble example."[85] He had acquired "an imperishable claim to the esteem of Catholics." And he had rendered France a great service as well by giving her a timely warning.[86] The following address to the hero of the day appeared in the *Union:*

> You have given to Catholic France a great example of national faith and personal independence. You teach Europe the rank which the sovereignty of the pope must hold. Your retirement is a most striking disavowal of the policy which abandoned the Holy Father to spoliation and insult. We beg you to receive the homage which we offer you as the guardian of the traditions of France, always worthy of being the well-beloved daughter of the church.[87]

The Bonapartists thoroughly sympathized with the attitude of the clerical-legitimist faction on this occasion. Bourgoing, they asserted, had refused to subscribe to "conditions humiliating for Catholics and for the Holy Father." The question at hand was to determine whether France was so republican as to forget that she was Catholic or so weak as to make concessions to the tyrannical Italian government which had victimized the supreme pontiff.[88]

The position of Thiers was distinctly unenviable. His relations with the parties of the right had of late been steadily growing worse, and this incident appeared to be ushering in the climacteric crisis. On January 7, General du Temple and Baron Belcastel, leading ultramontane members of the national assembly, filed notice of their intention to interpellate the government. The outcome of this discussion, which moderates deprecated in advance as wholly pointless,[89] would, it

---

[85] *Gazette de France*, December 29, 1872.

[86] *Union*, December 28, 1872.

[87] *Ibid.*, December 30, 1872.

[88] Cf. the *Pays*, December 29, 1872.

[89] Cf. *Journal des débats*, January 8, 1873.

seemed, determine Theirs's fate.[90] So strained did Franco-papal relations become that the appointment of Bourgoing's successor encountered real difficulties.[91] The president, however, proved equal to the situation. He sent Baron des Michels, an able diplomatist who had served as secretary of the embassy at the Vatican, to Rome with the mission of ascertaining the real state of affairs. After some rather desultory maneuvering by both sides, Thiers suggested that the pope select the new ambassador from a hand-picked list of four persons acceptable to the Holy See. Pius assented, and M. de Corcelles, a *persona gratissima* at the Vatican, was awarded the post.[92] But the government's difficulties were far from over. On January 12 a deputation representing the clerical-monarchist members of the national assembly called on the president and asked for an explanation of Bourgoing's action. In his reply, Thiers reiterated in some detail his views on Franco-Italian relations and the Roman question. He repeated that he too had favored the maintenance of the temporal power and regretted the unification of Italy. But it was imperative to face existing realities, which could be modified only by resorting to war. As for himself, he was determined to do nothing which might precipitate a conflict. The best interests of France dictated amicable relations with Italy. Did they, the members of the deputation, wish to push Italy into the arms of Bismarck, who was seeking an alliance with her? The French government respected the rights of the Holy See and wished to see the pope's independence preserved, but accomplished facts had to be recognized, and therefore nothing would be done to alienate Victor Emmanuel and his cabinet.[93]

Thiers hoped that the fulness of his statement might deter

---

[90] Hanotaux, *op. cit.*, I, 544.

[91] Cf. Lieutenant-Colonel Rousset, *La République conservatrice* (Paris, 1914), I, 430–31.

[92] Lecanuet, *op. cit.*, pp. 166–68; Hanotaux, *op. cit.*, I, 544–45.

[93] *Schulthess, 1873*, pp. 292–93; *Times*, January 14, 1873.

the clerical-monarchist deputies from going ahead with their
announced interpellation. But the champions of the papal
cause were not to be so easily shunted. On January 15 they
finally had their inning in the national assembly. Their
spokesman on this occasion was Belcastel. He contended
that the "Orénoque," which was a sort of "maritime extension" of the French embassy at the Vatican, enjoyed an
"absolutely exceptional" status. If Bourgoing had been ordered to felicitate the king of Italy, how, he asked, would
public opinion have reacted? The "Orénoque," which was
inseparable from the embassy, "must follow the same law."
He next inquired whether the incident was any indication
that the respectful and protective attitude hitherto assumed
toward the papacy was to be abandoned. "This protectorate
over the independence of the Holy See," he declared, "is very
dear to us. We regard it as more than ever necessary in view
of the present state of the world, in view of the particular
situation of France."[94] In the absence of Rémusat who was
ill, Dufaure, the keeper of the seals, undertook to answer
Belcastel. The instructions given the officers of the "Orénoque," he insisted, were intended only as a mark of courtesy
to a sovereign in whose waters a French warship was stationed. They portended no change in French policy toward
the Holy See. He defended the dual diplomatic representation in Rome. It was dictated, he contended, by very legitimate political considerations. No duplicity was involved.
The situation did, however, bristle with difficulties, and every
care had to be taken not to aggravate them. He reminded
the clericals that the present discussion might create serious
embarrassments for the government. If any confidence were
still reposed in the cabinet and in Corcelles, he pleaded, issues
such as these ought not be exploited for political advantage.[95]

The legitimists were unanimous in heaping extravagant
praise upon Belcastel. Dufaure, on the other hand, was
sharply censured for his failure to declare explicitly that

[94] *AAN*, XV (January 15, 1873), 150.   [95] *Ibid.*, pp. 151–52.

France's present Roman policy was a necessary evil and nothing else. This debate, the *Union* predicted, would be a useful warning to Thiers and a source of hope for the Catholics of France and of the world.[96] The *Gazette de France* observed that France was not yet ready to forget that in unifying Italy she had lost her high position in Europe. And she remembered too that her reward had been "the most unqualifiable ingratitude" on the part of the beneficiaries. Never, indeed, had France had more reason than now to show Italy "only a mediocre sympathy."[97] The ultramontanes accused Thiers of continuing the treacherous Roman policy of Napoleon III. "The last vestige of the recognition of the territorial rights of the papacy is being obliterated," wailed the *Univers*.[98] The *Monde* scored Dufaure's reply as "a vague declaration . . . . which clarifies nothing of the past and guarantees nothing for the future." Belcastel's protest, on the other hand, was eloquent and convincing.[99] The republicans loudly denounced the language of Belcastel, whose interpellation, they charged, was only calculated to keep alive Italian distrust of France. But their ire was directed primarily against the government. Dufaure, insisted the *République française*, should have been more emphatic in disavowing the remarks of the Catholic spokesman. His reply was "most inadequate and unfortunate." It revealed all too clearly a desire to indulge "the clerical passions" of the assembly.[100] The *Siècle* complained that Dufaure's address indicated no change in French policy vis-à-vis Italy.[101] Moderate opinion deeply deplored Belcastel's interpellation. But even more revolting to it was the campaign now launched by the ultramontanes to secure the recall of Fournier and a severance of diplomatic relations with Italy. Mazade warned

[96] *Union*, January 17, 1873.

[97] *Gazette de France*, January 17, 1873.

[98] *Univers*, January 17, 1873.

[99] *Monde*, January 17, 1873.

[100] *République française*, January 17, 1873.   [101] *Siècle*, January 17, 1873.

that Thiers, should he be further importuned, could bring the question before the national assembly and the country. He could ask the clericals whether they really wished to break with Italy and were prepared to face the consequences.[102]

The parliamentary repercussions of the Bourgoing affair were followed with feverish attention in Italy. The Sinistra, commenting on Dufaure's speech, urged the government to take a strong line and resist French "tyranny." The *Riforma* assailed Lanza and his colleagues for their failure to send the "Orénoque" back to France two years earlier. That vessel, it continued, had absolutely nothing to do at Civita Vecchia. The Italian government was very capable of protecting the spiritual power of the Holy Father.[103] The leftist organ besought the authorities to order the withdrawal of the ship within twenty-four hours, as its continued presence in the national waters was a permanent protest against and an intolerable insult to Italian unity and *Roma capitale*.[104] The Italian clericals discovered another hero in Belcastel. The *Voce della verità* extolled his "generous words." In them was to be found "the ancient love of France for the cause of her faith."[105] The *Osservatore romano* was no less enthusiastic. Belcastel's remarks, it said, were "dignified, frank, and solemn." The great papal organ was at the moment in a rather optimistic mood. On the eve of the Versailles debate, it had even ventured to predict that, before long, the majority of the national assembly would impose upon France a policy more favorable to the Holy See.[106]

The resignation of Bourgoing and the ensuing clamor of his clerical compatriots had the inevitable effect of accentuating the anti-French orientation of Italian foreign policy. Strong pleas for increased armaments once again resounded throughout the peninsula. And there were recurrent reports that an

[102] *Revue des deux mondes*, February 1, 1873, p. 713.

[103] *Riforma*, January 19, 1873.

[104] *Ibid.*, January 25, 1873.   [105] *Voce della verità*, January 22, 1873.

[106] *Osservatore romano*, January 15, 1873.

alliance between Italy and the central powers had been concluded.[107] These rumors, like their predecessors, were without foundation, but they bespoke a mood the significance of which was scarcely to be underestimated. Bismarck, who followed the course of the Italo-French feud with avid interest, was more than ready to strengthen the ties between Italy and Germany. In April he told Launay that he regarded the safety of Italy as one of the axioms of German policy in Europe. An alliance between the two countries was "predestined," he said, because they had the same enemies.[108] He himself helped promote the cause of Italo-German solidarity by appointing Robert von Keudell, formerly his righthand man in the foreign office and reputed to be his intimate and trusted friend, as head of the legation at the Quirinal. The new minister was very well received in Rome,[109] where he remained a popular figure and was regarded as an admirer and friend of the new Italy.[110]

Undeterred by the latest aggravation of Franco-Italian relations, the small but influential band of Italian Francophils continued to work for a *rapprochement* between the two Latin states. The labors of Bon-Compagni, who late in 1872 had resumed his plea for a durable Franco-Italian peace,[111] were materially aided by the persuasive pen of Bonghi. In an important article which appeared in the *Revue des deux mondes*, the famous journalist and statesman put his country's case before the educated classes of the neighboring republic. Italy, he wrote, wished to be the friend of France. She posed only one condition: that her position in Rome remain undisturbed. Catholics could rest assured that their church was

---

[107] Salvemini, "La Politica estera della Destra, 1871–1876," *Rivista d'Italia*, November 15, 1924, p. 370.

[108] *Ibid.*, p. 367.

[109] F. Gregorovius, *The Roman Journals of Ferdinand Gregorovius, 1852–1874* (London, 1907), p. 441.

[110] Cf. Bernhard Fürst von Bülow, *Denkwürdigkeiten* (Berlin, 1931), IV, 324; Ugo Pesci, *I primi anni di Roma capitale* (Firenze, 1907), p. 144.

[111] Bon-Compagni, *op. cit.*, p. 117.

in no danger. The law of guarantees, he complained, had not been adequately appreciated outside of Italy. He ridiculed the charge that it had not achieved its purpose because it had been rejected by the pope. "Since when," he queried, "do laws enacted by a sovereign state have to be accepted by those whom they concern?" Of importance alone was the fact that the statute of May 13, 1871, insured the spiritual freedom and independence of the Holy See.[112]

The endeavors of men like Bon-Compagni and Bonghi were destined, however, to be nullified by the march of events.

[112] R. Bonghi, "Le Gouvernement italien et la papauté," *Revue des deux mondes,* May 1, 1873, pp. 115-40.

CHAPTER IX
THE CHURCH-STATE FEUD CONTINUES

THE termination of papal rule in Rome gave the enemies of the church the opportunity for which they had long been waiting. In January, 1871, the Society of Free Thinkers issued a manifesto to the residents of the city which proclaimed that the destruction of the temporal power did not complete Italy's civilizing mission, that the "lie of religions" had still to be abolished.[1] To the saddened pontiff and his entourage, this was further proof, if any more were needed, of the perfidy of Italy's rulers. The *Civiltà cattolica* observed that the cynicism of this manifesto showed how vain was any hope of an Italo-papal reconciliation.[2] No less trying to the patience of the Vatican was the government's indulgent attitude toward press diatribes against the pope and Catholicism. Particularly galling was the failure of the authorities to forbid the dissemination of Protestant propaganda in Rome.[3] Everywhere, in the opinion of papalists, the forces of darkness seemed in the ascendant.

Immediately after the occupation of Rome, Italian Catholics had rallied to the defense of the Holy Father, without, however, any clearly defined program.[4] But early in February, 1871, Roman clericals took a first step toward remedying this situation when they organized the Society for Catholic

[1] Pietro Vigo, *Storia degli ultimi trent'anni del secolo XIX* (Milano, 1908), I, 6.

[2] *CC*, I (8th ser.; February 6, 1871), 491.

[3] It was reliably reported that those few members of the pope's inner circle who favored a *modus vivendi* with Italy would not hear of any reconciliation until some action had been taken to silence the anticlericals and halt the opening of Protestant churches in Rome (Camillo Manfroni, *Sulla soglia del Vaticano* [Bologna, 1920], I, 75–76).

[4] Ernesto Vercesi, *Il Movimento cattolico in Italia, 1870–1922* (Firenze, 1923), p. 2.

Interests.[5] Its object was stated to be the freeing of the pope from his captivity and the re-establishment, by legal means, of his spiritual independence.[6] The *Osservatore romano* hailed the formation of this society as an initial and significant move in the right direction. "While our enemies tremble over this," it triumphantly proclaimed, "the heart of every Catholic rejoices."[7] No less fervent was the *Unità cattolica* in welcoming the new organization as "the true means of combating the revolutionaries."[8] Moderates and leftists showed little inclination to take an alarmist view of these preliminary maneuvers. Italians, the *Libertà* remarked, had every reason to be satisfied. For the more openly Catholics opposed their country, the more tenacious and compact would all patriots be in its defense. The danger of resting overcomplacently upon past achievements would thus be averted.[9] The *Diritto*, after alluding to the "immoral" and "antinational" program of the new clerical organization, asked the government not to molest it. For it would now be possible to discern the enemy at home in the event of armed conflict with foreign ultramontanes.[10]

The peaceful counteroffensive of the Italian clericals quickly assumed more formidable proportions. Groups similar to the Roman Society for Catholic Interests were formed in other cities of the kingdom, and it was not long before they became an important and well-disciplined adjunct of the Vatican's forces. In March the *Civiltà cattolica* issued a call to all Italian Catholics to unite for the purpose of resisting the onslaughts of the radicals. It urged the creation of a nationwide association. Without union and proper organization, it warned, it would be impossible to deal effectively with the enemies of the church. It advocated the use of every avail-

[5] Cf. the *Unità cattolica*, February 2, 1871.

[6] *CC*, I (8th ser.; February 25, 1871), 626–27; Michele Rosi, *Vittorio Emanuele II* (Bologna, 1930), II, 195; Vigo, *op. cit.*, I, 39.

[7] *Osservatore romano*, February 4, 1871.   [9] *Libertà*, February 4, 1871.

[8] *Unità cattolica*, February 3, 1871.   [10] *Diritto*, September 10, 1871.

able instrumentality to combat legislation hostile to Catholicism. It adjured all Catholic laymen to join their priests in the struggle against the revolution.[11] This plea was seconded by the *Osservatore romano*. Inasmuch as Italian Catholics could not participate in political contests, the papal daily observed, they could accomplish much in behalf of religion and public morality by forming active associations.[12]

As the first anniversary of the occupation of Rome drew near, the Vatican's Jesuit spokesmen encouraged their supporters with the assurance that the events of September 20 were not irrevocable. In the meantime, they declared, war without quarter would have to be waged against the would-be destroyers of the church. The Holy Father had no choice but to defend his spiritual authority with all the means which God had placed at his disposal. Those anxious to preserve his independence were fully justified in resorting to strong measures, even to arms, to achieve that result.[13] The day itself passed without untoward incident. On October 2, the first anniversary of the plebiscite, the Black members of the Roman aristocracy presented Pius with an address which vigorously denounced the ecclesiastical policy of the government. The pontiff responded with a fiery tirade in which he voiced the hope that the miraculous events of Jericho would now be repeated at Rome. "The sacred ark," he said, "went around the walls of the city six times, but on the seventh, the walls crumbled and the city was taken and the people of God entered it in triumph. Let us then pray . . . . that we too, after long supplication and sacrifice, will be able to recover our city."[14]

The law of guarantees continued to be the principal target of papal censure. The Vatican accused the ministerial and Sinistra press of trying to convince the Catholic world that

[11] *CC*, II (8th ser.; March 20, 1871), 21.

[12] *Osservatore romano*, September 29, 1871.

[13] *CC*, III (8th ser.; September 1, 1871), 641-54.

[14] Vigo, *op. cit.*, I, 101.

the provisions of this statute were more effective than territorial sovereignty in insuring the freedom and independence
of the Holy Father. This contention, declared the *Civiltà
cattolica*, was founded on an absolute falsehood. The pope
was a prisoner in Rome, and his captivity, instead of dimin-
ishing in oppressiveness, was daily becoming more intolerable.[15] Pius himself, in an allocution on October 27, again
pronounced the law of guarantees wholly unacceptable.[16]
The text of the allocution appeared in every clerical journal
of Rome and was speedily reproduced in the sheets of all the
political parties. The passivity of the cabinet on this occasion
was in marked contrast with the severe treatment meted out
to those newspapers which had published the encyclical of
November 1, 1870.[17] Exactly a month later, on the inauguration of the first Italian parliament in Rome, Pius inveighed
fiercely against the government. He insisted that "no conciliation will ever be possible between Christ and Belial,
between light and darkness, between truth and falsehood."
So violent, too, was the outcry in the ultramontane press
that the ministry momentarily reverted to past practice and
ordered the sequestration of the *Osservatore romano*.[18]

The implacable hostility of the Vatican to the new order of
things in the peninsula spurred the Italian government to
take drastic measures against the church and its recalcitrant
hierarchy. Decisive, too, in the launching of this concerted
offensive was the eagerness of the country's rulers to acceler-
ate the secularization of Italian life. The treatment accorded
newly appointed bishops bespoke the mood of Lanza and his
colleagues. The retention of the *exequatur* for the assignment
of temporalities[19] placed in the hands of the cabinet a powerful weapon of coercion of which it now proceeded to make

---

[15] *CC*, IV (8th ser.; October 23, 1871), 257–58.

[16] *Ibid.*, November 4, 1871, pp. 385–90.

[17] This was enlarged upon by governmental apologists as evidence of the pope's
very ample freedom.

[18] Vigo, *op. cit.*, I, 108–9.   [19] See above, p. 120.

ample use. It filled the ultramontane camp with consternation by announcing that it would grant the *exequatur* only to those recipients of the miter who presented their bulls of appointment to the political authorities. The Vatican replied that, with the scrapping of the old concordats and the separation of church and state in Italy, ecclesiastical appointees were under no obligation to proffer such deference to the civil power.[20] This was the formal ground. More conclusive was the necessity of shunning any gesture, however innocuous, which might be construed as a recognition of the existing political order. Obeying the injunctions of the pope, new incumbents of episcopal sees late in 1871 refused to apply for the *exequatur*.[21] The government promptly retaliated by denying them possession of their benefices.[22] As a result, many bishops were constrained to take up quarters outside their official residences and depend upon subsidies from the Holy See.[23]

Moderate opinion, though deploring this situation, applauded the government's drastic procedure. Italian bishops, the *Opinione* pointed out, were free to secure recognition from the authorities. Their failure to do so fully justified the ministerial position. The Holy See was at liberty to choose whom it liked for episcopal honors. But it could not ignore with impunity the existence of Italian laws.[24] The authoritative journal warned the heads of the Roman hierarchy that their refractory attitude would bring down upon them reprisals of a most disconcerting nature. It alluded, in this connection, to the idea of intrusting the administration of preb-

---

[20] Cf. Stefano Castagnola, *Da Firenze a Roma: diario storico-politico del 1870-71* (Torino, 1896), pp. 209-11.

[21] Cf. the *Libertà*, November 23, 1871.

[22] Joseph Schmidlin, *Papstgeschichte der neuesten Zeit* (München, 1933-34), II, 119. The government meted out similar treatment to parish priests appointed by bishops who had failed to obtain the *exequatur* (cf. the *Unità cattolica*, January 5, 1872).

[23] Enrico Tavallini, *La Vita e i tempi di Giovanni Lanza* (Torino and Napoli, 1887), II, 93.

[24] *Opinione*, February 2, 1872.

ends to lay bodies.[25] The *Perseveranza* summoned the government to cut off bishops and priests from the revenues of their office until it had obtained "an act which implies on their part recognition of the legitimacy of the kingdom of Italy."[26] The *Libertà* went farther. It was not enough, it observed, to withhold the temporalities from recalcitrant bishops; the latter should be prevented from exercising their spiritual functions.[27] The Sinistra, which demanded maximum severity in dealing with this problem, complained that the clergy was getting off easily. It again drew attention to the fatal results which complete freedom for the ecclesiastical hierarchy might entail.[28] The government, it warned, was under obligation to enforce all laws voted by parliament. No relaxation of this principle was permissible.[29] It accused the authorities, and De Falco in particular, of pusillanimously acquiescing in episcopal violations of the *exequatur* clause.[30] The "free church in a free state" formula, it charged, cloaked "the vicious licence of the church within the servitude of the state." All the more imperative, therefore, was the unrestricted use of the right of patronage which alone among the erstwhile regalist safeguards was still intact.[31]

Some persevering spirits, undeterred by the apparent hopelessness of mediation, placed their good offices at the disposal of the government. One of these was Don Bosco, who was on excellent terms with certain members of the cabinet.[32] But even his efforts to bring about a settlement proved futile.[33] Ministerial circles professed little fear over the ultimate outcome of this trial of strength. They believed with

[25] *Ibid.*, February 9, 1872.

[26] *Perseveranza*, January 29, 1872.

[27] *Libertà*, September 24, 1872.

[28] *Riforma*, January 22, 1872.

[29] *Ibid.*, February 22, 1872; cf. also the *Diritto*, February 29, 1872.

[30] *Riforma*, April 23, 1872; *Diritto*, August 23, 1872.

[31] Cf. the *Riforma*, May 8, 1872.

[32] Cf. Ernesto Vercesi, *Don Bosco: il santo italiano del secolo XIX* (Milano, 1929), p. 185.

[33] Cf. De Vecchi di Val Cismon, "Don Bosco e Giovanni Lanza," *Rassegna storica del Risorgimento*, II (1934), 205–16; Tavallini, *op. cit.*, II, 94, 434–35.

Bonghi that, sooner or later, the bishops would submit.[34] The plight of the luckless prelates evoked sharp protests from the Vatican, but it had little hope of achieving any amelioration of their position. "We have the law," observed the *Civiltà cattolica*, "and according to it the bishops must die civilly; for that is the significance of the fact that the government not only denies them their temporalities but refuses to recognize their dignity and jurisdiction."[35] And the *Unità cattolica* sardonically remarked that the government, to be logical, would have to enforce the *exequatur* clause against Pius IX's successor in his capacity as the Bishop of Rome.[36]

No less drastic were the measures directed against the intrenched position of the church in the field of education. The first blows were struck in Rome. When the Italians occupied the city, they found the clergy in charge of all elementary instruction. The Jesuits established in the Collegio romano were the sole dispensers of secondary education, while the University of Rome had been ruthlessly purged of instructors suspected of liberal sympathies. The cabinet, aided by the Giunta, at once took up the question of secularizing the city's educational system. The new public schools were housed in the Collegio romano, with only a portion of that edifice reserved for the use of the Jesuits. The latter reopened their schools early in November, but the outcry which greeted this gesture led to the imposition of a ban on teaching by members of the hated order.[37] Visconti-Venosta, in a circular dated November 25, 1870, defended the closing of the Jesuit schools and invoked the law of the kingdom to justify the establishment, in their stead, of state-controlled institutions of secondary education.[38]

[34] *Nuova antologia* (February, 1872), p. 464.

[35] *CC*, V (8th ser.; February 8, 1872), 465-66.

[36] *Unità cattolica*, February 6, 1872.

[37] Ugo Pesci, *Come siamo entrati in Roma* (Milano, 1895), pp. 249-50, and *I primi anni di Roma capitale* (Firenze, 1907), pp. 499-500.

[38] *Libro verde*, No. 103, pp. 111-12.

Article XIII of the law of guarantees provided that Catholic seminaries in Rome and in the suburbicarian sees were to continue under the aegis of the Holy See, without any state interference at all.[39] However, the government was declared qualified to intervene whenever anything should be taught in them which was contrary to the laws of the land.[40] Difficulties speedily arose when these seminaries proceeded to admit large numbers of lay as well as clerical students. Moderates and radicals were at one in assailing this action. According to one eminent authority on constitutional law, Article XIII had reference only to the training of candidates for the priesthood. Were the seminaries to impart instruction to any and all students, they would forfeit their special immunity and become subject, like all other educational institutions, to the supervision of the state.[41] Acting on this interpretation of the article, the government dispatched inspectors to some of the seminaries. The latter, however, bolted their doors to these representatives of the civil power. The cabinet accepted the challenge. In August, 1872, it ordered the closing of the recalcitrant institutions. This produced results. The ecclesiastical authorities relented, and the ministerial order was revoked.[42] The following December the ministry of public instruction issued a circular which formally resolved the issue of the controversy. It laid down the principle that the ecclesiastical hierarchy was free to determine the curriculum of candidates for the priesthood. It added, however, that, whenever seminaries should be opened to lay and foreign students, the regulations of the civil educational authorities would have to be complied with.[43] Mod-

[39] Cf. Domenico Zanichelli, *Monarchia e papato in Italia* (Bologna, 1889), pp. 161–62.

[40] *Ibid.*, p. 164.

[41] Luigi Palma, "L'Insegnamento religioso nelle scuole primarie e i seminarii ecclesiastici," *Nuova antologia*, June, 1875, pp. 353–54.

[42] Manfroni, *op. cit.*, I, 103.

[43] Vincenzo Masi, "Istruzione pubblica e privata," *Cinquanta anni di storia italiana* (Milano, 1911) II, 23.

erate circles applauded the government's firmness. It was necessary, insisted the *Opinione*, to shield the youth from unpatriotic educational influences and to prevent the Catholic clergy from obtaining a monopoly in this all-important sphere.[44] The Vatican was furious. "The church is so free," the *Civiltà cattolica* mordantly remarked, "that the chains already binding it are never enough."[45] Not content with the promulgation of this regulation, moderates as well as leftist extremists demanded that the government concern itself with the course of studies offered in the episcopal seminaries.[46] They wished to see these institutions meet certain minimum general requirements with respect to the tone and content of the subject matters taught.[47]

Much more significant was the problem of religious instruction in public educational institutions. The secularism which inspired the government's attitude in this matter was clearly attested by the introduction of a bill abolishing the chairs of theology in all the state universities.[48] The enactment of such a measure had long been one of the objectives of Italian liberalism.[49] Now, however, a formidable nucleus of moderates interposed weighty objections. It was important, argued the *Opinione*, to have an "enlightened and cultured" clergy which participated in the "scientific movement" of the universities. The state was under obligation to make such educational opportunities available to priests, even though they were forbidden by the episcopate to attend university courses. Mingling freely with other students, Catholic clergymen would be in a better position to understand the tendencies of modern youth. They would thus be enabled to perform more effectively their work of moral and religious

---

[44] *Opinione*, December 4, 1872.

[45] *CC*, IX (8th ser.; January 25, 1873), 371.

[46] Cf. *Opinione*, January 24, 1873.   [47] *Ibid.*, September 17, 1873.

[48] For the text of this bill see *Atti*, CLXXI, No. 45.

[49] Cf. Marco Minghetti, *Stato e chiesa* (Milano, 1878), p. 156.

instruction.[50] The *Libertà* contended that the principal effect of the measure would be to surrender the education of the Catholic clergy to the exclusive influence of the Jesuits. This would close forever the way to any "beneficent contact" within the universities between young priests and young students of other disciplines. In short, nothing less was involved than the renunciation of the hope of seeing priests remain citizens. It was clear therefore that the chairs of theology ought to be retained as instrumentalities in the war against the errors and pretensions of the papacy and the church.[51]

The bill was discussed in the chamber late in April, 1872. Its opponents, led by Bonghi, made a valiant effort to defeat it. They warned that its effect would be to give the church a monopoly in the teaching of theology. This, they contended, was but one of the dire consequences that might be expected to ensue. Others were the destruction of the unity of the church and the decline of Catholic sentiment. On the other hand, retention of the chairs in question would redound to the advantage of both Italy and the church. Specifically, it would improve the prospects of a religious peace in the peninsula. The ministerial defenders of the measure, headed by Correnti, argued that church and state were distinct entities with well-articulated objectives of their own and that progress could be achieved only by allowing each to go its own way without interference from the other. Furthermore, the state, in accordance with the separatist principle proclaimed in the law of guarantees, was not qualified to have any hand in the teaching of theology. This proved to be one of the rare occasions on which the Sinistra saw eye to eye with the government,[52] and a somewhat heterogeneous majority was

[50] *Opinione*, April 21, 1872; Chiala, *Dina*, III, 322.

[51] *Libertà*, April 29 and May 2, 1872.

[52] The Sinistra had long been clamoring for the complete secularization of state-controlled education (cf. the *Diritto* of January 10, 1871). Now it sharply supported the proposed abolition of the chairs of theology in the universities of the kingdom (*ibid.*, November 22, 1871, April 24 and May 1, 1872; *Riforma*, April 26, 1872).

mustered to pass the bill.[53] The outcry in the clerical press was loud and sustained. The *Osservatore romano* made no effort to conceal the indignation of its august patrons. The suppression of the chairs of theology, it argued, was of a piece with the enactment of various measures aimed at enslaving the church. Now the money of taxpayers would be employed to subsidize the propagation of ideas destructive of "every true social principle." Indeed, this bill was nothing less than "a new step toward socialism."[54] The *Unità cattolica* decried the presumption of the government which had first despoiled the church of its temporalities and was now commanding it to educate its priests and teach theology at its own expense. Addressing itself directly to Lanza and his colleagues, the Turinese journal concluded: "Restore to the church its property, and it will be ready to renounce all your budgets."[55]

Correnti's concurrent attempt to eliminate religious instruction from the secondary schools of the country proved less successful, however.[56] The almost unanimous opposition which this bill encountered among moderates both in and out of parliament[57] led in May to its withdrawal by the cabinet and the resignation of the minister of public instruction.[58] The circumstances surrounding Correnti's departure and especially the failure of Lanza and Sella to support him on this issue gave rise in some quarters to the charge that the cabinet was seeking to ingratiate itself with the Vatican.[59] But

[53] *Atti*, CLXXXIII (April 30, 1872), 1821; cf. also Tullio Massarani, *Cesare Correnti nella vita e nelle opere* (Roma, 1890), pp.286–90; C. Hippeau, "L'Instruction publique en Italie," *Revue des deux mondes*, September 15, 1874, pp. 361–63; Saverio Cilibrizzi, *Storia parlamentare politica e diplomatica d'Italia* (Milano, 1925), II, 49–50. The measure became law on January 26, 1873 (cf. Francesco Ruffini, *Lineamenti storici delle relazioni fra lo stato e la chiesa in Italia* [Torino, 1891], p. 41).

[54] *Osservatore romano*, May 8 and 15, 1872.

[55] *Unità cattolica*, May 8, 1872.

[56] The text of the bill in question is to be found in *Atti*, CLXXI, No. 46.

[57] Cf., e.g., *Libertà*, May 19, 1872.

[58] Massarani, *op. cit.*, pp. 301–2; Tavallini, *op. cit.*, II, 114–15; Alessandro Guiccioli, *Quintino Sella* (Rovigo, 1887), I, 388–89; Cilibrizzi, *op. cit.*, II, 50.

[59] Pesci, *I primi anni di Roma capitale*, p. 106.

Lanza, after a hurried conference with the king, announced
to the chamber that the educational policy of the government would in no way be altered.[60] The Sinistra, which had
noisily supported the bill, refused to take this assurance seriously. It carried an appeal to the country and thus precipitated a nation-wide discussion of the whole question of religious instruction in the public schools. The various parties
to the controversy expounded their views with characteristic
pungency.[61] The anticlericals of the left demanded the adoption of an educational program which was in harmony
with the needs and institutions of the modern state. They
pointed to the apparent inability of lay instruction to com-
pete with the better-organized clericals schools which, they
said, exploited the religious sentiment of the masses. It was
therefore all the more necessary, they concluded, to strip the
clergy of any opportunity to do further harm within the
state-supported educational institutions.[62] The temper of the
Vatican was faithfully reflected in the strictures of the *Civiltà
cattolica*. The juridical separation of church and state, declared the indefatigable Jesuit journal, did not involve the
abolition of religious instruction in the schools of the land. It
went on to argue that all education should be placed in the
hands of the church and the family, since the training of the
young was not the proper function of the political authorities.[63]

The change recently instituted in the status of religious
instruction in the elementary schools was particularly galling
to the clericals. The famous Casati law of 1859 had made the
teaching of religion obligatory in all the primary educational
institutions of the state. Non-Catholics, however, were free

---

[60] *Atti*, CLXXXIII (May 18, 1872), 2155–57.

[61] A clear statement of the issues is to be found in A. Gabelli, "L'Insegnamento
religioso nelle scuole pubbliche," *Nuova antologia*, June, 1872, pp. 324–42.

[62] Cf. the discussion of these and other matters in *Riforma*, May 21 and June 5,
1872.

[63] *CC*, VII (8th ser.; June 21 and September 9, 1872), 5–18, 678–88.

to secure exemption for their children by declaring that they would furnish such instruction privately.[64] This arrangement had been the target of persistent criticism during the ensuing years. It had been argued that it was a flagrant violation of the freedom of conscience and utterly incompatible with the separation of church and state. Not infrequently, prefects and local school boards had advised the government that the teaching of religion was properly the function of the family and not of the state. These counsels finally prevailed. Circulars issued on September 29, 1870, and July 12, 1871, by the ministry of public instruction reversed the situation created by the Casati law. Religious instruction was hereafter to be imparted only to those children whose parents explicitly requested it. The teaching of religion in the elementary schools was thus relegated to a very subordinate place in the curricular hierarchy.[65] The government made ready to enforce this regulation, despite the loud protests of ultramontane spokesmen. The latter, however, did not confine themselves to ineffectual jeremiads. Making the most of the widespread resentment provoked by the government's program, they urged the various Catholic associations in the country to provide more schools of their own.[66]

No less severe was the government's treatment of monastic orders. Laws enacted in 1866 and 1867 and inspired in no small degree by financial considerations had proclaimed the suppression of all religious corporations in Italy.[67] No sooner had the remnants of the papal state conquered in 1870 been incorporated into the Italian kingdom than a great hue and

---

[64] Palma, *op. cit.*, pp. 334–35; Aristarco Fasulo, *Il primato papale nella storia e nel pensiero italiano* (Roma, 1924), p. 207; cf. Masi, *op. cit.*, p. 1, for an appraisal of the Casati law.

[65] Cf. Palma, *op. cit.*, p. 337; Gabelli, *op. cit.*, p. 332.

[66] Cf., e.g., the *Osservatore romano*, May 3, 1872.

[67] Cf. Mario Falco, "La Soppressione dei conventi," *Rivista d'Italia*, May, 1914, pp. 664–65; Lewis M. Hogg, "Politico-ecclesiastical Questions of the Day in Italy," *Contemporary Review*, April, 1866, pp. 642–43; Andrea Piola, *La Questione romana nella storia e nel diritto* (Padova, 1931), p. 32.

cry went up from anticlericals of every description in favor of the immediate extension of these laws to this most recent territorial acquisition. Once again, economic factors reinforced the doctrinaire zeal of these opponents of the church, for more than one-third of the land in the city and province of Rome was held in mortmain.[68] In March, 1871, a proposal sponsored by Mancini brought the issue before the chamber of deputies. The government, in its anxiety to spare as far as possible the susceptibilities of the Vatican, was resolved to proceed slowly in this delicate matter. It put Mancini off with the assurance that a bill dealing with the fate of the orders in Rome and in the suburbicarian sees would be presented at the earliest possible moment.[69] In reply to criticisms from other quarters, it asserted through the columns of its favorite organ that social rather than financial considerations motivated its desire to abolish mortmain and the juridical personality of religious corporations.[70] Simultaneously, it assured the Austrian government, which had advised more lenient treatment for the religious bodies in Rome, that the laws of 1866–67 would not be integrally applied in the capital of Catholic Christendom.[71]

The Sinistra continued to press for action. It bitterly assailed the cabinet's reported inclination to enact an exceptional law which would exempt the orders in Rome from the operation of the statutes of 1866 and 1867.[72] It re-emphasized the sole and complete authority of the state to determine the fate of monastic properties.[73] It assured its political adversaries that the powers, which had failed to aid the pope

---

[68] Cf. J. B. Bury, *History of the Papacy, 1864–1878* (London, 1930), p. 158.

[69] *Atti*, CLXV (March 18, 1871), 1219.

[70] *Opinione*, May 16, 1871. The *Opinione* reiterated on October 23, 1871, that financial considerations had no real part in the government's decision to do away with the Roman orders.

[71] Cf. Kálnoky to Beust, May 19, 1871, HHSA, Politisches Archiv (Rom), Fasz. XI/226, No. 29D, fols. 459*b*–460*b*.

[72] *Riforma*, July 26, 1871.   [73] *Ibid.*, August 20, 1871.

in September, 1870, would certainly not come to the rescue of the Roman monks.[74] Adverting to the special needs of the new capital, it observed that the buildings belonging to the orders could help alleviate the housing shortage there.[75] In the meantime, the juridical tangles of the question were being diligently canvassed by ministerial experts. Sources close to the government were at great pains to reiterate that the projected measure would do no more than suppress mortmain and divest religious bodies of their legal personality.[76] The treatment of the generals of the orders presented the knottiest problems. The Lanza cabinet was aware of the importance which the entire Catholic world attached to the fate of these powerful servants of the papacy. Even Andrássy, who resolutely refused to give any encouragement to those of his countrymen who demanded intervention in the Roman question, made no secret of his government's wish to see the generalships maintained.[77] It was his feeling that Italy should not abuse her power vis-à-vis the Holy See.[78]

The procrastination of the cabinet proved very trying to the exponents of immediate action. The patience of the Sinistra began to wear thin, and its spokesmen in and out of parliament adopted a more blustering tone. The ideal solution, the *Diritto* reiterated with peremptory finality, was the enactment of a measure based on the laws of 1866 and 1867.[79] The *Riforma* flayed the government for its apparent belief in the possibility of an eventual reconciliation with the papacy.[80] Any display of indulgence toward the religious corporations, the leftist journal warned, would prove of no avail,

[74] *Ibid.*, October 25, 1871.   [75] *Ibid.*, October 2, 1871.

[76] Cf. *Opinione*, October 12, 1871.

[77] Augusto Sandonà, *L'Irredentismo nelle lotte politiche e nelle contese diplomatiche italo-austriache* (Bologna, 1932), I, 98 n.

[78] Eduard von Wertheimer, *Graf Julius Andrássy: sein Leben und seine Zeit* (Stuttgart, 1910), II, 202.

[79] *Diritto*, November 29, 1871.

[80] *Riforma*, January 6 and May 16, 1872.

for the Curia's hatred of Italy would remain unaltered.[81]
Equally imperative, it insisted, was the necessity of pointing
out that no foreign power could regard the suppression of the
Roman orders as an offense against Catholicism. The right
so to deal with religious bodies was one which various states
had always exercised.[82] The restlessness of the anticlericals
was matched by the indignation which the demand for the
prompt suppression of the monastic orders evoked at the
Vatican. By yielding to this clamor, the *Civiltà cattolica* asserted, the government would be depriving the supreme
pontiff of one of his most useful instruments in governing the
universal church. The Jesuit organ charged that the attitude
of the political authorities in this matter revealed the inadequacy of the law of guarantees as a device to safeguard
the spiritual authority of the Holy See. The question, it argued, was international in character. Consequently, all governments which had Catholic subjects were entitled to intervene. It was unwearied in extolling the services rendered
the cause of civilization by the much reviled orders, and
warned that their extinction would constitute an unmitigated
calamity.[83] On June 16, 1872, in a strongly worded letter to
Antonelli, Pius himself directed a vigorous broadside against
the contemplated abolition of these pillars of the church.
He recapitulated all his woes beginning with the events of
September 20, 1870. The outrage now to be perpetrated, he
charged, was simply part of an infernal scheme to undermine
his position as head of the church. He alluded to the contin-
ual encroachments upon his jurisdiction and declared that
he could never enjoy freedom and independence as long as he
was subject to "the tyranny and caprice of a hostile authority." Everything that was happening in Rome, he asserted,
was convincing proof that the law of guarantees was a
ghastly joke. "Of what use is it," he queried, "to proclaim

[81] *Ibid.*, June 11, 1872.   [82] *Ibid.*, May 25, 1872.

[83] *CC*, III (8th ser.; September 1, 1871), 741–42; *ibid.*, IV (8th ser.; October 6
and November 4, 1871), 129–39, 408–21.

the immunity of the pope's person and residence, when the government is not strong enough to safeguard us from the daily insults to which our authority is exposed . . . . ? Of what use is it to proclaim the liberty of our pastoral ministry when all the legislation . . . . is in open conflict with the fundamental principles and universal laws of the church?" Antonelli was instructed to acquaint the diplomatic corps at the Vatican with the true state of affairs. He was to bring the sad predicament of the papacy to the attention of the powers in order that they might give the matter their serious attention. "Foreign governments," Pius wrote, "cannot forget that the pontifical throne, far from being a hindrance to the peace and prosperity of Europe, or to the greatness and independence of Italy, was always a bond between peoples and princes, and always a source of concord and peace. It was for Italy a source of real greatness, a guardian of her independence, and the constant defense and rampart of her liberty." If every Catholic had the right to ask his government to protect his own religious freedom, he was equally entitled to demand that it guarantee the liberty of the head of his church. It was incumbent upon all governments "to defend and protect the most legitimate cause on earth, certain, as they should be, that, in supporting the sacred rights of the Roman pontiff, they are defending and protecting their own."[84]

This passionate appeal made no little impression in foreign capitals, but the governments could scarcely do more than offer platonic expressions of commiseration. Typical was the reaction of Andrássy, who coolly remarked that Antonelli himself did not believe in the possibility of restoring the temporal power or of intervention on its behalf.[85] The defiant language of the papal document provoked furious retorts

[84] The text of the pope's letter is to be found in *ibid.*, VII (8th ser.; June 28, 1872), 93–99; Hubert Bastgen, *Die römische Frage* (Freiburg i.B., 1917), III (1), 98–101.

[85] Ludwig von Przibram, *Erinnerungen eines alten Oesterreichers* (Stuttgart and Leipzig, 1910), I, 351.

from the Sinistra,[86] whose clamor for legislative action against
the religious orders showed no sign of abating.[87] The moderate press was less acrimonious but no less firm. The *Opinione*
argued that no harm would be done religion by depriving the
monastic corporations of their juridical personality. What
was now in contemplation had already been accomplished in
all the liberal states of Europe and in the remainder of Italy.
Moreover, the properties of the suppressed orders would be
dedicated by the government to charitable and educational
ends, so that the latter could scarcely be accused of acting
from greed.[88] The temper of the country was accurately conveyed by one writer who declared that modern society, which
found the religious corporations incompatible with its own
ends, would reap important economic and moral advantages
from their extinction.[89] Matters were not aided by a report
that France had inspired the issuance of the papal letter and
had promised diplomatic action to prevent the suppression of
the orders in Rome.[90] No less irritating to Italian patriotism
was the rumor that Pius had appealed to Paris, Vienna, and
St. Petersburg for intervention.[91]

The cabinet's first impulse, on perusing the pope's missive,
was to draft a considerably harsher bill than the one which it
had originally planned.[92] But in the end it relented, partly
out of deference to the friendly representations of Austria and

[86] Cf. *Riforma*, June 21, 1872; *Diritto*, June 21, 1872.

[87] Cf. *Riforma*, July 22 and August 14 and 23, 1872; *Diritto*, July 27 and August
19, 1872. That indefatigable adversary of the church, Garibaldi, issued a manifesto urging, among other things, the immediate suppression of the religious orders
(cf. Michele Rosi, *I Cairoli* [Bologna, 1929], I, 243–44). The general was also
agitating for the suppression of Article I of the *Statuto* which declared Catholicism
the official religion of the state (cf. the *Opinione* of August 14, 1872). This agitation
was subsequently taken up by the Sinistra leadership (cf. *Riforma*, April 9, 1873).

[88] *Opinione*, June 21, 1872 Substantially the same language was employed by
other moderate sheets.

[89] Cf. A. Gabelli, "Il Progetto di legge sulle corporazioni religiose," *Nuova antologia*, October, 1872, pp. 267–86.

[90] Cf. *Diritto*, June 26, 1872.   [91] Cf. *ibid.*, September 22, 1872.

[92] Cf. Luigi Luzzatti, *Memorie autobiografiche e carteggi* (Bologna, 1931), I, 334.

France.[93] The second article of the bill which it submitted to parliament on November 20 made an exception in favor of the generals of the doomed orders. It permitted them to remain in the edifices which had hitherto served as their headquarters in Rome.[94] This significant concession, which the *Opinione* some months earlier had justified on the ground that the generalships were indispensable to the church in the performance of its spiritual duties,[95] was bitterly assailed by the Sinistra.[96] The *Riforma* contended that the orders would survive in other forms within the protective shadow of the generalship houses.[97] Indeed, it ventured to predict that from the retention of these houses would spring a wholesale revival of the monastic bodies.[98] Exhorting the government not to allow itself to be intimidated by foreign threats, it demanded a complete revision of the bill in order to exclude all special privilege.[99] The *Diritto* editorialized in similar vein to warn the cabinet against conferring an exceptional status upon the generalship houses.[100] The provisions of Article II were likewise decried by a considerable number of moderates, headed by Sella. The latter repudiated the contention that the continued residence in Rome of the generals of the orders was essential to the spiritual freedom of the Holy Father.[101] This dissident wing of the Destra was ably served by the *Libertà*, which from the outset strongly opposed preferential treatment for the heads of the monastic organizations. The

[93] Visconti-Venosta subsequently admitted in the chamber that certain foreign powers had urged the Italian government to deal gently with the pope (cf. *Atti*, CLXXXVIII [May 9, 1873], 6195).

[94] For the text of the bill see *ibid.*, CLXXV, No. 136, 45–52.

[95] *Opinione*, August 22, 1872.

[96] The Sinistra had repeatedly voiced its opposition to exceptional treatment for the generals of the orders (cf. *Riforma*, August 25, 1872; *Diritto*, September 22 and October 16, 1872).

[97] *Riforma*, November 24, 1872.   [99] *Ibid.*, January 21, 1873.

[98] *Ibid.*, January 4, 1873.   [100] *Diritto*, December 9, 1872.

[101] Guiccioli, *op. cit.*, I, 119; Mario Falco, *La Politica ecclesiastica della Destra* (Torino, 1914), p. 30.

government, it charged, was moved by an exaggerated generosity vis-à-vis its ecclesiastical adversaries.[102] It denied that the terms of the law of guarantees offered any legal justification for this deviation from the legislation of 1866–67.[103] It was in vain that the *Opinione* adjured this formidable array of opponents to think only of the basic provisions of the bill— the abolition of mortmain and the dissolution of the religious corporations as legal entities.[104] It was in vain, too, that it emphasized the political aspects of the question, that it counseled less preoccupation with juridical niceties and more with the general needs of the existing situation, that it held out the hope of an eventual suppression of the generalship houses.[105] Convinced that the exemption accorded the generals denuded the measure of all real effectiveness, the cabinet's adversaries stubbornly held their ground. Nothing less than the integral application to Rome of the laws of 1866–67 would satisfy them. The issue loomed large indeed to contemporary observers. Gregorovius noted in his Roman journal, under date of January 12, 1873: "The law concerning the convents is being prepared for the Italian Chambers. Within it lies a crisis for the entire development of the country."[106] The excitement was shared by foreign Catholics. The French clerical party made an abortive effort to bring the bill before the national assembly,[107] while an international deputation representing the Catholics of Europe and the United States bitterly denounced the proposed law in an

---

[102] *Libertà*, December 10, 1872.   [103] *Ibid.*, December 12, 1872.

[104] *Opinione*, December 8, 1872; Chiala, *Dina*, III, 340–41.

[105] *Opinione*, December 8 and 11, 1872.

[106] F. Gregorovius, *The Roman Journals of Ferdinand Gregorovius, 1852–1874* (London, 1907), p. 438.

[107] Cf. *Journal officiel de la République française*, CXCII (February 14, 1873), 1075–76. The Bishop of Versailles, in a letter to Thiers, demanded official action to save the generalship houses in Rome. The *Opinione*, in appraising this document, sarcastically observed that no Catholic power had chosen the Bishop of Versailles as its attorney. It did, however, assure the anxious prelate that the generalships would continue to exist and prosper even without recognition as juridical entities (cf. the issue of January 28, 1873).

address presented to the pontiff.[108] In Italy the Catholic press waged a spirited campaign. The *Osservatore romano* ascribed the bill to an implacable hatred of religion and to unabashed cupidity.[109] It charged that the Italian government was servilely executing orders from Bismarck.[110] The *Unità cattolica* went so far as to accuse Lanza of a sadistic desire to torture the Holy Father. It warned that grave disasters invariably attended all legislative measures directed against the religious orders.[111] The latter, it predicted, would reap great advantages from the impending persecution. Civil society alone would be the sufferer.[112]

The fate of the generals was the paramount issue of prolonged and acrimonious parliamentary debates in the spring of 1873. The chamber reporting committee proposed the retention of the generalship houses. They were indispensable, it held, to the Holy See in the discharge of its spiritual functions. But it recommended that only a portion of these buildings be allotted to the heads of the orders for the duration of their period of office.[113] The government somewhat reluctantly acquiesced in this modification. But the leftists refused to countenance any arrangement which would keep the generals and their staffs in Rome. They contended that the proposed concession was tantamount to treason because it would aid the church in continuing its struggle against the state. The *Riforma* deplored the committee's failure to subject the bill to substantial revision. It was convinced that the new version tended only to reduce the generalship quarters in size while leaving the way open for their subsequent re-enlargement.[114] Miceli's observations in the chamber sounded

---

[108] Vigo, *op. cit.*, I, 244–45.

[109] *Osservatore romano*, December 27, 1872.

[110] *Ibid.*, May 9, 1873.   [111] *Unità cattolica*, November 23, 1872.

[112] *Ibid.*, May 14, 1873.

[113] Cf. the text of the report of the parliamentary committee in the *Libertà* of April 5, 1873.

[114] *Riforma*, April 19, 1873.

the keynote of the Sinistra's position. The generalships, he asserted, represented "the concentration of religious power in the hands of the pontiff." They symbolized "the servitude of all the rest of religious society" and undermined the civil power. They were "the root from which, before long, the religious corporations will sprout again."[115] These contentions were echoed by Mancini. He, too, warned that the special treatment demanded for the generals would result in a wholesale recrudescence of the orders themselves.[116] The *Libertà* joined the leftists in denouncing the recommendations of the committee.[117]

Minghetti, who was destined very shortly to replace Lanza as premier, ably defended the ministerial view. There was universal agreement, he pointed out, that the religious orders should be abolished as juridical entities and that mortmain should be completely done away with. But it was also important to see that a rigid application of the laws of 1866–67 to Rome would be unwise. The exceptional circumstances in the former papal capital, together with the exigencies of the new church-state system inaugurated with the law of guarantees, called for a less drastic procedure. It was the necessity of giving the pontiff the most ample freedom in his relations with foreign Catholics that constrained the government to deal more leniently with the generals of the orders.[118] Visconti-Venosta spoke in like fashion. He explained that the cabinet, in order to be faithful to the spirit of the law of guarantees, had to ascertain whether any of the religious institutions now in Rome were essential to the government of the universal church. It was clear, he continued, that the generalships belonged in this category. They were, without a doubt, indispensable instruments of the pope's spiritual ministry and inseparable from his relations with the Catholic

---

[115] *Atti*, CLXXXVIII (May 8, 1873), 6155.

[116] *Ibid.*, May 13, 1873, p. 6289.

[117] *Libertà*, April 9, 1873.   [118] *Atti*, CLXXXVIII (May 8, 1873), 6147.

world.[119] Only the timely intervention of Baron Ricasoli averted a deadlock. With distracted deputies looking about for a Moses to lead them out of the parliamentary wilderness, he suggested a compromise which proved acceptable to the chamber. He proposed that the recommendations of the committee be made optional rather than mandatory in their effect. The government was to be authorized to permit the generals to occupy a section of their present quarters until their terms of office should expire.[120] But it was to be clearly understood that the minister in charge of this matter was to be entirely free in deciding whether or not to make use of this authority.[121]

Moderate opinion received the termination of the prolonged controversy with patent relief. The *Opinione* praised Ricasoli for his salutary action in the chamber and predicted that Italy would win prestige in Europe as a result of the concession vouchsafed the heads of the orders.[122] The Sinistra was furious. It bemoaned the new arrangement as equivalent to retention by the generals of their juridical personality.[123] But the ministerialists, declaring that they had no time for sterile recriminations, called for a minimum of delay in disposing of the remaining articles. With the thorniest issue disposed of, the bill moved swiftly forward to enactment. It received the approval of the chamber on May 27 and that of the senate on June 17. In thus divesting the religious corporations of their juridical personality, the Italian legislators believed that they were carrying into effect one of the logical

[119] *Ibid.*, May 9, 1873, pp. 6191–92.

[120] *Ibid.*, May 17, 1873, pp. 6463–72; Aurelio Gotti, *Vita del Barone Bettino Ricasoli* (Firenze, 1898), p. 384; Falco, *La Politica ecclesiastica della Destra*, p. 30. Only the general of the universally unpopular Jesuit order was denied this attenuated domiciliary privilege. The *Osservatore romano*, commenting on this compromise arrangement, accused the deputies of pursuing "a system of malignant and refined hypocrisy, simulating a desire to preserve the generalships of the orders while wishing to extirpate them entirely" (issue of May 18, 1873).

[121] Cf. *Libertà*, May 19, 1873.

[122] *Opinione*, May 19, 1873.   [123] *Riforma*, May 18, 1873.

consequences of the separation of church and state.[124] Actually, the most significant feature of the law was the destruction of the last vestiges of mortmain in the peninsula.[125] The Vatican had been worsted, but its loyal defenders came away from the struggle echoing the *Osservatore romano's* parting dictum that the law was "a horrible injustice and a violation of all rights."[126]

The attempts of the state to destroy the church's ancient monopoly in the field of marriage proved another fecund source of friction. Civil matrimony had been incorporated into the code issued in 1865 and put into effect on January 1, 1866. Openly flouting the terms of this statute, numerous devout couples contented themselves with the celebration of the religious rites and refused to appear before the civil magistrates. It was in vain that the *Opinione* exhorted the clergy to refrain from performing the religious ceremony if the civil formalities had not previously been complied with.[127] Defiance of the marriage law, instead of abating, assumed ever increasing proportions. Yielding to the clamor of anti-clericals in the chamber and in the country at large,[128] the government, in October, 1872, ordered the royal procurators to make a thorough investigation of the situation.[129] The data thus gathered convinced the cabinet that drastic intervention was required. In December of the following year it submitted to parliament a bill stipulating that the civil had always to precede the religious ceremony. Severe penalties for the infraction of this regulation were prescribed.[130] Vigliani, the minister of justice, made it very plain to the chamber just why the government was taking an action which was

[124] Cf. Falco, "La Soppressione dei conventi," *op. cit.*, p. 683.

[125] Cf. Cilibrizzi, *op. cit.*, II, 57.   [127] *Opinione*, May 19, 1872.

[126] *Osservatore romano*, June 3, 1873.   [128] Cf. *Riforma*, May 26, 1872.

[129] *Libertà*, October 28, 1872; Guido Padelletti, "Lo Stato ed il matrimonio ecclesiastico," *Nuova antologia*, May, 1874, pp. 5–6.

[130] The text of the matrimony bill of December 3, 1873, is in *Atti*, CXCIV, No. 48, 11.

clearly at variance with the separatist principle embodied in the law of guarantees.[131] He pointed out that during the period from January 1, 1866, to December 31, 1871, no fewer than 120,421 marriages had been solemnized with the church sacrament alone.[132] The Sinistra loudly supported the ministry. The *Riforma* defended the imposition of heavy penalties upon priests guilty of uniting in matrimony couples who had failed to comply with the civil formalities. It argued that such action was imperative in order to halt the increase in the number of illegitimate marriages.[133] The *Diritto*, which likewise defended the government's action, enlarged upon the necessity of averting social disorders and scandals. It too emphasized the urgency of dealing drastically with the law-flouting clergy.[134]

The bill, however, speedily encountered formidable opposition. The clericals were furious, and loud protest was registered by the Italian episcopate.[135] The *Osservatore romano* insisted that the clergy had faithfully endeavored to persuade all Catholics to comply with the law on civil matrimony. If that law was being ignored, it was not the fault of the priests. "The Italian people," the papal sheet went on to explain, "is profoundly Catholic. Believing that matrimony is a sacrament, it finds it difficult to understand what the magistrate has to do with it, and therefore to appear before him seems almost a sacrilege."[136] If Vigliani, remarked the *Unità cattolica*, cared to consult ancient Rome, it would tell him that religionless marriages were the origin of its fall. But of course Vigliani was not concerned about the sacrament of matrimony. Whether or not Italians lived in concubinage was a

---

[131] The measure was, as a matter of fact, symptomatic of the growing reaction against separatism (cf. Ruffini, *op. cit.*, pp. 41–42).

[132] *Atti*, CXCIV, No. 48, 5–6.

[133] *Riforma*, December 23, 1873.   [134] *Diritto*, February 3, 1874.

[135] *CC*, XII (8th ser.; December 6, 1873), 732; *ibid.*, II (9th ser.; May 2, 1874), 480; *Unità cattolica*, April 9, 1874.

[136] *Osservatore romano*, February 26, 1874.

matter of indifference to him. He was interested only in having them present themselves to the civil authorities. The results of his bill would soon be manifest in crime statistics. And all the while it was clear that in the past, when Italy did not know civil marriage, she was "great, rich, and powerful."[137] The *Voce della verità*, like the *Osservatore romano*, contended that the clergy could not be held responsible for the introduction of this measure. The episcopate, the priesthood, and the Catholic press, it declared, had behaved faultlessly. Ever since the promulgation of the civil matrimony law they had never ceased to advise couples to comply with the legal formalities once the religious rites had been celebrated. The clerical daily reminded its adversaries that the sacrament of marriage was regarded as holy by all peoples that had attained any degree of civilization. But the teachings of men like Maillet and Lamarck, it jeered, had changed all this. They had discovered that men originated from fish or Cete. And now it was being demonstrated that gorillas or macaques were the progenitors of the human species. In accordance with these notions, it was believed that matrimony too was something "bestial" and that the most sacred of unions could be consummated by a contract in exactly the same way that a horse was purchased or a house rented. The idea of having a contract solemnized in the presence of the mayor was "an egregious discovery of that dear French Revolution to which we owe immortal benefits," and the Italian government, with characteristic perversity, had imitated the French. It had borrowed from them civil matrimony and had completely ignored the religious sacrament. The Italian people had known how to answer. It was clinging to the religious ceremony and spurning the civil rites. This was the "just reply of an honest and pious nation to legislators who scorn the supreme law."[138]

The Catholic party was not alone in demanding the defeat

[137] *Unità cattolica*, December 10, 1873.

[138] *Voce della verità*, December 7 and 23, 1873.

of the bill. Large sections of moderate opinion, too, were outraged. They held that the proposed law was inconsistent
with the country's established policy of affording the maximum liberty to all citizens and in conflict with the principle
of the freedom of the church. Moreover, they were inclined
to believe that infractions of the civil marriage law were due
to ignorance and negligence rather than to ill will.[139] It was
in vain that the *Libertà*, which took up the cudgels in behalf
of the ministerial project, reminded its Destra friends that
the situation described by Vigliani called for effective remedi-
al action.[140] The quality of the opposition induced the government to reconsider the question, and the bill was allowed
to lapse.[141] Nor was the issue immediately revived with the
advent of the Sinistra in 1876. The latter sought to explain
its failure to deal promptly with this ticklish matter by alleging a reduction in the number of marriages contracted
without the civil formalities.[142] It was not until 1879 that the
entire problem was again discussed in the Italian parliament.

With the occupation of Rome, the question of the next conclave emerged as one of the paramount issues of Italo-papal
relations. Late in 1870 Trauttmansdorff wrote Beust that he
had good reason to believe that the cardinals would probably
decide not to stage the election in Rome were the pope's
death to occur in circumstances like those prevalent at the
moment and were a city in Austria to be made available to
the sacred college.[143] As early as the spring of 1871, Visconti-
Venosta brought another aspect of the matter to the attention of the French government. The various powers, he observed to Rothan, should lose no time in concerning them-

[139] *Opinione*, December 23, 1873; Chiala, *Dina*, III, 386–87; Padelletti, *op. cit.*,
p. 8.

[140] *Libertà*, December, 19, 1873.   [141] Cf. *ibid.*, April 28, 1874.

[142] Guido Padelletti, "La Politica ecclesiastica in Italia," *Nuova antologia*, February 15, 1878, p. 673.

[143] Trauttmansdorff to Beust, December 16, 1870, HHSA, Politisches Archiv
(Varia de Rome), Fasz. XI/225, fols. 47a–47b.

selves with the choice of a new pontiff. This was the more important now because Pius, who was notoriously under the influence of the Jesuits, might attempt to insure the elevation of an intransigent prelate by authorizing the cardinals present in Rome at the time of his death to dispense with the customary conclave formalities.[144] It was widely believed that a bull sanctioning an election *praesente cadavere*[145] had already been drafted.[146] Actually, the question of the next conclave had caused the gravest concern at the Vatican, and, before long, definite action was taken. The Holy Father's program was embodied in a bull entitled *In hac subi'ni* and dated August 21, 1871. This document prescribed certain rules designed to expedite the work of the future electors and to encourage them at the same time to assemble outside the peninsula. Those cardinals who happened to be in Rome at the time of the pontiff's decease were authorized to decide forthwith, without waiting until the expiration of the customary ten-day period, whether the election was to take place in the city or elsewhere. The document further specified that, inasmuch as the death of the pope might possibly occur outside of Rome, the election of his successor could be held in any part of the world in the presence of more than half of the

[144] Rothan to Favre, April 13, 1871, AMAE (Italie, mars-avril, 1871), Tome 381, fols. 411–12; cf. also Gustave Rothan, *Souvenirs diplomatiques: l'Allemagne et l'Italie* (Paris, 1884–85), II, 390–92.

[145] In an election *praesente cadavere* those members of the sacred college who chanced to be in Rome could proceed with the balloting for a new pope without awaiting the arrival of foreign cardinals.

[146] Manfroni, *op. cit.*, I, 113. After the outbreak of the Kulturkampf in Germany, the Bismarckian press repeatedly charged that such a bull had been secretly issued. In January, 1874, when the authoritative *Kölnische Zeitung* published the text of the alleged bull (cf. *Schulthess, 1874*, pp. 39, 431–32), the *Osservatore romano*, the *Civiltà cattolica*, the *Unità cattolica* and the Centrist *Germania* of Berlin joined in pronouncing the document apocryphal. Antonelli himself made a formal statement in the same sense (cf. *CC*, I [9th ser.; March 9, 1874], 726). The Sinistra, which insisted upon the authenticity of the bull, urged the country to take the proper precautions against this latest ultramontane maneuver (*Diritto*, January 18, 1874). At the same time, however, it complacently interpreted the alleged abrogation of the rules governing the conclave proceedings as a sign that the pontifical election had lost all importance (*Riforma*, January 14, 1874).

members of the sacred college.[147] There was no dearth of learned Catholic opinion to sustain the thesis that the Holy Father could modify at will the rules governing papal elections.[148] Nor were erudite churchmen loath to argue that the sacred college would do well to assemble outside of Rome.[149] Reports that the cardinals were planning to quit the former papal capital made Italian anticlericals more than ever apprehensive of foreign intrigues. There had even been an occasional warning in the Sinistra press that, should the next election take place in France, the new pontiff would be able to return to Rome only in the wake of a fierce war.[150]

Pius' advanced age and the persistent infirmities which often incapacitated him for weeks at a time were constantly giving rise to rumors of his impending demise; and friends and foes alike of the Vatican busily speculated on the outcome of the next conclave. No one was more interested than Bismarck. No one was more eager to see the throne of St. Peter occupied by a less intransigent churchman. In May, 1872, when his struggle with the Holy See was entering upon its most critical phase, he broached to the powers the idea of arriving at some agreement with respect to the recognition of Pius' successor. "The attitude of the supreme chief of the Catholic church," he urged, "has such importance for all the governments . . . . that it seems opportune to consider betimes the consequences of a change in the person of the pope." Those states which had Catholic subjects, he continued, were greatly interested in seeing the next papal election conducted

---

[147] Giovanni Berthelet, *La Elezione del papa* (Roma, 1891), pp. 184 and 187.

[148] Cf., e.g., Th. Granderath, "Die Papstwahl," *Stimmen aus Maria-Laach*, May, 1872, pp. 401–15.

[149] According to a Jesuit writer of considerable authority, one obstacle which stood in the way of staging the conclave in Rome was the fact that the Quirinal, the traditional site of papal elections, was in alien hands (Pachtler, "Ist der Papst frei unter der piemontesischen Heerschaft?" *Stimmen aus Maria-Laach*, April, 1872, p. 280).

[150] See one of the earliest of such warnings in *Diritto*, August 25, 1871.

in a fashion which would permit them to recognize it as "valid and regular." Before doing so, however, they were entitled to ask whether the choice and person of the new occupant of the pontifical throne offered satisfactory safeguards against abuse of the authority vested in his office.[151] A brochure on the same theme (entitled *Ein Wort über die Papstwahl*), written at Bismarck's instigation, intimated that the Curia would do well to seek an understanding with the major powers regarding the identity of the next pontiff.[152] Bismarck's overture to the powers met with no very encouraging response. Andrássy, though agreeing that an effort should be made to secure the election of a moderate pope, was averse to any international action.[153] The Italian government invoked its pledge, given in the law of guarantees, to protect the freedom of the conclave.[154] Bismarck himself confessed in July that only two major governments had returned a favorable answer.[155] Nevertheless, rumors of a collective *démarche* of the powers persisted, much to the annoyance of the Vatican. The *Civiltà cattolica* found all this talk about the next conclave "an outrage inflicted with refined cruelty" upon the present occupant of the papal throne.[156] But the unseemly discussion was apparently not confined to the governments. One report had it that even the sacred college was conducting a spirited debate of its own. According to one account, Cardinal Panebianco, the head of the intransigent party at the Vatican, was in favor of moving the conclave to non-Italian territory as a protest against the policies of the Lanza

---

[151] *Staatsarchiv*, second supplement to XXIII–XXIV, 266–68.

[152] Wertheimer, *Andrássy*, II, 212.

[153] *Ibid.*, pp. 212–13.

[154] Italy's sole preoccupation, declared the *Opinione* on July 5, 1872, was to make it possible for the next conclave to enjoy perfect autonomy. The Sinistra violently assailed the ministerialist attitude. According to the *Riforma*, it would be humiliating for Italy to abstain from all interference in the next papal election when other Catholic powers possessed the right of veto (issue of July 12, 1872).

[155] Moritz Busch, *Tagebuchblätter* (Leipzig, 1899), II, 365.

[156] *CC*, VII (8th ser.; July 23, 1872), 310–11.

cabinet. But his moderate colleagues, it was said, preferred to remain in Rome.[157]

Early in April, 1873, Pius contracted a severe rheumatic ailment. For ten days his condition remained dubious. But thereafter it showed decided improvement, and his recovery was pronounced certain. During the more critical phase of his illness, various and conflicting rumors received wide credence. The Italian government professed to know that the pope, if not already dead, was on the point of dying. Its besetting anxiety now was to prove to all Europe that the first conclave to be held after the fall of the temporal power would be absolutely free from external interference.[158] Certain precautions were actually taken to protect the Vatican in the event of the pontiff's death.[159] The Italian clericals were incensed by this wholesale rumormongering. They accused their political adversaries of desiring the death of Pius in the hope of seeing him succeeded by a less intransigent prelate who, never having possessed territorial sovereignty, might assume a more conciliatory attitude toward the existing political order.[160]

Shortly after the middle of May, the pope's condition took a sharp turn for the worse, and, for a time, his death seemed imminent. Again he recovered, but not before it had been reliably reported that the cardinals, finally convinced that a new pontiff could not be freely elected in Rome, were planning to hold the conclave elsewhere. Andrássy intervened at this point. He had consistently maintained that it would be unwise to stage the conclave outside of Italy, and he now urged this view upon the Vatican. He likewise declared himself opposed to an election *praesente cadavere*. At the same time he advised the Italian government to reaffirm its ability and determination to insure the absolute freedom of the next papal election.[161] He returned to the charge in the course of

[157] Manfroni, *op. cit.*, I, 99.

[158] *Ibid.*, pp. 121–25; II, 301.

[159] *Ibid.*, I, 125, 129.

[160] Vigo, *op. cit.*, I, 259–61.

[161] Sandonà, *op. cit.*, I, 99–100.

Victor Emmanuel's visit to Vienna in September.[162] He explained that he had refused and would continue to refuse to grant the Vatican's request for a site in Austrian territory which might serve as a meeting place for the conclave.[163] Francis Joseph likewise broached the subject to Victor Emmanuel, and the latter promised to do what he could to satisfy the scruples of the Catholic world in this matter. The ministers who accompanied the king also pledged themselves to give the question their attention on their return to Italy.[164] They were true to their word. On January 1, 1874, Visconti-Venosta issued a circular note which emphasized his government's readiness to insure the freedom and safety of the conclave in accordance with the pledge contained in the law of guarantees.[165] This assurance, explained the *Opinione*, would aid foreign governments in eluding certain difficulties concocted by their clerical subjects.[166] But Sinistra and Vatican organs gave the document scant praise. There was no need, averred the *Diritto*, to demonstrate the existence of ecclesiastical freedom in Italy. The circular was inopportune because all foreign governments had no lack of faith in Italy. Her resolve to give liberty to the church was already attested by the law of guarantees.[167] It was well enough, according to the *Riforma*, that the government should wish to evidence its readiness to respect the church's freedom. But it was wrong to forget that more thought ought to be given to the problem of freeing the government from the usurpations of the clergy than to ecclesiastical liberties.[168] In the opinion of the *Osservatore romano*, the circular did not merit "the honor of a serious and reasoned confutation." The Italian government

---

[162] Wertheimer, *Andrássy*, II, 213–14. This visit is fully discussed below, pp. 336–37.

[163] Francesco Crispi, *Politica estera* (Milano, 1912), p. 2.

[164] *DDF* (1st ser.), I, No. 237, 263.

[165] Cf. the text of this note in *AD, 1875*, III, 238–41.

[166] *Opinione*, February 10, 1874.

[167] *Diritto*, February 12, 1874.   [168] *Riforma*, February 11, 1874.

was the guarantor of the papal guarantees, and "the executioners of the September convention have no right to be believed by honest men."[169] The Quirinal, the *Unità cattolica* pointed out, was the meeting place of the conclave, and the cardinals could no longer assemble there. Consequently, Visconti-Venosta's note was simply "ridiculous."[170] The reaction of the powers was on the whole favorable, though some of them would have preferred a more explicitly worded document. Adverting to the Italian circular note, the French foreign minister wrote Gontaut-Biron on February 3: "It is entirely up to me to discuss and perhaps to secure some modification of its terms." But, he added, he could not allow himself to initiate such negotiations.[171] The other governments likewise remained inactive, and the matter was left in abeyance. The pope himself had no thought of accepting Visconti-Venosta's assurances. In a bull dated September 8, 1874, he signified his anxiety to frustrate in advance all proposals for any sort of arrangement with the Italian government during the forthcoming papal interregnum.[172]

[169] *Osservatore romano*, February 11, 1874.

[170] *Unità cattolica*, January 21, 1874.

[171] André Dreux, *Dernières années de l'ambassade en Allemagne de M. de Gontaut-Biron* (Paris, 1907), p. 40.

[172] Berthelet, *op, cit.*, p. 192.

CHAPTER X

THE ACCESSION OF MacMAHON AND THE ITALO-GERMAN *RAPPROCHEMENT*

FRANCO-ITALIAN relations, which for two years had suffered from pinpricks intermittently administered by the French ultramontanes, underwent a major shock when, on May 24, 1873, Thiers fell and was succeeded by Marshal MacMahon as president of the Third Republic. The new head of the state was a man of strong clerical-monarchist sympathies and his accession constituted a signal triumph for the rightist bloc.[1] Ultramontanes and royalists were jubilant.[2] It seemed that their long-awaited inning had at last arrived. The Orleanist leader, the Duke of Broglie,[3] formed a ministry composed of monarchists and drawing much of its political support from men known to desire the restoration of the temporal power.[4] The premier himself, who assumed personal charge of the foreign office, was notoriously favorable to the Holy See's territorial claims—a fact which was noted with no little satisfaction in Italian clerical circles.[5] The new cabinet was careful, however, to proclaim forthwith the pacific intentions of the marshal. On May 26, Broglie read to the national assembly a presidential message which declared that the good relations with the various pow-

---

[1] Cf. Hans Herzfeld, *Deutschland und das geschlagene Frankreich, 1871–1873* (Berlin, 1924), p. 259.

[2] Cf. *Univers*, May 26, 1873; the *Monde*, May 26 and 27, 1873; the *Union*, May 26 and 27, 1873; *Gazette de France*, May 26, 1873; *Journal de Paris*, May 26, 1873.

[3] See the characterization of Broglie in C. de Freycinet, *Souvenirs, 1848–1878* (Paris, 1914), pp. 360–61.

[4] *Le Premier Ministère de Broglie* (25 mai–26 novembre 1873), p. 9; Comte de Falloux, *Mémoires d'un royaliste* (Paris, 1888), II, 548.

[5] Cf., e.g., *Unità cattolica*, May 30, 1873.

ers would be maintained and that the foreign policy hitherto pursued would be continued.[6] Similar assurances were contained in his first circular note to the French diplomatic representatives abroad.[7] Legitimist and Orleanist organs echoed the government's declarations. The *Gazette de France* announced that peace would be the objective of the new cabinet's diplomacy.[8] The accession of MacMahon, asserted the now authoritative *Journal de Paris*, would in no way modify France's position vis-à-vis other powers.[9]

But Germany and Italy refused to be reassured. The fall of Thiers evoked surprise and distrust in Berlin. MacMahon was described as the "marshal of revenge."[10] His accession, in Bismarck's opinion, signified the advent of a militaristic and ultramontane France.[11] More than that, it enhanced the possibility of a Bourbon restoration which, the chancellor believed, might work irreparable harm to the German empire.[12] He held that a monarchical France would be a greater danger to Germany than a republican one. In any case, the papal sympathies of the legitimists made it impossible to go along with them. On the other hand, a republican regime in France would diminish her eligibility as an ally and thus render her less of a threat to Germany.[13] Bismarck foresaw,

---

[6] *AAN*, XVIII (May 26, 1873), 77–78.

[7] *DDF* (1st ser.), I, No. 207, 238–40; *AD, 1874*, I, 129–30; Le Duc de Broglie, *La Mission de M. de Gontaut-Biron à Berlin* (Paris, 1896), p. 101; Vicomte de Gontaut-Biron, *Mon ambassade en Allemagne* (Paris, 1906), pp. 347–48.

[8] *Gazette de France*, May 28, 1873.

[9] *Journal de Paris*, June 3, 1873.

[10] Gontaut-Biron, *op. cit.*, pp. 349–50.

[11] *Die Grosse Politik der europäischen Kabinette, 1871–1914* (Berlin, 1927), I, p. 189 n. (hereafter cited as *GP*).

[12] Otto Fürst von Bismarck, *Gedanken und Erinnerungen* (Stuttgart, 1898), p. 513.

[13] Cf. *GP*, I, Nos. 92, 95, pp. 155–56, 159–60, 161; cf. also Adalbert Wahl, *Deutsche Geschichte von der Reichsgründung bis zum Ausbruch des Weltkriegs* (Stuttgart, 1926), I, 22. Bismarck likewise believed that a republic in France would be a guarantee of European peace (Paul Matter, *Bismarck et son temps* [Paris, 1908], III, 349).

too, an aggravation of his difficulties with the Centrists.[14]
He was keenly alive to the dangerous potentialities of French
clericalism,[15] and he was all the more worried because he believed that a territoryless pope, who had nothing to lose,
would be restrained by fewer scruples in working for his
ends.[16] He suspected the Broglie cabinet of planning a thrust
on behalf of the pope.[17] Gontaut-Biron, the French ambassador in Berlin, made the seriousness of the situation clear to
his superiors. He pointed out that the clerical antecedents of
several members of the new French ministry had given rise to
reports of a forthcoming intervention in Italy. Many Germans, he added, placed credence in these reports.[18] "The attitude of the German press," he reported on May 29, "shows
a certain distrust as regards the direction of our policy in
religious matters, and it bases this on the private sentiments
of the marshal and of the members of his government." He
urged that the matter be given attention and counseled
greater prudence "in everything that relates to Italy."[19] Two
days later he again alluded to the advisability of exercising
the utmost care where that country was concerned. And, to
give point to this suggestion, he added: "I believe you do not
intend to replace M. Fournier."[20]

Such prudence seemed obviously dictated by the fear and
alarm with which the events of May 24 were received in the
peninsula. Only the papalists rejoiced in the fall of Thiers

[14] He was convinced that the events in France boded no good for the prospects of
the Kulturkampf (cf. Herzfeld, *op. cit.*, p. 276).

[15] Wahl, *op. cit.*, I, 23.

[16] Cf. Freiherr Lucius von Ballhausen, *Bismarck-Erinnerungen* (Stuttgart and
Berlin, 1921), p. 35.

[17] Georges Goyau, *Bismarck et l'église; le culturkampf* (Paris, 1911-13), II, 61.
The sympathies of Arnim, who had been promoted to the embassy in Paris, were
definitely with the French conservatives. But even he admitted that only the weakness of the Broglie government deterred it from reopening the Roman question (cf.
Herzfeld, *op. cit.*, p. 278).

[18] Gontaut-Biron, *op. cit.*, p. 381.

[19] *DDF* (1st ser.), I, No. 209, 241.   [20] Gontaut-Biron, *op. cit.*, p. 381.

and the advent of MacMahon.[21] The great bulk of the nation foresaw crucial difficulties. The *Riforma* conveyed the general mood when it seriously questioned MacMahon's ability to resist the pressure of his ultramontane compatriots.[22] As long as the papacy existed, the Sinistra journal dolefully predicted, Italy would be unable to relax her vigilance against French intrigues.[23] Visions of a monarchical restoration in France and of a subsequent attempt to reinstal papal rule in Rome began to haunt the peninsula. Bonghi was not exaggerating when he wrote that it would be difficult to convince most Italians that the Broglie-MacMahon regime really intended to continue the foreign policy inaugurated under Thiers. It was widely believed, he asserted, that the new rulers of France were only awaiting a favorable opportunity to embark upon a very different course. If they wished their pacific utterances to be taken seriously, they would do well to keep Fournier at his post.[24] Italy was now exposed to "a permanent danger," the *Libertà* remarked. MacMahon's protestations of peaceful intentions were scarcely compatible with his avowed determination to strengthen the French army.[25] Broglie's assurances of good will were likewise to be discounted. For everyone knew that the duke's friends would be happy to organize a crusade against Italy.[26] Indeed, according to the Destra journal, such a crusade was actually in the process of preparation.[27] Special note was taken of the fact that all the members of the Broglie cabinet were sympathetic toward the clerical program and that nearly all of them had supported the episcopal petitions.

The Italian government made no effort to dissemble its alarm. On May 30, Lanza declared to Fournier: "There is not a member of our parliament, to whichever party he might

---

[21] Cf. *Osservatore romano*, May 28, 29, and 30, 1873; *Unità cattolica*, May 28, 1873; *Voce della verità*, May 28, 1873.

[22] *Riforma*, May 23, 1873.

[23] *Ibid.*, June 2, 1873.

[24] *Nuova antologia*, June, 1873, pp. 506–7.

[25] *Libertà*, May 27 and 28, 1873.

[26] *Ibid.*, June 12, 1873.

[27] *Ibid.*, June 29, 1873.

belong, who has not come to express to me or to my colleagues
the secret apprehensions awakened in him by the names of
the persons so suddenly elevated to the government of
France." The record and speeches of these men had been
studied and were found to be distinctly unfavorable. "You
play politics with religious questions," he continued, "and
nothing could be more disturbing to us. We hope that the
statesmen who are in power in your country will see . . . . the
dangers which interference in these matters involves. They
will throw us, despite ourselves, into the arms of Prussia."[28]
Launay talked in a similar strain to Débains, the first secretary of the French embassy in Berlin. How, he queried, could
Italy fail to be frightened when one of the parties which gave
the Broglie ministry a majority in the assembly was stirring
up religious feeling against her?[29] Some comfort was taken
in the thought that Italy would not be alone should action
become imperative. "We believe," declared the *Opinione*,
"that we have the support of the civilized world and we
believe that we are able to rely always on the aid of those
powers which share our interests and enmities."[30] Specifically, there was the friendship with Germany which sprang
from common interests and was inspired by hostility to no
one.[31] Bonghi elaborated upon this theme. He pointed out
that the advent in France of a regime believed favorable to
the papacy had sufficed to revive reports of an Italo-German
alliance. While no formal pact had been concluded, there
subsisted between the two powers "a natural and necessary
understanding which springs from the very nature of existing
circumstances." As for the French, they could not and would
not act without allies.[32]

The fate of Fournier occasioned special anxiety. The
Italophil envoy's dismissal had been predicted by Veuillot

[28] *DDF* (1st ser.), I, No. 211, 243.

[29] Gontaut-Biron, *op. cit.*, pp. 398–99.

[30] Chiala, *Dina*, III, 354–55.

[31] *Opinione*, June 12, 1873.   [32] *Nuova antologia*, July, 1873, pp. 748–49.

on the morrow of MacMahon's accession.[33] Thereafter, clericals and legitimists made no secret of their impatience to see
him recalled forthwith.[34] The observations of the *Monde* were
eloquent of this attitude. France, it averred, needed a more
able representative in Rome.[35] And Catholics had every reason to be dissatisfied with a man who was so notorious an
enemy of the Vatican.[36] The republicans were equally emphatic in their demand that he be retained. Fournier, the
Siècle asserted, had succeeded in re-establishing friendly relations between Italy and France. His presence at the Quirinal
was now "more than ever necessary."[37] The radical *Rappel*
was likewise fearful lest he be removed from his post. "It is
important," it urged, "that the government keep M. Fournier
in Rome."[38] In July the much-discussed diplomatist quit the
Italian capital on an extended leave of absence. The Sinistra
press, in high dudgeon, wailed that he was being underhand-
edly relieved of his post and scored the growing arrogance of
France.[39] Ministerial journals in Paris countered with the
contention that Fournier was going on a short visit to his
country. He would return to Rome before long, they said.
But little confidence was placed in these assertions on either
side of the Alps. The *Temps* was not alone in believing that
Fournier's sojourn in France would be no brief one.[40]

French moderates and republicans wasted no time in warning their countrymen against the dangers of the new international situation. Alluding to the rumors of an Italo-German alliance, the *Journal des débats* declared that they were
to be expected following the assumption of power in France
by men "notoriously devoted to clericalism."[41] Editorializing
on the same theme, the *République française* remarked: "We

---

33 *Univers*, May 27, 1873.

34 *Ibid.*, July 7, 1873; *Union*, July 7, 1873.

35 *Monde*, June 17, 1873.

36 *Ibid.*, June 27, 1873.

37 *Siècle*, June 6 and 15, 1873.

38 *Rappel*, June 2, 1873.

39 Cf., e.g., *Riforma*, July 16, 1873.

40 *Temps*, July 20, 1873.

41 *Journal des débats*, June 15, 1873.

believe . . . . that the real danger for French diplomacy lies in the adoption of a clerical policy or of one suspected of clericalism."[42] The *Siècle* was even more outspoken. "We must know at once," it proclaimed, "whether our diplomacy is to be inspired by the Syllabus or by our international duties toward the Italian government and by the interests of France which forbid us to seal with our own hands the alliance between Italy and Prussia." The Broglie cabinet, it continued, was regarded by liberal Europe as the agent and instrument of ultramontane policies. Were not the well-known votes of several members of that cabinet in favor of the temporal power calculated to keep alive the apprehensions of those governments that were combating clericalism? The fact of the matter was that the rightist coalition of May 24 had succeeded in reviving Italian suspicions, in making Italians believe that France was "the soldier of the temporal power." The patriotism of French ultramontanes, the republican journal sneered, consisted in throwing their country into a new war in order to restore the pontifical government—"a government so detested and detestable that no nation in the world could tolerate it." It was the obligation of the French foreign minister to remove these "odious and ridiculous phantoms." Fortunately, impartial Italians knew that the French nation would give "neither a drop of its blood nor a centime" to re-establish the temporal power. If the present government of France entertained other ideas, it ought to state them publicly.[43] The *Rappel* summoned the new cabinet to adhere scrupulously to the Italian policy pursued under Thiers. It assured the statesmen of Italy that France had never been more hostile to the clerical party. Were the Vatican to beseech the republic for aid, it would receive a negative reply. Of decisive importance, too, the radical journal went on, was the fact that Germany could not be the permanent ally of the Italians because she threatened the Adriatic in her desire to

[42] *République française*, June 15, 1873.

[43] *Siècle*, May 30 and June 5 and 18, 1873.

become a great maritime power. France, on the other hand, was Italy's natural ally. "The Broglie ministry will pass on; but France will remain."[44]

The persistent reports of an Italo-German alliance did not deter the supporters of the MacMahon-Broglie regime from invoking the speedy redemption of the Holy Father. A leading legitimist organ expressed the hope of seeing "an army of crusaders cross the peaks of the Alps to deliver the pope and chastise Italy."[45] Pilgrims flocked to Paray-le-Monial to pray that God might liberate the prisoner of the Vatican and restore their country to its dominant position in Europe.[46] On June 29 an impressive demonstration was staged there when Belcastel, at the head of thirty other members of the national assembly, formally dedicated France to the Sacred Heart of Jesus in the chapel of St. Marie Alacoque. When the ceremonies were over, the deputies received a great ovation amid cries of "Long live Pius IX!" "Long live the Catholic national assembly!" "Long live France!" The enthusiasm of the pilgrims soared to fever pitch as they listened to a rousing sermon by Abbé Besson, the canon of Besançon. "The Zouaves," he shouted, "have laid down their flag at this holy place. Let us allow it to rest there for a moment; and when the hour shall have struck, we will all march, the Zouaves in the van, to restore the pope to the throne of St. Peter."[47] The proceedings at Paray-le-Monial, which evoked intense indignation and alarm in Italy,[48] were followed by other and

---

[44] *Rappel*, June 9, 1873.

[45] Cf. the *Année politique* (Paris, 1875–1906), issue for 1874, p. 20.

[46] R. P. Lecanuet, *Les dernières années du pontificat de Pie IX* (Paris, 1931), pp. 206–7.

[47] *Univers*, July 1, 1873; *Temps*, July 2, 1873; *Schulthess, 1873*, p. 324.

[48] The attitude of the *Libertà* was representative of this reaction. The Roman journal reiterated the charge that the French church was promoting a crusade against Italy. The pilgrimage to Paray-le-Monial, it went on, "must be a solemn warning to us." Italians would be guilty of unpardonable blindness if they should fail to perceive the significance of what was transpiring in France. Their reply would have to take the form of adequate military preparations (cf. the issue of July 4, 1873).

equally bellicose manifestations. At the close of July more than one hundred clerical-legitimist deputies sent the pontiff a stirring communication. It was their fervent hope, they told him, to see the church and France, "together and through each other," regain "well-being, peace, greatness and freedom."[49] A few weeks later the following address to Pius was circulated at the various shrines of France:

> Rome and France are inseparable. . . . . Because our country forgot its mission, it was humiliated, and . . . . you are a prisoner. Our misdeeds are the cause of your sufferings, and our misfortune is joined to yours. Your triumph will be ours. You alone can show us the way to victory. . . . . The salvation of France is the triumph of the church . . . . your liberation. To you the power of our country, ... the blood of our children![50]

Leading ultramontane organs of Paris were emboldened to discuss the possibility of reviving the September convention and of prevailing upon Italy to transfer her capital elsewhere. Less exalted spirits like Mazade warned that France would find herself severely alone in any crusade to rescue the pope;[51] and the redoubtable *République française* raged against those who were ready to sacrifice France "for a sterile demonstration in favor of the defunct temporal papacy."[52] But these admonitions went unheeded in the swift sequence of events which seemed to bode ill for the future of the Third Republic.

Early in August a formal reconciliation—the so-called "fusion"—was effected between the legitimist and Orleanist factions with the aid of the pope himself. This consolidation of the royalist forces evoked high hopes at the Vatican. The *Osservatore romano* pointed with keen satisfaction to the consternation with which news of the "fusion" was being received in Italy. The triumph of the legitimate monarchy in France, it prophesied, would prove "a mortal blow to the

---

[49] *Univers*, August 1, 1873; *Schulthess, 1873*, p. 328.

[50] *Temps*, August 16, 1873; *Schulthess, 1873*, p. 332.

[51] *Revue des deux mondes*, August 15, 1873, pp. 973–74.

[52] *République française*, August 22, 1873.

revolution in Europe."[53] France herself could be saved only by the return of the Bourbon dynasty. Her great objectives now were the restoration of the Catholic religion and the recovery of the military prestige lost at Sedan; and only the legitimate monarchy could enable her to attain them.[54] The papal organ sharply denied that the Catholics of the peninsula were trying to provoke foreign intervention on behalf of the pope.[55] It likewise denied that their position was in any real sense unpatriotic. One could be opposed to the unity of the state, it argued, and still be favorable to the unity of the nation. Consequently, adversaries of territorial unity could be hostile to the existing political order in Italy without being against the country and the nation.[56] Italian clericals were jubilant over the latest turn of affairs in France.[57] European liberalism, they gleefully proclaimed, was betraying its uneasiness.[58] They talked hopefully of the imminent "coming of the avenger." They even predicted that before the middle of September the French army, after disposing of Victor Emmanuel's battalions, would resurrect the temporal power.[59] The *Civiltà cattolica*, however, cautioned its readers against overoptimism. France, it pointed out, would have to prepare to fight Germany as well as Italy. And even if she did not have to recover Alsace-Lorraine and avenge the outrage of September 20, she would still be confronted with the necessity of humbling all those who were seeking to destroy her.[60]

The Jesuit organ's circumspect language deceived no one, least of all the Quirinal. The Italian cabinet did not underestimate the potential dangers of the situation and the dis-

---

[53] *Osservatore romano*, August 10, 1873.

[54] *Ibid.*, September 3, 1873.

[55] *Ibid.*, August 9, 1873.   [57] Cf. *Unità cattolica*, August 14, 1873.

[56] *Ibid.*, August 20, 1873.   [58] Cf. *Voce della verità*, August 13, 1873.

[59] Camillo Manfroni, *Sulla soglia del Vaticano* (Bologna, 1920), I, 143. This prophecy so irritated patriotic Romans that on September 20 they covered the city with paper figures representing French soldiers and bearing the derisive caption: "French Expeditionary Corps at Rome, 1873" (*ibid.*, p. 144).

[60] *CC*, XI (8th ser.; August 23, 1873), 520.

quietude which now possessed it was discernible in the language of ministerial journalists. The *Opinione* complained that the French government was permitting on its soil unpardonable manifestations of ill will toward Italy.[61] The tone of the *Libertà* was much more lugubrious. It predicted that France, regardless of the political views of her rulers, would always insist that she had a score to settle with the Italians, because the latter had come to Rome without her permission and at the low ebb of her fortunes. It compared the strength of the French and Italian armies and reiterated its demand for increased military appropriations.[62] Even Bonghi began to despair of witnessing a reconciliation between the two Latin nations. France, he wrote in his Milanese organ, the *Perseveranza*, would compel Italy to seek safety in an alliance with Germany. What was more, the triumph of ultramontanism in France would constrain Italy to assume a less indulgent attitude toward the clericals within her own borders. The influential journalist was even more emphatic in the *Nuova antologia*. He declared that Italy could maintain a strictly impartial position between Germany and France only if the latter were to abstain from a policy aimed at the destruction of the existing order in the peninsula. France would have to resign herself to the abolition of the temporal power and the establishment of the Italian capital in Rome. At the moment, he continued, it was clear that Italy could put her faith only in Germany and that the union of those two countries would serve as a barricade against French aggression. Joined in the struggle against the Vatican, they would be able to prevent the forces of reaction from undoing "the conquests of these last years."[63] Luzzatti, at this time one of the younger Destra statesmen, took an exceedingly pessimistic view of

[61] Especially shocking to the *Opinione's* sensibilities was the vituperative speech which De Charette delivered before his former papal Zouaves on August 25 (cf. *Opinione*, August 31, 1873).

[62] *Libertà*, August 14 and 21, 1873.

[63] *Nuova antologia*, September, 1873, p. 219.

the situation. He gave free vent to his fears in a letter to Minghetti, who had recently succeeded Lanza as premier. He pointed out that a clerical reaction was about to take place in France, that the hour of the royalists had arrived, and that, once the monarchy had been restored, the French would seek to destroy Italy. "We will be beaten," he wrote, "because we have neither soldiers nor money." He feared that Germany was not to be relied upon and that Austria, where an ultramontane victory in the forthcoming elections seemed likely, might join France in attacking Italy.[64] Minghetti refused to subscribe to these lugubrious reflections. "As much as I want to see black," he replied, "I do not go quite that far. If things were as you say they are, there would really be nothing to do. . . . . I see the dangers, and I assure you that I am not asleep. But I also believe in the power of my country to emerge from this new and critical phase."[65] Dina strongly disapproved of the premier's attitude. The influential editor of the *Opinione* wrote his well-placed friend, Castelli, that the Minghetti government was not taking the Bourbon-Orleanist fusion seriously enough. Italy, he insisted, must not stand alone.[66]

Minghetti, however, had not the slightest intention of forsaking the quest for powerful friends. Apart from his deference, as the head of a parliamentary government, to the pressure of public opinion which was unmistakably in favor of close co-operation with Germany, he was genuinely convinced that every consideration of prudence dictated such an alignment. Nor was he entirely immune from the apprehension that Austria might reverse her present liberal policy[67] and cast her lot with a monarchical and clerical France. It was imperative to counteract, if possible, this danger by seeking more cordial relations with the Hapsburg monarchy. An opportunity to make a first significant gesture in this direc-

---

[64] Luigi Luzzatti, *Memorie autobiografiche e carteggi* (Bologna, 1931), I, 377-78.

[65] *Ibid.*, p. 379.   [66] Chiala, *Dina*, III, 376.

[67] Cf. Giuseppe Gallavresi, *Italia e Austria, 1859-1914* (Milano, 1922), p. 123.

tion was already at hand. In the spring the Austrian government had invited Victor Emmanuel to pay a visit to Vienna on the occasion of the forthcoming universal exposition to be held in that city from May to November. Lanza had urged him to go. He had also advised acceptance of Emperor William's concurrent invitation to visit Berlin as a token of solidarity with the German government. Visconti-Venosta, who heartily indorsed the premier's position, had made his own attitude very plain to Count Wimpffen, the then head of the Austrian legation in Rome. He had requested the envoy to point out to Andrássy that cordial Austro-Italian relations constituted "one of the strongest guarantees of general peace." The foreign minister had likewise informed Wimpffen that he attached the greatest importance, in this connection, to a personal *rapprochement* between Victor Emmanuel and Francis Joseph.[68] For personal reasons and because he was reluctant to antagonize the French unduly, the king had hesitated,[69] and the Italian government, somewhat irked by his indecision, had found it none too easy to explain matters to the Austrian authorities. Victor Emmanuel, Andrássy had been informed, really desired to go to Vienna,[70] but his failure so far to make up his mind was to be explained by his "makeup and exceptional individuality."[71] Minghetti proved no less insistent than Lanza in urging the king to accept the Austrian government's invitation.[72] Though the new premier quickly discovered that his efforts were making but little impression upon his royal master, he did not despair.[73] He

[68] Wimpffen to Andrássy, June 28, 1873, HHSA, Politisches Archiv (Berichte aus Rom [Italien, 1873]), Fasz. XI/81, No. 21B, fols. 140a–140b.

[69] Pietro Vigo, *Storia degli ultimi trent'anni del secolo XIX* (Milano, 1908), I, 295.

[70] See Wimpffen to Andrássy, June 28, 1873, HHSA, Politisches Archiv (Berichte aus Rom [Italien, 1873]), Fasz. XI/81, No. 21A, fols. 138a–138b.

[71] *Ibid.*, No. 21B, fol. 141a.

[72] Cf Giovanni Maioli, *Marco Minghetti* (Bologna, 1926), p. 216.

[73] See Pusswald to Andrássy, August 9, 1873, HHSA, Politisches Archiv (Berichte aus Rom [Italien, 1873]), Fasz. XI/81, No. 26A, fols. 174b–175a.

requested Castelli, who was one of Victor Emmanuel's closest friends, to exert some salutary pressure on the still undecided monarch. He somewhat speciously contended that the Austrian emperor, in playing host to the king, would be sanctioning indirectly the establishment of the capital in Rome and the recently enacted law on religious corporations. This, the premier observed, would constitute a very valuable precedent. And the visit to Berlin was imperative in order to erase any lingering animosities on the score of the negotiations with Napoleon III in 1869 and 1870. He admitted that the fear of another French descent upon Rome was somewhat exaggerated. But he insisted that this fear was a factor which had to be taken into account.[74]

The king, however, was still unable to make up his mind. He continued to profess anxiety over the likelihood that a visit to Berlin would give umbrage to France, and he was unwilling to incur this risk without the certainty of tangible compensatory benefits from the voyage to the German capital.[75] Furthermore, he was aware that the negotiations of 1869–70 were known to the Berlin authorities,[76] and he foresaw some rather uncomfortable moments on meeting the German emperor. But on August 31 he finally yielded to Minghetti's pressure and resolved to accept the Austrian and German invitations.[77] The cabinet was distinctly relieved. The now impending trip, Visconti-Venosta remarked to one of Wimpffen's subordinates at the Austrian legation, was regarded by all Italian liberals as a most auspicious development for the consolidation of Austro-Italian friendship.[78] The announcement of Victor Emmanuel's decision to go to

---

[74] Luigi Chiala, *Dal 1858 al 1892; pagine di storia contemporanea* (Torino, 1892–93), I, 155–56; Vigo, *op. cit.*, I, 296–97; Gallavresi, *op. cit.*, pp. 123–24.

[75] Michele Rosi, *Vittorio Emanuele II* (Bologna, 1930), II, 204.

[76] Augusto Sandonà, *L'Irredentismo nelle lotte politiche e nelle contese diplomatiche italo-austriache* (Bologna, 1932), I, 102.

[77] See Pusswald to Andrássy, August 31, 1873, HHSA, Politisches Archiv (Berichte aus Rom [Italien, 1873]), Fasz. XI/81, No. 61/4726, fol. 200a.

[78] Pusswald to Andrássy, September 6, 1873, *ibid.*, No. 28B, fols. 209b–210a.

Vienna and Berlin was indeed received with the greatest satisfaction in Italy. Ministerial circles portrayed the forthcoming visits as evidence of the cordial relations between the three countries. They insisted that no ill will toward other powers was in any way implied. Italy, they said, continued faithful to her time-honored policy of neutrality in European feuds. But, in the face of any danger that might arise from ultramontane intrigues, her interests would be identical with those of the central empires. The king was rendering a signal service to his country, declared the *Libertà*. His journey was "the reply to a provocation." Frenchmen could scarcely be surprised to see Italy, mindful of their incessant threats, take the necessary diplomatic precautions.[79] The *Opinione* agreed that it was impossible any longer to remain indifferent to the activity of the French clericals. The danger from France had vanquished all hesitation about going to Vienna and Berlin. This voyage was not "merely an act of courtesy" but "a highly political act as well." Indeed, it was nothing less than the consecration of the occupation of Rome. The great Destra daily denied that any threat to or demonstration against France was intended. And wholly absurd was the charge that Italy was about to declare war on France. Italy desired only the republic's sincere friendship. The projected visits could be regarded as anti-French gestures only if the French government should embrace the clerical cause.[80] In a similar vein, Luzzatti wrote to Minghetti on September 3:

Either France does not threaten us with war and then we are her tranquil neighbor and she has no reason to be alarmed over the voyage of the king to Berlin; or she threatens us with war and then we have reason to ally ourselves with the power which renders impossible France's war against us. In any case, France must bear the responsibility for this reaction . . . . and her isolation will be her condemnation. Clericalism generates solitude.[81]

[79] *Libertà*, September 7 and 9, 1873.

[80] *Opinione*, September 2, 5, 6, and 13, 1873; cf. also Chiala, *Dina*, III, 378–79. The moderate *Italie* likewise insisted that the projected visits were not intended as a gesture of hostility toward France.

[81] Luzzatti, *op. cit.*, I, 378.

The Sinistra, which had feared that the Italian government, out of deference to France, might resolve to postpone the king's departure,[82] heaved a mighty sigh of relief. The expected dismay of its Catholic adversaries at home and abroad now became its principal source of delight. The French ultramontanes, the *Riforma* exultantly announced, would henceforth learn to fear Italy a little.[83] But this was not all. The royal voyage would mark the beginning of more resolute action against the Curia itself.[84] Leftist leaders viewed the monarch's impending journey to Berlin as an effective means of forestalling a resurrection of the pope's temporal claims.[85] The French government, they argued, was bent on making the Roman question a *casus belli*. It therefore would have no reason to complain if Italy should seek the co-operation of her natural ally.[86]

The one note of discord in the country's reaction was struck by the clerical party which had moved heaven and earth to prevent the visits.[87] Now, echoing the contentions of Veuillot,[88] it did its best to minimize their political significance. Victor Emmanuel's presence in Vienna and Berlin, declared the *Osservatore romano*, would change nothing. Italy, now as before, was merely tolerated by Austria and Germany, and a lasting alliance with the latter was absolutely impossible.[89] But though it persisted in this pooh-poohing attitude, the Vatican made no effort to conceal its bitterness, which was directed chiefly against Catholic Austria. It could not forgive her for lending herself to this unworthy transaction whose object it apparently was to frustrate France's desire

---

[82] Cf. *Riforma*, August 30, 1873.   [84] *Ibid.*, September 9, 1873.

[83] *Ibid.*, September 7, 1873.   [85] Rosi, *Vittorio Emanuele II*, II, 204.

[86] It was clear that the Minghetti government, by espousing the king's trip to Vienna and Berlin, had acquired much sympathy in Sinistra circles and had momentarily strengthened its political position.

[87] Enrico Tavallini, *La Vita e i tempi di Giovanni Lanza* (Torino and Napoli, 1887), II, 448.

[88] Cf. *Univers*, August 30, 1873.

[89] *Osservatore romano*, August 31 and September 4, 5, and 7, 1873.

to liberate the Holy Father. The *Voce della verità* was exceedingly caustic. It attributed the widespread elation evoked by the king's decision to the magnitude of the nation's fears and to a deep-seated sense of weakness.[90] The policy of *rapprochement* with Germany, it warned, would bring only harm to Italy. Bismarck was seeking to exploit his prospective ally for his own ends. Germany, moreover, was isolated in Europe, and this was an additional reason for regarding an alignment with her as scarcely wise.[91] The *Civiltà cattolica* sounded an even more pessimistic note. It charged that the forthcoming visits had a threefold objective. France was to be watched and, if necessary, dismembered. A restoration of the pope's temporal power was to be rendered impossible. And an arrangement was to be arrived at whereby the three powers were to co-operate in a war against Catholicism and the papacy.[92] Ultramontane organs in other countries were extremely indignant. The *Magyar allam*, the mouthpiece of the Hungarian episcopate, was easily the most outspoken. It made bold to hope that there would be an Orsini to wreak vengeance upon the German emperor should the latter return Victor Emmanuel's visit.[93] Republican opinion in France was at no loss to account for the projected voyage. "Our fusionists, our promoters of reaction, can now see the happy consequences of their policy," the *République française* bitterly remarked.[94] Their maneuvers had created in Italy a distrust which was taking shape "in a diplomatic demonstration whose importance can no longer be contested."[95]

The critical attitude of the Catholic press in Italy and France nettled the Italian government. The clericals were well aware, Visconti-Venosta remonstrated, that Italy demanded nothing better than to be on good terms with every-

---

[90] *Voce della verità*, September 10, 1873.

[91] *Ibid.*, September 6, 1873.

[92] *CC*, XII (8th ser.; September 26, 1873), 95.

[93] *Times*, September 24, 1873.

[94] *République française*, September 5, 1873.   [95] *Ibid.*, September 6, 1873.

one and above all with her neighbors. All her wishes and efforts were directed solely toward the preservation of peace.[96] But Minghetti and his colleagues were cheered by the thought that the steadily mounting blatancy of the ultramontane agitation, above all in France, was making the significance of Victor Emmanuel's imminent visits loom ever larger in the eyes of their liberal and patriotic countrymen. No less a person than Mgr. Guibert, the Archbishop of Paris, entered the lists with a booming pastoral which appeared in the *Univers* on September 8. The eminent prelate stigmatized the occupation of Rome as an unpardonable outrage against religion and society and violently upbraided the powers for their indifference to the perpetration of so heinous an act. The remissness of the European governments, he warned, would some day be punished by the avenging arm of revolution. Such a calamity could be forestalled only if Italy repented of her misdeeds and made atonement by returning the old papal domain to the Holy See. Guibert's pronouncement was deeply resented throughout the peninsula. The Sinistra, which boiled over with indignation, vented its spleen in excoriating diatribes.[97] Ministerial circles were scarcely less rabid. Notwithstanding the prelate's "pathetic exhortations" and lugubrious prophecies, declaimed the *Libertà*, Italy had no intention of abandoning Rome. She would cede the city to the pope on the day that France handed Paris over to Germany. In the meantime, the journal ironically queried, why did not Guibert work to secure the restoration of Avignon to the Holy See?[98] The feeling was general that, instead of lecturing foreigners on their alleged shortcomings, Guibert should have held forth to his own countrymen on the many wrongs which they had as yet failed to redress. This annoyance was not diminished by the suspicion that the pastoral was more than a fortuitous gesture. Under date of Sep-

---

[96] See Pusswald to Andrássy, September 6, 1873, HHSA, Politisches Archiv (Berichte aus Rom [Italien, 1873]), Fasz. XI/81, No. 28B, fols. 211*a*–211*b*.

[97] Cf., e.g., *Diritto*, September 11, 1873.   [98] *Libertà*, September 11, 1873.

tember 13, the correspondent of the *Times* reported from Milan:

There is something in the high rank and personal character of the Archbishop of Paris that gives his diatribe almost a political weight, as it convinces the Italians that this Prelate would scarcely allow himself expressions so offensive to a neighbouring nation, if his language did not find an echo in the hearts of many of his flock, and of the men at the head of it.[99]

In some quarters, responsibility for the outburst was placed squarely upon the Vatican. So intense was the bitterness that the Italian government, amid the applause of public opinion, confiscated the various clerical newspapers that had reproduced the objectionable document.[100] Official circles in Rome made much of the impunity with which Guibert had maligned a foreign government. And Launay did not conceal from a member of the French embassy at Berlin his surprise that no legal proceedings had been instituted against the archbishop.[101]

French moderates and republicans were scandalized by Guibert's action. The *Journal des débats* found this "aggressive" pastoral, in view of Victor Emmanuel's projected trip to Vienna and Berlin, exceedingly "inopportune."[102] The archbishop's broadside, it charged, was nothing less than a declaration of war on a sovereign and independent state which wished to be the friend of France.[103] The *Temps* described it as "a political document in which the hope of a speedy crusade in favor of the temporal power is expressed in the most unambiguous terms." The archbishop's language, the great daily continued, was identical with that of Chambord. Divine-right monarchy and ultramontanism were "two principles which have the same origin, aim, and aspirations."[104] It was true, Mazade observed, that Italy had little in common with the German empire. But when she saw so

[99] *Times*, September 17, 1873.

[100] Cf. *CC*, XII (8th ser.; September 26, 1873), 94.

[101] *DDF* (1st ser.), I, No. 236, 262.

[102] *Journal des débats*, September 12, 1873.

[103] *Ibid.*, September 19, 1873.   [104] *Temps*, September 12, 1873.

eminent a personage as the Archbishop of Paris throw down
the gage, she took fright and drew closer to her powerful
friend.[105] "The first pastor of the most important diocese of
France," stormed the *République française*, "has pronounced
an accusatory harangue, full of bitter recriminations and
violent menaces, against a friendly power." The moment
chosen for this outburst was one which found French public
opinion justly alarmed over the forthcoming visit of Victor
Emmanuel to Vienna and Berlin. The "imprudence" and
"injudiciousness" of such an exhibition could not be over-
emphasized.[106] The *Siècle* flayed the pastoral as "an almost
direct appeal" to Europe to terminate Italy's possession of
Rome. "And it is an old man, a bishop, a person charged
with the teaching of wisdom to others, who utters such follies
and heaps up these violences!"[107]

The incident was made the subject of an interpellation
in the permanent committee of the national assembly on
September 11. One deputy pointed out that the publication of the pastoral might compromise France's international position. Broglie replied that the government was
not responsible for the tenor of episcopal effusions. In any
case, he went on, his foreign policy had been made sufficiently clear in two presidential messages and in a diplomatic circular. That policy was one of "harmony and friendship" with all foreign powers. Batbie, the keeper of the seals,
followed with the terse reminder that bishops were not functionaries of the state.[108] The great majority of Frenchmen
applauded these declarations. Broglie's Orleanist friends insisted that his remarks "could only meet with the assent of
the committee, since they are in conformity with the principles consecrated by several votes of the assembly."[109] Even

[105] *Revue des deux mondes*, September 15, 1873, pp. 472–73.

[106] *République française*, September 9, 1873.

[107] *Siècle*, September 9, 1873.

[108] Cf. *Temps*, September 13, 1873; *Journal des débats*, September 13, 1873.

[109] See *Français*, September 13, 1873.

the legitimists agreed that he had spoken with "infinite reason."[110] Moderates, too, declared themselves satisfied. It was possible to infer from Broglie's reply, observed the *Journal des débats*, that the government repudiated the hostile language of the pastoral.[111] The clerical and leftist camps were divided. The more responsible ultramontane spokesmen found the premier's statement "wise and firm."[112] But the militants, led by Veuillot, attacked it as a piece of unmitigated heresy.[113] Among the republicans there were some who congratulated Broglie[114] and others who admitted that he had replied in a manner to satisfy "the men of good sense" who interrogated him.[115] The more authoritative leftist organs, however, found his utterance inadequate. The premier's response, declared the *République française*, was adroit strategy in France, but it would scarcely satisfy Europe. For, after all, the government was compromised by its avowed allies, the clericals.[116] Broglie, the *Siècle* conceded, had "implicitly disavowed" the anti-Italian policy demanded by Guibert. But such a rejoinder was not entirely satisfactory. It was not, vis-à-vis Italy, what it should have been. If only a question of internal policy had been involved, the reply would have been acceptable. But this was a question of foreign policy. Italy had been deeply offended by the pastoral. Consequently, it was not enough to say that this document was alien to the French authorities. It was necessary to go farther, to censure Guibert's manifesto. It was the duty of the government to intervene in this fashion.[117] Guibert

---

[110] Cf. *Gazette de France*, September 13, 1873.

[111] *Journal des débats*, September 13, 1873.

[112] *Monde*, September 13, 1873.

[113] The *Univers* went so far as to accuse Broglie of affirming the separation of church and state (cf. the issue of September 13, 1873).

[114] Cf. *Rappel*, September 13, 1873.

[115] Cf. *XIXe siècle*, September 13, 1873.

[116] *République française*, September 13, 1873.

[117] *Siècle*, September 13, 1873.

himself could well afford to ignore the government's implied disapproval. He was amply rewarded for his sensational gesture. In December he received the cardinal's hat from the grateful pontiff.[118]

The tone of Guibert's pastoral was rivaled by that of leading legitimist and ultramontane organs. The *Union* contributed the following blast:

What a great mistake to believe that one must set Europe on fire in order to compel the invaders of the Eternal City to pack up and go. . . . . Not a shot will be fired. . . . . The Piedmontese will withdraw under the pressure of the church's anathema, under the pressure of the hostility of the Catholics in Italy, under the prossuic of the judgment which the whole Christian world has passed against them. They will retreat before the abyss of the constantly growing deficit and before the absolute impossibility of going on. When Henri V will be where he should be, it will not be necessary for him to undertake an expedition to Rome in order to fulfil his duty as the eldest son of the church. . . . .[119]

The *Gazette de France* asserted that Italian unity, which was "absolutely artificial," the product of intrigue and violence, would have quickly succumbed without the self-seeking support of the powers. It existed solely by virtue of the favor of foreigners. Victor Emmanuel's forthcoming trip was "the manifestation of this dependence." And the day the legitimate monarchy was restored in France, the Italian question would be "easily solved."[120] Veuillot joyfully proclaimed that the restoration of the Bourbon monarchy would strengthen the clerical party in Italy, Austria, Bavaria, and other countries. The united influence of these powerful ultramontane groups, he predicted, would compel Victor Emmanuel to abandon Rome. If force should be required to expel the Italians, France would not hesitate to use it. "We do not fear war," he announced, "when it is undertaken on behalf of a just cause; we fear violence only when it serves the purpose of giving sanction to murderous attacks." He contended that

[118] A. Debidour, *L'Eglise catholique et l'état sous la Troisième République* (Paris, 1906), I, 109.

[119] *Union*, September 4, 1873.

[120] *Gazette de France*, September 15, 1873.

this position was the only truly patriotic one. "For history shows that our misfortunes began with the abandonment of Rome, and therefore our successes will return when we undertake the struggle on behalf of this cause." He assured his readers that "the liberty of Rome is necessary to the normal life of peoples" and that "the revolution will not last forever." Already Italy understood that she no longer had to do with the France which sent Sénard to Florence. Significant events were impending. "There will come a France of Christ. If Italy is wise, she will not wait until this happens."[121]

At this juncture, the Count of Chambord precipitated something of a sensation. Betraying a shrewdness which most people did not associate with the Bourbon mentality, he sought to disavow the joyous battle cry of his more irrepressible followers and disclaim any intention of plunging France into a war with Italy. In a letter to one of his adherents, dated September 19, he sharply decried the propaganda of his adversaries who, in an effort to discredit him, were raising the specter "of a war madly undertaken under impossible conditions, of a government of priests." The legitimists exulted. This "admirable" document, they contended, frustrated the endeavors of the radicals to misrepresent the count's views.[122] Henceforth, it would not be easy to link the re-establishment of the monarchy with such things as feudal rights and religious intolerance.[123] The *Journal des débats* was frankly skeptical. Chambord, it drily remarked, had principles, or rather "superstitions," of which he would never rid himself. "Rome and France will always be associated in his thinking."[124] The *Monde* joined the legitimists in lauding Chambord's letter as a satisfactory reply to "the nonsense and the calumnies of the radicals."[125] But the pre-

[121] *Univers*, September 7, 1873.

[122] Cf. *Gazette de France*, October 2, 1873.   [123] *Union*, October 3, 1873.

[124] *Journal des débats*, October 1, 1873.

[125] *Monde*, October 4, 1873. Shortly before the publication of Chambord's letter, the *Monde* had declared that the count, once he had become king of France, would

tender's disclaimers were hardly gratifying to Veuillot and his friends who were most impatient to see Henri V at the head of another Roman expedition.[126] The discreetly worded document took the republicans somewhat unawares, and their press, once recovered from the shock, hotly impugned its significance. Chambord, it was charged, knew "all the artifices of the language of the Jesuits." He cultivated equivocation and was adept in the art of concocting double meanings.[127] His assurances that he would not make war on behalf of the Holy Father were discounted as entirely futile.[128] His heredity, his past, and his education were declared to be altogether too familiar.[129] His earlier affirmations of undying loyalty to the cause of the pope-king were ironically recalled to prove the dictum: "Other times, other style."[130] Now he was warmly protesting against those who regarded him as capable of "madly undertaking" a war against Italy "under impossible conditions." The people of France could therefore relax, these critics sarcastically concluded. For if their future king should throw himself into an adventure for the benefit of the temporal power, he would do so "wisely" and under "possible" conditions.[131] These devastating strictures did

---

not pursue an aggressive foreign policy. He would not, it had continued, force his country, still weak from its recent wounds, into a war with Italy. The Holy See itself would not ask him thus to compromise his crown and risk new disasters (issue of September 7, 1873).

[126] The chagrin of the *Univers* was very imperfectly disguised behind half-hearted denials that Chambord was repudiating any part of his program (cf. the issue of October 2, 1873).

[127] *Siècle*, October 2, 1873. The *Siècle*, less than two weeks earlier, had contended that Chambord could have but one policy—"to re-establish the pope in the plenitude of his temporal power and in all the rights of his former kingdom in order to restore both the preponderance of France and the prestige of the legitimate monarchy." Were this program suppressed, the republican sheet concluded, the pretender would cease to have a *raison d'être* (issue of September 20, 1873).

[128] *Rappel*, October 2, 3, and 4, 1873.

[129] *République française*, October 3, 1873.

[130] *XIXe siècle*, October 2, 1873.   [131] *Ibid.*

not, however, deter French spokesmen from making the most of the count's letter to reassure the Italians.[132]

On September 17, Victor Emmanuel, accompanied by Minghetti and Visconti-Venosta, arrived in Vienna. His coming was preceded by attempts on the part of the Austrian clericals to rouse the populace against this alleged affront to their faith. The lead was taken by the Arch-fraternity of the Archangel Michael. It summoned all devout Catholics to assemble in commemoration of the papal Zouaves who three years earlier had died in defense of the Eternal City. But the violence of language with which these rites were announced and placarded throughout the city offended most Viennese, and the entire press, with the exception of the clerical organs, outdid itself in welcoming the royal guest. One ultramontane newspaper which ventured to appear in mourning was confiscated by the government. The clamor of his clerical compatriots made little impression on Andrássy. He even allowed a great military parade in honor of Victor Emmanuel to take place on September 20, the third anniversary of the occupation of Rome.[133] The Vatican was furious with Francis Joseph and his foreign minister. The Italians were naturally delighted,[134] and there was much rejoicing in Rome.[135] The emperor was indeed a most solicitous host, and the visit passed off very pleasantly. The Italians had ample reason to congratulate themselves. The appearance of their king in Vienna as the guest of the Hofburg constituted a signal vic-

[132] Cf., e.g., Gontaut-Biron's remarks to Launay in Gontaut-Biron, *op. cit.*, pp. 409–10.

[133] Przibram, *Erinnerungen eines alten Oesterreichers* (Stuttgart and Leipzig, 1910), I, 371.

[134] Minghetti, who came away with a lively sense of gratitude for the cordial reception given his sovereign (cf. Sandonà, *op. cit.*, I, 102–3), wrote Luzzatti: "But think: the emperor of Austria offers the king of Italy, at Vienna, a great military review on the day of September 20, the anniversary of the taking of Rome!" (Luzzatti, *op. cit.*, I, 380).

[135] Pusswald to Andrássy, September 20, 1873, HHSA, Politisches Archiv (Berichte aus Rom [Italien 1873]), Fasz. XI/81, No. 30A, fols. 246*b*–247*a*.

tory over Austrian clericalism.[136] More than that, Andrássy
assured them that he would in no way support the pope's
claims and would join France in no action affecting the
papacy.[137] This led Minghetti to believe that "they are persuaded at Vienna that there is no more turning back."[138]
Nor was the French ambassador at Vienna left in the dark as
to the motivation of the visit. Victor Emmanuel, though
avowing his friendliness toward France, did not hesitate to
speak to him of his apprehension over the likelihood of a
monarchical restoration in that country.[139]

The Italian party arrived in Berlin on September 22.[140]
Bismarck, like his visitors, believed that the Count of Chambord, once king of France, would pursue a reactionary, propapal policy, and that sooner or later conflicts with either
Italy or Germany would follow.[141] In his eagerness to consolidate the Italo-German accord, he told the Italians what
they wanted to hear. Their fears of a French coup to resurrect the temporal power were allayed by the promise that
Germany would not permit Italy to be attacked.[142] This

---

[136] Eduard von Wertheimer, *Graf Julius Andrássy: sein Leben und seine Zeit*
(Stuttgart, 1910), II, 201.

[137] Francesco Crispi, *Politica estera* (Milano, 1913), p. 2; cf. also Walter Schinner,
Der österreichisch-italienische Gegensatz auf dem Balkan und an der Adria (Stuttgart,
1936), p. 7.

[138] Luzzatti, *op. cit.*, I, 380. After Victor Emmanuel's visit to Vienna, some Italian observers were inclined to believe that Austria regarded the end of the temporal
power and the unity of the peninsula as accomplished facts (cf. Maioli, *op. cit.*,
p. 217).

[139] *DDF* (1st ser.), I, No. 237, 262.

[140] In his first conversation with the German emperor, Victor Emmanuel remarked that he had thought of taking up arms against Prussia in the summer of
1870. This frankness made a good impression on William (cf. Heinrich von Sybel,
Die Begründung des deutschen Reiches durch Wilhelm I [München and Leipzig, 1899],
VII, 406–7).

[141] Gontaut-Biron, *op. cit.*, p. 387; Hajo Holborn (ed.), *Aufzeichnungen und
Erinnerungen aus dem Leben des Botschafters Joseph Maria von Radowitz* (Berlin and
Leipzig, 1925), I, 282.

[142] Crispi, *Politica estera*, p. 3; William L. Langer, *European Alliances and Alignments, 1871–1890* (New York, 1931), p. 35; Luzzatti, *op. cit.*, I, 380; Schinner, *op.
cit.*, p. 7.

promise was all they needed to regain their self-assurance. Gontaut-Biron reported not long afterward: "Count Launay is courteously but frankly hostile. He impresses me, since the visit of his king to Berlin, as taking little airs of triumph which I had not seen him do till now."[143] Minghetti himself told a correspondent of the *Libertà* that he was "very satis-fied" with the outcome of the conversations with Bismarck.[144] The premier had much to say about the "complete success" of the voyage when he subsequently saw Wimpffen in Rome. Austria, he assured the envoy, could be very well satisfied with the tenor of the Italo-German conversations at Berlin. He continued:

> I have the conviction that an entente *à trois*, or *à quatre* if that is possi-ble, is in harmony with the interests of all. . . . . As between Austria, Prussia and Italy, we are certainly the most interested in the maintenance of peace, particularly as long as we have not reorganized our army and re-established equilibrium between our expenses and our revenue. . . . . I am of the opinion that in the event of occurrences menacing to the peace of Europe, the three of us should exchange views with perfect loyalty and frankness and make every possible effort to arrive at a common under-standing while consulting our individual interests.

Minghetti did not hide from Wimpffen the fact that the only dangers against which Italy had to fortify herself emanated from France. Though admitting the possibility that the Count of Chambord might shortly come into power, the veteran statesman did not believe that this scion of the House of Bourbon would of his own accord wish, immediately after his accession, to throw himself into an expedition against Italy. But there was reason to fear that sooner or later Chambord would fall victim to the influence of the cleri-cal party. Consequently, it was the duty of the Italian gov-ernment, in Minghetti's opinion, to be on the alert.[145] Vis-conti-Venosta agreed with his chief in attaching the greatest importance to the results of the voyage and of the conversa-

---

[143] Gontaut-Biron, *op. cit.*, p. 411.   [144] *Libertà*, September 30, 1873.

[145] Wimpffen to Andrássy, October 18, 1873, HHSA, Politisches Archiv (Berichte aus Rom [Italien, 1873]), Fasz. XI/81, No. 33, fols. 277*a*–279*b*.

tions at Vienna and Berlin. He regarded the entente established between the three countries as "the best guarantee of
peace and security."[146] The German government, which now
began to regard Italy as a dependable ally,[147] likewise had
reason to be gratified. No formal alliance, however, was concluded. One authoritative Berlin newspaper pointed out that
a treaty was not necessary, inasmuch as the two countries
would co-operate against their common enemies—France and
clericalism—without any written agreement. The *Provinzial-
Correspondenz* explained that the occasion for definite diplomatic pacts would arise only when peace should actually be
threatened.[148] Moreover, Visconti-Venosta was more optimistic than most of his colleagues about the prospect of an
eventual republican success in France. He believed that the
conclusion of an alliance at this time would be premature as it
would obstruct the Franco-Italian understanding to which he
doggedly looked forward.[149]

The Italian press descanted somewhat grandiloquently
upon the significance of the *pourparlers* at Berlin. The *Opinione* proclaimed that Italy and Germany were bound to each
other in self-defense against the depredations of that clericalism which was the mortal enemy of Italian and German
nationality. Italy would not abandon the struggle as long as
a political party which concealed its true aims beneath the
mantle of religion dared to challenge the liberal nations.[150]
In the reception accorded her ruler at Berlin, the *Libertà*
trimphantly announced, Italy perceived a guarantee of her
freedom and unity. Henri V ought now to realize that, even
if he should succeed in gaining the French throne, it would be
impossible for him to make himself "the executor of the
wishes of M. Veuillot." And always to be remembered was

---

[146] Wimpffen to Andrássy, November 1, 1873, *ibid.*, No. 35A, fol. 287*a*.

[147] Cf. Holborn, *op. cit.*, I, 279.

[148] Ludwig Hahn, *Fürst Bismarck* (Berlin, 1878), II, 607–8.

[149] Cf. Italicus, *Italiens Dreibundpolitik, 1870–1896* (München, 1928), p. 27.

[150] *Opinione*, September 24, 1873.

the fact that a different attitude on the part of France might have obviated the royal visits.[151] To all of this, the Vatican retorted by assuring its supporters that there was no cause for alarm. The *Osservatore romano* pointed out that, prior to Victor Emmanuel's departure, the Italian press had had much to say about impending alliances, treaties, and territorial pacts between Germany, Austria, and Italy. Nothing was said about them now. The bedrock of the whole business, it continued, was as follows: The voyage to Vienna and Berlin had been organized by the Italian cabinet under pressure from the revolutionary party in order to intimidate French public opinion and the Versailles assembly and thus to prevent the proclamation of the monarchy. But this maneuver had failed completely.[152] The *Voce della verità* was likewise convinced that nothing serious had been accomplished at Berlin. No treaty, it asserted, had been concluded. The trip to Vienna had also failed to improve Italy's international position. Indeed, the Austrian and Italian governments, far from having broken the ice, were becoming increasingly estranged. And the community of interests between Germany and Italy was not as great as might be supposed.[153]

Some observers in France were ready to believe that their country's diplomatic position had never been bleaker. In the opinion of one contemporary chronicler, the Italo-German *rapprochement* showed that, "if the republic isolated France, the monarchy would not necessarily attract to her the friendship of all European nations."[154] Nor were Frenchmen in any doubt as to one of the mainsprings of that *rapprochement*. Gontaut-Biron's observation that Germany and Italy were seriously disturbed by the increased possibility of a restoration of the temporal power[155] would have come as no surprise

[151] *Libertà*, September 24, 26, and 27, 1873.

[152] *Osservatore romano*, October 2, 1873.

[153] *Voce della verità*, October 1, 1873.

[154] Cf. *Année politique, 1874*, p. 35.   [155] *DDF* (1st ser.), I, No. 240, 266.

to his compatriots. For weeks, leftist newspapers in France had been hammering home the message that the legitimist-ultramontane agitation was exposing the country to disasters as great as those which had just overtaken it. The apparent severance of the bonds which made Italy the natural ally of France had given rise to disconsolate reflections which were rendered even more lugubrious by reports of an Austro-German-Italian alliance. Another German invasion and further dismemberment—notably the loss of Nice and Savoy—had been freely predicted;[156] and Broglie had been adjured to break with the ultramontane party and send Fournier back to Rome.[157] Even among the clericals there were some who did not disguise the fact that France's international position had taken a turn for the worse. Thus the *Monde*, which a few months earlier had declared in all positiveness that an anti-French alliance had been concluded by Italy and Germany,[158] had no choice but to concede the significance of Victor Emmanuel's voyage.[159] True, moderates were inclined to place little credence in the rumors of an anti-French alliance between Vienna, Berlin, and Rome. They kept insisting that the importance of Victor Emmanuel's visits had been exaggerated and that no *démarche* hostile to France had been intended. But even they did not question the reality of the Italo-German *rapprochement* vis-à-vis the common danger from the clericals.[160] Mazade, though he too professed to attach no very great political importance to Victor Emmanuel's visits, admitted that the agitation of French Catholics was thrusting their country into "a sort of moral isolation."[161] And the outlook for peace, in the opinion of Broglie's radical adversaries, seemed none too bright. They had been seeking

---

[156] *XIXe siècle*, September 3, 1873; *Rappel*, September 3, 1873; *Siècle*, September 2 and 18, 1873.

[157] *Rappel*, September 5, 1873.

[158] *Monde*, June 17, 1873.   [159] *Ibid.*, September 20, 1873.

[160] Cf. *Journal des débats*, September 3, 17, and 29, and October 1, 1873.

[161] *Revue des deux mondes*, October 1, 1873, pp. 713–14.

to convince the nation that the accession of Henri V would promptly be followed by a war in which Italy and Germany would join forces against France. They had pointed to the alleged alliance between the Bourbon pretender and the Jesuits as an adequate explanation of Italian belligerency. They had been summoning their country to decide whether it cared to renew "for the beautiful eyes of the papacy" an enterprise which had cost it "ten milliards and two provinces."[162] This extreme pessimism was by no means shared by all Frenchmen. But it was not unrepresentative of large sections of public opinion. For at no time had the Third Republic appeared more friendless.

The significance of Victor Emmanuel's visits to Vienna and Berlin was all too apparent to the French government. But there was little it could do except reaffirm the groundlessness of the fears which had sent the Italians to those capitals. In the course of a conversation with Arnim late in September, Broglie sought to minimize the importance of the clerical agitation and asserted that few Frenchmen had any desire to see the ultramontane program realized.[163] He too shared the view, he remarked to the German ambassador on October 16, that "the present political constitution of Europe was definitive. If disappointed ambitions, dispossessed princes, and His Holiness himself hoped for the fulfilment of their wishes from France, they would be bitterly disappointed."[164] He had no objection, he wrote a few days later to his ambassador in Vienna, to an Austro-Italian *rapprochement*. For friendly relations between those two states might make it easier for the Hapsburg monarchy to discharge a duty resting upon it as well as upon France, namely, that of protecting the freedom of the Holy Father.[165] MacMahon himself was convinced

---

[162] Cf. the *XIXᵉ siècle*, September 1 and 3, 1873; *Rappel*, September 13, 1873.

[163] *GP*, I, No. 134, 214.

[164] *Ibid.*, No. 136, p. 219.   [165] *DDF* (1st ser.), I, No. 241, 272.

that, in the end, he would be able to come to an understanding with the king of Italy, his former comrade in arms. On one occasion, he remarked to Broglie: "I will write to Victor Emmanuel. He knows me. We made war together. He will believe what I tell him."[166] Impending events were to bring that understanding much nearer than even the old soldier could have surmised.

[166] Broglie, *op. cit.*, pp. 146–47.

CHAPTER XI

THE RECALL OF THE "ORENOQUE" AND THE ITALO-FRENCH *DETENTE*

THE first weeks of October, 1873, were golden ones for the French royalists. Recent developments had altered both picture and prospect in their country, and they were firm in the belief that a monarchist victory was assured.[1] Chesnelong had gone as their emissary to see the Count of Chambord at Salzburg. What he was able to report seemed to bode well for their success. The pretender's insistence that he would never agree to any compromise where the flag was concerned[2] had been deplored by his followers as jeopardizing his chances. Now, however, he declared himself ready to defer action on this question until after his accession to the throne.[3] But the effect of this concession was promptly nullified by the prince himself. On October 31 the *Union* published a letter from Chambord to Chesnelong in which the former clearly indicated that the white ensign of his house was the only one acceptable to him.[4] This intransigent gesture wrecked the legitimist cause. The count's letter, Broglie wrote to Gontaut-Biron, had caused his followers to abandon the idea of restoring the monarchy.[5] Even the most ardent royalists were in despair,

[1] Comte de Falloux, *Mémoires d'un royaliste* (Paris, 1888), II, 567; Charles Chesnelong, *La Campagne monarchique d'octobre 1873* (Paris, 1895), pp. 170, 176, 236.

[2] This despite the fact that the pope, at the suggestion of Bishop Dupanloup, had advised him to yield on this issue (Vicomte de Meaux, *Souvenirs politiques, 1871–1877* [Paris, 1908] p. 169; Joseph Schmidlin, *Papstgeschichte der neuesten Zeit* [München, 1933–34], II, 128).

[3] Chesnelong, *op. cit.*, pp. 207–8.

[4] Cf. Falloux, *op. cit.*, II, 577–80; Chesnelong, *op. cit.*, pp. 366–70.

[5] Duc de Broglie, *La Mission de M. de Gontaut-Biron à Berlin* (Paris, 1896), p. 151.

and they agreed that, for the time being, nothing could be done to advance their plans.[6] Bonapartists and republicans were jubilant.[7] Rouher declared that Chambord's letter "buries the legitimate monarchy."[8] The sudden collapse of the legitimist movement profoundly saddened the pontiff and his court.[9] It was easily the severest blow yet administered their much checkered cause. But the resilience of the papalists was proof against even this shock. This demonstration of the pretender's incomparable qualities, they hastily insisted, was something to rejoice in. The count's pronouncement, according to the *Osservatore romano*, was "such a monument of nobility and greatness" that one felt proud "to support a principle which numbers among its foremost champions men of this loyal, magnanimous, and strong fiber." The situation had been thoroughly clarified. France could now "boast of having in the Count of Chambord the man chosen by Providence to preserve her from more terrible disasters."[10] The *Unità cattolica* vied with the great Roman daily in eulogizing the pretender. He was pictured as preferring exile to a throne secured through an unworthy bargain.[11] But though they agreed that the self-styled Henri V was everything he should be, the pope's supporters did not for a moment forget that his cause was, for the time being at least, very much under a cloud. Eschewing useless regrets, they transferred their hopes to Don Carlos of Spain.[12]

The Italian government was delighted. For the moment,

[6] Falloux, *op. cit.*, II, 580; Chesnelong, *op. cit.*, p. 393. They resolved, however, to make the best of a bad situation. The conservative majority in the national assembly voted to extend MacMahon's term of office for seven more years.

[7] Cf. Paul Deschanel, *Gambetta* (London, 1920), p. 179; Falloux, *op. cit.*, II, 583.

[8] Mme Juliette Adam, *Nos amitiés politiques avant l'abandon de la revanche* (Paris, 1908), p. 43.

[9] R. P. Lecanuet, *Les dernières années du pontificat de Pie IX* (Paris, 1931), p. 219.

[10] *Osservatore romano*, November 1 and 4, 1873.

[11] *Unità cattolica*, November 4, 1873.

[12] See Camillo Manfroni, *Sulla soglia del Vaticano* (Bologna, 1920), I, 150.

at any rate, it had been freed from a formidable incubus. Public opinion was no less elated. The despair which had pervaded Sinistra circles on the eve of Chambord's suicidal gesture[13] gave way to undisguised relief. Ministerial circles joyfully underlined the eclipse of the legitimist movement. Henri V, the *Libertà* observed with patent satisfaction, had destroyed all hope of establishing an accord between himself and his nation.[14] But though frustrated in the major issue, French clericals and their confreres in Italy had no thought of discontinuing the policy of pinpricks which in the past had proved so annoying to the Quirinal. An opportunity to resume that policy now presented itself. Lieutenant-Colonel de la Haye, the military attaché at the French legation in Rome, died late in December, 1873. He had fought with distinction at the battles of Magenta and Solferino, and numbered among his friends ranking officers of the Italian army. It was arranged that funeral honors should be paid him in the church of San Luigi dei Francesi, which was in the custody of French priests. But when a group of high army dignitaries, headed by the crown prince, announced their intention of attending the ceremony, the clergy of San Luigi dei Francesi declared that their church would not be available. The priest in charge insisted that he was merely obeying instructions from the French ambassador to the Holy See.[15] The incident created a painful impression in Italy. The *Riforma* as usual vented its irritation on the Italian cabinet. It accused Minghetti and his colleagues of submissiveness vis-à-vis France whose arrogance increased with every new instance of Italian

[13] This despair was reflected in the *Riforma's* prediction that a monarchical restoration in France would revive the hopes of European legitimists and reactionaries whose leader was the pope and whose tools were the diplomatists accredited to the Vatican (cf. the issue of October 26, 1873).

[14] *Libertà*, November 2, 1873. The *Libertà* scored Chambord's behavior as "a compound of egoism, arrogance, imbecile vanity and infantile wilfulness." It was truly fortunate, according to this influential sheet, that he and men of his ilk were powerless. For otherwise, "the times of Nero and Caligula would flourish again" (Issue of November 6, 1873).

[15] Cf. Ugo Pesci, *I primi anni di Roma capitale* (Firenze, 1907), p. 146.

pusillanimity.[16] The *Diritto* sarcastically queried whether the church of San Luigi dei Francesi was in French or Italian territory. The action of the directors of that church, it continued, was an insult to the Italian army and a gesture discourteous to the French legation at the Quirinal. In any case, there was reason to feel grateful to the French government for giving from time to time renewed indications of its hostility. Italians were thus enabled to convince themselves that the rights and claims of the two countries were incompatible. And the Italian government was far from blameless in this unpleasant business. It was still partial to France, even though recent events should have opened its eyes.[17] The *Opinione* was furious with the French authorities. "One must recognize," it declared, "that the government at Versailles is abetting . . . . the designs of the Italian clericals. It passes up no opportunity to offend the sentiments of Italians."[18] The *Unità cattolica* did not allow this aspersion to go unchallenged. It retorted by accusing the Italian government of wishing to convert the proposed funeral services in the church of San Luigi dei Francesi into a demonstration in favor of the recall of the "Orénoque."[19]

The French ultramontanes made the incident the signal for a characteristic arraignment of their republican adversaries. The *Univers* argued that the unpleasantness of the episode was entirely attributable to the leftist Parisian journals. If the latter had not constantly championed the Italian cause, the Quirinal would not have dared to complain of the action taken by the guardians of San Luigi dei Francesi.[20] The *Monde*, in a similar vein, accused the radicals of bad faith. It charged that the clergy of San Luigi dei Francesi had been calumnied "without reason and proof."[21] The *Français*, as became a ministerial organ, insisted that nothing irregular had happened. The obsequies had proceeded with-

[16] *Riforma*, January 4, 1874.

[17] *Diritto*, January 3 and 5, 1874.

[18] *Opinione*, January 4, 1874.

[19] *Unità cattolica*, January 6, 1874.

[20] *Univers*, January 5, 1874.

[21] *Monde*, January 5 and 6, 1874.

out detriment to the honor of De la Haye or of France. It therefore appeared impossible to turn this innocuous affair into an international incident.[22] The *Journal des débats* emphasized those features of the episode which were certain to prove most distasteful to the ultramontane party. It pointed to the Italian government's patent anxiety to prove that it wished to remain on good terms with France despite the efforts of those who were seeking to sow discord between the two countries. The Italian notables who attended the funeral—these included Crown Prince Humbert, the president of the chamber of deputies, and several generals—regarded it as an honor to accompany De la Haye to his last resting place. This demonstration, the moderate journal concluded, was "very significant."[23] More radical sheets minced no words. The republican *XIXe siècle* deplored the "unfortunate incident" and sharply assailed Corcelles.[24] The *Siècle* found the Roman clergy guilty of scandalous intolerance. "The body of one of our officers," it wailed, "is brutally put out of a church which bears the name of France."[25] Some well-informed observers professed no little alarm over the ultimate outcome of this campaign of pinpricks which the ultramontane party was waging with such tenacity. Thiers was one of them. He feared that the French government, despite the moderation of its new foreign minister, the Duke Decazes,[26] might be drawn into serious quarrels with Italy.[27] The former president's uneasiness was understandable enough, but it was an incontrovertible fact, as Arnim pointed out to Bismarck,

[22] *Français*, January 5, 1874.

[23] *Journal des débats*, January 4, 1874.

[24] *XIXe siècle*, January 5, 1874.   [25] *Siècle*, January 4, 1874.

[26] In the reorganization of the French cabinet following the extension of MacMahon's term of office, Decazes had been assigned to the foreign office (cf. Broglie, *op. cit.*, p. 154). He was an Orleanist whose moderate views separated him from the extreme right. He preferred an alliance with the left center (cf. Chesnelong, *L'Avènement de la République, 1873–1875* [Paris, 1934], pp. 5 and 7).

[27] *Staatsarchiv*, XXVIII, No. 5405, 184–85.

that the continued protection of the pope had become for France a question of honor.[28]

Even more exasperating to Italians than the De la Haye affair was the treatment meted out to Fournier. The Italophil envoy had failed to return to his post in the autumn of 1873, and this protracted absence was generally interpreted as the prelude to his removal. In the meantime, the French legation at the Quirinal remained without a titular head, much to the disgust of the Italian government. The latter, by way of reprisal, gave Nigra an indefinite leave of absence. At the beginning of December, however, the situation was clarified by an official announcement that Fournier had resigned. The latter's dismissal—such was the general interpretation placed upon this announcement—was sincerely regretted in Italy, where his friendly attitude had won him wide acclaim. His reputation as an anticlerical had endeared him particularly to the Sinistra. It sufficed to make him popular in leftist circles that he was accused by the ultramontanes of having instigated the suppression of the religious orders in Rome.[29] When Fournier appeared to present his letters of recall, Victor Emmanuel remarked: "I am angry with you for leaving us; we loved you." The Frenchman replied that his departure was not a voluntary one. It was because he loved Italy too much that he was being dismissed, the king quickly interjected. The latter went on to express his uneasiness over the future of Franco-Italian relations. He was anxious, he said, to ascertain the intentions of the present rulers of France. It was true that they said nice things to Italy, but so far they had failed to live up to these assurances. He feared that the faction now in power in France might commit too many mistakes while carried away by its passions.[30] "Do not," he queried, "certain parties in France know that

---

[28] *Ibid.*, p. 184.

[29] Pietro Vigo, *Storia degli ultimi trent'anni del secolo XIX* (Milano, 1908), I, 323.

[30] Daniel Halévy, *La Fin des notables* (Paris, 1930), pp. 479–80.

distrust and bad feeling toward Italy are desired by those who do not love France? . . . . It is truly deplorable that such blindness should find its origin and pretext in religious considerations."[31]

The announcement of Fournier's resignation prompted the French clericals to renew their demand that the government abstain altogether from filling the post at the Quirinal.[32] The *Univers* spun out an elaborate argument in defense of this position. The September convention still existed, it contended. Therefore, Italy's obligation vis-à-vis France and that of France vis-à-vis the Holy See had remained intact. The presence of a French minister at the court of Victor Emmanuel would consecrate the occupation of Rome and annul the convention. His absence, on the other hand, would not constitute a declaration of war against Italy. It would be only "a protest against facts accomplished in violation of a treaty." And though Italy might betray resentment, she could not make this a pretext for war.[33] But these contentions, which did not fail to evoke a sharp retort from the Italian ministerial press,[34] were of no avail. On December 6 the appointment of the Marquis of Noailles as Fournier's successor was announced in the *Journal officiel*.[35] The Italian government promptly instructed Nigra to return to Versailles. The new envoy to Italy, who was then serving as French minister in Washington, was known as a man of moderate views, and his appointment was applauded by his republican compatriots. If Fournier had to be sacrificed, they

---

[31] Vigo, *op. cit.*, I, 323–24; Giuseppe Massari, *La Vita ed il regno di Vittorio Emanuele II di Savoia* (Milano, 1910), II, 362. On this occasion, Victor Emmanuel paid tribute to Thiers. "Tell him," he said to Fournier, "that I have a strong feeling of friendship for him" (Henri Hauser [ed.], *Histoire diplomatique de l'Europe* [Paris, 1929], I, 83).

[32] *Univers*, December 3, 1873.   [33] *Ibid.*, December 4, 1873.

[34] The present government of France, the *Opinione* pointed out, was not entitled to consider the obligations of the imperial government as its own (issue of December 8, 1873).

[35] Cf. Vol. CXCVII, p. 7489 of this publication.

held, a better choice could not have been made.[36] The clericals were of course deeply mortified. "Jules Favre still directs our foreign relations," the *Univers* despairingly proclaimed.[37] But Veuillot and his friends were not yet disposed to consider the incident closed. Speaking in the name of his party, General du Temple declared that he would denounce this latest recognition of the Italian kingdom in an interpellation from the floor of the national assembly.[38] Moderates protested violently against this provocative gesture. It was necessary to tell the general and his associates, they urged, that France was sending a new minister to the Quirinal in order to free her relations with Italy of all equivocation.[39] One of their principal organs declared:

With all due deference to the clerical party, France and Italy ask only to live in peace with each other. We are therefore not disturbed over the outcome of the campaign which this party wages with so much fervor. . . . . The reply of the government and the attitude of the assembly will prove to these fanatics that France refuses to associate herself with the policy of hate and war pursued today by ultramontanism.[40]

Du Temple, nevertheless, persisted in his demand for a hearing. The government was at no loss for a reply. On January 20, 1874, the assembly listened to a forceful and reassuring speech by Decazes. The latter most emphatically stated that there was not the slightest dissension between Italy and France. No issue had been raised by either side "which might compromise the good relations which we are anxious to maintain with our neighbors." The present government was sending Noailles to Rome because it was resolved to adhere strictly to the policy hitherto pursued toward Italy. That policy had a double objective:

To surround the august pontiff . . . . with pious respect, sympathy, and filial solicitude, it being understood that this protection and this solicitude

---

[36] Cf. the *Siècle*, December 7, 1873.   [37] *Univers*, December 7, 1873.

[38] *Année politique, 1874*, pp. 85–86; Lieutenant-Colonel Rousset, *La République conservatrice* (Paris, 1914), I, 170.

[39] Cf. Mazade in *Revue des deux mondes*, January 1, 1874, p. 228.

[40] *Journal des débats*, January 4, 1874.

were to be extended to all interests connected with the spiritual authority, the independence and the dignity of the Holy Father; to maintain, without *arrière pensée*, harmonious, peaceful and friendly relations . . . . with Italy, such as circumstances have made her.

The government, he continued, desired peace because the greatness and prosperity of France required it. And, in order that peace might be assured, every effort would be made "to dissipate all misunderstandings and prevent all conflicts." The honor and dignity of France would be compromised not by such a policy but by one more adventuresome.[41] This appeal had the intended effect. In accordance with the orator's request, the assembly voted to shelve the interpellation.

Decazes's conciliatory statement was received with mixed feelings in France.[42] Ministerial organs were profuse in their praise of the foreign minister's statesman-like outlook. The observations of the *Français* were typical. The government, it explained, wished to avoid a "sterile" and "dangerous" discussion. Decazes had seized this opportunity to make some "very precise declarations" on foreign policy, and his auditors now understood that it was their duty to shunt the question posed by Du Temple.[43] Organs of the center and left hurried to claim the duke as a friend and ally. The *Temps* alluded to the "wisdom" which inspired his pronouncement. "Here," it declared, "is the claim of the temporal power solemnly removed from the program of the right."[44] Decazes's remarks, in the opinion of the *Journal des débats*, were "as satisfactory as possible." They confirmed the truth of the assertion that recently there had been no real dissension between the two governments.[45] The *République française* predicted that the foreign secretary's address would produce a favorable impression in other countries as well as in France.

[41] *AAN*, XXIX (January 20, 1874), 208.

[42] And not with general approval as Broglie asserts (cf. Broglie, *op. cit.*, pp. 179–80).

[43] *Français*, January 22, 1874.

[44] *Temps*, January 22, 1874.   [45] *Journal des débats*, January 22, 1874.

It remarked that Decazes had spoken, "as became him, of the factitious and noisy agitation carried on for some time past by the ultramontanes." It was none too soon, according to Gambetta's mouthpiece, "to signify to France and to Europe the necessary divorce of the government from the clerical faction."[46] The *Siècle* found the policy announced by the duke identical with that for long espoused in its own columns.[47] The *Rappel* joined the *Temps* in designating Decazes's remarks as "the final blow dealt the hopes of those who dreamt of a restoration of the temporal power."[48] The new foreign minister had indeed won many friends on the left, but this ephemeral popularity was somewhat offset by the strain which his declaration placed upon the government's relations with the legitimist-ultramontane coalition. The *Gazette de France* complained that Decazes had gone altogether too far in stressing his country's desire for friendly relations with Italy. The present condition of France, it conceded, did constrain her to maintain peace, but all possible declarations of amity could not obscure the fact that Italian unity had been achieved in opposition to the most precious interests of France. For the time being, war was out of the question. It was incomprehensible, however, that this duty to keep the peace should oblige France to sanction the results of the policy pursued by the empire and by the "Piedmontese" government.[49] The *Monde*, asserting that silence would have been better, sharply assailed the duke's pronouncement. But it hurried to reiterate that the Catholics of France had no thought of precipitating a war "against all Europe."[50]

Decazes's judicious utterance was warmly appreciated by most Italians.[51] The French chargé d'affaires at the Quirinal

---

[46] *République française*, January 22, 1874.

[47] *Siècle*, January 21, 1874.   [49] *Gazette de France*, January 22, 1874.

[48] *Rappel*, January 22, 1874.   [50] *Monde*, January 22, 1874.

[51] Cf. Luigi Chiala, *Dal 1858 al 1892; pagine di storia contemporanea* (Torino, 1892–93), I, 177.

reported that it had made a "very satisfactory impression" on Visconti-Venosta,[52] who hastened to convey his gratification to Decazes.[53] The *Opinione* acknowledged the latter's sincerity, although it could not refrain from pointing out that solicitude for the spiritual independence of the pope "is not the special prerogative of anyone."[54] But the irreconcilables of the left attached little weight to the duke's language and continued to proclaim their distrust of France.[55] The *Riforma* insisted that Decazes's declarations introduced nothing new into the situation and that they in no way altered Italy's position vis-à-vis France. Their only result, it predicted, would be to alienate from Italy the sympathies of Germany.[56] The *Diritto* concluded that the French were beginning to realize the significance of the united Italo-German front against clericalism. But words, it warned, were insufficient. The recall of the "Orénoque" would constitute a real earnest of good will.[57] It was felt in certain quarters, the Rome correspondent of the *Temps* reported, that Decazes might have been more explicit in announcing a change of policy in the Roman question.[58] Circles close to the Vatican held that the French ultramontanes had committed a tactical blunder. Antonelli himself decried Du Temple's action. In the cardinal's opinion, it was "unreasonable to raise questions which can only lead to the solemn affirmation of the sad situation of France and the Holy See."[59] The *Unità cattolica*, however, refused to dissemble its dissatisfaction with the language of the foreign minister. Could the French government, it asked, at one and the same time " 'surround the august pontiff . . . . with pious respect, sympathy and filial solicitude' " and maintain friendly relations with Italy, " 'such as circum-

[52] *DDF* (1st ser.), I, No. 270, 302.

[53] André Dreux, *Dernières années de l'ambassade en Allemagne de M. de Gontaut-Biron* (Paris, 1907), p. 39.

[54] *Opinione*, January 22, 1874.

[55] Vigo, *op. cit.*, I, 329.

[56] *Riforma*, January 27, 1874.

[57] *Diritto*, January 22, 1874.

[58] *Temps*, January 25, 1874.

[59] *DDF* (1st ser.), I, No. 274, 305.

stances have made her?' " This, it contended, was manifestly impossible.[60]

Decazes's speech ushered in a noticeable easing of the Franco-Italian tension. "Our relations with the Quirinal," the duke himself recorded early in February, "assume a distinctly tranquil character. . . . . All our consuls in Italy without exception report . . . . a swing of public opinion toward us."[61] Considerable attention was attracted in France by an article in the *Revue des deux mondes* urging a change in the country's Roman policy. The author warned that, if freedom to act were accorded those who spoke in the name of the French episcopate, France would suffer the most calamitous consequences. "It is time," he wrote, "to put an end to these compromising follies; they have prejudiced us all too much in the eyes of Europe. It is time to proclaim that the policy of France is not at the mercy of the passions of a sect." The cause of religious liberty was not at all bound up with that of the temporal power, and only the spiritual independence of the Holy Father, which "never was more real than now," was of importance to the Catholic world. He pleaded for resignation to accomplished facts. No serious Frenchman, he argued, could dream of embarking upon another Roman expedition. It was therefore unwise to talk and act in a threatening manner where Italy was concerned. If France, he significantly concluded, had to have an enemy, she ought to look elsewhere.[62]

Any lasting improvement in the relations between the two countries was impossible, however, as long as the "Orénoque" remained in Italian waters. The overwhelming majority of the Italian nation concurred in the *Riforma's* repeated assertion that the continued presence of the vessel at Civita Vecchia was "intolerable" and "a permanent insult to our

[60] *Unità cattolica*, January 23, 1874.

[61] Dreux, *op. cit.*, p. 40.

[62] P. Lanfrey, "La Politique ultramontaine," *Revue des deux mondes*, February 1, 1874, pp. 693, 697-98.

national dignity."[63] There were many, too, who shared the
Diritto's oft-expressed conviction that the French and the
Vatican were keeping the "Orénoque" where it was in order
to subject Italy to a standing provocation.[64] Of this, Decazes
and his colleagues were fully aware. But they were alive, too,
to the dangers which lurked in an attempt to remove this
formidable source of dissension. Their position, as Lord
Lyons, the British ambassador in Paris, pointed out to his
government, was indeed no enviable one. The veteran diplomatist, reviewing the various issues which might embroil
France with other powers, alluded to Italy as "the most dangerous neighbour from this point of view." The "ticklish
point," he continued, was the presence of the "Orénoque" at
Civita Vecchia. It was "a very delicate matter to touch; for
if the question came very prominently into notice, it might
raise one of the storms in the press of all countries, which are
so often the precursors of evil times."[65] The question was
canvassed in the Italian press at the close of December, 1873,
and early in January, 1874. The *Opinione* took a leading
part in this discussion. The retention of the "Orénoque" in
Italian waters, it remarked, was exceedingly inopportune,
and the French government, in recalling the ship, would be
giving proof of its fairness. The pope, it went on, had no need
of foreign vessels; and France had no interests to defend at
Civita Vecchia.[66] The Italian government, were it so minded,
could send a cruiser to Villefranche or Nice. It refrained
from doing so, but the French government, instead of being
grateful, persisted in maintaining this objectionable outpost
in Italian waters.[67] The papal thesis was vigorously sustained
by the *Unità cattolica*. The Holy Father, it contended, required the protection of a vessel for the eventuality of Italian

[63] Cf. *Riforma*, December 30, 1873, and January 2, 1874.

[64] *Diritto*, January 6, 1874.

[65] Lord Newton, *Lord Lyons: A Record of British Diplomacy* (London, 1913), II,
55.

[66] *Opinione*, December 30, 1873.   [67] *Ibid.*, January 4, 1874.

participation in a European war. As for France, she would be lost the day she recalled the "Orénoque." And in any case, by virtue of a sojourn of almost four years at Civita Vecchia, the vessel had acquired the right to stay there.[68] There were signs that a liquidation of the *vexata quaestio* was not far off. Late in January it was reported that a number of Italian deputies were planning to force a showdown by posing the question in an interpellation. The patience of French moderates and radicals was likewise nearing the vanishing-point. Mazade was reminding his countrymen that the retention of the vessel at Civita Vecchia had been the cause of recurrent difficulties and embarrassments.[69] The *Journal des débats* was showing equal insistence. The "Orénoque," it was saying, had outlived its usefulness; the Holy Father no longer required the service which it was designed to render.[70] The *XIXᵉ siècle*, in even stronger terms, complained that the frigate was being kept in Italian waters despite the fact that the pope was entirely free and had no intention of quitting Rome.[71] "We have the right to demand the recall of the 'Orénoque,'" the *Siècle* somewhat testily announced.[72] And the *Rappel*, after explaining to its readers that the ship was still anchored off Civita Vecchia because the clerical party was indispensable to the life of the present French cabinet,[73] adjured Broglie and his colleagues to satisfy Italy's demands. It was far better, the radical journal pointed out, to act now. Concessions made later in response to a diplomatic note from Italy would appear "an avowal of weakness."[74]

On March 23 all Italy joined in celebrating the twenty-fifth anniversary of Victor Emmanuel's accession.[75] The

[68] *Unità cattolica*, January 4, 1874.

[69] *Revue des deux mondes*, January 15, 1874, pp. 457–58.

[70] *Journal des débats*, February 15, 1874.

[71] *XIXᵉ siècle*, January 6, 1874.

[72] *Siècle*, January 4, 1874.

[73] *Rappel*, January 5, 1874.

[74] *Ibid.*, January 20, 1874.

[75] Cf. Pesci, *I primi anni di Roma capitale*, pp. 548–51.

French press, with the notable exception of the royalist and clerical organs, seized the opportunity to eulogize that monarch and enlarge upon the advantages of friendship with the neighboring kingdom. But this was not all. Noailles, acting on instructions from his government, ordered the officers of the "Orénoque" to commemorate the occasion by hoisting the Italian flag. Victor Emmanuel was distinctly gratified by this show of courtesy,[76] which did not fail to evoke anguished laments from the French ultramontanes.[77] The Italian cabinet was no less pleased. And it was led to expect more tangible evidences of good will. Its faithful mouthpiece, Bonghi, ventured to hope that the current improvement in Franco-Italian relations would be further consolidated by the recall of the "Orénoque."[78] Even the *Riforma* was encouraged to remind the French government that it could still manage, by its deeds, to prove its friendliness to Italy.[79] The fall of the Broglie government on May 16 and the advent six days later of another cabinet likewise dominated by Orleanists but deemed more friendly to Italy seemed to augur well for the future. The retention of Decazes at the foreign office enhanced the optimism on both sides. France, the *Libertà* happily announced, was realizing more and more the wisdom of maintaining friendly relations with Italy.[80] But the invariably Gallophobe Sinistra refused to relent. The moderates, it charged, were giving themselves false illusions about French amity. It mattered little that the rulers of France were liberals. Of far greater moment was the fact that they were availing themselves of the support of the ultramontanes. And as long as the French government remained unwilling to dissociate its cause from that of the Vatican, Italy could never repose confidence in it.[81] An intimate alliance with Germany was still the sole solution.[82]

[76] Vigo, *op. cit.*, I, 347–48.

[77] Cf. *Univers*, April 9, 1874.

[78] *Nuova antologia*, April, 1874, pp. 1019–20.

[79] *Riforma*, April 5, 1874.

[80] *Libertà*, June 11, 1874.

[81] Cf. *Diritto*, June 16, 1874.

[82] *Ibid.*, July 3, 1874.

French ultramontanes did what they could to mar the growing cordiality between Versailles and the Quirinal. In a letter addressed to Minghetti, Bishop Dupanloup served notice that the time had come for Italy to treat the pope more equitably. Unless she now proceeded to do so, he warned, she would some day come to grief. For Europe would remember its duties toward the Holy See. Italy herself had proclaimed the idea of a diplomatic understanding with the powers regarding a solution of the Roman question. It devolved upon the various governments to remind her of this solemn commitment.[83] But this epistle was stingless in comparison with the pastoral which Cardinal Guibert, fresh from a visit to the Vatican, issued in July. The document recorded the irrepressible prelate's wrath at seeing Rome become "the vulgar capital of a modern state." He contended that the church, to be properly governed, had to have at its head a pope who was absolutely independent.

The Italian revolution, in seizing Rome, has not only violated the sacred rights of justice; it has confronted the world with a formidable problem, whose solution can only be the failure of its sacrilegious enterprise or the suppression of the Catholic church, that is to say, of Christianity. . . . .[84]

The cardinal's broadside received extended attention in the Italian press. The French clericals, according to the *Opinione*, were spoiling their own game. They were alienating, by their excess of zeal, the sympathies of otherwise well-disposed compatriots. Even the legitimists, it contended, were becoming aware that their defeat was due to the partnership with the ultramontanes.[85] The *Libertà* showed less restraint. Miraculous indeed, it mocked, was the failure of Guibert to speak of the damp straw on which the pope supposedly lay and of the *bersagliere* who allegedly stood guard at the door of his prison. Somewhat more seriously, it explained that the cardi-

[83] Cf. the text of Dupanloup's letter, which was dated August 25, 1874, in the *Monde*, October 16, 1874; cf. also A. Debidour, *L'Eglise catholique et l'état sous la Troisième République* (Paris, 1906), I, 121–22.

[84] Cf. the text of the pastoral in *Univers*, July 27, 1874.

[85] *Opinione*, July 29, 1874.

nal needed the plaudits of the Jesuits who had helped him
secure the purple. And he had entirely succeeded in this
worthy endeavor.[86] Duplicating its procedure of the previous
year, the Italian government sequestered all newspapers
which had reproduced the bellicose pastoral.[87] This, strangely enough, infuriated the Sinistra. The authorities, it contended, should have posted the pastoral in every locality of
the country. The effect would have been most salutary. Italians would have been cured of hoping for the friendship of a
country which permitted such insulting language against
their king.[88] The government's action, the *Opinione* impatiently retorted, was inspired by the desire to apprise the
world of the painful impression produced by the document.[89]
But on this occasion Minghetti and his colleagues were determined to secure more ample satisfaction.[90] Nigra was instructed to demand of the French government a formal disavowal of the cardinal's language. Decazes was not unwilling
to make amends for his illustrious countryman's provocative
outburst. In response to Nigra's friendly representations, he
published the following communiqué: "The government has
seen with regret the publication of this letter. It is desirable
that it should not be much longer the subject of polemics."[91]
All this made little impression on Guibert. In a letter of con-
dolence which he addressed to the director of the *Osservatore
cattolico* of Milan, who had been sentenced to a fine and imprisonment for having published the pastoral,[92] he asserted
that pope and king could not be domiciled within the same
city and that, as long as Victor Emmanuel retained Rome as
his capital, he would find himself opposed by the entire

[86] *Libertà*, July 30, 1874.

[87] Cf. *ibid.*, July 31, 1874.

[88] *Diritto*, July 31, 1874.

[89] *Opinione*, August 1, 1874.

[90] DDF (1st ser.), I, No. 315, 342.

[91] *Journal officiel de la République française*, CCI (July 31, 1874), 5393; DDF (1st ser.), I, No. 316, 342; Gabriel Hanotaux, *Histoire de la France contemporaine* (Paris, 1903–8), III, 85.

[92] Cf. *Unità cattolica*, November 6, 1874.

Christian world.[93] Nor did the incident produce any greater impression upon Guibert's fellow-prelates.[94]

French moderates and leftists were thoroughly disgusted with the cardinal and his friends. "One asks," the *Temps* declared with unwonted sharpness, "what interest the church has in posing such a dilemma: the suppression of Italian unity or the suppression of Catholicism. Fortunately, the Italian government, wiser than its detractors . . . . does not think of taking them literally; it protects them against themselves."[95] Mazade complained that Guibert had involved himself in new recriminations with Italy and branded his action as "contrary to the cordial relations re-established between the two countries."[96] "Here we have the patriotism of the French clergy," the *Siècle* bitterly remarked. There was but one remedy for such abuses, according to this militant republican organ: the separation of church and state.[97] Pressensé, a political commentator of republican sympathies, wrote that the country was weary of the dangers to which it was being exposed "by an insensate clericalism which dares to give us patriotic counsels after having done all it could to aggravate the situation of France by its untimely petitions and its insulting pastorals." He alluded to the "unfortunate letter of the Archbishop of Paris . . . . which has created so much noise and perhaps so much evil."[98] The ministerial press was not silent on this occasion. Thus, the *Soleil* found Guibert's language "untimely in the present circumstances." It accused him of forgetting that the situation of France imposed upon her the greatest reserve and an unfailing respect for the precepts of prudence.[99]

[93] Vigo, *op. cit.*, I, 384.

[94] Thus, the notoriously Italophobe Bishop of Angers publicly exhorted Mac-Mahon to launch a crusade on behalf of the temporal power (cf. *Revue des deux mondes*, September 1, 1874, pp. 221–22; *Revue politique*, August 29, 1874).

[95] *Temps*, July 29, 1874.

[96] *Revue des deux mondes*, August 15, 1874, p. 939.

[97] *Siècle*, July 27, 1874.

[98] *Revue politique*, August 8, 1874.

[99] *Soleil*, August 2, 1874.

Decazes's communiqué did not entirely satisfy the Italians. The *Opinione* admitted that it was better than nothing. But, the Destra organ continued, "it is permissible to ask whether a mere manifestation of displeasure is really all that the cabinet of Marshal MacMahon could have and should have proffered."[100] "These good French ministers," jeered the *Libertà*, "must have sweated four shirts before deciding to make that little communication." Continuing in the same vein, it thanked the French government for its "supreme effort" and for its demonstration of "incomparable courage."[101] The *Diritto*, its eye always on the domestic scene, assailed the Italian government for its failure to demand more adequate amends.[102] Minghetti himself was far from satisfied. The communiqué, in his opinion, seemed to express "regret over the polemics provoked by the pastoral rather than censure of the contents of Mgr. Guibert's document." Nevertheless, the Quirinal agreed to consider the incident closed.[103] The ministerial press, making the most of Italy's favorable tactical position, proceeded once again to pose the question of the "Orénoque." The *Opinione* pointed out that the protracted stay of the vessel at Civita Vecchia had proved more embarrassing to France than to Italy. Originally, the "Orénoque" had indeed represented the last vestige of the French protectorate over the Holy See. Now, it was only "a puerile gratification" of French *amour propre*, an evidence of France's weakness vis-à-vis the clerical party. The whole business had certainly not enhanced French prestige.[104] The issue was indeed a very plain one, according to the *Libertà*. The recall of the frigate would dispose Italy to place more credence in French professions of good will. As long as the "Orénoque" remained anchored in the waters of Civita Vecchia, Italian suspicion would steadily grow.[105] The matter

---

[100] *Opinione*, August 1, 1874; cf. also Chiala, *Pagine*, I, 186.

[101] *Libertà*, August 2, 1874.

[102] *Diritto*, August 2, 1874.

[103] *DDF* (1st ser.), I, 343 n.

[104] *Opinione*, August 7, 1874.

[105] *Libertà*, August 6, 1874.

was hardly so simple, the Sinistra caustically remonstrated. Without an explicit repudiation by France of her present policy in the Roman question, it was now saying, the withdrawal of the "Orénoque" would be devoid of all value and definitely insufficient to eliminate Italian distrust.[106]

The Minghetti cabinet, which was determined to make the most of the French ministry's chastened temper, needed little prodding. For several months Visconti-Venosta had been intimating the intention of his government to demand the recall of the "Orénoque," but the Versailles authorities had steadfastly refused to engage in formal negotiations on the subject. The Italian foreign minister and his colleagues now decided that the psychological moment to put the question was at hand. Moreover, Minghetti was anxious to have the matter settled as quickly as possible. General elections were scheduled for the autumn, and he wished to face them with his own prestige and that of his party greatly enhanced by so signal a triumph.[107] The tone of certain influential French newspapers encouraged the Italians to believe that their *démarche* would be successful.[108] Decazes's reply, however, did not measure up to their expectations. His government, he said, was prepared to withdraw the "Orénoque" sometime in September. But he intimated that it was to be replaced by

---

[106] *Diritto*, August 12, 1874.   [107] Cf. Chiala, *Pagine*, I, 187.

[108] Early in August the *Temps* remarked: "As regards our relations with Italy, we are certain that in all conversations about the pastoral of the archbishop and the 'Orénoque,' Italian diplomacy has acted with the greatest reserve. It is in a friendly fashion and through official intermediaries that the attention of the French government has been drawn to these subjects." Even more significant were the concurrent observations of the ministerial *Soleil*. Italy, it declared, "has behaved with her usual prudence and finesse. . . . . This attitude does not pass unnoticed by our government. In our opinion, the moment seems to have arrived to remove even the slightest pretext for difficulties between Italy and ourselves. The recall of the 'Orénoque' would be . . . . an act of good policy. The presence of this vessel at Civita Vecchia can only serve the adversaries of a sensible entente between France and Italy." The *Univers*, of course, vehemently opposed such a step. "The recall of the 'Orénoque,' " it warned, "would be . . . . one of the greatest political mistakes." It would be "another humiliation for France." In relinquishing this "post of honor," France would be abandoning her role as a Christian nation (issue of August 4, 1874).

another warship to which the same destination and object would be assigned. Visconti-Venosta pointed out that this question was one of those which "do not allow of half-solutions." To substitute some other vessel for the "Orénoque" "is not," he insisted, "a solution worthy of France." Consequently, the French government was requested to recall the "Orénoque" "purely and simply."[109] Decazes and his colleagues declared that this was a bit too much; but they did agree to station the new guard ship outside Italian waters. In September, MacMahon formally notified the pope of the impending step. The latter, he wrote, had more than once reminded the French government that it must do nothing "which might provoke a conflict and trouble the general peace." The action now being taken, the marshal continued, would not "interrupt the mission which we have assumed, but would modify the conditions in which we have hitherto discharged it." Apart from the material difficulties involved in stationing a vessel at Civita Vecchia, it was more in accord with "our common dignity and independence" to anchor the successor to the "Orénoque" in a French port. This solution avoided foreign complications and enabled France to manifest, as always, "her religious attachment to the Holy Father." The missive closed with the hope that Pius, "appreciating the difficulty of our task," would receive this step "as a new proof of the devotion and the pious respect with which we implore the aid of his holy prayers."[110] The pontiff appeared very much touched by the marshal's letter.[111] He replied that his gratitude for the presence of the "Orénoque" forbade him to allow the prolongation of its stay in Italian waters to create any embarrassments for the French republic. The desire to preserve peace, which inspired the recall of the vessel, was not at all to be censured. Nor was this desire inconsistent with the mandates of filial piety. As a token of his "paternal benevolence," he imparted his blessing to Mac-

[109] *DDF* (1st ser.), I, No. 326, 349–50.

[110] *Ibid.*, No. 331, p. 354.   [111] *Ibid.*, No. 330, p. 353.

Mahon and the French republic.[112] The charitable mood displayed by the Holy Father was not shared by the editors of
the *Osservatore romano*. The latter hastened to declare that
the Vatican would be grieved were "the generous and Catholic French nation, through the fault of those who now govern
it, to be condemned to a new humiliation."[113]

Spurred by reports that the recall of the "Orénoque" was
in the process of negotiation, French moderates and leftists
exhorted their government to put aside all hesitation. The
Journal des débats remarked: "The 'Orénoque,' once back in
French waters, will find there the honor of the country and
the dignity of the government safe and intact."[114] The *Rappel* underscored the folly of antagonizing Italy by maintaining in her waters a vessel which was of no use to the pope and
only served the purposes of Prussia.[115] The *Siècle* emphasized
the nexus between the recall of the "Orénoque" and the re-
establishment of Franco-Italian friendship.[116] One anti-cleri-
cal writer prefaced his plea with a glowing allusion to the
historical and cultural bonds which united the two nations.
Italy, he went on, was "perhaps capable of ingratitude."
But her king "appears not to have forgotten our services."
The question of the "Orénoque" involved neither the honor
nor the territorial integrity of France. Moreover, the pope
was in no danger from Italy, "a Catholic power like ourselves." The entire business had cost France whatever benefits she might have derived from "an opportune and resolute
renunciation of chimerical pretensions."[117] In other quarters
it was urged that the "Orénoque" would be powerless to aid
the pope, should he really need assistance, as long as the territory between Rome and Civita Vecchia remained under
Italian control. In any case—so ran this argument—France

[112] *Ibid.*, No. 332, p. 355.

[113] *Osservatore romano*, October 6, 1874.

[114] *Journal des débats*, September 24, 1874.

[115] *Rappel*, September 25, 1874.

[116] *Siècle*, October 1, 1874.   [117] *Revue politique*, September 26, 1874.

did not have to prolong so meaningless a gesture in order to assure the Holy Father of her veneration and protection. The warning was likewise sounded that the defenders of the existing arrangement regarded the ship as "a last protest against the presence of King Victor Emmanuel in Rome." They were working, it was charged, to keep alive Italo-French discord in order to facilitate a legitimist-clerical restoration.[118]

Ministerial spokesmen were not inactive. They underlined the fact that the government, weighed down by the disasters of 1870–71, enjoyed no freedom in this delicate matter.[119] The authoritative *Soleil* broke its silence to brand as "an anomaly" the presence of the "Orénoque" in Italian waters. "We are no longer the powerful France of earlier days," it asserted. But it hurried to add that the government, far from yielding to threats, was inspired exclusively by the desire to remove a pretext for action against France.[120] On this occasion, the Bonapartists, though denouncing the antipapal attitude of the republicans,[121] pronounced the government's position the only tenable one under existing circumstances. They lauded the pope's reasonable attitude. He knew, they said, that France, "weakened by the republic," had been constrained to submit to the violation of the September convention. He knew too that for the time being France was powerless to improve his position. But it was not to be doubted that "a force superior to that of men . . . . will restore to the Holy See its former splendor."[122]

The clerical-legitimist bloc, perceiving that the game was up, vented its grief in long and poignant jeremiads. Veuillot proclaimed in the deepest despair:

Let history . . . . engrave these ineffaceable words: . . . . "A vessel remained in the waters of Civita Vecchia as a last protest by France. It was

[118] *Revue des deux mondes*, October 1, 1874, pp. 714–16.

[119] Cf. *Français*, October 4, 1874.   [121] Cf. the *Pays*, September 28, 1874.

[120] *Soleil*, October 7, 1874.   [122] *Ibid.*, October 7, 1874.

withdrawn, and nothing serves to recall that France, ever since the days of Clovis, had had the glory of protecting the Catholic church."[123]

Why, queried the *Monde*, was the French government bringing "this last sorrow" upon the already bereaved pontiff? Why was it severing "the last link between him and a free country?" The world would interpret the removal of the "Orénoque" as "an abandonment of our policy toward the Holy See."[124] Even weak countries, it warned, had to guard their honor. The protection of the papacy was the century-old mission of France. No power contested her right to place at the pontiff's disposal "a poor, inoffensive vessel . . . . the sad symbol rather than the effective instrument of the filial devotion of the eldest daughter of the church to the vicar of Jesus Christ."[125] The *Union*, which was joyously predicting the not-too-distant collapse of Italian unity,[126] interrupted its musings to denounce the government's decision to eliminate "this last vestige of the protective mission which France has discharged vis-à-vis the church and its head." It maintained that the country, though mutilated by Prussia, had not lost "the heritage of moral grandeur bequeathed to us by our fathers." Had Frenchmen fallen so low that they themselves were going to destroy the bond which joined the pope's destiny to their own? Was France about to hear Decazes invoke diplomatic difficulties in order to justify this new humiliation? The recall of the "Orénoque," it concluded with magisterial solemnity, would mark the end of French honor and independence.[127] Equally lugubrious was the tone of the *Gazette de France*. The withdrawal of the frigate, it admonished, would be "a new and regrettable concession," another victory for the anticlerical and anti-French policy of Bismarck. One act of weakness would lead to another, and be-

[123] *Univers*, September 28, 1874.

[124] *Monde*, September 17, 1874.

[125] *Ibid.*, September 23, 1874.

[126] *Union*, September 2, 1874.

[127] *Ibid.*, September 5 and 23 and October 1, 1874.

fore long France would be asked to suppress her embassy at the Vatican.[128]

The promptings of moderate and republican journalists were quite unnecessary in this instance. The French government, reassured by the pope's gracious reply to MacMahon, was prepared to act. On October 13 it announced that the "Orénoque" was being recalled to Toulon. The departure of the vessel, an official communiqué explained, "implies no change in the sentiment of devotion and solicitude which France entertains for His Holiness." Another ship was to be placed at his disposal. Stationed in a French port, it would be at his beck and call at all times. These measures had been brought to the attention of the Holy Father, who "has deigned to receive them with confidence."[129] On the same day the "Orénoque" quit Civita Vecchia, and its successor, the "Kléber," armed with very explicit instructions, set out for its base at Ajaccio. Journals close to the government promptly recapitulated all the now familiar arguments adduced at one time or another in defense of the official thesis. They stressed, too, the pope's acquiescent attitude, the superior wisdom of stationing a guard ship in French waters, and the unimpaired devotion of France to the Holy See.[130] They likewise seized the opportunity to take a spirited fling at both the Second Empire and Thiers. The latter were saddled with exclusive responsibility for the present plight of the papacy. The former president of the republic drew some very harsh strictures. He was assailed for his failure to regularize the presence of the "Orénoque" in Italian waters. He might have obtained, it was urged, "the recognition of our right to maintain a vessel in Civita Vecchia, as a supplement to the law of guarantees."[131] Finally, the ministerial apologists pointed to the announced intention of the Sinistra to exploit the entire

[128] *Gazette de France*, September 23 and 24, 1874.

[129] *Journal officiel de la République française*, CCII (October 13, 1874), 6995.

[130] Cf. *Soleil*, October 14, 1874; *Presse*, October 14, 1874.

[131] *Français*, October 14, 1874.

"Orénoque" affair in the forthcoming Italian elections. Had
the leftists of the peninsula been enabled to do this in consequence of inaction by the Versailles authorities—so ran this
argument—the result might have been unfortunate for
France. It was with this eventuality in mind that the French
government had conceived a solution "which could not . . . .
give rise to any claim based on international law or furnish
any pretext for conflict, diplomatic or otherwise."[132]

Moderates were all applause. The *Temps* tersely remarked:
"The 'Orénoque' was merely a means of transport for an
eventual voyage. For this there was no need of a special vessel or of its being anchored in Italian waters. . . . . The
Mediterranean is full of warships able to fulfil this mission."[133] The *Journal des débats* observed that the government was "extricating itself from a position which in the long
run might have involved it in serious difficulties." It regretted, however, that this action had been taken so tar-
dily.[134] The republicans were agreed that the government
had waited too long,[135] but many of them were ready to subscribe to the verdict: "Better late than never."[136] They were
not entirely satisfied with the wording of the official communiqué. That document created the impression, they insisted, that the recall of the "Orénoque" in no way modified
the existing relations between the Vatican and the French
government. It would have been better, in their opinion, to
say frankly that the vessel was being withdrawn "because it
had become impossible not to obliterate this last vestige of
the French occupation."[137]

The legitimists and the ultramontanes, though convinced
of the futility of further protest, registered loud indignation.
"Here is a French question," wailed the *Union*, "settled by a

[132] *Ibid.*

[133] *Temps*, October 14, 1874.

[136] *Rappel*, October 15, 1874.

[134] *Journal des débats*, October 15, 1874.

[135] Cf. *Siècle*, October 15, 1874.

[137] *République française*, October 15, 1874.

French minister against the interests of French policy"[138]— settled, indeed, "on orders from the holy atheist empire of Berlin."[139] If this decision had been come to voluntarily, reasoned the *Gazette de France*, it implied a resumption of the disastrous policy pursued under Napoleon III.[140] Catholic hearts would be deeply moved by this "short and singular note," the *Monde* predicted in alluding to the official communiqué. This fateful document, the clerical sheet continued, could be likened to a tombstone placed upon the glorious and historic mission of France as the protector of the church.[141] Veuillot was desolate. The pope, he lamented, was being "disarmed and despoiled." The honor of France had been irretrievably sullied.[142] The "Orénoque," he proclaimed in the *Univers*,

had served as a silent protest against facts, accomplished indeed, but accomplished according to the passions of men, not according to the justice and honor of France. France had been an impotent witness . . . . and not a . . . . party to the iniquity. She had been in the position of a son at the door of his father's prison. She now assumes that of a pitying and resigned friend.

The dispatch of the "Kléber" to Ajaccio, he sorrowfully added, "will not very sufficiently replace the 'Orénoque' at Civita Vecchia."[143] On October 15, M. de la Bouillerie, a Catholic member of the permanent committee of the national assembly, drew attention to the recall of the vessel and declared that he and his friends deplored the disappearance of this "last material attestation of the respect and affection of France for the Holy See." He wished to know, he continued, whether the government's action was the result of foreign pressure. Decazes briefly replied that he was willing to assume entire responsibility for this step, which he had recommended to his ministerial colleagues in the interests of

[138] *Union*, October 14, 1874.   [140] *Gazette de France*, October 14, 1874.

[139] *Ibid.*, October 16, 1874.   [141] *Monde*, October 14, 1874.

[142] Debidour, *op. cit.*, I, 123; Manfroni, *op. cit.*, I, 186.

[143] *Univers*, October 14, 1874.

France.[144] The *Presse*, which was reputed to be the foreign minister's organ, sought to forestall a clerical interpellation by pronouncing the accord between France and Italy "definitive" and "absolute." It asserted that Decazes and Nigra had tranquillized public opinion on both sides of the Alps. "All those," it continued, "who have at heart the interests of France and are solicitous of her prosperity, her strength, and her future, will welcome the success of the policy of appeasement and concord." This policy was all the more praiseworthy because it enabled France to remain on the best of terms with the Holy See. The sovereign pontiff, who had taken account of France's position, was much too noble to wish to keep alive the causes of her difficulties with Italy.[145] This oblique admonition had the desired effect. No interpellation on the recall of the "Orénoque" was presented.

The Minghetti government made no secret of its profound satisfaction. Artom, the general secretary of the Italian foreign office, voiced the official attitude when he declared to the French chargé d'affaires that the departure of the "Orénoque" eliminated "a subject of recriminations" and "an eventual cause of disagreeable incidents."[146] The comments in the ministerial press were inspired by a similar sense of relief.[147] The Sinistra attempted to mar this complacency. It reiterated that France's gesture was without significance as long as she failed to renounce her claims to a protectorate over the Holy See.[148] But most Italians were less pessimistic. Their fear of foreign intervention was for the time being allayed.[149] One political commentator was encouraged to declare that the seal had been placed upon the country's unity and upon the transfer of the capital to Rome.[150] Italian cleri-

---

[144] *Temps*, October 17, 1874; *République française*, October 17, 1874; *Presse*, October 17, 1874.

[145] *Presse*, October 19, 1874.   [146] *DDF* (1st ser.), I, No. 336, 358.

[147] Cf. *Opinione*, October 14, 1874; *Libertà*, October 15, 1874.

[148] Cf. *Diritto*, October 19, 1874.   [149] Vigo, *op. cit.*, I, 381.

[150] Cf. *Nuova antologia*, November, 1874, p. 762.

cals were furious with MacMahon and his subordinates.[151] The *Voce della verità* inveighed against the "moral debility" of France in yielding in such abject fashion to pressure from the Quirinal. "It is with profound sadness," lamented the *Osservatore romano*, "that we give our salute to the vessel which sailed . . . . from Civita Vecchia, carrying far from us the honored and glorious flag of France." The presence of the "Orénoque," it continued, had, it was true, brought no real advantage to the papal cause. But it was nevertheless painful to witness "this new and immense act of weakness" on the part of the French government. It was now clear that in the liberal Catholicism professed by the present rulers of France, "the spirit of dignity and national independence is lower than in Voltairianism and in demagogy itself." The journal closed with the solemn reminder that the fortunes of France were linked inseparably with those of the church.[152] Pius himself was now inclined to take a less indulgent view of the French government's action.[153] He showed Cardinal Bonnechose the letters exchanged with MacMahon. "I did not ask for the 'Orénoque,'" he said. "Let them recall it if they wish. Civita Vecchia is rather far from here. The 'Orénoque' was twenty-four hours away from the Vatican. It would have been of little help to me. But the humiliation of France is great, and I groan at the thought of it."[154] In a note to the Bishop of Montpellier, he sharply denied the truth of a report that he himself had requested the withdrawal of the guard ship.[155]

The recall of the "Orénoque" was a signal triumph for the

---

[151] Manfroni, *op. cit.*, I, 186–87.

[152] *Osservatore romano*, October 15, 1874.

[153] Cf. Pesci, *I primi anni di Roma capitale*, p. 16.

[154] Hanotaux, *op. cit.*, III, 86.

[155] Cf. Debidour, *op. cit.*, I, 122, and note on p. 123. The attitude of the pope, according to Broglie, was most exemplary at this trying moment. "Nothing," he records, "equals the touching resignation with which Pius IX saw this last mark of her [France's] impotent sympathy disappear" (Broglie, *op. cit.*, p. 175 n.).

Minghetti cabinet, and it proceeded to make the most of it in the parliamentary elections which occurred on November 8. Nevertheless, the Destra emerged from this contest with a reduced majority,[156] and signs were not wanting that dissatisfaction with the ministerial party on other scores—principally economic and financial—was steadily mounting.[157] But there was no gainsaying the almost universal approbation enjoyed by the foreign policy of Visconti-Venosta. The astute minister was credited with having been able to exploit the friendly attitude of Decazes to effect a notable improvement in Franco-Italian relations. The likelihood of a war over the temporal power now appeared reassuringly remote.[158] Victor Emmanuel indirectly alluded to the Franco-Italian *détente* when he opened the sessions of the new parliament on November 23.[159] French moderate opinion was also disposed to view the future hopefully. Its tireless spokesman, Mazade, declared that between Italy and France, between the policy of Visconti-Venosta, which had been ratified in the recent elections, and that of Decazes, there was only cordial understanding.[160] All seemed quiet on the Franco-Italian diplomatic front. But the Vatican did not cease to remind its despoilers that the day of reckoning could not be evaded. "Rome is not with you," the *Osservatore romano* warned the "men of the revolution."[161] For Rome was "the Alsace of Italy, ... a city conquered by force," and it would have to be returned to its rightful owners.[162]

[156] On the results of the elections see Pesci, *I primi anni di Roma capitale*, p. 115.

[157] Sinistra radicals were especially jubilant over the electoral victory scored by Garibaldi, the archenemy of the Roman Curia (cf. the *Diritto*, November 15, 1874).

[158] Vigo, *op. cit.*, I, 396.

[159] Cf. Massari, *La Vita ed il regno di Vittorio Emanuele II di Savoia*, II, 572–73.

[160] *Revue des deux mondes*, December 1, 1874, p. 708.

[161] *Osservatore romano*, November 17, 1874.

[162] *Ibid.*, November 20, 1874.

CHAPTER XII
TESTING THE LAW OF GUARANTEES

DURING the initial months of 1874, rumors of an impending peace between Quirinal and Vatican caused something of a stir throughout the peninsula. Unquestionably, many devout Catholics would have welcomed an Italo-papal understanding. They were aware that a final settlement of the issues involved would necessarily require much time, but they hoped that at least some preliminary steps in the right direction might be taken without undue delay.[1] The activity of Don Bosco, who had not abandoned his efforts on behalf of a termination of the *exequatur* controversy,[2] was decidedly cheering to the peacemongers. It was reported in the press that he had conversed with the leading personalities in both camps in an attempt to find some acceptable basis for discussion.[3] But well-informed circles refused to repose any great confidence in the outcome of these negotiations. Thus the *Libertà* predicted that efforts to promote a *modus vivendi* were premature, owing to the continued intransigence of the Vatican. The latter, according to the ministerial journal, would agree to a peace only on one condition: the destruction of Italian unity.[4] The *Perseveranza* agreed with its Roman contemporary that no positive result

[1] Pietro Vigo, *Storia degli ulitimi trent'anni del secolo XIX* (Milano, 1908), I, 348.

[2] It is interesting to note that Bishop Bonomelli of Cremona, the future champion of Italo-papal reconciliation, betrayed his patriotic proclivities as early as 1874, when he asked for and obtained the *exequatur*. Mussolini alluded to this circumstance in the course of his speech of May 14, 1929 (cf. *Scritti e discorsi di Benito Mussolini* [Milano, 1934], VII, 58–59).

[3] Vigo, *op. cit.*, I, 348–49; *Libertà*, January 13, 1874; Ernesto Vercesi, *Don Bosco: il santo italiano del secolo XIX* (Milano, 1929), pp. 186–87.

[4] *Libertà*, January 14, 1874.

could be expected under prevailing circumstances.[5] Clerical circles ridiculed the entire business.[6] The Vatican itself finally put an end to the wishful speculation of those hardy optimists who still refused to admit defeat. On April 14 the *Osservatore romano* stated in the most unequivocal terms that the Holy Father had made no proposals to the Italian government. He was, as before, determined to reject any overtures whose only result would be to give legal sanction to the great injustice he had suffered.[7] And the venerable Turinese ecclesiastic found himself the target of acrid criticism for his exertions on behalf of reconciliation.[8]

It was shortly after this reaffirmation by the Vatican of its unyielding position that Italian clericals gave an imposing demonstration of their discipline. On June 12, 1874, Venice was host to the first Italian Catholic congress.[9] The rationale of this new departure had long before been clearly stated by the *Voce della verità*. As long as church and state co-operated on behalf of social well-being, the influential Roman organ had declared, there was no need for individuals to meet in congresses and assemblies to reinforce this unity of purpose and action. But when the state, far from giving the proper support to the church, violated the latter's rights and launched a fierce offensive against it, it became imperative to create associations of the faithful in order to guarantee, through collective effort, "the immortal interests of religion

---

[5] *Perseveranza*, January 14, 1874.

[6] Cf. *Unità cattolica*, January 16, 1874.

[7] Cf. also *CC*, II (9th ser.; April 20, 1874), 355; Vigo, *op. cit.*, I, 349.

[8] Friedrich Fuchs, "Der römische Friede: seine Propheten, Pseudo-propheten, Vorläufer u. Märtyrer," *Hochland*, June, 1929, p. 240.

[9] The idea of convoking such a body in Italy goes back to 1871. In October of that year Venice celebrated the third centenary of Lepanto. On this occasion a young publicist from Bologna, Carlo Cazzani, announced that the supreme council of the Italian Catholic Youth was organizing itself as a committee to promote the formation of an Italian Catholic congress. He invited the co-operation of all the associations represented at the Lepanto commemoration (cf. F. Crispolti, "I Congressi e l'organizzazione dei cattolici in Italia," *Nuova antologia*, October 16, 1897, p. 663; Vercesi, *Il Movimento cattolico in Italia* [Firenze, 1923], pp. 13–14).

and morality."[10] Armed with the pope's benediction, the delegates at Venice sought to give cohesion, unity, and a more comprehensive program to the ultramontane forces of the country. They studied, among other things, methods of defending the rights of the church and problems of the press and of education. Three important resolutions were adopted at this initial parley. One of these recommended that Catholics who had secured the requisite permission from the ecclesiastical authorities should not reject membership on the governing boards of charitable institutions. Another urged participation in local elections in order to Christianize the municipal schools,[11] while the third proposed the organization of a committee to prepare plans for the founding of institutions of higher learning.[12]

Many Italian clericals, inspired by a sense of their growing strength, believed that the moment had come to discard the *nè eletti nè elettori* formula. Parliamentary elections, the first since the transfer of the capital to Rome, were scheduled for November, and during the preceding months not a few influential Catholics pronounced themselves in favor of mass participation. They contended that abstention, though it represented a logically consistent course, only worked injury to the real interests of the church. On the other hand, much good might come from recourse to the polls. It would be possible, once a considerable number of chamber seats had been captured, to frustrate the machinations of the anticlericals. But the Vatican was adamant in its refusal to countenance such a *volte-face*. It was frankly skeptical of its ability to

[10] *Voce della verità*, May 22, 1873.

[11] A distinction was made by the Vatican between local, administrative elections and parliamentary ones. The former, classed as nonpolitical, and involving no recognition of the existing regime in Italy, were declared open to Catholics.

[12] Cf. "Il primo congresso cattolico in Italia," *CC*, III (9th ser.; June 22, 1874), 5–36; *Osservatore romano*, June 13, 16, 18, 19, 23, 1874; *Unità cattolica*, June 17, 18, 20, 1874; Crispolti, *op. cit.*, p. 663; Vercesi, *Il Movimento cattolico in Italia*, pp. 14–17; "Ueber das politische Verhalten der Katholiken in Italien," *Historisch-Politische Blätter für das katholische Deutschland*, 1878, pp. 691–92.

secure, by parliamentary methods, any appreciable improvement of its position.[13] The papal attitude was faithfully stated by the *Unità cattolica*. The abandonment of the abstentionist policy, the Turinese journal held, was a matter which could not be discussed.[14] It was true that Catholics, if they so desired, could obtain a majority of the seats in the chamber. But they were unwilling to see their spokesmen engage in legislative activity in the city that was still the papal capital. And loyal sons of the church, if elected deputies, would stay away from Rome and renounce their mandates.[15] The Destra argument that the continued abstention of Catholic voters would facilitate a Sinistra triumph could scarcely be taken seriously, according to this authoritative clerical sheet. The church entertained no illusions about the nature of Destra rule. Mazzini and his fellows had done the church no more harm than the party now in power. And the Sinistra was at least more frank than its rival in manifesting its anticlericalism.[16] Pius himself would not hear of any departure from the formula of Don Margotti. On October 13 he silenced the dissidents within the flock by publicly reaffirming the *non expedit*. He could not, he said, permit Catholics to accept seats in the chamber of deputies. For one thing, the elections were not free, owing to the interplay of political passions. And, even if this were not so, there was the insuperable obstacle of the oath required of all deputies—an oath which signified acquiescence in the existing political order. Therefore, he concluded, Catholics would have to continue to stay away from the chamber.[17] The *Civiltà cattolica*, commenting authoritatively on the meaning of the papal

---

[13] Cf. Humphrey Johnson, *The Papacy and the Kingdom of Italy* (London, 1926), pp. 35–36.

[14] *Unità cattolica*, June 23, 1874.

[15] *Ibid.*, August 20, 1874.   [16] *Ibid.*, October 4, 1874.

[17] *Ibid.*, October 16, 1874; *CC*, IV (9th ser.; October 23, 1874), 353–54; Vigo, *op. cit.*, I, 388–89; Saverio Cilibrizzi, *Storia parlamentare politica e diplomatica d'Italia* (Milano, 1925), III, 289; "Ueber das politische Verhalten der Katholiken in Italien," *op. cit.*, pp. 600–601.

pronouncement, declared that the ban imposed upon the acceptance of seats in the chamber was equally applicable to voting in parliamentary elections.[18] And the *Osservatore romano*, alluding to the government's plea for support against the ever growing leftist threat, followed the *Unità cattolica* in pronouncing the Destra as bad as the Sinistra. "They are all sectarians," it charged, "all enemies of the pope, all oppressors of religion."[19]

The Italian government was keenly disappointed, as it had hoped to the last for electoral support from Catholic conservatives. But despite the defection of these potential allies, it was determined to persist in the moderate ecclesiastical policy inaugurated after the fall of the Lanza cabinet. Of this determination it was now to give striking proof. On February 5, 1875, Pius issued an encyclical which declared the May laws[20] null and void and released Prussian Catholics from obedience to them. At once there was a great outcry in Germany.[21] The ministerial and liberal press declaimed in the strongest language against the pontiff and deplored the impunity with which this bold gesture had been made. One writer close to Bismarck pronounced the encyclical a declaration of war which dissolved all previous compacts between Prussia and the Roman see.[22] The semi-official *Kölnische Zeitung* regretted that Civita Vecchia was no longer a papal port; for then German soldiers could have gone to fetch the Holy Father and bring him to Wilhelmshöhe or Stettin as a prisoner of war. At either of those places he would have had ample leisure to ponder the sanctity of laws.[23] Bismarck's

---

[18] *CC*, IV (9th ser.; October 23, 1874), 354.

[19] *Osservatore romano*, November 11, 1874.

[20] Laws enacted in Prussia in May, 1873, to expand the control of the state over the Catholic hierarchy.

[21] Cf. Joseph Schmidlin, *Papstgeschichte der neuesten Zeit* (München, 1933–34), II, 186.

[22] *Preussische Jahrbücher*, March, 1875, p. 327.

[23] This evoked from the *Fanfulla* of Rome the ironic remark that the German government was considering the idea of demanding the extradition of Pius IX (cf.

indignation was directed as much against the Italian government as against the Holy Father. For this incident was a
forcible reminder of Italy's failure to follow his example and
wage a Kulturkampf of her own. He felt that Minghetti and
his colleagues had been altogether too gentle with the Vatican. And now it had become incontrovertibly clear that the
law of guarantees endowed the pontiff with an altogether
dangerous degree of freedom and immunity. The latter, he
had complained to Minghetti and Visconti-Venosta in September, 1873, was now inaccessible. Before the occupation of
Rome, a German warship at Civita Vecchia would have
brought him to his senses. Minghetti had promptly replied
that no higher praise of the law of guarantees was possible.
For that statute was apparently effective in shielding the
pope from even the most powerful governments.[24] Throughout 1874 the alleged meekness of the Italian government vis-
à-vis the Vatican in such matters as the recognition of episcopal appointments, the assignment of temporalities, and the
execution of the civil marriage law had drawn much acrid
comment from the German press;[25] and these complaints had
been pronounced justified by leftist circles in the peninsula.[26]
It was reported that the chancellor had protested to the
Quirinal against the anti-German language of certain Italian
bishops. According to the same source, Visconti-Venosta had
very bluntly replied that he did not know of the pastorals in
question and that in any case he could do absolutely noth-

---

the issue of March 8, 1875). The *Diritto* took the German press attacks on the encyclical very seriously. It reproached the Destra for not giving sufficient attention
to this new assault of "theocracy" against "civilization." It insisted that the law of
guarantees should operate to protect liberty from the "excesses" of the Vatican
(issue of March 5, 1875).

[24] Jean Lulvès, "Bismarck und die römische Frage," *Hochland*, June, 1929, p.
273; Luigi Luzzatti, *Dio nella libertà: studi sulle relazioni tra lo stato e la chiesa*
(Bologna, 1926), pp. 180, 452–53.

[25] Adalbert Wahl, *Deutsche Geschichte von der Reichsgründung bis zum Ausbruch
des Weltkriegs* (Stuttgart, 1926), I, 346.

[26] Cf. the *Diritto*, January 16 and September 28, 1874.

ing.[27] The controversy provoked by General La Marmora's book on the events of 1866 had widened the rift between the two governments.[28]

Bismarck was now determined to impress upon the Italian cabinet that it would have to assume responsibility for the incitements to resistance contained in the encyclical of February 5. He believed that that cabinet was under obligation to tolerate upon its soil no acts hostile to a friendly power.[29] In this he was supported by such learned contemporaries as Treitschke[30] and the noted political theorist, J. K. Bluntschli.[31] He was also anxious to ascertain the truth of current reports that Italy was secretly negotiating an accord with the Vatican. More than that, he was beginning to suspect a *rapprochement* of the Catholic powers under ultramontane auspices.[32] His first concern was to clear the atmosphere by sounding out the Italian government. Accordingly, Keudell was instructed to point out informally to Visconti-Venosta that Germany would no longer tolerate threats from the pope. Military action, he was to say, would have been resorted to in former days. But now that such reprisals were impossible, the Italian government would have to be held responsible for

[27] Cf. André Dreux, *Dernières années de l'ambassade en Allemagne de M. de Gontaut-Biron* (Paris, 1907), p. 40; Franz Xaver Schmitt, *Bismarcks Abkehr vom Kulturkampf* (Neu-Ulm, 1931), p. 13.

[28] La Marmora's volume contained documents which were calculated to compromise Bismarck in the eyes of Austria. The German government had demanded an investigation. The Italian press had defended La Marmora, and Minghetti had refused to make the investigation (cf. Schmitt, *op. cit.*, p. 16).

[29] Lulvès, *op. cit.*, pp. 272–73.

[30] Cf. Heinrich von Treitschke, *Zehn Jahre deutscher Kämpfe* (Berlin, 1897), II, 336–37.

[31] In an important article which appeared in the *Gegenwart* in 1876, Bluntschli argued that legal responsibility for papal attacks on foreign states devolved upon the Italian government. He subsequently developed this position in a more elaborate study. He contended that the law of guarantees could not be invoked to protect the pope when he went beyond the discharge of his spiritual functions. Foreign governments, he insisted, were within their rights in demanding that the Holy Father refrain from abusing his asylum in Rome to assail the institutions of other countries.

[32] Lucius von Ballhausen, *Bismarck-Erinnerungen* (Stuttgart and Berlin, 1921), p. 73; Schmitt, *op. cit.*, pp. 34 and 36.

his behavior.[33] It was therefore incumbent upon it to curb his excesses of language. This could be best achieved by modifying the law of guarantees, under whose protection the pope was attacking foreign states with impunity.[34]

Keudell executed his delicate mission in the course of a court ball at the Quirinal. After some reflection, Visconti-Venosta replied that he would have to bring this matter to the attention of Minghetti and the king. But, speaking unofficially, he could say that the kind of pressure demanded by Bismarck was out of the question. It would be at variance with both the Catholic sentiment of the Italian nation and the law of guarantees.[35] Bismarck was exasperated by this refusal,[36] and he was not quick to forget it.[37] It strengthened his suspicion that Italy was flirting with the Vatican behind his back.[38] "We have become absolutely indifferent toward

---

[33] Bülow, *Denkwürdigkeiten* (Berlin, 1931), IV, 329.

[34] Gaetano Salvemini, "La Politica estera della Destra, 1871–76," *Rivista d'Italia*, February 15, 1925, pp. 186–87; Schmitt, *op. cit.*, p. 31; Dreux, *op. cit.*, p. 76.

[35] Bülow, *op. cit.*, IV, 329–30.

[36] Cf. Salvemini, *op. cit.*, p. 187.

[37] More than two years later he complained to Crispi that the Italian government had "packed the pope away in cotton wool, and no one can touch him." As early as 1875, he continued, "we pointed out . . . . the threats to other powers which the law of guarantees contains. The question, however, was dropped" (Crispi, *Politica estera* [Milano, 1912], p. 46).

[38] A political observer familiar with the views of the chancellor voiced the same suspicion. He remarked that Italy, though willing to make the most of the Kulturkampf, was loath to take part in it. She was working on the theory that the growing intensity of that struggle would facilitate her quest for a reconciliation with the papacy. Minghetti and his colleagues were too much under the spell of their Francophil sympathies and the Cavourian *free church in a free state* formula to make Germany's cause their own. In annexing the Patrimony of St. Peter, this writer continued, the government of Victor Emmanuel had rendered it impossible for the powers to chastise the Holy Father for flagrant abuse of his spiritual authority. It had bestowed sovereignty upon him without providing some mode of redress against attempts on his part to incite foreign Catholics to rebellion, and Germany was the victim of this serious oversight. He concluded on a somber note. The unity of Italy, he claimed, was dependent for its continued existence on that of Germany. But should the Italians cease to regard their interests as identical with those of Germany, the latter would have no reason to assist them in frustrating the designs of the Holy See (*Preussische Jahrbücher*, April, 1875, pp. 454–56).

Italy," he remarked to Károlyi, the Austrian ambassador.[39]
He did not hesitate to speak in the most derogatory fashion
about the object of his ire. "Italy," he said to Prince Hohenlohe, Arnim's successor as German ambassador to France, "is
of no importance. That country has no weight, because it has
a poor army and pursues a policy absolutely unworthy of
trust."[40] He went so far as to indicate to Hohenlohe that he
would welcome an understanding with the Vatican and instructed him to discuss the question of the temporal power
with Decazes.[41] Even the ardently Germanophil Launay admitted that Visconti-Venosta's reply on this occasion had
created a tension in Italo-German relations.[42] Decazes
watched all this with understandable satisfaction. On March
12 he explained to Corcelles that "the representations made
to Italy . . . . are believed to have as their object the very
liberties left to the Holy See by the law of guarantees."[43] He
professed to know that the impression produced on the Italian government was a most painful one. On April 3 he wrote
to his ambassadors in London, Vienna, St. Petersburg, and
Berlin that the Quirinal was "keenly preoccupied with the
difficulties of which it has a presentiment. . . . . The Italian
cabinet has understood, like everyone else, that it was under
the menace of a dangerous blow."[44]

Bismarck's designs upon the law of guarantees—as conveyed in somewhat confused and garbled press dispatches—
were not kindly received by most Italians. The ministerial
press declared without hesitation that compliance with his
request—assuming that it really had been made—was unthinkable. The *Opinione*, in an elaborate but rather evasive
defense of the government's ecclesiastical policy, was reduced

[39] Eduard von Wertheimer, *Graf Julius Andrássy: sein Leben und seine Zeit*
(Stuttgart, 1910), II, 220.

[40] *Denkwürdigkeiten des fürsten Chlodwig zu Hohenlohe-Schillingsfürst* (Stuttgart
and Leipzig, 1906), II, 152.

[41] *Ibid.*

[42] Dreux, *op. cit.*, p. 77.

[43] *DDF* (1st ser.), I, No. 369, 382.

[44] *Ibid.*, No. 375, p. 390.

to the admission that the territoryless pope was virtually invulnerable. It pointed out that a friendly invitation from Germany to co-operate in repressing clerical excesses could not embarrass the Italian cabinet. When the law of guarantees was enacted, no one believed that the freedom it granted the Holy Father would be abused. But the apparent futility of this expectation could not affect the situation. The inviolability of the pope's person and utterances remained unaltered, although his responsibility was in direct proportion to his freedom.[45] This responsibility, however, was spiritual rather than political in nature, in keeping with the new status of the Holy See.[46] Moreover, Pius' position was to be likened to that of monarchs in exile who plotted with impunity against the masters of their erstwhile principalities. Not Krupp cannon, but spiritual arms, had to be employed in replying to papal broadsides. In any case, the Destra journal somewhat illogically concluded, the exceptional position of the pontiff was to be attributed not to the law of guarantees but to the European states which continued to maintain needless diplomatic agents at the Vatican.[47] The *Libertà* was blunter and less defensive. Bismarck, it drily observed, was not in the habit of making useless gestures. Hence, until conclusive proof to the contrary was available, it could be assumed that reports of his *démarche* were untrue. It was difficult to believe that so sagacious a statesman could not have foreseen that a negative reply was inevitable.[48] For a modification of the law of guarantees was wholly unfeasible.[49] Some there were who believed that the chancellor had conveyed his demands in a formal note,[50] but this the cabinet categorically denied.[51] The *Opinione* hastened to explain that

45 *Opinione*, March 12, 1875.

46 *Ibid.*, March 18, 1875.

47 *Ibid.*, April 8, 1875.

48 *Libertà*, March 24, 1875.

49 *Ibid.*, April 1, 1875.

50 Cf., e.g., *DDF* (1st ser.), I, No. 362, 377.

51 *Ibid.*, No. 377, p. 392; Charles Gavard, *Un Diplomate à Londres* (Paris, 1895), p. 232.

"in reality there had been only a verbal request by the prince, to which a verbal reply had been given reaffirming the liberal intentions of the Italian government."[52] Circles close to the Vatican refused to take this denial seriously.[53] And the lurking fear that the law of guarantees might be in jeopardy helped to soften their attitude toward that much reviled statute. Indeed, some clerical newspapers guardedly admitted that it was not so bad after all.[54] The irony of the situation did not elude certain observers. The privileges granted the pope, one of them pointed out, were intended to reassure the powers that he was in no danger of becoming Italy's vassal. Now the authors of the law of guarantees were being reprimanded because they had done their job too well. The pope was so free that he was endangering the independence of other states. And the latter, powerless to defend themselves against him, were looking to the Italian government to curb his excesses.[55]

On the heels of Bismarck's fruitless *démarche* at Rome came word of the forthcoming meeting of Francis Joseph and Victor Emmanuel in Venice. The secrecy with which the Austrian and Italian governments had conducted their preliminary conversations on this theme was regarded by the chancellor as an unhappy omen.[56] He was inclined to suspect the worst. He had visions of a clerical conspiracy hatched under the pope's aegis. He saw Italy, Austria, and France arrayed against Germany, the first of these enticed into the combination by papal recognition of the new order of things in the peninsula.[57] He had before him ultramontane press re-

[52] Chiala, *Dina*, III, 433.

[53] *CC*, VI (9th ser.; March 23, 1875), 15 n.

[54] Camillo Manfroni, *Sulla soglia del Vaticano* (Bologna, 1920), I, 218.

[55] *Nuova antologia*, April, 1875, p. 1040.

[56] Schmitt, *op. cit.*, p. 31. Schweinitz records that Andrássy informed him of the impending visit "rather late" (*Denkwürdigkeiten des Botschafters General v. Schweinitz* [Berlin, 1927], I, 309).

[57] Wahl, *op. cit.*, I, 354.

ports to the effect that such a Catholic league was actually in existence.[58] Most alarming of all was the recent strengthening of the French military forces. The news from Vienna completed the dismal picture. According to Schweinitz, influential army, church, and court circles there were working for a war to avenge the defeat of 1866. Their objective at the moment was to get rid of Andrássy and instal a clerical, anti-German cabinet.[59] The immediate danger was that the conferees at Venice might conclude an arrangement on the ecclesiastical issue which would not be to Germany's liking.[60] These fears were expressed in a "Vienna Letter" written by the press chief of the German foreign office, Professor Ludwig Aegidi, and published in the *Kölnische Zeitung* on April 5.[61] The reorganization of the French army, the anti-German machinations of the Austrian ultramontanes, and the possibility of an Italo-papal reconciliation were noted as the foci of danger.

The appearance of this article synchronized with the arrival of Francis Joseph in Italy. The Minghetti government had hoped to the last that he might be induced to come to Rome. But this the emperor had declined to do out of regard for the Holy Father and because of the attitude of the Vatican. Moreover, as he was traveling to Dalmatia anyway, the choice of Venice could be represented as a natural one.[62] Though deeply disappointed, the Italian cabinet proceeded to make the best of the situation. Visconti-Venosta assured Wimpffen of Victor Emmanuel's gratitude for the Austrian emperor's "generous intention" of coming to Ven-

[58] Cf. Hajo Holborn (ed.), *Aufzeichnungen und Erinnerungen aus dem Leben des Botschafters Joseph Maria von Radowitz* (Berlin and Leipzig, 1925), I, 315–16.

[59] Johannes Ziekursch, *Politische Geschichte des neuen deutschen Kaiserreiches* (Frankfurt-am-Main, 1925), II, 40.

[60] Wertheimer, *Andrássy*, II, 218.

[61] Ziekursch, *op. cit.*, II, 41; Wahl, *op. cit.*, I, 354.

[62] Cf. Eduard Ritter von Steinitz, *Erinnerungen an Franz Joseph I* (Berlin, 1931), p. 286; Wertheimer, *Andrássy*, II, 217; Ludwig Ritter von Przibram, *Erinnerungen eines alten Oesterreichers* (Stuttgart and Leipzig, 1910), I, 391; *DDF* (1st ser.), I, No. 313, 340.

ice.[63] The popular reaction to the news of Francis Joseph's forthcoming arrival was one of intense satisfaction. Most Italians, Wimpffen reported, regarded the impending event as "the crowning of the work of peace and reconciliation" which had caused the past to be forgotten and had brought about friendly relations between the two sovereigns and their countries. According to the Austrian minister, it was the choice of Venice—erstwhile possession of the Hapsburg monarchy—which evoked the greatest public enthusiasm.[64] There were some who refused to overlook the slight to *Roma capitale*. But even these malcontents directed their ire against the Italian government rather than against the imperial visitor.[65] The latter was everywhere very well received.[66] He proved a most complaisant guest. It was reported in quarters close to the cabinet that he improved the occasion to voice his approval of Italy's ecclesiastical policy.[67] He remarked to the patriarch of Venice that, if he was satisfied and was giving proof of this by coming to Italy, the Vatican too should be content.[68] It was widely believed that the two rulers agreed not to join Bismarck in his struggle against the Catholic church[69]—an agreement which was entirely consistent with the views of Minghetti and Andrássy.[70]

[63] Wimpffen to Andrássy, March 12, 1875, HHSA, Politisches Archiv (Berichte aus Rom [Italien: Januar bis August 1875]), Fasz. XI/83, No. 7532/45, fol. 94a.

[64] Wimpffen to Andrássy, March 20, 1875, *ibid.*, No. 10A, fols. 100a–101a.

[65] Cf. particularly the *Diritto*, March 23, 1875. The leftist organ assailed Minghetti and his colleagues for their alleged failure to bestir themselves sufficiently to bring Francis Joseph to Rome. All Italians, it taunted, were still asking themselves which of their cities was their capital.

[66] Michele Rosi, *Vittorio Emanuele II* (Bologna, 1930), II, 209; Giuseppe Massari, *La Vita ed il regno di Vittorio Emanuele II di Savoia* (Milano, 1910), II, 575–76.

[67] Cf. *Nuova antologia*, May, 1875, p. 222.

[68] Chiala, *Dina*, III, 433 and note.

[69] Cf., e.g., Decazes's letter of April 9, 1875, to Harcourt (Gabriel Hanotaux, *Histoire de la France contemporaine* [Paris, 1903–8], III, 236); cf. also Georges Goyau, *Bismarck et l'église; le culturkampf* (Paris, 1911–13), II, 211–12.

[70] Andrássy, like Minghetti, disapproved of Bismarck's Kulturkampf (cf. Wertheimer, *Andrássy*, II, 220).

The meeting was variously appraised in Italy. The *Opinione* described it as "a solemn sanction given by the emperor of Austria-Hungary . . . . to all the accomplished facts." Indeed, it demonstrated that "the present state of affairs in the peninsula is regarded by the emperor himself as necessary to the European political system."[71] It was, in the opinion of the *Libertà*, an event which history would record with "the greatest pleasure and admiration." Two nations and two sovereigns, formerly adversaries, had promised each other sincere friendship.[72] The real purpose of the meeting, according to still other sections of moderate opinion, was to bring Italy into the Three Emperors' League.[73] Visconti-Venosta himself, upon his return to Rome, apprised the Austrian chargé d'affaires of the great pleasure he had experienced in witnessing the "cordial understanding" between the two monarchs. This meeting and its consequences, the foreign minister remarked, would contribute effectively to the well-being and prosperity of the two countries.[74] The Sinistra was jubilant. It joined the *Opinione* in hailing the proceedings at Venice as a confirmation of the new order of things in the peninsula, and it echoed the *Libertà* in welcoming the presence of the imperial guest as a significant step in the consolidation of Italo-Austrian amity.[75] The clericals made light of the visit. They dismissed it as a formal gesture of courtesy. Furthermore, they underscored the emperor's failure to come to Rome.[76] This, they proclaimed, was attributable to his un-

[71] The *Opinione*, replying to clerical assertions that Francis Joseph was planning to shun Rome, Florence, and Naples in order not to sanction the "usurpations" perpetrated in those places, had stated that such contentions were puerile in view of the emperor's recognition of the Italian kingdom (cf. issue of March 30, 1875).

[72] *Libertà*, April 6, 1875.

[73] Cf. *Nuova antologia*, May, 1875, p. 220.

[74] Gravenegg to Andrássy, April 10, 1875, HHSA, Politisches Archiv (Berichte aus Rom [Italien: Januar bis August 1875]), Fasz. XI/83, fols. 13a–14a.

[75] Cf. *Diritto*, April 9, 1875.

[76] *Osservatore romano*, April 6, 1875; Manfroni, *op. cit.*, I, 219.

willingness to do anything which might be construed as acquiescence in the outrage of September 20, 1870.[77]

The cordiality which marked the Austro-Italian parley was noted with misgiving in Berlin, where there was no tendency to minimize the danger of an international clerical conspiracy.[78] This uneasiness was again reflected in the tone of the famous "War in Sight?" article which appeared in the Berlin *Post* on April 9. It raised the bogey of a Franco-German war, discussed the ultramontane intrigues in Austria and Italy, and alluded to the joy manifested by the French clerical press at the prospect of Francis Joseph's visit to Venice, as if thereby an Austro-Italian alliance were assured.[79] The scare which it engendered proved of short duration, for the German authorities, impressed by the attitude of the Russians and of the British, quickly put a damper on the war talk. Bismarck declared that the articles in the *Kölnische Zeitung* and the *Post* had taken him by surprise.[80] "There is no question of war," he told his friend, Baron Lucius von Ballhausen, on April 11.[81] An article in the authoritative *Norddeutsche Allgemeine Zeitung*, written at the instigation of the German general staff,[82] asserted that the *Post* had been mistaken in its appraisal of Germany's relations with Austria and Italy. It was erroneous, it observed, to assume the existence of an Austro-Italian conspiracy. It pointed out that, though a Jesuit party hostile to Germany did exist in both those countries, it was not sufficiently powerful to disturb the good relations between Vienna, Rome, and Berlin.[83] On April 15 the emperor himself remarked to the French military attaché:

---

[77] *CC*, VI (9th ser.; April 19, 1875), 261.

[78] Cf., e.g., *Preussische Jahrbücher*, April, 1875, p. 448.

[79] Cf. Wahl, *op. cit.*, I, 355–56; *GP*, I, 253 n.

[80] Cf. Pearl Boring Mitchell, *The Bismarckian Policy of Conciliation with France, 1875–1885* (Philadelphia, 1935), p. 27.

[81] Ballhausen, *op. cit.*, p. 72.

[82] Cf. Ziekursch, *op. cit.*, II, 42.

[83] *Times*, April 12, 1875; Wahl, *op. cit.*, I, 356; Schmitt, *op. cit.*, p. 41.

"They have wished to embroil us. . . . . Now, it is all over."[84] The tranquil aftermath found France and Germany conversing on the possibility of ironing out their difficulties, and the status of the Holy See was one of the questions discussed.[85] Bismarck, eager to conciliate France and avert, if possible, a Franco-Russian *rapprochement*,[86] fell in with Decazes's overtures. On April 30 the German foreign secretary drafted a note for Hohenlohe's use which explored the conditions of a Franco-German accord. Among the questions reviewed was that of defining the position of the pope.[87] But Decazes refused to commit himself on this issue,[88] though he did seem to share the German view that an agreement could be reached only with a peace-loving pope.[89] It has been suggested that Decazes's diffident attitude was inspired by the fear that peace between Bismarck and the Catholic church might have deprived the French government of its strongest talking-point and thus paved the way for its defeat at the hands of the leftist republican opposition.[90]

The *alerte* of April, 1875, further aggravated Italo-German relations.[91] Many Italians interpreted the *Post* article as a warning to Rome and Vienna.[92] No great surprise was there-

[84] Dreux, *op. cit.*, p. 87. There is no agreement among historians as to Bismarck's real intentions in connection with the "scare" of 1875. It is clear, however, that the French government, feigning great alarm over Germany's attitude, achieved a diplomatic victory by appealing to the Russians and warning the British. Cf., on the "scare" of 1875, Bernadotte E. Schmitt, *Triple Alliance and Triple Entente* (New York, 1934), pp. 7–8.

[85] Late in April, Decazes informed Hohenlohe that he would welcome an understanding with Germany. He indicated, however, that France could not be expected to join in the struggle against the Holy See. Even if anticlericals like Gambetta were in power, he said, they would be unwilling to do this, as it would mean civil war in France (*GP*, I, No. 167, 261–62).

[86] Cf. Mitchell, *op. cit.*, pp. 48–49; Franz Xaver Schmitt, *op. cit.*, p. 41.

[87] *GP*, I, No. 168, 263.

[88] For Decazes's report of his conversation with Hohenlohe see Dreux, *op. cit.* p. 110.

[89] *GP*, I, No. 172, 271.   [90] Cf. Franz Xaver Schmitt, *op. cit.*, p. 43.

[91] Salvemini, *op. cit.*, February 15, 1925, p. 192.

[92] Cf., e.g., *Nuova antologia*, May, 1875, p. 222.

fore occasioned by the announcement that the German emperor had decided to postpone his visit to Italy.[93] In circles close to Bismarck, this action was linked with Italy's waning enthusiasm for an alliance with Germany.[94] There was reason, too, to believe that it was motivated in part by the apparent hopelessness of inducing Italy to modify her ecclesiastical policy. On April 13, Morier talked at some length with the German Crown Prince. The question of the emperor's visit to Italy, he learned, had been discussed for weeks. Various plans had been considered. Finally Bismarck had declared that "unless he could come back with a treaty in his pocket"—by which, according to Morier, was meant "a treaty in the matter of the Pope"—he would "expose himself to appearing to have gone on a fool's errand, and there was at present no prospect of concluding such a treaty."[95] Some amends, however, were made by arranging that the Crown Prince should go to Italy. But even this compensatory gesture gave rise to no little rancor. For Frederick, out of deference to the attitude of the Holy Father, refused to meet Victor Emmanuel in Rome, while the Italian government, egged on by its supporters,[96] insisted on receiving him there.[97] In the end, the prince had his way, and he saw the king in Naples. He also conferred with Minghetti. They discussed, among other things, the question of the next conclave, and the premier, according to Frederick, envisaged the election of "some broken-down old cardinal whose business it would be to tide over the next few years, leaving all things in *statu quo*."[98]

[93] This was the second postponement, the first having occurred in October, 1874. On both occasions the emperor's ill-health was given as the reason.

[94] Cf. *Preussische Jahrbücher*, April, 1875, p. 449.

[95] *Memoirs and Letters of the Right Hon. Sir Robert Morier* (London, 1911), II, 337.

[96] Cf. *Opinione*, April 9, 1875.

[97] Cf. *Memoirs and Letters .... Morier*, II, 337–38.

[98] *Ibid.*, p. 340.

Bismarck's criticism of Italian ecclesiastical policy spurred the Sinistra to force a showdown on the church-state issue. For several months, charges of inexcusable submissiveness and laxity vis-à-vis the Holy See had been directed at the government.[99] Official acquiescence in attempts by the church to overstep the bounds of its authority had been alleged.[100] Not a few moderates had joined their leftist compatriots in denouncing the excessively indulgent attitude of the political authorities toward clerical defiance of existing ecclesiastical legislation.[101] The *Opinione*, taking up the cudgels in behalf of the government, had retorted that Bismarck's treatment of the Catholic clergy could not be emulated in Italy.[102] But the accusations against the government had diminished neither in frequency nor in virulence. They were now pressed with greater energy by anticlericals in and out of parliament. Destra malcontents once again joined in the hue and cry. They too continued to attack the government's "passive and resigned attitude" toward the Vatican and warned that public opinion demanded a more vigorous ecclesiastical policy.[103] There were two important counts in this indictment. One was the alleged failure of the authorities to withhold the temporalities from those bishops who had refused to comply with the *exequatur* clause of the law of guarantees.[104] The other was the do-nothing attitude of the government in the face of papal efforts to foment revolution in Germany.[105] The cabinet's critics insisted further that the clergy was being permitted to plot with impunity against the national interests. Bismarck's dissatisfaction with the law of guarantees, they urged, proved two things. It showed that the church, if left alone, might succeed

99 Cf., e g., *Diritto*, June 21, 1874.

100 *Ibid.*, July 25, 1874. 102 *Opinione*, July 20, 1874.

101 *Libertà*, July 5 and 30, 1874. 103 Cf. *Libertà*, April 1, 1875.

104 Cf. S. William Halperin, "Church and State in Italy during the Last Years of Pius IX," *Church History*, March, 1936, p. 73; *Libertà*, April 19 and 30, 1875.

105 Cf. *Diritto*, April 6, 1875.

in destroying Italo-German friendship. And it demonstrated the suicidal generosity of the terms of the law. One anticlerical deputy, Petruccelli, even proposed that the statute be abrogated on the death of Pius IX.[106] This motion, however, was not even admitted to a reading in the chamber.

The major offensive was launched by Deputy La Porta on May 1. In presenting his interpellation on the law of guarantees, he reminded the chamber that the Sinistra had combated that measure on the ground that the state was supreme over all entities within its borders. This opposition had proved inefficacious, and the civil power had ended by sacrificing many of its prerogatives in the name of ecclesiastical freedom. But the situation, fortunately, was not irremediable. Parliament could always modify this law like any other whenever the interests of the nation should require it.[107] In the subsequent course of the debate, La Porta charged that the government was deliberately ignoring episcopal violations of the *exequatur* clause. The ecclesiastical policy now in vogue, he said, was "the abandonment of all the prerogatives of the civil authority in order to effect a reconciliation with the papacy."[108] Two days later, the redoubtable Mancini followed with an interpellation of his own. He accused the government of flirting with the Vatican and compromising thereby the sacred rights of the state. He doubted whether this peace-at-any-price policy had brought any comparable benefits. It was hopeless, he urged, to expect a church armed with the Syllabus of Errors and the dogma of papal infallibility to reconcile itself with the modern world. Actually, the church was waging an ever fiercer war against the modern liberal state.[109] He next turned to a careful examination of the law of guarantees. He cited with approval the adverse judgment

---

[106] The *Civiltà cattolica* remarked, apropos of this proposal, that the conviction was gaining ground among Catholics that the law of guarantees was a temporary expedient which would not survive the next conclave (*CC*, V [9th ser.; May 3, 1875], 486).

[107] *Atti*, CCXVIII (May 1, 1875), 2831.

[108] *Ibid.*, pp. 2843-47.   [109] *Ibid.*, May 3, 1875, pp. 2864-66.

which leading foreign jurists had pronounced upon it. He declared, however, that he could not subscribe to Petruccelli's proposal. In his opinion, the law had not been fairly enforced. Its real merits and flaws were therefore a matter of uncertainty. Indeed, he was now ready—so far had he moved from the position he had assumed in 1871—to consider it almost an extension of the *Statuto*. And though constitutions could be modified, such action, he cautioned, should be taken only in very exceptional cases.[110] But these considerations, he went on, could not obscure the fact that the government had been guilty of flagrant failure to enforce the *exequatur* clause. Nor could they divert attention from the Holy Father's misuse of his new freedom to incite to rebellion against the existing political regime in Italy.[111]

The Sinistra press enthusiastically elaborated upon the accusations of La Porta and Mancini and echoed the demand for a stronger ecclesiastical policy.[112] The state, argued the *Diritto*, must endeavor "to educate" the church.[113] This program could be realized within the existing statutory framework. The law of guarantees, despite its shortcomings, was therefore acceptable on two conditions: its integral observance and maintenance of the rights of the state vis-à-vis papal "tyranny."[114] The *Opinione* was once again the government's principal and most eloquent defender. In appraising the La Porta interpellation, it reminded the Sinistra that the struggle against the church was of greater moment than the single *exequatur* issue. It conceded that this struggle would have to be continued. But it underlined the fatuity of believing that the feud would cease once the church had submitted to the state.[115] The government, it argued, had been well advised to show prudence and moderation in the granting of the *exequatur*. Prevailing circumstances counseled magnanimity. At the same time, however, the authorities

---

[110] *Ibid.*, pp. 2867–69.

[111] *Ibid.*, pp. 2870, 2875–79.

[112] Cf. especially *Diritto*, May 3, 1875.

[113] *Ibid.*, May 4, 1875.

[114] *Ibid.*, May 5, 1875.

[115] *Opinione*, May 3, 1875.

would do well to indicate that they had no intention of making any deals with the enemies of national unity. As for the
program of the Sinistra, it was not altogether comprehensible.
But the interpellations had this merit: they afforded the cabinet an opportunity to proclaim that, though it abhorred
violence, it was determined to safeguard the rights of the
state.[116]

In the subsequent course of the debate, Professor Pasquale
Villari, the noted historian, emphasized the importance which
liberals attached to the outcome of the chamber's deliberations. How long, he asked, would the government's weak ecclesiastical policy, inspired, as it was, by a mistaken anxiety
to mollify the church, be continued? Moderates, he said, had
no desire to see the civil and ecclesiastical powers at war.
But they did want the state to maintain its position and
dignity and impress upon its denigrators that it too had
rights which were inviolable.[117] He warned that the strength
of the Roman hierarchy was being greatly underestimated.
Unencumbered by the temporal power, it was now preparing
to wage its struggle against modern civilization with weapons
more formidable than ever. It behooved Italy to prepare herself for this assault against her basic institutions. Above all,
she had to protect her schools, where the church was using
its new liberty to recruit the young for the impending trial of
strength.[118] Equally pungent were the remarks of Miceli. He
enlarged upon the international repercussions of the government's pusillanimity vis-à-vis the Vatican. It was clear, he
said, that the Italian nation, as distinguished from its rulers,
deplored the recent aggravation of Italo-German relations.
For it knew that Germany, in fighting the papacy, was fighting Italy's battle too. The German people, as well as its government, had registered its protest against the behavior of
the Italian cabinet, and both were now distrustful of their
natural ally. The inference from all this was plain: Italy had

[116] *Opinione*, May 6, 1875.

[117] *Atti*, CCXVIII (May 6, 1875), 2976.   [118] *Ibid.*, pp. 2977–78.

to abandon a policy based upon the "unfortunate" law of guarantees.[119]

The hard-pressed premier proved more than equal to the occasion. He affected to oppose irrefutable fact to the partisan charges of his adversaries. With considerable flourish he cited figures purporting to show that all was well with the enforcement of the *exequatur* clause. He sought to appease his less factually minded listeners with the promise that a bill for the reorganization of ecclesiastical properties would speedily be introduced. He reminded the house that its purpose in enacting the law of guarantees had been to effect the separation of church and state. And to that purpose his government had remained steadfastly loyal. The Italian people, he went on, wanted neither religious nor civil intolerance. It was averse to ecclesiastical intervention in civil affairs, but it was equally averse to civil interference with the church.[120] Addressing himself to Miceli's observations, he denied most emphatically that any note on ecclesiastical matters had been received from Berlin. The relations between the two countries had never been better. He had no intention, he said in conclusion, of altering his ecclesiastical policy. The law of guarantees would, as heretofore, be rigidly enforced.[121] Minghetti's oratorical effort was rewarded with an indorsement by the chamber of the ministerial position.

Once again the government had emerged victorious, and its supporters were jubilant. The *Opinione* remarked that the Sinistra's strictures had been recognized as wholly unfounded. Minghetti and his colleagues had been charged with violation of the law of guarantees, whereas the real issue simmered down to a mere question of judgment in applying it. It had further been alleged that the cabinet was seeking a reconciliation with the Vatican. But it was generally con-

[119] *Ibid.*, May 8, 1875, pp. 3052–53.

[120] *Ibid.*, May 7, 1875, pp. 3015, 3017–19, 3021–23.

[121] *Ibid.*, May 8, 1875, pp. 3080, 3082–83; cf. also, on Minghetti's defense of his ecclesiastical policy, Giovanni Maioli, *Marco Minghetti* (Bologna, 1926), pp. 208–9.

ceded that such a reconciliation was impossible, and this the
government knew as well as anyone else. Finally, the ministers had been accused of being reactionary. Actually, however, they were constantly combating reaction. "The vote of
the chamber," the Destra sheet continued, "serves as a warning to some and as a reassurance to others. It is a warning to
those who believe that Italy should modify her policy toward
the papacy and the church. It is a reassurance to those who
feared a change of policy which would usher in a new period
of perplexities and uneasiness." The country's good sense
stood revealed in this stability of outlook and purpose. And
the party in power, it emphatically concluded, would remain
adamant in its refusal to identify itself with the anticlericalism espoused by its adversaries.[122] The *Civiltà cattolica*
viewed the incident in a very different light. The government, it claimed, had been in a most uncomfortable dilemma.
Bismarck had demanded more severe measures against the
church. Minghetti, convinced that he could neither yield to
this pressure nor disregard it, had taken the easiest way out.
He had decided to promote a debate in the chamber on the
subject. He would give the deputies a chance to vent their
rage against the church and the papacy and thus appease
Bismarck, who did not discount the effect of anticlerical
demonstrations. And the ministry, in the course of the debate, would have an opportunity to defend its policy and
promise something better for the future. It would thus avoid
the appearance of surrendering to foreign pressure. Indeed,
it would give the impression that it was complying with the
wishes expressed by the national legislative body. In this
way, not alone Bismarck's good will, but its own prestige as
well, would be salvaged.[123] The *Osservatore romano* was no less
outspoken in denouncing the "senseless perfidy" of the Sinistra interpellants and the "hypocrisy" of the government. It,

[122] *Opinione*, May 10, 1875; cf. also Chiala, *Dina*, III, 435–36.

[123] *CC*, VI (9th ser.; June 5, 1875), 641–42.

too, was convinced that Italy had received "orders" from her German "masters."[124]

The considerations which inspired the ministerial strategy continued to be a matter of dispute. But it was abundantly clear from the temper of the debate that the Italian nation would not brook further temporization in punishing clerical defiance of the statutes of the realm. The discussion, according to the *Libertà*, had demonstrated that the Destra was averse to a reconciliation with the Vatican. The ministry would have to remember this.[125] And, indeed, Minghetti lost little time in giving effect to his pledge to protect the rights of the state. During the next few months the government commenced a wholesale expulsion from their sees of those prelates who had refused to comply with the *exequatur* clause.[126] The Vatican indignantly countered with the charge that this "persecution" was being carried out at the behest of Berlin.[127] The lull in the Italo-papal feud which had followed the accession of Minghetti was clearly at an end.

It was in the midst of this revitalized campaign against recalcitrant members of the episcopate that announcement was made of the German emperor's impending journey to Italy. This bit of news helped to dispel the concern occasioned by the recent deterioration of the Italo-German friendship. The imminent arrival of the German emperor, the *Libertà* remarked, was "a happy event" for Italy. It was "the confirmation of the good and cordial relations which prevail between the two courts . . . . between the governments of the two countries, and between the two nations."[128] The *Opinione*, which likewise registered its satisfaction, had some sharp words for those who had been announcing a cooling-off between the two countries as a result of Italy's refusal to

---

[124] *Osservatore romano*, May 10, 1875.   [125] *Libertà*, May 10, 1875.

[126] Halperin, "Church and State in Italy during the Last Years of Pius IX," *op. cit.*, p. 73.

[127] *CC*, VII (9th ser.; August 9, 1875), 479–80.

[128] *Libertà*, October 1, 1875.

emulate Germany in matters of ecclesiastical policy.[129] It was consequently with no little disappointment that Italians learned that Milan and not Rome was to receive the distinguished guest. They had hoped that this Protestant sovereign, whose government was still waging war against the Catholic church, would not hesitate to set foot in the Eternal City.[130] The Sinistra was somewhat embarrassed by this defection of the man whose praises it had for years been singing. It hastened to explain that his refusal to come to Rome was not due to any unwillingness to recognize Italy's claims to the city—an attitude which would have been in flat contradiction with German policy.[131] The Romans were very much disgruntled. Their municipal council sent Minghetti a telegram which read in part: "Rome, were it possible, would have been happy and proud to receive . . . . the first German emperor within her historic walls."[132] The premier, however, could scarcely be reproached for want of zeal in pressing the claims of the capital. So impressed had Keudell been with his arguments that he had offered to go to Berlin to present the Italian case to Bismarck. But the latter had made short shrift of Minghetti's plea. The German government, he said, did of course recognize Rome as the Italian capital. But domestic considerations precluded the choice of that city. The emperor had to take account of the feelings of his fourteen million Catholic subjects, who would not forgive such an affront to the head of their church.[133]

On October 18, William, accompanied by foreign secretary Bülow, arrived in Milan and was given a cordial reception. The local Giunta issued a proclamation which declared that "William and Victor [Emmanuel] together represent unity of

[129] *Opinione*, October 2, 1875.   [130] Rosi, *Vittorio Emanuele II*, II, 210.

[131] Cf. *Diritto*, October 3, 1875.

[132] Vigo, *op. cit.*, II, 65; *Schulthess, 1875*, p. 403.

[133] Luigi Chiala, *Carteggio politico di Michelangelo Castelli* (Torino, 1890–91), II, 587; Chiala, *Dal 1858 al 1892; pagine di storia contemporanea* (Torino, 1892-93), I, 189-90; Vigo, *op. cit.*, I, 378.

country and freedom of thought, the first having conquered the clerical hydra, the second having shaken off and overthrown the last stronghold of theocracy, the temporal power."[134] Bismarck's decision to forego the trip to Milan was keenly disappointing to the Italian government. According to an official German announcement, he had abandoned the idea of accompanying the emperor on the advice of his physician.[135] The chancellor himself, in a letter to Visconti-Venosta, alleged ill-health as the reason for his failure to come.[136] Nevertheless, his absence was reliably attributed in part to political considerations.[137] Of the many rumors to which it gave rise, the most persistent had it that he was evincing in this way his dissatisfaction with Italian ecclesiastical policy. This was the explanation noisily advanced by the Sinistra. The men of the left charged that the "timid" and propapal policy of the government had estranged Bismarck, who accordingly was not at all desirous of meeting the leaders of the Destra.[138] The *Opinione* sharply dissented. It was impolite, it said, to reject the official explanation. Moreover, no considerations of a political nature demanded Bismarck's presence in Italy. The emperor's visit was entirely one of courtesy, and new alliances were scarcely concluded on such occasions.[139] The only serious conversation which actually took place during William's stay in the Lombard capital was that between Bülow and Minghetti. The former had instructions from Bismarck to warn the Italian premier that the destruction of the Italian state would ensue if greater energy were not shown in dealing with the Curia. Italians, Minghetti replied, had been treating with the papacy for centuries. They therefore understood that institution better than foreigners and they would continue on the same

[134] Vigo, *op. cit.*, II, 62.

[135] Ludwig Hahn, *Fürst Bismarck* (Berlin, 1878–91), II, 781.

[136] *Aus Bismarcks Briefwechsel* (Stuttgart and Berlin, 1901), pp. 473–74.

[137] Cf. Dreux, *op. cit.*, p. 362.

[138] Cf. *Diritto*, October 17, 1875.   [139] *Opinione*, October 18, 1875.

tolerable footing with it long after Bismarck had revised his May laws and beaten a retreat.[140]

The emperor's presence in Milan evoked warm plaudits from the Italian press. The language of the *Libertà* was exceptionally fervid. This visit, the Roman daily triumphantly proclaimed, placed "a new and solemn seal on the policy which produced the contemporaneous renascence of Germany and Italy and which is founded on an intimate and lasting friendship." William was being cheered at Milan because it was understood that "his name guarantees to us forever the possession of the Tiber."[141] These claims were ridiculed by the Vatican. It was difficult, the *Osservatore romano* pointedly remarked, to explain away certain very obvious facts. Victor Emmanuel had voyaged to Berlin, but the German emperor had been careful to stay away from Rome. It was very easy to see, the papal organ concluded, that William's sojourn in Italy was devoid of political importance and would change nothing.[142] This was all quite unfair, the ministerialists retorted. The *Opinione* explained that the German monarch had avoided Rome only because he was unwilling to visit the Vatican. All the princes of Europe, it pointed out, were bound by personal ties to the venerable pontiff, and it would have been discourteous to go to Rome without calling on him. It was certain, however, that under Pius' successors foreign sovereigns would not fail to visit the Italian capital.[143]

Following the emperor's departure, Italians awaited with more than usual interest the government's next move in the church-state feud. The hopes of the anticlericals—they had been greatly bolstered by William's visit—were dashed by the premier himself. In an address before his constituency at the close of October, he ridiculed the idea that the Milan meeting would usher in any change in Italian ecclesiastical

[140] Bülow, *op. cit.*, IV, 330–31.   [141] *Libertà*, October 19, 1875.

[142] *Osservatore romano*, October 20 and 22, 1875.

[143] *Opinione*, October 27, 1875.

policy. That policy, he said, rested on the principle of the separation of church and state. And the results so far achieved with that principle offered no reason for any deviation from it.[144] The adroit statesman was careful, however, to disclaim any intention of abandoning the recently inaugurated campaign against episcopal flouters of the *exequatur* clause. More than that, he assured the country that before long a law defining the status of ecclesiastical properties would be placed upon the statute-books.[145] Minghetti's moderate supporters were elated,[146] while the Vatican, inured though it was to governmental strategems, professed to be extraordinarily disgusted. It did not seem possible, according to the *Osservatore romano*, that Minghetti would dare to make fun of the Italian public quite so boldly. His speech, at bottom, rested upon "nothing except hypothetical calculations, chimerical presumptions, and an absolute lack of precise data—nothing, in short, that was clear and positive except the imperturbable frankness of an individual famous for his stupidity in economic matters."[147]

The premier's preoccupations were cut short by the swing of the political pendulum. In March, 1876, Destra rule finally came to an end when the Minghetti government went down to defeat on a motion relating to the unpopular *macinato* or flour tax.[148] A parliamentary revolution of the first magnitude occurred with the advent of a Sinistra cabinet headed by Agostino Depretis, the veteran politician who had succeeded Rattazzi as the leader of the opposition. The antecedents of the country's new rulers were well calculated to fill

---

[144] Vigo, *op. cit.*, II, 67.

[145] Influential Destra circles had for months been urging him to submit such a bill to parliament (cf. the *Libertà*, August 1, 1875).

[146] Cf. the *Opinione*, November 4, 1875.

[147] *Osservatore romano*, November 11, 1875.

[148] Cf. Ugo Pesci, *I primi anni di Roma capitale* (Firenze, 1907), p. 122.

the Vatican with profound foreboding.[149] Depretis himself was a Freemason and a staunch liberal. His program, as he had stated it the previous autumn, comprised the extension of secular education, the defense of the state's traditional prerogatives, the prosecution of clerical calumniators, and the lay administration of ecclesiastical properties.[150] Mancini, whose devastating tirades against the ecclesiastical policy of the Destra were well remembered, was the new minister of justice. Hardly less hostile to the church was Professor Michele Coppino, who assumed the portfolio of public instruction. The key ministry of the interior was intrusted to Giovanni Nicotera, erstwhile republican conspirator and Garibaldian legionnaire.[151] The *Diritto*, which speedily came to be regarded as the new premier's special mouthpiece, minced no words in proclaiming that the era of halfway measures was past. "Germany," it predicted, "will find Italy . . . . aiding her vigorously to carry on the course she has adopted." The Depretis cabinet, according to the Sinistra journal, was determined to safeguard the civil authority against clerical abuses. It was likewise interested in certain sweeping reforms. It wished to secularize the administration of ecclesiastical properties, emancipate the lower clergy, and develop public instruction. But it was resolved, at the same time, to preserve the law of guarantees.[152] And it had no thought of impeding in any way the convocation of the next papal conclave.[153]

The program foreshadowed in this newspaper pronouncement boded ill for the future of church-state relations. And indeed, with the accession of the Sinistra, Italian ecclesiasti-

---

[149] The *Osservatore romano* did, it is true, insist that there was little to choose between the two parties in matters of ecclesiastical policy. But it sadly conceded that the Sinistra government would probably outdo its predecessor (issue of March 31, 1876).

[150] Cilibrizzi, *op. cit.*, II, 92.

[151] Cf. Jessie White Mario, *In Memoria di Giovanni Nicotera* (Firenze, 1894), chaps. i–v.

[152] *Diritto*, March 25 and 28, 1876.   [153] *Ibid.*, April 1, 1876.

cal policy became definitely more severe.[154] Late in March, Depretis himself intimated in the chamber of deputies that darker times were ahead for the church. His government, he said, would be neither aggressive nor hostile in its ecclesiastical policy. But it likewise had no intention of being conciliatory. The existing laws would be firmly enforced, even though they were dictated by "a political prudence which experience has shown to be excessive but which in any case should not be repudiated without grave and new reasons." That was not all, however. He and his ministerial colleagues felt obliged to take legislative action to protect "freedom of conscience and the rights of society" against abuses, committed in the exercise of the spiritual office.[155] This declaration of policy left the clericals with few illusions. Depretis, the *Unità cattolica* charged, was initiatng "an era of tremendous persecution." But there was some merit, it went on, in his frank repudiation of any reconciliation with the papacy. "We prefer," it concluded, "the clear language of Depretis to the fictions and hypocrisies of his predecessor, Minghetti."[156] The *Osservatore romano* heartily concurred. True it was, it conceded, that a more active offensive against the church could now be expected. But, after all, the Sinistra would only be doing openly what the Destra had been doing clandestinely.[157] The *Opinione*, now a leading mouthpiece of the opposition, found the premier's statement quite acceptable. Confessing surprise at his moderation, it declared that it agreed with him in rejecting both hostility to and reconciliation with the church.[158] But moderates were quickly to discover that their evaluation of the Sinistra's program was a bit wide of the mark.

The new cabinet wasted no time in demonstrating its

[154] Cf. Francesco Scaduto, *Guarentigie pontificie e relazioni tra stato e chiesa* (Torino, 1884), p. 335.

[155] *Atti*, CCXXIX (March 28, 1876), 235.

[156] *Unità cattolica*, April 1 and 2, 1876.

[157] *Osservatore romano*, April 5, 1876.   [158] *Opinione*, March 30, 1876.

mettle. Late in March, Pius felicitated Bishop Dupanloup for having protested against the recently enacted law abolishing the exemption of Italian clerics from military service. The papal letter contained some very unflattering allusions to the Italian government, and a ministerial decree was issued forbidding its publication in Rome. The *Osservatore romano* disregarded the ban and reproduced the document in its issue of April 23, 1876. It was promptly confiscated by the authorities, much to the indignation of the clericals, who signalized the incident as still another proof of the futility of the law of guarantees.[159] Bismarck, they wailed, was exerting pressure upon his Sinistra friends in an effort to get them to wage war against the Catholic church. But the latter, they reiterated, preferred "open persecution to a feigned and deceitful peace." And if Mancini should follow "the sacrilegious example" of Bismarck, Italian priests would know how to emulate the "most noble" conduct of their German colleagues.[160] This outcry, however, made little impression upon Depretis and his associates. They had only begun the long-deferred task of subjugating the ecclesiastical hierarchy. Late in July, Nicotera forbade outdoor religious processions, alleging that they were deleterious to the maintenance of public order.[161] This measure, according to the Sinistra apologists, was entirely defensible.[162] The government possessed the right to prohibit religious processions in the interests of public health, safety, and tranquillity. In any case—so ran

---

[159] Vigo, *op. cit.*, II, 110. Who, queried the *Unità cattolica* on July 20, 1876, could prevent the present Italian government from proposing the abolition of the law of guarantees? Such action hinged only upon the will of the ministers and the sanction of parliament. Hence, the guarantees guaranteed nothing, and Pius had been wise to reject them.

[160] *Unità cattolica*, July 19, 1876.

[161] Vigo, *op. cit.*, II, 128–29; Manfroni, *op. cit.*, I, 264. He did stipulate, however, that exceptions might be made from time to time whenever permission to stage such processions had been secured from the local prefect a fortnight in advance.

[162] Leftist spokesmen had repeatedly demanded the outlawing of religious processions prior to their party's assumption of power (cf., e.g., *Riforma*, April 22, 1872, and April 15, 1873).

the argument—religious processions were unnecessary. They were reminiscent of pagan celebrations and had been discontinued in many civilized countries.[163] The Destra decried this violation of the principle of religious freedom. Nicotera's action was distinctly inopportune, declared the *Opinione*. In view of the strength of religious sentiment in many of the cities, it would have been better to leave such matters to the discretion of the prefects. The latter could have been relied upon to decide when and if disciplinary action should be taken against the processioners.[164] The clericals once again complained of religious persecution.[165] Nicotera could scarcely have chosen a less opportune moment for his hateful action, the *Unità cattolica* asserted. Religious processions were being banned, but a recent procession at Genoa in honor of the minister of the interior had been allowed to take place without the slightest interference. As a matter of fact, the Catholic organ contended, religious processions never gave rise to disturbances of public order. So it was clear that not love of public tranquillity but a desire to molest the church had inspired the objectionable circular.[166] Was it true, demanded the *Osservatore romano*, that cabinet ministers and prefects possessed authority to prescribe rules forbidding that which was "permissible and virtuous?" Obviously, the papal organ concluded, Nicotera's decree was devoid of validity.[167] Pius himself protested against the ban in an address before a group of Savoyard pilgrims.[168]

This clamor, too, went unheeded. The offensive against the church was pushed with unabated ardor. In September the minister of the interior ordered drastic action to halt the

[163] Cf. the elaborate contentions in *Diritto*, December 4, 1877.

[164] *Opinione*, August 18, 1876.

[165] Manfroni, *op. cit.*, I, 264–66.

[166] *Unità cattolica*, August 5, 1876.

[167] *Osservatore romano*, September 8, 1876.   [168] Cf. *ibid.*, September 20, 1876.

stealthy resurrection of religious orders.[169] It was the duty of
the state, explained the *Diritto*, to defend itself against this
danger to its security.[170] The Destra again objected. It
charged that Nicotera's decree was ambiguous, illogical, and
inefficacious.[171] Despairing moderates were still shaking their
heads when the third Catholic congress which had convened
in Bologna came to an unceremonious and premature end.
The local prefect, acting with governmental authorization,
ordered its dissolution on the ground that it had given rise to
public disturbances. These disturbances, however, were the
work of anticlerical demonstrators, and consequently the
action of the authorities, which penalized the victims and not
the culprits, evoked vitriolic criticism. In the opinion of the
Libertà, the prefect's decree constituted a most unpardonable
violation of freedom because it had come as a result of mob
clamor. And the papal party, the Destra organ charged, had
been presented with a triumph. It could now accuse the
government of wanting liberty for itself and of denying it to
everyone else.[172] The clericals naturally made the most of the
cabinet's blunder. The *Osservatore romano* was full of commiseration for the congress, "so villainously dissolved" by
"the despotism of the *piazza* and of the government."[173] The
Unità cattolica accused the church's enemies of indulging in
brutal violence in order to prevent the faithful from exercising their legal rights. "The Catholic congresses frighten the
Revolution," it asserted. The incident at Bologna would con-

---

[169] Cf. *Libertà*, September 7, 1876; *Osservatore romano*, September 12, 1876;
Schulthess, 1876, pp. 390–91. This revival of religious corporations in Italy was aided
by the retention of the generalship houses and by the influx of large numbers of foreign monastics put to flight by recent legislative action against their orders (cf.
Biagio Brugi, "Giurisprudenza e codici," *Cinquanta anni di storia italiana* [Milano,
1911], II, 18).

[170] *Diritto*, September 11, 1876. The authoritative Sinistra journal went on to
suggest the enactment of a special law to deal with this problem.

[171] Cf. *Opinione*, September 10 and 12, 1876.

[172] *Libertà*, October 13, 1876.

[173] *Osservatore romano*, October 13 and 27, 1876.

stitute "a beautiful page in the story of Italian freedom under Nicotera and Depretis."[174]

This storm of protest made no very great impression upon the anticlerical zealots who dominated the cabinet. It was now the turn of church-controlled schools to come under the hostile scrutiny of the authorities. "About ten years have elapsed since the religious corporations were suppressed," the ministerial *Diritto* observed, "and the ecclesiastical institutions dedicated to instruction still exist and prosper and threaten to prosper even more." It concluded with a plea for the complete abolition of all clerical schools.[175] The step urged by the premier's organ was not taken, much to the relief of the ecclesiastical authorities. But a very telling blow —the most devastating of all—was reserved for the episcopate. The Depretis government had pledged itself, among other things, to the rigid enforcement of the *exequatur* clause.[176] Mancini undertook to implement this pledge. He informed the procurators of the kingdom that refractory bishops were to be deprived not only of their temporalities but of their spiritual prerogatives as well. This brought results. Fearful lest further resistance be followed by the complete disruption of the functions of the church, the Vatican finally yielded and authorized compliance with the requirements of the law.[177]

Satisfied that the drift of public opinion was favorable to his party's chances, Depretis announced new chamber elections for November 5. Throughout the ensuing campaign, he kept the ecclesiastical question in the foreground as one of the issues on which the nation and the Sinistra were in entire accord. The law of guarantees, he told his constituency early in October, represented "a transition or a transaction . . . . between the past and the future"—a dictum with which few

[174] *Unità cattolica*, October 13, 1876.

[175] *Diritto*, September 30, 1876.   [176] Mario, *op. cit.*, p. 104.

[177] *CC*, I (10th ser.; January 20, 1877), 359–60; Vigo, *op. cit.*, II, 158–59.

of his countrymen could disagree. Religion, he triumphantly continued, had been whittled down to its proper stature—that of an abstract bond.[178]

> Let us not delude ourselves. There is in Italy and in Europe a party which conceals its worldly aims and its thirst for dominion under the mantle of religion. The traditions of Gregory VII are not yet extinct within the papal Curia; the Syllabus is still its *modus agendi;* and it is a formidable power because of its new despotic constitution, its complete and perfect organization, the breadth of its ramifications, the great influence which it continues to exert over the masses. . . . . I am a defender of religious liberty . . . . but when religious sentiment turns against the political organization of the state, it is time to sound the alarm in order that provision might be made for the latter's defense. The war has begun, and it will be necessary to wage it *à outrance.*[179]

The oratorical broadsides of the premier and of his lieutenants, coupled with skilful electioneering, contributed significantly to the triumph of the ministerialists. The popular tendency to associate the rule of the moderates with onerous tax burdens did the rest. The bulk of the nation, which had had its fill of Destra finance, was of no mind to oust its new rulers, and the Depretis government emerged with a decisive victory at the polls.[180] The offensive against the church could now be resumed with far better prospect of complete success. Moreover, the cabinet's tactical position seemed greatly strengthened by the death of Antonelli early in November. With his passing, the Vatican lost its most resourceful diplomatist. Cardinal Simeoni, the papal nuncio in Madrid, was named his successor. He possessed little of Antonelli's shrewdness and finesse, and it was not long before he was called upon to cope with a crisis which would have taxed the abilities of a far more capable statesman.

On November 20, Victor Emmanuel informed the new parliament that Italy was about to embark upon a Kul-

---

[178] Vigo, *op. cit.,* II, 137.   [179] Cf. *Libertà,* October 9 and 10, 1876.

[180] Cf. Alessandro Guiccioli, *Quintino Sella* (Rovigo, 1887), II, 129. Many Destra notables went down to defeat in these elections. The outcome, as one prominent rightist put it, was a "real disaster" (cf. "Nuove pagine del diario di Alessandro Guiccioli: 1876," *Nuova antologia,* July 1, 1935, p. 93).

turkampf of her own. "It remains for us," he said, "to face
a problem hitherto not dealt with. The freedom conceded the
church in our kingdom far exceeds that enjoyed by it in any
other Catholic state. But it cannot be so exercised as to violate public liberty or infringe upon the national sovereignty."[181] These words evoked great applause from the government benches. They foreshadowed that abridgment of ecclesiastical liberties which Mancini and others had consistently championed prior to the accession of the Sinistra.[182] The
import of the royal announcement was all too clear to the
Vatican. The *Osservatore romano* warned its readers that they
could now expect "an aggravation of the war against the
church, more sectarian greed to be appeased at public expense, further larcenies, and more extended propaganda in
favor of public corruption."[183] On November 25 the so-called
clerical abuses bill made its appearance in the chamber of
deputies. It imposed severe penalties upon priests guilty of
abusing their spiritual functions to disturb the "public conscience" and the "peace of families," censure the laws and
institutions of the state, and encourage resistance to the acts
of the public authorities.[184] A special statute was preferable

---

[181] Massari, *La Vita ed il regno di Vittorio Emanuele II di Savoia*, II, 583.

[182] Cf. Mario, *op. cit.*, pp. 111-12; Manfroni, *op. cit.*, I, 279.

[183] *Osservatore romano*, November 22, 1876.

[184] Cf. the text of the bill in *Atti*, CCXXXII, No. 20-A, 45-46. The principal features of this measure had been embodied in the Sardinian penal code approved by
royal decree on November 20, 1859 (cf. Vilfredo Pareto, "Il Disegno di legge contro
gli abusi del clero," *Nuova antologia*, January, 1877, p. 139 and note; Francesco
Ruffini, *Lineamenti storici delle relazioni fra lo stato e la chiesa in Italia* [Torino,
1891], p. 38). In June, 1871, in keeping with the principle of freedom proclaimed in
the recently enacted law of guarantees, these articles of the penal code were replaced by milder provisions, although the principle of disciplinary action by the
state was retained (cf. Pareto, *op. cit.*, p. 140 and note; *Nuova antologia*, February,
1877, p. 433; Ruffini, *op. cit.*, p. 41; Stefano Castagnola, *Da Firenze a Roma: diario
storico-politico del 1870-71* [Torino, 1896], p. 98 n.). This indulgence, however, was
not of long duration. The incurable hostility of the clergy to the existing political
order impelled the government to retrace its steps. Early in 1875 the then minister
of justice, Vigliani, submitted to parliament a new penal code which revived the
penalties suppressed in 1871. Simultaneously, he warned that the government,
though resolved to respect the freedom of the church, would tolerate no abuse of

to modifications of the penal code, the *Diritto* declared with solemn finality. In taking this position, it went on, it was voicing the sentiment of the great majority of deputies who had applauded Victor Emmanuel's recent proclamation of war against clerical abuses.[185]

The Vatican was ready for a fight to the finish against a measure which it branded as mischievously ambiguous and "essentially persecutory." The *Osservatore romano* ridiculed the allusion to "public conscience." The latter was one of those phrases, "as devoid of sense as grandiose in sound, with which the Mazzinian philosophy of our government is replete." The bill, as a whole, was "tyrannical" and "odious" because it robbed clergymen of their freedom of speech and offended the susceptibilities of the great majority of Italians.[186] The *Unità cattolica* professed to be convinced that a new kind of religious persecution was now to begin. The state was asserting its right to define clerical abuses in order that it might eventually relegate even prayers to that reprehensible category. No one knew, the Turinese organ complained, what these alleged abuses were. But the evil doings of the brigands who continued to plague Italy with impunity required no elucidation.[187] The pontiff himself was all defiance. He denounced the "internal seditionaries" and "external enemies" who were molesting not only the properties of the church but its most sacred rights as well.[188] This pronouncement was only a foretaste of the verbal lashing he was shortly to administer, but it sufficed to indicate that the ineluctable trial of strength between the Vatican and the Sinistra was

---

that freedom (cf. *Osservatore romano*, February 14, 1875; *CC*, V [9th ser.; February 22, 1875], 610–12; Vigo, *op. cit.*, II, 15–16). It remained for the Sinistra cabinet, pending the adoption of the new penal code, to give effect to this warning by introducing the clerical abuses bill.

[185] *Diritto*, January 22, 1877.

[186] *Osservatore romano*, December 15, 1876.

[187] *Unità cattolica*, November 28 and December 6, 1876.

[188] Manfroni, *op. cit.*, I, 279–81.

well on its way to a climax. The former, in this instance, found the bulk of the Destra arrayed on its side.[189] That party's leading organs were at the outset agreed in denouncing the bill. The *Opinione*, though conceding the duty of the state to assert its sovereignty vis-à-vis any insubordination on the part of the clericals, insisted for a time that the proposed law was justified by no extraordinary circumstances. The statutes of the kingdom, it held, made adequate provision for the maintenance of public order. No convincing arguments could be adduced in favor of an exceptional law. The articles of the bill could very properly be incorporated into the new penal code, so that their enforcement would affect all citizens alike without distinction of class or party.[190] "All our convictions, all our ideas of freedom for everyone, all our principles regarding the functions of the state," declared the *Libertà*, "induce us to hold that this bill, unjust in principle, is inconclusive in actuality." The basic error involved was to believe that one could combat ideas with prison terms and fines. For it was clear that the clergy could never be reduced to silence or reason by repressive measures.[191] Substantially the same language was employed by other moderate sheets.[192] Some influential Destra spokesmen invoked the Cavourian formula to justify their opposition to the proposed muzzling of the Catholic hierarchy.[193] Others warned that Italy was not ready for a Kulturkampf.[194] Still others

[189] Cf., for the Destra criticism of the clerical abuses bill, Pareto, *op. cit.*, pp. 161–62; *Nuova antologia* (February, 1877), pp. 434–35.

[190] *Opinione*, January 4 and 16, 1877.

[191] *Libertà*, December 4, 1876.   [192] Notably the *Perseveranza*.

[193] The attitude of this group was well represented by Minghetti. The erstwhile premier maintained that, once the state had invaded the province of the church, the old, discredited regalism would virtually be restored (cf. his elaboration of this view in his *Stato e chiesa* [Milano, 1878], pp. 144–45).

[194] The leading exponent of this view was Lanza. A few years earlier he had written Dina that he was opposed to any law designed "to discipline the clergy." The Italian government, he had observed, did not have the power of a Bismarck. In any event, "a religious struggle in Italy would be very dangerous" (cf. Chiala, *Dina*, III, 424).

shared the feeling of Alessandro Guiccioli, a prominent member of the conservative wing of the Destra, whose conscience rebelled against voting in favor of a law which was "excessively evil."[195] But Sella, now the leader of the Destra opposition in the chamber,[196] favored the enactment of the measure and ranged himself on the side of the ministry.[197] He admitted that the introduction of the bill was a serious error, but he insisted that parliament would commit an even greater one by rejecting it.[198] Dina, whose attitude hitherto had been indistinguishable from that of the majority of his moderate friends, now reversed his stand and rallied to Sella's support. The influential editor of the *Opinione* likewise began to belabor the necessity of subordinating doctrinaire scruples to practical exigencies.[199] In accordance with this train of thought, the *Opinione* parted company with the majority of its Destra confreres and proceeded to enlarge upon the folly of scrapping the proposed measure despite its admitted shortcomings.[200]

The chamber debate opened on January 18, 1877. The anticlericals who now dominated the lower house seized the opportunity to attack the pope, the church, and the Catholic faith in language of unprecedented violence. Petruccelli led the onslaught. "The church," he asserted, "has always been subversive. After the Vatican council, it became aggressive. After September 20, it became hydrophobic." He could write a volume, he said, were he to record all the "antisocial, immoral, perverse doctrines of the church, the Holy Father, and the Vatican." He would vote for the bill, even though it was not sufficiently drastic. For it did, after all, consecrate "the

[195] "Nuove pagine del diario di Alessan[.].:o Guiccioli: 1877," *Nuova antologia*, July 16, 1935, p. 216.

[196] Sella had been chosen head of the Destra on July 1, 1876 (cf. "Nuove pagine del diario di Alessandro Guiccioli: 1876," *Nuova antologia*, July 1, 1935, p. 91).

[197] "Nuove pagine del diario di Alessandro Guiccioli: 1877," *Nuova antologia*, July 16, 1935, p. 216.

[198] Guiccioli, *Quintino Sella*, II, 138–39.

[199] Cf. Chiala, *Dina*, III, 489.   [200] *Opinione*, January 23, 1877.

principle of the sovereignty of the state."[201] Another inveterate anticlerical, Giovanni Bovio, used his caustic wit with telling effect. The issue, he declared, was: "Should priests die of their own abuses, or should they survive under repressive laws?" He preferred the first of these alternatives. "Abuse," he went on, "has exhausted them; it should also extinguish them." Penal laws, prison terms, or fines would not destroy them. They would come to grief "poisoned by the buffoons of Leo X, the bastards of Alexander VI, the Jesuits of Paul IV." In a word—so ran his argument—the clergy, if left alone, would exterminate itself. Moreover, repressive measures were powerless in the face of such things as auricular confession, traffic in indulgences, and the punishments of a next world. The present bill was therefore to be rejected as misdirected and futile.[202] The debate was enlivened by the valiant attempt of the conservative deputy, Bortolucci, to restrain his radical colleagues. He deplored the irreverent tone of the preceding speakers who had spared neither the church nor its venerable head. He denied that the papacy aspired to universal dominion. He recalled the Italian government's promise, made before the occupation of Rome, to preserve the freedom of the Holy Father. That promise was enshrined in the law of guarantees, which constituted something of a pact with the Catholic world. But now past pledges were being indiscriminately forgotten. The present measure was ample proof of this. It exposed the clergy, whose only offense was obedience to the mandates of conscience, to the whims of the authorities. The state, he urged, could not intervene in ecclesiastical matters without infringing upon the spiritual sphere and transgressing the separatist principle. He closed with a plea for real religious liberty.[203]

Mancini, however, was ready for this and other criticisms. The present bill, declared the persuasive minister, was "modest" and "innocuous." More than that, it was opportune and

---

[201] *Atti*, CCXLIV (January 18, 1877), 657–61.

[202] *Ibid.*, CCXLIV (January 19, 1877), 692.   [203] *Ibid.*, pp. 702–6.

just. The claim, he said, was made in some quarters that the clergy was no longer abusing its spiritual functions. He cited some recent examples to prove the absurdity of that contention. Equally absurd, in his opinion, was the charge that parliament was being asked to sanction an exceptional law. The freedom of individuals and that of private associations, he observed, "have a rational and legitimate limit in the conservation of the social order. Therefore, they are necessarily subordinated to the freedom of all, to the rights of all." To hold that religious liberty was a thing apart from the jurisdiction of the state would be "to admit a state within a state, or rather, a state above the state." A vote against the proposed measure would mean, accordingly, a vote for the theocratic principle.[204] Mancini's utterance provoked sharp retorts from moderates and clericals alike. Even the minister's most sincere admirers, the *Libertà* charged, confessed that his speech was "very weak." For it was obvious that he visualized a state of affairs which in reality did not exist. The journal adjured the chamber to reject the bill as an inefficacious and dangerous gesture. Its enactment would have but one consequence: that of intensifying the hostility of the papal party.[205] The *Voce della verità* stigmatized Mancini's oratorical effort as the "unhappiest" of his speeches, replete, as it was, with "petty sophisms," "subtleties," and "banal rhetorical arguments."[206] Catholic groups throughout the country threw themselves into the fray with resounding protests against the abusive language of the anticlerical parliamentarians.[207] But this outcry proved of no avail. Most of the deputies required little urging to heed the *Diritto*'s entreaty to approve the measure in order not to embolden the perennially vigilant ultramontanes.[208] On January 24 the

---

[204] *Ibid.*, CCXLIV (January 20, 1877), 723–28.

[205] *Libertà*, January 22, 1877.   [206] *Voce della verità*, January 23, 1877.

[207] Cf. *ibid.*, January 24, 1877, and *Osservatore romano*, January 28, 1877.

[208] Cf. the admonition in *Diritto*, January 24, 1877.

chamber gave its sanction to the bill. It now awaited indorsement by the senate to become law. The ministerialists had
won an impressive initial victory, and the likelihood of ultimate success in bringing the measure through the upper
house seemed enhanced by the continued support of such
Destra notables as Sella and Dina. Though reiterating its
belief that the bill was inopportune, the *Opinione* joyfully
signalized the considerable majority which the government
had secured in the chamber. Greater audacity on the part of
the clericals, it claimed, had thus been rendered impossible.[209]

[209] *Opinione*, January 26, 1877.

CHAPTER XIII

THE BATTLE OVER THE CLERICAL ABUSES BILL AND THE ECLIPSE OF THE FRENCH ULTRAMONTANE THREAT

THE chamber vote of January 24, 1877, was a challenge, and the Vatican was not loath to accept it. There was nothing urgent to justify the presentation of the bill in question, declared the *Civiltà cattolica*. It was clearly an exceptional measure and as such contrary to the principle of freedom to which Italy's rulers paid unfailing lip service. In view of the impossibility of defining the "abuses" which were the object of official ire, the government's action could be interpreted only as the prelude to tyrannical violence.[1] There was no reason to be dismayed, the *Voce della verità* assured its readers. The bill was too stupid and ambiguous to be taken seriously. It was impossible to believe that the Italian people would condemn a priest or a bishop simply because he performed his duty. The slogan of Catholics had to be: "Keep calm and carry on!"[2] Throughout the peninsula the defenders of the church rallied to ward off the impending blow. Protest after protest against the clerical abuses bill appeared in all the ultramontane newspapers. One of the most telling broadsides came from the spokesmen of the Roman Society for Catholic Interests. The burden of their indictment was that one class, the clergy, was being penalized and persecuted, that an attempt was being made to silence the pope as well as his subordinates, and that revolt against the legitimate ecclesiastical authorities was being shamelessly fomented.[3] Pius himself, in a stirring allocution

[1] *CC*, I (10th ser.; February 6, 1877), 390–99.

[2] *Voce della verità*, January 25 and 26, 1877.   [3] *Ibid.*, February 25, 1877.

delivered on March 12, lashed out furiously against the ecclesiastical policy of the Quirinal and appealed to Catholics
throughout the world to induce their governments to intervene on his behalf.[4] This consistorial pronouncement—easily
the most violent of the many utterances which had emanated
from the Vatican since the occupation of Rome[5]—was in a
sense the aged pontiff's political testament. Never before had
he so unequivocally asserted that the existence of a united
Italy was incompatible with the independence of the Holy
See.[6] It was his purpose to proclaim a sort of crusade against
Italy. The Catholic powers, with France, so he hoped, in
their van, were to be prevailed upon to throw themselves into
this holiest of enterprises.[7] Copies of the papal address were
sent to the members of the diplomatic corps accredited to the
Vatican. They were also the recipients of a note from Cardinal Simeoni expressing the hope that they would convey to
their governments the facts cited by the Holy Father.[8]

So bellicose was the language of the allocution that it made
even some of the cardinals squirm. One of them was reputed
to have exclaimed: "Here are the consequences of the death
of Antonelli! Here is the triumph of the party which he had
always fought."[9] But the well-disciplined minions of the Vatican were assailed by neither scruples nor doubts. The Catholic world, proclaimed the *Voce della verità*, now had an opportunity to promote the most sublime of causes. This it
could do by securing the removal of existing limitations upon
the pope's independence.[10] Whoever spoke in the manner of
Pius IX "cannot be vanquished," the *Unità cattolica* boasted.
The pope's invocation of foreign aid against Italy loosed a

[4] *CC*, II (10th ser.; March 26, 1877), 5–25.

[5] Ugo Pesci, *I primi anni di Roma capitale* (Firenze, 1907), p. 525.

[6] A. Leroy-Beaulieu, "Un Roi et un pape: II. Pie IX et le Saint-Siège," *Revue des deux mondes*, May 15, 1878, p. 401.

[7] Cf. Camillo Manfroni, *Sulla soglia del Vaticano* (Bologna, 1920), I, 287.

[8] *AD, 1876–1877*, IV, 163–64.

[9] Manfroni, *op. cit.*, I, 287.   [10] *Voce della verità*, March 18, 1877.

barrage of withering criticism from moderates and radicals
alike. The political commentator of the *Nuova antologia* observed:

It is true that the law of guarantees confers upon the pontiff the prerogatives of a sovereign. But there is no sovereign who is permitted as much
within the confines of our country. The freedom of which the Holy Father
makes such extensive use is superior to that which all men of this world,
including the monarchs of all the Russias and of the Celestial Empire, enjoy, although he modestly declares that it does not suffice for him.

The pope would now find it difficult, this writer concluded,
to persuade the world that his independence was being restricted by the Italian government.[11] Pius' gesture, according
to the *Libertà*, signalized the hopelessness of attempting an
equitable and peaceful solution of the Roman question. The
allocution, it held, would prove a boomerang. For it was not
so much a declaration of war against Italy as against the
papacy itself.[12] The Sinistra once again pointed an accusing
finger at its predecessors in office. The attitude of the pope,
it claimed, was the logical result of excessive Italian generosity in the past. For it was the law of guarantees which enabled him to vilify the fatherland and invite foreign intervention. However, in the opinion of ministerialists, the latest
turn of affairs was not altogether regrettable. They felt that
a serious struggle provoked by the Holy See would prove a
healthful experience for the Italian people. The latter, in
combating the "artificial" religion of the Vatican, might witness the resurgence of its own pure and strong faith.[13] Welcome, too, was the fact that those optimists who had continued to hope for a change of heart on the part of the pontiff
were now completely disillusioned. There could henceforth
be no doubt that Pius was deaf to all counsels of moderation;
and there was reason to fear that his successor would emulate
him.[14]

Mancini's first impulse was to order the sequestration of

---

[11] *Nuova antologia*, April, 1877, pp. 905–6.   [13] *Diritto*, March 17, 1877.

[12] *Libertà*, March 17, 1877.   [14] *Ibid.*, March 30, 1877.

those newspapers which had published the text of the allocution. But he quickly changed his mind, for the reverberations of such a tactical blunder were not hard to foresee.[15] Something, however, had to be done to counteract the effect of the papal broadside in other countries and appease the anticlericals at home who were demanding severe reprisals. Moreover, the Quirinal was disturbed by rumors that the allocution was part of a prearranged international campaign to secure a re-examination of the Roman question.[16] After a hurried conference, the cabinet agreed upon a vigorously worded circular which Mancini addressed to the procurators of the kingdom. The allocution, the minister charged, was an expression of revolt against the sovereignty of the national state. It demonstrated the ingratitude of the church which had been accorded concessions and privileges unparalleled elsewhere in the Catholic world. It was evidence, too, of the pontiff's intention to destroy the monarchy and recover that temporal power which the Italian nation regarded as inconsistent with its freedom and well-being. The government viewed the occasion as a propitious one to give the world proof of its self-reliance and tolerance. Newspapers which reproduced the text of the allocution were not to be molested. Only those which ventured comments or evaluations favorable to the papal pronouncement were to be prosecuted. This forbearance, Mancini observed, would provide Europe with "a new and luminous demonstration of the fact that the pope in Rome not only enjoys complete liberty and independence in the exercise of his spiritual ministry, but experiences likewise the generosity of the Italian government even when . . . . he descends into the political arena to vilify Italian sover-

[15] Cf. Pietro Vigo, *Storia degli ultimi trent'anni del secolo XIX* (Milano, 1908), II, 171.

[16] It was said that letters from Francis Joseph and MacMahon promising the pope their support in case Italy should violate the law of guarantees so inflated the Vatican that it felt it could throw down the gage to the Italian government. This act of defiance was to be part of a comprehensive plan in the execution of which France was to have the major role (cf. Franz Xaver Schmitt, *Bismarcks Abkehr vom Kulturkampf* [Neu-Ulm, 1931], p. 64).

eignty and attack the solidity of our national edifice." For the rest, he concluded, the dangerous example offered the Italian clergy by the pontiff's language afforded ample justification for the proposed law against clerical abuses.[17]

Mancini's circular was bitterly attacked by both moderates and clericals. Destra newspapers called it arbitrary, contradictory, and politically inopportune. They claimed that it obscured "the state's sentiment of decorum" and substituted "the spirit of party for reasons of national policy."[18] Mancini was assailed for engaging in polemics with the Holy See. He was reminded that "the voice of an Italian keeper of the seals compares with that of the pope like the sound of a horn with the roar of cannon." Though the Libertà conceded that the permission granted the press to publish the allocution was "a happy inspiration," it insisted that it would have been much better to withhold the clerical abuses bill altogether.[19] The Opinione admitted that the cabinet had been subjected to strong provocation. But it nevertheless reproved Mancini for vouchsafing a reply which was unworthy of the Italian government. It preferred to see the Vatican given complete freedom to continue in the false, superannuated, and self-destructive course it had adopted.[20] The circular spurred the ultramontanes to recapitulate all the counts in their long indictment against the Italian government. Here was "proof" of the pope's spiritual freedom and of the "generosity" of the political authorities, the Unità cattolica ironically observed.[21] The Voce della verità complained that Mancini had replied to "the words of the vicar of Christ" with "a slap in the face." The real effect of the minister's action, it charged, was to permit liberal newspapers to vilify the allocution and to prevent Catholic sheets from defending it.[22] The Vatican found

[17] AD, 1876–1877, IV, 164–67; Vigo, op. cit., II, 172–75.

[18] Manfroni, op. cit., I, 292.

[19] Libertà, March 21 and April 1, 1877.

[20] Opinione, March 21, 1877.

[21] Unità cattolica, March 21, 1877.   [22] Voce della verità, March 21, 1877.

the ministerial document entirely of a piece with past official pronouncements. It was totally devoid of logic, truth, and honesty, in the opinion of the *Osservatore romano*.[23] The *Civiltà cattolica* made much of its "false suppositions," its "pestiferous principles," and its "insolence."[24] Another appeal to the powers seemed the most effective way of striking back. On March 21, Simeoni instructed the nuncios to bring the current Italo-papal controversy to the attention of the various governments and to make clear to them their obligation to concern themselves with it.[25] Little, however, came of this diplomatic overture. It was the attitude not of the governments but of their Catholic subjects that cheered the Vatican. The allocution of March 12 had stirred the masses of the faithful everywhere, and impressive indeed were the manifestations of loyalty which poured in upon the Holy Father in response to his request for aid. Spanish Catholics proclaimed their solidarity with the pontiff and adjured their government to recall its minister from the Quirinal.[26] On April 2 the Catholic Union of Great Britain plunged into the fray with a formidable protest against the clerical abuses bill.[27] The Belgian episcopate, headed by Cardinal Des-

[23] *Osservatore romano*, March 28, 1877.

[24] *CC*, II (10th ser.; March 26, 1877), 116; *ibid.*, II (10th ser.; April 9, 1877), 131; cf. also, on the ultramontane reaction, Manfroni, *op. cit.*, I, 297; Michele Rosi, *Vittorio Emanuele II* (Bologna, 1930), II, 219.

[25] *AD, 1876–1877*, IV, 167, 170; Vigo, *op. cit.*, II, 180–82.

[26] Cf. *Univers*, April 21, 1877; Manfroni, *op. cit.*, I, 294.

[27] British Catholics, it was explained, were taking this action "1. Because the proposed legislation, by forbidding the clergy to criticize the laws or institutions of the country, either by public speech or writing, debars them from the exercise of the rights conceded to all classes in free countries. 2. Because its provisions, whereby the clergy are subjected to fine and imprisonment for 'disturbing the public conscience or the peace of families,' would seem to be expressly intended to strike at the essential functions of the sacred ministry, the chief sphere of which is in the conscience, individual and public. 3. Because the vagueness of the terms in which it is framed is inconsistent with the acknowledged principles of criminal legislation, and provides a constant pretext for harassing the ecclesiastical order. 4. Because it is avowedly aimed at the Sovereign Pontiff whom, as has been stated by an Italian minister, it is sought to punish in the person of his subordinates and is incompatible with that free exercise of the authority of the Holy See which is essential to Catholic

champs, the Archbishop of Malines, implored King Leopold II to bestir himself in the pope's behalf.[28] German clericals vented their indignation in a fiery manifesto which denounced the Mancini circular as "a direct attack against the rights of the church" and as "a monstrous and infamous assault upon the Catholics of all nations."[29] On May 1 the first general assembly of Austrian Catholics unanimously pledged itself to work for "the termination of the pope's sufferings." After a discussion in which less intrepid spirits were given a perfunctory hearing, it decided to send an address to the emperor invoking his aid.[30] These gestures, in themselves of no extraordinary account, assumed special significance in the light of the current Austro-Italian tension over Balkan affairs.[31]

Nowhere was the agitation more intense and more anti-Italian in character than in France. For some time French ultramontanes had had little cause for rejoicing. Their country's relations with Italy had continued to improve after the *détente* of 1874. The republican victory in the chamber elections of February, 1876, had further consolidated this amity with the neighboring kingdom.[32] MacMahon had been constrained to appoint republicans to several ministerial posts. In October of the same year the French and Italian govern-

---

interests throughout the world. 5. Because many of its supporters in the Italian Parliament have openly declared that it is intended as an attack, not only upon the liberty of the church, but upon the existence of the Christian religion itself in Italy" (*Times*, April 4, 1877).

[28] Cf. *Osservatore romano*, April 24, 1877; *Univers*, April 20, 1877. The Catholic laity of Belgium likewise petitioned King Leopold.

[29] *Osservatore romano*, April 22, 1877; Vigo, *op. cit.*, II, 183–84.

[30] Cf. *Schulthess, 1877*, pp. 210–11.

[31] Cf. Walter Schinner, *Der österreichisch-italienische Gegensatz auf dem Balkan und an der Adria* (Stuttgart, 1936), p. 12.

[32] The outcome of these elections was described by Charles Chesnelong as "almost a disaster for the conservatives" (cf. his *L'Avènement de la République, 1873–1875* [Paris, 1934], p. 196). The monarchists did, however, retain a small majority in the senate.

ments had raised their respective legations to embassy rank.[33] The following month a leftist deputy had proposed the suppression of credits for the maintenance of the embassy at the Vatican. The motion had been defeated, but it was nonetheless symptomatic of a trend which gave the clericals no little uneasiness.[34] It was therefore with extraordinary fervor that the latter now responded to the papal appeal of March 12. Decazes was the first object of their attention. A group of ultramontane senators and deputies called on him for an explanation of his position.[35] But all they were able to elicit from the cautious foreign minister was a paraphrase of his declaration of January 20, 1874.[36] Hardly disposed to let the matter rest there, they announced they would interpellate the government when parliament should resume its sessions. Their disappointment was somewhat assuaged by a widely publicized report that Charette had forwarded to the pope an album containing the names of thirty thousand volunteers who were ready for a fight to the finish on behalf of the temporal power and the Catholic church.[37]

The battle began in earnest when the general assembly of French Catholics early in April issued a call for a nation-wide campaign. In a petition addressed to the president, the senate, and the chamber of deputies, it insisted that the pope, bereft of his territorial sovereignty, was finding it increasingly difficult to discharge his spiritual functions. There was a real danger, it warned, that he might soon be prevented from communicating with his flock throughout the world. "In

[33] Gabriel Hanotaux, *Histoire de la France contemporaine* (Paris, 1903–8), III, 620. Germany had preceded France in making such an arrangement with Italy. The other great powers had taken similar action.

[34] Symptomatic, too, of this trend was the attitude of Gambetta. One of his great ambitions, he wrote a friend in February, 1877, was "to draw Italy nearer to France" (Paul Deschanel, *Gambetta* [London, 1920], p. 224).

[35] *Temps*, March 28, 1871; *Journal des débats*, March 29, 1877; Hanotaux, *op. cit.*, III, 691.

[36] Cf. *Univers*, April 2 and 3, 1877; Edmond Hippeau, *Histoire diplomatique de la Troisième République* (Paris, 1889), p. 321.

[37] Cf. *République française*, April 5, 1877; *Schulthess, 1877*, p. 265.

view of so serious a situation," it continued, "French citizens and Catholics . . . . feel it their duty to appeal to you. They ask you to employ all the means which are in your power to make the Holy Father's independence respected, to protect his administration, and to insure to the Catholics of France the indispensable enjoyment of a liberty dearer than all others—that of their conscience and faith."[38] The *Monde* hastened to underline the importance of the issue raised by these spokesmen of French Catholicism. The Holy Father's protest, it proclaimed, deprived his despoilers of the prescriptive right created by the *fait accompli*. The allocution marked "a solemn date, the point of departure of a new period," in the history of the church's sufferings. The duty of the Catholic nation, it urged, was traced with "precision" and "sovereign authority" in this momentous utterance. Such an appeal could not encounter "hesitating spirits" or "lukewarm and inactive souls." France, the journal concluded, had to be the first to respond.[39] But this was a responsibility she shared with others. Every power that possessed Catholic subjects was equally obliged to safeguard the latter's religious rights; and, certainly, international diplomatic intervention at Rome could scarcely be regarded as a purely French threat to Italy.[40]

Even stronger was the language of certain French prelates.[41] Mgr. Besson, the Bishop of Nîmes, ventured the following prophecy:

> The Revolution guards the pope as its prey. Italian unity has not been consummated; Pius IX is still king; the temporal power will exist again. . . . . After a great crash, in which perhaps many armies and crowns will go under, there will be a single voice in the policy of the nations which will call out from one end of Europe to the other: "Return Rome to its former ruler; Rome belongs to the pope; Rome belongs to God!"[42]

[38] Cf. the text of the petition in *Univers*, April 10, 1877; cf. also R. P. Lecanuet, *Les dernières années du pontificat de Pie IX* (Paris, 1931), p. 526.

[39] *Monde*, April 13, 1877.   [40] *Ibid.*, April 16 and 17, 1877.

[41] On the agitation inaugurated by the French episcopate see *Univers* of May 3 and 5, 1877.

[42] Cf. *Journal des débats*, April 30, 1877; Hanotaux, *op. cit.*, IV, 154.

The broadsides of Mgr. de Ladoue, the Bishop of Nevers, quickly established him as the spearhead of this agitation. The pope, he declared, was either sovereign or slave in Rome. No intermediate status was possible.[43] In a letter dated April 7, 1877, he vouchsafed the following advice to MacMahon:

The best measure to take is distinctly and at once to declare that you accept no solidarity with the Italian revolution, and that, so far as you can, you redeem the France of Charlemagne and St. Louis from all connivance with that revolution. . . . . Such a declaration . . . . will have a weight in the councils of Italy much greater than all the *jamais* pronounced by one of the highest representatives of the imperial system.[44]

Ladoue likewise addressed a letter to all the mayors of his diocese, in which he besought their co-operation in urging these views upon the government.[45] More astute spokesmen of the ultramontane party attempted to soften the effect of these bellicose utterances. The Catholics, they were careful to insist, did not wish a war against Italy in order to restore the temporal power.[46] Some other action, presumably diplomatic, was their goal. But the radical-republican press, making the most of its opportunities, accused the clerical party of working for another Roman expedition. The *XIXe siècle* denounced the members of the Catholic general assembly as "maniacs drunk with holy water" who, on leaving "a congress of tolerance," tried to drag the country into "an immoral and stupid adventure."[47] The *République française* claimed that the ultramontanes' insistence upon the restoration of the temporal power was tantamount to a demand for war. But France, it grimly concluded, did not regard the pope as a captive and had no desire to become embroiled with Italy.[48] The *Siècle* found the Catholic assembly's petition "ridiculous." It contended that the pope was free in every respect and that the attitude of the Italian government had been

[43] Cf. *Temps*, April 15, 1877.

[44] Cf. *Univers*, April 14, 1877.   [45] *Ibid.*, April 20, 1877.

[46] Cf. *Revue des deux mondes*, May 15, 1877, p. 469.

[47] *XIXe siècle*, April 12, 1877.   [48] *République française*, April 1, 1877.

extremely correct. There was not a man in France, however ardently Catholic, who would subscribe to a declaration of war issued with the idea of resurrecting the temporal power.[49] And yet the clericals were already placing their swords at the disposal of the pope-king![50] The assembly, the *Rappel* acidly remarked, wished France to say to the Italians: "The pope wants your capital; I ask you to give it to him." Suppose, it continued, that the Italians were to invite France to deprive herself of Paris. Her reply would differ not at all from that which the Italians would give to an invitation to surrender Rome.[51] Distressing indeed, echoed the *Siècle*, was the Catholic party's refusal to understand that the dictates of patriotism commanded an immediate cessation of the anti-Italian agitation.[52] The Bishop of Nevers received his meed of attention. His letter to the mayors of his diocese was termed "an astounding and scandalous circular,"[53] an unprecedented and audacious violation of all the rules of French public law,[54] an unabashed summons to enrol in a crusade against Italy.[55] The moderate press was scarcely less outspoken. The clerical abuses bill, averred the *Temps*, was none of France's business. It was the exclusive concern of the Italian government, and no foreign state had any right to interfere.[56] The great daily lauded the Mancini circular. That document, it contended, revealed an attitude which could only strengthen "the liberal and wise government of King Victor Emmanuel."[57] Very different was the *Temps'* appraisal of the allocution. It was frankly critical of that pronouncement, particularly of its

[49] *Siècle*, April 11, 1877.   [50] *Ibid.*, April 16, 1877.

[51] *Rappel*, April 13, 1877.

[52] *Siècle*, April 26, 1877. According to the *Petit parisien*, the Catholic assembly's petition was a piece of criminal effrontery; and the *Allobroge*, a journal of the extreme left, was moved to declare: "The priests demand war. At a time when France, more than ever, needs peace and tranquillity, ... a party arises and asks the government to send our children to the slaughter."

[53] *Siècle*, April 22, 1877.

[54] Cf. *République française*, April 21, 1877.   [56] *Temps*, March 28, 1877.

[55] *Rappel*, April 21, 1877.   [57] *Ibid.*, March 21, 1877.

recriminatory language and its appeal for foreign aid.[58] The petition of the Catholic general assembly, it said, was a grave error. It warned the clericals that their efforts would prove futile, that the bulk of the nation was not with them. True, they had ruled out war. But the diplomatic intervention they wanted would only alienate Italy without benefiting the pope.[59] The *Journal des débats* took a very similar line. It, too, praised the Italian government's conduct in dealing with the allocution. In its opinion the authorities at Rome had acted with "extreme moderation."[60] It reiterated with emphasis that Italian unity was an accomplished fact and that the pope was entirely free.[61] And it urged its own government to disavow all complicity in the ultramontane agitation.[62]

Jules Simon, the premier and minister of the interior, was a staunch liberal who had little in common with MacMahon and his clerical-monarchist allies. His sympathies were distinctly pro-Italian.[63] It was at his insistence that the cabinet decided to rebuke Mgr. Ladoue for his importunate counsels. The prelate was informed that the government, "perfectly resolved to maintain good relations with the king of Italy and convinced that in doing so it serves the interests of the Holy Father as well as those of France," could not help but disapprove of his language.[64] The prefect stationed in the bishop's diocese was instructed to inform Ladoue that the law of France did not give him the right to address circulars to mayors.[65] Simon further signified his determination to give

[58] *Ibid.*, March 26, 1877.
[59] *Ibid.*, April 11, 1877.
[62] *Ibid.*, April 29, 1877.

[60] *Journal des débats*, March 29, 1877.
[61] *Ibid.*, April 23, 1877.

[63] Early in April, Simon, accompanied by Léon Say, the minister of finance, visited Italy in quest of a commercial treaty. While there, he received the decoration of the order of St. Maurice and St. Lazarus. Circles close to the Vatican, commenting on the impending arrival of the French statesmen, had predicted that the Roman question would very likely figure in their conversations with the Italian government (cf. *Voce della verità*, April 1, 1877).

[64] Cf. *Times*, May 8, 1877.
[65] *Univers*, May 5, 1877.

no quarter to clerical mischief-makers by forbidding the circulation of petitions denouncing the clerical abuses bill. The dissemination of such objectionable documents, he explained, "cannot enjoy the immunities which cover the legitimate exercise of the right of petition." The government could under no circumstances allow its citizens to be incited "to intervene in the internal affairs of a foreign nation."[66] When the cabinet learned, through its ambassador at the Vatican, that Simeoni planned to request its intercession on behalf of the pope, it authorized Decazes to write back that such a *démarche* would not be well received in Paris.[67] It likewise empowered the minister of justice to appeal to the bishops to desist from further agitation. Nevertheless, the radical parties felt that the authorities had not been sufficiently severe in dealing with the ultramontane propagandists.[68] At the beginning of May a group of republican deputies aired their dissatisfaction in the chamber. Simon replied in a slashing address which dealt fully with the laments and demands of his clerical compatriots. He denied that the pope was in any sense a prisoner. Declarations to that effect, he charged, were, "Shall I say false? Shall I say untrue? I confine myself to saying that they are strangely exaggerated." To substantiate this position, he read the principal articles of the law of guarantees. The Italian government, he went on, had done everything possible to preserve the freedom and independence of the Holy Father. It had, in fact, renounced in his favor rights which France herself, under all regimes, had never relinquished. It had accorded the august inmate of the Vatican "the most entire, the most complete, the most absolute liberty." And the clerical abuses bill represented no "aggravation" of the law of guarantees. Its purpose was not to alter the existing relations between the pope and the king

66 *Temps*, April 28, 1877; *Année politique, 1877*, p. 28; Lecanuet, *op. cit.*, p. 527.

67 Lecanuet, *op. cit.*, p. 529; A. Debidour, *L'Eglise catholique et l'état sous la Troisième République* (Paris, 1906), I, 169 n.

68 Cf. *République française*, April 24, 1877; *Siècle*, April 28, 1877.

of Italy. It was intended simply to regulate the relations between the monarchy and the episcopate and was therefore an "internal law."[69]

This declaration, which failed to satisfy the premier's leftist friends,[70] was welcomed by Italian public opinion.[71] But the French ultramontane agitation continued to be bitterly resented as a gratuitous interference in a matter which was deemed the peninsula's exclusive concern. Those moderates who had urged the enactment of an admittedly imperfect bill as the lesser evil could now claim that the wisdom of their position had been entirely vindicated. The issue, as they saw it, was stated by the *Opinione* when it declared that the dignity of the state, the independence of the government, and the freedom of parliament were at stake.[72] The Destra journal called attention to the maneuvers of the clericals who allegedly were seeking to provoke a conflict between the two branches of the Italian parliament. Behind the ultramontane party, it warned, stood the champions of the temporal power, and certainly nothing should be done which might strengthen their hand.[73] Even the *Libertà*, which had consistently opposed the bill, was inclined to temporize now. The great majority of Italians, it remarked, wished their government to pursue a prudent and moderate policy vis-à-vis the Vatican. But they were determined, too, to protect the independence and unity of their country.[74] This view was expressed even more forcefully by the political commentator of the *Nuova antologia*. He did not dissemble his conviction that the intro-

[69] *Annales du sénat et de la chambre des députés*, III (May 3, 1877), 23–26 (hereafter cited as *Annales*). Simon's remarks deeply offended Pius, who complained to a delegation of French pilgrims that he had been accused of lying. He also called the attention of the French ambassador to this "outrage" (*Univers*, May 7, 1877; Lecanuet, *op. cit.*, p. 532; Debidour, *op. cit.*, I, 172–73 n.; Deschanel, *op. cit.*, pp. 228–29).

[70] They decried it as deficient in firmness and clarity (cf. the *Rappel*, May 5, 1877; *XIXe siècle*, May 5, 1877; *Siècle*, May 4, 1877).

[71] Cf. the representative comments in *Libertà*, May 6, 1877, and in *Diritto*, May 7, 1877.

[72] *Opinione*, April 29, 1877.   [73] *Ibid.*   [74] *Libertà*, April 24, 1877.

duction of the bill was both inopportune and imprudent.
But now, he observed, the question was no longer the same.
It had come to be this: Did the Italian government or the
French episcopate rule the peninsula? Hence, the dignity of
the Italian nation was inseparable from the outcome of the
present controversy. In view of the demonstrations in other
countries, any "suspensive proposal" would be tantamount
to showing the white flag. It would constitute, in the eyes of
the world, evidence of Italy's weakness. If the machinations
of foreign clericals should be permitted to defeat the bill, the
Vatican would exploit the ensuing situation to promote its
own ends. Firmness now would avert difficulties, while rejection of the measure could not fail to undermine the legislative authority and sovereignty of the Italian state.[75] On
May 4 the issue was raised by an interpellant in the chamber.
Melegari, the foreign minister, briefly stated the government's position. He refused, he said, to subscribe to the widespread fear of international intervention. The agitation in
question would have been "scarcely perceptible had not interested newspapers sought to magnify it." It was, in any
case, the work of a few die-hards and consequently did not
merit serious consideration. None of the states represented
in Rome had made any observations to the foreign office.
There was therefore no ground for the fear that any of them
would be disposed to participate in an anti-Italian crusade
"promoted by their own enemies . . . . under the banner of
the Catholic religion."[76]

All eyes were focused on the Italian senate, in whose hands
lay the fate of the much-discussed bill. The clamor of foreign
Catholics had not facilated the task of the opposition.
Senators of moderate sympathies who from the first had
doubted the wisdom of exceptional laws against any section
of the population were repelled by the spectacle of alien
bishops and priests inciting their governments to intervene

[75] *Nuova antologia*, May, 1877, pp. 252-53.
[76] *Atti*, CCXLVI (May 4, 1877), 3069.

in the affairs of Italy. The *Opinione* played upon the sensibilities of these vacillating members of the upper house. It was true, it repeated, that the government had acted rather tactlessly. But, in view of the battle being launched by clerical reactionaries throughout Europe, it would be reprehensible to give them a victory in this particular test. In a state of war all citizens had to do their duty, even if their government were guilty of committing an error.[77] But, despite the efforts of Sella[78] and the split within the ranks of the Destra,[79] the measure was defeated on May 7 by a majority which persisted in regarding it as both untimely and tyrannical.[80] According to one reliable source, word of this unexpected denouement evoked from the pontiff a laconic "Thank God!"[81] The clerical press, however, was less restrained. The *Voce della verità* jubilantly announced:

> The proverbial good sense of the Italians has again triumphed. We who do not expect good from evil nor invoke catastrophe have reason to congratulate ourselves. The government has again been able to see that Catholic Italy is not dead, that the impotence of the "poor clericals" is not, after all, so great as it pretends. . . . . The less deranged members of the liberal party . . . . have been obliged to realize that it is necessary to reckon with the Catholic world. . . . . And they have been compelled to bow their arrogant heads.[82]

The *Osservatore romano* contributed the observation that the independence of the senate was the more meritorious because it was not habitual and because it had been asserted in the face of tremendous pressure from the radicals. In any case, it concluded, the enactment of the measure, instead of silencing foreign Catholics, would have spurred them to even greater activity.[83] The comment of the *Unità cattolica* was pitched on a more sardonic note. A miracle had occurred in

[77] *Opinione*, May 3, 1877.

[78] Alessandro Guiccioli, *Quintino Sella* (Rovigo, 1887), II, 142.

[79] Cf. Chiala, *Dina*, III, 490 n.

[80] *Atti*, CCXLIX (May 7, 1877), 1019. The vote was 105 to 92.

[81] Cf. Pesci, *I primi anni di Roma capitale*, p. 526.

[82] *Voce della verità*, May 9, 1877.   [83] *Osservatore romano*, May 9, 1877.

the senate, "which always approves," it jeered. "Oh! Rome is fatal also to the Mancinis."[84]

That section of moderate opinion which had steadily refused to support Sella in his advocacy of the bill was no less pleased with the outcome of the prolonged controversy. The senate, it believed, had helped the country avoid a serious blunder.[85] Sella himself was exceedingly disgruntled, and Destra circles were for a time fearful that he would relinquish his post as the head of the party. But the veteran statesman finally yielded to the insistence of his confreres and consented to remain the leader of the opposition in the lower house.[86] The *Opinione*, which continued to see eye to eye with Sella, was loud in its condemnation of the senate's action. The vote, it charged, was contrary to the real interests of the nation. In the current situation, with clericals everywhere on the offensive, the representatives of the Italian people should have given their unstinted support to the government.[87] The *Libertà* confessed that it would not have complained overmuch if the senate had voted otherwise. But, now that the bill had been rejected, it went on, it would be wholly senseless to interpret the incident as a victory for the clerical party. For the senate had exercised its power of veto not to please the clericals but because it was convinced that the executive authority already possessed, in the statutes of the realm, efficacious means of punishing clergymen guilty of abusing their spiritual functions.[88] But the Sinistra, which had expected to muster a majority in the upper house,[89] refused to be consoled and vented its wrath upon the aborters of its pet project. It denounced them as shameless traitors who had

[84] *Unità cattolica*, May 9, 1877.

[85] Cf., e g., Bonghi's appraisal of the senate's action in his "Pio IX e il papato," *Nuova antologia*, July, 1877, p. 547.

[86] "Nuove pagine del diario di Alessandro Guiccioli: 1877," *Nuova antologia*, July 16, 1935, pp. 223–24.

[87] *Opinione*, May 9, 1877.

[88] *Libertà*, May 9, 1877.   [89] Cf. *Diritto*, March 2, 1877.

dared to challenge the government's ecclesiastical policy and flout the popular will. The senate, it complained, had demonstrated its indifference to the interests of the nation at a moment when foreign ultramontanes were working feverishly to stir up feeling against Italy. The moral was clear: the senate had to be reformed. It was clear too that the Destra was a pack of unscrupulous schemers allied with the clericals and virtually indistinguishable from them. The only fitting reply to these unpatriotic machinations was to proceed boldly with the anticlerical program.[90] To give point to this suggestion, radical leaders in Rome staged a noisy protest meeting in which the dissatisfaction with the senate's action was freely aired.[91] Depretis and his colleagues, however, needed little urging. They were already girding for a new effort. So much, at least, was clear from the ominous language of the *Diritto*. The rejection of the bill, it remarked, was a formidable challenge. The ministry, in retaliation, would have to prepare to carry its ecclesiastical program into complete execution. It would have to devote its attention to such matters as the relation of civil to religious marriage and the treatment of episcopal seminaries which had become a permanent threat to the nation and to civilization. The Destra had given the church a law of guarantees. The Sinistra, now that its turn had come, would endow the state with a similar statute.[92]

Italy was still resounding with the reverberations of the senate's *tour de force* when alarming news arrived from France. On May 16, McMahon, disregarding the wishes of the majority in the chamber, forced the resignation of Simon and commissioned Broglie to form a new cabinet. The marshal's republican adversaries promptly raised the cry that he was avenging the chamber's recent condemnation of the ultramontane agitation.[93] It was the country's belief, they as-

[90] Vigo, *op. cit.*, II, 195–97; *CC*, II (10th ser.; June 5, 1877), 736–37.

[91] Cf. Pesci, *I primi anni di Roma capitale*, p. 527.

[92] *Diritto*, May 10, 1877.　　　　　[93] Cf. *XIXᵉ siècle*, May 18, 1877.

serted, that the clerical coalition, beaten in the lower house, powerless in the senate, and everywhere hated, had availed itself of a *coup de palais* to overthrow Simon.[94] The latter, it was generally supposed, had not been forgiven for his anti-papal allegations in the chamber. His fall, according to all appearances, was the work of the Vatican.[95] Decazes, who remained at his post on the strength of the president's promise that the friendly relations with the powers would be maintained,[96] lost little time in apprising the various governments that the foreign policy of France would undergo no change and induced the Italian ambassador to write in a reassuring sense to Rome.[97] "We have been and we remain the sincere friends of Italy," he asserted in instructions to his envoy at the Quirinal.[98] A presidential message read to the French parliament on May 18 reaffirmed the peaceful intentions of the new cabinet.[99] A letter from MacMahon addressed to Victor Emmanuel[100] was designed to give Italy further earnest of France's friendliness.[101] But these efforts to allay Italian alarm were largely unavailing. Public opinion in the peninsula readily indorsed the charge of French republicans that the ultramontane party, irked by Simon's spirited rejection of the papal thesis, had encompassed his fall.[102] The "specter of clericalism," Noailles reported, was again being raised, and to Italians "clericalism is the destruction of

[94] Cf. *Siècle*, May 17, 1877.   [95] Hanotaux, *op. cit.*, IV, 155.

[96] Cf. MacMahon's letter of May 17, 1877, to Decazes in the *Journal officiel de la République française*, CCXVIII (May 18, 1877), 3730. It was asserted that Decazes had agreed to serve in the Broglie cabinet in return for a written pledge to the effect that the "ultramontane maneuvers" would be repressed (cf. Hanotaux, *op. cit.*, IV, 36).

[97] *DDF* (1st ser.), II, No. 166, pp. 171–72 and note on p. 172.

[98] *AD, 1876–1877*, IV, 177.   [99] *Annales*, III (May 18, 1877), 251.

[100] It is not known, however, whether this letter was actually sent to the Italian sovereign.

[101] *DDF* (1st ser.), II, No. 174, 179.

[102] The Vatican itself readily admitted that Simon's fall was due to his anticlerical policies and utterances (cf. the *Osservatore romano*, May 19, 1877).

Italian unity, it is the temporal power forcibly reestablished by France."[103] There was, moreover, the disconcerting fact that many Frenchmen were now encouraged to look forward to a speedy restoration of the monarchy.[104] The behavior of the marshal evoked some rather uncharitable appraisals even among the more conservative members of the Destra. The attitude of Guiccioli was typical. On May 18 he wrote in his diary: "In France, MacMahon, by means of a real coup d'état, has formed a Broglie cabinet, clerical-Orleanist with some Bonapartist elements. In short, full reaction. If the marshal wished to go as far as this, he is a great fool. If he wished to stop halfway, he is an imbecile."[105]

Leading organs of the two major parties of the peninsula vied with one another in regaling their readers with lugubrious interpretations of the May 16 coup. The *Diritto* warned that MacMahon was openly identifying himself with the aspirations of the French episcopate. It accused the Italian senate of having contributed, by its rejection of the clerical abuses bill, to Simon's fall. For the latter, the Sinistra journal explained, had been charged by his adversaries with being more anticlerical than the members of the Italian upper house.[106] The marshal's message to the French parliament, observed the *Libertà*, had in no way modified the painful impression created by his unconstitutional action. He had believed, it went on, that he was saving France by yielding to the pressure of the clericals. But he would soon perhaps realize that he had succeeded only in "ruining himself."[107] The *Opinione*, betraying unusual acerbity, flayed the French ultramontanes for their alleged desire to wage war against

[103] *DDF* (1st ser.), II, No. 173, 177.

[104] On May 25, Lord Lyons wrote Lord Derby: "The upper ten thousand in Paris are indulging in all sorts of illusions and the Paris shopkeepers are dreaming of the restoration of a Court and of a great expenditure on luxuries" (Lord Newton, *Lord Lyons: A Record of British Diplomacy* [London, 1913], II, 115).

[105] "Nuove pagine del diario di Alessandro Guiccioli: 1877," *op. cit.*, p. 225.

[106] *Diritto*, May 18, 1877.   [107] *Libertà*, May 22, 1877.

Italy and Germany. The forced resignation of Simon was an initial victory for these would-be disturbers of the peace. The Italian government, it urged, would therefore be well advised to move carefully in order to curry even greater favor with the liberals of France and of all Europe.[108]

This admonition was scarcely necessary. For it was not easy for Italians to forget that the support of the clerical party was indispensable to the life of the new French cabinet. And there were some who believed that the pretext for the war which that party was supposedly planning would be furnished by the current crisis in the Near East.[109] Suspicious, too, was the elation with which the papal organs received the news of MacMahon's coup. The *Osservatore romano* hailed the president's "courageous policy" which, it claimed, had received the approval of "all those who hold dear the cause of tranquillity and social order."[110] The *Voce della verità* rejoiced over the dismissal of Gambetta "in the person of his 'prisoner,' Simon."[111] MacMahon, declared the *Unità cattolica*, had "nobly" rectified the "error" he had committed in allowing Simon to serve as premier.[112] The Depretis government, once the initial shock had worn off, professed to view the situation calmly. But it was clearly disturbed by the possible international repercussions of the French crisis. It had the feeling that Italy's position was going to become much more difficult.[113] On May 23 the alarmists had their inning in the chamber. One interpellant reminded the government that Italy could not remain indifferent to the recent developments in the neighboring republic. "The ideas which today are triumphant in France," he warned, "may, in the not distant future, threaten us, our independence, our unity."[114] Another

[108] *Opinione*, May 18, 1877.

[109] *Nuova antologia*, June, 1877, pp. 499, 503–4.

[110] *Osservatore romano*, May 23 and June 17, 1877.

[111] *Voce della verità*, May 22, 1877.   [112] *Unità cattolica*, May 19, 1877.

[113] Cf. *DDF* (1st ser.), II, No. 173, 177.

[114] *Atti*, CCXLVII (May 23, 1877), 3575.

worried deputy pointed out that all Europe interpreted MacMahon's gesture as an act of aggression against both Italy and Germany. He accused the marshal of allying himself with a party which had made the destruction of Italian unity "the first article of its syllabus." The existence of such an alliance opened up all sorts of black possibilities, and it therefore behooved Italy to give thought to the problem of self-defense.[115] The government, scrupulously cloaking its own uneasiness, gave very little encouragement to these scaremongers. Melegari pronounced the fears of Europe greatly exaggerated. He alluded to the spontaneous assurances of good will received from both MacMahon and Decazes. These, he said, had convinced the cabinet that no change in Franco-Italian relations was in the offing. It was inconceivable that France would "turn against herself and destroy the most beautiful achievement of modern times, the creation of Italy." He admitted that the French clergy was demanding rights for the Holy See which were incompatible with Italian sovereignty. But the unity of the peninsula was in no real danger, for any attempt to impair it would be frustrated by the Italian people rising as one man to save its freedom.[116] Depretis spoke in a similar vein. The government, he admitted, had for a time been disturbed by events in France. But Italy had survived many a trial. In any case, there was reason to be completely reassured by the declarations of MacMahon and Decazes. No change had occurred in the relations with France. "We all know," he continued, "that there is a sect which makes religion an instrument of mundane power, and this sect is our enemy." But it was a familiar enemy. And the government, which was not without a religion of its own—"the religion of civilization and progress"—would act to defend the freedom and sovereignty of the state. Buoyed by popular support, it could not fail in this struggle against the national foe.[117]

[115] *Ibid.*, p. 3580.   [116] *Ibid.*, p. 3583.   [117] *Ibid.*, pp. 3584–85.

Italian public opinion received these statements with considerable skepticism.[118] Nor was it any more impressed by Decazes's pacific address in the French chamber on June 18.[119] There was no gainsaying the fact, observed the *Opinione*, that Broglie's clerical supporters were hailing the new government as one created in their own image. And it was no less obvious that they were a constant threat to peace and freedom.[120] Even the ministerial *Diritto* refused to accept the official view. It felt moved to remind its readers that Broglie had always been an outspoken defender of the temporal power. The sympathies of Italians, it somewhat superfluously concluded, were entirely with the French liberals.[121] The fear persisted that the MacMahon-Broglie regime would have to seek the aid of the papacy, with the result that clericalism, triumphant within France, would come to dominate that country's foreign policy as well.[122] This suspicion of an impending deal between the new rulers of the Third Republic and the Vatican was strengthened by the imprudent remarks of one high in the councils of the Holy See. Early in June, Mgr. Vanutelli, the nuncio at Brussels, told a deputation of Belgian ex-Zouaves:

> Whether it will or not, Europe is driven by the instinct of self-preservation to seek a remedy which can only lead to the triumph of the papacy. You are legitimately entitled to hope that the hour is drawing near when the help of your strong arm will be required to achieve this triumph and when you will be enabled to resume the combat where it was prematurely broken off.[123]

---

[118] The Italian foreign minister made a very sorry impression on some of his Destra auditors. One of these was Guiccioli, who wrote in his diary under date of May 23: "Poor Melegari embarks upon a long speech to prove that France is animated by the best of intentions, he gets lost on the way and after inexpert maneuvering, runs into shoals and is shipwrecked on the shore of things ridiculous" ("Nuove pagine del diario di Alessandro Guiccioli: 1877," *op. cit.*, p. 225).

[119] Decazes declared that the intentions of the French government were well known and properly appreciated in Italy. He went on to read two of his recent dispatches to Noailles in an effort to prove that Franco-Italian relations were most friendly. The explanations contained in these dispatches, he asserted, had been pronounced "fully satisfactory" by Melegari (*Annales*, III [June 18, 1877], 287-88).

[120] *Opinione*, June 21, 1877.   [122] Cf. *DDF* (1st ser.), II, No. 185, 189.

[121] *Diritto*, June 24, 1877.   [123] *Times*, June 6, 1877.

These words produced a real sensation in Italy. It was generally assumed that they would never have been uttered had not recent developments in France greatly bolstered the Vatican's territorial ambitions.[124]

On June 22, in the face of strong minority opposition, the French senate voted to dissolve the chamber.[125] New elections were fixed for October. The ensuing contest was followed with intense interest by all Europe. Arrayed against the ultramontane-monarchist supporters of MacMahon and Broglie were the various republican factions. The latter had for the moment put aside their differences in order to present a united front against the common enemy.[126] Charges and denials flew thick and fast. The leftists accused their clerical adversaries of preparing "to offer the kingdom of France to the pope as compensation for the kingdom he has lost."[127] They derided the pacific assurances of the government. They even offered further light on the origins of the May 16 coup. At the outbreak of hostilities in the Near East, they said, the pontiff had caressed the hope of seeing the war spread to the rest of Europe and of witnessing thereupon the restoration of his ancient throne.[128] And the advent of a reactionary government in France was essential to the achievement of this unhappy result. No less persistent were Broglie's foes in denouncing his government as clerical and as one, in consequence, which exposed France to the peril of war.[129] In thus re-emphasizing the nexus between clericalism and war, the republicans revived the specter of a "government of priests" which, in its anxiety to resurrect the monarchy, was ready to incur the danger of most serious foreign complications.[130] They warned that an ultramontane victory made

---

[124] One month earlier, a leading Roman newspaper observed, Vanutelli would not have dared to speak as he did.

[125] Cf. C. de Freycinet, *Souvenirs, 1848-1878* (Paris, 1914), pp. 366-67; Hanotaux, *op. cit.*, IV, 44-45.

[126] Cf. the *République française*, May 20, 1877; Hanotaux, *op. cit.*, IV, 3-4, 8.

[127] *Rappel*, August 2, 1877.   [129] Hanotaux, *op. cit.*, IV, 150.

[128] *Ibid.*, September 20, 1877.   [130] Cf. *ibid.*, p. 32.

another expedition against Rome a certainty. Did the peasants of France, they queried, wish to see their sons go off to be killed in order that the pope might sit on his throne again? And almost as persuasive was the oft-repeated contention that the possibility of a rightist triumph had led Italy to seek protection in an entente with Germany.[131] In an effort to bolster this contention, republican spokesmen publicized the following passage from an editorial comment in a widely read Italian newspaper: "What would be the significance of the triumph of Marshal MacMahon's policy in the forthcoming elections? Abroad, this triumph would have but one significance: war. Indeed, if France should hesitate, prudence would counsel Germany and Italy to take the initiative in a struggle which no human force can avert."[132] To all these allegations and maneuvers, Broglie and his aides replied with ringing disavowals of warlike intentions.[133] Fourtou, the very unpopular minister of the interior, was the premier's principal mouthpiece in assuring the country that war and clericalism were alien to the present government.[134]

In Italy conjectures as to the outcome of the French electoral contest became the order of the day. Moderate circles were inclined to believe that the republican parties would emerge victorious if they succeeded in remaining united.[135] Papal organs were busy exhorting the various conservative factions in France to submerge their dynastic quarrels and co-operate to secure a decisive triumph at the polls. Such a triumph, they repeatedly contended, could not fail to ma-

[131] Cf. Lecanuet, *op. cit.*, pp. 541–43.

[132] Hanotaux, *op. cit.*, IV, 165.

[133] On the eve of the dissolution of the chamber Broglie had attempted to forewarn the country against misrepresentations of his position on foreign affairs. He had denied most vehemently that his government was the instrument of a party which desired "to drag France . . . . into the horrors of a new war" (cf. De Broglie, *Discours du Duc de Broglie* [Paris, 1909], pp. 275–76).

[134] Cf. *Temps*, August 25, 1877.

[135] Cf. *Libertà*, August 2, 187⁻

terialize once the rightists had closed their ranks.[136] The Holy
Father himself did not hesitate to tell a group of pilgrims
from Angers that he hoped to witness a victory for those who,
"before all else, have in view God and his church."[137] And
the *Osservatore romano*, on the eve of the elections, proclaimed
that a conservative majority in the chamber was needed to
safeguard "the cause of order and real liberty" in France.[138]
The Italian government, none too sanguine over the outcome
of the electoral struggle, ordered a strengthening of the Roman fortifications. But its main preoccupation was to consolidate the country's international position. The prospect of
meeting unaided a French attack was not one to be faced
with equanimity. An alliance with Germany was therefore
imperative. Austrian hostility and the imminence of territorial
changes in the Balkan peninsula as a result of the Russo-
Turkish conflict pointed the same moral.[139] Especially inauspicious for the future of Austro-Italian relations was the
encouragement given to Italian irredentism ever since 1875
by the Near Eastern crisis which had erupted in that year.[140]
Crispi, who was then the president of the chamber of deputies, was intrusted with the mission of sounding out Bismarck. He was to propose to the chancellor a treaty of alliance which would take account of the danger from France
and the possibility of Austrian territorial expansion at the
expense of the Ottoman Empire. He was also to point out
that Italy and Germany had to match each other in their

---

[136] Cf. *Osservatore romano*, June 21 and July 3 and 26, 1877; *Voce della verità*, July
3 and 13, 1877. The papalists' hope for unity within the French conservative camp
was destined to be cruelly disappointed. The discord among the rightists in the summer of 1877 is described by Hanotaux in his *La France contemporaine*, IV, 148.

[137] *Univers*, September 14, 1877.

[138] *Osservatore romano*, October 13, 1877.

[139] Cf. Francesco Crispi, *Politica estera* (Milano, 1912), p. 6; Italicus, *Italiens
Dreibundpolitik, 1870–1896* (München, 1928), p. 31.

[140] Cf., for the Irredentist movement of these years, C. Grove Haines, "Italian
Irredentism during the Near Eastern Crisis, 1875–78," *Journal of Modern History*,
March, 1937, pp. 23–47; cf. also, for the effect of irredentism on Austro-Italian rela-
tions in 1877, Attilio Simioni, *Vittorio Emanuele II* (Milano, 1911), p. 155.

determination to defend their national unity.[141] The nominal purpose of his mission was to secure international acceptance of the principle contained in Article III of the Italian civil code.[142]

Late in August Crispi embarked upon an extended voyage which took him to France, Germany, England, and Austria. He had a pleasant interview with Decazes in Paris. The latter assured him that no party in France would commit the folly of making war on Italy. He expressed some concern over Italian military preparations, alluding specifically to the strengthening of the fortifications about Rome.[143] It was clear, Crispi reported, that the French government was anxious to prove its friendliness.[144] But he was also impressed with the extent of the clerical influence at the Elysée.[145] His conversations with republican leaders, notably Gambetta, only served to confirm this impression. What he saw and heard convinced him that the French conservatives would seize any pretext to plunge their country into a war with Italy.[146] He pointed out in a letter to Victor Emmanuel that an antirepublican coup d'état would owe its success to the clergy and the army. The former, he wrote, would make the restoration of the temporal power its first objective. The army, in turn, would seek to re-establish its prestige by some resounding victory. And Italy was the field best adapted to "this reactionary enterprise."[147] On September 17 he con-

---

[141] Crispi, *Politica estera*, pp. 8–9; Schinner, *op. cit.*, pp. 15–16, 17; Luigi Chiala, *Dal 1858 al 1892; pagine di storia contemporanea* (Torino, 1892–93) I, 261–62; Franz Xaver Schmitt, *op. cit.*, p. 75; Gualterio Castellini, *Crispi* (Firenze, 1915), p. 129; Rosi, *Vittorio Emanuele II*, II, 224.

[142] This article dealt with the rights of foreigners in Italy (cf. Schinner, *op. cit.*, pp. 14–15).

[143] Crispi, *Politica estera*, pp. 10–11; cf. Decazes's report of the conversation in *DDF* (1st ser.), II, No. 202, 207–8; cf. also Castellini, *op. cit.*, p. 130.

[144] Crispi, *Politica estera*, p. 12.   [145] Cf. Chiala, *Pagine*, I, 273.

[146] Crispi, *Politica estera*, p. 14.

[147] *Ibid.*, p. 19. He spoke in a similar vein to Gambetta, remarking that the army and clergy were dangerous to popular government (cf. F. Crispi, "La Conferenza pel disarmo," *Nuova antologia*, May 16, 1899, p. 364). Gambetta reported to his friends

ferred with Bismarck at Gastein. The chancellor had been not a little disturbed by the latest news from Paris. He was reported to have remarked recently: "France is in the hands of the clericals; we demand nothing better than peace in order to consolidate our conquests, but will we be able to preserve it? We ought to make the pope the king of the French with his capital at Avignon."[148] He still believed that a monarchical restoration in France would menace the peace of Europe.[149] He therefore listened sympathetically as Crispi stated the purpose of his visit. The Italian explained that his government was worried by the possibility of hostilities in the event of a conservative triumph in the French elections. He likewise alluded to the uneasiness caused by Austria's unfriendly attitude. He asked the chancellor if he were ready to conclude an alliance with Italy for the contingency of a war with either France or Austria. Bismarck replied that, if Italy were attacked by France, Germany would come to her assistance. But he refused to give a similar assurance where Austria was concerned. He declared he could not regard her as an enemy and did not wish to provide for such an eventuality.[150] He subsequently stated, however, that, if Austria should make herself the protector of Catholicism, Ger-

---

that he and the Italian statesman were at one in their anticlericalism (Mme Juliette Adam, *Après l'abandon de la revanche* [Paris, 1910], p. 29), and a writer in the *République française* was careful to point out that Crispi was the adversary not of France but of "theocracy and Caesarism" (cf. the issue of September 7, 1877).

[148] "Nuove pagine del diario di Alessandro Guiccioli: 1877," *op. cit.*, p. 234.

[149] Hajo Holborn (ed.), *Aufzeichnungen und Erinnerungen aus dem Leben des Botschafters Joseph Maria von Radowitz* (Berlin and Leipzig, 1925), I, 369. Crown Prince Frederick entirely agreed with Bismarck. He feared that the new masters of France would be unable to resist the clericals' demand for a war to restore the temporal power (cf. André Dreux, *Dernières années de l'ambassade en Allemagne de M. de Gontaut-Biron* [Paris, 1907], p. 281). This view was zealously propagated by the German press.

[150] Crispi, *Politica estera*, pp. 22–23; Schinner, *op. cit.*, p. 20; Chiala, *Pagine*, I, 274–75; Castellini, *op. cit.*, p. 131. For Bismarck's remarks on Italo-Austrian relations see Gaetano Salvemini, "Alla vigilia del Congresso di Berlino," *Nuova rivista storica*, January–February, 1925, pp. 75–76.

many would modify her position.[151] The intrigues of the Vatican, which inspired this reservation, visibly disturbed him. He did not hesitate to tell Crispi that the Holy See was exercising excessive influence in Italy.[152] He still suspected the ultramontanes of trying to overthrow Andrássy and attributed the present situation in both Austria and France to the allocution of March 12.[153] There was always the danger, he wrote several weeks later, that, after a coup d'état in France, the French army would be asked to wage war against Germany on behalf of the Vatican.[154]

Crispi's presence in Germany and the strongly Germanophil tenor of the speeches he delivered during his sojourn there were generally interpreted as proof of an intimate accord between Berlin and Rome. The Italian statesman was not at all reticent about the current European situation. Thus, on leaving the German capital late in September, he unburdened himself in an interview with the director of the *Deutsche Montagsblatt*. He hoped, he said, for a republican victory in the French elections, inasmuch as a government which took orders from the Vatican could scarcely be considered friendly to Italy.[155] He next visited Vienna and Budapest. His conversations with Andrássy ranged over the territorial questions which were threatening to precipitate an Italo-Austrian crisis.[156] He derived some comfort from the Magyar's explicit repudiation of the ultramontane pro-

[151] Crispi, *Politica estera*, p. 25.

[152] Salvemini, "Alla vigilia del Congresso di Berlino," *op. cit.*, p. 87.

[153] Eduard von Wertheimer, *Graf Julius Andrássy: sein Leben und seine Zeit* (Stuttgart, 1910), III, 18–20; Schmitt, *Bismarcks Abkehr vom Kulturkampf*, p. 71.

[154] *Aus Bismarcks Briefwechsel* (Stuttgart and Berlin, 1901), pp. 496–97.

[155] Chiala, *Pagine*, I, 282. This broadside did not pass unchallenged in French ultramontane circles. Had Crispi, the *Univers* sardonically queried, acquired his pro-German enthusiasm in the course of his recent conversations with leftist leaders in Paris? Public opinion, it warned, would remember that the "patriots" who feted this avowed enemy were the spokesmen of the republican party (cf. the issue of October 5, 1877).

[156] Cf. Salvemini, "Alla vigilia del Congresso di Berlino," *op. cit.*, p. 73.

gram.[157] He came away, according to the Vienna correspondent of the *Allgemeine Zeitung*, with the impression that Italy
had no reason to fear Austrian intervention in favor of the
temporal power.[158]

Crispi's sojourn in foreign capitals was widely commented
upon in the Italian press. Sinistra journalists paid tribute to
this proof of official prescience in the face of serious international complications. The *Diritto* pointed triumphantly to
the splendid reception accorded the cabinet's special emissary in Berlin. Italo-German friendship, it declared, would
be greatly strengthened. Crispi, in affirming the solidarity of
the two countries vis-à-vis their common enemies, had merely
given expression to the feeling which prevailed in Italy, Germany, and, for that matter, France. For it was worth re-
membering, the ministerial journal added with significant emphasis, that Italy would always be the ally of *liberal* France.[159]
Moderate and clerical sheets adopted a less flattering tone.
The *Libertà* censured the envoy's Gallophobe statements. It
contended somewhat sharply that one could scarcely ignore
the present state of Franco-Italian relations, which were, in
its opinion, "perfectly friendly."[160] It did not, however, go so
far as to say that Crispi had accomplished nothing. For this
voyage was, after all, a "frank, cordial, friendly" warning to
France that, if she should attempt to restore the old order of
things in the peninsula, she would find Italy and Germany
united against her. No treaty had been concluded with Bismarck, but France was well aware that, should the need arise,
its consummation would be instantaneous.[161] The *Opinione*
made the most of the occasion to lament the alleged failures
of the Sinistra's foreign policy. It accused the government of
alienating the sympathies of many Italophils and of showing
little decorum in maintaining the friendship with Germany.
It violently assailed Crispi's injudicious utterances. Every-

[157] Crispi, *Politica estera*, p. 65; Schinner, *op. cit.*, p. 29.

[158] Chiala, *Pagine*, I, 290.

[159] *Diritto*, October 4, 1877.

[160] *Libertà*, October 3, 1877.

[161] *Ibid.*, October 11, 1877.

one was aware, it continued, that he was the most eminent leader of the Sinistra. It was therefore futile to attempt to tranquilize the French by trumpeting the fact that he was not a member of the cabinet.[162] The *Osservatore romano* accused the Italian government of prostrating itself at Bismarck's feet in the hope of securing thereby his much solicited aid. This policy, it argued, had little to recommend it. Germany was in danger of finding herself isolated vis-à-vis a possible alliance of Great Britain, France, Austria, and Turkey. Should such an alliance ever materialize, what would happen to Italy, united, as she was, with Germany and confronted by the same foes?[163]

As the day of the elections drew near, the French government redoubled its efforts to combat the persistent report that a rightist victory would precipitate serious foreign complications. The premier and the minister of the interior ordered the prefects and the royal procurators to take action against anyone guilty of disseminating such a report. "An effort is being made"—so ran the instructions—"to spread the rumor of an offensive and defensive alliance concluded or contemplated by Germany and Italy against France and to present a war with these powers as the possible consequence of elections favorable to the candidates of the government. The government most formally denies these rumors."[164] No less sustained was the French cabinet's endeavor to discredit the report that it was secretly preparing a Roman expedition. MacMahon, Broglie, and Fourtou were kept busy issuing spirited *démentis*. "Nobody," the premier declared before the members of the Paris conservative committee, "will believe . . . . that Italy . . . . would have the slightest anxiety were the man who has the honor to be named the Duke of Magenta to be declared in the right."[165] The marshal himself solicited votes with an eleventh-hour assurance that his government would

---

[162] *Opinione*, October 3, 1877.

[163] *Osservatore romano*, October 6, 1877.

[164] Hanotaux, *op. cit.*, IV, 178.

[165] *Temps*, October 12, 1877.

not be drawn into any course which might jeopardize the peace of Europe.[166] But these fervent disclaimers were nullified by the declamations of the aroused episcopate. From the pens of leading prelates came a series of strongly worded pastorals urging the voters to go to the polls.[167] The Cardinal-Archbishop of Cambray affirmed the undying determination of the Catholic hierarchy of France to protect the freedom of the Holy Father. The Archbishop of Chambéry, though proclaiming the pope's aversion for war, insisted upon the necessity of the temporal power.[168] The Archbishop of Bourges summoned legitimists, Orleanists, and Bonapartists to regard the impending success of MacMahon's candidates as a mandate to save the church and liberate the prisoner of the Vatican. "Catholics should not hesitate," he proclaimed. "They have no right to be uninterested in this decisive struggle."[169] He even ordered the priests of his diocese to conduct prayers in behalf of a conservative triumph.[170] It was accordingly easy for republican journalists to convince the greater part of the nation that clericalism was the principal issue[171] and that the danger of complications with Italy was a very real one. The Holy Father, they knowingly pointed out, was becoming more and more interested in the success of the conservative candidates.[172] They kept constantly before their readers the suspicion and alarm which were forcing the neighboring kingdom to align itself with the enemies of France. The Depretis cabinet's decision to strengthen the fortifications of Rome impelled the *XIXe siècle* to exclaim: "It is against us, against a French invasion, against ultramontane France, that the Italians feel it necessary to fortify their capital!"[173] The participation of the pope and the French clergy in the elec-

---

[166] *Journal officiel de la République française*, CCXX (October 12, 1877), 6757.

[167] Hanotaux, *op. cit.*, IV, 177.

[168] Cf. *Temps*, October 4, 1877.

[169] Hanotaux, *op. cit.*, IV, 177.

[170] *Univers*, October 1, 1877.

[171] Cf. *Siècle*, October 3, 1877.

[172] Cf. *ibid.*, October 1, 1877.

[173] *XIXe siècle*, September 2, 1877.

toral struggle, echoed the *Rappel*, made Italy's inclination to doubt France's peaceful intentions quite understandable.[174] Particularly effective were the disquieting inferences which leftist newspapers drew from Crispi's presence in Germany.[175] A people which had so many reasons for being the "sister" of France, one of the radical organs wailed, was throwing itself into the arms of Prussia. Italy perceived that the government of the Third Republic was dominated by a party eager to aid the pope in destroying her unity. She would return to her friendship with France only when the latter was ruled by men who could not be suspected of subservience to the Vatican.[176] Italians, asserted another anticlerical sheet, believed themselves menaced by a double calamity: invasion and the restoration of the temporal power. It was impossible to overlook the complex of factors which constrained the Italian government to solicit German assistance against the Black International. France alone was guilty of keeping alive ultramontane illusions and Italian fears. "To vote for the government of priests," this journal concluded, "is to invite war. And war today . . . . would be the end of France."[177] The organs of the Broglie cabinet countered with the assurance that Crispi was invested with no official mission. In moderate circles, however, the tendency to take a serious view of the Italian statesman's visit to Germany persisted.[178] And even the *Monde* admitted that Frenchmen would have attached importance to that visit if they had been less busy with the forthcoming elections.[179]

The zeal with which dignitaries of the church espoused the conservative cause was as embarrassing to French minis-

---

[174] *Rappel*, October 9, 1877.

[175] Cf. *République française*, October 11, 1877; *Siècle*, October 1, 1877.

[176] *Rappel*, September 27, 1877.   [177] *XIXᵉ siècle*, October 5, 1877.

[178] Cf. *Journal des débats*, October 9, 1877.

[179] The *Monde* went on to argue that the enthusiastic reception given Crispi signified that the German government, now that Russia had become less valuable to it from a military point of view, was seeking to assure itself of the aid of another ally whose forces were still intact (issues of October 1 and 2, 1877).

terialists as it was helpful to the propagandists of the left. Broglie and his colleagues were not slow to recognize the clamorous aid volunteered by the prelates as a boomerang which might jeopardize the government's electoral chances. Something had to be done to restrain these ecclesiastical well-wishers and prevent them from working further harm to their political friends. On October 3, Brunet, the minister of public instruction and worship, telegraphed the following message to the prefects: "With an intention that is excellent but entirely contrary to the very aim pursued, a certain number of prelates have ordered general prayers on the occasion of the forthcoming elections and they have given every publicity to their pastoral letters. . . . . I request you to see the bishop of your department and tell him that the government asks him to maintain and recommend the most absolute silence. Any other attitude would be imprudent and harmful."[180] Three days later a second circular was issued. "In all the dioceses," it ran, "ask the bishop to instruct the priests and curates to say nothing in the pulpit about the elections; the government attaches the greatest importance to these instructions."[181]

The electoral activity of the French episcopate was bitterly assailed in Italy. The opposition press joined readily in this sustained outcry. Priests had engineered the May 16 coup, fumed the *Libertà*, and now they were seeking to derive exclusive profit from that bold stroke. The Destra journal vented its disgust at seeing the pope "converted into an election agent" and the Catholic religion degraded to the status of "an instrument in the hands of a political faction." The French government, it went on, labored under the delusion that it was the master of the situation. In reality, it was the puppet of the clericals. Hence its friendly assurances to Italy, however sincerely vouchsafed, were worth but little.[182] The *Opinione*, in tones scarcely less acrimonious, continued to be-

[180] Hanotaux, *op. cit.*, IV, 177.

[181] *Ibid.*   [182] *Libertà*, October 6 and 9, 1877.

wail the fact that France was throwing herself into the arms of the clericals. No one, it sadly remarked, would have imagined that such a fate could overtake the mother of modern liberties. Italy had no choice but to remain forever vigilant, for she had the most to fear from the maneuvers of ultramontanes and reactionaries.[183] There were some Destra stalwarts, however, who found it difficult to choose between the French conservatives and their radical compatriots. Thus Guiccioli very candidly noted in his diary: "For us, the absolute triumph of Marshal MacMahon or of Gambetta will be equally harmful. With one there is the probability of war. With the other there is radicalism and republican propaganda."[184] The papal press betrayed no reluctance to acknowledge the existence of an intimate alliance between the Vatican and the French conservatives. If society should be saved, the *Unità cattolica* proclaimed, it would owe this beneficent result to a great pope and to a valorous soldier. "The cross of Pius IX and the sword of MacMahon," it predicted, "will restore order in France and elsewhere." God had made France clerical, and she would have to remain clerical if she wished to escape the fate that had overtaken Poland. Clericalism was the source of France's greatness and her hope at the present juncture.[185]

On October 14, Frenchmen went to the polls, and their verdict was unmistakable. The republicans emerged from the battle of ballots with a clear-cut victory. Although royalists and Bonapartists increased their representation in the chamber, they obtained only a minority of the seats.[186] The monarchist cause, and with it that of the Italophobe ultramontanes, seemed hopelessly compromised. For a time it was feared that the disavowed president might attempt to con-

[183] *Opinione*, October 6, 1877.

[184] "Nuove pagine del diario di Alessandro Guiccioli: 1877," *op. cit.*, p. 236.

[185] *Unità cattolica*, October 13 and 14, 1877.

[186] Cf. *Temps*, October 17, 1877. The legitimists fared better than their allies in the conservative camp (cf. Hanotaux, *op. cit.*, IV, 188).

tinue with a regime of his own choice in defiance of the popular will. Events, however, quickly dispelled this apprehension. On November 16 the Broglie cabinet resigned, and the
following month a liberal ministry boasting no fewer than
five Protestants was formed under M. Dufaure.[187] The Vatican was inclined to agree with Veuillot that the outcome of
the elections was enough "to discourage hope itself."[188] It
had left little undone to promote MacMahon's success, and
its faith in a conservative victory had persisted despite the
failure of the rightists to achieve a united front. Priests im-
bued with a wishful sense of the impending had been urging
errant souls to make their peace with the church ere Rome
returned to its former masters. So contagious had this confidence become that business circles had begun to reject erstwhile ecclesiastical properties as collateral in mortgage transactions.[189] MacMahon's defeat came therefore as a great
shock to the Vatican and brought this self-deception to a
sudden end.[190] The *Osservatore romano* sadly confessed that
"the principle of order" had been defeated. But it found some
consolation in the thought that "the authority and strength
of the man who at present rules the French nation, if not enhanced, were certainly not destroyed."[191] Moreover, the result of the elections clearly demonstrated the inadequacy of
popular rule. "To base governments on the decisions of the
multitude," the papal organ concluded, "amounts to founding them on the tumult of passions fomented and directed
by a handful of radicals."[192] The *Voce della verità* agreed
that the triumph of the republicans was due to the mainte-

---

[187] One of these Protestants was Waddington, Decazes's successor at the foreign office.

[188] *Univers*, October 17, 1877. The *Monde* (October 17, 1877) managed to argue that the "revolutionaries" had lost ground. But the government, it conceded, could not be "very satisfied" with the outcome of the elections. Though it had "defeated" its adversaries, its "victory" had fallen short of its hopes and of the needs of the situation.

[189] Cf. *Schulthess, 1877*, p. 339.

[190] Manfroni, *op. cit.*, I, 317.

[191] *Osservatore romano*, October 19, 1877.

[192] *Ibid.*, October 23, 1877.

nance in the French constitution of "that great lie: universal suffrage." In the same breath, however, it attributed the disappointing showing of the conservative parties to the divisions within their ranks and to the excessive number of abstentions from the polls.[193] The *Unità cattolica* found it more difficult to explain away the stark significance of what had transpired in France. Barabbas, it wailed, had triumphed. Pius had been "abandoned and cursed."[194] The pontiff himself was deeply disappointed. But his more resilient Jesuit advisers made the best of a bad situation and insisted that Catholicism would have stood to gain but little from a triumph of the conservative forces.[195]

Italian public opinion was frankly exultant. It hailed the discomfiture of the rightists as a disavowal of all interventionist velleities in the Roman question.[196] Domestic freedom and international peace had won a notable victory, observed the *Diritto*, and they would be even further assured once the influence of the ultramontanes had completely disappeared within France.[197] The triumph of the republicans was the triumph of peace and progress, according to the *Opinione*.[198] And Italy, now that a formidable threat to her existence had disappeared, would do well to proclaim her desire for peace.[199] It was now clear, the *Libertà* announced, that in France, too, "the ascendancy of the papalists was scant and inefficacious." The defeat of the French ultramontanes was "the victory of liberty in all Europe."[200] Gambetta's visit to the peninsula at the beginning of January, 1878, brought further assurances of French good will. The republican leader was strongly of the opinion that his country ought to detach itself from its papal connections and resume the old ties with

[193] *Voce della verità*, October 18, 1877.

[194] *Unità cattolica*, October 20, 1877.

[195] *CC*, IV (10th ser.; November 6, 1877), 401.

[196] Chiala, *Pagine*, I, 297; *Times*, October 17, 1877; Vigo, *op. cit.*, II, 217.

[197] *Diritto*, October 17, 1877.   [199] *Ibid.*, November 19, 1877.

[198] *Opinione*, October 17, 1877.   [200] *Libertà*, October 17, 1877.

Italy. He had some very pleasant interviews with the heads of the Sinistra[201] and with the king himself.[202] The latter alluded with satisfaction to the results of the October 14 elections. As long as France refrained from attempts to restore the temporal power, he said, Italy could be only her friend.[203] Now that France had embraced liberalism, echoed the *Diritto*, Italy could hope for an alliance with her without in any way renouncing the ties with Germany.[204] The battle-scarred foes of the Vatican were at last ready to believe that the danger of a French descent upon Rome had been permanently averted.

[201] Particularly gratifying was his conversation with Crispi (cf. Pearl Boring Mitchell, *The Bismarckian Policy of Conciliation with France, 1875–1885* [Philadelphia, 1935], pp. 72–73). In his talks with Italian political leaders, Gambetta denounced the French expeditions of 1849 and 1867 to the peninsula as crimes against France and Italy (Vigo, *op. cit.*, II, 230). Gambetta's presence in Rome gave rise to a host of rumors. One of these evoked a statement denying that he had come in order to take up the question of the forthcoming pontifical election (cf. Hanotaux, *op. cit.*, IV, 258 n.).

[202] Gambetta was reported to have said, after his interview with Victor Emmanuel, that, if he were living in Italy under such a ruler, he too would be a monarchist (cf. Pesci, *I primi anni di Roma capitale*, p. 241; Vigo, *op. cit.*, II, 231). Guiccioli wrote in his diary, under date of January 1, 1878: "Gambetta is in Rome and he has expressed himself very tactfully about our country. He has faith in our monarchy" ("Nuove pagine del diario di Alessandro Guiccioli: 1878," *Nuova Antologia*, August 1, 1935, p. 416).

[203] Adam, *Après l'abandon de la revanche*, pp. 124–25.

[204] *Diritto*, January 23, 1878.

CHAPTER XIV
THE END OF A PONTIFICATE

LESS publicized than the clerical abuses bill, but an even more telling gesture against the power of the church in Italy, was the measure announced by Coppino in the spring of 1876. It called for the establishment of compulsory instruction for all children who had attained the age of six.[1] It thus placed the state in direct competition with the ecclesiastical hierarchy as the dispenser of primary education.[2] The outcry in the clerical press was loud and sustained. "Italian liberty," prophesied the *Osservatore romano*, "will receive a new and lethal blow through the law on obligatory instruction, which is destined . . . . to violate the most sacrosanct of rights, that exercised by parents over the education of their children."[3] But that was not all, in the opinion of the papal organ. State-controlled education would mean the prevalence in Italy of the most abysmal ignorance.[4] Even more violent was the language of the *Unità cattolica*. The proposed measure, it raged, was "such an enormity that we can scarcely find words strong enough to designate it properly." It was part of a scheme "to corrupt the minds and hearts" of Italian children. For obligatory in-

---

[1] For the text of this bill, which was not submitted to parliament until December, 1876, see *Atti*, CCXXXIII, No. 42C, 3–6; cf. also Vincenzo Masi, "Istruzione pubblica e privata," *Cinquanta anni di storia italiana* (Milano, 1911), II, 2.

[2] Private education on all levels was largely in the hands of religious bodies. The greatest problem confronting Italian ministers of public instruction for more than a decade had been that of transferring this virtual monopoly to the lay community (cf. C. Hippeau, "L'Instruction publique en Italie," *Revue des deux mondes*, September 15, 1874, p. 339). A bill similar to the one sponsored by Coppino had been defeated in the chamber in January, 1874. Its opponents had argued that it infringed upon personal freedom and would work economic harm (cf. Saverio Cilibrizzi, *Storia parlamentare politica e diplomatica d'Italia* [Milano, 1925], II, 69).

[3] *Osservatore romano*, May 3, 1876.   [4] *Ibid.*, September 5, 1876.

struction was nothing less than the offspring of modern socialism.[5]

The chamber debate occurred early in March, 1877. The extremist fringe of the Sinistra majority was not altogether satisfied with the terms of the bill. Led by Petruccelli and Bovio, it urged the total exclusion of religious instruction from the schools of the state. The *Diritto* heartily indorsed this position. It demanded that only secular instruction be imparted in the nation's schools, alleging that the clergy was intent upon exploiting its teaching functions to recruit supporters for the ultramontane party.[6] But the cabinet, though its sympathies were with these militants, appreciated the difficulty of completely laicizing public education and persuaded the chamber to reject that proposal. It accepted with alacrity the alternative one offered by Benedetto Cairoli, another notorious anticlerical. He suggested that religious instruction be made purely optional and that it be given only at the request of the parents and at special hours.[7] Thus, the law, which was finally promulgated on July 15, reaffirmed the principle already laid down in the circulars of 1870 and 1871.[8] Throughout the parliamentary discussion of the bill the moderate press gave the ministry its unstinted support. It hailed the chamber's approval of the measure as a victory for a government "which proposes something just and wise" and urged prompt senatorial indorsement.[9] The Vatican's organs, continuing their spirited campaign against Coppino's project, decried the attempt to secularize all elementary instruction as an assault against freedom. Modern liberalism, one of them charged, "rejects liberty in fact because it feels it cannot live . . . . by liberty, because it itself is really the worst of tyrannies." The idea of obligatory education was

[5] *Unità cattolica*, September 22, 1876. [6] *Diritto*, March 11, 1877.

[7] *Atti*, CCXLV (March 9, 1877), 1914 and 1926.

[8] Cf. Aristarco Fasulo, *Il primato papale nella storia e nel pensiero italiano* (Roma, 1924), p. 208; Cilibrizzi, *op. cit.*, II, 118 and note.

[9] Cf., e.g., *Libertà*, March 12 and May 13, 1877.

again vehemently arraigned, and the political authorities were warned that "honest" heads of families preferred religious instruction for their children.[10]

But the Coppino law was neither the sole nor the principal source of preoccupation in high Vatican circles. The aged and constantly ailing pontiff was not likely to live much longer,[11] and certain matters connected with the forthcoming conclave were the subject of anxious speculation. It was feared that the situation created by the occupation of Rome might give rise to serious incidents and thus compromise the freedom of the electors.[12] There was uneasiness, too, regarding the cabinet's behavior on the occasion of the next papal election. "How will it be possible," Simeoni wrote in March, 1877, "to prevent regrettable disorders if, in the event of a conclave, the government of King Victor Emmanuel should attempt . . . . to create an anti-pope who, naturally, will only be the creature of the ministry which happens to be in power?"[13] It was the feeling in Vatican circles that the entire question ought to be seriously examined and suitable precautions taken beforehand. A committee of cardinals was organized for the purpose. It held many meetings and carefully discussed all the various contingencies that might arise apropos of the next conclave. And it finally concluded its labors by adopting certain measures deemed appropriate in the circumstances.[14]

Irksome indeed to the dignitaries of the church was the evident relish with which the pope's enemies disseminated reports of his impending demise. Some of these rumormongers

---

[10] *Voce della verità*, March 8 and 9, 1877.

[11] Guiccioli noted in his diary under date of December 3, 1877: "The pope no longer gets out of bed. I believe his days are numbered" ("Nuove pagine del diario di Alessandro Guiccioli: 1877," *Nuova antologia*, July 16, 1935, p. 239).

[12] Card. Dominique Ferrata, *Mémoires* (Roma, 1920), I, 31.

[13] *AD, 1876–1877*, IV, 163. For the rumors attributing certain sinister designs to the Italian government which were to be executed upon news of Pius' death, see Eduardo Sodèrini, *Il Pontificato di Leone XIII* (Milano, 1932), I, 35–37.

[14] Ferrata, *op. cit.*, I, 31, 32.

had Pius on the point of death. Others had him dead and impersonated by a priest who resembled him. It was explained that the purpose of this deception was to make possible a clandestine papal election. The credulity of the public balked at this tale, but the cabinet, feeling that it could not be too careful, busied itself with the necessary precautions.[15] It was something of a relief to the Quirinal to know that the French government professed no anxiety in the matter. Decazes told Crispi when the latter visited Paris that he was sure the next conclave "will function in the Vatican with the most complete freedom."[16] The attitude of Bismarck was not a little surprising. His eagerness to insure the accession of a more moderate pontiff, Crispi discovered, had apparently given way to complete indifference on this score. He cared little, he told the Italian statesman late in September, about the identity of Pius' successor. "A liberal pope," he said, "will perhaps be worse than a reactionary one. The evil is in the institution, and the man, whoever he is and whatever his opinions and tendencies, can influence but little or not at all the action of the Holy See."[17]

Italians were scarcely inclined to agree with their powerful friend. They were certain that the character of the next wearer of the tiara would play no small part in shaping the course of Italo-papal relations. Influential circles wishfully observed that the new pontiff would scarcely be able to pose as a prisoner once he had been freely elected.[18] Here and

[15] Camillo Manfroni, *Sulla soglia del Vaticano* (Bologna, 1920), I, 313–14.

[16] Francesco Crispi, *Politica estera* (Milano, 1912), p. 12. Late in November, 1876, the papal nuncio to France had written from Paris: "Regarding the measures to be taken à propos of the future conclave, ... and in the event that Rome was still occupied, the Duke (Decazes) thinks that the Catholic governments should reach an accord in order to enforce respect for the liberty of the church and the independence of the sacred college. He is unable to believe that the Italian government would wish to violate the residence of the Vatican and interfere or place any obstacles in the way of the meeting of the cardinals in conclave, inasmuch as it is to its interest to make it clear to the Catholics that in Rome the church is free in spiritual matters and that the government recognizes the inviolability of the Roman pontiff and of the sacred college." Soderini, *op. cit.*, I, 23 n.

[17] Crispi, *Politica estera*, p. 46.   [18] Cf. *Diritto*, September 26, 1877.

there it was predicted that he would fare worse than his predecessor should he prove intractable. One very persistent report had it that the Italian government would deny him recognition unless he formally accepted the new order of things in the peninsula. This train of thought emerged from the anonymous stage when G. M. Bertini, a noted writer on ecclesiastical subjects, made it his own. He advised the cabinet not to acknowledge the election of Pius' successor until it had elicited from him a condemnation of the doctrine that the temporal power was indispensable to the pope's spiritual independence.[19] But this counsel met with no very favorable response,[20] and no less authoritative a sheet than the *Diritto* vouchsafed the assurance that the government's policy would not be affected by the attitude, whether conciliatory or intransigent, of the next pope.[21] Bonghi helped keep the discussion alive by contributing some timely observations on the next conclave.[22] He was mainly concerned with the problem of placing the papal election in the hands of conciliatory prelates whose choice would fall on someone favorable to a *modus vivendi* with Italy. Of more practical moment, in the opinion of official circles, was the possibility that the sacred college might yield to the pressure of the Jesuits and decide to hold the conclave outside Italy. Apprehensions were somewhat stilled when it became known that Pius had appointed Cardinal Pecci, the Archbishop of Perugia, camerlingo of the Holy See.[23] For this prelate, who had long been kept from the inner councils of the Vatican by the jealousy of Antonel-

[19] Cf. Bertini's *Il Vaticano e lo stato* (Napoli, 1877).

[20] Cf. Marco Minghetti, *Stato e chiesa* (Milano, 1878), p. 210, for the reaction of leading Destra circles.

[21] *Diritto*, November 15, 1877.

[22] Cf. his *Pio IX e il papa futuro* (Milano, 1877).

[23] Pesci's appointment as camerlingo occurred in September, 1877. The holder of this office wielded supreme authority during the interregnum following the death of a pontiff. His was the task of arranging for the conclave and assuring its absolute liberty (cf. Ernesto Vercesi, *Pio IX* [Milano, 1930], pp. 243–44).

li,[24] was reputed to be a man of conciliatory and moderate views.[25]

But popular optimism in this instance was wide of the mark. For in a bull (*Consulturi ne post obitum nostrum*) which bore the date of October 10, 1877, the pontiff, obviously alarmed over the possibility that the sacred college, for reasons which he could not foresee, would deem it wiser to convoke the conclave in Rome or in some other part of Italy, urged the cardinals to make even the slightest disturbance or untoward incident the pretext for staging the papal election in non-Italian territory.[26] This pronouncement was decided upon despite the fact that certain powers had repeatedly advised the Curia not to abandon Rome on the occasion of the election of Pius' successor.[27] The Italian cabinet's cue, now as before, was to reiterate its honorable intentions. The Italian minister in Madrid was authorized to inform the Spanish authorities that his government felt "perfectly able to assure the complete freedom of the conclave in Rome."[28] Melegari told Baron Haymerle, the Austrian ambassador to the Quirinal, that the Italian government wanted the forthcoming conclave to be "free, independent and safe."[29] The attitude of the new French government encouraged still another protestation of benevolent regard for the safety and tranquillity of the sacred college. On December 17, Waddington told Cialdini, the Italian ambassador, that what made the return to a cabinet of the left "galling and deplorable" to MacMahon was "the supposed imminence of the death of the pope." The French ministry, Waddington

---

[24] Cf. Raffaele de Cesare, *Il Conclave di Leone XIII con aggiunte e nuovi documenti e il futuro conclave* (Città di Castello, 1888), p. 4.

[25] Cf. *ibid.*, pp. 4–5.

[26] Soderini, *op. cit.*, I, 30–31. Cf. also Giovanni Berthelet, *La elezione del papa* (Roma, 1891), p. 199.

[27] Cf., for the advice of these powers, Soderini, *op. cit.*, I, 37 and note on pp. 37–38.

[28] De Cesare, *Il Conclave di Leone XIII*, p. 300.

[29] Soderini, *op. cit.*, I, 40.

continued, would therefore desire to be able "to appease MacMahon's scruples of conscience" by giving him the assurance that the Italian government "will respect and will enforce respect for the liberty of the future conclave." He said he would be very grateful to Cialdini if the latter were to request his government to make "a new and explicit declaration in this sense."[30] Melegari promptly vouchsafed the desired assurances in a note to Cialdini.[31] A few days later, Waddington again alluded to this theme in the course of a conversation with the Italian chargé d'affaires. France, he declared, wanted the conclave to meet in Rome and the election of a new pontiff to occur "in the freest, most regular . . . . manner, in order that the validity of the . . . . election might under no circumstances be contested." It was likewise the wish of the French government that the successor of Pius should be "a man of moderate sentiments who would render possible a reconciliation with Italy." Waddington added that he had had occasion to discuss the question of the future conclave with the representatives of other Catholic countries and that the latter shared his government's wishes regarding the site of the next papal election.[32] These were gracious and reassuring words, and the authorities at Rome welcomed them as a further earnest of French good will.

In other sectors of church-state relations the feud between the two powers showed no sign of abating. Early in 1877, Pius categorically reaffirmed the *non-expedit*. Some persons who called themselves Catholics, he told a group of Italian pilgrims, wished to see the church draw closer to the state and resign itself to the loss of its temporal domain. He, however, found it impossible to discard the oaths he had taken.[33] Under no circumstances, therefore, would he permit Catholics

[30] De Cesare, *Il Conclave di Leone XIII*, p. 301.

[31] *Ibid.*, p. 25.

[32] *Ibid.*, pp. 302–3.

[33] *CC*, I (10th ser.; January 20, 1877), 355.

to accept seats in the chamber of deputies.[34] Later that year, Simeoni made the ban on outdoor religious processions the theme of a strong note to the members of the diplomatic corps at the Vatican.[35] A collision loomed over the appointment of a new Neapolitan primate to succeed the late Cardinal Riario Sforza. By the laws of the former kingdom of Naples, the archbishopric in question was in the gift of the crown, and the Quirinal now made ready to challenge the validity of any action taken independently by the pope to fill the vacancy. The Vatican in turn insisted that, by virtue of the unification of Italy and the enactment of the law of guarantees, the special concordat with Naples, upon which the royal right of patronage rested, had ceased to be operative.[36] In the north, at Turin, a great outcry went up from the clerical camp when the authorities of that city, complying with the requirements of the Coppino law, refused point-blank to allow religious instruction in the elementary schools during the regular teaching hours.[37] The *Osservatore romano* issued the warning that Catholics would not be satisfied until their church had resumed the teaching function conferred upon it by its divine founder.[38]

The hopelessness of mediation was fully attested by the fate which overtook Father Carlo Maria Curci. The latter was one of the most learned and eloquent members of the Society of Jesus. He had helped found the *Civiltà cattolica* and had been instrumental in organizing the Roman Society

[34] *Ibid.*, February 6, 1877, pp. 385–89. The *Osservatore romano* a few months earlier had declared that a chamber of deputies which met in Rome could be either Destra or Sinistra; it could never be Catholic. Were it Catholic, "it would not and could not meet in Rome" (issue of October 27, 1876).

[35] *AD, 1876–1877*, IV, 194–95.   [36] *Schulthess, 1877*, p. 340.

[37] Pietro Vigo, *Storia degli ultimi trent'anni del secolo XIX* (Milano, 1908), II, 220–21.

[38] *Osservatore romano*, November 17, 1877. The *Opinione*, though declaring itself opposed to obligatory religious instruction, was moved to point out on this occasion that it would be deplorable if the youth of the country should become habituated to the skeptical, anticlerical point of view (cf. the issue of November 18, 1877).

for Catholic Interests.[39] For years he had distinguished himself as an uncompromising foe of Italian unity and as a most zealous champion of the papal cause.[40] His troubles began with the occupation of Rome. That event left him with the conviction that the temporal power was irrevocably lost. He wanted the church to admit this and act accordingly.[41] He developed these views in a pamphlet which made its appearance shortly after September 20, 1870.[42] He argued that the pope could expect no aid from the great powers. He ridiculed the idea, entertained at the time in influential Vatican circles, that help might come from King William of Prussia. At Pius' command, however, he recanted.[43] But four years later, in the Preface to a biblical study,[44] he again urged acceptance of the *fait accompli*. "God has permitted the robbery," he wrote, "in order to sanctify his church. . . . . We must free ourselves of all illusions and submit to God's will."[45] He returned to the charge the following year in a letter to the pope. Italy, he pleaded, could not be compelled to relinquish the former papal domain. By insisting upon the recovery of its territorial sovereignty, the Holy See would ultimately undermine its own position and that of the Catholic church in Italy. In his opinion, the wisest course was to come to an understanding with Victor Emmanuel. The latter, it was to be expected, would reciprocate by appointing a Christian cabinet, dissolving the chamber, and ordering new elections; and there was little doubt that, with the aid of the conserva-

[39] Cf. Soderini, *op. cit.*, II, 13.

[40] Cf., for some interesting personal information about Curci, Ugo Pesci, *I primi anni di Roma capitale* (Firenze, 1907), pp. 503-4.

[41] Cf. "Ueber das politische Verhalten der Katholiken in Italien," *Historisch-Politische Blätter für das katholische Deutschland*, 1878, p. 423.

[42] It was entitled: *La Caduta di Roma per le armi italiani, considerata nelle sue cagioni e nei suoi effetti.*

[43] The letter of retraction was published in *Unità cattolica*, November 12, 1870.

[44] Entitled *Lezioni sugli evangeli.*

[45] Cf. Friedrich Fuchs, "Der römische Friede: seine Propheten, Pseudo-propheten, Vorläufer u. Märtyrer," *Hochland*, June, 1929, p. 230.

tive elements in the country, a majority of Catholic candidates would be returned. In the regime that would thus emerge, the church would be supreme.[46]

This letter, which had remained a secret between Curci and the Holy Father, appeared in the columns of the *Univers* in July, 1877. It became overnight the center of an acrimonious controversy. It was reprinted in all the Italian newspapers, which elaborated upon it with understandable gusto. Curci insisted that its publication had occurred without his knowledge and was to be attributed to the indiscretion of others.[47] But his superiors, who professed to be scandalized by this heterodoxy, were not to be so easily placated. In October he was summarily expelled from the Jesuit order.[48] This martyrdom promptly endeared him to patriotic circles. The ideas expounded by Curci, declared the *Libertà*, were those of "an intelligent, learned, experienced man." The journal did not fail to comment on the strange twist of fortune which had made this erstwhile reactionary and fierce adversary of Italian unity the object of papal displeasure. The heartening moral of the episode, it concluded, was that "we liberals can from now on count on allies whose existence we had not even dreamt of."[49]

Undismayed by the ire of his superiors, Curci utilized his enforced leisure to prepare a fuller exposition of his views. The product of his labors was *Il moderno dissidio fra la chiesa e l'Italia*, which appeared early in January, 1878. In it he declared himself opposed to the *nè eletti nè elettori* formula and urged that Catholics be authorized to vote in parliamentary elections. It was entirely possible, he argued, to

[46] Manfroni, *op. cit.*, I, 229–30; "Ueber das politische Verhalten der Katholiken in Italien," *op. cit.*, p. 424; cf., for an excellent discussion of the theocratic objectives of Curci's program, *Libertà*, November 6, 1877.

[47] Manfroni, *op. cit.*, I, 318.

[48] On Curci and his position see R. Bonghi, "I Dissidii del partito clericale e le proposte del Sacerdote Curci," *Nuova antologia*, January 1, 1878, pp. 5–28.

[49] *Libertà*, October 27, 1877.

compose the ancient quarrel between Italy and the church.[50]
The Vatican was deeply irked by this persistent insubordination. Curci's volume, the *Osservatore romano* contended, was
in large part "an inexact and slovenly piece of bungling."
Stripped of its platitudes, it stood revealed as a mass of con-
tumely heaped upon the heads of the author's superiors.
The papal organ sharply denied that Catholic participation
in political elections would make it easier for the church to
hold the Italian government in check. "First make us free,"
it proclaimed, "and then we will vote."[51] Pius promptly demanded a complete retraction. He ordered the refractory ex-
Jesuit to embrace the orthodox view on the temporal power,
the boycott of political elections, and the incompatibility of
papal and Italian claims. This Curci refused to do. Mean-
while, his book was causing a considerable stir. His critics
suggested that he was animated by no very high motives.
The *dissidio*, one of them caustically observed, was not between Italy and the church, but between Curci and the general of the Society of Jesus. If the learned father had been
allowed to retain his membership in the order, so argued this
writer, his pen would have remained inactive.[52] In other
quarters he was lavishly praised. Those who had been predicting that isolation from the political life of the peninsula
would ultimately bring disaster upon the church cited his
volume in support of their position.[53] There was even some
agitation in favor of a concordat between Italy and the Holy
See based upon a recognition of the *status quo*.[54]

[50] Pp. 74–75, 78–94. A similar attitude inspired Canon Giuseppe Cerruti's *La
Chiesa cattolica e l'Italia*, which preceded Curci's study by a few months. Cerruti
indirectly suggested the idea of reconciliation with Italy by pointing out that the
church had always made its peace with the changing conditions of various eras.

[51] *Osservatore romano*, January 8 and 12, 1878.

[52] Palmiro Billeri, "Il moderno dissidio tra la chiesa e l'Italia di C. M. Curci,"
Rivista Europea, January 16, 1878, pp. 301–11.

[53] Cf. De Gubernatis, "Contemporary Life and Thought in Italy," *Contemporary
Review*, March, 1878, p. 846.

[54] Enrico Tavallini, *La Vita e i tempi di Giovanni Lanza* (Torino and Napoli,
1887), II, 59.

It was in the midst of these lively polemics that Victor Emmanuel was fatally stricken. He died on January 9, after he had received the last sacraments of the church from his chaplain, Mgr. Anzino.[55] "I die like a Catholic," the monarch was reported to have said during these closing lugubrious moments. "I have never done anything with the idea of offending the church. I regret that the decisions I have had to make in the interests of Italy should have been the cause of sorrow to the pope."[56] He was reputed to have added that, in everything he had done, he had been certain in his own mind that he was fulfilling his duties as a citizen and as a ruler.[57] His death came as a great shock, and intense indeed was the grief of the nation.[58] The pontiff himself partook of the general mourning. On first learning of the king's illness he had asked to be kept minutely informed as to his condition.[59] According to the *Osservatore romano*, he had even hurried to send a "respectable" ecclesiastic to the Quirinal not only to ascertain the status of the royal invalid but also to minister to the latter's spiritual wants. But this ecclesiastic, the papal organ was careful to add, had not been conducted into the king's chamber,[60] much to the relief of those who believed that the papal emissary had been sent to elicit a formal retractation from Victor Emmanuel.[61] On the morning of the ninth, when the bulletins from the Quirinal indicated that the end was near, Pius said to one of his at-

---

[55] Cf. *Gazzetta ufficiale*, January 10, 1878; Vigo, *op. cit.*, II, 235; Attilio Simioni, *Vittorio Emanuele* (Milano, 1911), p. 158. The clericals were very zealous in pointing to the fact that the king had received the sacraments (cf. Michele Rosi, *Vittorio Emanuele II* [Bologna, 1930], II, 228).

[56] Cf. *Libertà*, January 15, 1878.   [57] Cf. Vigo, *op. cit.*, II, 236.

[58] Pesci, *I primi anni di Roma capitale*, pp. 592–94.

[59] *Ibid.*, p. 589.

[60] *Osservatore romano*, January 11, 1878.

[61] Guiccioli noted in his diary that, according to the story which had come to his attention, various pretexts had been found to prevent the papal emissary from seeing the king because it was believed that he wished to demand a recantation ("Nuove pagine del diario di Alessandro Guiccioli: 1878," *Nuova antologia*, August 1, 1935, p. 419).

tendants that the passing of Victor Emmanuel would be a misfortune for everyone, including the Vatican.[62] When informed that his royal adversary was no more, he was reported to have exclaimed: "He died like a Christian, like a sovereign, and like an honorable man!"[63] The charity displayed by His Holiness on this occasion was emulated by the more responsible ultramontane journals. The *Voce della verità* spoke highly of the deceased ruler's ability and acknowledged his moderation. He combined, in its opinion, "courageous intelligence, prudent courage, and strength of purpose in any path with a clearly traced and firmly pursued aim." He possessed, too, all the proverbial Italian finesse and political good sense. It remained to be seen, however, whether this good sense failed him "in his last and most hazardous enterprise"— the occupation of Rome and the establishment there of the capital of the kingdom.[64] The *Osservatore romano* declared that Catholics, in accordance with the example given them by the Holy Father, "will have only one word before the tomb of Victor Emmanuel: that of compassion and peace."[65] But not all the clerical sheets showed such generosity. So abusive was the language of some of them in commenting upon the death of the king that even certain members of the sacred college protested to the pope. The most flagrant offender was the *Osservatore cattolico* of Milan, and it drew a sharp rebuke from the clergy of that city. The outraged ec-

[62] Manfroni, *op. cit.*, I, 326–27.

[63] Massari, *La Vita ed il regno di Vittorio Emanuele II di Savoia* (Milano, 1910), II, 591; Humphrey Johnson, *The Papacy and the Kingdom of Italy* (London, 1926), p. 39; Cilibrizzi, *op. cit.*, II, 138–139. According to a report which reached Guiccioli, Pius declared in the presence of a great many visitors: "The king died like a Christian and like an honorable man. I know that there are people who speak otherwise, but those persons are scoundrels and I wish it to be known that I regard them as such" ("Nuove pagine del diario di Alessandro Guiccioli: 1878," *Nuova antologia*, August 1, 1935, p. 420).

[64] *Voce della verità*, January 11, 1878.

[65] *Osservatore romano*, January 11, 1878.

clesiastics found the journal's language offensive to "the most noble sentiments of priest, Christian, and citizen."[66]

Rome was decided upon as the site of interment, in the face of bitter opposition from the citizens of Turin. The latter insisted that the king's remains should be preserved in the mausoleum of the Superga, just outside the Piedmontese capital, which housed the tombs of all of Victor Emmanuel's Savoyard ancestors. But grave political considerations, apart from the attitude of the Romans themselves,[67] impelled the government to ignore the claims of the Turinese.[68] One contemporary observer justly appreciated the situation when he wrote:

> It was feared that taking the body of Victor Emmanuel from Rome might give rise to the idea at the Vatican that the House of Savoy did not consider itself sufficiently secure of its permanent tenure of Rome. The good sense of the Italian people comprehended the evil which might accrue had the clerical party a pretext of affirming that the House of Savoy carried away their dead from the field of battle like an acknowledgment of their defeat.[69]

The majority of the Destra supported the government. According to the *Opinione*, the choice of Rome as the site of the royal burial was a fitting confirmation of Italy's hallowed right to the city.[70] It constituted, in the opinion of the *Libertà*, "a sacred and more intimate bond between the dynasty and the nation."[71] The Turinese sent a deputation to the capital to plead the claims of the Superga.[72] They were supported by Sella, who disagreed with his party confreres in

[66] Cf. the *Libertà*, January 17 and 20, 1878; Manfroni, *op. cit.*, I, 329–30. The Archbishop of Milan associated himself with the protest of his ecclesiastical subordinates.

[67] The municipal government of Rome published an address demanding that the king be buried in the capital.

[68] The Italian cabinet had lost no time in taking up this delicate issue (cf. "Nuove pagine del diario di Alessandro Guiccioli: 1878," *Nuova antologia*, August 1, 1935, p. 419).

[69] De Gubernatis, *op. cit.*, p. 844.

[70] Chiala, *Dina*, III, 503.

[71] *Libertà*, January 15, 1878.   [72] Cf. *Voce della verità*, January 18, 1878.

this matter.[73] But Humbert, the new ruler, refused to give way. He declared that national sentiment and the welfare of the country made it imperative to confer this honor on Rome.[74] The body of Victor Emmanuel remained in the Eternal City "as the sacred seal of national unity."[75] The outcome of the controversy was very much in accord with the spirit of the new Italy, but the Turinese received the news of their defeat with ill grace.[76]

The funeral rites were most imposing.[77] The procession to the Pantheon, which had been selected as Victor Emmanuel's final resting-place, lasted more than three hours. Patriotic Italians had little cause to complain of the conduct of the Holy See on this solemn occasion. In compliance with orders from the pontiff himself, the ecclesiastical authorities had done nothing to obstruct the celebration of the customary ceremonies.[78] Negotiations between the government and the Curia, conducted through intermediaries, had produced this happy result.[79] The archbishops of northern Italy had even been instructed to hold a requiem mass for the late monarch and permission to attend the obsequies in Rome had been granted the clergy. However, only thirteen priests of low rank appeared to take their places in the great procession. Bishops and dignitaries of the church were conspicuously absent, although a number of them publicly voiced their

[73] Alessandro Guiccioli, *Quintino Sella* (Rovigo, 1887), II, 179–80.

[74] Vigo, *op. cit.*, II, 242.

[75] Rosi, *Vittorio Emanuele II*, II, 227.

[76] Nuove pagine del diario di Alessandro Guiccioli: 1878," *Nuova antologia*, August 1, 1935, p. 420.

[77] Cf. Joseph Schmidlin, *Papstgeschichte der neuesten Zeit* (München, 1933–34), II, 100.

[78] Guiccioli noted in his diary on January 12, 1878: "The pope, on his own initiative, has permitted the royal obsequies to be celebrated in any church that is not a basilica. . . . . The fact of the pope's assent . . . . is most important. The new reign begins under the best of auspices" ("Nuove pagine del diario di Alessandro Guiccioli: 1878," *Nuova antologia*, August 1, 1935, p. 420).

[79] De Cesare, *Il Conclave di Leone XIII*, p. 135.

sorrow over the death of Victor Emmanuel.[80] The tolerance shown by the Holy See in this moment of national bereavement was gratefully noted. The behavior of the papacy, the *Libertà* remarked, "is the sanest since 1870."[81] One competent student of Italian affairs was moved to write:

> In truth, this death and these Christian funeral services for the usurper, these solemn rites celebrated in numerous cathedrals of the peninsula, take us quite far from the Middle Ages. . . . . Certainly, there is here a sign of the times, a proof that amid all its resistance and protests, the church can on occasion reconcile itself to accomplished facts.[82]

But thoughts of peace with Italy were as remote as ever from the mind of Pius. On the very morrow of Victor Emmanuel's death he issued a regulation prescribing rules to be observed by the members of the sacred college during the papal interregnum. The document specified that the attitude of the cardinals toward the Italian government was to undergo no change. The diplomatic corps at the Vatican, it went on, was to be informed that the sacred college could do nothing to alter the situation bequeathed by the late pontiff.[83] On January 17, Pius addressed a letter to the editors of the *Osservatore cattolico* praising them for having admonished their readers to beware of the sophisms of those who were preaching Italo-papal reconciliation.[84] Simultaneously, Cardinal Simeoni, in a note to the nuncios, renewed the protest against the seizure of Rome and the alleged maltreatment of the church. The papal attitude required reiteration, he explained, because Humbert, in assuming the title of king of Italy, had presumed to sanction the usurpation perpetrated

[80] Cf. *Libertà*, January 17, 1878.   [81] *Ibid.*, January 19, 1878.

[82] A. Leroy-Beaulieu, "Un Roi et un pape: I. Le Roi Victor Emmanuel et la monarchie italienne," *Revue des deux mondes*, April 15, 1878, p. 868.

[83] Berthelet, *op. cit.*, pp. 214, 217.

[84] Vigo, *op. cit.*, II, 254. The pope's gesture provoked the following comment from Guiccioli: "The Vatican always has the amiability to free us from embarrassment when we find ourselves in a delicate position, and above all to release us from the burden of gratitude" ("Nuove pagine del diario di Alessandro Guiccioli: 1878," *Nuova antologia*, August 1, 1935, p. 423).

by his father.[85] Notice was thus served upon the country that the intransigent party at the Vatican was more firmly than ever in the saddle. The ministerialists were quick to adduce Simeoni's declaration in vindication of their implacably antipapal position. Even the blindest person, they caustically observed, could now discern the true nature of the pope's aspirations. Italy's future course was clear. She would have to persist in her legislative program without bothering about the Holy See, whose friendship it was futile to seek.[86] Destra circles professed deep concern over the Vatican's unyielding attitude. The *Opinione* felt impelled to remind the country that the Italian clericals were stronger than ever and that it was imperative to oppose them strenuously.[87] The ascendancy of the irreconcilables at the Vatican was further signalized by the report that the pope had been persuaded to countermand an earlier order and forbid the use of the Church of the Lateran for services in honor of Victor Emmanuel.[88] Equally symptomatic was Pius' resolute refusal to receive the princely personages who had come to Rome to pay homage to the departed sovereign. Among those denied an audience were the Queen of Portugal[89] and the Austrian Archduke Regnier.[90]

Feeble and ailing as he was, the indefatigable pontiff girded himself for a devastating pronouncement on the subject of Humbert's accession. But he did not live to make it. He died on February 7, leaving to his successor the grim business of

[85] *AD, 1876–1877*, IV, 262–63; Vigo, *op. cit.*, II, 255; Cilibrizzi, *op. cit.*, II, 139.

[86] *Diritto*, January 25, 1878.

[87] *Opinione*, January 30, 1878.

[88] De Cesare, *Il Conclave di Leone XIII*, p. 135; Manfroni, *op. cit.*, I, 328–29.

[89] The pope refused to receive her because, he said, she was staying at the Quirinal (cf. "Nuove pagine del diario di Alessandro Guiccioli: 1878," *Nuova antologia*, August 1, 1935, p. 423).

[90] The treatment accorded the archduke made a painful impression on the Austrian government (cf. De Cesare, *Il Conclave di Leone XIII*, pp. 33 and 34).

continuing the feud which he had waged so relentlessly.[91] Thus ended a pontificate which one writer has called "the most tempestuous in the entire history of the church."[92] On this occasion, the press and public opinion, irrespective of party, gave an exemplary demonstration of tact and fair-mindedness. Journals of every description paid the deceased warm tribute. The *Opinione* made itself part of the general chorus when it referred to him as a pontiff "whom Catholicism venerated and all the civilized world revered." It predicted that his successor would scarcely be able to achieve a comparable prestige unless there should ensue a complete reversal of papal policy.[93] The great service he had rendered the national cause during the first years of his pontificate was recalled.[94] The *Libertà* reminded its readers that Pius, in separating himself from that cause, had only done what he could not avoid doing. It was therefore not just to accuse him of treason. And it was only fair, too, to remember that he had been less intransigent than his counselors.[95] Even the *Diritto* adopted a less hostile tone in appraising the career of its eminent adversary.[96] Italians were now ready to forget his opposition to the unification of the peninsula. They remembered only that he had blessed the principle of nationality.[97] The cabinet proved itself fully alive to the solemnity of the moment. It expressed its sympathy in these generous terms:

[91] Pius did indeed bequeath a sad legacy to his successor. The feud with Italy was only one small part of it. In Germany the Kulturkampf was still in progress. Since October 20, 1877, all relations with Russia had been severed. In Belgium a party opposed to the claims of the church was in power. England was resentful over papal support of the Irish. The relations with Austria, already strained because of ecclesiastical disputes, had been aggravated by Pius' recent refusal to grant an audience to Archduke Regnier. The situation in Spain was far from satisfactory, and in France a resolutely anticlerical policy was being inaugurated (cf. Vercesi, *Pio IX*, p. 258).

[92] Cilibrizzi, *op. cit.*, II, 139.

[93] *Opinione*, February 9, 1878; Chiala, *Dina*, III, 628.

[94] Cf. Marco Tabarrini, "Il Papa Pio IX," *Nuova antologia*, February 15, 1878.

[95] *Libertà*, February 9, 1878.   [96] Cf. *Diritto*, February 9, 1878.

[97] Pesci, *I primi anni di Roma capitale*, pp. 621–22.

To the mourning of Catholicism for the death of its august and venerated chief is joined the regret of the secular world at witnessing the disappearance of one of the great figures of our century. The pontificate of Pius IX has left an ineffaceable mark upon the history of Italy and of Europe.[98]

The prefects were reminded that sovereign honors were due the deceased.[99] King Humbert, through one of his adjutants, conveyed his sorrow to the camerlingo.[100] It was even rumored that Their Majesties would be disposed to attend the funeral services if the proper place were accorded them.[101] All public theatrical performances were ordered suspended. The one discordant note was struck by sporadic demonstrations in favor of the repeal of the law of guarantees.[102] The government, however, quickly put a stop to this unseemly activity. By a queer turn of fate it devolved upon Crispi, the archadversary of that law in 1871, to act now in its defense. The former Garibaldian, who had succeeded Nicotera as minister of the interior in December, 1877, sent the following instructions to the prefects on February 9:

At this solemn moment, when the conclave is to be convoked and proof should be given to the civilized world that Italy grants the cardinals the most complete freedom to elect a new pontiff, nothing is more absurd and more unpatriotic than to promote and stage popular demonstrations against the law of guarantees.[103]

He asked Garibaldi to intervene, and the latter consented to advise his masonic and republican friends, who had fomented the agitation, to hold their peace.[104]

On February 13, Pius was buried in the Vatican basilica. There his remains were to be preserved until San Lorenzo outside the Walls, which he had designated in his testament

---

[98] *Gazzetta ufficiale*, February 8, 1878.

[99] Crispi, *Politica interna* (Milano, 1924), p. 88.

[100] Schmidlin, *op. cit.*, II, 105.

[101] "Nuove pagine del diario di Alessandro Guiccioli: 1878," *Nuova antologia*, August 1, 1935, p. 424.

[102] Vigo, *op. cit.*, II, 271.

[103] Crispi, *Politica interna*, p. 87.   [104] *Ibid.*, pp. 90–91.

as his permanent sepulcher, had been made ready to receive them.[105] But already the grandeur and pathos which had marked his reign had become a receding memory. For attention was now riveted on the throne which he had vacated. A new pope was awaited, the first to don the tiara since the fall of the temporal power. Would a new era commence with his accession? Would new ideas inspire the policies of the Holy See under his leadership? These were the questions which agitated Italy and the world as the sacred college assembled in conclave to elect another supreme pontiff.

[105] Cf. the text of the testament in the *Osservatore romano*, February 17, 1878.

INDEX

INDEX